SOCIAL WORK S1

NASW POLICY STATEMENTS   *4TH EDITION*

NASW PRESS

National Association of Social Workers
Washington, DC

Jay J. Cayner, ACSW, LISW, *President*
Josephine Nieves, MSW, PhD, *Executive Director*

First impression January 1997
Second impression February 1998

Linda Beebe, *Executive Editor*
Nancy Winchester, *Director, Editorial Services*
K. Hyde Loomis, *Production Editor*
Louise R. Goines, *Copy Editor*
Kathy Savory, *Proofreader*
Shenandoah Publications, *Proofreader*
Bernice Eisen, *Indexer*

Printed in the United States of America

ISBN 0-87101-273-1

Contents

Policy Statement Topic Areas v

Foreword ix
By Jay J. Cayner and Josephine Nieves

Public and Professional Policy Statements

Abortion 3
Adjudication 4
Adolescent Pregnancy 8
Affirmative Action 12
Aging 16
Aid to Families with Dependent Children Reform 23
Alcohol, Tobacco, and Other Substance Abuse 31
Alternative Work Patterns 39
Case Management in Health, Education, and Human Services Settings 42
Child Abuse and Neglect 45
Civil Liberties and Justice 50
Client Self-Determination in End-of-Life Decisions 59
Community Development 63
Confidentiality and Information Utilization 68
Cultural and Linguistic Diversity in the United States 72
Cultural Competence in the Social Work Profession 75
Declassification 79
Deinstitutionalization 84
Disasters 88
Drug Testing in the Workplace 95
Early Childhood Care and Services 100
Economic Policy 103
Education of Children and Youths 108
Electoral Politics 115
Energy 120
Family Planning 124
Family Policy 127
Family Violence 132
Foster Care and Adoption 136
Full and Equitable Employment 141
Gender-, Ethnic-, and Race-Based Workplace Discrimination 146
Health Care Financing 155

HIV/AIDS 159
Homelessness 164
Hospice Care 169
Housing 172
Immigrants and Refugees 177
The Impaired Professional 185
International Policy on Human Rights 188
Juvenile Justice and Delinquency Prevention 192
Lesbian, Gay, and Bisexual Issues 198
Long-Term Care 210
Managed Care 216
Mental Health 223
National Health Care 228
Occupational Social Work 235
Parental Kidnapping 240
Peace and Social Justice 244
People with Disabilities 250
Physical Punishment of Children 255
Public Child Welfare 259
Racism 261
Role of Government, Social Policy, and Social Work 267
Role of Social Work in Health Maintenance Organizations ... 272
School Dropout Prevention 275
Social Services 283
Social Work in Home Health Care 288
Social Work in Rural Areas 292
Social Work Practice in the Health Care Field 297
Tax Reform 301
Third-Party Reimbursement and Consumer Choice 306
Volunteers and Social Services Systems 310
Voter Participation 314
Women in the Social Work Profession 316
Women's Issues 323
Youth Suicide 332

NASW Code of Ethics 337

Index 353

Policy Statement Topic Areas

Adolescents

Adolescent Pregnancy
Education of Children and Youths
Juvenile Justice and Delinquency
    Prevention
School Dropout Prevention
Youth Suicide

Aging

Aging
Client Self-Determination in
    End-of-Life Decisions
Hospice Care
Long-Term Care
Social Work in Home Health Care

Child Welfare

Aid to Families with Dependent Children
    Reform
Child Abuse and Neglect
Family Policy
Family Violence
Foster Care and Adoption
Physical Punishment of Children
Public Child Welfare

Community

Community Development
Disasters
Energy
Housing
Social Services
Volunteers and Social Services Systems

Discrimination and Equity Issues

Affirmative Action
Civil Liberties and Justice
Cultural and Linguistic Diversity in the
    United States
Cultural Competence in the Social Work
    Profession
Full and Equitable Employment
Gender-, Ethnic-, and Race-Based Workplace
    Discrimination
Immigrants and Refugees
International Policy on Human Rights
Lesbian, Gay, and Bisexual Issues
Peace and Social Justice
People with Disabilities
Racism
Women in the Social Work Profession
Women's Issues

Education

Case Management in Health, Education, and
    Human Services Settings
Early Childhood Care and Services
Education of Children and Youths
Physical Punishment of Children
School Dropout Prevention

Employment

Alternative Work Patterns
Drug Testing in the Workplace
Economic Policy
Full and Equitable Employment
Gender-, Ethnic-, and Race-Based Workplace
    Discrimination

Homelessness
Housing
Occupational Social Work

Ethnicity and Race

Affirmative Action
Civil Liberties and Justice
Cultural and Linguistic Diversity in the
    United States
Cultural Competence in the Social Work
    Profession
Full and Equitable Employment
Gender-, Ethnic-, and Race-Based Workplace
    Discrimination
Immigrants and Refugees
International Policy on Human Rights
Racism

Families and Children

Adolescent Pregnancy
Aid to Families with Dependent Children
    Reform
Alternative Work Patterns
Child Abuse and Neglect
Early Childhood Care and Services
Family Planning
Family Policy
Family Violence
Foster Care and Adoption
Homelessness
Housing
Parental Kidnapping
Physical Punishment of Children
Public Child Welfare
Women's Issues
Youth Suicide

Family Planning

Abortion
Adolescent Pregnancy
Family Planning

Gender Issues

Affirmative Action
Civil Liberties and Justice
Family Violence

Full and Equitable Employment
Gender-, Ethnic-, and Race-Based Workplace
    Discrimination
International Policy on Human Rights
Lesbian, Gay, and Bisexual Issues
Women in the Social Work Profession
Women's Issues

Health

Abortion
Adolescent Pregnancy
Aging
Alcohol, Tobacco, and Other Substance Abuse
Case Management in Health, Education, and
    Human Services Settings
Client Self-Determination in End-of-Life
    Decisions
Deinstitutionalization
Early Childhood Care and Services
Family Planning
Family Violence
Health Care Financing
HIV/AIDS
Hospice Care
Long-Term Care
Managed Care
Mental Health
National Health Care
People with Disabilities
Role of Social Work in Health Maintenance
    Organizations
Social Work in Home Health Care
Social Work Practice in the Health Care Field
Third-Party Reimbursement and Consumer
    Choice

Macro Issues

Economic Policy
Energy
Family Policy
Full and Equitable Employment
Health Care Financing
Housing
Immigrants and Refugees
International Policy on Human Rights
National Health Care
Peace and Social Justice
Role of Government, Social Policy, and
    Social Work

Social Services
Tax Reform

Political Action

Civil Liberties and Justice
Electoral Politics
Role of Government, Social Policy, and
    Social Work
Tax Reform
Voter Participation

Social Work Professional Statements

Adjudication
Confidentiality and Information Utilization
Cultural Competence in the Social Work
    Profession
Declassification

The Impaired Professional
NASW Code of Ethics
Occupational Social Work
Public Child Welfare
Third-Party Reimbursement and Consumer
    Choice
Women in the Social Work Profession

Substance Abuse

Alcohol, Tobacco, and Other Substance Abuse
Drug Testing in the Workplace
The Impaired Professional

Violence

Child Abuse and Neglect
Family Violence
Physical Punishment of Children
Youth Suicide

Policy Statements Approved by the 1996 Delegate Assembly

Affirmative Action
Alcohol, Tobacco, and Other Substance Abuse
Child Abuse and Neglect
Cultural Competence in the Social Work
    Profession
Disasters
Early Childhood Care and Services
Education of Children and Youths
Electoral Politics
Gender-, Ethnic-, and Race-Based Workplace
    Discrimination
HIV/AIDS
Homelessness
Immigrants and Refugees
Lesbian, Gay, and Bisexual Issues
Long-Term Care
Racism
Role of Government, Social Policy, and Social
    Work
School Dropout Prevention
Women in the Social Work Profession
Women's Issues
Youth Suicide

Title Changes from the 3rd Edition

AIDS/HIV is now HIV/AIDS
Alcoholism and Other Substance Abuse–
    Related Problems is now Alcohol, Tobacco,
    and Other Substance Abuse
Elimination of Sex- and Race-Based Wage
    Discrimination is now Gender-, Ethnic-, and
    Race-Based Workplace Discrimination
Lesbian and Gay Issues is now Lesbian, Gay,
    and Bisexual Issues
Preschool, Elementary, and Secondary Educa-
    tion is now Education of Children and
    Youths

Statements Deleted

Children and Youths—A Bill of Rights
Environmental Issues
NASW: Relationships with Other
    Organizations and Disciplines

Foreword

The social work profession was born in social change. Early social workers advocated effectively for better housing, more employment opportunities, peaceful solutions to conflict, education as a means of advancing people and society, and empowerment for disenfranchised populations. Over the past 100 years, social workers have continued to hone their advocacy skills, both as individuals and collectively as a profession.

The involvement of social workers, with our value systems and our expertise, in policy development and implementation is more critical today than at any other juncture in our history. On the one hand, our universe has expanded. The world today is truly a global village. In the United States, our population is more diverse, culturally, ethnically, and racially. We must deal with a rapidly aging population and a widening gap between affluent and poor people. At the same time, we are witnessing an unprecedented dismantling of social programs, a broad and dramatic turn to more conservative viewpoints, and a consequent reduction in services to people in need of them.

We believe that this book can be very helpful to social workers in three areas:

1. development of organizational responses to policy issues

2. policy analysis and study, particularly in schools of social work

3. action by individual social workers, particularly in coalitions.

The fourth edition of *Social Work Speaks* presents the results of the profession's most systematic approach to policy development. Since its inception in 1955, NASW has incorporated policy statements into its governance process. NASW's Delegate Assembly, an elected body of 300 professional social workers representing NASW's diverse membership, meets at regular intervals (every three years since 1981) to set broad parameters for the association's program, to determine bylaws issues, and to agree on policy statements that will be used to guide NASW's advocacy efforts in social policy. *Social Work Speaks, 4th Edition* includes all the new and revised policies approved by the 1996 NASW Delegate Assembly, as well as those approved by previous assemblies.

THE PROCESS

Any individual member or group of members may propose that a particular Delegate Assembly approve a policy statement. Before the Delegate Assembly meets, all proposed statements are circulated to chapters and national units for review and recommendations; most policy statements also undergo revision during the Assembly process, either in coalition meetings before the Delegate Assembly or in hearing panels during the Assembly. Consequently, policy statements represent the collective thinking of thousands of experienced social work practitioners from all fields of practice. As products of a political process in which different views are reconciled, the statements are useful for political action and the study of policy in many areas.

Until 1990 policy statements, once passed, remained in effect unless a constituency group proposed a revision. Concerned about the datedness of some of its policies, the association instituted a new process for the 1990 Delegate Assembly that was followed in the 1993 and 1996 Assemblies as well. Each Assembly reviews all the policy statements adopted six or more years earlier to determine whether each statement should be reconfirmed, eliminated, or referred for revision to the next Assembly. The revisions subsequently are screened by the Delegate Assembly Planning Committees and placed on the agenda by the NASW Board of Directors.

In 1993 the association also introduced hearing panels to improve the quality of debate on statements. Each hearing panel considered the policy statement in question in depth, listening to testimony from delegates and reworking statements in response to the debate on substantive issues. Altogether in 1996, 20 statements (13 revisions and seven new statements) were considered in hearing panels. The 1996 Delegate Assembly subsequently approved all 20 statements.

Recognizing that the policy statements are used extensively in schools of social work, the association has encouraged a scholarly approach to writing the statements and has emphasized the need for appropriate documentation of facts and ideas in the background and issue statement sections. The 1996 Delegate Assembly Planning Committee extensively revised the instructions for the development of policy statements and worked directly with teams of authors on revisions to ensure the usefulness and quality of each new statement. Policy statements, they noted, should be NASW's statement of policy about social issues, not practice guidelines or calls to action. Further, the statements should be easily accessible, in terms of language and organization, to social workers and policymakers.

ORGANIZATION OF THE BOOK

Social Work Speaks, 4th Edition contains 66 statements, 20 approved by the 1996 Delegate Assembly and 46 approved by previous assemblies. They are offered in strictly alphabetical order to make finding a specific policy easier. However, to assist readers who seek policy statements in related areas, NASW has added a new feature. Immediately following the table of contents is a compilation of topic areas that lists policy statements in 16 topic areas. We hope that these guides will add to the usefulness of the book. Although most of the policies address broad issues of public concern, a few, such as the Adjudication and Declassification statements, pertain to intraprofessional issues.

In general, policy statements include four components: background, issue statement, policy statement, and references. At the end of each statement, readers will find a complete legislative history. For example, the Foster Care and Adoption statement includes the following: "Policy statement approved by the NASW Delegate Assembly, November 1987; reconfirmed by the Delegate Assembly, August 1993. This statement supersedes the policy statement on Foster Care and Adoption approved by the Delegate Assembly in 1979."

ASSOCIATION IMPLEMENTATION

NASW relies on these policy statements to guide policy advocacy and legal action. Over the past several years, the association has substantially increased its presence in federal and state debate on policy issues and has expanded its scope from acting almost solely in the legislative arena to active outreach to the executive and judicial branches. In addition, NASW has expanded its role in developing social work alliances such as the Action Network for Social Work Education and Research (ANSWER), which comprises the Baccalaureate Program Directors, the Council on Social Work Education, the Group for the Advancement of Social Work Education, the National Association of Deans and Directors, and the National Association of Social Workers.

Policy Advocacy

Before taking a position on legislation or action with the federal executive branch, the NASW national office compares the proposed policy with policies in *Social Work Speaks*. If the proposed legislation or regulation is consistent with the thrust of an NASW policy statement or if it contradicts an NASW policy, NASW's position will be readily apparent. However, in many cases federal proposals contain some provisions that support NASW's policy and some that are inconsistent with or only partially support NASW recommendations. In these cases, there is no easy decision. NASW considers all the factors, weighing the potential for revising the proposed legislation or regulation, the overall value of possible policy gains, political concerns, and other variables before deciding which course of action to take.

NASW chapters also use *Social Work Speaks* to guide action at the state level. When chapters are considering whether they should take action on state or local policy matters or join in coalition activity, they review the relevant NASW policy statement to ensure that their actions are in congruence with NASW policy.

The NASW national office and state chapters work closely together to ensure that NASW is heard as one voice. The national office coordinates advocacy efforts at the national, chapter, unit, and member levels with Congress and the federal executive branch. Action may include endorsements for or opposition to a bill before Congress, letters to Congress requesting action on a bill, or participation in coalition actions for or against legislation, as well as a wide variety of communications with the president and federal agencies.

Legal Action

NASW also initiates or participates in a number of *amicus curiae* (friend-of-the-court) briefs on critical social and professional issues. For example, NASW was a major participant in the *Jaffee v. Redmond* Supreme Court case in 1996, which determined the right of confidentiality for social work services. In deciding which briefs to submit or join at the federal or state level, NASW looks to policy statements for guidance.

POLICY STATEMENT AND ANALYSIS

As an articulation of what one Delegate Assembly viewed as an ideal policy, individual statements are useful for analysis and review. They are excellent resources for classroom discussion and debate, and they can be used to raise questions such as the following:

■ What important issues have practitioners raised in the subject area?

■ Are the issues ones I deem critical?

■ In my opinion, are there major issues that were not considered?

■ Do I concur with NASW's policy stance?

■ What documentation did NASW provide for the conclusions?

■ On what course work, research, other readings, or practice experience have I based my stance?

■ How do the positions compare with the public positions of other groups and organizations on the same subject?

■ How might the statements be amended?

■ What purposes might the statements serve?

Social Work Speaks may be used as a text or as supplementary reading for overview, introductory, or macro courses in social policy. The book may also serve as an adjunct to a wide range of specialty courses, as so many of the policy statements address specific fields of practice.

For lobbying or analysis, policy statements should be considered in the context of their purpose and the time in which they were adopted, keeping in mind that each policy statement is the product of a specific Delegate Assembly. Social workers developed the statements to serve as broad parameters for advocacy work and to help professionals who are concerned with social issues focus their thinking. As NASW has systematically reviewed and revised statements, they have become increasingly useful. Nonetheless, because of the breadth of issues and the constantly emerging new information, readers may find that they need more specificity than the statements contain. Contemporary professional literature will serve as an important extension of the policy statements, and NASW national and chapter offices may also provide updated information in many areas.

As readers use these statements, they may also want to consider new statements that could be presented to the 1999 Delegate Assembly. Whether you are involved in policy analysis, advocacy for social policies, or the formulation of future policy statements, we hope that you will find *Social Work Speaks, 4th Edition* useful in your professional work.

Jay J. Cayner, ACSW, LISW
President, NASW

Josephine Nieves, MSW, PhD
Executive Director, NASW

PUBLIC AND PROFESSIONAL POLICY STATEMENTS

Abortion

BACKGROUND

In acknowledging and affirming the profession's commitment to respecting diverse value systems in a pluralistic society, it is recognized that the issue of abortion is controversial because it reflects the different value systems of different groups. Consequently, the National Association of Social Workers (NASW) does not take a position concerning the morality or immorality of abortion.

POLICY STATEMENT

The profession's position concerning abortion services is based on the principle of self-determination. Every individual (within the context of his or her value system) must be free to participate or not participate in abortion services. Women should have the right to participate in or refrain from abortion counseling.

In the event that a woman chooses to consider abortion, the following services should be available to her:

■ counseling and referral of patients provided by professionally trained staff who are knowledgeable of the social and psychological dynamics of unwanted pregnancy and abortion

■ safe surgical care, including pre- and postoperative services

■ counseling regarding the use of contraception and the prevention of further unwanted pregnancies

■ provision of appropriate contraceptive devices. These devices should be available to all women.

Every effort should be made to extend all options and support services (for example, pre- and postabortion counseling, postnatal counseling, counseling for single parents, and adoption counseling) to women at all economic levels and to ensure their availability to those women who wish to keep their child, place the child for adoption, or choose other alternatives. In states where abortion services are not available, as one option, those members of NASW who so desire may work toward the legalization, planning, funding, and implementation of such services.

If a social worker chooses not to participate in abortion counseling, it is his or her responsibility to provide appropriate referral services to ensure that this option is available to clients. In addition, the profession supports the development of public education and information services designed to inform people about the current legal, medical, and social aspects of abortion. A system also should be established for listing the services that are available.

Policy statement approved by the NASW Delegate Assembly, 1975; reconfirmed by the Delegate Assembly, August 1990. Referred to the 1999 Delegate Assembly, to be combined with the policy statement on Family Planning and renamed Family Planning and Reproductive Choices. For further information, contact the National Association of Social Workers, 750 First Street, NE, Suite 700, Washington, DC 20002-4241. Telephone: 202-408-8600 or 800-638-8799.

Adjudication

BACKGROUND

In reflecting on the philosophical base of the adjudication process for the violation of personnel standards, it is necessary to consider social workers' perception of their profession. As the profession has evolved and matured, its knowledge base, which encompasses the parameters of the person-in-situation paradigm, has been explicitly and more specifically defined. Similarly, its humanistic value base has been elaborated. Development of the person-in-group and person-in-community as an analytic perspective as well as social justice (viewed as necessary to this development) are central value orientations. Such values require social workers to take into serious account the structures, processes, and institutions that make up the social milieu. This value base has been operationalized in the *NASW Code of Ethics* (NASW, 1993), the accepted conceptual standards of professional behavior.

Social workers are committed to a fourfold set of covenant relationships with the community, the client, NASW, and the agency or employing organization. Competent services are an expression of the purposes of the profession. Because service delivery can be compromised seriously by unjust personnel practices, NASW's involvement in personnel practices is grounded in the nature of the profession. Models of personnel practices are thus a reflection of our perception of the profession and its role in society.

Social work is concerned with systems' interactions, that is, the person with the environment. Social work organizations necessarily have a special concern for the social worker, as well as the client, although this responsibility is moral rather than legal. Likewise a social worker has responsibilities to his or her employing organization. As stated in the *NASW Code of Ethics*

(VI, P6): "The social worker should advocate changes in policy and legislation to improve social conditions and to promote social justice" (p. 10). Also, the *Code* states (IV, L1): "The social worker should work to improve the employing agency's policies and procedures, and the efficiency and effectiveness of its services" (p. 8).

The social work perspective emphasizes mutuality, interdependence, and integration. Models of collaboration are applied to negotiate and confront conflict situations. Using the principle of least conflict to resolve differences, social workers would choose education, consultation, negotiation, and advocacy models, in that order. The latter model would be engaged when others were inappropriate or failed.

The *NASW Chapter Guide for Adjudication of Grievances* (NASW, 1989a) explicitly grounds the basis of personnel standards complaints in the authority of the profession. From this authority flow the rights and obligations to the community—the right for NASW to carry out purposes, to preserve integrity and credibility, and the obligation to carry out these purposes competently. To carry out these purposes, the services of the profession must be carried out by competent staff, and staff must work under conditions of employment that are conducive to maintaining and enhancing high-quality performance.

NASW Standards for Social Work Personnel Practices (NASW, 1989b) state that personnel standards

are based on the principles that (1) effective social service depends on qualified staff and (2) staff members can give their best service when they work under conditions of employment that are conducive to the maintenance of high quality and quantity of performance. Since the provision of responsible services to individuals, groups, and communities is the paramount concern of the social work profession, these standards are issued with the understanding that they will always be applied within this fundamental concern of the profession.

These standards describe competent services. One might hold that any set of standards should have a threefold focus: (1) competent service, (2) the integrity and credibility of the profession, and (3) the protection of the profession. (This focus is explicit in the *NASW Procedures for the Adjudication of Grievances* [NASW, 1988].) NASW recognizes that these standards are not based on legal authority, but because the profession has moral force, it therefore has moral responsibility in this area.

ISSUE STATEMENT

Because NASW is an association of individual members and not of employing organizations, it therefore has no jurisdiction over agency employers. Central questions include the following: What model of protection is appropriate for the profession and congruent with its nature? How does NASW implement its duty? What should be the nature of interprofessional relationships?

Initial discussions of problems with the personnel standards grievance procedure surfaced at the 1984 Leadership Meeting. Several chapter leaders informally expressed strong sentiment that change was needed urgently. As a result, the California chapter volunteered to prepare a statement of concerns, which was forwarded to NASW's president in May 1984. President Stewart requested a review of the statement by the National Committee on Inquiry (NCOI), whose chairperson presented a statement that detailed and integrated those concerns and others of NCOI to the board in June 1984. At that meeting, the board instructed the president to appoint a board task force to study the questions raised and to report to the board the recommended action in June 1985. The task force, chaired by then-President-elect Dorothy Harris, met at each

of the 1984–85 board meetings and concluded that a substantial problem existed and that an association-wide task force should be appointed to examine comprehensively the nature and extent of the identified problems and prepare recommended changes. Any policy revisions were to be ready for consideration by the board in time for presentation to the 1987 Delegate Assembly. The board adopted the task force report in June 1985 and instructed that such a new, broad-based task force be appointed.

The earlier task force appointed to study issues of adjudication posed the following six questions:

1. Do the current procedures achieve their stated purpose? (The intent of grievances regarding personnel standards is to promote the observance of professional standards in the employment of social workers and thereby to protect the quality of services to clients.)

2. Do members receive the protection sought for them as individual claimants through the current policies?

3. What moral or social power or responsibility does NASW have to effect the purposes of the policies? What is the effect of imposing sanctions?

4. What legal grounds does NASW have to adjudicate these matters, and what legal vulnerability does adjudication expose NASW to?

5. Has the external, societal situation changed with regard to laws governing personnel practices or the existence of alternative mechanisms for aggrieved social workers to use in pursuing their complaints?

6. Are there alternative strategies that might be effective in working toward the same ends?

Two research projects were undertaken to address the issues. A content analysis of case records on personnel standards from 1980 through 1986 yielded the following:

■ The largest number of filed complaints were concerned with violations of agencies' stated personnel procedures regarding discharge from employment without reason or due process, or both.

- The most important barrier to fact finding in the course of adjudication was the respondent's refusal to cooperate.

- The revision of agencies' personnel practices was the most frequently cited recommendation.

- Satisfaction with the adjudication process (in 25 cases) was noted by 10 complainants and three respondents. Dissatisfaction was noted by seven complainants and six respondents.

- Ten cases were decided in favor of the complainant and three in favor of the respondent; nine were unresolved as "pending," "suspended," or "withdrawn."

- Among the surveyed cases, which noted change as a result of adjudication, three-quarters indicated favorable outcomes and one-quarter indicated no apparent influence.

Responses to a task force-initiated survey of chapter presidents, chairs of chapter Committees on Inquiry, and executive directors yielded the following information:

- The general attitudes of chapter members toward adjudication in personnel standards grievances were 29.3 percent negative, 17.0 percent neutral, 48.8 percent positive, and 4.9 percent very positive. The attitudes among the three groups of respondents were not notably different.

- Of all respondents, 24.5 percent found that the procedures unequivocally accomplished the intended goal; 69.5 percent answered positively to some extent. The percentage of all respondents who perceived that the procedure had a positive effect on NASW's working relationship with agencies is equal to those who perceived it as negative. Most believed that it has no effect.

Because NASW is a voluntary association whose members freely affiliate and accept the *NASW Code of Ethics* as developed by NASW, members have rights to be protected as well as duties to fulfill these obligations. The organization also has a right to become involved in areas of concern to the members and the profession and an obligation to protect its members and become involved in areas that impede the performance of social workers. NASW clearly has the right to inquire into the conduct of its membership in areas of professional performance, which embraces personnel practices. NASW also would be involved collegially with non-social workers in carrying out its responsibilities. Moral responsibility and legal responsibility need to be differentiated carefully. NASW is clear on the nature of its duty. The question that arises is: What models are appropriate for the profession and are congruent with its nature in carrying out this responsibility on behalf of its members?

POLICY STATEMENT

In keeping with its purpose "to promote the quality and effectiveness of social work practice in the United States of America," under conditions of nondiscrimination, with respect to race, color, creed, or national origin, in personnel practices and in the provision of services, the National Association of Social Workers (NASW) has the responsibility to study and adjudicate complaints of alleged practices detrimental to this purpose and to do the following:

- educate the NASW membership, the agency leadership, and the larger professional community about standards of ethical professional practice and fair personnel practices

- ensure the responsible use of facts in making judgments about the actions of agencies or individuals

- protect its members against exploitation and injustice

- promote sound and equitable personnel administration

- protect the agencies and the public from unethical practice by social workers

- discipline its members when unethical conduct is found to exist.

To fulfill this obligation, NASW has developed adjudication procedures governing the handling of grievances resulting from alleged violations of social work personnel practices or the *NASW Code of Ethics* and alleged instances of penalties imposed as a consequence of social or political action. These procedures shall consistently be designed to do the following:

- make the NASW chapter the initial unit of the association to receive and act on a complaint

- provide an opportunity for prospective parties to an adjudication to confer with a chapter-appointed consultant who also is a member of NASW for the purposes of exploring alternative resolutions, mediating the differences, or preparing a complaint

- provide for reasonable promptness in filing and adjudicating complaints for the protection of the parties to a complaint

- ensure objective, factual, and confidential consideration of the situation under adjudication

- permit both parties to a complaint to be heard and to defend their positions

- provide for judicious handling of appeals from chapter decisions to the NASW National Committee on Inquiry (NCOI) and final appeal to the Board of Directors

- make possible the waiver of chapter jurisdiction and referral of a case to NCOI in either one of two instances: when the chapter (1) chooses to disqualify itself or (2) fails to comply with the stipulated time limits for acting on a complaint.

Revisions in procedures growing out of the experience of the association shall meet the criteria stated previously. They shall be made by the Board of Directors on recommendation of NCOI with the approval of the Cabinet of the Division of Professional Standards.

Any member or group of members may initiate revision of the procedures by submitting suggestions to NCOI. The committee may circulate to the chapters and other groups revisions that it suggests and may ask for reactions and suggestions before making its recommendations to the division cabinet and Board of Directors. NCOI shall report to the membership annually on its work.

REFERENCES

National Association of Social Workers. (1988). *NASW procedures for the adjudication of grievances* (rev. ed.). Silver Spring, MD: Author.

National Association of Social Workers. (1989a). *NASW chapter guide for the adjudication of grievances* (rev. ed.). Silver Spring, MD: Author.

National Association of Social Workers. (1989b). *NASW standards for social work personnel practices* (rev. ed.). Silver Spring, MD: Author.

National Association of Social Workers. (1993). *NASW code of ethics.* Washington, DC: Author.

Policy statement approved by the NASW Delegate Assembly, November 1987; reconfirmed by the Delegate Assembly, August 1993. For further information, contact the National Association of Social Workers, 750 First Street, NE, Suite 700, Washington, DC 20002-4241. Telephone: 202-408-8600 or 800-638-8799.

Adolescent Pregnancy

BACKGROUND

More than 1 million teenage girls ages 10 to 19 years become pregnant, and approximately 517,000 give birth annually (Ventura, 1991). Ventura (1991) found that 67 percent of those giving birth were unmarried. Pregnancy rates of nonwhite adolescents exceed those of white adolescents, although pregnancy rates for white adolescents have been increasing faster than those of nonwhite adolescents (Office of Technology Assessment, 1991). Most young mothers who give birth decide to parent their babies rather than release them for adoption (Hayes, 1987).

Adolescent pregnancy and parenthood are both a cause and a consequence of school dropout. Recent studies have documented that pregnancy continues to be a significant determinant of high school graduation for adolescents age 17 years and younger. In 1986, 50 percent of young women with a first birth at age 17 years or younger graduated from high school; of those who did not give birth, 88 percent graduated (Upchurch & McCarthy, 1989). Graduation rates for younger adolescents who become pregnant were less than 50 percent. Although there are fewer data available concerning adolescent fathers, extant studies demonstrated that early parenthood limits opportunities to complete high school and obtain job skills (Card & Wise, 1978; Smollar & Ooms, 1987).

School dropout and a lack of requisite employment skills are commonly recognized as factors contributing to risk of welfare dependence. Nationally, 71 percent of mothers younger than 30 years receiving Aid to Families with Dependent Children (AFDC) began their childbearing as teenagers, compared with 37 percent of all mothers in the same age group (Children's Defense Fund, 1987). The poverty of teenage parents extends to their children who compose an increasing share of the one in five children living in poverty in the United States (Children's Defense Fund, 1989). Although recent studies have documented that, over time, women who began their childbearing as adolescents were employed and socially secure, their incomes were significantly lower than women whose childbearing began after completion of high school (Furstenberg, Brooks-Gunn, & Morgan, 1987).

Low birthweight is the principal threat to the survival and later good health of infants born to adolescents. Adolescent mothers are more likely to have a low-birthweight (under 5.5 pounds) infant than mothers ages 20–24 years (Ventura, 1991). Adolescents younger than age 15 years and black adolescents give birth more often to low-birthweight infants than do other adolescents. Other factors associated with low birthweight include socioeconomic status, lack of early and continuous prenatal care, poor nutrition, smoking, alcohol use, and poor maternal health.

Many adolescent parents lack maturity, understanding, and knowledge of child growth and development necessary to parent their children successfully. These deficits sometimes result in an increased risk of abuse and neglect or developmental delays to infants in these young families. Without systems of support the physical, cognitive, and psychosocial growth of the children born to teenage mothers may be jeopardized.

Comparisons of teenage pregnancy rates in the United States with those in other industrialized nations show that adolescent pregnancy is not an inevitable consequence of increased adolescent sexual activity (Jones et al., 1985). Instead, high teenage pregnancy rates stem from a lack of policies and programs to address adolescent sexual activity and social and economic conditions that contribute to the risk of pregnancy. Reducing adolescent pregnancy requires an investment in child, adolescent, and family services that bolster teenagers' motivation to prevent early sexual activity, as well as increase their capacity to do so (Children's Defense Fund, 1986). NASW supports the adoption of a policy that will address the complex factors that contribute to adolescent pregnancy.

ISSUE STATEMENT

Adolescent pregnancy is part of a complex web of social, health, and economic problems experienced by individuals and families in the United States. The issue has been linked through research to biological and developmental factors, such as earlier onset of puberty, and to social and economic factors, such as poverty; changing social values; changing patterns of family formation and composition; racism; sexual abuse; and access to health care, social services, and education. Although policymakers at the state and national levels generally agree that out-of-wedlock pregnancy during adolescence is undesirable, no specific national policy has been formulated and implemented to reduce pregnancy rates. Concurrently there has been considerable advocacy to reduce teenagers' access to abortion. Furthermore, progress is slow in reducing and eliminating poverty, family stress and dysfunction, family isolation, and poor health—all conditions that increase the risk of adolescent pregnancy.

Inherent in the issue of adolescent pregnancy are access to and availability of education and services to prevent pregnancy, access to abortion services, and access to and availability of health care and social services to strengthen and support adolescents who give birth.

POLICY STATEMENT

Pregnancy Prevention

To prevent adolescent pregnancy, young people and their families need access to a range of services that begin long before children reach puberty. Parents need information about child growth and development, education on psychosocial and physiological aspects of adolescent development, and guidance and support in communicating to their children age-appropriate sexuality information and family values concerning sexuality.

Youths need access to a range of services that include age-appropriate sex education, preferably not later than the middle grades; family life education; and programs that build youths' capacity to make decisions and plan for the future. Adolescent health care should be comprehensive with a range of services that promote physical and mental wellness. Adolescents need easy and confidential access to reproductive health care services that include pregnancy testing, birth control, screening and treatment for sexually transmitted diseases, reproductive health education, and information and referral to agencies that provide abortion options counseling and abortion services. All services provided to adolescent clients must respect their need for and right to maintain confidentiality, to participate in decision making, and to have complete information concerning their treatment or service options. Whenever possible parents should be involved, and adolescents must be given the support necessary to involve parents. When parental involvement is unrealistic or is counter to the health and safety of adolescents, then nonparental mentoring should be provided.

Pregnancy and Parenting

Adolescents and their families should have access to a range of social and health services as soon as possible after pregnancy is suspected and confirmed. Essential services include case management, pregnancy options counseling, family counseling, adoption counseling, prenatal care, and postpartum follow-up and support. Adolescents who choose to parent need a range of services to help them complete the developmental tasks of adolescence while assuming the adult responsibilities required to care for themselves and their children. These services depend on extant family support, availability of financial resources, and the adolescent's cognitive development. Such services include, but are not limited to, parenting skills training, relationship counseling and mediation, counseling and support services to continue or return to school or complete a general equivalency diploma, AFDC or other financial aid, employment training and placement, health care for young parents and their babies, family planning, ongoing education and information about child growth and development, legal aid, housing, transportation, and education and support in life skills and decision making. Services should be school based and also should be provided in community agencies and centers that are used by young people.

Multidisciplinary Approach

A pregnant and parenting adolescent benefits from a multidisciplinary approach that uses the skills and perspectives of the social work, health care, education, and psychology professions. Volunteer and peer counseling services may also contribute to ameliorating the negative consequences of early pregnancy and parenting. However, assessment, planning, counseling, monitoring, and evaluation services provided by professional social workers who practice in social agencies, schools, health settings, or independent private practice are often the core of interventions that mobilize and support pregnant and parenting adolescents. These services, provided as long as needed, help young parents to cope with the immediacy of parenthood while they gain the competence to manage the future successfully for themselves and their children.

Outreach

Many barriers to adolescents' access to services exist. A primary barrier is the adolescents' inexperience. Other barriers are embarrassment, fear, lack of awareness of services, and reluctance to seek assistance. Adolescents often are powerless in an adult-oriented social services and health care system that views them as dependent and legally unable to act on their own behalf. Outreach is essential to ensure access for adolescents in need of the range of services from pregnancy prevention to parenting support. Social workers must advocate for outreach as a component of any program of service to this vulnerable population and their families.

Legislation

Adolescents and children are powerless in a political process that is predicated on the influence of an electorate. Parents of the most vulnerable children and youths often lack the time, skills, and sophistication to advocate on behalf of their children. Social workers have professional expertise with an insight into the individual, family, and societal complexities that contribute to the prevalence of adolescent pregnancy. Social workers can use their professional skills to empower these families and adolescents to advocate for needed programs and services. Social workers also can and should take a leadership role in speaking on behalf of pregnant and parenting adolescents and those adolescents who are at risk of becoming pregnant or parents too soon. Action is required at the local, state, and national levels to ensure legislation, policies, and programs that enable adolescents to obtain information, education, and services that reduce their risk of early pregnancy and provide the full range of options, including safe and legal abortion when pregnancy occurs. NASW urges the adoption of the following:

■ national economic and social policies that end poverty and set a standard of living sufficient to support families

■ access to health care that respects and responds to the developmental issues of adolescents and includes early periodic screening, diagnosis, and testing; mental health treatment; wellness programs, including smoking cessation and substance abuse prevention and treatment; nutrition and weight control; and reproductive health care that includes pregnancy prevention

■ early prevention programs that acknowledge and address the multiple problems of youths, such as child sexual abuse, school failure and dropout, delinquency, and substance abuse

■ age-appropriate sexuality education and family life education for youths, beginning in the early grades, as well as training and education for teachers and parents to help them competently provide sexuality education and family life education

■ access for adolescents to specific early comprehensive prenatal care, medical case management, postpartum follow-up, and reproductive health care, including family planning

■ adherence to federal statutes and guidelines (Title IX of the National Education Act) that protect pregnant and parenting adolescents from discrimination in the public schools, denial of access to education, and exclusion from participation in school activities because of pregnancy or parenting

■ programs and services that provide parenting skills, training, and ongoing support to help adolescent parents develop confidence and competence to care for and nurture their children

■ access to legal services that assist adolescent mothers and fathers with paternity, adoption, child support, custody, care, and control of their children

■ school-based, community-linked services such as child care, case management, parenting skills training, family counseling, information and referral, health care, and career planning that support and assist pregnant and parenting adolescents to remain in or return to school

■ family counseling, mediation, and support services when appropriate for young fathers of babies born to adolescent mothers.

REFERENCES

Card, J. J., & Wise, L. (1978). Teenage mothers and teenage fathers: The impact of early childbearing on the parents' personal and professional lives. *Family Planning Perspectives, 10*(4), 199–205.

Children's Defense Fund. (1986). *Adolescent pregnancy: Whose problem is it?* Washington, DC: Author.

Children's Defense Fund. (1987). *Adolescent pregnancy: An anatomy of a social problem in search of comprehensive solutions.* Washington, DC: Author.

Children's Defense Fund. (1989). *A vision for America's future.* Washington, DC: Author.

Furstenberg, Jr., F. F., Brooks-Gunn, J., & Morgan, S. P. (1987). Adolescent mothers and their children in later life. *Family Planning Perspectives, 19*(4), 142–151.

Hayes, C. D. (Ed.). (1987). *Risking the future: Adolescent sexuality, pregnancy and childbearing* (Vol. 1). Washington, DC: National Research Council.

Jones, E. F., Forrest, J. D., Goldman, N., Kenshaw, S. K., Lincoln, R., Rosoff, J. I., Westoff, C. F., & Wulf, D. (1985). Teenage pregnancy in developed countries: Determinants and policy implications. *Family Planning Perspectives, 17*(2), 53–63.

Office of Technology Assessment. (1991). *Adolescent health: Summary and policy options, Volume 1.* Washington, DC: U.S. Government Printing Office.

Smollar, J., & Ooms, T. (1987). *Young unwed fathers: Research review, policy dilemmas and options.* Washington, DC: Catholic University of America.

Upchurch, D. M., & McCarthy, J. (1989). Adolescent childbearing and high school completion in the 1980's: Have things changed? *Family Planning Perspectives, 21*(5), 199–202.

Ventura, S. J. (1991). Advance report of final natality statistics, 1989 (Suppl.). *Monthly Vital Statistics Report, 40*(8).

Policy statement approved by the Delegate Assembly, August 1993. This policy statement supersedes the policy statement on Adolescent Pregnancy approved by the Delegate Assembly in 1984. For further information, contact the National Association of Social Workers, 750 First Street, NE, Suite 700, Washington, DC 20002-4241. Telephone: 202-408-8600 or 800-638-8799.

Affirmative Action

BACKGROUND

The concept of affirmative action in this country can be traced to the passage of the Civil War amendments to the U.S. Constitution (Thirteenth, Fourteenth, and Fifteenth Amendments). The Freedman's Bureau Bill of 1865 created a system for the distribution of provisions, clothing, and land for lease or sale specifically to the descendants of slaves. It was argued that such measures were needed not because of race but because the beneficiaries were men who for generations had been deprived of their rights (U.S. Commission on Civil Rights, 1995). Since that time, affirmative action plans and policies have emerged in a variety of contexts to assist historically disadvantaged racial and ethnic groups and women.

Affirmative Action in Employment

In employment, affirmative action programs encourage recruitment and outreach efforts to include qualified women and people of color in the talent pool when hiring decisions are made and training programs to give all employees a fair chance for promotions. In some cases, flexible goals and timetables are used as benchmarks by which to measure progress toward eliminating severe underrepresentation of qualified women and people of color in specific job categories (National Women's Law Center, 1995).

Title VII of the Civil Rights Act of 1964 requires both public and private employers in traditionally segregated job categories to support the establishment of voluntary affirmative action plans. It further requires that the plans be flexible in application and temporary in duration.

Employment issues have been further addressed through legislation, court interpretations, and executive orders. Executive Order No. 11246 (1964–1965) consolidated and extended to women earlier executive orders barring employment discrimination by federal contractors and subcontractors and the construction industry.

Despite affirmative action regulations and laws against discrimination, disparity in rates of employment and earnings continues. Pay inequities between women and men are commonplace.

Affirmative Action in Education

Brown v. Board of Education I (1954) eliminated the separate but equal clause from *Plessy v. Ferguson* (1896) and mandated that all schools be desegregated with all deliberate speed. The federal government, President Eisenhower in Little Rock, and President Kennedy in Mississippi enforced this ruling with the aid of federal troops. President Johnson's executive order for affirmative action further expanded educational opportunity for women and people of color.

By 1975 the proportions of African Americans and white people attending college were nearly equal. However, these gains were lost by 1986 as evidenced in Illinois, New York, and Mississippi, where 89 percent of African American children attended segregated schools. Clearly, the playing field is not level, and affirmative action continues to be needed in education.

Affirmative Action in Housing

The federal government has a long history of involvement in affirmative action in housing. Executive Order No. 11063, issued by President Kennedy in 1962, acknowledged that discriminatory policies and practices in housing produce other forms of discrimination and segregation. The order directed all federal agencies to prevent discrimination based on race, color, creed, or national origin in the disposition of property, including sales, leasing, or rental and in the lending practices of institutions with moneys insured or guaranteed by the federal government.

The Fair Housing Act of 1968 and the amendments of 1988 addressed housing discrimination and provided a basis for affirmative action policies in housing. The Housing and Community Development Act of 1974, amended in 1981, required affirmative efforts by states and localities receiving community development block grants to further fair housing practices. In January 1994, President Clinton issued Executive Order No. 12892, which retained the mandate to ensure fair housing and expanded President Kennedy's Executive Order No. 11063 to provide protection against discrimination in programs of federal insurance or guaranty to people with disabilities and to families with children.

Between 1970 and 1980 the number of African American suburbanites grew from 5.4 million to 8.2 million. Between 1986 and 1990, 73 percent of African American population growth occurred in the suburbs. However, organized efforts on the part of the federal government to eradicate housing discrimination clearly continue to be much needed. A 1991 study by the Department of Housing and Urban Development found that Hispanics were more likely to live in overcrowded housing and housing in disrepair. In 1993 the *Chicago Tribune* reported that African Americans are twice as likely to be denied mortgages as white people at the same economic level. Home Mortgage Disclosure Act data for 1990 "indicated that within each income category and for every type of loan, Hispanics were significantly less likely to receive loan approvals than non-Hispanic whites with similar income" (Cintron, 1995).

Affirmative Action in Contracting

Employment rules governing federal contractors and the Small Business Administration's Minority Enterprise Program have had some of the broadest impact of any federal affirmative action program (Savage, 1995). The Department of Labor's Office of Federal Contract Compliance Programs (OFCCP) requires contractors and subcontractors with 50 or more employees and $50,000 or more in federal contracts to develop and maintain affirmative action programs for people of color, women, and people with disabilities ("Supreme Court Ruling," 1995; U.S. Commission on Civil Rights, 1995).

An OFCCP study of 77,000 companies with more than 20 million employees showed that minority employment increased by 20 percent and female employment by 15 percent after the implementation of affirmative action plans (National Council of La Raza, 1995). Affirmative action programs in contracting have worked.

All of American society benefits from affirmative action. Despite the individualism characteristic of American society, attention to diverse, collective interests will determine its future.

ISSUE STATEMENT

The profession of social work is committed to equality and justice. NASW has always fought discrimination. Social work values, belief in the worth and dignity of each individual, history of practice, and advocacy on behalf of oppressed people require that social workers speak out at this critical juncture in our nation's history.

Although measurable gains have been made as a result of affirmative action, "color blind" policies cannot survive racist biases still prevalent in U.S. society. Affirmative action has been an effective tool in forcing changes in entrenched patterns of segregation and prejudice. It is best understood as a tool with which to create change. Proportional representation, numerical quotas, women and minority set-aside programs, and other efforts are tools that can be used to implement affirmative action.

The complexity of affirmative action regulations and practices and the problems they are designed to address often lead to affirmative action being misunderstood and misrepresented. Discussions of affirmative action regulations are often marred by fear of misuse, ignorance, and at times willful intent to preserve discrimination and prejudice. Social workers must clarify the facts, indicate that discrimination continues to be a problem, and unmask the myths and untruths that too often cloud the issues.

NASW has long recognized that people who are "different" have yet to achieve equal opportunity. NASW's affirmative action commitment was first made in 1973, when the Delegate Assembly instructed the Board of Directors to make a conscious effort to increase the representation of women, African Americans, Latinos, Asians and Pacific Islanders, American Indians, and Alaska Natives within the association. The 1975 Delegate Assembly mandated the development of an affirmative action plan. This plan was adopted by the national Board of Directors in June 1976, and an affirmative action officer was appointed. In February 1977 the Board of Directors adopted the chapter section of the plan and total program goals and established a three-year timetable for implementation. In April 1980 NASW adopted affirmative action as a permanent program, amended it to increase women's representation from 50 percent to proportional representation matching their percentage in the membership, and established goals for women and people of color in NASW's elected bodies. NASW's affirmative action plan has undergone several revisions since 1980 that have strengthened and reinforced the association's commitment.

The 1996 Delegate Assembly chose affirmative action as one of the four social policy priorities requiring aggressive action by NASW over the next three years. This formal policy statement declares NASW's commitment to affirmative action and enables social work practitioners to vigorously advance affirmative action programs. Although critics of affirmative action have questioned its effectiveness and even the continued existence of discrimination, social workers must not lose their way in this controversy. NASW stands in firm support of the mandated inclusions afforded by affirmative action.

POLICY STATEMENT

The intent of affirmative action is to correct the present effects of past discrimination and exclusion from opportunities (Myers, 1995) and to achieve future parity. Its purpose is to provide opportunities to a class of qualified individuals who have either historically or actually been denied opportunities and to prevent recurrence of discrimination (U.S. Commission on Civil Rights, 1977, 1981). Affirmative action has been effective in a broad spectrum of U.S. society's activities including, but not limited to, employment, education, housing, and federal contracting.

NASW supports affirmative action as a viable tool for upholding its ethical code to act to prevent and eliminate discrimination. NASW supports the following principles:

■ full endorsement of local, state, and federal policies and programs that give all people equal access to resources, services, and opportunities that they require—everyone should be given equal opportunity regardless of age, disability, gender, language, race, religion, or sexual orientation

■ social workers joining others to denounce attempts to end affirmative action initiatives

■ changes in affirmative action that will strengthen practice and policy aimed at ending discrimination and its impact

■ a firm commitment to protect the gains realized by affirmative action

■ working with others to develop more effective and cogent policies and strategies to guide society and communities to that end.

REFERENCES

Brown v. Board of Education I, 347 U.S. 483 (1954).

Brown v. Board of Education II, 349 U.S. 294 (1955).

Cintron, D. (1995, Fall). Hispanic's housing conditions: Poor participation in federal housing programs. *Fair Housing Report,* p. 12.

Civil Rights Act of 1964, P.L. 88-352, 78 Stat. 241.

Fair Housing Act of 1968, P.L. 90-284, 82 Stat. 81.

Fair Housing Act Amendments of 1988, P.L. 100-430, 102 Stat. 1619.

Freedman's Bureau Bill, 13 Stat. 507 (1865).

Hacker, (1992). (Complete ref.)

Housing and Community Development Act of 1974, P.L. 93-383, 88 Stat. 633.

Housing and Community Development Act Amendments of 1981, P.L. 98-181, 97 Stat. 1164.

Myers, S. L., Jr. (1995, July/August). Equity, fairness, and race relations. *Emerge, 6,* 48–52.

National Council of La Raza. (1995). *Fact sheet on affirmative action and Latinos*. Washington, DC: Author.

National Women's Law Center. (1995). *Affirmative action and what it means for women*. Washington, DC: Author.

Plessy v. Ferguson, 163 U.S. 537 (1896).

Savage, D. (1995, April 2). Plan to boost firms owned by minorities is assailed. *Los Angeles Times*, pp. A14, A19.

Supreme Court ruling imperils U.S. programs of racial preference. (1995, June 13). *Wall Street Journal*, pp. A1, A10.

U.S. Commission on Civil Rights. (1977). *Statement on affirmative action* (Clearinghouse Publication No. 54). Washington, DC: Author.

U.S. Commission on Civil Rights. (1981). *Affirmative action in the 1980s: Dismantling the process of discrimination* (Clearinghouse Publication No. 70). Washington, DC: Author.

U.S. Commission on Civil Rights. (1995). *The legislative, executive and judicial development of affirmative action*. Washington, DC: Office of the General Counsel.

SUGGESTED READINGS

Adarand v. Pena, 16 F.3d 1537 (10th Cir. 1994), cert. granted, 115 S.Ct. 41 (1994).

Biskupic, J. (1995, June 13). Court toughens standard for federal affirmative action. *Washington Post*, pp. A1, A6.

City of Richmond v. J. A. Croson, 488 U.S. 469 (1989).

Civil Rights Act Amendments of 1988, P.L. 92-318, Title IX, 86 Stat. 375, 20 U.S.C. §§1681–1688.

Civil Rights Act of 1991, P.L. 102-166, 105 Stat. 1071.

Emergency School Aid Act of 1972, P.L. 92-318, 86 Stat. 354.

Fullilove v. Klutznick, 448 U.S. 448 (1980).

Gibelman, M., & Schervish, P. H. (1993). *Who we are*. Washington, DC: NASW Press.

Local 28, Sheet Metal Workers' International v. Equal Employment Opportunity Commission, 478 U.S. 421 (1986).

National Association for the Advancement of Colored People Legal Defense and Education Fund. (1995). *Fact sheet on discrimination and affirmative action*. Washington, DC: Author.

National Association of Social Workers. (1993). *NASW code of ethics*. Washington, DC: Author.

National Organization for Women Legal Defense and Education Fund. (1995, July 24). *Legal basics on affirmative action*. New York: Author.

Public Employment Works Act of 1977, P.L. 95-28, 9 Stat. 116 (codified as amended at 42 U.S.C. §§6701, 6705–6708, 6710 1988 & Supp. V 1993).

Regents of the University of California v. Bakke, 438 U.S. 265 (1978).

Rehabilitation Act of 1973, P.L. 93-112, 87 Stat. 355.

Small Business Investment Act of 1958, P.L. 85-699, 72 Stat. 689.

United States v. Paradise, 480 U.S. 149 (1987).

U.S. Department of Labor, Women's Bureau. (1993). *Women workers: Trends and issues*. Washington, DC: Author.

Yzaguirre, R. (1995, June 13). Statement of Raul Yzaguirre on Adarand Constructors, Inc. v. Pena [News Release]. *National Council of La Raza*, p. 1.

Policy statement approved by the NASW Delegate Assembly, August 1996. For further information, contact the National Association of Social Workers, 750 First Street, NE, Suite 700, Washington, DC 20002-4241. Telephone: 202-408-8600 or 800-638-8799.

Aging

BACKGROUND

NASW policy on aging is predicated on the following demographic and social characteristics and political and professional concerns.

Demographic Characteristics of Older People

Between 1900 and 1990, the percentage of the U.S. population aged 65 years and older increased from 4 percent to 13 percent (24 million). Among these older people, the 85-plus population is one of the fastest growing groups. In 1970, 0.7 percent (145,000) of the elderly population was over 85; by 2000, 1.4 percent (3.9 million) will be in this age group. The growth in this segment of older Americans has far-reaching implications for social and health policy. Older women outnumber older men three to two. This disparity, largely a result of women living longer than men, is expected to continue. Twenty-eight million elderly men and women are veterans, and the number of frail elderly veterans will increase fourfold by 2000. By 2030, the elderly will constitute at least 20 percent of the population, with the proportion of young and elderly people being almost equal. This phenomenon has been referred to as "squaring of the population pyramid." The increasing proportion of elderly people will have a significant impact on America's economic and social institutions.

Epidemiological data suggest that the aging of the population is an international phenomenon. Underdeveloped, or Third World, countries are also experiencing rapid rates of growth in their elderly populations, which are increasing three times faster than are the elderly populations in the "First World." These countries will be challenged to stretch meager resources to meet the needs of their elderly populations.

At birth, on the average, people of color have a shorter life expectancy than do white people. In some ethnic groups (African Americans, for example) there may be what has been termed an "ethnic crossover." Some research suggests that by age 65, black men and women will outlive white people. As the life expectancy of people of color increases, there will be more elderly people in these groups. To be a person of color is to be in double jeopardy, for there is less likelihood of survival into old age and a greater likelihood of becoming a crime victim or of having an impoverished existence in later years. For example, 33 percent of elderly blacks live below the poverty line.

Economic Characteristics of Older People

The interrelationship between economic security and the capacity to meet basic living needs, particularly among impaired elderly people, makes people of color, the very old (age 88 and older), and women especially vulnerable. Although the economic status of the elderly has improved since 1960 as a result of policy changes, the poverty rate for people aged 65 and older is still 14 percent (people of color have rates more than two times higher). This rate does not include the "hidden poor," the homeless elderly, and those living in nursing homes or with their families. In addition, a larger percentage of older people are just above the poverty line and thus at risk of poverty, often for the first time in their lives, because of the loss of income entailed by retirement, the inadequacy of private pension or social security benefits, the devastating consequences of the costs of health care and long-term care, or the loss of a spouse.

The median income of families headed by people aged 65 years or older is about two-thirds that of families headed by younger people. Such reduced income is not necessarily accompanied by a decreased need for food, housing, and health care, especially for elderly people who face inflation on a fixed income. Elderly people depend more heavily on social security than on any other source for their income.

Economic marginality is even more pronounced among elderly people who are women, who live alone, who are people of color, who live in rural areas, or who are older than age 75. It is also more pronounced for elderly people with chronic disabilities, who are mentally ill, or who have developmental disabilities. For example, women, particularly widows, constitute nearly 75 percent of the elderly poor. Of older people who are living alone, 43 percent are either poor or nearly poor. Among those older than age 85, nearly 40 percent are poor. The median income of older black and Hispanic men is about half that of white men age 65 and older, and the poverty rate is highest among minority women living alone. Of the population older than age 65, 11 percent receive some type of public assistance through Supplemental Security Income (SSI) or Medicaid.

Social Characteristics of Older People

Older adults are a heterogeneous group with a wide range of physical and mental capabilities, financial resources, and preferences. Many elderly people ages 65 to 75 are healthy, experienced people with time and energy to participate in volunteer or paid activities, although some of them need training and support to undertake these activities. However, as they age, older Americans often have needs and problems that are related to their living arrangements, economic conditions, and physical limitations. Nearly two-thirds of older people live with family members, but more than one-third live alone or with nonrelatives. Living alone is especially a problem for older women, who represent 77 percent of the elderly who do so.

The likelihood of living alone increases with age, and almost half those who are older than age 85 live alone. For some older people, living alone reflects their desire to remain independent and in their own homes. Unfortunately, this desire often is thwarted by the lack of adequate, affordable housing and in-home support services.

Although most older people live in their own households, most see a family member at least weekly. Despite myths that adult children have abandoned the elderly, families provide approximately 80 percent of the in-home care to those older than age 75 with chronic health problems. Often, younger and middle-aged family members, usually women, are forced to curtail or give up jobs to care for their elderly relatives. With the decline in the proportion of younger family members and the growth of four- and five-generation families, many family caregivers are themselves elderly, of low economic status, and in poor health. They frequently lack supports that would reduce the economic, physical, and emotional burdens they face from providing care. As the number of women in the work force continues to rise, the availability of caregivers may diminish.

Vulnerability of Older People

As a group, elderly people constitute one of the highest at-risk populations in the United States. Compared with younger people, the elderly are disproportionately vulnerable to chronic illness, functional disabilities, inadequate housing, crime, the loss of their spouses, and the loss of their social role. For example, of the top four chronic medical problems affecting the elderly, arthritis affects 500 out of 1,000 elderly people; hypertension, 400 out of 1,000; hearing problems, 300 out of 1,000; and heart problems, 300 out of 1,000. General use of medical care increases with age. Moreover, those within the overall population of people aged 75 years and older have extraordinary needs because frailty or functional disability frequently accompanies increasing age. For example, the proportion of elderly people who report difficulty with personal-care activities increases from 15 percent for those ages 65 to 69 to nearly 50 percent for those aged 85 years and older.

Elder abuse is now seen as being a major problem for the elderly. Although there is no unified definition of abuse, statistics indicate that there are 100,000 new cases of abuse each year. It is also suggested that only one out of six cases is reported. Some figures suggest that 500,000 to 1.5 million older people are abused or neglected.

There are other major health–mental health problems for the elderly. Five percent of the elderly abuse substances, mostly alcohol. Twenty-five percent of the suicides in the United States are by elderly people. Two to four million elderly people have a progressive dementia. Accidental death rates for the elderly are twice the rate of all other groups; each year 23,000 elderly people die as the result of accidents. The number one cause of accidents in the elderly is falls, 25 percent of accidents are caused by motor vehicles, and 10 percent are from burns. The elderly currently receive only 6 percent of the nation's mental health services.

Response of Society

This society has failed to address adequately the needs of older Americans. Some 95 percent of people older than age 65 now receive social security, SSI, or both, and Medicare and Medicaid help to pay for some acute health care costs, but many elderly people, when faced with the loss of a spouse or with chronic health problems, are unable to maintain an adequate standard of living. Although services have been made available to elderly people through the Social Services Block Grant (Title XX) of the Social Security Act (P.L. 89-73) and the Older Americans Act, they are often insufficient to meet the needs of many older people, particularly those who are most vulnerable in terms of their health, economic, and social status.

The problems and inadequacies of these well-intentioned benefits and services are well known. Funding is insufficient to serve adequately those who are in need. In some instances, a person's increase in benefits from one program eliminates his or her eligibility for other programs. Furthermore, older people frequently are unaware that they are eligible for certain benefits and services, and those who are nearly poor are often not poor enough to qualify for some finan-

cial benefits. Also, services are often fragmented and are not systematically coordinated.

The delivery of health care services to elderly people is also a concern. Health care dollar expenditures indicate that 13 percent of the elderly population utilize 30 percent of the health care dollars. Advances in medical technology have created ethical dilemmas related to who should live and for how long. There is also insensitivity to the social and psychosocial dimensions of illness. The development of long-term-care facilities has resulted in a dual system of care—institutionalization versus community-based care—without adequate funding for a continuum of care. Research has indicated that nursing home placement is based more on the characteristics of the family-caregiver system than on the characteristics of the patient. Although institutionalization affects only 25 percent of the over-80 population, it is often feared as an end to personal autonomy and to a meaningful social role.

ISSUE STATEMENT

The social work profession is challenged to respond to the needs of a growing and changing heterogeneous elderly population. Although the socioeconomic circumstances of the elderly have improved to the extent that they no longer constitute the poorest age group, a significant number of older people are at high risk, particularly the burgeoning over-80 population, single women, and minorities. Impairing chronic illness, inadequate income, and the loss of social supports are the greatest threats to these groups. In contrast is the growing number of able older people who, in the future, will be healthier and better educated than their predecessors. They are a resource to be tapped, and productive opportunities for them must be forged. Negative attitudes about aging by the professional and lay communities continue to have an unfavorable impact on both able and disabled elderly people. Unless aggressively counteracted, these attitudes will forestall the implementation of effective changes.

Although the importance of gerontological social work is increasingly acknowledged in the literature, the social work profession must recognize its unique contribution to improving the quality of life for older Americans. Identifying the strengths of elderly people; providing supports to enhance functioning; and viewing the whole person from a combined biological, psychological, and social perspective, within the context of the family and larger environment, are social work values with applicability for the elderly. Specifically, the social work profession, in its practice, research, planning, and social policy formulations, must address the following issues:

■ the urgency of developing and funding a coherent system of a long-term continuum of care that encompasses therapeutic, rehabilitative, and supportive goals in a variety of community and institutional settings

■ the need for social supports, including social services and housing, to maintain older people in their homes and communities

■ disparities among the older population in the distribution of and access to health and social services

■ disparities between the older and younger populations with regard to the provision of mental health services

■ the underutilization of the elderly as a resource to society

■ the need to educate the public, professionals, and service providers on attitudes toward aging

■ recognition of the mutuality of support now enjoyed by the multigenerational family and the need to provide supports that enhance this reciprocity

■ recognition of the cultural heterogeneity among the elderly population and the need to provide culturally appropriate services

■ broadening the work force of gerontologically trained social workers

■ recognition of the constructive role that can be played by retirees within the profession and the need for long-range planning to ensure the security and participation of the growing number of retired social workers.

POLICY STATEMENT

A first guiding principle in policy development should be recognition of the intergenerational stake in providing adequate support for all dependent populations, including disabled, impoverished, and isolated elderly people. Such a perspective recognizes the interdependence of generations across the life span. It also acknowledges the importance of intergenerational alliances in obtaining public support to benefit the most needy, regardless of age, as well as to institute preventive and early intervention strategies to forestall social, economic, and health problems for all age groups. For example, social workers must vigorously oppose strategies that are designed to pit one generation against another as a means of dealing with the national budget deficit. A second guiding principle is that all generations, including the elderly, should be afforded opportunities for vocational pursuits and personal growth.

Work Force Needs

There is a great need to invest in the training of social workers and to "train the trainers" on social work faculties. More opportunities must be provided for social workers trained in gerontology in state departments of aging and area agencies on aging and other related public and private entities.

Economic Security

As declared by the 1971 and 1981 White House Conferences on Aging, there should be a minimum standard of income for elderly people, based on the intermediate budget as developed by the Bureau of Labor Statistics. Although social security should be the universal basic system for providing retirement income, other programs of retirement should be encouraged and integrated with it. The "retirement test" for social security, which penalizes recipients who want to continue employment, should be liberalized for older people who need or wish to augment their incomes. Any proposed changes in the Older Americans Act or other programs to implement fees for service should protect the access of low-income and minority elderly people to free and low-cost services.

The government must work to ensure the integrity of public, private, and commercial systems of economic security for elderly Americans. Efforts should be made to examine the merits of increasing, on an actuarial basis, the social security payments of those who retire after age 65. Efforts must be aimed at eliminating the adverse effects of interactions among programs that often result in an overall loss of benefits to people who are receiving assistance from two or more government-financed programs with separate and different requirements for eligibility. Social workers must also be sensitive to economic-security issues related to pension reform. Company takeovers, bankruptcies, and a change in marital status must not be allowed to threaten lifelong benefits to which workers are entitled.

Social and Support Services

A continuum of social services should be available to older people to enhance the functioning of and provide support to a diverse population. Services should be available to meet the needs resulting from the normal aging process, including life care and retirement planning. In addition, a range of services should be available to help elderly people with the losses of work, income, spouse, or friends that they may face. Such services as job programs, volunteer opportunities, senior centers, and support groups should be available. Older people should have the opportunity to participate in the widest range of civic, educational, recreational, and cultural activities.

Older people who are isolated, lonely, depressed, frail, or physically disabled also will require a range of social and supportive services, including counseling, advocacy, case management, and outreach. Protective services are needed to ensure that older people who are vulnerable to victimization receive the support and assistance they need.

Both individual and group services should be available. Services also should be available to help family members of elderly people cope with the aging process. A broad range of services should be available to family caregivers, including respite care, support groups, and assistance with direct care.

Social workers should play a leadership role in planning and providing this broad range of social and supportive services. Programs should use informal helping networks, when possible. Multipurpose senior centers and day care centers should be maintained as focal points for services for the involvement of elderly people.

Rural Elderly People

Programs that address the special needs of elderly people in rural areas should be designed to fit their lifestyles. Because growing old in rural America presents unique problems in the design and delivery of services and outreach programs, broad service programs of income support, employment, housing, health care, legal and protective services, and transportation, among others, must be provided in ways that are compatible with rural conditions, patterns, and traditions.

Minority Elderly People

A special effort must be made to ensure that services to elderly people meet the needs of minority populations. Many minority elderly people are unable to gain access to the social service system because of linguistic and cultural barriers. Therefore, the system must be flexible and comprehensive enough to meet the social, cultural, and care needs of minority elderly people. Minority representation must be increased at all levels of the social service system, and programs must recognize and reflect differences in language, culture, and demographic and social characteristics so that minority elderly people are not systematically excluded from services. Furthermore, special efforts must be made to eliminate the extreme poverty levels of minority elderly people.

Employment and Retirement

Although federal law specifies that discrimination on the basis of age is illegal, many forms of discrimination limit the use of older people's talents, skills, and experience for the good of themselves and their communities. With the "squaring of the population pyramid," older people will represent a valuable pool of workers. Efforts should be made to better use the skills of older people as employees and volunteers. Training and employment programs must continue to address the needs of displaced homemakers—women who are too old to qualify for Aid to Families with Dependent Children but who do not yet qualify for social security. Compensation for elderly people who remain employed should be based on the prevalent community wage scale for comparable work. Benefit programs should allow for part-time jobs and volunteer jobs. Preretirement planning should be readily available to all employees. Special attention should be paid within the profession of social work to the needs of retired members of the National Association of Social Workers (NASW) and their full participation in the association's activities.

Health Care

An adequate system of health care for elderly people—going beyond Medicare, which is essentially a system of insurance for part of the cost of acute health care; catastrophic health insurance, which is limited to the cost of acute care; and Medicaid, which is a system of welfare medicine—must be developed as an integral part of a universal program of comprehensive health care available to all Americans. Such a comprehensive system should include full rehabilitative and preventive services, protection against overpayment, and funding for pharmaceuticals and prostheses. The vast resources of the Department of Veterans Affairs should be included as an integral part of the universal program.

Elderly people need to be informed about their rights and options regarding medical treatment. Social work, along with the other health care professions, must confront the ethical issues related to the use of life-sustaining medical technology.

Social work must develop clear policies related to euthanasia and must resist using chronological age as a criterion for withholding treatment. Support for the development of living wills will clarify individuals' wishes regarding the use of technology as a means to prolong life.

Long-Term Care

Social work must recognize that the long-term-care system cannot wait until society develops a comprehensive acute-care system. There is a critical need for long-term care that is available, affordable, and accessible in communities throughout the United States. Long-term care should encompass a continuum of care, including both institutional and community settings. The point of entry into the system must include a psychosocial assessment of the person, in which a professional social worker plays a major role and in which services and facilities are provided for those who are being screened. In assisting in the development of the continuum of care, the social worker must address the issues of maintenance of independence, self-determination, appropriate support systems, and the provision of adequate protective services. The goal is to develop and implement a long-term-care system that meets the needs of chronically impaired people, the majority of whom are elderly.

Older people should be sustained to the extent possible in their own environments. Thus, home health care, day programs, case management, and respite care must be available. Placement in an institution should be based on a person's need for health care, not on a simple calculation of costs. The quality of institutional care, when needed, must be maintained by adequate reimbursement and the regular review and monitoring of community-based board-and-care facilities, as well as the families of such people. All long-term care and health services, including hospice services, should include a prominent social work component to help elderly people and their families cope. The importance of family caregivers as providers of long-term care must be recognized through education and support services, family and medical leave for relatives who care for elderly people, and tax and other financial benefits.

Mental Health

The mental health needs of elderly people should receive attention that is proportionate to their number through a comprehensive health care system. Community-based facilities must provide elderly people with equal access to mental health services. Adequate screening systems should be instituted to prevent inappropriate placement, and screening should be the gateway to available, appropriate services and facilities. Discharge planning and follow-up services should ensure the humane care and treatment of mentally impaired elderly people. The long-term-care needs of older people with mental impairments should be addressed within appropriate facilities. Staff, including nursing home staff, must receive training to meet the mental health needs of elderly people. This training should place special emphasis on cultural diversity.

Living Arrangements

A wide range of living arrangements should be available, designed, and located with reference to special needs and at costs that older people can afford. Sufficient housing should be available to provide older people with a choice. The public housing supply for lower- and middle-income older people must be increased. Funds for the maintenance and repair of housing should be readily available through a combination of grants and subsidized and conventional loans, as well as public funding of incentives for private investment. Laws must be developed to protect the assets of elderly people who choose to reside in retirement homes.

A range of supportive health and social services, such as home health, personal care, homemaker, friendly visiting, meals, and telephone reassurance, should be available to maintain older people in their homes and communities. Fire and safety codes should be established and enforced in all congregate facilities for older people. Subsidized congregate housing for elderly people should include social and supportive services. The public sector must fund incentives for the private sector to increase the supply of available housing.

Transportation

If elderly people are to benefit from available health and social services and other resources in a community, adequate transportation is necessary. Barrier-free transportation services must be established or expanded in urban and rural communities. Accessible low-cost mass transit and special-purpose programs for the elderly should be coordinated in the interest of serving the mobility requirements of elderly people.

Involvement of the Elderly

Older people should be involved in every aspect of the planning, policy development, administration, and evaluation of programs, including the deliberations of NASW. They should be represented on all governing boards of agencies that are designed to deliver services to the elderly. They must be actively involved in the development of laws dealing with ethical issues and the prolongation of life, as well as laws and programs that are designed to prevent elder abuse and to enhance health.

Policy statement approved by the NASW Delegate Assembly, August 1990. Referred to the 1999 Delegate Assembly for revision. This statement supersedes the policy statement on Aging approved by the Delegate Assembly in 1977. For further information, contact the National Association of Social Workers, 750 First Street, NE, Suite 700, Washington, DC 20002-4241. Telephone: 202-408-8600 or 800-638-8799.

Aid to Families with Dependent Children Reform

BACKGROUND

Aid to Families with Dependent Children (AFDC) is a federal program that provides grants-in-aid to states for the provision of cash aid to income-needy families whose heads are typically not disabled or elderly. Dating from the New Deal era, the program now serves almost 4 million families with approximately 11 million individuals. The program's objective of assuring a minimum level of aid to deprived children, even when their caretakers are able-bodied adults, has been consistently controversial, causing repeated impassioned debate about the possibility that AFDC will decrease the recipients' efforts to achieve personal discipline and self-reliance. Because states have considerable discretion in setting critical levels of eligibility and payment, the program always has reflected the historical idiosyncrasies of the individual state governments—as evidenced principally by wide disparities in payment levels for families in similar circumstances. Much general dissatisfaction with AFDC for many years has resulted in countless amendments, but efforts to restructure the program comprehensively by Presidents Nixon, Ford, Carter, and (in a much different way) Reagan all failed or resulted in considerably less change than was proposed.

In the mid-1980s, a coalition of concerned interest groups mounted a new effort to "reform" AFDC. The coalition allied itself with interested political leaders, the most prominent of whom was Senator Daniel Patrick Moynihan, a Democrat from New York who had been associated with the issue for more than 20 years. This latest drive was fueled by intense, angry debate over changes initiated by the Reagan administration in 1981 that resulted in tighter regulations and the loss of eligibility for several hundred thousand families. The efforts were fueled as well by the growing national embarrassment over the increasing proportion, approximately one in five, of the nation's children who live in families whose incomes are below the poverty level. The political strategy adopted by the coalition was to propose that the first goal of the revised program would be to extract from the absent parent who was responsible for child support (almost invariably the father) as large a payment as possible through a revised and strengthened Child Support Enforcement Law. If that effort did not produce sufficient income, public assistance (AFDC) would then be used to supplement or sustain the family. Added to this inverted sequence would be a genuine effort to help the custodial parent (almost invariably the mother) to obtain work and personal earnings. To make this plan feasible, the government would provide a set of services, including education, training, work experience, child care, Medicaid, and social services. To ease the transition to work status, child care and Medicaid would be continued for several months after employment began. The constructive promise of such a strategy motivated NASW to join the coalition of interest groups and to develop the policy statement on welfare reform adopted by the Delegate Assembly in 1987.

The states are now in the process of implementing the Family Support Act of 1988. NASW monitors that process at the national level and urges chapters to follow developments in their own states. Although the bill, as enacted, is less than NASW desired, it does make five improvements:

1. It strengthens child-support enforcement provisions and, if implemented conscientiously, promises to make the setting of support awards

and their prompt and regular collection more likely and consistent across the country.

2. It recognizes that enabling recipients to enter the mainstream labor market and become self-sustaining requires the provision of education, training, or appropriate work experience: States are required to offer an array of such opportunities, and the federal government provides new money to help with their development.

3. Child care and Medicaid are guaranteed accompaniments to the required work or training, and if regular employment is obtained, child care and Medicaid are guaranteed for several additional months to ease the transition and to reduce the disincentives that giving up such vital benefits may cause.

4. The act also allows states to use federal funds to provide "case managers" to coordinate the provision of services needed by individual recipients.

5. In a long-sought step, the act requires that all states offer AFDC-UP (AFDC for unemployed parents), an optional program of aid for intact families that is currently offered by only about one-half the states.

On the other hand, the new act did nothing to require states to improve their monthly payment levels, did not mandate a complete mix of education and skills training, and did not require the use of case managers. Furthermore, the bill mandated rates of participation that will likely force states to spread their resources too thin and included a provision mandating states to require at least one parent of an eligible AFDC-UP family to spend a minimum of 16 hours per week in "work supplementation, Community Work Experience Program or on-the-job training." In spite of these and other shortcomings, NASW believes that the act represents a net gain in opportunity for those it will affect. NASW will continue to advocate for the other recommendations enunciated in 1987, as well as additional ones incorporated into this statement (see Harris, 1989).

However, NASW policy statements must reflect the reality that "welfare" includes a wide array of concepts and programs for the nonpoor, as well as for the poor. In fact, all U.S. citizens receive benefits from provisions of laws aimed at producing desired behavior and promoting the "general welfare." AFDC is only a tiny part of a total system of benefits to citizens that include not only direct public transfers but an intricate set of tax provisions and fringe benefits. Provisions other than public income transfers constitute a kind of "shadow system" of welfare that many citizens refuse to recognize as such. Included are such items as mortgage-interest and other housing-related deductions; employer-paid health and life insurance, and pension premiums on which the employee is not taxed; child- and dependent-care tax credits, and so forth. Indeed, many citizens will not even consider such provisions as the public schools, social security, veterans' benefits, unemployment insurance, and workers' compensation as forms of "welfare" protection for commonly shared needs and risks. When this total picture is considered, "welfare state" provisions cost the nation more than $1 trillion annually, through either direct government outlays or the loss of tax revenues. All AFDC expenditures (federal, state, and local) total less than 2 percent of the total "welfare state" costs, the majority of which benefit nonpoor individuals and families. NASW policy statements should reflect this reality and not allow the poorest of the poor to bear an unfair burden of blame for the high costs of "welfare" (Abramovitz, 1983; Karger & Stoesz, 1987).

It has become increasingly clear that the objectives of the Family Support Act—to move parents of AFDC children into the mainstream labor market and to enable families to leave AFDC and move beyond the poverty level of income—will prove difficult to achieve. In fact, the Congressional Budget Office (1989) predicted that nationwide the program will remove only about 50,000 families (1 percent of the welfare rolls) from AFDC in its first five years. The most obvious barriers to subsidy-free status are the lack of jobs in the labor market and the wage levels of available jobs, a phenomenon that reflects national and international trends in the labor force of the past two decades. Low wages are further complicated by the growing shortage and rising costs of low-income housing, plus the fact that low-wage jobs often have few, if any, fringe benefits. With short time limits on the continuation of essential child care and medical coverage and the difficulty of transportation arrangements, even a highly motivated parent may become discouraged if the effort to work makes her less secure and only slightly better off with regard to cash resources than she was when receiving AFDC (Berlin, 1988; Graham, 1988; Kaus, 1989; Mathews, 1989).

It is not correct to assume that there will be no "good jobs" with adequate pay and solid fringe benefits, but experts predict that those jobs increasingly will require higher levels of literacy and social skills than are possessed by most of those who come from deprived circumstances. For most of them, it may well prove to be too expensive and too time consuming to undergo the level of reeducation that is required to equip them even to be considered for such jobs. U.S. companies, with a few exceptions, have shown little interest in the development of "human capital" that must begin with a "raw" product (Whitman et al., 1989).

To offset the seemingly inevitable permanent status of "working but poor" for these families and their children and to counter the strong work disincentives, several congressional proposals have been aimed at the goal of "making work pay." The mechanism proposed for pursuing that objective is an expansion of the Earned Income Tax Credit (EITC), in existence since 1975 and already providing a cash subsidy of up to $910 per year to families in which a parent works. The subsidy peaks when earnings reach $6,500 and begins to decline when earnings reach $10,240; the reduction is gradual until it ends at $19,340. The new proposals not only would expand the amount of the credit, but would adjust it upward for the number of children in the family. Such a revision in the EITC, coupled with a raise in the minimum wage, would bring many of the "working poor" families near or above the poverty level (Shapiro & Greenstein, 1989).

Such changes would help ameliorate the fundamental need for "cold cash," without which other social and educational services, no matter how sophisticated, are not likely to succeed. Nevertheless, a long-range approach to child-

hood poverty must invest in a broad spectrum of developmental services and protections: early childhood education, developmental day care, improved public schools and colleges, access to high-quality health care, affordable housing, child protective services, protection against job discrimination toward minorities and women, layoff and worker-retraining assistance, and so forth. Supplying these services is a vital task, since demographic trends indicate that our future economy will be highly dependent on new entrants to the labor force from groups who are growing up in deprived circumstances. Even more important, our cohesiveness as a nation is threatened by the continued growth in the inequality of incomes and the development of an ever larger segment of the population that has lost hope of achieving the minimum standards of living to which all Americans have historically aspired.

ISSUE STATEMENT

Description of the Problem

The current rate of 31.9 million people living below the poverty level is intolerable (U.S. Department of Commerce, 1988). Poverty rates for the 1980s were much higher than those for the 1970s, no matter how poverty is measured. The situation for the young, women, the elderly, and minorities is particularly grim:

■ One child in four is born into poverty, and one in every five—13 million children—lives in poverty (American Public Welfare Association, 1987).

■ Annually, 700,000 young people drop out of school, 500,000 teenage girls give birth, and 1.4 million young people who may lack job skills seek employment (Evans, 1986). Without special assistance, all these individuals have little hope of entering the job market.

■ Nearly 12.5 million women live in poverty (U.S. Department of Commerce, 1988).

■ Of the women who live in poverty, 3.5 million are single heads of households, and their households account for 47 percent of all families in poverty (U.S. Department of Commerce, 1988).

■ The poverty rate for black people is 2¾ times the poverty rate for whites; the poverty rate for Hispanics is 2½ times the poverty rate for whites (Gabe, 1986).

In addition, 3.5 million elderly people live in poverty, and vast numbers of seniors live on the edge of poverty (U.S. Department of Commerce, 1988). Finally, although poverty disproportionately affects certain groups, potentially it can affect anyone. Research suggests that one in every four families will live below the poverty line for at least one year in a given 10-year period as a result of transitional situations such as unemployment, divorce, illness, or childbearing (Dunkin, 1984).

Statistics demonstrate that poverty is multifaceted, and it touches those in every age, sex, and racial category. The welfare system must also be multifaceted to provide a range of approaches that will meet the needs of poor people, including single adults. The current welfare system fails to provide an appropriate range of approaches, and the programs it does provide are inadequate in a variety of ways. Inconsistent and insufficient benefits, inaccessible and inadequate social services and community support systems, and limited opportunities, particularly for women, to develop economic self-sufficiency are primary deficiencies in the current income maintenance system.

As a major cash publi1c assistance program for families with children, Aid to Families with Dependent Children (AFDC) has been the focus of much of the debate about welfare reform. Unlike some other governmental benefit programs, AFDC benefits are not indexed for inflation. Despite the enactment of some improvements through the Family Support Act, many AFDC families will continue to lack basic supports. Even those individuals who are given work and training opportunities may never have the chance to fill jobs that provide a decent standard of living. For example, a woman who works for the minimum wage (approximately $7,000 a year) and pays $3,000 a year for day care will endure more financial hardship working than she would if she remained on AFDC (Dunkin, 1984).

The problems in the public assistance system were described in a report published by the National Association of Social Workers (NASW) in February 1987. *Helping the Strong, An Exploration of the Needs of Families Headed by Women* (Miller, 1987, p. 13) stated that "the use of public assistance was, with few exceptions, reported to be humiliating and frustrating. Parents are stymied by the rules and feel that they are trapped and unable to get ahead." Respondents cited problems such as the restriction on resources and work and education disincentives. In fact, the problems in the system can be viewed primarily as problems of omission, not of commission. AFDC, as it exists, is an inadequate system that makes a minimal effort to provide income support. Programs for job preparation must not become a substitute for the provision of sufficient support to meet the basic needs of food, clothing, and shelter.

Recommended Solutions

Using its knowledge and experience, the social work profession must advocate for major reform of the AFDC system. The knowledge and experience of social workers are unique in that they include seeing the homes of poor families and hearing the personal stories of racial oppression and the lack of protection of children's basic rights to continuous care, food, housing, and safety. Social workers must use this unique database to advocate for families' needs in light of severe funding cuts. The system must, at a minimum, be adequately funded, provide for federally established eligibility requirements and minimum benefit levels tied to standards of need, be comprehensive and multifaceted in approach, facilitate long-term sustained employment, and provide educational and employment opportunities for individuals on the basis of their circumstances. It is understood that reform must address a complex set of interacting factors, such as public assistance, health care, education, housing, and employment. Furthermore, it is assumed that the impact of any reform will be greatest if the programs include those individuals whose long-term dependence already is established or highly likely, as well as those who move quickly out of the system.

Specifically, AFDC reform should include the following basic elements:

Provision of National Standards and Safeguards. Although states and localities should be encouraged to assume leadership in experimenting with bold, innovative approaches to AFDC reform, the federal government must maintain an integral role and must establish and enforce adequate national eligibility standards and minimum benefit levels that are tied to standards of need. The program must recognize household compositions that include two parents, single parents, and others. States should be allowed to diverge from the national base only if they scale benefits upward from it. An adequate system also will provide stringent oversight of state and local experiments to ensure sufficient access to programs and continuity of services, so that no one is deprived of benefits for which he or she would be eligible under the current policy.

Provision of a Comprehensive, Meaningful, Adequately Funded Employment Program That Includes Education, Training, and the Creation of Jobs. Although the Family Support Act was an important first step in ensuring that states prepare AFDC recipients to enter the job market, an acceptable AFDC system must guarantee adequate education, training, and job preparation that are geared to long-term sustained employment. The federal and state governments and the private sector must cooperate, through such strategies as private-public partnerships, in the development and creation of jobs. Sufficient jobs that pay a living wage must be available because preparatory services alone do not lead to economic self-sufficiency. A job without adequate compensation will not remove a family from poverty. A parent who works at a full-time, year-long job that pays the minimum wage remains below the poverty line if she or he has even one child. People should be trained in marketable skills to match the emerging needs for a skilled labor force. Health insurance and child care benefits, both during training and for a sustained period following employment, are essential supports if true self-sufficiency is to be attained.

Voluntary work programs for AFDC recipients have been successful in various locations. Underpinning voluntary work efforts is the assumption that recipients share a value system with the larger population and will strive to improve their circumstances and their children's future. Voluntary programs also eliminate issues about the ages of the children involved, because participation is self-selected. NASW supports the position that voluntary participation should be a priority in any AFDC reform program. NASW opposes the imposition of any compulsory work requirement for AFDC recipients.

Provision of Nondiscriminatory Employment Opportunities That Recognize Women's Role as Primary Caregivers. Women's distinctive needs must be reflected in AFDC reform. All women face employment barriers, and the barriers are particularly significant both for women who are caregivers in two-parent families and for female heads of households. The system must address the barriers that make it difficult for women to become participants in the labor force. Among the issues to be addressed are discriminatory hiring and promotion practices, the gender gap in wages, and inappropriate working conditions that do not include flexible work hours, maternity leave, on-site child care, job sharing, and adequate leave for individuals who care for dependent family members.

Coordination of Human and Economic Development Programs and Services. An acceptable public assistance policy must provide a logical, coherent, coordinated system of education, employment, transportation, housing, child care, health care, and other support services. For example, human and economic development, the creation of jobs, and support services all must be linked to reform so that changes are directed at both reducing poverty and improving the quality of life of AFDC families. Basic education, as well as vocational education, job training, and job preparation, are prerequisites if people are to be productive in an increasingly complex work world. Because of the inadequate education provided in many schools, the high dropout rate, and the large number of people for whom English is a second language, job preparation skills must begin with basic literacy. Educational programs also must include the provision of financial assistance to give the poor access to higher education. The vehicle for coordination of these various services is the case management model.

Provision of Comprehensive Transitional and Support Services. When recipients lose public assistance benefits because they work too many hours, they also lose other services, such as Medicaid. Many AFDC recipients are discouraged from seeking work because of the potential loss of health insurance; many jobs do not offer health coverage, and many employers have a waiting period before an employee becomes eligible for a workplace health plan.

An acceptable AFDC system must recognize that job training and employment opportunities alone will not provide sufficient resources and support for many individuals to climb from poverty. It is critical that policies and regulations eliminate all disincentives to employment. Services, such as safe, affordable, high-quality child care; transportation; health care coverage; and, as needed, income support, also are required to ensure the transition out of poverty. Without these services, a job becomes an unattainable goal for many.

To ensure the successful transition to economic self-sufficiency, the AFDC system also must provide psychological and social support services to help people succeed in work or training endeavors. Support services could include outreach, assessment, case management, personal and career counseling, motivation training for parenting and living skills, problem solving, nutrition counseling, home and money management, and health care. Such services must also include access to safe, decent housing, transportation, child care, and health care. In the absence of these services, the transition from a public assistance program to work may be overwhelmingly stressful.

Recognition of Individual Circumstances. To help people achieve economic self-sufficiency, the AFDC system should provide a range of op-portunities for individuals to exit from poverty. For example, the range of opportunities for young mothers must include education, child care, and job training so that these women can start preparing for their entry into the job market. The system also must permit individuals to maintain an adequate standard of living if they are unable to work toward economic self-sufficiency.

Recognition That, for Reasons Beyond Their Control, Some of This Nation's Poorest, Most Disadvantaged Citizens Will Not Attain Economic Self-Sufficiency. Our public assistance system must include more effective programs for all the poor, not just those who are able to work. The population in poverty includes elderly, young, and disabled people, as well as unemployed men and women, many of whom may not be able to work, but all of whom are entitled to an adequate standard of living. An acceptable system must provide a full range of appropriate and humane services to maintain, compassionately and safely, those citizens who, temporarily or permanently, cannot achieve economic self-sufficiency. Minimum services include food, shelter, clothing, medical care, and transportation costs.

Provision of a Comprehensive Impact Evaluation Component. Even small changes in public assistance programs can affect people's lives profoundly. Reform should include provisions for the ongoing analysis of how people are affected by the changes and provide for rapid redress, if necessary. The process and outcomes of new programs should be evaluated. Reform also must be considered in the context of today's society and must not be viewed as the only solution to this nation's major economic and social problems. Social workers should be leaders in discussions that deal creatively with broader solutions to society's ills.

POLICY STATEMENT

NASW believes that the level of poverty in this nation is intolerable. NASW is committed to working vigorously at the local, state, and federal levels for Aid to Families with Dependent

Children (AFDC) reform based on the principle that an effective system is an investment in the future of the nation and must be funded adequately. In addition, NASW will seek reform that incorporates the following:

■ minimum national benefit standards for AFDC recipients, based on the intermediate budget as developed by the Bureau of Labor Statistics, adjusted annually to the cost of living, as well as national eligibility criteria that include the largest number of low-income people

■ improved access to a coordinated system of education, employment, housing, health care, nutrition, and social-support services, including child care, health insurance, and transportation

■ social work services that address needed supports and services and their effective integration

■ a nationwide system to enforce child support payments

■ a comprehensive, meaningful, adequately funded, nondiscriminatory employment program with particular emphasis on the creation of sufficient jobs that pay living wages and the development of job conditions appropriate to the needs of women

■ educational opportunities that provide academic and vocational training that is geared to individuals' needs, skills, and capabilities, to range from basic education to college education and preparation for jobs

■ services that support psychological and social needs

■ educational, training, and employment opportunities that accommodate individual circumstances

■ an appropriate range of services for all poor individuals, regardless of their ability to become economically self-sufficient

■ adequate access to and continuity of services so that no one is deprived of benefits for which he or she would be eligible under the current policy

■ provision for the stringent oversight of experiments and demonstration programs

■ provision for comprehensive process and impact evaluations and the immediate redress of negative consequences

■ an improved Earned Income Tax Credit that includes an amount adjusted upward according to the number of children in the family

■ the presentation in understandable language, both in writing and orally, of procedures for appeal of decisions affecting families on AFDC.

REFERENCES

Abramovitz, M. (1983). Everyone is on welfare: "The role of redistribution in social policy" revisited. *Social Work, 28.*

American Public Welfare Association. (1987). *Investing in poor families and their children: A matter of commitment. Final report, Part 1.* Washington, DC: Author.

Berlin, G. (1988). The permanence of poverty. *Ford Foundation Newsletter, 19*(2).

Congressional Budget Office. (1989, January). *Work and welfare: The Family Support Act of 1988* (Working paper). Washington, DC: Author.

Dunkin, G. J. (1984). *Years of poverty, years of plenty.* Ann Arbor: Institute for Social Research, University of Michigan.

Evans, A. (1986, December). *Families at risk.* Washington, DC: Education and Public Welfare Division, Congressional Research Service.

Gabe, T. (1986, September). *Progress against poverty (1959 to 1985) and the poverty debate.* Washington, DC: Education and Public Welfare Division, Congressional Research Service.

Graham, M. (1988, November 21). Good jobs at bad wages. *New Republic.*

Harris, S. (1989, February). *A social worker's guide to the Family Support Act of 1988.* Silver Spring, MD: National Association of Social Workers.

Kaus, M. (1989, June 19). Revenge of the softheads. *New Republic.*

Karger, H. J., & Stoesz, D. (1987, June). Welfare reform: Maximum feasible exaggeration. *Tikkun Magazine, 4*(2).

Mathews, J. (1989, June 19–25). Mixed reviews for California's job-training program. *Washington Post Weekly.*

Miller, D. (1987). *Helping the strong, an exploration of the needs of families headed by women.* Silver Spring, MD: National Association of Social Workers.

Shapiro, I., & Greenstein, R. (1989, March 21). *Making work pay: A new budget agenda for poverty policies.* Washington, DC: Center on Budget and Policy Priorities.

U.S. Department of Commerce, Bureau of the Census. (1988). Consumer income: Money income and poverty status in the United States: 1988 (advance data from the March 1989 Current Population Survey). *Current Population Reports,* Series 60, No. 166. Washington, DC: Author.

Whiteman, D., et al. (1989, June 26). The forgotten half. *U.S. News and World Report.*

Policy statement approved by the NASW Delegate Assembly, August 1990. Referred to the 1999 Delegate Assembly for revision. This statement supersedes the policy statement on Welfare Reform, approved by the Delegate Assembly in 1987. For further information, contact the National Association of Social Workers, 750 First Street, NE, Suite 700, Washington, DC 20002-4241. Telephone: 202-408-8600 or 800-638-8799.

Alcohol, Tobacco, and Other Substance Abuse

BACKGROUND

There are more deaths, illnesses, and disabilities from alcohol, drugs (including illicit, over-the-counter, and prescribed drugs), and tobacco use and abuse than from any other preventable health condition. Of the 2 million deaths in the United States each year, more than one in four is attributable to substance-related disorders (Robert Wood Johnson Foundation, 1993). Every day millions of Americans use alcohol, tobacco, and other psychoactive substances; however, not everyone experiences a problem as a result of such use. It is therefore helpful to conceptualize alcohol, tobacco, and other drug use as ranging on a continuum from nonproblematic experimental and social use to abuse and finally to dependence or addiction (Lewis, Dana, & Blevins, 1994; Straussner, 1993).

Most people who occasionally drink alcohol, take drugs, or smoke do not experience problems from using these substances (although it is possible to have a serious injury or even to die from a single episode of alcohol or drug use). However, with heavier, more frequent consumption, occasional users are at greater risk for experiencing problems with health, family members and other people, school, work, or the law (Lewis et al., 1994; Robert Wood Johnson Foundation, 1993).

Substance abuse refers to patterns of use that result in health consequences or impairment in social, psychological, and occupational functioning. The essential feature of substance abuse is a "maladaptive pattern of substance use" (American Psychiatric Association, 1994, p. 182) manifested by recurrent and significant adverse consequences related to repeated use of substances. Substance dependence also involves compulsive use and craving and may include withdrawal and increased tolerance (American Psychiatric Association, 1994).

Although some people may be able to stop or diminish their use of a substance, for most people substance dependence is a chronic, relapsing condition that makes it difficult to quit or curtail use. A common characteristic of dependence on alcohol, tobacco, and other drugs is "denial"—the difficulty the abuser has in realistically assessing the impact of the substance on his or her life and the lives of others (Fewell & Bissell, 1978; Miller & Rollnick, 1991). The process of recovery includes the likelihood of relapse and additional treatment.

Scope of Alcohol, Tobacco, and Other Drug–Related Problems

No population group is immune from substance abuse and its effects. Men and women of all ages, racial and ethnic groups, and levels of education and income smoke, drink, and use illicit drugs (Robert Wood Johnson Foundation, 1993). Social workers are not immune from the problems of substance abuse. In a survey of members of the New York City chapter of NASW, 43 percent of the random sample of 198 reported knowing one or more social workers impaired by alcohol or drug abuse. Seventy-five percent of that group knew two or more impaired social work colleagues (Fewell, King, & Weinstein, 1993). In a survey conducted by the Indiana chapter of NASW, 25 percent of 1,005 respondents indicated that they knew of a social worker with an alcohol or drug problem that had adversely affected job performance (Elpers, 1992).

Nearly 13.4 million Americans have problems with drinking, including 8.1 million people who are alcoholic (National Institute on Alcohol Abuse and Alcoholism [NIAAA], 1994). The most recent data from the 1994 National Household Survey on Drug Abuse (Substance Abuse and Mental Health Services Administration [SAMHSA], 1995) indicate that the rate of heavy alcohol use (five or more drinks per occasion on five or more days a month) has not changed since 1990. Thirteen million Americans (6.2 percent of the population) are heavy drinkers (SAMHSA, 1995). Moreover, 2.7 percent of people over 12 years of age are affected by illicit drug use, 2.5 million Americans are dependent on drugs, and another 3 million are drug abusers (Gerstein & Harwood, 1990). One of every three U.S. adolescents uses tobacco by age 18 years (U.S. Department of Health and Human Services [DHHS], 1994).

Tobacco-related causes account for more than 400,000 deaths a year—20 percent of all U.S. deaths. Nearly 90 percent of lung cancer deaths result from smoking, surpassing the death rates from all other kinds of cancer including prostate cancer in men and breast cancer in women. Smoking also is a major contributor to coronary heart disease; chronic bronchitis and emphysema; poor pregnancy outcomes; and cancers of the pancreas, trachea, bronchus, and larynx. Most deaths associated with smoking occur among the smokers themselves; however, exposure to environmental tobacco smoke also is an acknowledged health hazard, and each year some 50,000 deaths occur among nonsmokers as a result of cancer and other diseases caused by tobacco smoke (Glantz & Parmely, 1991).

The abuse of alcohol, tobacco, and other substances also is associated with a wide variety of illnesses and social problems. A minimum of three of every 100 deaths are attributed to alcohol-related causes, including liver and pancreas diseases, cancer, and cardiovascular problems (Williams, Grant, Hartford, & Noble, 1989). The synergistic effect of tobacco and alcohol use increases the risk of cancer of the esophagus, pancreatitis, and cirrhosis (Orleans & Slade, 1993). Nearly half of all violent deaths (accidents, suicides, and homicides), particularly of men under the age of 34, are alcohol-related (DHHS, 1990), and alcohol has been found to be a consistent factor in reports of child abuse including

incest (Straussner, 1989), domestic violence (Hindman, 1979; Wright, 1985), and date rape among young adults (New York State Division of Alcoholism and Alcohol Abuse, 1988; Straussner, 1993).

In the 1980s and early 1990s, professionals became aware of the increasing prevalence of substance abuse and co-occurring psychiatric disorders (Orlin & Davis, 1993). People with dual disorders are often difficult to treat and have a poor prognosis.

Of those people arrested for serious crimes in major urban areas during 1988, 75 percent tested positive for illicit drugs (DHHS, 1991). Of the estimated 500,000 to 1 million chronic intravenous drug abusers in the United States, about 25 percent have tested positive for the human immunodeficiency virus (HIV), and approximately 28 percent of all reported acquired immune deficiency syndrome (AIDS) cases occur among members of this risk group (DHHS, 1991). Intravenous drug abuse or sexual contact with intravenous drug abusers accounts for more than 80 percent of AIDS cases in women, and 80 percent of pediatric patients with AIDS have a parent who abuses intravenous drugs. Among the adult population of intravenous drug abusers with AIDS, more than half are African American, and nearly one-third are of Hispanic origin (DHHS, 1991).

In addition to AIDS, the use of dirty, shared, and reused needles results in various systemic infections. Illnesses such as anemia, tuberculosis, heart disease, diabetes, pneumonia, and hepatitis are common among heroin abusers, whereas cocaine use affects the cardiovascular system, resulting in blockages in blood circulation, abnormal heart rhythms, and strokes. Prostitution, a frequent means of support for drug-dependent women, leads to a high incidence of sexually transmitted diseases (Strom, 1993).

An issue among women who abuse alcohol, tobacco, or drugs is the prenatal impact of these substances on their children. During 1985 an estimated 50,000 babies were born affected by prenatal alcohol exposure leading to fetal alcohol syndrome, a common and preventable cause of mental retardation and related defects (Brody, 1986). Maternal smoking during and after pregnancy triples the risk of sudden infant death syndrome (DiFranza & Lew, 1995). Infants born to women addicted to cocaine or heroin have health and socialization problems that will result in high costs for health, education, and other services delivery ("Care of Babies," 1991; MacGregor et al., 1987).

For many people with sensory, cognitive, or physical developmental disabilities, alcohol, tobacco, and other drug dependency may impose far greater limitations than their disability. Until recently, the need for alcohol, tobacco, and other drug abuse treatment and the benefits of recovery for people with disabilities have not been acknowledged by society, the medical community, families, and peer groups. Failure to adequately address alcohol, tobacco, and other drug abuse as a primary health care issue may lead to increased medical complications from the disability and interfere with other aspects of living.

According to the 1993 National Household Survey on Drug Abuse, millions of Americans both abuse illicit drugs and drink and smoke heavily (SAMHSA, 1994). Of 11 million heavy drinkers in 1993, 26 percent also had used illicit drugs within the past 30 days. Among 50 million current smokers, 12 percent were illicit drug users (American Medical Association, 1994). In addition, for adolescents, substance abuse typically proceeds in stages. Tobacco, alcohol, and marijuana are considered "gateway drugs," that is, substances that frequently precede the use of other drugs.

A growing body of research on the costs of untreated alcohol, tobacco, and other drug addiction to employers, insurers, and the criminal justice system has evolved. Numerous studies demonstrate high health care use by untreated alcohol- and nicotine-dependent people for a variety of addiction-related illnesses, accidents, and injuries. Although addiction treatment resulted in marked reductions in health care utilization, the health care costs for individuals who abuse alcohol and go untreated are at least 100 percent higher than for individuals who do not abuse alcohol (Langenbucher, McCrady, Brick, & Easterly, 1993). Without treatment, the individual with an addiction continues to deteriorate, leading to high health care utilization and increased welfare, Medicaid, and Medicare costs.

Impact on Family

The concept of family as a system has long been accepted in substance abuse literature and practice. When one family member becomes a substance abuser, profound and significant implications for the rest of the family can be anticipated (Straussner, 1994). According to a 1988 national survey, 38 percent of adults in the United States have a relative with an alcohol problem, and an unknown number are affected by familial use of other substances (Harford, 1992). Forty-five percent of adolescents live in a household in which someone smokes cigarettes (DHHS, 1994). Families with alcohol, tobacco, and other substance abuse problems experience myriad financial, medical, and social problems such as compulsive gambling, violence, child abuse and neglect, death or disability from fires in the home, and a higher likelihood of raising children who themselves become substance abusers (Vaillant, 1983). Research has shown that health care utilization by families with members who abuse alcohol and go untreated is roughly twice that of families without a member who abuses alcohol (Langenbucher et al., 1993).

Such problems affect not only social work clients but also social workers themselves. A 1987 survey of 250 first-year graduate students at a major school of social work found that 27 percent had a substance-abusing parent and 15 percent had a substance-abusing sibling (Straussner, 1993). A random sample survey of the members of the New York City chapter of NASW found that 39 percent of the 198 respondents had a nuclear family member who had a problem with alcohol or other drug abuse (Fewell et al., 1993).

Practice Wisdom

Social workers need to view alcohol, tobacco, and other drug addictions as primary problems, rather than as symptoms of other problems. To effectively treat clients' problems rather than symptoms, all social workers must develop basic knowledge and skills to identify, assess, treat, and refer clients with alcohol, tobacco, and other substance abuse problems. Some individuals may be treated for alcohol misuse and later return to social drinking patterns (Sobel & Sobel, 1993). For people who have become chronically dependent on alcohol, tobacco, and other drugs, practice experience supports the need for abstinence as a treatment goal. Practice wisdom also has led social workers to recognize that 12-step approaches have benefited many people. Other approaches to treatment also must be made available.

Sometimes members of families with an individual who is a substance abuser are able to respond to the dysfunction of the individual without lasting personal impairment, although practice wisdom has shown that frequently each member of such families may develop his or her own maladaptive defense system to survive (Zelvin, 1993). Therefore, all family members must be considered and, when appropriate, included in treatment efforts. Treatment approaches should be individualized to meet the needs of the clients (Miller, 1989). Prevention strategies need to be customized for individuals, groups, and communities.

ISSUE STATEMENT

The enormous day-to-day impact of substance abuse on the lives of children and adults is in stark contrast to the low priority these issues receive on the national agenda. Americans continue to deny the full impact of alcohol, tobacco, and other drug-related disorders on individuals, families, and society. Despite the tremendous social costs, alcohol and other drug abuse has been seen either as a criminal practice or as an individual moral or psychological problem. Although smoking control regulations have increased, the addictive nature of nicotine continues to be minimized, and treatment options are limited. The federal "war on drugs," with its attention to interdiction and law enforcement, has minimized funding for comprehensive alcohol and other drug prevention and treatment efforts.

Current treatment capacity is limited, and treatment programs vary widely in quality. Moreover, insurance coverage for substance-abusing clients varies depending on the community or on private insurance riders. Social workers should advocate parity with other health conditions for benefit coverage. Managed care companies are dictating treatment on an ad hoc basis, necessitating the need for national policy guidelines.

A comprehensive public health approach that addresses the availability and nature of abused substances (the agent); the individuals affected by the substances; the vectors that bring the drugs into communities; and the economic, physical, cultural, and social environment of alcohol and drug abuse would allow for the development of a more comprehensive range of preventive and interventive approaches.

POLICY STATEMENT

Social workers believe that the abuse of alcohol, tobacco, and drugs (illicit, over-the-counter, and prescribed) is a significant public health problem, and as such the focus should be on prevention in addition to treatment. Social, economic, and environmental factors contribute to alcohol, tobacco, and other drug abuse. Consequently, social workers support a broad range of intervention approaches focused on addressing the causes and manifestations of substance abuse. These interventions include strengthening communities and individuals through community empowerment; economic development; mutual aid; and group, family, and individual treatment. Social workers need to rely on accurate scientific information for understanding the complex causes of abuse and dependence and on empirically tested intervention for designing effective problem solving.

NASW supports responses to problems related to the abuse of alcohol, tobacco, and other drugs in four major areas: (1) social policy; (2) professional issues; (3) prevention, intervention, and service delivery; and (4) research, including program evaluation.

Social Policy

In the late 1980s and early 1990s, U.S. policy toward controlled substances emphasized reducing the availability of illicit drugs and made treatment less of a priority. In 1991 treatment received 14 percent of the $10.5 billion federal drug budget compared with 25 percent 10 years earlier (American Bar Association, 1994). Although enforcement is an important component of an overall substance abuse strategy, the reliance on a "war on drugs" has been ineffective (Drug Strategies, 1995).

Adopting a comprehensive public health approach will enable social workers to focus on the prevention and treatment of alcohol, tobacco, and other drug problems. This focus will prevent unnecessary stigma and will combat substance-related diseases, disabilities, and premature death. Intervening at the earliest opportunity can prevent other problems that often accompany alcohol, tobacco, and other drug abuse such as physical deterioration, the disintegration of the family, and substance-related violence. Finally, a public health approach to illicit drugs permits the development of more sensible policies with respect to diseases such as AIDS, tuberculosis, and hepatitis B that are related to drug use.

NASW advocates that comprehensive insurance coverage for alcohol, tobacco, and drug addiction treatment be mandated for all insurance policies at the federal and state levels. Treatment coverage, including the treatment of nicotine dependence, should be made available without arbitrary time limits and should cover a range of treatment settings and modalities. Such comprehensive insurance should include coverage for the treatment of the substance abusers and their children (minors or adults), spouses, parents, and significant others who are affected. Treatment for the consequences of alcohol, tobacco, and other drug abuse should be covered for family members whether or not the substance abuser is in treatment.

NASW supports the development of uniform practice guidelines and patient outcome measures for all managed care and other insurance companies. Social workers as well as other health professionals should be involved in the development of such guidelines.

Professional Issues

NASW supports the principle that all social work practitioners should possess general knowledge about the range of alcohol, tobacco, and other drug problems; about the impact of these problems on individuals, families, significant others, and communities; and about the processes of prevention and intervention. Graduate and undergraduate social work education

programs should develop, reinforce, and strengthen the study of alcohol, tobacco, and other drug problems. Specifically, each graduate and undergraduate program should include content in that area as a part of the core curriculum. Substance abuse prevention and treatment should be offered as a field of social work practice in graduate programs. The profession should support and encourage the inclusion of education regarding substance abuse in traditional in-service training programs offered by agencies that employ social workers. Education on substance abuse should include training on prevention, assessment, and treatment as well as the specific assessment and treatment issues of dually diagnosed clients. Recognizing that there are many different treatment modalities in the addictions treatment arena, social work education must include the full range of treatment goals and modalities.

NASW supports the continued well-being and health of social workers. NASW recognizes that social workers have a duty to help colleagues suffering from substance abuse and other physical or emotional impairments and to intercede when colleagues' professional roles are adversely affected by their impairments. NASW recognizes the responsibility of social work administration and management (per the NASW Code of Ethics, NASW, 1996) to cultivate work environments conducive to healthy functioning. NASW supports the use of external consultation services to assess the functioning of social work administration and management with regard to alcohol and other substances abuse issues. Entry into the recovery process should be confidential and nonpunitive. Social workers should be enabled to reenter the profession following recovery as accountable and reliable professionals (NASW, 1994b).

Prevention, Intervention, and Service Delivery

Prevention, intervention, and treatment programs should reflect the interrelationships among substance abusers, their families, and problems such as economic difficulties and poverty, poor health, unemployment and underemployment, homelessness, and mental illness. It must therefore be recognized that because alcohol- and other substance-related disorders are multifaceted, prevention approaches and treatment programs should be comprehensive, culturally and ethnically sensitive, and integrated to meet the multiple needs of the diverse populations to be served.

NASW supports policies that address the development of comprehensive prevention and early intervention programs that meet the unique needs of individuals and families from various racial, ethnic, and socioeconomic groups throughout their entire life span. NASW supports community-based prevention strategies aimed at children, adolescents, pregnant women, gay men and lesbians, and older people. Harm-reduction strategies should be aimed at those already affected by tobacco, alcohol, and other drug use and those who have HIV/AIDS. Workplace prevention strategies should be promoted, including employee assistance programs. Emphasis should be placed on promoting changes in public attitudes and increased support of alcohol, tobacco, and other drug abuse prevention and treatment programs.

The incidence and severity of problems have been shown to be influenced by the manner and extent to which substances are made available to the population. Therefore, NASW supports public policy measures that take a public health approach to addressing alcohol, tobacco, and other drug problems in society. These policy measures should address public safety and alcohol and tobacco marketing practices. Attention should be devoted to the development of policies aimed at reducing the availability of and harm done by illicit drugs.

Social workers should assume an active advocacy role at the local, state, and national levels for obtaining funding to expand services. The full range of appropriate and coordinated treatment options should be made available to match clients' needs and be included as part of any comprehensive health care delivery system.

Research

NASW recognizes and supports the need for research in alcohol, tobacco, and other drug abuse and dependence. A clear understanding of the social, economic, psychological, spiritual, and biological relationships involved in substance use and abuse is needed. Research efforts should continue to explore the impact of alcohol, tobacco, and other drugs on diverse populations. The social work professional should support research on the effectiveness of various treatment approaches and modalities and on matching treatment with different populations. Social workers should maintain current knowledge of new research findings on the etiology, course, and consequences of substance abuse, including the biochemical linkage between use and addiction. The profession should support research on prevention and treatment needs for underserved groups such as women; gay men and lesbians; older people; people of color; and members of various racial, cultural, and ethnic groups. NASW supports ongoing research on the impact of alcohol, tobacco, and other drug dependence on family members, especially the short-term and long-term effects on children. More research devoted to prevention is needed. In addition, social work research should include identification of biopsychosocial risk factors of alcohol, tobacco, and other drug abuse to provide prevention and early intervention strategies. Finally, NASW supports research on the role and contribution of social workers in the field of alcohol, tobacco, and other drugs.

REFERENCES

American Bar Association. (1994). *New directions for national substance abuse policy.* Washington, DC: Author.

American Medical Association. (1994). *Policy compendium on tobacco, alcohol and other harmful substances affecting adolescents.* Chicago: Author, Department of Adolescent Health.

American Psychiatric Association. (1994). *Diagnostic and statistical manual of mental disorders* (4th ed.). Washington, DC: Author.

Brody, J. E. (1986, January 15). Personal health. *New York Times*, p. C6.

Care of babies for cocaine is put at $504 million a year. (1991, September 19). *New York Times*, p. B4.

DiFranza, J., & Lew, R. (1995). Effect of maternal smoking on pregnancy complications and sudden infant death syndrome. *Journal of Family Practice, 40,* 1–10.

Drug Strategies. (1995). *Keeping score.* Washington, DC: Author.

Elpers, K. (1992). *Social work impairment: A statewide survey of the National Association of Social Workers.* Indianapolis: Indiana Chapter, NASW.

Fewell, C. H., & Bissell, L. (1978). The alcohol denial syndrome: An alcohol-focused approach. *Social Casework, 59,* 6–13.

Fewell, C. H., King, B., & Weinstein, D. (1993). Alcohol and other drug abuse among social workers and their families: Impact on practice. *Social Work, 38,* 565–570.

Gerstein, D. R., & Harwood, H. J. (Eds.). (1990). *Treating drug problems* (Vol. 1). Washington, DC: National Academy Press.

Glantz, S.A., & Parmley, W.E. (1991). Passive smoking and heart disease: Epidemiology, physiology, and biochemistry. *Circulation, 83,* 1–12.

Harford, T. D. (1992). Family history of alcoholism in the United States: Prevalence and demographic characteristics. *British Journal of Addictions, 87,* 931–936.

Hindman, M. (1979). Family violence: An overview. *Alcohol Health and Research World, 4*(1), 2–11.

Langenbucher, J. W., McCrady, B. S., Brick, J., & Easterly, R. (1993). Addictions treatment in general clinical populations. In *Socioeconomic evaluations of addictions treatment* (Vol. 11, Chapter 4). New Brunswick, NJ: Rutgers Center of Alcohol Studies.

Lewis, J. A., Dana, R. Q., & Blevins, G. A. (1994). *Substance abuse counseling: An individualized approach* (2nd ed.). Pacific Grove, CA: Brooks/Cole.

MacGregor, S. N., Louis, G. K., Chanoff, I. J., Rosner, M., Chisum, G. M., Shaw, P., & Minogue, J. P. (1987). Cocaine use during pregnancy: Adverse perinatal outcome. *American Journal of Obstetrics & Gynecology, 157*(3), 686–690.

Miller, W. R. (1989). Matching individuals with interventions. In R. K. Hester & W. R. Miller (Eds.), *Handbook of alcoholism treatment approaches: Effective alternatives* (pp. 261–272). Boston: Allyn & Bacon.

Miller, W. R., & Rollnick, S. (1991). *Motivational interviewing: Preparing people to change addictive behavior.* New York: Guilford Press.

National Association of Social Workers. (1994b). *Helping social workers who have alcohol and other drug problems: Intervening with colleagues.* Washington, DC: NASW Press.

National Association of Social Workers. (1996). *NASW code of ethics.* Washington, DC: Author.

National Institute on Alcohol Abuse and Alcoholism. (1994). *Alcohol Health and Research World, 18*(3), 243–248.

New York State Division of Alcoholism and Alcohol Abuse. (1988). *Alcohol problems prevention/intervention programs: Guidelines for college campuses.* Albany, NY: Author.

Orleans, E. T., & Slade, J. (Eds.). (1993). *Nicotine addiction: Principles and management.* New York: Oxford University Press.

Orlin, L., & Davis, J. (1993). Assessment and intervention with drug and alcohol abusers in psychiatric settings. In S.L.A. Straussner (Ed.), *Clinical work with substance-abusing clients.* New York: Guilford Press.

Robert Wood Johnson Foundation. (1993). *Substance abuse: The nation's number one health problem.* Boston: Institute for Health Policy, Brandeis University.

Sobel, M. B., & Sobel, L. C. (1993). *Problem drinker: Guided self-change treatment.* New York: Guilford Press.

Straussner, S.L.A. (1989). Intervention with maltreating parents who are drug and alcohol abusers. In S. Ehrenkranz, E. Goldstein, L. Goodman, & J. Seinfeld (Eds.), *Clinical social work with maltreated children and their families: An introduction to practice.* New York: New York University Press.

Straussner, S.L.A. (1993). Assessment and treatment of clients with alcohol and other drug abuse problems: An overview. In S.L.A. Straussner (Ed.), *Clinical work with substance-abusing clients.* New York: Guilford Press.

Straussner, S.L.A. (1994). The impact of alcohol and other drug abuse on the American family. *Drug and Alcohol Review, 13,* 393–399.

Strom, D. P. (1993). AIDS and intravenous drug users: Issues and treatment implications. In S.L.A. Straussner (Ed.), *Clinical work with substance-abusing clients.* New York: Guilford Press.

Substance Abuse and Mental Health Services Administration. (1994, Summer). *1993 house-*

hold survey: Good and bad news. Washington, DC: U.S. Department of Health and Human Services.

Substance Abuse and Mental Health Services Administration. (1995). [Advance Report #10], *Preliminary Estimates from the 1994 National Household Survey on Drug Abuse.* Author, Office of Applied Studies. Washington, DC: U.S. Department of Health and Human Services.

U.S. Department of Health and Human Services. (1988). *The health consequences of smoking: Nicotine addiction.* Washington, DC: U.S. Government Printing Office.

U.S. Department of Health and Human Services. (1990). *Seventh special report to the U.S. Congress on alcohol and health.* Washington, DC: U.S. Government Printing Office.

U.S. Department of Health and Human Services. (1991). *Drug abuse and drug abuse research: The third triennial report to Congress from the Secretary, Department of Health and Human Services.* Washington, DC: U.S. Government Printing Office.

U.S. Department of Health and Human Services (1994). *Preventing tobacco use among young people.* Washington, DC: U.S. Government Printing Office.

Vaillant, G. (1983). *The natural history of alcoholism.* Cambridge, MA: Harvard University Press.

Williams, G. D., Grant, B., Hartford, T. C., & Noble, J. (1989). Population projections using DSM-III criteria: Alcohol abuse and dependence 1990–2000. *Alcohol Health and Research World, 13*(4), 366–370.

Wright, J. (1985). Domestic violence and substance abuse: A cooperative approach toward working with dually affected families. In E. Freeman (Ed.), *Social work practice with clients who have alcohol problems* (pp. 26–39). Springfield, IL: Charles C Thomas.

Zelvin, E. (1993). Treating the partners of substance abusers. In S.L.A. Straussner (Ed.), *Clinical work with substance-abusing client.* New York: Guilford Press.

Ziedonis, D., Kosten, T. R., Glazer, W. M., & Frances, R. J. (1994). Nicotine dependence and schizophrenia. *Hospital and Community Psychiatry, 45,* 204–206.

SUGGESTED READINGS

Goldstein, E. G. (1993). The borderline substance abuser. In S.L.A. Straussner (Ed.), *Clinical work with substance-abusing clients.* New York: Guilford Press.

McKelvy, M., Kane, J., & Kellison, K. (1987). Substance abuse and mental illness: Double trouble. *Journal of Psychosocial Nursing, 25,* 20–25.

National Association of Social Workers. (1994a). *NASW code of ethics.* Washington, DC: Author.

National Association of Social Workers. (1994c). *The impaired professional.* In *Social work speaks: NASW policy statements* (3rd ed., pp. 149–151). Washington DC: Author.

Policy statement approved by the NASW Delegate Assembly, August 1996. This policy supersedes the policy statement on Alcoholism and Other Substance Abuse–Related Problems approved by the Delegate Assembly in 1987, the policy statement on Alcoholism approved in 1979, and the policy statement on Substance Abuse approved in 1975. For further information, contact the National Association of Social Workers, 750 First Street, NE, Suite 700, Washington, DC 20002-4241. Telephone: 202-408-8600 or 800-638-8799.

Alternative Work Patterns

BACKGROUND

Supporting and strengthening the family has been a major concern of the social work profession throughout its history. Today, changes in conceptions of the roles of women, as well as an increased divorce rate and economic pressures, have led to increased participation of women in the work force. In 1980, 51 percent of American women worked outside the home, compared with 43 percent in 1970 ("The Superwoman Squeeze," 1980). Six million mothers with children under age six worked, and the Urban Institute predicted that 14 million would be in the labor force by 1990 (Smith, 1979).

Although the impact of working mothers on families has been positive in many ways, it has produced a new source of stress. Because the increase in the number of women working has not been accompanied by a decrease in the number of men working, children spend less time with their parents. From their clinical experience, social workers know how important it is for parents to nurture and pay attention to the development of their children, especially very young children (Fraiberg, 1977).

The provision of adequate child care is a problem for many families. The lack of adequate day care centers for preschool and school-aged children has forced many families to make unstable, makeshift arrangements for their children or to leave children unsupervised after school. In addition, women who work full-time often continue to carry the main burden of child care and household management. The result is that these women become exhausted and tense and virtually have no time for themselves (Curtis, 1976).

Given the stresses and difficulties involved in trying to combine work and family responsibilities, many women stay home until their children are finished with school; however, staying home may create stresses of a different kind. Work, social and financial recognition, and the ability to develop and use one's abilities are important for maintaining self-esteem. Despite the lip service that our culture pays to the importance of motherhood, full-time housewives are a low-status group that is highly vulnerable to depression, alcoholism, loneliness, and frustration. Reentry into the job market also may be difficult if a woman has been out of the work force for too many years. Also, many families simply cannot manage on one paycheck.

For many women, and for men who wish to spend more time with their families, a partial solution to the problems just described is part-time or flex-time work. Flex-time refers to full-time work outside the standard hours—7 A.M. to 3 P.M., for instance. It is much more common in Europe and Japan than in this country. In Germany, 50 percent of the white-collar work force is on flex-time schedules, but only 6 percent of full-time jobs in the United States are flex-time jobs ("The Superwoman Squeeze," 1980).

There are an estimated 17 million part-time jobs in this country, but the demand far exceeds the supply ("The Superwoman Squeeze," 1980). The unemployment rate of people who are looking actively for part-time work, for instance, is almost double that of people who are seeking full-time jobs (*Geographic Profile of Employment and Unemployment*, 1978). Moreover, unemployment figures do not account for full-time workers who would work part-time if they could or for other people who are not seeking work actively because of the lack of part-time opportunities.

Part-time work tends to be concentrated in low-paying, unskilled jobs. In large segments of American industry, such as manufacturing, part-time work hardly exists. Many part-time jobs also lack benefits, job security, or opportunities for advancement.

The lack of good part-time job opportunities has a negative impact on two of the groups that social work serves: the handicapped and welfare recipients. Some people with physical, mental, or emotional handicaps are not able to take the stress of full-time work but could work part-time. Welfare recipients with child care responsibilities could work their way out of economic dependence and its associated problems if more and better-paying part-time jobs were available.

In the 1970s government and industry began to show some interest in alternative work patterns. They are responding, in part, to the many studies that have found a relationship between the implementation of part-time and flex-time schedules and increased productivity, increased employee morale, and decreased absenteeism (*Flexitime: Kentucky Takes a Second Look,* 1979; Nollen, 1979; *A Report on Alternative Work Schedules; Report on the Part-Time Employment Pilot Project*). Commuting time can be reduced, which may relieve congestion and save energy, if flex-time can be implemented more widely (*Association for Public Transportation Survey Results: Transportation and Energy Impacts of Flexitime;* Salvin, Ott, & Ward, 1979). Interest also has been expressed in shortening the workweek to prevent layoffs in industries faced with recession (Singer, 1980). Although organized labor is wary of such a move, such a change may be a fairer and more humane way to distribute the burden of unemployment, particularly if unemployment compensation is broadened to provide income protection for workers whose hours are reduced.

Within the social work profession, there is a need for more alternative work patterns. Although certain social work jobs require full-time workers because of organizational or service needs, many do not. There is much underutilized talent among social workers who cannot work full-time because of family responsibilities. Some agencies are finding imaginative ways to expand their services by hiring part-time workers, often on a contract basis. The number of such agencies is still small, however, and the use of flex-time is rare, despite its obvious advantages in serving clients who cannot keep appointments during standard working hours.

ISSUE STATEMENT

The world of work has a major impact on all individuals in this society and on the quality and character of family life. Work patterns, however, have not been sufficiently responsive to the changing needs of families, especially the needs of children and of women who wish to or must work but who still carry the main or sole responsibility for child care and housework. There is a large discrepancy between the demand for and the supply of part-time and flex-time jobs. The result is that women, particularly poor women, and the handicapped are discriminated against. Furthermore, the part-time job market primarily has low-level jobs that lack benefits, security, or opportunities for advancement.

Alternative work patterns have many advantages for employers and the general public, including social agencies and their clients. More widely publicized experimentation is needed to determine which arrangements best suit the needs of employers and employees.

POLICY STATEMENT

NASW believes that work patterns in this society should be more responsive to the needs of families and handicapped individuals. Therefore, NASW strongly supports the expansion of opportunities for part-time and flex-time jobs in the public and private sectors. Such jobs should have benefits and protections that are prorated to those of full-time jobs. Social service agencies, in particular, should make more extensive use of alternative work patterns that are consistent with the needs of clients and of the organization.

REFERENCES

Association for Public Transportation survey results: Transportation and energy impacts of flexitime. Boston: Commonwealth of Massachusetts, Division of Personnel Administration.

Curtis, J. (1976). *Working mothers.* Garden City, NY: Doubleday.

Flexitime: Kentucky takes a second look. (1979). Lexington, KY: Council on State Governments.

Fraiberg, S. (1977). *Every child's birthright—In defense of mothering*. New York: Basic Books.

Geographic profile of employment and unemployment: States 1978 (Report No. 571). (1978). Washington, DC: Bureau of Labor Statistics, U.S. Department of Labor.

Nollen, S. D. (1979). Does flexitime increase productivity? *Harvard Business Review, 57.*

A report on alternative work schedules. Albany, NY: Office of Employee Relations.

Report on the part-time employment pilot project. Sacramento: California State Personnel Board.

Singer, J. W. (1980, February 9). Sharing layoffs and jobless benefits—A new approach is attracting interest. *National Journal.*

Salvin, H., Ott, M., & Ward, D. (1979, August 10). *The behavior impacts of flexible working hours.* Cambridge, MA: U.S. Department of Transportation Research.

Smith, R. E. (Ed.). (1979). *The subtle revolution: Women at work.* Washington, DC: The Urban Institute.

The superwoman squeeze. (1980, May 19). *Newsweek,* 72–79.

Policy statement approved by the NASW Delegate Assembly, 1981; reconfirmed by the Delegate Assembly, August 1990. Referred to the 1999 Delegate Assembly, to be combined with the policy statement on Economic Policy. For further information, contact the National Association of Social Workers, 750 First Street, NE, Suite 700, Washington, DC 20002-4241. Telephone: 202-408-8600 or 800-638-8799.

Case Management in Health, Education, and Human Services Settings

BACKGROUND

Case management has been uniquely a social work role for more than 100 years. Social work is the only profession in which education and training maintain a dual focus on the client and the environment, enabling the client to use agency services and linking and coordinating agency services to meet clients' needs. Within the past 10 years, policy makers have appropriated case management tasks and assigned them to nonprofessionals in the interest of cost containment. It is our obligation to our clients to arrest a movement that deprives clients of professional psychosocial assessment, skilled counseling, mediating interventions with service providers at each stage of the process, and advocacy efforts that will increase clients' options.

Case management is an approach to service delivery whereby clients with complex, multiple problems and disabilities efficiently receive all necessary services. Case management is a facilitative process within the framework of assessment, planning, linking, monitoring, and advocacy. Components of case management have been a traditional part of social work practice since the days of Mary Richmond, who stressed the importance of case coordination. Since the mid-1970s, case management has increased in popularity in the delivery of social services to clients with complex situations that place them at risk of diminished capacity. Case management services have been used in many practice fields, including chronic mental disability, aging, physical and developmental disabilities, and child welfare.

Case management is the link between the client and the service delivery system. It is a process based on several tenets and functions, which include but are not limited to the following:

■ functions of assessment, planning, linking, and monitoring services

■ recognition that a trusting and enabling relationship is needed to expedite the utilization of services along a continuum of care and to promote, restore, or maintain the independent functioning of clients

■ advocacy on behalf of clients to ensure that clients receive appropriate and continuous care despite inadequacies of the service system

■ assurance that clients of health and human services systems receive the prescribed services, treatment, and care.

At the center of the service delivery system is the case manager. The case manager's activities are aimed primarily at enhancing the quality of life of the client in the community; serving as the client's representative; keeping individuals from being overlooked; making the system work consistently and coherently for the client; and, from a clinical perspective, reducing the hospitalization rate and length of stay of clients, should hospitalization become necessary.

Social work concepts, especially in the generalist social work theoretical practice model, emphasize four processes:

1. enhancing the developmental, problem-solving, and coping capacities of people

2. promoting the effective and humane operation of systems that provide resources and services to people

3. linking people with systems that provide them with resources, services, and opportunities

4. contributing to the development and improvement of social policies.

Accordingly, the social worker as a case manager will establish a helping relationship, assess clients' needs and available resources, select problem-solving interventions, and help clients to function. Professional values regarding the recognition of the inherent worth and capacity of the individual, the individual's right to self-determination, and the right to confidentiality, along with the *NASW Code of Ethics* (NASW, 1996), interact with the tenets of case management.

With the underlying interaction of the person and the environment in case management and social work, it is appropriate that the profession of social work take an active role and leadership position in advancing case management.

ISSUE STATEMENT

Social workers are the primary providers of case management services to many health, education, and human services systems. The case management model evolved and developed from the concepts and practices of promoting the social welfare of individuals, groups, and populations. Inherent in social work practice is the organization of resources to resolve immediate problems of society, the community, the family, and the individual as the practitioner (or case manager) seeks solutions and strategies to reduce the risk of further harm.

The generic model for the delivery of case management services grew from the experience and expertise of professional social workers involved in all aspects of health, education, and human services programs—that is, service delivery, planning, evaluation, research, and policy development. Recently, we have witnessed an emergence of case management models in a variety of human and health service settings—including those for chronically mentally ill people; substance abusers; and, most recently, people with acquired immunodeficiency syndrome (AIDS). With this, we see a movement toward the use of people other than social work professionals in the design, development, implementation, and administration of case management services. Other professionals are cognizant of the concepts of case management, its

cost-effectiveness (as demonstrated through evaluation research), and its potential efficacy in organizing resources for the delivery of human services.

Only the professional social worker receives the rigorous education and training required to provide and administer case management services. Furthermore, professional licensing and certification demand that the professional social worker demonstrate a thorough knowledge of concepts and practices required by applications of case management models. The demonstration of this knowledge involves not only the successful completion of cognition tests, but a demonstrated ability to apply this knowledge in actual practice. Social workers, therefore, represent the primary source of experience and expertise in case management; social work is a profession with a tradition of promoting minorities, women, people with disabilities, and the recovered into its ranks of management, research, and direct services and the only profession that requires all practitioners to obtain professional education and training in the concepts of case management and to demonstrate the ability to apply these concepts successfully before recognition as social work professionals.

We believe the quality of case management services is highly dependent on the professionals who are responsible for applying the models, organizing the resources for services to clients, and evaluating the outcome. We also believe there is a sufficient supply of experienced social work professionals to plan, manage, and evaluate case management service models and applications. The demand for experienced professionals depends, in part, on how well their peers advocate for representation of the social work profession in all aspects of the administration and delivery of case management services.

POLICY STATEMENT

NASW strongly urges the use of professional social workers in all aspects of the delivery of case management services. NASW views the use of qualified social work professionals in case management as the primary means of ensuring the quality and comprehensiveness of services to clients. The use of social work professionals also assures that approaches to case management are applied effectively and appropriately.

The emergence of case management applications in health education and human services management requires that NASW support the use of professional social workers in the delivery, planning, and evaluation of services. In settings where case management models are used, NASW recommends that organizations and institutions employ professional social workers as service managers and providers.

NASW strongly urges organizations to recruit, select, and retain professional social workers to assume responsibility for case management services. In less populous geographic regions and rural areas and in cases in which organizations are unable to hire and retain adequate numbers of professional social workers and social work managers, NASW recommends that organizations use qualified and experienced social work professionals to act as consultants until such time that others can be recruited to serve as principals in the delivery of case management services.

NASW strongly urges schools of social work at the baccalaureate and graduate levels to include the specific knowledge, methods, and techniques of the case management models in their curricula.

NASW encourages adequate compensation of case managers to attract the best qualified and trained professional social workers in case management.

NASW Standards for Social Work Case Management (NASW, 1992) should be recognized as the standard for professional case management practice.

REFERENCES

National Association of Social Workers. (1992). *NASW standards for social work case management.* Washington, DC: Author.

National Association of Social Workers. (1996). *NASW code of ethics.* Washington, DC: Author.

Policy statement approved by the NASW Delegate Assembly, November 1987; reconfirmed by the Delegate Assembly, August 1993. For further information, contact the National Association of Social Workers, 750 First Street, NE, Suite 700, Washington, DC 20002-4241. Telephone: 202-408-8600 or 800-638-8799.

Child Abuse and Neglect

BACKGROUND

In 1874 a court petition was filed for legal protection and removal of nine-year-old Mary Ellen from her stepmother, who brutally beat and neglected her. The petition argued that Mary Ellen, being human, was a member of the animal kingdom and therefore entitled to protection under the laws protecting animals. Public outrage over the highly publicized case helped lead to the establishment of the Society for the Prevention of Cruelty to Children. Child protection efforts focused on cruel employers and adoptive and foster parents. Biological parents were rarely charged with child abuse, because children were considered the property of parents. The failure of the courts and society to recognize children as individuals with inherent basic rights hampered efforts of child advocates to protect children from their caretakers.

In 1962 *The Battered-Child Syndrome*, published by C. Henry Kempe and his colleagues, identified child abuse as a serious problem and was a catalyst for a new social movement to protect children. In 1963 Colorado was the first state to pass a child abuse law requiring physicians to report suspected cases of child abuse.

By the end of the 1960s, legislation was passed mandating child abuse and neglect reporting in every state (Pagelow, 1984). The Child Abuse Prevention and Treatment Act (CAPTA) was signed into law in 1974 and established the National Center on Child Abuse and Neglect (NCCAN), with the mission to assess the extent of the problem, to examine models for prevention and treatment, and to act as a catalyst for change. NCCAN focused its efforts on encouraging states to pass child protection legislation, including reporting requirements; to educate law enforcement professionals in investigating and prosecuting child abuse cases; and to create coordinated child protection systems sensitive to the needs of children and families. NCCAN provided guidance to professionals involved in the child protection system and stressed multidisciplinary collaboration as a method to expand and coordinate services to children and families.

NCCAN became a valuable source of funding for research into the causes of child abuse and neglect and modalities of treatment and prevention. Since that time, a proliferation of research has expanded the original medical model to include other variables such as economic and social stressors and individual coping skills among people who maltreat children.

In 1980, the Adoption Assistance and Child Welfare Act of 1980 (P.L. 96-272) was enacted to create an individual entitlement for foster care and adoption assistance and to establish a national program of child welfare services for children who were victims of abuse and neglect. The act not only authorized funding for these programs but also provided safeguards and standards for states' intervention on behalf of children endangered by intrafamilial abuse and neglect. As a condition of funding, it required reasonable efforts to prevent out-of-home placements of children, reunify families, and establish permanent plans within specified time limits. Finally, the act provided funds for staff and foster parent training; subsidies to help to assure adoption, particularly for hard-to-place children who would otherwise remain in foster care; and "independent living program" services for children being emancipated from foster care.

During the 1980s NCCAN began to focus on prevention. In 1985 it provided the first Challenge Grants to states to establish Children's Trust Funds for community primary prevention programs. Ray E. Helfer, a Michigan pediatrician and vice-president of the National Committee for the Prevention of Child Abuse, proposed a nationwide network of funds dedicated to the prevention of child abuse and neglect in 1979. Kansas was the first state to establish a Children's Trust Fund in 1980. There are currently 51 trust and prevention funds established by state legislative action. As public–private partnerships, trust and prevention funds work closely with public agencies and the private sector.

The 1988 amendments to the CAPTA (P.L. 100-294) established the U.S. Advisory Board on Child Abuse and Neglect. The board's mission is to evaluate the nation's efforts to accomplish the purposes of CAPTA and to recommend ways to improve those efforts for the benefit of children, families, and society at large. In its 1990 report, the board concluded that "child abuse and neglect in the United States now represent a national emergency" (U.S. Advisory Board on Child Abuse and Neglect, 1990). The board based its conclusions on three findings: (1) Each year hundreds to thousands of children are starved, abandoned, burned, severely beaten, raped, sodomized, and berated; (2) the system the nation has devised to respond to child abuse and neglect is failing; and (3) the United States spends billions of dollars on programs that deal with the results of the nation's failure to prevent abuse and neglect.

A 1995 U.S. Advisory Board on Child Abuse and Neglect report stated that abuse and neglect in the home is a leading cause of death for children age four and under. The federal advisory panel concluded that at least 2,000 children per year, or five children every day, die at the hands of their parents or caretakers. More preschool-age children die at the hands of parents than from falls, choking on food, suffocation, drowning, fires, or street violence. The board found that child deaths are often wrongly attributed to accidents or natural causes because police, physicians, or coroners are largely untrained in identifying evidence of inflicted trauma and severe neglect in children. These problems, combined with inaccurately completed death certificates, have resulted in a long-standing underestimation of the nature and extent of this national crisis. The report makes 26 recommendations for saving children by improving accountability for identifying and reporting child abuse fatalities, promoting prevention services, ensuring more effective prosecution of caretakers who murder children, increasing training of legal and medical professionals, ensuring that children's safety is a priority in all child and family service programs, and developing a structure for a national focus to prevent fatalities.

In fall 1993 Congress enacted the Family Preservation and Family Support Services Act (part of the Omnibus Budget Reconciliation Act of 1993), which offered states and communities an opportunity to reform their child and family services systems fundamentally. The act called for broad-based and ongoing planning to identify needs, resources, and capabilities in states and communities and recommended improvements in services delivery. The act also provided new funding to assist in the implementation of community-based prevention and supportive services to strengthen families to help them avoid crisis and cope better when crisis does occur. The goals of the act are to contribute to the development of a more responsive, collaborative, family-centered child and family services system.

The Center for the Study of Social Policy and the Children's Defense Fund issued a guide for planning in October 1994, noting that the lives and prospects of many children and families are poor and getting worse. The traditional approach to categorical programs often requires families to demonstrate failure before assistance is provided. Child welfare professionals need a more comprehensive array of services, including preventive services, before problems are manifest.

Social workers can provide assistance that protects children by helping families recognize and build on their own strengths and the strengths of their communities. Building this kind of comprehensive, family-centered, and community-based system of services requires the broad and deep involvement of every agency serving children, of parents and communities, and of other groups and institutions that play important roles in protecting children (Center for the Study of Social Policy and Children's Defense Fund, 1994).

ISSUE STATEMENT

Abuse and neglect are leading causes of death for young children in the United States. Each year, hundreds of thousands of children are subjected to abuse and neglect. Social workers play key roles in the prevention, identification, investigation, treatment, and administration of services for children and their families. The profession of social work should facilitate child protection through comprehensive efforts to ensure the healthy development of children.

Societal response to the protection of children has been an evolutionary process complicated by diverse ideologies, contradictory political forces, economic trends, divergent laws, and widespread differences in child-rearing practices (National Association of Public Child Welfare Administrators, 1988). Child maltreatment occurs in all cultural, ethnic, occupational, and socioeconomic groups but is most often reported among poor, single-parent families of color. For this reason, a culturally sensitive approach is required based on a clear understanding of the influences of poverty, racism, and sexism in U.S. society.

Families are the first caregivers for children. Families have the first responsibility for the physical and emotional well-being of children. Families, however, are bombarded daily with stresses that make it difficult to provide adequately for their children. Rising poverty, fewer living-wage jobs, increasing unemployment and underemployment, inaccessible health care, reductions in mental health and drug rehabilitation services, inadequate housing, and increased crime and violence are all taking their toll on families. Preventive child and family services have been scaled back in both the public and voluntary sectors. Public resources have become severely inadequate, particularly in impoverished communities. Child welfare priorities have focused on intervention after abuse and neglect have taken place. Crisis responses and out-of-home placements have become the most routine interventions rather than consumer-driven, preventive services. The complex issues in understanding child abuse and neglect demand that social workers explore ethical, legal, and clinical issues in prevention, investigation, intervention, and treatment of child abuse and neglect.

The U.S. Advisory Board on Child Abuse and Neglect (1993) listed the following findings:

■ Each year, hundreds of thousands of American children are subjected to abuse and neglect. Approximately 2.3 million children were reported in 1993 as suspected victims of abuse and neglect.

■ Often the child protection system fails to protect such children from further maltreatment or to alleviate the consequences of maltreatment.

■ The child protection system has developed largely in an unplanned fashion, with resulting failure to reach many of the children in need of protection and to provide effective services to children and their families.

■ Substantial gaps exist in knowledge about child abuse and neglect, the diffusion of that knowledge, and the development of a pool of trained professionals who specialize in child protection.

■ Tolerance of child abuse and neglect threatens the integrity of the nation because of its inconsistency with core American values: regard for individuals as worthy of respect, reverence for family life, concern for one's neighbors, and competence in economic competition.

■ Failure to provide an effective system of child protection also imperils the nation by increasing the risk of crime and physical and mental illness.

■ The link between child abuse and substance abuse has strengthened over the years. Parental abuse of alcohol and use of other drugs have been identified as major factors contributing to child maltreatment and death.

■ Consequences of child abuse and neglect cost the nation billions of dollars each year in direct expenditures for health, social, and special educational services.

POLICY STATEMENT

NASW believes that children have a right to protection from all forms of child maltreatment. Child abuse and neglect include physical, emotional and sexual abuse, neglect, and exploitation. Children have a right to be treated with respect as individuals and to receive culturally sensitive services from professionals who are trained in the ethnic and linguistic backgrounds of their client populations.

The profession of social work should continue its historic commitment to child protection through comprehensive efforts to ensure the safety and healthy development of children. In promotion of these efforts, NASW supports the following principles:

■ Public and private agencies and systems that serve children and families should work collaboratively to maximize their resources and effectiveness in preventing child abuse and neglect and effectively treating victims and their families. Such a collaborative network would include child protective services; courts and law enforcement agencies; medical, education, and mental health providers; and national boards and commissions.

■ A comprehensive approach to the prevention of child abuse and neglect should include increased public awareness and availability of family support services, parenting education, and training for staff in the identification of risk factors for children and families. A comprehensive approach to prevention must also address the stressors that precipitate family violence. Community-based services to enhance and support healthy family life include day care, recreation and leisure activities, parent education, counseling, case management, job training, health and mental health services, and adequate financial support for families.

■ A continuum of services should be available to all families, beginning with prenatal care and parent education.

■ Public policy and resource allocation to protect children should support specialized law enforcement, child abuse investigative units, child advocacy services, mandatory reporting of suspected child neglect and abuse, development and use of risk assessment tools, continued professional training of staff working with children and families, and community-based efforts toward identification and early intervention in situations of suspected child abuse and neglect.

■ Social work education and training should emphasize effective treatment for victims of child abuse and neglect, the psychological impact of trauma on a child's development, the specialized treatment needs of abused children, family-focused intervention, and community-based approaches toward prevention.

■ Bachelor's and master's degrees in social work (BSW and MSW) are the most appropriate educational requirements for child protection workers. Undergraduate and graduate schools of social work should include competency-based course work and field placements in child abuse and neglect. Financial incentives and educational leave should be available for staff in the field of child protection to obtain BSW and MSW degrees.

■ Child maltreatment and prevention should be included in the undergraduate and graduate curricula for social work, education, psychology, law, medicine, nursing, and other disciplines that work with children and families.

■ Children are generally protected best by strengthening the child's family and kinship network. Children should remain with their families with appropriate and adequate supports when their safety and well-being can be ensured. Clear criteria and professional judgment should be used in making decisions regarding the maintenance, removal, and return of children to their biological or adoptive families.

■ Services must recognize and address the special needs of vulnerable populations such as people with disabilities and very young children.

■ Professionally trained social workers should take leadership roles in developing and strengthening policy, legislation, and child protection programs. School social workers in particular have a role in educating teachers, administrators, and support staff in identifying suspected child abuse and neglect.

■ The National Research Council (1993) research agenda on child abuse and neglect should be implemented.

■ Government, community, and workplace policies should facilitate positive parent and child relationships that build on the strengths in each individual and family and kinship network.

- Sufficient public and private funding, staff, and resources should be provided to meet the needs of abused and neglected children and their families. Child protective services staff should be professionally educated, adequately trained, administratively supported, and legally protected.

- Standards for caseload or workload size among child protection workers need to be established that ensure the provision of effective case management services to each at-risk child and family.

- Management information systems that track the status of children and families should be developed and used in a way that protects children and supports families.

- Specialized treatment for juvenile and adult sex offenders should be mandated.

REFERENCES

Adoption Assistance and Child Welfare Act of 1980, P.L. 96-272, 94 Stat. 500.

Center for the Study of Social Policy and Children's Defense Fund. (1994, October). *A guide for planning: Making strategic use of the family preservation and support services program.* Washington, DC: Authors.

Child Abuse Prevention and Treatment Act, P.L. 93-247, 88 Stat. 4 (1974).

Child Abuse Prevention and Treatment Act, P.L. 100-294, Title I, §101, 102 Stat. 102 (1988).

Kempe, C., Silverman, F., Steele, B., Droegmueller, W., & Silver, H. (1962). The battered child syndrome. *Journal of the American Medical Association, 181,* 17–18.

National Association of Public Child Welfare Administrators. (1988). *Guidelines for a model system of protective services for abused and neglected children and their families.* Washington, DC: American Public Welfare Association.

National Research Council. (1993). *Understanding child abuse and neglect.* Washington, DC: National Academy Press.

Omnibus Reconciliation Act of 1993, P.L. 103-66, 107 Stat. 312.

Pagelow, M. D. (1984). *Family violence.* New York: Praeger.

U.S. Advisory Board on Child Abuse and Neglect. (1990, August). *Child abuse and neglect: Critical first steps in response to a national emergency.* Washington, DC: U.S. Department of Health and Human Services, Administration for Children and Families.

U.S. Advisory Board on Child Abuse and Neglect. (1993, April). *The continuing child protection emergency: A challenge to the nation.* Washington, DC: U.S. Department of Health and Human Services, Administration for Children and Families.

U.S. Advisory Board of Child Abuse and Neglect. (1995. April). *A nation's shame: Fatal child abuse and neglect in the United States.* Washington, DC: U.S. Department of Health and Human Services, Administration for Children and Families.

Policy statement approved by the NASW Delegate Assembly, August 1996. For further information, contact the National Association of Social Workers, 750 First Street, NE, Suite 700, Washington, DC 20002-4241. Telephone: 202-408-8600 or 800-638-8799.

Civil Liberties and Justice

BACKGROUND

The *NASW Code of Ethics* (NASW, 1993) requires social workers to make the interests of clients their primary responsibility. It states not only that social workers "should not practice, condone, facilitate or collaborate with any form of discrimination" (p. 5) but that they "should not condone or engage in any dual or multiple relationships with clients or former clients in which there is a risk of exploitation of or potential harm to the client" (p. 5). In the final section, "The Social Worker's Ethical Responsibility to Society," the *Code* goes beyond describing proscriptive behavior and establishes an affirmative obligation for social workers to take action "to prevent and eliminate discrimination . . . to ensure that all people have access to resources, services, and opportunities which they require . . . to expand choice and opportunity for all people, with special regard for disadvantaged or oppressed groups and people . . . [and to] advocate changes in policy and legislation to improve social conditions and to promote social justice."

The *Code*, therefore, regards the attainment of the individual well-being of clients and the achievement of the common good as complementary pursuits. Under the guise of promoting traditional values, however, ascendant political and religious leaders have undermined the preservation of individual liberties and set back long-standing societal efforts to broaden the application of social justice principles, particularly for oppressed and disadvantaged groups, which are the focus of social work's historical concern. These setbacks have occurred in five vital areas: (1) the criminal justice and penal systems; (2) access to justice; (3) restrictions on First Amendment rights, particularly freedom of expression, and on the separation of church and state; (4) the due process and equal protection clauses of the Fourteenth Amendment; and (5) the right to privacy and its effects on social services.

ISSUE STATEMENT

Throughout the 1980s and early 1990s, the fragile gains in civil liberties and social justice obtained by the social movements of the 1950s, 1960s, and 1970s were steadily eroded by executive order, legislation, voter referenda, and judicial decisions. In an era in which the triumph of freedom and democracy has been hailed by U.S. political leaders, it is ironic that in the United States the legal rights of women, people of color, gay and lesbian people, and people with low incomes have been abrogated by federal cutback policies and abridged by administrative neglect at all levels of government. Each of these groups has been increasingly stigmatized as a means to distract attention from the socioeconomic issues that afflict the entire society. Recently, under the guise of promoting family values, concerted political and ideological attacks have been targeted at the changing roles of women in U.S. society, the growing acceptance of alternative sexual lifestyles, and the consequent evolution of increasingly varied family constellations in the United States.

Simultaneously the civil liberties of many constituent populations, including people with AIDS or HIV-related illness, deinstitutionalized mental patients, welfare recipients, juvenile and adult offenders, union members, immigrants and refugees, and substance abusers, as well as social workers who work with them, have been denied or severely limited by changes in government policy or cutbacks in government programs. For example, federal gag rules not only denied women their reproductive rights, but also denied health and human services workers their right of free speech. Restrictions on the confidentiality of case records similarly affect the well-being of clients and the professional integrity of social workers.

Furthermore, the assault on civil liberties has also involved growing demands for the censorship of books and other forms of cultural expression; restrictions on the rights of people to bring suit against the government; increased incidents of police brutality, particularly in communities of color; punishment of whistle-blowers who expose government misconduct; and redefinition of many individual and social problems in criminal terms. These developments create a fertile soil for the spread of dangerous trends already visible on the nation's cultural landscape, such as increases in racially or religiously motivated hate crimes, crimes against women, and restrictions on people's right to privacy. If social workers, who have long championed the cause of individual and social rights, and social workers' allies do not take action to reverse these trends, the freedoms social workers have taken for granted for so long may be seriously curtailed in the decade ahead.

The Criminal Justice System

Social workers share the increasing concern of citizens over the rise in crime, particularly violent crime, in the United States. The increase in attacks on social workers in the workplace has underscored the dangers that social workers face in their daily work. Nevertheless, the focus of politicians and the media on crime and the criminalization of many activities has masked the social problems that lie behind the growing crime rate. However, the emphasis on public fear has served as a rationale for diverting resources from programs that address those problems toward the construction of prisons and the expansion of police power. They also have provided the justification for the infringement of defendants' rights and the erosion of many of the protections guaranteed in the Bill of Rights. The beating of Rodney King by Los Angeles police officers was a highly visual example of increasing police violence in communities of color.

No-Knock Entry. The expanded use of no-knock entry allows police to break into homes without warrants if they suspect that needed evidence is on the premises. This tactic, justified as part of the necessary arsenal of police in the war on drugs, encourages police to consider too many situations as "emergencies" and constitutes a clear invitation to violate the constitutional prohibition of illegal searches and seizures. Police and prosecutors have used similar arguments to chip away at defendants' rights established by the Warren Court, most notably the *Miranda* decision (*Miranda v. Arizona*, 1966), which protects an individual accused of a crime from self-incrimination and guarantees all defendants the right to legal counsel before interrogation.

Preventive Detention. Preventive detention is a procedure for incarcerating allegedly dangerous defendants between their arrest and trial. Those who support such procedures point out that many crimes of violence are perpetrated by people who are out on bail and awaiting trial. The growing use of this procedure, however, violates the historic principle of Anglo-American common law that an individual is considered innocent until proven guilty. Preventive detention places accused people and their families in jeopardy in that it may prevent them from locating witnesses and preparing their cases. The procedure deprives families of the accused of economic support and unfairly stigmatizes them before they have been convicted by a jury of their peers. Low-income people and people of color are more likely to be affected by such intimidating measures.

Proposed Federal Legislation. Federal reform legislation currently under consideration would have devastating effects on individual rights, particularly on the most vulnerable segments of the population. The proposed legislation would extend the death penalty to some 51 offenses, including those that do not involve either murder or unintentional deaths. It would restrict access to the federal courts by all but eliminating the opportunity to review a state prisoner's claim that his or her constitutional rights had been violated. (This proposal would virtually abolish the principle of *habeas corpus*.)

It would impose a new set of harsh mandatory minimum sentences for drug and gun offenses. It would require expensive drug testing of all people convicted of federal crimes before they are released on probation, parole, or supervised release, regardless of whether drug use was a factor in their commission of a crime. Furthermore, the proposed legislation would prohibit the use of research data to prove the prevalence of racial discrimination in capital cases, although data demonstrate that the racial background of defendants, victims, and juries significantly influences the outcome of trials and the severity of sentences (U.S. General Accounting Office, 1991).

Although the legislative proposals are still pending, the effects of changes already made in the criminal justice system have been profound. The United States now has the highest percentage of its population incarcerated of any nation in the world. Currently more than 2,500 people are on death row in U.S. prisons (NAACP Legal Defense Fund, 1992). A higher percentage of defendants are sent to prison for longer terms, often for minor, first offenses, because of mandatory sentencing requirements (U.S. Department of Justice, 1992). The increased sentencing rates have produced significant overcrowding in jails and prisons, itself a violation of prisoners' rights, as well as the diversion of resources from social programs that could prevent crime and recidivism toward prison construction.

African Americans compose a disproportionate number of criminal defendants and inhabitants of death row (Children's Defense Fund, 1993; National Center on Institutions and Alternatives, 1993). More than 25 percent of African American men aged 18 to 29 years are in prison, jail, on probation, or on parole. More African American men are in prison than in college, and death from homicide, which is six times more frequent among African American men, is the number one cause of death for African American men between the ages of 15 and 44 years. African American youths are also overly represented in the juvenile court system. The juvenile court traditions of rehabilitation and diversion, especially for first offenders, are rapidly being replaced by emphasis on punishments of increasing severity.

Access to Justice

Although the Fourteenth Amendment guarantees all members of society equal protection under the law and due process, actions by executive and judicial branches of government have severely diminished these constitutional guarantees, especially for low-income, low-power groups. Three developments illustrate the impact of such decisions at the executive level.

First, the attempts by the Reagan and Bush administrations to eliminate Legal Aid Services for the poor and the subsequent underfunding of this program resulted in a severe lack of lawyers for low-income defendants (a violation of the Sixth Amendment) and the inability of low-income plaintiffs to file suits for damages when the program literally ran out of money (a possible violation of the Fourteenth Amendment). At the same time federal budgets increased the resources provided to prosecutors, further tipping the balance of power in the court system. These events combined with recently imposed restrictions on class action suits have severely curtailed the ability of low-income people and low-power groups to seek redress for civil grievances.

Second, Presidents Reagan and Bush named a majority of members to the current Supreme Court and nearly two-thirds of all current federal judges—a majority in nine of the 13 appellate circuits, where most decisions affecting federal laws and public policies are made. Pending appointments would create a majority in all 13 circuits. These courts bear the major responsibility for the increase in executions in the United States. Even when Congress "acts to undo court rulings—as it did with the hard-fought Civil Rights Act of 1991—those new laws return to the federal courts to be interpreted by the same judges whose views prompted the laws in the first place" (Mauro, 1992, p. 7). Because only two of the Reagan-Bush appointments to appeals courts are African Americans, and an ideological litmus test was applied to those nominated, it is not surprising that "the losers in this ideological battle are those who most need the protection of the courts: minorities, criminal defendants, the downtrodden" (Mauro, 1992, p. 10).

Third, in 1983, the Reagan administration issued Rule 11, which asserted that individuals or groups bringing "frivolous" suits against the government could be fined. The aim of this regulation was to discourage lawsuits trying to stop illegal actions by the government. Recently this rule has been applied in an attempt to stop an action filed by the Center for Constitutional Rights on behalf of Haitian refugees seeking political asylum, whose efforts to obtain legal counsel were blocked by the Justice Department.

In the 1980s numerous judicial decisions also restricted the access of individuals and groups to the legal system to seek a redress for specific grievances. In the *Patterson* case (*Patterson v. McLean Credit Union*, 1989), for example, the Supreme Court severely limited the use of the Civil Rights Act of 1966 to remedy workplace discrimination in private businesses. After this decision more than 300 pending suits were dismissed and a number of judgments already won were reversed. In *Los Angeles v. Lyons* (1983), the Court ruled that the plaintiff could not sue for an injunction, although he suffered permanent physical damage because of the use of illegal choke holds by police officers, on the grounds that the plaintiff could not prove "that he was likely to be the victim of an illegal choke hold in the future" (Mauro, 1992, p. 11). Since then, virtually every circuit court of appeals has adopted the reasoning used in *Lyons* to decline to take actions against allegations of police brutality. Furthermore, in Supreme Court cases, such as *City of Richmond v. Croson* (1989) and numerous lower court cases subsequent to this decision, the courts have eroded the principle of affirmative action as it has been applied to a board range of programs, including the awarding of government contracts and Federal Communications Commission licenses, the hiring and promotion policies of corporations, and the admissions and financial aid policies of colleges and universities.

Restrictions on First Amendment Rights

The test of civil liberties is not how people treat others who express only majority opinions; it is how we treat what Justice Oliver Wendell Holmes called the "opinions we loathe" (cited in Glasser, 1991, p. 12). Dissent is a critical part of the process of democratic dialogue and an integral component of social change. The right to dissent, embodied most clearly in the First Amendment of the Constitution, is perhaps the most precious of civil liberties. When those in power refuse to listen to dissenters or refuse to allow dissenting opinions and values to be expressed, people's faith in the integrity of the political system is undermined. More than just the freedom to dissent is at issue. The system itself will be in jeopardy unless it is able continually to adapt to new ideas and new imperatives. In the final analysis the preservation of liberties depends on the willingness of people to put those liberties into practice. In the words of Judge Learned Hand, "When liberty dies in the hearts of men and women, no constitution, no court can save it" (cited in Glasser, 1991, p. 12).

Yet the threats to these precious liberties are greater now than at any time in the past half century. These threats have taken several distinct forms on several distinct fronts:

■ repression of political dissent by policy, particularly during the demonstrations that accompanied the Gulf War and that erupted in the aftermath of the verdict in the Rodney King trial.

■ attempts to ban acts of symbolic protest, such as flag burning, student speech, and expressions in public forums, through legislation, judicial ruling, or constitutional amendment.

■ restrictions on artistic freedom, for example through the revocation of grants to artists from the National Endowment for the Arts based on new "decency" standards; attempts to legislate the censorship of lyrics of popular songs, especially by rap groups, on the grounds that they are "obscene" or "inflammatory"; and the closure of museum exhibits because of allegations that they offended local standards of morality.

■ increased incidents of book banning by local school boards and library committees.

■ attacks on labor unions and government-imposed restrictions on workers' rights to organize and to strike.

- laws restricting panhandling by indigent and homeless individuals.

- punishment of whistle-blowers in institutions as varied as the Pentagon and local departments of social services.

- erosion of the constitutional separation of church and state, for example through the government's support of tax breaks for private sectarian colleges, promotion of tax credits for private school tuition, support for religious groups seeking to use public schools for meetings, and promotion of official school-sponsored prayer.

- restrictions on free speech in the area of women's reproductive rights, most notably through the institution of a gag rule, upheld by the Supreme Court in *Rust v. Sullivan* (1991). This executive order forbade health and human services professionals in any clinic that receives federal funds "to discuss or offer information about abortion, or to indicate where such information might be available, even for women who specifically ask to discuss abortion and have no other access to medical advice" (Dworkin, 1991).

Fourteenth Amendment Rights

The most significant of the civil rights amendments, the Fourteenth Amendment, states, "No state shall make or enforce any law which shall abridge the privileges or immunities of citizens of the United States; nor shall any state deprive any person of life, liberty, or property, without due process of law; nor deny to any person within its jurisdiction the equal protection of the laws." In the 1950s and 1960s, this amendment was used as legal justification for the expansion of civil rights and liberties, particularly to people of color, women, and low-income people. In the 1980s and early 1990s, however, the gains fostered by the amendment were diminished by executive and judicial actions at the federal and state levels. These actions include

- failure by states and localities to comply with court-ordered desegregation plans

- violations of the civil rights of recent immigrants and refugees by local police departments, the Immigration and Naturalization Service, and the Internal Revenue Service

- unwillingness of courts to protect the rights of former mental patients who have been denied essential services because of the underfunding of community mental health programs

- failure of the Justice Department to enforce the provisions of the Civil Rights Act and dilution of its original intention by assertions that plaintiffs must prove the *intention* to discriminate in instances of demonstrated employment or housing bias

- decisions by state and federal courts that reject lawsuits attempting to overturn existing patterns of school funding, which place low-income, largely minority districts at a considerable resource disadvantage

- repeal of local gay and lesbian rights ordinances and the introduction of anti–gay and lesbian referenda in several states.

The Right to Privacy

Because the 1965 *Griswold v. Connecticut* decision upheld the right of adults to purchase contraceptives, the right to a "zone of privacy" has been regarded as implicitly guaranteed by the First, Fourth, Ninth, and Fourteenth Amendments to the Constitution. This guarantee, which served as the foundation for the expansion of women's reproductive rights, the rights of workers, and the rights of social services clients, has been steadily attacked by policy initiatives and judicial decisions that upheld the initiatives.

- Reproductive rights have been curtailed so sharply by state legislatures and the Supreme Court—in the *Webster* (*Webster v. Reproductive Health Services*, 1989) and *Casey* cases, for example—that the rights guaranteed to women in *Roe v. Wade* (1973) are in serious jeopardy. Growing numbers of legislative initiatives have attempted to impose "fetal murder" charges on women who obtain abortions and on their physicians. There have been proposals to deny women on probation the right to become pregnant. In addition, many recent welfare "reforms" in effect deny the right of women to have children when they desire through sanctions imposed by the state in the provision of benefits.

■ Corporate and government surveillance of workers has increased markedly in the past decade under the guise of promoting greater worker efficiency and productivity and rooting out drug and alcohol abuse. The imposition of electronic and computer surveillance and random drug tests are but a few examples of this practice, which has created a climate of fear and suspicion in many organizations. Pre-employment health screenings and background checks of job seekers have been used to deny employment to applicants and health benefits to employees.

■ In Wisconsin and other states, welfare clients have been subject to random home visits to determine whether violations of eligibility requirements have occurred. Such checks are not only demeaning to clients, but they also jeopardize the social worker–client relationship and the integrity of social workers required to implement them.

■ The growing use of computer networks to store and share information about clients threatens the confidentiality of these records, particularly when police authorities and the courts demand access to them. On a broader scale the development of computerized data banks, which store information on virtually all people in the United States, has already had serious consequences for privacy rights and civil liberties. Errors, inaccuracies, and misinterpretation or exaggeration of youthful activity and lawful dissent from the accepted views of the majority could distort facts and have permanent consequences for individuals involved.

■ The use of mandatory HIV testing as a prerequisite to obtain essential services has endangered the well-being of many clients and subjected many people to discrimination in other arenas, such as employment and housing.

POLICY STATEMENT

In its historic role as an agent of social change, the social work profession has achieved its greatest successes when it has regarded change in a broad perspective, linking the improvements sought through social and economic reforms with the larger cultural, legal, political, and ideological dimensions of the issues it has addressed. NASW calls on the social work profession to reaffirm its long-standing commitment to individual liberties and social justice. NASW considers the protection of individual rights and the promotion of social justice essential to the preservation of our collective well-being as a society. NASW urges social workers and other policy makers to focus on the following areas.

Criminal Justice Reform

Abolition of the Death Penalty. There is no evidence that the death penalty serves as a deterrent to violent crime. In fact the recent increase in homicides in the United States has occurred despite the reinstitution of capital punishment in most states. The abolition of the death penalty would bring the United States' penal system in line with those of other modern industrialized societies. As it is currently used, the death penalty violates the constitutional prohibition against cruel and unusual punishment. In addition, the unequal application of the death penalty deprives many people of color and low-income people of the Fourteenth Amendment's guarantee of "equal protection under the law."

Protection of the Rights of Criminal Defendants. Although legitimate police activities are justified to protect human life and property, recent expansion of police and prosecutorial powers seriously infringes on the rights of the accused and violates the basic common law principle of presumed innocence. NASW opposes all legislation that would permit no-knock entry by police into homes without a proper warrant, the use of preventive detention by the courts, and the steady erosion of *Miranda* rights by the judiciary. NASW also opposes the use of mandatory sentencing requirements, particularly for first-time offenders, on the grounds that it substitutes an emphasis on punishment for one on rehabilitation within the criminal justice system and that it virtually eliminates judicial discretion to factor in environmental circumstances in determining the severity of sentences.

Protection against Self-Incrimination. The Fifth Amendment to the Constitution grants individuals protection from self-incrimination. People cannot be forced to testify against themselves. In *Grunewald v. United States* (1957), the Supreme Court stated, "Recent examination of the history and meaning of the Fifth Amendment has emphasized anew that one of the basic functions of the privilege is to protect *innocent men*" [emphasis added].

Currently, police and courts at all levels of government abuse this privilege. Grand juries use subpoenas to force journalists to divulge confidential sources; social workers are pressured to reveal confidential information about their clients; and mandatory drug and HIV testing is imposed on employees, prospective employees, and criminal defendants for actions with no direct relation either to drug abuse or HIV status. The principle of *habeas corpus* is under direct attack by proposed federal policy. The use of electronic and computer surveillance has expanded considerably, and computer surveillance in particular has the potential for virtually infinite intrusion into the lives of innocent people.

NASW holds that these actions constitute a misuse of government authority and should not be permitted. Although protection against crime is a legitimate police function, more can be done to fight crime by devoting greater resources to the elimination of its causes than by repressive measures that jeopardize the well-being of innocent people.

Civilian Review of Police Activity. Because the increasing number of incidents of abuse of police authority creates greater distrust of government institutions, particularly in communities of color, and threatens to generate growing civil unrest, closer scrutiny of police activities is needed. NASW supports the establishment of civilian review boards to monitor police conduct and to investigate allegations of excessive use of force by police officers.

Access to Justice

Restoration of Legal Assistance Funds. Because the constitutional right to legal counsel is one of the cornerstones of the U.S. system of justice, low-income defendants and plaintiffs in civil actions must be provided with ade-

quate legal assistance. NASW supports the restoration of full funding for legal aid services and opposes any attempts by the federal government to eviscerate this vital program any further.

Judicial Appointments. Because the courts, particularly at the federal level, constitute the last resort of protection for the rights of the people, NASW supports the appointment of judges who are committed to the maintenance of civil liberties as guaranteed by the Constitution. NASW also supports the appointment of judges who reflect more accurately the demographic diversity of the United States, particularly in regard to people of color and women.

Due Process Issues. NASW opposes any executive or legislative initiatives that would restrict the rights of individuals to file class action suits, either against the government or corporations. NASW supports the unimpeded application of individuals' civil rights through the courts in such areas as sexual harassment, employment discrimination, and housing bias.

First Amendment Rights

The Right to Dissent. The right to dissent from prevailing opinions of the majority—in political and cultural arenas—is a fundamental principle of a democratic society. NASW supports the following four principles regarding political and cultural expression:

1. All individuals should exercise their right to dissent with responsibility and with respect for the opinions of others.

2. No individual should be denied funds from federal or state agencies, or access to services to which he or she would be otherwise entitled, on the basis of his or her participation in lawful protest and dissent.

3. No individual should be arrested for the lawful exercise of his or her First Amendment rights of free speech and free assembly. Individuals who are arrested in the course of infractions of ordinary law should be fully informed of their rights. Such individuals also have a right not to be subjected to undue force by the law

enforcement officer or officers making the arrest. Pretrial treatment, trial, and sentencing should be the province of the judicial system, following the constitutional principle of due process.

4. Pending action on any charges, the status of individuals participating in any acts of dissent should not be altered, particularly in regard to employment, access to services, and other legal entitlements; nor should the work or eligibility status of individuals be suspended prior to the institution of formal charges.

Freedom of Expression. NASW opposes all executive, legislative, or judicial actions that restrict freedom of speech, assembly, or cultural expression. Specifically, NASW opposes attempts to limit artistic freedom through the withholding of government grants (for example, by the National Endowment of the Arts); the imposition of any form of censorship by local authorities in regard to museum exhibits, library holdings, or school reading lists; and any government restrictions on the rights of individuals or groups to protest policies or actions to which they are opposed.

Workers' Rights. The social work profession has long recognized the importance of the labor movement as an ally in its struggle for civil rights and social justice. NASW reaffirms its support for the right of workers to organize, to engage in collective bargaining to improve their working conditions, and to strike to draw attention to their grievances. NASW opposes any abrogation of these rights by administrative regulation, legislation, or judicial action. NASW also opposes the use of medical screenings to deny workers access to health benefits, the imposition of mandatory drug testing in the workplace, and the use of electronic or computer surveillance of employees to monitor job performance. Furthermore, NASW supports the courage of whistleblowers in the public and private sectors and opposes the use of sanctions that discourage or punish such behavior.

Separation of Church and State. NASW strongly supports the constitutional principle of separation of church and state. NASW avers that the expression of religious beliefs is a personal and private matter that should be neither con-strained nor promoted by the government in any way. Therefore NASW opposes the use of tax policy, administrative regulations, or the distribution of government funds to support organized religion in any manner.

Equal Protection under the Law

Events of the past decade have demonstrated that the existence of legislative or judicial rights does not guarantee their implementation by the executive branch of government, particularly when the resistance of that branch is abetted by the judiciary. NASW strongly supports the *full* implementation of existing civil rights legislation and its application to women, people of color, and gays and lesbians. NASW also strongly supports the expansion of these rights to include immigrants and refugees, people who are mentally ill—both inside and outside institutions—and recipients of public assistance and their families. NASW opposes all efforts to deny or retract these rights from *any* individuals or groups in the United States.

The Right to Privacy/Social Services and Civil Rights

The *NASW Code of Ethics* (NASW, 1996) emphasizes that social work's practices, as well as its goals, must include an affirmative obligation to offer protection against excesses of authority that violate the rights of people whom social workers serve. In many states, counties, and cities, the following practices, supported by law, official regulation, or bureaucratic imperatives, continue to curtail the civil liberties of those who are least able to resist them. In particular, NASW strongly supports the preservation of the constitutional right to privacy, especially in its application to health and human services settings, and strongly condemns the following:

■ any attempts by the federal government to reimpose the gag rule and its affirmation by the Supreme Court in *Rust v. Sullivan* (1991).

■ any efforts by state legislatures, Congress, the executive branch of the federal government, or the courts to restrict access to information about abortion, contraception, or family planning, or to restrict access to any of these services.

NASW specifically opposes the current ban on Medicaid funding of abortion and government efforts to erode and, ultimately, overturn the right of women to seek an abortion established in *Roe v. Wade* (1973), on the grounds that such actions constitute an unwarranted invasion of privacy.

■ mandatory HIV, DNA, or drug testing as a precondition for employment or the receipt of services for which an individual would be otherwise eligible.

■ violation of the confidentiality of welfare rolls or of case records of individuals who seek assistance because of drug/alcohol abuse or HIV-related illness, or the use of computer-stored information for purposes other than the enhancement of service delivery to clients.

■ unannounced inspections of homes, made without warrants, at inappropriate times with the ostensible purpose of checking on continuing eligibility for public assistance or on the "desirability" of the home.

■ the use of degrading and humiliating methods to determine eligibility for public assistance or social services by investigators whose practice violates some of the basic principles of the profession.

■ state legislation to sterilize welfare recipients or deny them benefits if they have more than a certain number of children.

■ legislative or administrative actions that involve the imposition of punitive sanctions to deny the right of women on probation to become pregnant.

■ the eviction of tenants designated as "undesirable" in low-income public housing, for vaguely defined reasons, without providing such tenants with administrative or judicial due process.

REFERENCES

Children's Defense Fund. (1993). *The state of America's children.* Washington, DC: Author.

City of Richmond v. J. A. Croson Co., 488 U.S. 469 (1989).

Dworkin, R. (1991, July 18). The Reagan revolution and the Supreme Court. *New York Review of Books*, pp. 23–28.

Glasser, I. (1991). The Bill of Rights at 200: Remembering what it all means. *Civil Liberties, 374,* 1, 12.

Griswold v. Connecticut, 381 U.S. 479 (1965).

Grunewald v. United States, 352 U.S. 866, 353 U.S. 391 (1957).

Los Angeles v. Lyons, 461 U.S. 95, (1983).

Mauro, T. (1992, September 20). High stakes in the lower courts. *San Francisco Chronicle,* pp. 7, 10–11.

Miranda v. Arizona, 384 U.S. 436 (1966).

National Association for the Advancement of Colored People (NAACP) Legal Defense Fund. (1992). *Report on the criminal justice system and African-Americans.* Baltimore: Author.

National Association of Social Workers. (1996). *NASW code of ethics.* Washington, DC: Author.

National Center on Institutions and Alternatives. (1993, October). *Statistical report.* San Francisco: Author.

Patterson v. McLean Credit Union, 491 U.S. 164 (1989).

Roe v. Wade, 410 U.S. 113 (1973).

Rust v. Sullivan, 111 S. Ct. 1759 (1991).

U.S. Department of Justice. (1992). *Statistics for 1990.* Washington, DC: U.S. Government Printing Office.

U.S. General Accounting Office. (1991). *Criminal justice statistics.* Washington, DC: U.S. Government Printing Office.

Webster v. Reproductive Health Services, 492 U.S. 490 (1989).

Policy statement approved by the NASW Delegate Assembly, August 1993. This policy statement supersedes the policy statement on Civil Liberties and Justice approved in 1967 and revised in 1971. For further information, contact the National Association of Social Workers, 750 First Street, NE, Suite 700, Washington, DC 20002-4241. Telephone: 202-408-8600 or 800-638-8799.

Client Self-Determination in End-of-Life Decisions

BACKGROUND

End-of-life decisions are the choices made by a person with a terminal condition regarding his or her continuing care or treatment options. These options may include aggressive treatment of the medical condition, life-sustaining treatment, palliative care, passive euthanasia, voluntary active euthanasia, or physician-assisted suicide. For the purposes of this policy statement, these terms are defined as follows:

Terminal and irreversible condition means a continual profound comatose state with no reasonable chance of recovery or a condition caused by injury, disease, or illness, which, within reasonable medical judgment, would produce death within a short time and for which the application of life-sustaining procedures would serve only to postpone the moment of death. There is no universally accepted definition of "a short time," but in general it is considered to be less than one year (American Hospital Association, 1991).

Client self-determination means the right of the client to determine the appropriate level, if any, of medical intervention and the right of clients to change their wishes about their treatment as their condition changes over time or during the course of their illness. Self-determination assumes that the client is mentally competent.

Incompetent means lacking the ability, based on reasonable medical judgment, to understand and appreciate the nature and consequences of a treatment decision, including the significant benefits and harms of and reasonable alternatives to any proposed treatment decision.

Advance health care directive is a document in which a person either states choices for medical treatment or designates who should make treatment choices if the person should lose decision-making capacity. Although the term "advance directive" generally refers to formal, written documents, it may also include oral statements by the patient (American Hospital Association, 1991).

Life-sustaining treatment is medical intervention administered to a patient that prolongs life and delays death (American Hospital Association, 1991).

Medically inappropriate life-sustaining procedures means life-sustaining procedures that are not in accord with the patient's wishes or that are medically futile.

Palliative care is medical intervention intended to alleviate suffering, discomfort, or dysfunction but not to cure (American Hospital Association, 1991).

Passive euthanasia is the withholding or withdrawing of life-sustaining treatment. It is the forgoing of treatment, sometimes called "letting die." The right-to-die rulings such as in the Karen Ann Quinlan case establish the right under certain circumstances to be disconnected from artificial life support.

Voluntary active euthanasia is a physician's administering a lethal dose after a clearly competent patient makes a fully voluntary and persistent request for aid in dying. This is the active termination of a patient's life by a physician at the request of the patient.

Physician-assisted suicide is a patient's ending his or her life with the means requested of and provided by a physician for that purpose. The physician and the patient are both involved. Nurses or significant others may also be involved, but the physician has the responsibility for providing the means. In all cases, the patient will have been determined competent to make such a decision.

Some argue that little distinction exists between euthanasia and physician-assisted suicide other than mechanical or technical difference as to who—the patient or the physician—triggers the event. Others (for example, Quill, 1991) maintain the difference is significant in that in assisted suicide the final act is the patient's; the risk of subtle coercion from doctors, family, or other social forces is reduced; the balance of power between patient and physician is more equal; and there is less risk of error, coercion, or abuse.

There has been a proliferation of state legislation related to assisted suicide, including Washington State's "Death with Dignity" initiative, which was narrowly defeated in a referendum in 1991, and bills that were in progress in 1993 in the California, Iowa, Maine, Michigan, and New Hampshire state legislatures. (The Michigan bill required social work counseling to qualified applicants for assisted suicide.) Currently, 37 states outlaw actively helping a patient to die (Brody, 1992).

The Patients' Self-Determination Act of 1990, included in the Omnibus Budget Reconciliation Act of 1990, requires all hospitals participating in Medicare or Medicaid to ask all adult inpatients if they have advance directives, to document their answers, and to provide information on state laws and hospital policies. Other health agencies such as home health and hospice have instituted similar requirements (American Hospital Association, 1991). In many of these facilities, social workers are called on to work with patients regarding advance health care directives and end-of-life decisions.

ISSUE STATEMENT

Advances in medical capabilities and technology have made it possible to extend life through artificial means that were heretofore unimaginable. Although this level of care often provides enormous benefits for patients, it may also present difficult and increasingly complex ethical choices for patients, their families, and health care professionals. Inappropriate or unwanted utilization of medical technology may lead to lessened quality of life, loss of dignity, and loss of integrity of patients.

State and federal legislation related to advance health care directives has raised public awareness about the right of patients to participate in medical decision making, including end-of-life decisions. The individuals most immediately facing end-of-life decisions are those with a terminal and irreversible condition, a progressive chronic illness, or chronic intractable pain.

As advocates for the rights of individuals; as providers of mental health services; and as workers in hospitals, hospices, nursing homes, and crisis centers, social workers regularly deal with quality-of-life issues and choices related to life and death. Social workers have requested guidelines that are compatible with professional and personal ethics, legal parameters, and respect for client self-determination. Furthermore, other professionals look to social work for guidelines on these complex issues:

> Social work values, our traditional role as advocates and enablers, and our self-awareness and conscious use of self should serve as justification for engaging people in open and honest debate, recognizing the biases that society and the health care system have had with respect to the backgrounds, lifestyles, and illness of different groups of patients. . . . The social work community has the opportunity and the obligation to educate, organize, and advocate for a more widespread and extensive debate of these life and death matters. (Mizrahi, 1992)

In acknowledging and affirming social work's commitment to respecting diverse value systems in a pluralistic society, end-of-life issues are recognized as controversial because they reflect the varied value systems of different groups. Consequently, NASW does not take a position concerning the morality of end-of-life decisions, but affirms the right of the individual to determine the level of his or her care.

It is also recognized that de facto rationing of health care based on socioeconomic status, color, ability to pay, provider biases, and government policy differentially affects people's right to choose among viable service alternatives and their ability to give truly informed consent. The social worker should work to minimize the effect of these factors in determining the care options available to individuals.

In examining the social work role in working with clients concerning end-of-life decisions, the following issues must be addressed:

■ the legal parameters that affect social work practice (for example, limits of confidentiality, state laws prohibiting assisted suicide, the potential for civil liability)

■ the potential conflict of social work values with those of other health care professionals

■ the emerging pressures for cost control and rationing of health care (for example, temptation of health care institutions and insurers to encourage use of end-of-life practices to control costs)

■ the possibility of patients feeling obliged to choose death rather than becoming a burden (Brock, 1992)

■ the societal limits on individual self-determination and autonomy

■ the necessity to define safeguards to protect individuals and society in the implementation of end-of-life practices.

POLICY STATEMENT

NASW's position concerning end-of-life decisions is based on the principle of client self-determination. Choice should be intrinsic to all aspects of life and death.

The social work profession strives to enhance the quality of life; to encourage the exploration of life options; and to advocate for access to options, including providing all information to make appropriate choices.

Social workers have an important role in helping individuals identify the end-of-life options available to them. This role must be performed with full knowledge of and compliance with the law and in accordance with the *NASW Code of Ethics* (NASW, 1996). Social workers should be well informed about living wills, durable power of attorney for health care, and legislation related to advance health care directives.

A key value for social workers is client self-determination. Competent individuals should have the opportunity to make their own choices but only after being informed of all options and consequences. Choices should be made without coercion. Therefore, the appropriate role for social workers is to help patients express their thoughts and feelings, to facilitate exploration of alternatives, to provide information to make an informed choice, and to deal with grief and loss issues.

Social workers should not promote any particular means to end one's life but should be open to full discussion of the issues and care options. As a client is considering his or her choices, the social worker should explore and help ameliorate any factors such as pain, depression, need for medical treatment, and so forth. Further, the social worker should thoroughly review all available options including, but not limited to, pain management, counseling, hospice care, nursing home placement, and advance health care directives.

Social workers should act as liaisons with other health care professionals and help the patient and family communicate concerns and attitudes to the health care team to bring about the most responsible assistance possible.

Because end-of-life decisions have familial and social consequences, social workers should encourage the involvement of significant others, family, and friends in these decisions. Social workers should provide ongoing support and be liaisons to families and support people (for example, caregivers, significant others) with care to maintain the patient's confidentiality. When death occurs, social workers have an obligation to provide emotional and tangible assistance to the significant others, family, and friends in the bereavement process.

Social workers should be free to participate or not participate in assisted-suicide matters or other discussions concerning end-of-life decisions depending on their own beliefs, attitudes, and value systems. If a social worker is unable to help with decisions about assisted suicide or other end-of-life choices, he or she has a professional obligation to refer patients and their families to competent professionals who are available to address end-of-life issues.

It is inappropriate for social workers to deliver, supply, or personally participate in the commission of an act of assisted suicide when acting in their professional role. Doing so may subject the social worker to criminal charges. If legally permissible, it is not inappropriate for a social worker to be present during an assisted suicide if the client requests the social worker's presence. The involvement of social workers in assisted suicide cases should not depend on race or ethnicity, religion, age, gender, economic factors, sexual orientation, or disability.

NASW chapters should facilitate their membership's participation in local, state, and national committees, activities, and task forces concerning client self-determination and end-of-life decisions. Education and research on these complex topics should be included in the social work role.

REFERENCES

American Hospital Association. (1991). *Put it in writing*. Chicago: Author.

Brock, D. W. (1992). Voluntary active euthanasia. *Hastings Center Report, 22*(2), 10–22.

Brody, J. E. (1992). Doctor-assisted suicide: Ever acceptable? *New York Times*.

Mizrahi, T. (1992). The direction of patients' rights in the 1990s: Proceed with caution. *Health & Social Work, 17*, 246–262.

National Association of Social Workers. (1996). *NASW code of ethics*. Washington, DC: Author.

Patients' Self-Determination Act of 1990, P.L. 101-508, 104 Stat. 1388 et seq.

Quill, T. (1991). Death and dignity: A case of individualized decision making. *New England Journal of Medicine, 324*, 691–694.

Policy statement approved by the NASW Delegate Assembly, August 1993. For further information, contact the National Association of Social Workers, 750 First Street, NE, Suite 700, Washington, DC 20002-4241. Telephone: 202-408-8600 or 800-638-8799.

Community Development

BACKGROUND

Irving Spergel (1987) has referred to community development as "a deliberate intervention into the social network or structure of relations among people and organizations in a local area or interest community to facilitate social problem solving and improve patterns of service delivery and sociopolitical functioning" (p. 300). The development of strong communities is a basic goal of the social work profession.

Early in the profession's history, Bertha Reynolds (1982) suggested that survival of the community depends on its ability to meet the social development and social welfare needs of its residents. It is social work's simultaneous focus on the interrelationship of the individual's and the community's development that sets it apart from other professions in the United States.

The emphases of community development have varied considerably in the past 40 years. In the 1950s, the primary focus was on developing and coordinating agency direct services. In the 1960s, partially as a result of the civil rights movement and community action programs, emphasis shifted to community control and social reform. In the 1970s, the focus was on the administration of agency programs in which citizen participation was mandated by federal legislation, such as the Economic Opportunity Act of 1964, the Model Cities Program, and Community Development Block Grants. In the 1980s and early 1990s, the focus has been on helping communities survive economically and socially amidst decreased federal funding to state and local governments and the decline in the overall national economic strength. The present challenge is to advocate for meaningful social development policy and to engage in long-term planning while in a crisis management mode.

The social work profession achieves the goal of community development by helping community residents and all interacting institutions (political, economic, educational, religious, family, and the social welfare system) find ways to improve the community's, and thereby the individual's, social, physical, and economic well-being. The methods used by social workers to reach the profession's goal include, but are not limited to, identifying the community's problems or needs and resources; creating opportunities or organizational mechanisms; establishing goals, objectives, and strategies; collecting and analyzing data; studying alternatives; selecting a course of action; implementing this action; training and developing staff and community leadership; developing funding sources; and establishing ongoing evaluations and feedback mechanisms.

NASW lobbies for policies and legislation that promote the development of competent communities, characterized by equality and justice for all population groups. Undergraduate and graduate schools of social work instruct students in the area of community organization and development.

Demographic Changes

Demographic changes profoundly affect community life. By 2020, almost 20 percent of the U.S. population will be older than age 65 years, compared with 14 percent in 1990 (U.S. Bureau of the Census, 1989). Community-based long-term health care (for example, home health care and homemaker services) and social services (for example, housing, transportation, and adult care) must be developed to meet the needs of the growing number of elderly people. In 1991, NASW submitted to Congress a proposal on national health care. This legislation would provide long-term care services at a reasonable cost.

By the year 2000, there will be almost as many women as men in the work force (Shank, 1988). With women working, communities must find ways to provide affordable and quality child care and adult care services for frail or disabled people. The lack of these services results in "latch-key children," isolated and unattended frail or disabled adults, stressed family caregivers, and decreased work productivity. At the community level, partnerships are needed between the government, the workplace, community service agencies, and family members to solve the dependent care dilemma. Occupational social workers and social workers affiliated with community planning bodies and direct practice are in a position to advocate for family policies and services that support the needs of working families.

The racial and ethnic composition of the United States is changing. The percent of the total population that is white declined from 88.6 percent in 1960 to 84.1 percent in 1990, whereas the percentage of the population that is African American increased from 10.6 percent to 12.4 percent, and other-race populations (primarily consisting of Asians and Pacific Islanders and Native Americans) grew from less than 1 percent to 3.5 percent for the same period (U.S. Bureau of the Census, 1989). Immigrants compose an increasing share of the population changes. New arrivals are primarily of Asian and Hispanic descent. The Eurocentric or other extreme nationalistic perspectives of many Americans do not prepare them to live harmoniously in an increasingly diverse society. Consequently, many communities have experienced increased racial tensions.

Positive steps toward improving racial and ethnic relations include changing state and local educational systems to reflect a multicultural perspective that supports cultural pluralism. At the neighborhood level, we must develop opportunities for diverse ethnic groups to come together to increase their understanding of each other's differences, as well as their common humanity.

The traditional family form is changing. Current households include more single people, more couples without children, more gay and lesbian couples, more unrelated single adults, more couples with children in which the mother is in the work force, and more one-parent families (U.S. Bureau of the Census, 1990). Yet laws and regulations, community activities, business practices, and housing structures address the traditional family as if it were still the majority.

Economic Changes

The structure and function of jobs are changing. Work tasks increasingly require a highly skilled and educated work force. By 2000, 80 percent of new jobs will be filled by women and minorities (U.S. Department of Labor, 1987). To remain competitive and productive, work organizations must improve management–labor relations and workers' involvement in decision making. Local communities need to interact with business and industry to improve the educational preparation of all workers, help integrate minority or racial/ethnic workers and women fully into work organizations, and assist workers in gaining more job autonomy and participation in work decisions.

New Federalism

The Bush and Reagan administrations' position on the limited and distorted role of government was particularly damaging to the economic and social strength of communities. Their conservative policies supported the business sector (for example, deregulation and reduction of the capital gains tax) but shrank social welfare funds for community development and social services for middle-class and disadvantaged groups. State and local communities were expected to assume more financial responsibility for health and human services, given the decrease in national and federal resources.

Federal policies are particularly damaging to local communities with a weak tax base. Grassroots organizing is needed to pressure the government to implement more realistic and fair policies and budget allocations.

ISSUE STATEMENT

With communities undergoing significant economic, social, and environmental changes, community development is imperative for our nation's survival. Local communities and sub-populations (for example, farmers, women, black youths, Hispanics, Native Americans, Asians, the elderly, adolescents) are directly and indirectly affected by world events, demographic changes, environmental changes, social attitudes, catastrophes, economic changes, and unique attributes of community life. These conditions can significantly affect the physical, economic, and social health of community residents.

Threats to community life include, but are not limited to, deterioration of neighborhoods; lack of affordable housing; homelessness; social disorganization; high crime rates; high rates of high school dropouts; underachievement among students enrolled in school from kindergarten through grade 12; increased domestic violence; unwanted teenage pregnancies; high infant mortality rates; increased racial tensions; and increased discrimination against diverse groups, including people of color, gay and lesbian people, older people, and women. Instead of the community fostering social well-being, protection, and an enhanced quality of life, it has fostered or allowed disharmony and destructiveness to prevail. With citizen participation and focused planning and commitment, however, communities can thrive within an increasingly complex and interdependent world.

Two major interactive approaches must be used to deal with profound threats to community life. One approach involves the grassroots organization, or the "bottom-up" approach. This approach calls for local community activism and solidarity, based on the mobilization of citizen, neighborhood, and civic groups and resources to effect desired changes. A second related approach requires operating within the larger structure of city, county, state, national, and international arenas to effect wide-range change for and with the local community and socially disadvantaged groups.

POLICY STATEMENT

In an effort to implement the social work goals and objectives of community development, NASW supports the following policy initiatives:

■ the right of citizens to contribute significantly to the destiny of their local communities.

Social workers who assist communities in gaining access to information and resources, develop local and participatory organizational mechanisms, and help citizens make socially responsible decisions can encourage these contributions.

■ multiculturalism. NASW advocates open communications, tolerance, and expanded educational curricula that reflect the influence and participation of diverse groups in American society.

■ local, state, and federal legislation responsive to the needs of communities and diverse populations. NASW supports legislation related to national health insurance, medical and family leaves, antidiscrimination, civil rights, fighting crime, and youth development programs.

■ an increased federal government role in distributing funds more adequately to state and local governments. NASW supports renewed federal efforts in community development and social services coordination strategies. NASW believes that federal funding is crucial to communities with a weak tax base that need continuous support.

■ effective societal change for the following imperatives:

Black Male Youths. This population group has experienced more deaths by violence and illness, with the possible exception of Native Americans, than any other group in the United States. Increased efforts must be made to improve their educational and employment opportunities, family functioning, self-esteem, and confidence in their future.

Educated Work Force. Employment opportunities for people without a high school education are rapidly declining. Everyone should receive an equal and enriched education. Presently, children and adolescents in low-income areas receive a less adequate education than those in more affluent areas, primarily because local property taxes are school systems' primary funding source. Efforts must be made to equalize funding for schools in low-income areas. In addition to these educational goals, retraining opportunities for adults of working age must be expanded to address the increasing techno-logical complexity of work.

Children Living in Poverty. One in five children live below the poverty line (U. S. Bureau of the Census, 1990). Communities need more government assistance to provide adequate financial, housing, medical, and social services to impoverished children and their caretakers.

Environmental Pollution and Destruction. Government regulations and enforcement procedures are needed to protect community residents from government, business, and even professional or agency opportunists. Education is needed on the community level to educate people about how to access services and obtain legal assistance in maintaining a healthy environment.

Housing Problems. Impoverished, low- and moderate-income individuals are struggling to locate and maintain adequate and affordable housing. Renewed advocacy efforts are needed to facilitate the development of local community advisory groups and to reach the housing goal set forth by the Housing Act of 1949, which called for a decent and suitable home for every American family.

HIV/AIDS. The National Commission on AIDS (1991) stated that AIDS is the domestic crisis of the 1990s. The commission predicted that every American will soon know at least one person with AIDS. Local community as well as state and federal efforts to prevent, treat, and assist in determining the cause of AIDS must be aggressively pursued by NASW and its members.

Impact Areas. When anticipated business expansion and population growth is expected to result in high levels of community upheaval and stress, private developers and the government should be required to design and implement plans for community development and enhanced social services. On the other hand, when business shifts bring about plant closings, government intervention is needed to slow down this occurrence and help communities engage in long-term planning and funding ventures to prepare for future economic changes.

Land Use. Patterns of land development in the United States frequently have been wasteful and harmful. Agricultural land has been removed unnecessarily from production, and suburban and exurban areas have sprawled. In the future, all levels of government should encourage a more compact and intense use of land for industrial and commercial development, as well as preservation of open spaces, to minimize the resultant costs, including ever-increasing transportation costs.

Management Information Systems and Other Forms of Technical Assistance. Computerization is essential to manage large data sets, communicate effectively, and coordinate service delivery systems. Small private firms, local governments, and local nonprofit institutions should be provided with technical assistance in management, environmental studies, and new project development.

Strengthened Social Work Curricula Related to Community Development. All social work students should be knowledgeable about the ways that social policy can affect direct practice and the ways in which communities and disadvantaged populations can become more involved and competent in solving their problems and enhancing the quality of their lives. Social work community developers should have a broad view of the community so that they can raise the consciousness of local citizens, provide and develop local leadership, and participate in the coordination of the multidisciplinary efforts of a variety of community groups. Community organization practice must be developed within a strategic policy framework in which social workers can have an affect on both local and larger community interactivity.

REFERENCES

National Commission on AIDS. (1991). *America living with AIDS*. Washington, DC: Author.

Reynolds, B. C. (1982). *Between client and community: A study in responsibility in social casework*. Silver Spring, MD: National Association of Social Workers. (Original work published in 1934).

Shank, S. E. (1988). Work and the labor market: The link grows stronger. *Monthly Labor Review, 111,* 3–8.

Spergel, I. A. (1987). Community development. In A. Minahan (Ed.-in-Chief), *Encyclopedia of social work* (18th ed., Vol. 1, pp. 299–308). Silver Spring, MD: National Association of Social Workers.

U.S. Bureau of the Census. (1989). *Projections of the population of the United States, by age, sex, race: 1988 to 2080.* (Current Populations Reports, Series P-25, No. 1018). Washington, DC: U.S. Government Printing Office.

U.S. Bureau of the Census. (1990). *Changes in American family life.* (Current Populations Reports, Series P-23, No. 163). Washington, DC: U.S. Government Printing Office.

U.S. Department of Labor. (1987). *Workforce 2000* (Executive summary). Washington, DC: U.S. Government Printing Office.

Policy statement approved by the NASW Delegate Assembly, August 1993. This policy statement supersedes the policy statement on Community Development approved by the Delegate Assembly in 1981. For further information, contact the National Association of Social Workers, 750 First Street, NE, Suite 700, Washington, DC 20002-4241. Telephone: 202-408-8600 or 800-638-8799.

Confidentiality and Information Utilization

BACKGROUND

Problems involved in the use of information—privacy, confidentiality, and privileged communication—have commanded increased attention in both the public and private sectors of U.S. society in recent years. Many factors have combined to make an information policy a primary concern of civil libertarians, a subject for legislation, and an area of expanding legal action: the information explosion of the past generation, the advent of the computer, the revolution in data processing and storage, the expanded role of government, the growth of consumer credit, the requirements of the insurance industry, and the growth of giant corporate enterprises. Officially sanctioned governmental invasions of privacy, insurance company exchange of data, credit blacklisting, and countless other incursions into the personal affairs of virtually every citizen are cause for alarm. The danger of even greater abuses, deliberate or inadvertent, in the collection, maintenance, and use of personal data by government and industry poses a threat of unprecedented dimensions to Americans' basic civil liberties.

The confidential nature of communications between social workers and their clients has been a cardinal principle of the social work profession from its earliest years and, indeed, undergirds the therapeutic worker–client relationship. Legislative protection for social work information in adoption and juvenile court records dates back half a century: the Social Security Act of 1935 (P.L. 74-271), as amended in 1939, required state public assistance plans to "provide safeguards which restrict the use or disclosure of information concerning applicants and recipients to purposes directly connected with the administration of [the program]" (Title IV, Section 502[a][8]). The Office of Vocational Rehabilitation issued regulations during the 1940s requiring similar safeguards. Subsequently, legislation, regulations, and guidelines dealing with various health, welfare, and educational programs in varying degrees have recognized the need for limiting and safeguarding the collection and use of personal data.

In both public and private agency practice, confidentiality has been a continual concern. Although pressures toward gathering, preserving, and, at times, revealing personal information are greater in the public sector, both public and private agencies have had to contend with the same basic issues and dilemmas: How is personal privacy to be balanced against the public's need for information, the need for accountability, and, at times, the need for protection? How is the client's privacy to be maintained when there is a need to share information with third parties, obtain consultation, or otherwise divulge information in conjunction with professional purposes related to the client's interest? To what extent must the protection of individual privacy be balanced against the needs of research, the development of knowledge, and teaching?

Many of the same issues and dilemmas are present in private practice, although external pressures for sharing information are likely to be less on private practitioners than on agency practitioners. However, insurance carriers and managed care firms often demand detailed diagnostic and other personal data in the name of accountability; private practitioners as well as agency social workers are often subpoenaed to testify and reveal clients' confidences in divorce and custody proceedings, in child abuse cases, and in other domestic lawsuits; and law enforcement agencies occasionally seek information from case records. In the face of societal demands regarding the use of information, the strictures of the *NASW Code of Ethics* (NASW, 1993) are insufficient guides:

II. H. Confidentiality and Privacy—The social worker should respect the privacy of clients and hold in confidence all information obtained in the course of professional service.

1. The social worker should share with others confidences revealed by clients, without their consent, only for compelling professional reasons.

2. The social worker should inform clients fully about the limits of confidentiality in a given situation, the purposes for which information is obtained, and how it may be used.

3. The social worker should afford clients reasonable access to any official social work records concerning them.

4. When providing clients with access to records, the social worker should take due care to protect the confidences of others contained in those records.

5. The social worker should obtain informed consent of clients before taping, recording, or permitting third-party observation of their activities.

The concepts of respect for privacy and responsible use of information must be elaborated more fully in the context of an explicit NASW public social policy.

ISSUE STATEMENT

In the most basic sense, the issue of confidentiality and use of information pits the individual's right to privacy against society's need to know. The issue involves individual's and society's needs to ensure accountability, to protect other individuals, and to amass information for a variety of social welfare needs, such as disease control, research, and community planning. The social worker's central role as the recipient and custodian of personal information places a particularly heavy responsibility on the social work profession and on individual practitioners to

weigh consequences, balance equities, and assume responsibility for action taken.

Social workers, agency administrators, clients, and legislators must be educated about the implications of computer technology and must become aware of both its beneficial and harmful potentials. Social workers must be especially mindful of the threat to confidentiality posed by the development of electronic data processing and storage. Precautions that once sufficed to ensure the safety of agency case records are no longer sufficient when correspondence is sent by telephone facsimile machines and data are fed into computer banks or linked to other information systems beyond the social worker's and client's control. The social work profession must re-examine its practices with regard to gathering information and maintaining, sharing, and using case records.

The profession also must reassess its policies and ethical base regarding privacy issues. It must consider the need to assume a more vigorous and active posture in this area, including the assumption of new advocacy roles.

In addition, social workers are constrained to some degree by privileged communication. Whereas confidentiality is a professional mandate, privileged communication is a legal issue in which a client's right to privacy is protected by state law. Many courts have held that the right belongs to the client and that only the client can waive the protection (Perlman, 1988; Schwartz, 1989). Privacy laws, however, vary by state statute, and it behooves social workers to be familiar with the applicable laws in their states.

POLICY STATEMENT

NASW policy addresses three levels: (1) the government–regulatory agency–business sector, which includes the several levels of government, law enforcement agencies, insurance carriers, and other institutions and systems that collect, maintain, and use personal data banks; (2) the public and private social agency sector; and (3) the individual social work practitioner. In many other areas of broad federal involvement, other than health, education, and welfare (for example, census data and tax return information from the Internal Revenue Service), restrictions are placed on usage and disclosure of personal information.

Government–Regulatory Agency–Business Sector

For government units, agencies, and institutions that use automated personal data, the principles of a code of fair information practice should be adopted along the lines recommended by the Advisory Committee on Automated Personal Data Systems (U.S. Department of Health, Education and Welfare, 1973). Therefore, NASW recommends that, as appropriate, legislation should be enacted, regulations promulgated, and policies adopted to ensure the following:

■ No personal data record-keeping systems whose existence is secret should be permitted.

■ Individuals should be able to learn what information is maintained about them and how it is used.

■ Information obtained about individuals for one purpose should not be used or made available for other purposes without the individual's explicit informed consent.

■ Individuals should have the right to and be able to correct or amend a record of identifiable information about them.

■ Efforts should be made to curb the proliferation of universal identifiers, including the use of social security numbers, whenever not currently mandated by law.

■ Any organization creating, maintaining, using, or disseminating records of identifiable personal data must assure the reliability of the data for their intended use and must take precautions to prevent misuse of the data.

Public and Private Social Welfare Agencies

NASW recommends that each social welfare agency develop and disseminate policies and guides that will cover at least the following: (1) what information is to be sought and from whom; (2) what information is to be recorded and in what form; (3) who has access to information about cases and under what cir-

cumstances; (4) means for assuring the accuracy of records and for noting differences; (5) plans for disposing of records; (6) when and how the social worker has a "duty to warn" regarding danger to the public (refer to the *Tarasoff*, 1976, decision), including guidance about handling HIV-positive clients' information; and (7) in-service training to help social workers understand the policy.

Certain kinds of data, such as political beliefs or opinions, should not be recorded at all, even if they are assumed to have some tangential relevance to the case. Process recording, if used for teaching purposes, should be promptly disposed of as soon as it has served its purpose— either summarized or expunged. In addition, the agency has the obligation to ensure that the client understands what is being asked, to determine why and what uses will be made of the information, and to assure informed consent for specific purposes and to specific other parties in situations in which the client signs a release of information. Clients also must be helped to understand the possible consequences of refusing to give information required by governmental agencies under law. Therefore, NASW recommends the following:

■ Information about an individual client should not be shared with any other individual or agency without the individual's express informed consent.

■ Case records and related files should not be transferred to another agency or individual without the express informed consent of the client or client's guardian or legal agent, and then only under rules requiring that the receiving agency provide the same guarantee of confidentiality as the transferring agency.

■ Case records should be maintained in a safe and secure area and, when computerized, appropriate security measures for access should be developed (see *NASW Guidelines on the Private Practice of Clinical Social Work*, 1991).

Social Work Practitioners

Whether as independent or agency-based practitioners, social workers should have available for all new clients information in written form about records, release of records, and the legal and ethical limits of confidentiality/privileged communication, and should ensure that clients understand the issues. Social workers should be guided by the following five principles vis-à-vis clients:

1. Clients should be used as the primary source of information about themselves.

2. Only information that is demonstrably related to the solution of clients' problems should be received, recorded, or released.

3. Clients should understand fully the implications of sharing personal information, including the ethical and legal obligations of the social worker to respect privacy and protect the confidentiality and legal constraints and limitations that impinge on both the client and the social worker.

4. Clients' informed and express consent should be a prerequisite to transmitting information to or requesting it from third parties.

5. Clients should be apprised of the kind of records maintained by the social worker or agency and should have the right to verify the accuracy of the records personally.

REFERENCES

National Association of Social Workers. (1991). *NASW guidelines on the private practice of clinical social work.* Washington, DC: NASW Press.

National Association of Social Workers. (1993). *NASW code of ethics.* Washington, DC: Author.

Perlman, G. L. (1988). Mastering the law of privileged communication: A guide for social workers. *Social Work, 33,* 425–429.

Schwartz, G. (1989). Confidentiality revisited. *Social Work, 34,* 223–226.

Social Security Act of 1935, P.L. 74-271, 49 Stat. 620.

Tarasoff v. Regents of the University of California, 551 P.2d 334, 131 Cal. Rpt. 14 (1976).

U.S. Department of Health, Education and Welfare. (1973). *Records, computers and the right of citizens* (Report of the Secretary's Advisory Committee on Automated Personal Data System, DHEW Publication No. OS 73–94). Washington, DC: U.S. Government Printing Office.

Policy statement approved by the NASW Delegate Assembly, August 1993. This statement supersedes the policy statement on Information Utilization and Confidentiality, approved by the Delegate Assembly in 1975. For further information, contact the National Association of Social Workers, 750 First Street, NE, Suite 700, Washington, DC 20002-4241. Telephone: 202-408-8600 or 800-638-8799.

Cultural and Linguistic Diversity in the United States

BACKGROUND

In the 1980s a movement that identifies itself under the banner of English-Only or English First emerged. The purpose of this movement is to ensure the survival of the English language and to preserve the linguistic unity of the United States against the influence of foreign tongues. Adherents of this movement present a fearful image of an American "Tower of Babel," in which the English language is submerged in an ocean of immigrants, refugees, and aliens speaking foreign languages. Such fears have led many well-intentioned individuals to support and advocate the adoption of English as the official language of nation, state, and municipality.

The decade of the 1980s brought about a powerful and profoundly disturbing resurgence of American xenophobia. Throughout its history, the United States has held an ambivalent attitude toward immigrants, refugees, and other foreign-born people. America, the "nation of immigrants," symbolized by the Statue of Liberty with its noble inscriptions, also has a darker history of hostility to people and ideas that are considered un-American. Fear and hostility toward foreign populations have been a constant if inconsistent stream in the great river of American history. Slavery, racism, and anti-Catholic and anti-Semitic currents all have been a part of this stream. At times, this chauvinism has found expression in political parties or secret organizations. The Know-Nothing Party, which existed before the Civil War, and the Ku Klux Klan, which arose after 1865, are but two examples of this stubborn strain of nativism.

When people believe that traditional values are being attacked, they sometimes respond with symbolic gestures. The English-Only movement appears to be such a case. When the nation's founding fathers drafted the Constitution in 1787, they did not establish an official language for the United States. For more than 200 years, English has been the common and accepted form of speech in the United States without a constitutional amendment or Supreme Court decision. It is significant that such a movement should emerge at a time of highly restrictive immigration policy. If fear of domination by foreign languages were the actual concern, such legislation would have been more appropriate in 1890, when a flood of immigrants entered the United States.

The convergence of patriotism and nativism has created a climate of fear that most thoughtful Americans have been slow to recognize and confront. During the past decade, the English-Only movement has united with a newly expressed patriotism and at times with religious fundamentalism to create a powerful political force advocating "traditional American values." In this process, adherents have fanned the flames of negativism toward non-Americans, a negativism marked by racist and biased values. This political force, aided by a highly restrictive national immigration policy, has created an atmosphere in which words such as *foreign* and *alien* have been transformed into negative or pejorative labels.

The ultimate goal of the English-Only movement is to amend the U.S. Constitution to declare English the official language of this nation. In the meantime, supporters of the movement have worked energetically for and have succeeded in obtaining the passage of legislation that declares English the official language of individual states. As of August 1990, 15 states have adopted English-Only legislation: Arizona, Arkansas, California, Colorado, Florida, Georgia, Idaho, Illinois, Indiana, Kentucky, Mississippi, North Dakota, South Carolina, Tennessee, and Virginia. Some of these states are among the largest and most populous in the country.

ISSUE STATEMENT

NASW and the social work profession have a mandate to advocate for those groups in our society whose rights and welfare are being attacked or undermined. Indeed, this mandate is the core of the social welfare profession.

To limit the provision of human services to those who speak one particular language is, in effect, to deny services. English-Only legislation that restricts the government to communicating with its citizens and residents only in English creates discrimination in the delivery of services. Likewise, preventing governmental employees from delivering basic health, social welfare, legal, or other services to people who are not proficient in English denies such people services and places them at risk. The danger is especially great for newly arrived immigrants and refugees, who are often in immediate need of basic human services and whose health or general welfare may be threatened without these services. Many English-Only laws would restrict or prevent the publication of materials or directives in languages other than English. Therefore, the ability of non-English-speaking individuals to use public health materials and medication would be affected.

Such legislation could restrict the use of foreign-language interpreters in courts, medical settings, or social service agencies. These laws prevent bilingual staff from communicating or offering professional services in languages other than English. In geographic areas with large populations of non-English-speaking people (especially refugees), such mandates would have a devastating impact on the service delivery system. Also, limiting the availability of social services is in direct contradiction to the traditional social work ethic of advocacy and empowerment. Politically and economically, such legislation would have its greatest impact on the poor, the disenfranchised, and racial and cultural minorities.

POLICY STATEMENT

The National Association of Social Workers (NASW) affirms that language is a source and an extension of personal identity and a discrete representation of self. A guiding principle of the profession is to accept the individual person in his or her totality. To limit or deny language is to reject that aspect of a human being that helps to define who he or she is.

NASW recognizes the potentially dangerous and destructive implications of establishing an official language in the United States. The potential negative impact of English-Only legislation on the social welfare service delivery system is obvious; no sector of the system would be safe from its possible ramifications. Therefore, NASW's response must be broad based and inclusive. We must defeat this movement in the arenas of public opinion and social policy development by implementing the following principles:

■ NASW repudiates any hostility toward foreign-born or foreign-language-speaking individuals. The association condemns and rejects such racially and culturally biased xenophobia.

■ NASW condemns the suggestion that those who are not fully proficient in English are second-class or otherwise less-deserving individuals. The association rejects as abusive the psychological and educational damage done to children who are raised in bilingual or bicultural communities under such circumstances.

■ NASW and individual social workers should advocate for and ensure the provision of information, referrals, and services in the language the client understands.

■ NASW supports the concept of follow-up studies of the actual impact of English-Only legislation on the delivery of social services in areas where the legislation exists.

■ NASW supports bilingual and bicultural educational programs with an English-as-a-second-language (ESL) component and advocates adequate funding levels for the programs. By supporting such programs, we will help disprove the claim that foreign-language-speaking individuals are not motivated to learn English. In fact, ESL classes are oversubscribed and underfunded.

■ NASW supports the inclusion of foreign language study at the earliest grades of public education. NASW recognizes that we live in a world of instantaneous communication and that children need to be multilingual, not monolingual, to be prepared for the future.

■ NASW urges that the curricula of all schools of social work include course work designed to increase cultural awareness and sensitivity to languages in all students.

■ The NASW Political Action for Candidate Election (PACE) should endorse and vigorously support candidates who oppose English-Only legislation and who can articulate the potential negative and destructive effects of such legislation.

■ NASW should activate campaigns to educate the public and elected officials about the potential impact of what may seem to be patriotic legislation. Educational campaigns should be carried out at the federal, state, and local levels.

■ NASW supports legislation prohibiting employers from making rules requiring that English be spoken in the workplace unless the rules are justified by safety concerns.

■ NASW opposes any legislation that prohibits businesses from displaying signs in languages other than English.

■ NASW understands that the United States must maintain its capacity to compete economically in the international market. The advocacy of the English-Only movement does not make us more competitive; it makes us less competitive. The rise in economic power of the Pacific Rim countries, the reunification of Europe, and the political reorganization of the Soviet Union suggest that we should place more emphasis on multiculturalism and multilingualism in a global economy.

Policy statement approved by the NASW Delegate Assembly, August 1990. Referred to the 1999 Delegate Assembly, to be combined with the policy on Affirmative Action or Immigrants and Refugees. For further information, contact the National Association of Social Workers, 750 First Street, NE, Suite 700, Washington, DC 20002-4241. Telephone: 202-408-8600 or 800-638-8799.

Cultural Competence in the Social Work Profession

BACKGROUND

The elements of cultural competence have received wide and far-ranging attention in the social work literature. Whether directed at the client or worker, the question of cultural competence places major emphasis on the effective use of knowledge and skill application within an ecological context and transactional dimensions of motivation, skill, and empowerment (Breton, 1994). Cultural competence implies a heightened consciousness and analytical grasp of racism, sexism, ethnocentrism, class conflict, and cross-cultural and intracultural diversity.

Professional interest in cultural competence among social workers is predated by a rich and varied history on the subject and many decades of discourse regarding the profession's response or lack of response to the service needs of diverse clients. In the 1960s the Council on Social Work Education (CSWE) began to address the issues of racial and ethnic diversity in the recruitment and training of social work students and faculty, as well as in the content of social work curricula. Schools emphasized the "dual perspective," or the concept that all people are part of two systems: the larger societal system and their immediate environment (Norton, 1978). Solomon (1976) defined empowerment as facilitating clients' connection with their own power and, in turn, being empowered by the very act of reaching across cultural barriers. Gallegos (1982) provided one of the first conceptualizations of ethnic competence as "a set of procedures and activities to be used in acquiring culturally relevant insights into the problems of diverse clients and the means of applying such insights to the development of intervention strategies that are culturally appropriate for these clients" (p. 4).

Green (1995) identified some of these culturally competent procedures: clarification of the worker's personal values concerning "minority" people; articulation of personal and professional values and ways they may conflict with or accommodate the needs of clients of color; development of interviewing skills that reflect the worker's understanding of the role of language in ethnically distinct communities; development of the ability to relate to professionals of color in ways that enhance their effectiveness with clients; development of the ability to use resources on behalf of communities of color; development of the mastery of techniques for learning the history, traditions, and values of an ethnic group; development of the ability to communicate information on the cultural characteristics of a given group to other professionals; and gaining knowledge of the impact of social policies and services on clients of color.

The concept of cultural competency has moved through a progression of ideas and theoretical constructs favoring cultural pluralism, cultural sensitivity, multiculturalism, and most recently a transcultural orientation to social work practice (Gould, 1995). A brief review of the social work literature in the past few years points to the range of content areas present in cultural competence, including racial identity formation; the interrelationship between race, gender, class, and ethnicity; HIV/AIDS among Hispanics; work with poor families; work with poor African American or Puerto Rican families; sexual identity and sexual orientation; gay adolescents; acculturation and immigration; spirituality and religious diversity; biculturalism; cross-racial practice considerations; work with people with disabilities; reaching American Indian and Asian American clients; empowerment; intermarriage; racially mixed clients; biracial children; mental health services for Chinese, Cuban, Indochinese, and West Indian clients; sociocultural models of practice; and training of culturally sensitive practitioners.

U.S. society is constantly undergoing major demographic changes that heighten the diversity confronting social workers. For example, despite anti-immigration sentiment and concerted efforts to limit immigration, Latinos, Asians, and Africans are expected to constitute 47 percent of the U.S. population by the early part of the 21st century (Brimelow, 1995). Immigration patterns from Asia, Eastern Europe, Russia, Africa, and Latin America can be expected to dramatically intensify the diversity social workers will witness in their agencies. Social workers will increasingly need to consider the question of culturally competent social work practice.

As more heterosexual, gay, lesbian, bisexual, and transgender women and men demand fair treatment and inclusion in all aspects of American life, social workers of all sexual orientations will need to be prepared to bridge the cross-cultural experiences of people of different sexual orientations. People with disabilities also want more than empathy and accommodation. They wish to be recognized as bicultural people with the right to seek inclusion in both mainstream and their own cultures. Social workers need sophisticated skills and abilities to advocate for clients against the underlying devaluation of cultural experiences related to difference and oppression. This mandate includes white social workers as well as social workers of color, because the need to master culturally competent knowledge and skills is a social reality in a pluralistic society (Gould, 1995).

The quest for authentic cultural competence is a process stage of becoming more attuned to how clients experience their uniqueness, deal with their differences and similarities, and cope with a sociopolitical environment which is less and less concerned with the welfare of its people, however diverse their needs may be. Culturally competent social work practice needs to start with the driving assumption of individual uniqueness interconnected to human universality, and the cultural specificity of individual existence through which reality is seen and meaning interpreted (Congress, 1994). Social workers' self-awareness of their own cultures is as fundamental to practice as the informed assumptions about clients' cultural background and experiences in American society.

ISSUE STATEMENT

The complexities associated with cultural diversity in the United States affect all aspects of professional social work practice requiring social workers to strive to deliver culturally competent services to a broad range of clients. Social workers using a person-in-environment framework for assessment need to include to varying degrees important cultural factors that have meaning for clients and reflect the culture of the world around them. In U.S. social work, cultural diversity is primarily associated with race and ethnicity, but social workers are also aware of the need to develop culturally competent skills, knowledge, and values when working with people of a different gender, social class, religion or spiritual belief, sexual orientation, age, and disability. This kind of sophisticated cultural competence does not come naturally to any social worker and requires a high level of professionalism. This policy statement speaks to the need for definition, support, and encouragement of a heightened level of social work practice that encourages cultural competence among all social workers so that they can respond effectively, knowledgeably, and sensitively to the diversity inherent in the agencies they work in and with the clients and communities they serve.

Cultural competence is a vital link with the theoretical and practice knowledge base that defines social work expertise. Increasing cultural competence within the profession requires demonstrated efforts to recruit and retain as diverse a group of social workers as possible, many of whom would bring some "indigenous" cultural competence to the profession, as well as demonstrated efforts to increase avenues for the acquisition of culturally competent skills by all social workers. Indigenous cultural competence is a result of absorbing positive and negative cultural memories through lifelong experiences which can be an advantage as well as an obstacle when the workers confront the subjective qualities of sharing the same cultural experiences as their clients. Cultural competency should not be equated with cultural identity or consciousness. For example, a Latino social worker is not inherently culturally competent when working with Latino clients; he or she must also consider the context of class, race, gender, sexual orientation, religion, age, and abilities. When social workers have little contact with people who are distinctly different from themselves, they must acquire cultural competence through a process of turning cognitive learning into affective insight. The profession needs to enhance culturally competent social work practice by addressing the needs of both indigenous workers and those struggling to acquire competency.

Cultural competence builds on the professional's valued stance on self-determination and individual dignity and worth, adding inclusion, tolerance, and respect for diversity in all its forms. Social workers have been made aware of the importance of developing ethnic-sensitive practice when working with people of similar or different races, nationalities, language proficiencies, and immigration or migration experiences. Social workers are keenly aware of the deleterious effects of racism, sexism, ageism, anti-Semitism, homophobia, and xenophobia on clients' lives and the need for social advocacy and social action to better empower diverse clients and communities. This policy statement reinforces this awareness but moves the discussion toward the development of clearer guidelines, goals, and objectives for the future of social work practice in which cultural diversity will increase in complexity.

POLICY STATEMENT

Social workers have an ethical responsibility to be culturally competent practitioners, as the *NASW Code of Ethics* (NASW, 1996) suggests. The social work profession needs to clearly define what is meant by culturally competent social work practice. *Cultural competence* is a set of congruent behaviors, attitudes, and policies that come together in a system or agency or among professionals and enable the system, agency, or professionals to work effectively in cross-cultural situations. The word "culture" is used because it implies the integrated pattern of human behavior that includes thoughts, communica-

tions, actions, customs, beliefs, values, and institutions of a racial, ethnic, religious, or social group. The word "competency" is used because it implies having the capacity to function effectively. A culturally competent system of care acknowledges and incorporates at all levels the importance of culture, the assessment of cross-cultural relations, vigilance toward the dynamics that result from cultural differences, the expansion of cultural knowledge, and the adaptation of services to meet culturally unique needs (Cross, Bazron, Dennis, & Isaacs, 1989).

Cultural competence requires social workers to examine their own cultural backgrounds and identities while seeking out the necessary knowledge, skills, and values that can enhance the delivery of services to people with varying cultural experiences associated with their race, ethnicity, gender, class, sexual orientation, religion, age, or disability. Furthermore, culturally competent practice is a critical component of professional social work expertise in all practice settings, whether urban or rural.

A policy statement alone cannot fully define the values, knowledge, and skills required for culturally competent practice. Cultural competency is an important ingredient of professional competency, as important as any component that forms the basis of the theoretical and clinical knowledge that defines social work expertise. This policy statement supports and encourages the development of standards for culturally competent social work practice, a definition of expertise, and the advancement of practice models that have relevance for the range of needs and services represented by diverse client populations. As advocates for the providers and consumers of social work services, social workers need to promote cultural competence by supporting the evaluation of culturally competent service delivery models and setting standards for cultural competence within the profession. Monitoring cultural competence among social workers should include establishing mechanisms for obtaining direct feedback from clients. The social work profession should be encouraged to take more proactive measures to ensure cultural competence as an integral part of social work practice and to make efforts to increase research and scholarship among its professionals.

REFERENCES

Breton, M. (1994). Relating competence, promotion and empowerment. *Journal of Progressive Human Services*, 5(1), 27–44.

Brimelow, P. (1995). *Alien nation: Common sense about America's immigration disaster.* New York: Random House.

Congress, E. P. (1994). The use of culturagrams to assess and empower culturally diverse families. *Families in Society, 75*(9), 531–540.

Cross, T. L., Bazron, B. J., Dennis, K. W., & Isaacs, M. R. (1989). *Towards a culturally competent system of care.* Washington, DC: Child and Adolescent Services Program, Technical Assistance Center.

Gallegos, J. S. (1982). The ethnic competence model for social work education. In B. W. White (Ed.), *Color in a white society* (pp. 1–9). Silver Spring, MD: National Association of Social Workers.

Gould, K. H. (1995). The misconstruing of multiculturalism: The Stanford debate and social work. *Social Work, 40*(2), 198–205.

Green, J. (1995). *Cultural awareness in the human services: A multiethnic approach* (2nd ed.). Boston: Allyn & Bacon.

National Assocation of Social Workers. (1996). *NASW code of ethics.* Washington, DC: Author.

Norton, D. G. (1978). *The dual perspective.* New York: Council on Social Work Education.

Solomon, B. (1976). *Black empowerment.* New York: Columbia University Press.

Policy statement approved by the NASW Delegate Assembly, August 1996. For further information, contact the National Association of Social Workers, 750 First Street, NE, Suite 700, Washington, DC 20002-4241. Telephone: 202-408-8600 or 800-638-8799.

Declassification

BACKGROUND

NASW's policy statement on the issue of its relationship with other social work organizations and human services disciplines, adopted by the 1981 NASW Delegate Assembly and reconfirmed by the 1990 NASW Delegate Assembly, reported that, "Of the 375,000 positions that are classified as social work jobs, only 33 percent are filled by people with graduate social work degrees and 15 percent are held by people with the BSW. Over one-half of the current social work labor force does not have social work training" (NASW, 1991).

Carol Meyer (1983) cautioned that, "In every field of practice, on every level of government, and in the voluntary sector, the declassification of professional social work positions has become a dismal reality" (p. 419). Ten years later, declassification continues to pose a formidable challenge for social workers in all practice fields.

Early in the 1980s, NASW (1984) undertook a major study to investigate the dynamics of reclassification (the term authors preferred to declassification). The final report noted that an "ever increasing number of state social service agencies and private social service providers have undertaken revisions to their personnel system so that preference has no longer been given to job applicants who have social work training" (p. 1). Other investigators reached similar conclusions (Gilbert, 1975; Ginsberg et al., 1989; Kahn, 1981; Karger, 1983; Pecora & Austin, 1983).

Declassification is the result of reduction in the standards of professional education and work-related experience for social service jobs (Pecora & Austin, 1983). Karger (1983), in his discussion of the reclassification phenomenon, concurred with Kahn (1981), who described it as a trend that results in "reduction in educational requirements for entry level jobs, assumption of interchangeability of bachelor's degrees, reorganization of jobs to reduce educational requirements, nonrecognition of the exclusivity of bachelor's or master's of social work (BSW and MSW) skills, and equating education with experience" (p. 3).

At times, under various declassification and reclassification schemes, public sector agencies have used job or task analysis as a basis to create generic job classifications, such as clinical case manager, case management specialist, or social services worker that eliminated the title of social worker. The combined effect of the declassification and reclassification movement has been civil service systems that permit hiring of unqualified and uncredentialed staff members for social work positions. Another consequence has been the eradication of chief social worker positions and functions in major agencies and departments. In 1992, observers "guesstimate" that more than half of social work positions are filled by untrained non–social workers who are performing social work tasks.

The NASW policy statement on declassification, adopted by the 1981 NASW Delegate Assembly, identified several contributing factors that have eroded the legitimacy and sanctioning of social work positions (NASW, 1991). The following factors were listed:

■ Because there are insufficient numbers of MSWs and BSWs or a lack of interest in public services agencies, vacancies are filled by untrained staff, staff with undifferentiated undergraduate degrees, or "human services" staff; the result is that agencies emphasize on-the-job training.

■ State employee unions have emphasized promotion via experience and do not support professional education.

■ Quantitative accountability, that is, the number of clients served, rather than qualitative intervention, and effectiveness of services, has become the objective.

■ Proliferation of legislation and administrative rules has allowed equivalence to social work education.

■ Fewer resources and budget cuts have led to a justification to lower social work standards and to fill jobs with less-qualified personnel who fit lower salary standards.

Several investigative reports support NASW's position that social work education provides the beginning-level practice knowledge and skills necessary for entry-level positions and that experience alone is an unreliable indicator of job performance (Gilbert, 1975; Karger, 1983). A study of social services jobs in Maryland concluded that social work education (specifically, the master of social work degree) is the best predictor of performance (Booz-Allen & Hamilton, 1987).

Although the importance of social work education has been denigrated and social work functions have been redefined in such a manner as to eliminate them, the job performance requirements and some critical tasks, such as psychosocial assessment, treatment planning, and discharge planning, have remained unchanged. Paraprofessionals, counselors, or human services personnel are considered as qualified as trained social workers and, at times, are sanctioned to function under the title "social worker." Thus, noncredentialed social workers are held responsible for delivering social services although they lack the social work knowledge base, skills, and values necessary to perform such tasks.

The problem of declassification persists. Public-sector agencies continue to hire unqualified staff personnel to perform complex social services tasks, which remain unchanged. The social work profession must develop forceful solutions and strategies to reverse this trend. To do so will require a thorough understanding of the dynamics of declassification. This analysis must focus on factors external and internal to the social work profession and on the value of social work education. Some of the factors external to the profession are the relaxation of social services standards, at both federal and state levels; reduction in federal and state funding for social services programs; radical changes in public social services agency personnel policies; and the diminishing number of social workers in administrative and policy making positions. Increasingly, other human services disciplines are competing with social workers who have bachelor's and master's degrees in social work for jobs that once exclusively required social work education.

Factors internal to the social work profession include redefinition of tasks and responsibilities by speciality groups and a preference by social workers for status agencies. Meyer (1983) gave examples of areas in which social workers gave up tasks in some instances and of fields where social workers once flourished. In recent years, hospital social workers have given up or shared the discharge planning function with nurses. Social workers have almost abandoned the courts and the probation field. Workers with MSWs are less attracted to public social services departments. Many new MSW graduates prefer private practice, and the drive for pay equity has pressed social workers in mental health agencies into accepting the title of mental health therapist.

Trends in social work education indicate that students interested in social policy, social research, or social services administration opt for other professional degrees, and workers with MSWs often must enroll in doctoral programs to specialize in these fields. As a result, non–social workers occupy decision-making positions and make policies that affect the status of social workers and social work practice.

Since 1981, NASW has enhanced its capability to address declassification and other professional issues. Frequently, NASW has accomplished results in cooperation with schools of social work and coalitions with other social work and related professional associations. The association has strengthened its research capacity by establishing the National Center for Social Policy and Practice. NASW has intensified legislative capabilities and lobbying activities at federal and state levels. With the establishment of the automatic check-off for the Political Action for Candidate Election (PACE) fund, NASW has further increased its legislative effectiveness and political clout.

NASW designated social work licensing a high-priority action; as a result, 49 of 50 states have some form of licensing or regulation. NASW also achieved landmark legislative goals, such as the inclusion of social workers as payees under Part B and other sections of Medicare and standards for social services staffing in nursing facilities. NASW has supported projects in North Carolina and South Carolina to increase the number of trained staff in child welfare. NASW also sponsored research and cooperated with other research organizations to determine the relative efficacy of social work training and made widely available research reports such as the *Maryland Social Work Services Job Analysis and Personnel Qualification Study* (Booz-Allen & Hamilton, 1987). The association has intervened to prevent dilution of social work standards and in other instances fostered training programs in public social services agencies.

Additional accomplishments include NASW actions to block legislation in North Carolina and South Carolina that would have required social workers to obtain other than social work licensure or certification to practice in fields that are traditionally part of social work practice, such as family therapy. In 1993, NASW also helped expand vendorship opportunities for social workers in North Carolina. The association has provided educational programs on peer review and other managed care issues, as well as on occupational social work and other relatively new practice fields. Finally, in recent years, NASW has moved to stop the news media from using the term *social worker* to apply to people who in fact are not social workers. As a result of NASW actions since the 1990 Delegate Assembly, the *New York Times* has changed its stylebook so that the title social worker is used to apply only to social workers who have MSW degrees.

NASW has increasingly demonstrated its effectiveness in promoting the social work profession by assuming a leadership role in the social policy and political arena. Chapter and unit-level activities and an increasing membership have further strengthened NASW. The Council on Social Work Education's accreditation of un-

dergraduate and graduate social work programs has significantly standardized social work education to assure quality and educational preparation for practice. Nevertheless, the solutions and the strategy to counteract declassification continue to elude the profession.

ISSUE STATEMENT

Public social services departments have failed to recognize the social work profession as a major contributor to effective social services and as an advocate for social welfare policies and programs in the United States. Systematically, social workers are being eliminated from direct services, supervision, policy making, and administrative positions. This elimination is being accomplished by declassifying and reclassifying traditional social work positions in public-sector agencies.

Increasingly, public agencies are hiring staff members who are uncredentialed, inadequately trained, and not qualified to fill social work positions. These people, who lack social work practice knowledge, values, and skills, are required to perform such complex tasks as psychosocial assessment, treatment planning, interviewing, and acting as change agents within the parameters of public social services agency policies and procedures. The national trend is to consider work experience or undifferentiated college education as equivalent to social work education. This equivalence assumes that people without social work degrees have the knowledge and intervention skills necessary to help individuals and families deal with complex problems. Such staffing trends are equally harmful to clients and to the social work profession. It is critical to the protection of clients and to the survival of the profession that this national declassification and reclassification trend be reversed.

POLICY STATEMENT

Professional social workers possess the specialized knowledge necessary for an effective social services delivery system. Social work education offers a unique combination of knowledge, values, skills, and professional ethics for which there is no exact equivalent and that cannot be acquired by on-the-job training, by experience only, or by possession of related degrees. Further, social work training is consistent with the tasks to be performed in helping clients solve problems that bring them to public social services departments and human services agencies.

NASW affirms that, in any social services delivery system, there must be a career ladder that recognizes the place of preprofessional workers and those with bachelor's and master's degrees in social work. In the program delivery system, social work professionals must have the authority and the responsibility for providing services to the clients and for supervising entry-level social workers and preprofessionals. Promotional opportunities and advancement to positions of greater responsibility and more complex tasks must be based on the level of social work education and experience. Social workers must also have promotional opportunities for policy-making and administrative positions.

NASW supports client-service ideology that emphasizes the *NASW Code of Ethics* (NASW, 1996), client interests, and the dignity of recipients of social services (Brager & Holloway, 1978). NASW supports the client's right to expect and to receive a high standard of professional services. Under the equal protection law, as in the case of private agency clients, public agency clients have the right to ask for and to receive the same quality care that is provided by trained social workers at private agencies.

NASW opposes declassification and reclassification of social work positions in public social services agencies. Declassification and reclassification have jeopardized the quality of social services because unqualified and uncredentialed staff are employed in social work positions.

NASW must develop a more aggressive multifaceted strategy to include the following actions:

■ clearly delineate and actively communicate social work expertise and knowledge and the skills of social workers with bachelor's and master's degrees in social work; demonstrate how social work education is distinctly different from other human services disciplines such as counseling, clinical psychology, marital counseling, and psychiatric nursing.

■ develop a national strategy to ensure title protection for social work.

■ identify the distinguishing features of social work education that prepare social workers to perform entry-level tasks—psychosocial assessment, treatment planning, interviewing, discharge planning, and so forth—that are intrinsic to social services provided by public agencies.

■ support social work validation studies to demonstrate the relevance of social work education content to the tasks performed at entry-level positions in public social services.

■ support studies that demonstrate the cost-benefits of hiring trained social workers at entry-level and middle-management positions.

■ encourage schools of social work to increase the number of field placements in public social services agencies and include in the social work curriculum policy and practice content related to child welfare, child and adult protective services, adoption, income maintenance programs (Aid to Families with Dependent Children and Supplemental Security Income), Food Stamp, and Medicaid programs.

■ work cooperatively with public-sector agencies to provide non–social workers currently employed in entry-level positions access to graduate social work education.

■ recognize different levels of social work practice, which requires teamwork necessary to provide comprehensive services to the consumers of social services and develop standards of ethics and practice specific to all such settings.

■ develop constructive and cooperative relationships with other human services organizations and state employee organizations (unions or associations) to promote personnel and professional service delivery standards necessary to provide quality service to clients of public-sector agencies.

■ work toward a national policy that will require, as a condition to receive matching federal funds, a uniform standard of professional service in public social service agencies. NASW should work toward a federal standard for human service programs that includes minimum professional social work degree requirements for entry-level positions.

■ increase the development of cooperative working relationships with state and local agency administrators to address declassification and the general trend to hire less-qualified staff in times of budget cuts and fewer resources.

■ develop an organizational strategy to review state legislation and existing policies that have allowed equivalence to accredited social work education and the replacement of social workers by staff having less experience and undifferentiated college degrees.

REFERENCES

Booz-Allen & Hamilton. (1987). *The Maryland social work services job analysis and personnel qualification study.* Annapolis: Maryland Department of Human Resources.

Brager, G., & Holloway, S. (1978). *Changing human service organizations.* New York: Free Press.

Gilbert, B. (1975). *An analysis of hiring requirements for social service classifications in merit systems.* Washington, DC: National Association of Social Workers.

Ginsberg, L., et al. (1989). *Social workers in public social services: A review of the literature.* Silver Spring, MD: National Association of Social Workers, National Center for Social Policy and Practice.

Kahn, T. (1981). *Chapter action guide on declassification.* Lansing: National Association of Social Workers, Michigan Chapter.

Karger, J. H. (1983). Reclassification: Is there a future in public welfare for the trained social worker? *Social Work, 28,* 427–433.

Meyer, C. M. (1983). Declassification: Assault on social workers and social services [Editorial]. *Social Work, 28,* 419.

National Association of Social Workers. (1984, May). *Classification validation processes for social service positions, executive summary.* Silver Spring, MD: Author.

National Association of Social Workers. (1991). *Social work speaks* (2nd ed.). Silver Spring, MD: NASW Press.

Pecora, P. J., & Austin, M. J. (1983). Declassification of social service jobs: Issues and strategies. *Social Work, 28,* 421–426.

Policy statement approved by the NASW national Board of Directors, October 1993, following recommendations from the NASW Delegate Assembly, August 1993. This statement supersedes the policy statement on Declassification approved by the Delegate Assembly in 1981. For further information, contact the National Association of Social Workers, 750 First Street, NE, Suite 700, Washington, DC 20002-4241. Telephone: 202-408-8600 or 800-638-8799.

Deinstitutionalization

BACKGROUND

The depopulation of mental hospitals and other human services institutions has continued unabated since the mid-1950s. Deinstitutionalization was intended to return institutionalized individuals to the community and to prevent unnecessary or traumatic institutionalization. The aims of deinstitutionalization, therefore, involve pivotal social work values, such as normalization, empowerment, and interdependency.

However, patients frequently have been denied inpatient or residential services or have been discharged before adequate community supports and services could be developed. Although progress has been made, there have rarely been sufficient community support systems, partly because of budgetary constraints. Implementing deinstitutionalization has varied widely according to the problem area and the quality of social concern in the community and at the state and federal levels, but the underlying funding limitations persist.

People with Developmental Disabilities

Developmental disabilities include mental retardation, epilepsy, autism, or organic impairment; people with these disabilities constitute approximately 1.8 percent of the general population (Center on Residential Services and Community Living, 1993). The deinstitutionalization movement for this population continues to be stimulated by court actions, by P.L. 101-496, and by advocacy groups, such as the Association for Retarded Citizens (formerly the National Association for Retarded Citizens). In addition, the Medicaid ICF-MR program, established in 1971, has contributed significantly to deinstitutionalization of people with mental retardation and

related conditions. The normalization ideology, in which residential conditions and settings replicate as much as possible the norms and patterns of everyday life, drives deinstitutionalization for these people. The ideology has led to an increase in community-based foster homes, group homes, and supported living and employment programs. However, the lack of adequate numbers and fragmentation of community resources, lack of proper interagency coordination, and the failure of communities to comply with zoning ordinances continue to be major problems in availing people with developmental disabilities of their basic legal and human rights.

People with Mental Illness

Between 1955 and 1990, the population of state and county mental hospitals and residences in the United States declined by 83.5 percent, from 558,922 to 92,054 (National Institute of Mental Health, 1955, 1990). During the 1980s, the impact of deinstitutionalization spread to the private sector as well. Between 1980 and 1990, the census of all public and private psychiatric units and hospitals dropped by almost 50 percent, from 245,029 to 128,530 (U.S. Bureau of the Census, 1980, 1990b). Much of the decline has been fueled by a rapidly diminishing length of stay and the spread of managed care. A variety of factors have stimulated the decline: the provision of psychotropic drugs, the belief that patients should be treated in the least restrictive environment, the emphasis on community-based treatment and rehabilitation, court decisions on the rights of mental patients, state laws making involuntary hospitalization more difficult, the rising costs of hospital care, and the effort to transfer the costs of long-term care from state budgets to federally subsidized maintenance and medical assistance programs.

Federal and state agencies have developed a variety of community service programs as alternatives to institutional care. These programs are designed to enable people with mental illness to remain in or return to their community and to lead as normal and as independent a life as possible. The transition from institution to community-based treatment has been difficult. Thousands of patients enter institutions and remain there or reenter them because of the lack of appropriate community support services. Thousands of other people are in community settings that do not serve their needs. In many cases, the community settings are worse environments than the institutions. These community settings include jails and prisons, nursing homes, board and care homes, and homeless shelters. In addition, it has been estimated that there are approximately 200,000 severely mentally ill people homeless on any given day (Manderscheid & Rosenstein, 1992).

The most difficult task in deinstitutionalization is to develop adequate services and residential facilities for people with serious mental illness, who have always been vulnerable to neglect and abuse. Without improved federal leadership, full and coordinated support from state and local agencies, and adequate financing for appropriate facilities and services in the community, people with serious mental illness will continue to suffer and their needs will not be met.

Dependent Children

There has been a widespread movement to transfer children from large, overcrowded institutions, such as preparatory schools and correctional facilities, to resources in their communities. These resources include children's homes with assistance provided by the parents, foster care, and group homes. During the 1980s, there was an additional movement to transfer children from foster care and group homes back to their families, or if this was not possible, to adoptive families.

There are many benefits for children as a result of deinstitutionalization. Children feel less alienated if they are closer to their homes and families. Community-based care is less expen-

sive because transportation, communications, and other logistical items cost less. In addition, the family system remains open when the children are close enough for frequent visits. Although the rationale for deinstitutionalization is valid, the fast rate with which it was accomplished in the 1980s stretched community resources severely and resulted in relaxed screening procedures, less-stringent placement procedures, and insufficient family preservation services.

Juvenile Offenders

Courts without detention facilities detain juveniles less frequently than courts that have detention facilities, although juveniles in both types of courts have similar backgrounds and commit similar types of crimes. Courts that have detention facilities often err in their use of detention. Courts that do not have detention facilities must be more selective and discriminating about the juveniles they detain. This fact suggests that all courts could be more selective. Most juveniles appear for their court hearing, and only a small percentage commit a second crime before their hearing. Thus, the rationale that detention ensures a court appearance and protects the safety of the community is not valid for most juvenile offenders. Offenders who are detained, have a formal hearing, and receive diagnostic services are more likely to be institutionalized than those who are not detained. Courts warn and release a significant number of juvenile offenders in a perfunctory way. Furthermore, courts do not refer a sufficient number of offenders to community agencies.

Older Adults

People age 65 and older constitute 12.6 percent of the population (U.S. Bureau of the Census, 1990a). Currently 1.8 million people (0.7 percent of the U.S. population) reside in nursing homes. Of these, 1.5 million are older adults who represent 4.9 percent of the over 65 population (U.S. Bureau of the Census, 1990a). Institutional services for the aged increasingly have focused on services for older people who are unable to maintain independent living arrangements and who require personal care. Although home health care can provide an alternative to nursing homes for many elderly people, the system is undeveloped in many communities.

ISSUE STATEMENT

Deinstitutionalization should not be thought of as a goal in itself. Simply moving clients from one setting to another is no guarantee that their life situation or functional capacities will improve. If deinstitutionalization is to benefit the seriously mentally ill, a broad network of community resources and services must be provided over an extended period. Broad networks of community supports cannot be the responsibility of any single services system—health, mental health, or social services. Developing and maintaining adequate supports must involve many agencies, including those for public health, medical assistance, social services, income maintenance, transportation, employment, housing, and vocational rehabilitation.

The social work profession should take a leadership role in helping the various human services agencies provide the services to which people with mental illness or other mental handicaps or disabilities are entitled.

The states must tackle issues related to funding, clarification of roles, and coordination of services for people who have long-term disabilities. The use of federal and state funds for these purposes must be adequately monitored.

POLICY STATEMENT

Therapeutically appropriate, not merely convenient, methods of deinstitutionalization should permit people to maintain their independence, dignity, and quality of life in their own homes or in appropriate congregate residential settings.

It is the policy of NASW that people with developmental disabilities, individuals with mental illness, and other people who have been institutionalized should have their legal and human rights affirmed, their potential developed, and the quality of their lives enhanced. Clients, their families, and significant others should be included in treatment planning.

Professional social workers should complete differential and independent assessment and planning with clients before their initial admission and before their discharge. Clients who are now institutionalized should receive the same services.

Standards for a range of community-based services should be developed and resources for their full implementation should be provided. A comprehensive system of interrelated services should be established. This system should include a full range of alternative facilities and support services, adequately financed to meet the changing needs of deinstitutionalized people and the families who care for them and to help prevent institutionalization. The services system should consist of a full continuum of programs for primary prevention, early intervention, intensive treatment, rehabilitation, and sustaining care, and it should include both temporary and long-term residential services.

There should be adequate funding for alternative community-based facilities and support for people and the families who care for them. Facilities should be located throughout a community to avoid concentrations in low-income areas.

The social work profession should develop standards to guide the planning and implementation of institutional change and closures. Standards should require that no institution can be closed without comprehensive needs assessment, program evaluation, public hearings, and the provision of transitional services and alternative programs.

The policy of providing federal and state programs to ensure the right of people with mental illness to be treated in the least restrictive setting appropriate to their needs should be used as a model for other populations. Public policies should include the following:

■ Services should be organized to promote the continuity of supportive relationships. For case management, one person or team should be responsible for establishing and maintaining contact with the client on a continuing basis. The total number of clients assigned to the professional or to the team should be small enough to ensure that each client is treated as a unique individual in a supporting, caring relationship.

■ All services should be organized to help clients become or remain part of a network of caring relationships of a personal support system. As a result, clients will be able to develop capacities for mutual and self-help, and unnecessary dependence on organized services systems can be reduced.

■ All programs for these client groups should subscribe to the principle of normalization.

To ensure that public policies incorporate these principles, social workers should advocate for their clients and the clients' families.

REFERENCES

Center on Residential Services and Community Living, Institute on Community Integration/ UAP, College of Education, University of Minnesota. (1993, January). *Residential services for people with developmental disabilities: Status and trends through 1991.* Minneapolis–St. Paul: Author.

Manderscheid, R., & Rosenstein, M. (1992). Homeless people with mental illness and alcohol or other drug abuse: Current research, policy, and other prospects. *Current Opinions in Psychiatry, 5,* 273–278.

National Institute of Mental Health. (1955). *Patients in mental institutions.* Washington, DC: U.S. Government Printing Office.

National Institute of Mental Health. (1990). *Additions and resident patients at end of year, state and county mental hospitals, by age and diagnosis, by state, United States, 1990.* Bethesda, MD: Author.

U.S. Bureau of the Census. (1980). *Statistical abstract of the United States, 1980.* Washington, DC: U.S. Government Printing Office.

U.S. Bureau of the Census. (1990a). *Standard tape file 1C.* Washington, DC: U.S. Government Printing Office.

U.S. Bureau of the Census. (1990b). *Statistical abstract of the United States, 1990.* Washington, DC: U.S. Government Printing Office.

Policy statement approved by the NASW national Board of Directors, October 1993, following recommendations by the NASW Delegate Assembly, August 1993. This statement supersedes the policy statement on Deinstitutionalization approved by the Delegate Assembly in 1977. For further information, contact the National Association of Social Workers, 750 First Street, NE, Suite 700, Washington, DC 20002-4241. Telephone: 202-408-8600 or 800-638-8799.

Disasters

BACKGROUND

Definitions

Several definitions are frequently applied to disaster. A *disaster* can be an event that causes extensive destruction, death, or injury and that produces widespread community disruption and individual trauma (Hartsough & Myers, 1987). Disasters may be occurrences of nature such as a hurricane, tornado, storm, flood, high water, tidal wave, earthquake, volcanic eruption, drought, blizzard, pestilence, or fire (American Red Cross, 1991); they may have a technological cause such as hazardous waste contamination or nuclear accident; or they may be the result of human error or equipment failure such as transportation accidents, industrial accidents, dam breaks, or building or structural collapse. In addition, acts of terrorism, riots, kidnapping, and random acts of violence may be viewed as disasters. The disaster may be either sudden or slow and insidious over several months; it may be unexpected or have some degree of predictability .

For policies related to the social work profession, it is important to conceptualize disasters in a framework that encompasses the breadth of responses compatible with social work knowledge and skills at the macro, mezzo, and micro levels. Disasters are but one subcomponent of extreme stress situations. This overall category of phenomena—extreme stress situations— may be subdivided into two major areas: (1) situations that affect individuals (such as rape or other violent crime, a serious home fire, or a tragic accident) and (2) extreme, collective situations. A *collective stress situation* is one in which a social system fails to provide expected life conditions for its members. Collective stress situations are divided into disasters and conflicts; conflicts include such events as wars, riots, and terrorist attacks (Quarantelli, 1985). Using this framework, disaster trauma exists at two levels: individual and collective. Disaster creates trauma for entire communities by virtue of massive disorganization, immobilization of infrastructure, and hiatus of customary leadership, all of which produce trauma, grief, and a sense of helplessness in individuals, families, and small groups owing to losses, severe disruption, and frustrated attempts to obtain assistance and solve problems.

Across the duration of a disaster, four stages have been identified that provide chronological targets for social work responses: (1) preimpact, beginning when a disaster poses no immediate threat but prompts mitigation and preparedness activities; (2) impact, or the period when the disaster event takes place; (3) postimpact, or the period immediately after the impact up to the beginning of recovery; and (4) recovery, or the period in which disaster survivors are working toward restoration of their predisaster state (American Red Cross, 1993). It is useful to services delivery to recognize the short- and long-term stages of recovery; the latter sometimes require years. For example, nearly three years after the assault of Hurricane Andrew on South Florida in August 1992, the *Miami Herald* reported that more than 1,000 families continued to live in severely damaged structures (Arthur, 1995).

Populations at Risk and Outcomes

Within a community affected by disaster, several categories of victims can be defined: *Primary* or *impact victims* are those who have experienced direct physical, material, and personal losses from the disaster; *context victims* are those who have witnessed the destruction of the disaster (such as the death or material losses of family or friends and the sociocultural disorganization of the postimpact environment) but have not directly experienced the specific impact; *entry victims* are people who enter the impact area during the postdisaster crisis period (such as police and military personnel, rescue workers, government officials, and volunteers) and who are exposed to the death and destruction; and *peripheral victims* are those who were not directly affected by the disaster but who suffer distress and uncertainty over the safety and well-being of family and friends (Bolin, 1986; Dudasik, 1980). Among these categories of disaster survivors and victims are the vulnerable populations of central concern to the social work profession: poor people; older people; people with disabilities; people who are isolated, institutionalized, or otherwise at risk; and all exposed children. These populations may be among the most vulnerable disaster survivors and may require special attention during preparedness, immediate relief, and recovery.

The course of recovery is patterned and predictable, with steps that include (1) heroism, (2) honeymoon, (3) response, (4) recovery, and (5) reconstruction (American Red Cross, 1992). Effective interventions are tailored to the phase of recovery. During these recovery phases, it is common for a second disaster to occur: The emergency bureaucracy's uncoordinated, ineffective, and at times misguided response and unwieldy procedures often inadvertently create or magnify difficulties and impose barriers to problem solving.

The outcomes of disaster events have immediate and long-term biological, psychological, social, and environmental consequences, that social workers from all fields of practice will need to consider in their response activities. Outcomes for victims and survivors, particularly those who are most vulnerable, also include extensive damage to property and possessions, dislocation, unemployment, health and coping problems, and death. There are a range of reactions to the stress that are universal, normal for the situation, and widely shared and that abate naturally (Cohen & Ahearn, 1980). Typical reactions include feelings of distress, grief, diminished role functioning, problems in living, irritability, frustration, guilt, and disillusionment.

But most disaster survivors' individual behavior is organized, controlled, and adaptive. Survivors often exhibit selflessness and personal strength. A strengths model (as opposed to pathology and deficit models) should guide disaster-related interventions.

A significant percentage of survivors develop profound, debilitating posttraumatic stress reactions requiring extended mental health interventions rather than short-term disaster assistance. These extreme stress reactions include fear and irrational behavior, shock, immobilization, withdrawal, denial and intrusive thoughts, hypervigilance, easy startle, insomnia, decreased attention and concentration, and psychophysiological reactions (Cohen & Ahearn, 1980; Forster, 1992). Children are especially vulnerable and often display stress reactions such as fear, sleep disturbances, separation anxiety, confusion, disruptive classroom behavior, and aggressiveness (Farberow & Gordon, 1986; Forster, 1992). Older people, who tend to be more resilient than younger disaster survivors (Bell, 1978; Huerta & Horton, 1978), also include a frail and vulnerable subgroup who may be displaced from extended-care facilities in the disaster impact area. Other high-risk survivors include people with physical disabilities; people with histories of stressful life events and dysfunctional coping patterns (Forster, 1992); and people with intense exposure to the disaster's impact, including emergency workers, first responders, and rescue teams. Rescue workers, working under a high degree of concentration and physical demand, witness firsthand the breadth of destruction, identify and remove the deceased, and are exposed to situations that compromise their physical safety. Disaster personnel, especially those who themselves are primary victims, therefore experience the additive effects of the disaster event, the aftermath, and unique occupational stressors (Hartsough & Myers, 1987).

Some survivors experience the reactivation of distress at anniversary points. Furthermore, the phases of a disaster widely accepted by the emergency response institutions—mitigation and preparation, response, and recovery—fail to emphasize the long-term recovery stage, during which a segment of survivors continue to struggle to reestablish their homes or other predisaster circumstances at two, three, and four years after the disaster. For some, especially those who were highly exposed and bereaved, the experience of distress persists past the disaster event for some time, even as long as 14 years (Green et al., 1990). In many cases, the people or families plunged into precarious economic situations as a result of the disaster or whose situations were marginal before the disaster become substantially worse off because of the disaster.

Research

Research on the human services aspects of disaster has focused on mental health outcomes. In a review of research on the effects of disaster on mental health, Green (1993) found 131 quantitative empirical studies of people exposed to natural or technical disasters. Many of these studies were descriptive. The number of studies using control group designs was fewer than 25. Natural prospective (single-group pretest–posttest) and retrospective designs with large numbers of subjects were few. Intervention research (assessing program or treatment outcomes) was virtually nonexistent, as was research informing disaster response services systems and structures (Dodds & Nuehring, in press). The scarcity of disaster-related research is a result, in part, of limited access to subjects (survivors) who receive postdisaster services.

Social work research on disasters is only now beginning to emerge (Ager & Zakour, 1995; Cherry & Cherry, 1995; Dodds & Nuehring, in press; Gillespie, Sherraden, Streeter, & Zakour, 1986; Rogge, 1995). Furthermore, little has been done to disseminate information systematically about disasters and disaster response to social workers through the established journals and communication channels of the profession.

Management of Disasters

The social disorganization surrounding a disaster and the number and types of responding organizations and groups create the need for a well-ordered mass response system. For routine, daily emergencies, local public and private entities have responsibilities typically determined by charters and laws. A disaster, in contrast, may be viewed as an occurrence of such magnitude that it cannot be managed by a single entity or routine procedures. Consequently, a complex organizational environment has developed to respond in disaster situations.

Federal laws (in particular, the Disaster Relief Act of 1970, the Disaster Relief Act Amendments of 1980, and the Robert T. Stafford Disaster Relief and Emergency Assistance Act) grant authority to the federal government to provide assistance in defined disasters. The Federal Emergency Management Agency (FEMA) administers the federal natural disaster relief programs and civil defense systems. FEMA supplements state and local governments in emergency response operations and may order any other federal agency (for example, the Departments of Agriculture, Defense, Health and Human Services, or Justice) to directly help state and local governments. These agencies, in turn, mobilize such functions and services as emergency transportation, communications, emergency food distribution and mass care, housing, direct financial assistance, emergency medical care, crisis counseling programs, search-and-rescue operations, mortuary services, and construction management (Myers, 1994).

To mobilize these organizations, a declaration of disaster is initiated according to an increasing level of emergency. A local emergency is declared when the governance of a city or county deems conditions to pose an extreme threat to the safety of people and property within that jurisdiction. When the disaster conditions threaten the safety of people and property within a state, the governor may proclaim a state of emergency, making mutual aid assistance mandatory from other cities, counties, and state authorities. When damage exceeds the resources of local and state governments, the president may declare a disaster, which may activate two types of federal assistance as provided for in the Stafford Act. Individual assistance may include low-interest loans, individual and family grants, temporary housing, and crisis counseling. Public assistance in a disaster declared by the president may include search-and-rescue operations, repair and replacement of public property such as roads, and debris clearance. The president also may declare a state of emergency, which authorizes emergency mass care, search-and-rescue operations, and emergency transportation (Myers, 1994).

In addition to FEMA and state and local governments, several volunteer agencies assume defined roles and responsibilities in disaster situations. Chief among these is the American Red Cross. In 1905 a congressional charter (reaffirmed by the Disaster Relief Act of 1970 and the Stafford Act, as amended in 1988) designated the American National Red Cross to conduct a system of national and international relief to mitigate the suffering caused by pestilence, famine, fire, floods, and other great national calamities and to develop and execute measures for preventing these events (American Red Cross, 1991). Using voluntary contributions, the Red Cross coordinates with local, state, and federal resources to disseminate official warnings, conduct voluntary evacuation, provide emergency shelter and services, and coordinate a trained volunteer rescue corps.

A host of other key volunteer organizations are involved in disaster response, including the Salvation Army (bulk food distribution, mass shelter facilities, trained staff and volunteers, crisis intervention, financial assistance), Volunteers of America (ambulances and air transportation and rescue), the United Methodist Church, the Southern Baptist Convention, the National Catholic Conference and Catholic Charities, the Mennonite Disaster Services, and the Christian Reformed World Belief (Myers, 1994).

Following two major airline crashes in the mid-1980s, the Dallas branch of the Texas chapter of NASW, in cooperation with the Dallas area chapter of the American Red Cross, submitted a request for mental health disaster services that was later implemented by the National Red Cross. As a result of this policy decision, several professional organizations have entered into a statement of understanding with the American Red Cross. NASW entered into such an agreement in 1990 (NASW & American Red Cross, 1990). The California chapter of NASW, Los Angeles County regions, developed a statement of understanding with the American Red Cross in 1993. These agreements were developed to facilitate social worker participation in the planning, training, and provision of mental health services to disaster victims and Red Cross personnel as needed (NASW & American Red Cross, 1993). Various NASW chapters have developed agreements with other volunteer organizations, such as the North Carolina chapter's agreement with the Salvation Army.

ISSUE STATEMENT

Disasters are collective, communitywide traumatic events that cause extensive destruction, death, or injury and widespread social and personal disruption. They apparently are becoming more frequent as populations concentrate in coastal areas at high risk for natural disasters such as hurricanes (Freedy, Resnick, & Kilpatrick, 1992) and in urban centers at high risk for technological and industrial disasters (Baum, 1987; Freedy et al., 1992). Additionally, a changing global political climate has led to an increase in terrorism and random acts of violence. Striking whole locales, disasters may endanger and overwhelm already vulnerable members of the community, such as children and people who are older, disabled, isolated, institutionalized, in out-of-home care, or living in compromised housing.

In addition to empirical studies that have accumulated on the effects of disasters, much practice wisdom has evolved around the delivery of disaster assistance. Even though an immense emergency response system of voluntary and government organizations has become established, disasters continue to be undermitigated, not prepared for, and significantly mismanaged. This "second disaster" is cited as creating more long-lasting and severe stressors for survivors and victims than the original disaster (Cohen & Ahearn, 1980; Myers, 1994). Much remains to be understood, and many systems and policies require significant refinement, if not reconceptualization, if disaster response is to advance in quality and effectiveness.

NASW has adopted a disaster policy at the national level for four primary reasons:

1. Disasters are large-scale catastrophes that affect whole communities or multiple communities in geophysical, social, and psychological ways.

2. The trauma and deprivation resulting from disasters often are magnified for those with few resources and reduced opportunities to rebuild homes and replace losses. As such, vulnerable populations, such as children, older people, or people with disabilities, are likely to be among those especially affected by disasters.

3. Of all the allied health and human services professions, social work is uniquely suited to interpret the disaster context, to advocate for effective services, and to provide leadership in essential collaborations among institutions and organizations. Individuals, families, groups, neighborhoods, organizations, schools, interorganizational networks, and whole communities require intervention. Furthermore, compatible with social work epistemology, disaster assistance must be construed holistically, encompassing the physical, developmental, psychological, emotional, social, cultural, and spiritual needs of survivors. Finally, respected disaster response modalities readily translate to the language of empowerment and classic, generalist social work practice.

4. Although social workers have been quick to respond to need in the immediate aftermath of disasters, they have largely provided direct casework and, at times, community organization services to survivors and have received little recognition for their efforts. Social work's input in planning for disaster response at national, state, and local levels has usually been negligible; social work research on disaster is only now emerging (Ager & Zakour, 1995; Cherry & Cherry, 1995; Dodds & Nuehring, in press; Gillespie et al., 1986; Rogge, 1995). Practically no intervention research has been done to date on the outcomes of disaster assistance efforts. The importance of the potential contribution and role of social work warrants more than ad hoc, intuitive, spontaneous responses on a disaster-by-disaster basis. Effective disaster leadership and a proactive presence on the part of the profession require preparation, direction, training, and rehearsal.

POLICY STATEMENT

NASW supports participation in and advocates for programs and policies that serve individuals and communities in the wake of disaster. NASW supports

■ the prevention or mitigation of the adverse consequences of disaster and effective preparation for disaster by individuals, families, social networks, neighborhoods, schools, organizations, and communities, especially where vulnerable populations are concentrated

■ enhancement of the efficiency, effectiveness, orchestration, and responsiveness of disaster relief and recovery efforts to prevent the second disaster phenomenon that magnifies the trauma of the initial catastrophe

■ the provision of mental health and social services to survivors in a context of normalization and empowerment, with sensitivity to the phases of disaster recovery and with understanding of the unique cultural features of the affected community and its populations

■ attention to the protracted recovery phase of disasters that leaves substantial numbers of people without resources, without resolution of their losses, and with little opportunity to restore their predisaster quality of life

■ attention to the special and critical training, stress management, and support needs of disaster workers in all capacities, from administrative to field staff, and the need to respond to their circumstances as victims and survivors

■ education of social workers and social work students in the specialized knowledge and methods of trauma response and critical incident stress debriefing

■ the development of rigorous disaster research, especially intervention effectiveness research

■ the development of a cadre of well-trained disaster professionals committed to effective interdisciplinary and interorganizational collaboration in disaster planning and disaster response, at both the administrative and direct services levels

■ the presence, commitment, and leadership of social workers in disaster services

■ the provision of accurate and effective public information on the normal stages of disaster reaction, functional coping methods, and strategies for accessing and successfully using the disaster assistance bureaucracy.

REFERENCES

Ager, R. D., & Zakour, M. J. (1995, March). *Network exchange and the coordination of disaster relief services.* Paper presented at the Annual Program Meeting of the Council on Social Work Education, San Diego.

American Red Cross. (1991). *Statement of understanding between the American Psychological Association and the American Red Cross* (ARC Publication No. 4468). Washington, DC: Author.

American Red Cross. (1992). *Disaster mental health services I: Glossary of terms* (ARC Publication No. 3077-1A). Washington, DC: Author.

American Red Cross. (1993). *Disaster services regulations and procedures* (ARC Publication No. 3077-1A). Washington, DC: Author.

Arthur, L. (1995, April 6). Two S. Dade cities angered over vote on hurricane relief fund. *Miami Herald*, p. 28.

Baum, A. (1987). Toxins, technology, and natural disasters. In G. R. VandenBos & B. K. Bryant (Eds.), *Cataclysms, crises, and catastrophes: Psychology in action* (pp. 9–53). Washington, DC: American Psychological Association.

Bell, B. D. (1978). Disaster impact and responses: Overcoming the thousand natural shocks. *Gerontologist, 18*, 531–540.

Bolin, R. (1986). Disaster characteristics and psychosocial impacts. In B. J. Sowder (Ed.), *Disasters and mental health* (pp. 11–36). Washington, DC: American Psychiatric Press.

Cherry, A. L., & Cherry, M. E. (1995, March). *Research as social action in the aftermath of Hurricane Andrew*. Paper presented at the Annual Program Meeting of the Council on Social Work Education, San Diego.

Cohen, R. E., & Ahearn, F. L. (1980). *Handbook for mental health care of disaster victims*. Baltimore: Johns Hopkins University Press.

Disaster Relief Act of 1970, P.L. 93-288, 88 Stat. 164.

Disaster Relief Act Amendments of 1980, P.L. 96-563, 94 Stat. 3334.

Disaster Relief and Emergency Assistance Amendments of 1988, P.L. 100-707, 102 Stat. 4689 to 4711.

Dodds, S. E., & Nuehring, E. M. (in press). Preparation for disaster: A formula for social work research. *Journal of Social Service Research*.

Dudasik, S. (1980). Victimization in natural disaster. *Disasters, 4*, 329–338.

Farberow, N. L., & Gordon, N. S. (1986). *Manual for child health workers in major disasters* (DHHS Publication No. ADM 86-1070). Washington, DC: U.S. Government Printing Office.

Forster, P. (1992). Nature and treatment of acute stress reactions. In J. H. Gold (Series Ed.) & L. S. Austin (Vol. Ed.), *Clinical practice: Volume 24. Responding to disaster* (pp. 25–52). Washington, DC: American Psychiatric Press.

Freedy, J. R., Resnick, H. S., & Kilpatrick, D. G. (1992). Conceptual framework for evaluating disaster impact: Implications for clinical intervention. In J. H. Gold (Series Ed.) & L. S. Austin (Vol. Ed.), *Clinical practice: Volume 24. Responding to disaster* (pp. 3–23). Washington, DC: American Psychiatric Press.

Gillespie, D. F., Sherraden, M. W., Streeter, C. L., & Zakour, M. J. (1986). *Mapping networks of organized volunteers for natural hazard preparedness* (Publication No. PB87-182051/A09). Springfield, VA: National Technical Information Service.

Green, B. L. (1993). *Mental health and disaster: Research review* (Report to NIMH, Requisition 91MF175040). Washington, DC: Georgetown University Medical Center, Department of Psychiatry.

Green, B., Grace, M., Lindy, J., Gleser, G., Leonard, A., & Kramer, T. (1990). Buffalo Creek survivors in the second decade: Comparison with unexposed and nonlitigant groups. *Journal of Applied Social Psychology, 20*, 1033–1050.

Hartsough, D. M., & Myers, D. G. (1987). *Disaster work and mental health: Prevention and control of stress among workers* (DHHS Publication No. ADM 87-1422). Washington, DC: U.S. Government Printing Office.

Huerta, F., & Horton, R. (1978). Coping behavior of elderly flood victims. *Gerontologist, 18*, 541–546.

Myers, D. (1994). *Disaster response and recovery: A handbook for mental health professionals* (DHHS Publication No. SMA 94-3010). Washington, DC: U.S. Government Printing Office.

National Association of Social Workers/American Red Cross. (1990). *Statement of understanding between National Association of Social Workers and the American Red Cross*. Washington, DC: Authors.

National Association of Social Workers/American Red Cross. (1993). *Statement of understanding between the California chapter of the National Association of Social Workers, Los Angeles County regions and the American Red Cross*. Los Angeles: Authors.

Quarantelli, E. L. (1985). An assessment of conflicting views on mental health: The consequences of traumatic events. In C. R. Figley

(Ed.), *Trauma and its wake: The study and treatment of post-traumatic stress disorder* (pp. 173–215). New York: Brunner/Mazel.

Robert T. Stafford Disaster Relief and Emergency Assistance Act, P.L. 93-288, 88 Stat. 143.

Rogge, M. E. (1995, March). *Reducing community vulnerability to technological and natural hazards: Tool for empowerment.* Paper presented at the Annual Program Meeting of the Council on Social Work Education, San Diego.

SUGGESTED READINGS

Austin, L. (Ed.). (1992). *Clinical practice: Responding to disaster.* Washington, DC: American Psychiatric Press.

Green, B., Grace, M., Lindy, J., Titchener, J., & Lindy, J. (1983). Levels of functional impairment following a civilian disaster: The Beverly Hills Supper Club fire. *Journal of Consulting and Clinical Psychology, 51,* 573–580.

Holen, A. (1991). A longitudinal study of the occurrence and persistence of post-traumatic health problems in disaster survivors. *Stress Medicine, 7,* 11–17.

Lima, B., Pai, S., Lozano, J., & Santacruz, H. (1990). The stability of emotional symptoms among disaster victims in a developing country. *Journal of Traumatic Stress, 3,* 497–505.

Phifer, J., & Norris, F. (1989). Psychological symptoms in older adults following natural disaster: Nature, timing, duration, and course. *Journal of Gerontology: Social Sciences, 44,* S207–S217.

Shore, J., Tatum, E., & Vollmer, W. (1986). Psychiatric reactions to disaster: The Mount St. Helens experience. *American Journal of Psychiatry, 143,* 590–595.

Weisaeth, L. (1989). A study of behavioral responses to an industrial disaster. *Acta Psychiatrica Scandinavica, 355* (80 Suppl.), 131–137.

Policy statement approved by the NASW Delegate Assembly, August 1996. For further information, contact the National Association of Social Workers, 750 First Street, NE, Suite 700, Washington, DC 20002-4241. Telephone: 202-408-8600 or 800-638-8799.

Drug Testing in the Workplace

BACKGROUND

The testing of employees for the presence of exogenous substances is an area of emerging concern to employers and employees, to the legal and social environment, and to professional practice. Increasingly, the idea of drug testing demands that social workers make professional, ethical, and even personal decisions. It is of gravest concern to those practicing in employee assistance programs (EAPs), which include member assistance programs and other employer- or union-sponsored programs of intervention at work sites.

The abuse of exogenous substances is common in our society. The most visible and perhaps the most damaging substances are tobacco and alcohol, both legal (see the policy statement on Alcohol, Tobacco, and Other Substance Abuse). The purpose of this policy statement is to propose ethical guidelines on drug-testing initiatives (DTIs) at work sites that are aimed at detecting the illicit use of controlled substances or the use of illegal substances.

Other issues of testing at work sites pose equally troubling ethical dilemmas for social workers. Although polygraphs and testing for HIV/AIDS and for genetic predisposition are not covered in this statement, similar ethical guidelines should be established for all testing situations at work sites.

Since the inception of the industrial/occupational social work field of practice, practitioners have been concerned about the lives of workers, their conditions of employment, the structures and cultures of their workplaces, and the relationships among these elements. The following sections outline urgent ethical conflicts that are posed by drug testing in everyday practice.

Defining the Client

The *NASW Code of Ethics* (1993) emphasizes the primacy of the client's interests. In most traditional practice environments, the client who seeks services is an individual, family, group, or community. At work sites, however, the client also may be the employing organization.

Defining the Best Interests of the Client

If the client is an employee who is abusing substances, it is in his or her best interest to become and to remain free from substance abuse. If the client is the employing organization, it is in its best interest to have a healthy work site. It is also in the best interest of other employees to have their co-workers free from substance abuse.

The Individual Client's Right to Confidentiality

Individual clients receiving treatment for substance abuse clearly are protected by federal confidentiality statutes. The *NASW Code of Ethics* (1993) states that "the social worker should respect the privacy of clients and hold in confidence all information obtained in the course of professional service" (p. 1).

The Employing Organization's Right to Privacy

Social workers who are employed by organizations as staff members or consultants should respect the privacy of information obtained in fulfillment of their professional responsibilities, except for compelling reasons affecting the public welfare. There is no precedent for this statement in the *NASW Code of Ethics*.

Conflicts between Individual and Societal Rights

When rights clash, the social worker needs to determine whose rights take precedence. Agency-based practice follows the dictum of primacy of the client's interests. As stated in the *NASW Code of Ethics* (1993, p. 5), "The social worker's primary responsibility is to clients." However, the *NASW Code of Ethics* also requires a social worker to be ethically responsible to employers and employing organizations; thus, "The social worker should adhere to commitments made to the employing organization" (p. 8). If the employing organization adheres to a policy of individual drug testing, the social worker should assess the ethics of the DTI and its value (positive or negative) to both the employer and the employees. Having weighed how best to promote the client's best interests, the social worker then should decide whether to support or oppose the DTI.

The Social Worker's Ethical Responsibility to Society

There may be a conflict between the social worker's ethical responsibility to society and the primacy of service to clients, whether people or organizations. The social worker's responsibility to society may conflict with the client's right to self-determination. Social workers should work to promote the general welfare of society, which may have a different meaning from the welfare of the individual who requires the protections of due process, nondiscrimination, and civil rights. In fact, the *NASW Code of Ethics* (1993, p. 10) mandates that social workers "act to prevent and eliminate discrimination against any person or group. . . ." A DTI that appears to promote the general welfare also may discriminate against substance-abusing individuals, for whom services must be an ethical focus.

ISSUE STATEMENT

This section outlines the social worker's response to work site issues raised by the eventuality of a drug-testing initiative (DTI). It neither resolves nor explores all the social, legal, scientific, and ethical issues posed by drug testing in the workplace.

Social workers must take an active role in promoting a harmonious, healthy society. They also must scrutinize the ethics of their own work environments. As in all areas of professional work, the social worker facing DTIs should be guided by the *NASW Code of Ethics*, as well as by reason and the law, to balance the interests of the employer, the employees, and the public. Although the social worker is expected to observe the law, this expectation, in itself, does not mean that an employer's legal rights harmonize with social work ethics. Each social worker must evaluate each situation on its own merits and make informed decisions on whether to promote a DTI, acquiesce to it, challenge it, or even withdraw from the organization in protest.

Social workers should be concerned primarily with helping substance-abusing individuals find successful treatment and should work to preserve jobs within the Rehabilitation Act of 1974 and other employee protection regulations.

To negotiate through the institutional denial of chemical dependence as a disease, social workers should advocate specific job descriptions and accurate reviews of the work performance of employees. In some situations, however, employers may be justified in implementing DTIs to protect their organizations, their customers, other employees, or society.

Employers are entitled to maintain healthy workplaces and to want their products and services to be free from defects resulting from employee substance abuse. Employers should expect that the employees whom they hire will be able to carry out the responsibilities of their jobs. Employees are entitled to expect substance-abusing coworkers to be appropriately treated when it is probable that the abusers will injure other employees or their interests. The public is entitled to expect protection from defects in products and services resulting from substance abuse. Each situation compels the social worker to formulate his or her own ethical evaluation, abiding by the *NASW Code of Ethics.*

The social worker should promote a comprehensive and ethical approach to the problem of substance abuse at the work site. This approach should cover treatment, education and prevention, and consultation with the employing organization. When a DTI is the sole approach to substance abuse, the employer strongly risks punishing individual workers without helping them obtain treatment. Within a humane and comprehensive approach to employee assistance, a DTI may have a useful place. Conditions under which DTIs could merit the support of social workers are described in the policy statement, followed by procedural criteria.

NASW reaffirms the merit of the comprehensive EAP, preferably as a cooperative labor–management initiative. People who have been identified as abusers of substances should be given access to treatment through an EAP. Providing access to treatment is in accord with the *NASW Code of Ethics* (1993, p. 10), which states that "The social worker should act to ensure that all people have access to the resources, services, and opportunities which they require."

The social worker has a responsibility to advocate for and educate employers on the EAP approach to substance abuse, including advocacy for public information and prevention efforts about the risks of alcohol and drug usage on the job. Social workers should advocate for clients' access to treatment and insurance coverage. Social workers should also work to see that community treatment programs anticipate obstacles to treatment, for example, child care for one of the most untreated groups, women with children. The EAP can link troubled employees with community-based treatment resources. Referrals to the EAP must be confidential. Self-referrals should be encouraged. Sharing information with management must be consistent with federal laws on confidentiality.

Whether or not the employing organization has an EAP, the social worker should be aware of the following potential problems:

Harmful Resistance by Supervisors

Supervisors may sympathize with staff or with management or may be affected by substance abuse themselves. This resistance may compromise the supervisory referral process and procedures.

Negative Perceptions

DTIs are considered punitive in workplaces where companies do not clearly communicate the rationale, procedures, laboratory methods, and consequences of a negative test. EAPs are generally viewed as helpful.

Threat of Lawsuits by Employees

Proceedings based on a range of constitutional and other legal issues are now pending in a number of state and federal courts.

Inaccuracy of Drug Testing

False positives are relatively unheard of when a GCMS (gas chromatography mass spectrophotometry) confirmation test is done by a certified laboratory. The potential of non–substance abusers being stigmatized by the false positive results of tests is low, with the biggest source of error being the human factor, somewhere in the custody chain.

Danger of Tying the Positive Results of Drug Tests to Automatic Dismissal

Policies and practices should link the positive results of tests to assessment and evaluation and referral to company EAPs or to treatment and other resources, when appropriate.

Class, Race, Age, and Gender Bias

Substance abuse is not restricted to any one group of employees, but afflicts people at all levels of the organization. Any DTI should be bias free to preclude resentment, morale problems, and discrimination.

POLICY STATEMENT

General Policy

Because of the potential for abuse by employers, discriminatory behavior, and the risk of unreasonable search, the National Association of Social Workers (NASW) opposes random drug testing of individuals. NASW supports the use of a drug-testing initiative (DTI) as a preventive or deterrent tool with a selected class of employees, under clearly defined circumstances of national security or public safety when actual danger of the loss of life exists.

NASW reaffirms the merit of the comprehensive EAP as the first and basic approach to substance abuse at work sites. When an EAP is available, social workers should make an informed, personal decision to support or not to support a DTI. The possibility of making this decision assumes that all testing procedures can be shown to be fair to employees and that well-argued reasons and precedents establish clear justification for a DTI.

Drug testing of an employee *is warranted* under the following circumstances:

■ when the employee's work performance is suffering, as measured against his or her work history, contractual agreements, or other accepted standards, or

■ when the employee's behavior at the work site has a significant likelihood of physically harming the person or seriously damaging the product of a co-worker, and

■ when there is a reasonable suspicion of substance abuse, when a company's policy and procedures clearly allow for intervention at the work site, and when the consequences have been communicated in writing to employees.

The employer should establish clearly defined policies and procedures with regard to drug testing in the workplace. Whenever possible, referral to an EAP should be made and all employees encouraged to use EAP services before intervention at the work site or a DTI. The termination of employment should be based solely on unsatisfactory job performance or the violation of a company's DTI.

Implementation of a DTI

If a DTI is implemented, NASW recommends the following procedures:

Drug testing of employees. A written policy outlining the employer's drug-testing procedures should be distributed to all employees. It should include all circumstances under which an employee may be required to submit to a drug test, as well as the consequences of a positive test result. When applicable, such a policy should be developed jointly by labor and management.

The employer should use a licensed laboratory exclusively, ensure chain-of-custody safeguards, use split samples, and conduct confirmation testing to limit the possibility of erroneous test reports and human error.

There should be no disciplinary action or procedures for firing initiated against an employee solely on the basis of a positive drug test result. Referral to an EAP should be made. An employer may, however, temporarily suspend an employee when substance abuse poses a threat to public safety or the national security until an employee participates in an EAP. Actual termination of employment should be based solely on unsatisfactory work performance.

Pre-employment drug testing. The employer should inform an applicant in writing of drug-testing policies and procedures and of the consequences of a positive test result before administering the test. The employer should inform the applicant of the results of the test. All reports must remain confidential.

The employer should offer information and referrals for treatment to an applicant who is not hired solely on the basis of a positive drug test result. The applicant should be permitted to reapply without prejudice for the same position at a future date. In addition, an appeal process should be made available to the employee.

In fulfillment of his or her ethical responsibilities, the social worker should advocate these procedures.

A Policy of Education and Awareness

Although the most recent surveys would indicate a significant drop in the non-addictive, casual use of illicit drugs, the number of drug-dependent users continues to increase. Social workers have a responsibility to educate themselves on the broader issues of drug testing, including its impact on civil rights.

The law and the literature in this field are changing rapidly. In an ongoing educational effort, social workers should monitor and publicize research, law, and practice on drug testing issues. When deemed necessary, appropriate political action should be taken to challenge and change the existing laws. Schools of social work and all graduate and undergraduate programs are urged to develop comprehensive curricula on substance abuse that include relevant theory, practice, and policy issues.

Education is a viable way to combat substance abuse. Whether practicing alone, in social ser-vice agencies, or in employing organizations, social workers must educate themselves in the etiology of substance abuse, its course, and its impact on individuals and family systems. However, social workers also have a mandate to educate society at large about the nature of substance abuse, its far-reaching impact, the importance of treatment, and the best ways to link substance abusers with treatment. When treatment facilities are insufficient, social workers have an obligation to advocate vigorously for improved services.

REFERENCE

National Association of Social Workers. (1993). *NASW code of ethics.* Washington, DC: Author.

Policy statement approved by the NASW Delegate Assembly, August 1990. Referred to the 1999 Delegate Assembly, to be combined with the policy on Civil Liberties and Justice. For further information, contact the National Association of Social Workers, 750 First Street, NE, Suite 700, Washington, DC 20002-4241. Telephone: 202-408-8600 or 800-638-8799.

Early Childhood Care and Services

BACKGROUND

The diverse field of early childhood is unified by a common core of knowledge that children from birth through eight years of age require special attention to begin the developmental process in an optimal fashion. The growing awareness of the critical nature of experiences during these years requires the social work profession to be involved in setting policies that ensure that young children and their families are successful and ready to enter the 21st century. The United States remains the only technologically developed nation that lacks a national policy regarding the early childhood years.

During the past 20 years, demographic changes have moved early childhood care and child care to the forefront of the public policy agenda. More women with children below school age are entering the workforce, growing from a third in 1967 to 70 percent in 1993. Second, the divorce rate has grown rapidly, resulting in a growing number of single-parent families. In addition, married couples increasingly need two paychecks to maintain a middle-class standard of living. Consequently, most American children spend some time during their early years in the care of people outside of the family. Many of these children are enrolled in some form of group care, such as public or private day care centers, Head Start, nursery schools, family day care, or before- and after-school child care.

According to the Children's Defense Fund, (1996), many American parents rely on child care providers to care for their children while they work to support their families. In 1991 over 7 million children younger than five years whose mothers were employed were cared for by someone other than a parent while their mothers were working. In 1994, 60 percent of women with children younger than 6¾ years and 76 percent of women with children ages six to 17 were in the labor force. Moreover, a growing percentage of preschool children attend early childhood programs regardless of their mother's employment status. Quality early childhood programs provide important educational and nurturing experiences to young children.

Welfare reform cannot succeed without significant investments in child care assistance. One-quarter of the families on the waiting list for child care turned to Aid to Families with Dependent Children (AFDC) to survive (Children's Defense Fund, 1995). If parents are to increase their participation in education, training, and work activities, there must be an infusion of new child care funds.

ISSUE STATEMENT

The National Association for the Education of Young Children (NAEYC, 1994) has advocated for the need to strengthen child care quality standards. They reported that the public regulation of early childhood programs, when well-designed and effectively administered, can help ensure that early childhood programs will nurture, protect, and educate young children.

The development of knowledgeable and competent professionals to work with young children and their families is a continuous process. The NAEYC *Guidelines for Preparation of Early Childhood Professionals* (1994) recognize that programs must prepare early childhood professionals to establish and maintain positive, collaborative relationships with families and involve families in planning for individual children, including children with disabilities, developmental delays, or special abilities. Professionals who work in early childhood education must understand differences in family structure and social and cultural backgrounds. Families must know that professionals who are concerned about their children and their family are able to communicate effectively with other professionals and with agencies in the larger community to support children's development, learning, and well-being. NAEYC further stated that an interdisciplinary approach must be applied in the area of early childhood. Children with special needs must have access to appropriate therapeutic interventions provided by competent professionals.

Parent involvement and support are a critical component of any good quality early childhood program. By supporting parents in their role as their children's primary educators and main source of emotional, social, and financial support, early childhood programs can simultaneously help children enter school ready to succeed and strengthen and support their families. Parents are the constant in their children's lives. Professionals come and go. Family-centered care is an integral part of any high-quality early childhood and child care program. Numerous programs have begun to emphasize this approach because research on family support programs indicates that they improve social skills and school performance as well as parent–child relationships.

POLICY STATEMENT

It is the policy of NASW that

■ early childhood be recognized as including a broad age range from birth through 8 years (NAEYC, 1994).

■ early childhood programs and services occur in diverse settings: families' homes, public and private schools, family day care homes, and group child care centers. Programs should be designed to include children from various ethnic and socioeconomic backgrounds.

■ comprehensive prevention, intervention, and support services be provided for infants and young children, with and without special needs, and their families.

■ services be integrated and include perinatal services, family support services, health and mental health services, educational services, day care (full- and part-time), respite care, parenting education, and before- and after-school care.

■ effective services be based on a family-centered multidisciplinary approach that includes social workers as members of the team.

■ families, as the constant in their children's lives, should be supported in actively participating in the development and implementation of services and programs affecting their children.

■ social workers support national, state, and local policies that use the principles of child development and early childhood education and meet the physical, social, emotional, and educational needs of young children and their families.

■ social workers support equal access to high-quality, culturally and developmentally appropriate, affordable early childhood services and programs.

■ social workers support the continuing implementation of existing legislation to ensure appropriate early childhood programs and services for all infants and young children, including children with special needs and their families.

■ social workers support programs and services that address factors that place children at risk, including health and nutrition, environmental, psychosocial, economic, ethnic, cultural, and linguistic factors.

■ social workers advocate for high-quality standards with adequate safeguards for very young children and their families in all settings.

■ social workers support efforts to ensure continuity for infants and young children receiving services.

■ social workers advocate for family leave policies that are equitable, affordable, and universal.

■ early childhood programs and services reflect the needs of a variety of family configurations and have as their basis sound principles of child development theory.

■ early childhood services be provided by appropriately trained, qualified, and licensed providers.

■ services for young children be provided in a timely manner so that children are more likely to be healthy, have better developmental outcomes, and experience more secure attachments.

REFERENCES

Children's Defense Fund. (1995). *Welfare reform briefing book*. Washington, DC: Author.

Children's Defense Fund. (1996). *Child care briefing book*. Washington, DC: Author.

National Association for the Education of Young Children. (1994). *Position statement: Guidelines for preparation of early childhood professionals*. Washington, DC: Author.

SUGGESTED READINGS

Adams, G., & Sandfort, J. (1994). *Children's Defense Fund: First steps, promising futures: State prekindergarten initiatives in the early 1990s*. Washington, DC: Children's Defense Fund.

Behrman, R. (Ed.). (1994). *Critical health issues for children and youth: The future of children* (Vol. 4, No. 3). Los Altos, CA: Center for the Future of Children, David and Lucille Packard Foundation.

Bishop, K. K., Woll, J., & Arango, P. (1993). *Family/professional collaboration for children with special health needs and their families*. Burlington: University of Vermont.

Dunst, C. J. (1990). Family support principles: Checklist for program builders and practitioners. *Family systems intervention monograph series*, 2(5). Morganton, NC: Family, Infant and Preschool Program, Western Carolina Center.

Hartman, A., & Laird, J. (1983). *Family-centered social work practice*. New York: Free Press.

Powell, D. (Ed.). (1988). *Parent education as early childhood intervention*. Norwood, NJ: Ablex.

Shelton, T., & Stepanek, J. (1994). *Family centered care for children needing specialized health and developmental care* (3rd ed.). Bethesda, MD: Association for the Care of Children's Health.

Policy statement approved by the NASW Delegate Assembly, August 1996. This policy supersedes the policy statement on Early Childhood Care and Education approved by the Delegate Assembly in 1987. For further information, contact the National Association of Social Workers, 750 First Street, NE, Suite 700, Washington, DC 20002-4241. Telephone: 202-408-8600 or 800-638-8799.

Economic Policy

BACKGROUND

A society's economic institutions and practices influence how well individuals and groups fulfill their needs and achieve optimum development. People's health and well-being reflect how much their intrinsic needs are fulfilled. Consistent frustration of these needs tends to cause physical, emotional, and social problems. To correct these problems at their roots, social and economic policies must be transformed from needs-inhibiting to needs-fulfilling ones.

Economic systems should be evaluated according to their consequences for the fulfillment of people's intrinsic needs rather than judged by the claims, jargon, and slogans of their advocates. Economic systems should be understood as means toward consciously chosen social and financial ends rather than as ends in themselves. Examining the actual output of given economic systems in relation to the fulfillment of human needs helps avoid the fallacy of considering economic growth as a self-evident "good," regardless of the quality and distribution of economic product, its impact on the environment, and the conditions and quality of life of all people in a society. By these standards, the U.S. economy is in deep trouble, because the basic human needs of an ever-increasing number of people are not being met.

ISSUE STATEMENT

NASW historically has promoted public policies on a range of issues related to the economy. However, before 1990 the economy itself had not been the focus of a policy statement. In light of current economic situations, which significantly affect social workers and their clients, NASW has given priority to the relationship between social and economic policy.

Thurow (1985) eloquently argued that if present trends continue, America's standard of living and economic superiority will continue to decrease compared with other world economic powers, and our relative strength will be weaker than it has been at any time since World War II. Average household income and the poverty rate verify that economic recovery is shallow and uneven. In analyzing 1988 economic data, the Center on Budget and Policy Priorities (personal communication, press releases, 1989) found that the income gaps between rich and poor and between the upper class and middle class were wider than they had been at any other time since the end of World War II. Furthermore, the number of poor people in 1992 increased by 1.2 million people to 36.9 million. The 1992 poverty rate of 14.5 percent is the highest poverty rate since the 15.2 percent recorded in 1983, and nearly as high as the 17.3 percent recorded in 1965 (Pear, 1993). It is even more alarming that the poor population has become poorer. Forty-seven percent of all poor children—6.8 million of the 14.6 million poor people under age 18—lived in households where incomes were less than half the official poverty level ($14,335 for a family of four, $11,186 for a family of three) (Pear, 1993).

Compared with wealthy Americans, middle- and low-income groups are experiencing the greatest income difference ever recorded. In 1992, the wealthiest 20 percent of the population had incomes averaging 8.4 times the poverty level, versus six times the poverty level in 1967. The least affluent one-fifth of all families had incomes averaging 91 percent of the poverty level in 1992, down from 97 percent in 1967 (Pear, 1993). The middle- and lowest-income groups—80 percent of the population—received only 32 percent of the total income, the highest and lowest levels, respectively, ever recorded (Center on Budget and Policy Priorities, personal communication, 1989). For the working poor, this decline is largely the result of decreasing wages and a sharp drop in the purchasing power of the minimum wage. From the 1960s through the late 1970s, a minimum-wage income for one worker in a family of four was enough to lift a family above the poverty line. Today's minimum wage, including scheduled increases, would keep the same family of four below the poverty threshold of $14,335.

Many families have adjusted to this situation by having the second parent, usually the mother, work outside the home. The Children's Defense Fund (1989) noted that the vast majority of women work for economic survival. Two out of three women in the labor force are either single, are heads of households, or have husbands who earn less than $20,000 per year.

When they work outside the home, women earn significantly less than do men. The Rand Corporation (Smith & Ward, 1984) optimistically estimated that by the year 2000 women will earn 74 cents for each dollar earned by men. Thus, many two-earner, two-income families still do not make enough to support a middle-class lifestyle. These conditions have an even greater adverse effect on people of color, single parents, female-headed families, elderly people, and other disadvantaged groups.

Rather than ensuring the nation's economic prosperity and families' financial security, today's economy has created financial insecurity and poverty for many people. The marketplace traditionally has been posited as the preferred means for achieving financial self-sufficiency. Those who fail to provide for themselves must seek help through the public or private social welfare systems and pay a big price in social stigma, feelings of failure, and a vastly diminished standard of living.

American society has debated the issue of residual and institutional concepts of social welfare as originally articulated by Wilensky and Lebeaux (1958) in their classic work *Industrial Society and Social Welfare*. According to this formulation, the U.S. social welfare system was designed to come into play only after the natural helping systems of the family, community, and

market economy proved unable to meet individual needs. The changes that have occurred in the family and community are similar in their impact on the capacity of individuals to meet their needs. The economy as it currently is structured makes it impossible to ensure economic and material sufficiency for the total population. Despite the marketplace's proven inability to ensure economic and material sufficiency, in 1988 Congress adopted a welfare "reform" package that narrowly defined reform and success as the movement of recipients from the welfare rolls to the marketplace.

A major expected outcome of most social programs has been to produce self-sufficiency. The more we examine our nation and its social and economic policies, we must ask whether anyone can be totally self-sufficient and free of government subsidies, given our current tax structure. We are all part of an interrelated whole, admittedly or not; what happens to one person affects all of us.

The economic system's inability to meet the needs of individuals and families has created economic uncertainty and insecurity. As Harvey Brenner and others have documented (cited in Bluestone & Harrison, 1982), economic insecurity can be statistically correlated with a number of physical and mental health problems. In addition, as economic conditions worsen, our confidence weakens as well. Society's reluctance to face these problems directly leads us to believe that if the government would loosen its grip on the economy, or if workers would work harder and be better prepared, the economic slowdown would be corrected by presuming the entrepreneurial spirit of "rugged individualist" capitalism would rescue us.

The assumption was that letting the rich get richer at the expense of the middle class and the poor would, as it had before, revitalize our economy. Furthermore, we have relied too much on massive military defense expenditures, financed by huge cuts in social and domestic spending, along with previously unheard of federal borrowing and increasing deficits. The decade of the 1980s was a time of massive national denial of reality and introduced an economic policy that continues to be disastrous to society's well-being.

National economic policy has virtually ignored social needs. The social well-being of all members of our society must be affirmed as the unaltered basis of our national social and economic policies.

POLICY STATEMENT

NASW believes that the pursuit of profit can not be the only motivator within the U.S. economy. To further this belief, NASW must actively work with other like-minded groups—economists and politicians, labor unions, the larger service community, and allied think tanks—to design, advocate, implement, and evaluate policies and programs that deal with our economic troubles and that promote social and financial well-being of individuals and families.

Recognizing that we are all interdependent, NASW has identified the following principles and policies to provide an essential framework for understanding the relationship between the social and economic needs of our world, nation, communities, and workplaces.

Global Issues

■ To strengthen the United States within the global economy, the nation must expand efforts at international economic cooperation and develop a comprehensive international industrial policy.

■ Private profit must be reexamined as the sole criterion for motivating economic activity. The U.S. government must ensure that basic necessities are available to all people at a level that promotes human dignity, whether or not the production and distribution of those necessities are profitable.

■ To compete in the world economy, the U.S. government, in cooperation with state and local governments, must form a partnership with the private sector to ensure a well-trained labor force. A highly educated society requires a vastly improved educational and training system. Education and training must become a life-long enterprise.

■ Some people in the United States believe that the distribution of income and wealth is more equal than it really is, and that those with the lowest income levels are responsible for their

unequal status. We must continue to educate the public about the unequal and irrational distribution of income and wealth, with particular attention to its effects on communities and people of color. NASW supports efforts to help the public understand that it is in everyone's interest to reduce the inequalities, because there are few, if any, examples of democratic societies that have survived in the face of extreme disparities in income and wealth (Thurow, 1985).

■ To compete in a global economy, we must support economic policies that affirm spending on social services as an essential part of creating a strong nation. Social services spending generates significant economic productivity.

■ Open and free trade with other countries must be conducted on a level playing field that does not lead to exploitation of U.S. workers or those of our trading partners.

National Issues

■ A thoughtfully designed government and private sector strategy is needed to foster research, promote the greater availability of capital, and coordinate the movement of resources to areas of the economy that are in the greatest need.

■ Unique forms of state-sponsored public-private cooperation that exist in various sectors of the economy must be adapted for areas such as the public financing of low- and moderate-priced housing and environmental protection and restoration efforts.

■ As much as possible, social and economic choices can and must be made to avoid recession and inflation and to mitigate their impact.

■ Federal minimum-wage legislation should ensure that the minimum wage enables families to live above the poverty line. The minimum wage must be indexed to increases in the cost of living.

■ The formula for calculating the unemployment rate must be revised to provide an accurate picture of the number of people who have lost their jobs, who are seeking employment for the first time, or who have given up on finding a job. In addition, those who are temporarily or partially employed should be represented in this figure. (For further discussion see "Full and Equitable Employment" in *Social Work Speaks*.)

■ The importance of work cannot be overlooked as a means of providing financial support to individuals and families as well as meeting other needs. Especially during times of depressed economies, people need alternatives when being laid off, displaced, or otherwise detached from the workplace. In addition, people who lack the resources to work or to provide for themselves should be able to count on a guaranteed annual income, including long-term support if needed, that provides for their basic needs and some form of medical coverage. Implementing programs that remove the stigma of welfare restores dignity to many people who, through no fault of their own, find themselves depending on the government for support.

■ The United States must institute a more comprehensive, progressive, fair, and equitable tax system that reflects a combination of personal income and loophole-free corporate and inheritance taxes as well as user taxes and fees. Comprehensive tax reform is needed to ensure adequate financing that does not require the government to borrow to pay for the policies previously listed. Tax reform should establish a tax-exempt basic income corresponding to the actual cost of living; income beyond this level, regardless of its source, would be subject to progressive taxation.

■ Opportunities for higher education should be made in the form of increases in financial assistance to those individuals most in need.

■ Special initiatives must be undertaken to ensure full economic participation for traditionally disadvantaged groups, especially targets of racism, sexism, homophobia, ageism, and classism and those who are discriminated against because they are physically challenged.

■ Federally legislated guarantees of employment are needed that are suited to individual capacities and compensated at wage levels that provide a decent standard of living. Full employment can be achieved by adjusting the legal length of the workday or workweek to the number of positions in the economy or to the number of individuals who require work. Another

approach includes publicly sponsored projects designed to meet community and human needs often overlooked by private enterprise, for example, housing, highways and bridges, hospitals, schools, and parks.

■ A national, federally financed, comprehensive system of preventive, rehabilitative, and curative health care must be adopted as a component to ensure a strong economy.

■ Federally financed construction and maintenance of housing stock, infrastructure, and public transportation within and between cities and towns are required as a component to ensure a strong economy.

Community Issues

■ Community redevelopment must be a major component of economic reform to provide opportunities for employment, training, and investment. Community residents must be involved in planning and implementing community revitalization efforts.

■ Workers and communities must be protected from the impact of corporate downsizing, plant closures, the conversion of full-time employees to part-time status, and the excessive use of overtime through tougher legislation. These measures must be carefully regulated and accompanied by early and adequate notice. Compensation and benefits for displaced workers should be in proportion to the monetary advantage of the closures or downsizing.

Workplace Issues

■ The wage gaps between workers, managers, and owners must be reduced. An effective way to ensure regular and adequate salary increases for workers would be to make managers' wages proportional to workers' wages.

■ Federal and state laws must ensure wage equity. Wage discrimination must be illegal, and work of comparable value must be equitably remunerated.

■ In addition to adequate wages, workers should be able to rely on their employers to provide comprehensive and family-friendly benefits to cover job loss, child care, and parental leave. Employers also should provide training and retraining and programs to combat discrimination and promote affirmative action for all targets of oppression.

■ The care of children and elderly or of disabled relatives in the home must be redefined legally as socially necessary work. In addition, the federal government should sponsor a system of high-quality public child care.

Implicit in this economic policy agenda is an unequivocal rejection of the notion that the people of the United States cannot afford economic reform. Contrary to common assumptions these ideas are economically possible— albeit sometimes politically unpopular. They are likely to revitalize economic activity and human resources and to enrich the quality of life and human relations. They involve the full use and development of available productive and creative human capacities and they also imply the equitable redistribution of available resources and wealth.

Implementing the proposed policies would make possible further stages of social and economic development that were unrealized during the 1980s. Full employment and the elimination of poverty would reduce the dynamics of individual and intergroup competition and would thus reduce economic sources of discrimination by race, gender, age, and other factors.

Because of our professional exposure to the daily, intimate, and devastating effects of poverty on people's lives, social workers must supply the qualitative data needed to guide social activism and economic reform. Social workers must tell the stories of people affected by unjust economic policies. Social workers hear and see the drama of private terror and the depletion of families by domestic violence, chemical dependence, insufficient education, and hopelessness—the direct results of poverty. Therefore, social workers must be strong advocates for needed economic changes.

REFERENCES

Bluestone, B., & Harrison, B. (1982). *The deindustrialization of America*. New York: Basic Books.

Children's Defense Fund. (1989). *A vision for America's future*. Washington, DC: Author.

Pear, R. (1993, October 5). Poverty in U.S. grew faster than population last year. *New York Times*, p. A5.

Smith, J., & Ward, M. (1984). *Women's wages and work in the twentieth century* (Report No. R-3119). Santa Monica, CA: Rand Corporation.

Thurow, L. C. (1985). *The zero-sum solution*. New York: Simon & Schuster.

Wilensky, H., & Lebeaux, C. (1958). *Industrial society and social welfare*. New York: Russell Sage Foundation.

Policy statement approved by the NASW Delegate Assembly, August 1993. This policy statement supersedes the policy statement on Economic Policy approved by the Delegate Assembly, 1990. For further information, contact the National Association of Social Workers, 750 First Street, NE, Suite 700, Washington, DC 20002-4241. Telephone: 202-408-8600 or 800-638-8799.

Education of Children and Youths

BACKGROUND

Need for Change

Schools must be responsive to the changing needs of students regardless of economic, racial, cultural, and ethnic background. The judicial system has created the groundwork for changes in the interpretation of state and federal legislation on education, particularly in affirming the rights of students with disabilities. All branches of government must remain committed to fostering educational change to meet the ongoing needs of the people.

Students with Disabilities

The passage of the Education for All Handicapped Children Act of 1975 (P.L. 94-142) brought a major shift in responsibility for educating people with disabilities. This landmark legislation mandated a public education for every child, including children with disabilities. Subsequent reenactments of this legislation have expanded coverage to children from three to five years, encouraged programs for children from birth to three years, and included additional specific disabling conditions for coverage.

This legislation resulted initially in the segregation of children with disabilities from the regular education classrooms for some or all of the school day for specialized instruction and therapy. Currently, a new movement, originally called the Regular Education Initiative (McDonald, 1996) and currently known as "inclusion," is reversing this trend. Schools are now being encouraged to deliver services in the regular classroom with classmates not identified as special education students. Nevertheless, students who are able also now benefit from personalized instruction in small groups or with specialized coinstructors assigned to the regular classroom to support other students' specialized learning needs (McDonald, 1996). Accommodation of students with severe disabilities in pull-out programs should continue to be available when the individualized educational plan identifies the need.

Funding

Since 1980 many of the most important categorical programs for school aid have been combined in block grants and cut significantly across the board at the federal level. State and local governments have been interested in holding taxes down. The result has been a scramble for the remaining money, which has pitted various educational constituencies against each other. This trend is accompanied by a steady decline in the percentage of the total budget of a school district being supported by state-administered funds. Many states are either voluntarily or through court mandates switching the funding of public education in their states to an income tax revenue base instead of the currently more popular property tax base. The property tax funding source is inherently unequal, which is the usual basis for court rulings requiring the change.

Relationship of Federal Government to Education

The problems confronting the public school system require the federal government to recognize and exercise its leadership role in public school education. Despite rhetoric about "full-service goals," the dollar gap between legislated authorization and actual appropriations remains enormous. As a result, educators are directed to initiate new programs with insufficient local funds. Further, because of the lack of broad policy development and planning, what happens in one part of the total system often is unconnected with what happens in other parts. In consideration of "related services," such as social work, psychology, nursing and other specialized credentialed personnel (for example, in behavior disorders, communication delays or disorders, learning disabilities, mental retardation, and other more specialized categories in the severe and profound range of disability), proposals continue to recommend the use of "mixed category" classrooms called for by the inclusion movement. Even more seriously, some proposals want to dismantle the Department of Education.

High-Risk Students

There is an urgent need to better identify and provide services to vulnerable student groups, such as children with disabilities, poor rural youths, children of migrant laborers, other economically disadvantaged children, children of color, pregnant adolescents, children of adolescent single parents, gifted children, new immigrants, abused and neglected children, truant children, drug-dependent children, latchkey children, and children who move frequently. For example, children who have limited English skills have a four times greater chance of graduating from high school if they participate in bilingual programs, yet these programs are threatened constantly with cutbacks (Committee on Education and Labor, 1986). Many of the reforms of the 1960s, such as the War on Poverty's attempts to raise family incomes and to provide school breakfasts and health programs, were based on the recognition that students who are hungry, sick, or worried about their families cannot achieve as well in school as students who are free of these cares. These reforms are continuously threatened by budget cuts. There is currently a movement to develop a full-ranging curriculum focused on children's health and mental issues to be offered from kindergarten through high school, but such a curriculum is hollow without the provision of concrete services, such as school breakfast and lunch programs and counseling for anxiety-producing problems in students' lives.

Safe, Positive, and Secure Schools

Potential dropouts and push-outs represent a high-risk group in the educational system. In too many cases, discipline involves suspensions or expulsions that deny access to school for students who most need positive school experiences, placing them in nonsupervised atmospheres. These students have already shown that their ability to maintain self-control and anticipate consequences is limited. Consequently, the risk of negative behaviors such as crime and misuse of alcohol and other drugs increases. Further, students of color experience a disproportionately high incidence of suspensions and expulsions. Alternatives to out-of-school suspension are being actively investigated and implemented in many districts, and the results of these experiences need to be documented and evaluated (Gay, 1989).

Many states continue to use corporal punishment as a primary disciplinary measure, even though research and experience prove it to be counterproductive and harmful in the long term (Strauss, 1991). As many studies have shown, positive expectations of success have a positive effect on how well students do. Students can be provided with a safe, positive, and secure school climate by valuing all students for the positive contributions they make, whether disabled or not; promoting the cultural sensitivity and competence of faculty and staff; ensuring a nonsexist educational climate; establishing rational and humane disciplinary policies and alternatives to suspension and expulsion; and eliminating corporal punishment, intimidation, and scapegoating from public school education.

Alternative Education

Millions of youths are underserved or not served at all by the educational system. It is estimated that 30 percent of children who start first grade do not finish high school. Of those who complete 12th grade, many do not have the requisite skills and behaviors to enter the labor market successfully. Many become marginal participants in society and heavy users of health, welfare, rehabilitation, and penal resources (Children's Defense Fund, 1990; Hare & Sullivan, 1996). Any program of reform in public education must include alternative routes to becoming educated and finding successful roles as adults. However, these alternatives must be provided not to isolate undesirable students from the mainstream, but rather to enable them to find sufficient support to meet their unique behavioral and situational needs.

Relationship of School to Home and Community

Parents and school personnel often have mistaken perceptions of each other because of problems negotiating the bureaucratic maze and because of feelings of blame and antagonism regarding students' problems. Effective communication among school, home, and community is vital to reach the goals set for each student. Coordination of services is critical to the efficient and effective use of resources and the attainment of goals. Making school buildings available for use as community centers and early childhood education sites is key to building schools' relationships with home and community. Providing services to parents after school and at night gives the school a position in the community as a provider of services and not just a caretaker and educator of students.

Need for Comprehensive Sex Education

Although more young people are sexually active at an earlier age than in the past, in general they lack adequate knowledge and motivation to protect themselves from the hazards of premature sexuality, including pregnancy and disease. Sexually active adolescents and preadolescents who are experimenting with drugs are particularly vulnerable. Too few school districts are providing any sex education.

In 1986 Surgeon General C. Everett Koop called for AIDS education to be included in sex education curricula beginning in elementary schools (Koop, 1986). At the time, NASW commended Koop for this brave stand on the urgent need for AIDS education. The need still exists. Public schools have been loath to comply with Koop's

call because of public dissent. A few exceptions have led the way, but much still must be done to support young people in dealing with their emerging sexuality knowledgeably and maturely. Otherwise, AIDS will be a continuing legacy.

Social Workers in Public Schools

School social workers are one of the few resources in schools for addressing personal and social problems that inhibit students' ability to learn. School social workers constitute a stable and growing force within the field of education. Approximately 9,300 school social workers serve students in 37 education jurisdictions across the country (Torres, 1996). But the distribution of social workers is uneven and inequitable; school social workers tend to be clustered in greater proportions in industrial states and in school districts with greater resources. The skills and competencies of school social workers enable schools to carry out their primary functions of educating all pupils more effectively. The following are the primary skills of school social workers:

■ assessing and intervening in the social and emotional needs of students in relation to learning

■ understanding, evaluating, and improving the total environment of pupils and thus contributing to a positive school climate

■ strengthening the connections with home, school, and community by identifying and linking these components to create the best learning environment for the student and to personalize and make education relevant to all constituents of a pluralistic society

■ building mutual communication and support among all participants in the school system, including parents, students, staff, and the community

■ developing preventive and remedial intervention programs for systemic problems

■ providing meaningful and relevant consultation and in-service programs to teachers and school administrators concerning student needs and counterproductive school policies

■ providing group and individual counseling for students and, when necessary, for the family

■ ensuring that students with disabilities receive appropriate educational services

■ providing training and support for conflict resolution programs and other student support programs, such as drug use prevention, sex education, alternative suspension programs, and parent education programs.

ISSUE STATEMENT

The education of our nation's children will continue to be a top priority of NASW. NASW has been very active in advancing legislation to promote the role of school social workers, and several NASW publications have highlighted the role of school social workers in education. Additionally, in 1995 NASW established the first specialty practice section for school social work.

Public education is a primary institution that shares with the family responsibility for raising and training children and youths. Furthermore, public education is a vital socializing force that, with the family, promotes the total development of the child—intellectually, socially, and physically. To nurture the full potential of children and youths, our nation's public schools are an excellent forum to ensure equal opportunity; ensure excellence; provide a physically and emotionally sound environment; promote transitional steps to the areas of work, community living, and civic responsibility; accomplish the early identification of disadvantaged students, students with disabilities, and students at risk of truancy, failure, and early withdrawal from school; develop and provide appropriate educational programs for students with disabilities; and provide factual information about human sexuality and sexually transmitted diseases within the context of a comprehensive health and family life education course.

POLICY STATEMENT

Components of Education

Education is a continuing maturational process that promotes the intellectual, physical, and social development of students in their environments. It is the position of NASW that the educational system has a responsibility to provide all students with free, appropriate, quality education and to help students cope effectively with their education so that they attain full vocational and career skills and concomitant behaviors conducive to success and lifelong learning; increased self-awareness and self-actualization; empathy for others; understanding and acceptance of differences in race, culture, ethnicity, and sexual orientation; understanding of the personal realities of individuals with disabilities and how to help them to participate more fully in normal daily activities; and an awareness that health-compromising behaviors, particularly sexual, substance abuse, and violent behaviors, can have lifelong and life-threatening consequences.

NASW emphasizes the following educational components:

1. *Pupil Services Teams.* The policy of NASW is that the model of collaboration used by multidisciplinary teams, including pupil services personnel, teachers, administrators, and families, in the identification and evaluation of students for special services is optimal for the delivery of services to all students. The school social worker provides expertise in coordinating home, school, and community resources to enhance learning objectives, in assessing students' adaptive behaviors, and in describing cultural history. The multidisciplinary team can also implement intervention and prevention strategies for at-risk students prior to a special education referral as a result of the diagnostic assessment team process.

2. *Least-Restrictive Environment.* Every student has the right to a free, appropriate public education in the least restrictive environment. NASW supports the least-restrictive environment concept as it is determined individually for each student. The school social worker on the multidisciplinary team plays a key role in determining the least-restrictive setting for each student and in assisting both parents and students in being involved in the decision-making process. Although at all times NASW supports the regular education environment as the first placement consideration, NASW strongly supports placement for students in the setting that best meets the student's needs, with the appropriate continuum of services, staffing, and assistive devices, and re-placement in a more restrictive setting if so determined by student need.

3. *Family, School, and Community Linkages.* Strengthening the relationship among the family, school, and community is a fundamental principle of any educational policy. NASW encourages linking the school to community resources as sound public policy and encourages further policy development focused on bringing schools, families, and communities together for mutual support and problem solving as well as for cultural and celebratory events. School–community centers, which facilitate the participation of families and the wider community in school activities, allow opportunities for community-based social workers to collaborate with school social workers in working with teachers and families.

4. *Early Childhood Education.* It is the policy of NASW that early childhood education should continue to be expanded and made available to all children through federal and state support (Bishop, 1996; see NASW policy statement on Early Childhood Care and Services in this volume). Significant research supports the position that early intervention for children with disabilities of all types benefits their later ability to succeed educationally. In addition, such programs promote total learning for all children through their emphasis on early stimulation of children within the home, recognition and use of parenting skills, provisions for adequate nutrition and medical care, and the introduction of important social skills needed for later school success.

5. *Career and Vocational Education.* NASW affirms that the primary function of education is to prepare students for life tasks, specifically the world of work. Preparation should include instilling the attitudes and behaviors that will ensure successful entry into the labor market. American children must be prepared to compete in a global society that offers opportunities for all nations to share the resources of the world. It is the policy of NASW that transitional experiences and entry structures should be available throughout the educational ladder. To accomplish this, schools, postsecondary educational institutions, communities, and businesses should continue to form articulation and linkages that will provide opportunities into the labor market. Career and vocational programs should have the same economic and academic investment from school facilities and administrations as do college prepara-

tory programs (see NASW policy statement on School Dropout Prevention in this volume).

6. *Comprehensive Health and Mental Health Education.* It is the policy of NASW that educating students about their health and physical needs and about optimal health practices, including sexual conduct and AIDS education, is a necessary and appropriate function of public schools. Such programs should be developed by multidisciplinary teams that include, but are not restricted to, social workers, health care providers, educators, and parents. The programs developed by these teams should begin in early childhood programs or kindergarten and should continue throughout students' formal public education. Such programs should provide information that will enable students to make responsible choices about their bodies and emotions.

To make responsible choices, students need access to basic facts about human physiology and psychology, including information on reproduction, family planning, pregnancy prevention, responsible parenting, AIDS and venereal diseases, substance abuse, healthy eating, exercise, and general lifestyle decisions. A comprehensive life education program should involve parents and should promote open communication among parents, students, and schools. With increasing attention to children suffering physical and sexual abuse, it is imperative that students learn how to defend themselves against violence and abuse. Social work services must be made available for the education and counseling of affected students. Prevention programs that build self-esteem, teach conflict mediation skills, and help students develop protective behaviors to guard against victimization should be provided in schools.

7. *Nonsexist and Integrated Education.* The right to equal educational opportunity requires a nonsegregated, nonsexist environment and a curriculum that reflects a pluralistic society. Further, NASW views the optimal goal of integration as a requisite for a positive, pluralistic educational experience. Integration should provide for and facilitate interaction among students and faculty of diverse racial, cultural, and ethnic backgrounds. An integrated environment will promote understanding, knowledge, and acceptance of racial, cultural, and ethnic differences. Bilingual education programs will promote greater understand-

ing of the educational process to those experiencing language and cultural barriers.

8. *Discipline.* It is the policy of NASW that disciplinary policies in schools, including detention, suspension, and expulsion policies, must reflect the desire to shape students' behavior toward productive participation in schools and society. Many such policies are clearly punitive in intent and thus do not reflect the school's concern for retaining and successfully graduating students involved in their disciplinary system. The focus of school discipline should be on helping students accept responsibility for their own behavior, rather than punishment, through a shared problem-solving process with parents and guardians. NASW subscribes to the following recommendations as policy initiatives related to disciplinary actions:

■ Students should be guaranteed due process procedures in serious disciplinary actions.

■ Social workers should be used as advocates in promoting the best interests of the students and schools.

■ Alternative education programs should be developed based on students' unique educational needs.

■ The use of corporal punishment in schools should be abolished in the remaining states that still approve such practices, and social work services should be made available to train teachers to teach children conflict resolution techniques, including improved interpersonal communication skills.

9. *Full Funding for Education.* All legally mandated educational programs must be funded at a level that will ensure effective implementation. Such programs include P. L. 94-142 and its future reauthorizations; P. L. 99-457 (Education of the Handicapped Act Amendments of 1986), including Part H; P. L. 101-476 (Individuals with Disabilities Education Act); the Rehabilitation Act of 1973, especially section 504; the Americans with Disabilities Act of 1991; and Title IV, VI, and VII of the Civil Rights Act. Programs must not be weakened because of politically shortsighted initiatives or economic recession by changing or eliminating key rules and regulations. Rights of students and families should not be eliminated or reduced to foster a more controlling and in some cases oppressive environment. Mandating educational programs without allocating the full cost of implementing such programs is not good public policy.

10. *Evaluation and Research.* Evaluation of school social work services is critical in documenting effectiveness. Federal, state, and local education agencies as well as school social workers should conduct research related to the effectiveness of social work services in the schools. Research that examines both the short-term and long-term effectiveness of innovative prevention programs must be supported.

11. *Role of School Social Workers.* NASW encourages legislation and funding at the federal and state levels to substantially increase the number of social workers available in schools to serve both students with identified disabilities and students in the general school population. Because of the inequitable distribution of social workers both nationally and within individual states, NASW recommends that pupil services teams in every state include school social workers on the elementary and secondary levels who graduated from a Council on Social Work Education-accredited program. Further, school social workers are qualified to implement interagency agreements between school districts and human services agencies, both public and private, to promote collaboration in the provision of services to all pupils. Human services agencies include protective services, juvenile courts, mental health facilities, family services agencies, and rehabilitative resources. School social workers are the professionals who help ensure that students have access to necessary components of education. These components enable students to acquire the academic skills and the ability to function in and contribute to a multicultural society.

REFERENCES

Americans with Disabilities Act, P.L. 101-336, 104 Stat. 327 (1990).

Bishop, K. (1996). Part H of the Individuals with Disabilities Education Act: Analysis and implications for social workers. In R. Constable, J. Flynn, & S. McDonald (Eds.), *School social work: Practice and research perspectives.*

(3rd ed., pp. 116–131). Chicago: Lyceum Press.

Children's Defense Fund. (1990). *Children, 1990: A report card, briefing book and action primer*. Washington, DC: Author.

Civil Rights Act of 1957, P. L. 86-387, Title IV, Sec. 401, 73 Stat. 724.

Civil Rights Act of 1964, P. L. 88-352, 78 Stat. 241.

Committee on Education and Labor, House of Representatives. (1986). *The report on bilingual education of the 99th Congress, 2d session*. Washington, DC: U.S. Government Printing Office.

Education for All Handicapped Children Act of 1975, P. L. 94-142, 89 Stat. 773.

Education of the Handicapped Act Amendments of 1986, P. L. 99-457, 100 Stat. 1145.

Gay, G. (1989). Ethnic minorities and educational equality. In J. A. Banks & C. A. Banks (Eds.), *Multicultural education: Issues and perspectives*. Boston: Allyn & Bacon.

Hare, I., & Sullivan, K. (1996). The economic, political and social world of school social work. In R. Constable, J. Flynn, & S. McDonald (Eds.), *School social work: Practice and research perspectives* (3rd ed., pp. 66–84). Chicago: Lyceum Press.

Individuals with Disabilities Education Act, P. L. 101-476, 104 Stat. 1142 (1990).

Koop, C. E. (1986). *The Surgeon General's report on acquired immune deficiency syndrome*. Washington, DC: U.S. Government Printing Office.

McDonald, S. (1996). The trend toward inclusion. In R. Constable, J. Flynn, & S. McDonald (Eds.), *School social work: Practice and research perspectives* (3rd ed., pp. 147–155). Chicago: Lyceum Press.

Rehabilitation Act of 1973, P. L. 93-112, 87 Stat. 355.

Strauss, M. A. (1991). *Beating the devil out of them*. New York: Lexington Books.

Torres, S., Jr. (1996). The status of school social workers in America. *Social Work in Education, 18*, 8–18.

Policy statement approved by the NASW Delegate Assembly, August 1996. This policy supersedes the policy statement on Preschool, Elementary, and Secondary Education, approved by the Delegate Assembly in 1987. The original policy statement was approved by the NASW national Board of Directors in June 1985 following recommendations by the Delegate Assembly in 1984. For further information, contact the National Association of Social Workers, 750 First Street, NE, Suite 700, Washington, DC 20002-4241. Telephone: 202-408-8600 or 800-638-8799.

Electoral Politics

BACKGROUND

In every society the political system is the determining vehicle for expressing human values and for the provision of resources, and social workers are experts in the areas of human needs and human services delivery. Since the early part of the 20th century, social workers have lobbied the legislative and executive branches of government, advancing policy recommendations and offering information. The social work profession was active in the administration of the New Deal and later in the Great Society. Unfortunately, the Hatch Political Activity Act, passed in 1939, became until recently both a real and perceived barrier, causing some public sector social workers to abandon their political activity. Whenever the participation of social workers is diminished or absent in the political arena, the quality of public policy deteriorates.

Social work practitioners have always participated vigorously in electoral politics. The social work profession grew out of the political action of its founders, from Jane Addams and Jeannette Rankin in the early 1900s to Harry Hopkins, Frances Perkins, and Molly Dewson in the New Deal era to Ron Dellums, Barbara Mikulski, Ed Towns, and Maryann Mahaffey now, and social workers have held prominent political offices (NASW, 1995). In recent decades social workers have moved toward greater participation in political activity (Weismiller & Rome, 1995).

Two recent studies fortify the perception that social workers are active in campaigns and elections and vote at much higher rates than the general public. The first study, conducted in 1984, replicated a 1968 survey designed to access the level of activism by social workers (Reeser & Epstein, 1990). Among measures of electoral participation, the 1984 study found increases in specific behaviors such as giving money to campaigns, volunteering for candidates, and encouraging political activity among clients. Reeser and Epstein's historical comparison of social workers' political behavior suggested fundamental increases in the profession's political activism profile.

The second study looked at social workers' electoral participation in the 1988 presidential campaign (Sherradan & Parker, 1991). More than 92 percent of the 222 social workers who responded reported voting in that election, a turnout rate 1.62 times that of the general public. In the same study, social workers reported making campaign contributions, going to meetings and rallies, and working for candidates or political parties at a rate twice that of the general public. The authors concluded that these high participation levels provide a foundation from which the profession can exert increased political influence.

NASW has promoted the broad concept of political action in various ways throughout its 40-year history. Political activity is approved in the *NASW Code of Ethics* (NASW, 1996), and successive Delegate Assemblies have encouraged social worker involvement. On the practice level, valuable program initiatives have included the following activities:

■ operating federal and state political action committees

■ organizing national, regional, and chapter training programs

■ providing a checkoff system on annual membership renewal forms to enhance voluntary candidate contributions

■ mobilizing association support for political candidates who will advance NASW's professional and program agenda

- encouraging social workers to seek public office

- promoting voter registration.

Through its support of practitioners who have spent decades securing legal and commercial recognition of the profession through licensing and vendorship campaigns, NASW has steadily built elements of political action into its program. However, social work practitioners and educators have been more equivocal in their approach to electoral politics (Salcido & Seck, 1992; Weismiller & Dempsey, 1993). The ambivalence of educators is reflected in social work education programs with a dearth of either electoral political field placements or specific curriculum material about campaigns, elections, political parties, or other important electoral institutions and processes (Wolk, Weismiller, Dempsey, & Pray, 1994). The intent of this policy is to initiate a synthesis that fills the present lack of policy.

Electoral Political Institutions and Processes

Electoral politics are the formal and informal systems by which citizens and groups in a democracy contest for the power to run government (Plano & Greenberg, 1989). Primary electoral political institutions include political parties, interest groups and coalitions, candidate campaign organizations, political action committees (PACs), the campaign industry (businesses that provide management, polling, fundraising, and communication services to candidates), and the media. Electoral political processes encompass candidate nominations, party conventions, primaries, caucuses, campaigns, elections (primary, general, and special), voter registration, voting (including absentee and special voting programs), ballot measures, and transitions.

Some aspects of electoral politics that require special attention by NASW are political parties, PACs, transitions, and political education. Participation in these processes amplifies the political influence of a group. *Political parties* are voluntary groups of voters with some shared ideology who organize to try to win elections, control government, and influence public policy. Political party activity increases organizational

electoral power. A person who holds firmly to a party or its cause is a *partisan*, hence the term "partisan politics." Partisan politics are about working with or within major political parties to achieve desired public policy goals. Whatever partisan choices an individual or organization makes, it is still possible and often necessary to have civil and constructive relationships with political partisans of other parties.

Confusion often occurs about the terms "bipartisan" and "nonpartisan." *Bipartisan* means relating to or involving members of two parties such as, for example, when Republicans and Democrats present a united front in the face of a serious foreign threat to the country. *Nonpartisan* usually refers to elections in which candidates have no party designations and political parties are prohibited from entering candidates.

Federal election law refers to a corporate political committee as a separate, segregated fund (SSF), although it is more commonly called a PAC. As the name implies, money contributed to an SSF is held in a separate bank account from the general corporate treasury. These accounts hold money voluntarily contributed by association members that can legally be used for candidate contributions (Plano & Greenberg, 1989). NASW maintains such an account, called the Political Action for Candidate Election (PACE), in accordance with the federal election law. Authority to make decisions about candidate endorsements and disbursements from the PACE fund has been delegated by the NASW board of directors to the PACE board of trustees.

Transition refers to the time between election to an office and the assumption of the office. Successful candidates use transition time to prepare to hold office. This presents an opportunity for organizations and campaign activists to shape the development of a new administration.

Political education is how an organization develops a sense of the framework in which its political activity takes place. It involves making members more aware of specific policy issues, candidates, parties, and electoral processes and how these relate to the economic, political, and social situations in local, state, and national elections (Kahn, 1991). Political education also includes helping members develop an understanding of the relationship between politics and economics that they can explain easily to others.

In asking rhetorically, "What makes politics so important?" Jesse Jackson answered: "The political order is the distribution system for the economic order. Politics determines who gets what, when, where, and how" (National Rainbow Coalition, 1994, p. 1).

NASW Involvement in Electoral Politics

Current tax and campaign election laws permit corporations such as NASW to use their dues-generated funds to support all electoral activity of their members except for direct contributions to candidates. Although these laws make much activity legally permissible, the availability of funds limits what is organizationally feasible. NASW has numerous demands on its resources and must balance many needs in its program planning and budgeting process.

National Level

Elections provide a vehicle for accomplishing diverse association agendas. NASW has focused on electing progressive candidates to public offices for three decades. Since 1984 NASW and PACE have made it a priority to support the candidacies of women and people of color seeking election to federal offices. The composition of Congress shows some increased diversity, and social workers can be proud of the role NASW has played in that change.

Elections can also be used to gain power for the profession. The 1993 Delegate Assembly made support of social worker candidates for public offices a priority. Between 1991 and 1995 the association published three editions of the directory *Social Workers Serving in Elective Offices* (NASW, 1995). Each edition showed a marked increase in the number of social workers holding public offices at all levels.

State Level

NASW electoral activity in states originated primarily from chapter legislative initiatives on professional issues such as licensing and vendorship. Acquiring the means to support or oppose legislators spurred the creation of chapter PACs. Once they were in the electoral arena,

the value of trying to influence the outcome of statewide office races, particularly the governor's office, quickly became apparent. Ballot measures are also a growing electoral tool that chapters are learning to use.

Only recently has NASW paid more attention to state ballot measures. These measures include the *initiative*, a mechanism by which citizens can propose legislation or constitutional amendments; the *referendum*, a mechanism by which voters can veto a bill passed by their legislature; and the *recall*, a procedure enabling voters to remove an elected official from office before his or her term has expired (Plano & Greenberg, 1989). Ballot measures are another way to exercise electoral power at the state level.

Recent election cycles have seen important referenda on abortion in Maryland (in 1992) and on public school financing in Michigan (in 1994). Initiatives on welfare reform in California, anti–gay and lesbian proposals in Oregon and Colorado, and tax limitations in Washington State occurred in 1992. In the 1994 election cycle, several states authorized anti–gay and lesbian proposals, and California presented restrictive immigration legislation, an initiative on a single-payer health care system, and a recall vote on a state senator who supported gun control restrictions (Priest, 1994). Ballot measures present major threats and opportunities in the electoral arena (Pear, 1994).

Issues Raised by Electoral Political Participation

Candidate Endorsements. A candidate endorsement is a public statement of support and commitment to provide resources and mobilize members to promote, work, and vote for the candidate. NASW has authorized PACE to make such endorsements on behalf of the association. Endorsement decisions are based on established process and criteria (NASW, 1994a).

Candidate Contributions: Through PACE, NASW provides financial support to endorsed candidates. Current federal law and most state laws require that money given to candidates by corporations such as NASW come only from monies voluntarily contributed by members and disbursed by PACs. NASW may also make other campaign support available to candidates such as recruiting volunteers; mailing information to members; publicizing a candidate's record on policy issues; and using an endorsement by NASW, photo opportunities, letters of support, and assistance with position papers and issue development.

Fairness. The social work professional value of fairness requires that the association maintain procedures for candidate endorsements that are open and fair. To maintain credibility with candidates and its own members, NASW and PACE follow a clearly defined endorsement process with criteria that are applied fairly to all candidates who wish to go through the process.

NASW can promote inclusion of members in its political activities by respecting the diversity of political positions they hold. PACE is committed to endorsing political candidates only on the basis of their support for NASW policy positions, not on the basis of political party affiliation. It is PACE's responsibility during its endorsement deliberations to give fair consideration to all candidates (Kendall, 1994).

Communication with Power versus Exercise of Power. Having readily available communication with a public official is often confused with having power to influence that official. Having readily available communication with a decision maker is not a synonym for power. Social workers frequently view a friendly political relationship as a successful relationship, whether or not it advances the agenda of the profession or of that professional. The goal of NASW is to build political relationships with elected leaders that will result in a favorable action on its policy priorities (Kendall, 1994).

ISSUE STATEMENT

Social work is inextricably linked to electoral politics in a myriad of ways. The political authority of decision makers confers ability to determine access to and distribution of vital resources. Political power sets, limits, and defines quality of life for all citizens, affecting almost every aspect of daily life.

Social workers possess a continuum of knowledge about human needs and behavior, services delivery, systems that affect individuals and groups, and the effects of public policy. Therefore, social workers are in a unique position to participate in electoral politics to advocate for candidates, laws, and policies that promote NASW's agenda. As a profession it is imperative that social workers become informed about and involved in all levels of electoral politics.

Social workers frequently approach electoral politics with great caution because of its potential for divisiveness. The major cause for division occurs around the concepts of partisanship and political parties. Some members of the profession believe that NASW should be nonpartisan in terms of candidates for office or that NASW should take positions only on issues, not candidates. Other members think that NASW should be aligned with only one of the major parties, and still others favor a bipartisan or multipartisan approach.

There are two practical difficulties with NASW either adopting a nonpartisan approach to candidates or taking positions on issues instead of candidates. For most political offices in this country, partisanship is unavoidable. Only a few offices, such as those on school boards and some municipal and judicial positions, are contested on a nonpartisan basis. Virtually all other elective offices involve partisan contests. If an individual or group wants to be able to influence electoral outcomes, it will have to make partisan choices. Campaigns and elections in the U.S. political system are, by and large, about choices among candidates, not issues. Social workers must be involved in the election of candidates who support NASW values and issues to advance the profession's values, issues, and ethics.

POLICY STATEMENT

1. NASW reaffirms that participation in electoral politics is consistent with fundamental social work values such as self-determination, empowerment, democratic decision making, equal opportunity, inclusion, and the promotion of social justice.

2. NASW's ability to achieve public policy goals and other political objectives depends on participation in the full spectrum of legitimate electoral activities, and these activities should be thoroughly integrated into other association programs.

3. NASW's primary organizational strength lies in the involvement and mobilization of its members in all aspects of electoral politics, with particular emphasis on campaigns and elections, electoral coalitions, fundraising, and the seeking of public office.

4. NASW reaffirms that members seeking and serving in appointive and elective public offices are rendering community service consistent with the profession's code of ethics.

5. NASW encourages its members to participate in all facets of electoral political activity and recognizes the right of individual members to make their own choices about electoral participation and candidate support.

6. NASW seeks to work collaboratively with the Council on Social Work Education and social work education programs to develop appropriate curriculum material on and field placements in electoral politics and expand opportunities for political social work practice.

REFERENCES

Kahn, S. (1991). *Organizing: A guide for grassroots leaders.* Silver Spring, MD: NASW Press.

Kendall, J. (1994). *Report and recommendations: Midwest PACE project meeting and focus group.* Washington, DC: National Association of Social Workers, Political Affairs Department.

National Association of Social Workers. (1994a). *Candidate endorsements* (PACE Tip Sheet Series No. 4). Washington, DC: Author.

National Association of Social Workers. (1995). *Social workers serving in elective offices* (3rd ed.). Washington, DC: Author.

National Association of Social Workers. (1996). *NASW code of ethics.* Washington, DC: Author.

National Rainbow Coalition. (1994, June 10). *Jax Fax, 2*(23).

Pear, R. (1994, November 7). Debate on whose voice is heard on initiatives. *New York Times,* p. B11.

Plano, J. C., & Greenberg, M. (1989). *The American political dictionary* (8th ed.). Fort Worth, TX: Holt, Rinehart, & Winston.

Priest, D. (1994, November 2). Ballot names may yield to ballot measures. *Washington Post,* p. A9.

Reeser, L. C., & Epstein, I. (1990). *Professionalization and activism in social work: The sixties, the eighties, and the future.* New York: Columbia University Press.

Salcido, R. M., & Seck, E. T. (1992). Political participation among social work chapters. *Social Work, 37,* 563–564.

Sherradan, M., & Parker, M. D. (1991). Electoral participation of social workers. *New England Journal of Human Services, 11*(23), 23–28.

Weismiller, T., & Dempsey, D. (1993). NASW becoming a dynamic political force [Letter]. *Social Work, 38,* 645–646.

Weismiller, T., & Rome, S. H. (1995). Social workers in politics. In R. L. Edwards (Ed.-in-Chief), *Encyclopedia of social work* (19th ed., Vol. 3, pp. 2305–2313). Washington, DC: NASW Press.

Wolk, J. L., Weismiller, T., Dempsey, D., & Pray, J. L. (1994, November 12). *Political practicums: Educating social workers for policy making.* Paper presented at the Baccalaureate Program Directors Meeting, San Francisco.

Policy statement approved by the NASW Delegate Assembly, August 1996. For further information, contact the National Association of Social Workers, 750 First Street, NE, Suite 700, Washington, DC 20002-4241. Telephone: 202-408-8600 or 800-638-8799.

Energy

BACKGROUND

The world energy crisis has had a profound effect on all segments of the population. From the early 1970s to the mid-1980s, there was a drastic shift in the economic and political power bases of the world. The interruption of energy supplies to the United States and increased oil prices weakened the national economy. Rapidly rising energy costs contributed heavily to the already high inflation rates and increased our economic vulnerability. Today, energy experts question how the United States can maintain economic growth in the 1990s with zero energy growth.

It was evident in the early 1970s to mid-1980s that the time had come to reduce our dependence on imported oil. There was an increased emphasis on developing conventional sources of domestic energy (oil, natural gas, nuclear power, and coal), an immediate response to the energy needs. However, we did not work toward alternative opportunities in nonconventional methods of conservation, renewable sources of energy, and solar power.

All Americans currently live with the problems created by the national drive toward self-sufficiency in energy. The rapid development of energy resources (for example, oil, gas, coal, shale, and uranium) in the United States in the 1970s and 1980s required large numbers of construction, mining, and transportation personnel. The resulting boomtowns offered economic benefits, but these benefits were accompanied by a large number of social problems, such as increased population, crimes against property, family disturbances, substance abuse, and a dramatic increase in crimes against people, including child neglect and abuse. Characteristically, small communities also suffered from gender stratification, which created an added burden on women. The

combination of these massive changes was a special hardship for rural communities.

Boomtowns usually lacked the fiscal and professional wherewithal to plan adequately for and to cope with such growth and attendant problems. Part-time town officials, nonexistent or limited planning staffs, and a general reliance on natural helping systems were no match for explosive growth. Rural communities suffered from a lack of attention, from under-financing, and from unplanned and uncoordinated efforts by federal and state government units, energy companies, universities, and professional organizations.

In addition, inequitable energy-related burdens often were the result of regional differences. For example, the West has borne the cost of reclaiming strip-mined land for agricultural purposes; the industrial Northeast has experienced a rapid rise in electricity costs and a heavy dependence on oil; metropolitan areas have suffered negative environmental effects from the deregulation of power-producing facilities; the coal mining area of Appalachia has faced the danger of health and safety hazards in the mines (for example, black lung disease, increases in cancer, and inadequate equipment standards); and rural areas throughout various regions and areas where people of color reside have become sites for nuclear dumping and avenues for transporting hazardous wastes.

Rural minority populations, like Native Americans on reservations, are enticed to welcome the dumping of hazardous wastes in an attempt to boost their local economies. These communities may embrace becoming the site of a depository without understanding the health, economic, and social risks. Conversely, rural and Native American communities that do not welcome such development may not possess the information or resources to thwart such an endeavor.

Today, the energy crisis, compounded by inflation and deregulation, inflicts a special hardship on traditional groups at risk, such as older, poor, and unemployed people, and people of color, who already are paying a disproportionate share of their income for energy-related items, such as heating fuels and transportation. Inadequate public and private funds have been spent on technical assistance, educational, and outreach programs to assist the poor with their energy problems. Consumers at all socioeconomic levels have had limited access to the resources of public and private utilities.

Both private and public social services organizations, faced with inflation-caused budgetary crunches, find it difficult to maintain the necessary levels of staff and services. Clients' access to services, which is affected by transportation costs, is being curtailed severely.

All too often, environmental impact statements are poorly developed, are focused on the physical and economic environment, and have little or no effect on social policy. These statements are usually of scant value to anyone who is planning, directing, delivering, or evaluating human services in communities that are affected by an energy crisis.

The United States lacks a strong national commitment to equitable conservation policies in the industrial and domestic sectors. A strong commitment would reduce the need for additional energy resources, slow the energy-fueled inflation rate, ease economic pressures on low-income people, and reduce the negative effects of unplanned energy development. There has been no national leadership in conserving or developing alternative resources. Increased experimentation and use of ethanol could reduce costs, increase efficiency, and provide distressed farmers with an additional outlet for their cash crops.

ISSUE STATEMENT

Rising energy prices have forced vulnerable groups, such as the aged, minorities, and the poor, to pay a disproportionate part of their income for energy-related expenditures. In ad-

dition, increased energy prices adversely affect the ability of human services organizations to provide and deliver services.

During the 1970s and 1980s, the national drive toward energy self-sufficiency resulted in hundreds of boomtowns and attendant social problems as some areas were inundated by people rushing in to develop energy resources. Communities were ill-prepared to manage such growth. Because they did not receive adequate assistance from the federal and state governments, energy companies, universities, and professional organizations, communities bore a disproportionate and unequal amount of the burden created by the energy crisis.

Furthermore, standards of health and safety often were low during critical times of rapid development. Environmental impact statements for major energy developments have been weighted too heavily in favor of the physical and economic environment at the expense of human problems.

The inevitable "bust" occurred in the mid-1980s when the United States began relying on overseas energy resources again. We did not appear to learn much from relying too heavily on foreign oil and began to revert to pre-mid-1980s practices. When the Persian Gulf crisis demonstrated the vulnerability of the United States to unstable international conditions, the Bush administration felt compelled to send in troops to protect our energy-related interests. Many lives were disrupted because revenues needed for domestic causes were diverted to the war effort.

There is an immediate need for a balanced and equitable energy system that uses conventional energy resources and new, safe alternatives. Conservation, renewable energy sources, and solar power deserve a fair chance in attempts to reduce our dependence on fossil fuels. Decision-making structures in the public and private sectors inadequately represent the consumer. Helping consumers gain access to the process is essential. New legal mechanisms to allow consumers to advocate and negotiate for their communities are long overdue.

There is considerable confusion about the appropriate roles and responsibilities of local, state, and national governments; energy companies; universities; and lay citizens in addressing and resolving the energy crisis. The lack of a strong, equitable consumer- and conservation-oriented national energy policy accentuates all the previously stated problems.

POLICY STATEMENT

NASW supports strategies that promote the following aims:

■ analyze the socioeconomic costs and effects of current policies, especially as they affect traditional groups at risk and the delivery of social services.

■ ensure that no group or region bears an inequitable part of such costs and burdens, if at all possible.

■ ensure that any group or region that does bear an inequitable part of such costs and burdens is reimbursed accordingly.

■ preserve and promote high standards in health, safety, and environmental regulations in the continued production of domestic energy.

■ promote the development of programs that provide income support, assistance with conservation, social work, and other community services to people who are at risk because of the inflationary rise in the cost of energy and the attendant social consequences of the energy crisis and of energy development.

■ support the funding of such programs by federal, state, and local governments and by the energy industry.

■ support the production of safe fuels and other unconventional sources of energy, including cash crops.

■ advocate that independent consumer groups become part of the decision-making and planning processes with public utility commissions and private utility providers.

■ ensure that the negative environmental consequences of energy development, such as water and air pollution, soil destruction, defoliation, and radioactive and chemical contamination, do not diminish the quality of life in affected areas.

■ support the development of a strong and equitable national commitment to conservation in both the industrial and domestic arenas.

■ encourage social workers to participate in energy-related alliances as a means of achieving social equity in energy policy.

■ promote the safe handling, transportation, and storage of energy resources and wastes. Promote equity in the selection of communities.

■ develop skills in solving energy problems through social work education. Field placements should be established in areas that are affected by or deal with the social consequences of the energy crisis.

■ determine the appropriate roles and responsibilities of local, state, and national governments; energy companies; universities; and lay citizens in addressing and resolving the energy crisis.

■ reduce the reliance on foreign energy resources so that the United States will be less vulnerable to government instability in various parts of the world.

■ provide advance information to groups, such as Native Americans, about the possible hazards of locating depositories for toxic waste on their lands.

■ promote active participation by social workers in the development of the national energy plan to ensure equity, safety, and an enhanced quality of life.

SUGGESTED READINGS

Department of Health and Human Services, Office of Human Development Services, Region VIII, and Loretto Heights College. (1980). *Toward the 80's: Women and energy.* Denver: Author.

Haynes, T. L. (1983). The socioeconomic impacts of resource development on the elderly. In S. Yarie (Ed.), *Alaska symposium on the social, economic, and cultural impacts of natural resource development* (pp. 160–166). Fairbanks: University of Alaska.

Hurley, K. (1983). Research on the impacts of resource development on women. In S. Yarie (Ed.), *Alaska symposium on the social, economic, and cultural impacts of natural resource development* (pp. 158–160). Fairbanks: University of Alaska.

Hurst, J. B., & Shepard, J. W. (1992). The dynamics of plant closings: An extended emotional roller coaster ride. In M. Bloom (Ed.), *Changing lives: Studies in human development and professional helping.* Columbia: University of South Carolina Press.

Knox, M. L. (1985, November 17). Town grapples with growth as boom days hit. *Atlanta Journal and Constitution.*

Larson, S. S. (1980). The elderly: Victims of the energy venture. In J. Davenport & J. A. Davenport (Eds.), *The boom town: Problems and promises in the energy vortex* (pp. 33–41). Laramie: University of Wyoming.

Midwest Research Institute. (1992). *Economic impact analysis of AECI compliance options.* Macon, MO: Associated Electric.

Robbins, L. A. (1980). Native Americans' experiences with energy developments. In J. Davenport & J. A. Davenport (Eds.), *The boom town: Problems and promises in the energy vortex* (pp. 21–32). Laramie: University of Wyoming.

Western Gerontology Society and U.S. Department of Health and Human Services. (1980). *Energy and aging: A symposium.* Denver: Author.

Policy statement approved by the NASW Delegate Assembly, August 1993. This policy statement supersedes the policy statement on Energy approved by the Delegate Assembly in 1981. For further information, contact the National Association of Social Workers, 750 First Street, NE, Suite 700, Washington, DC 20002-4241. Telephone: 202-408-8600 or 800-638-8799.

Family Planning

BACKGROUND

The unique importance of the family in the development and maintenance of the physical, mental, and emotional health of its members underpins the determination of social workers to support social institutions and welfare programs that enhance and buttress effective family functioning. Our respect for the dignity and worth of each individual human being commits us to work toward fulfillment of the highest potential in every person. Although society has the responsibility to facilitate the well-being of each person, the individual, in turn, must assume some responsibility for the welfare of the community.

Within this philosophical framework, NASW directs attention to the individual and social consequences of unplanned and unwanted pregnancies. We believe that potential parents should be free to decide for themselves, without duress and according to their personal beliefs and convictions, whether they want to become parents, how many children they are willing and able to nurture, and the opportune time for them to have children. These decisions are crucial not only for the parents but also for the unborn children, the community, the nation, and the world. For the parents, unwanted children may present economic, social, physical, or emotional problems. If the birth occurs out of wedlock, the problems are compounded for everyone. The tragedy of the unwanted child born in or out of wedlock often is dramatized by cases of abuse and abandonment.

Advances in the United States in the standard of living, urbanization, medical technology, and understanding of both family and individual needs have produced a corresponding demand for family planning services. Many married people and engaged couples using private physicians have had fairly ready access to medically approved methods of contraception. Until re-

cently, many medically indigent people have been able to obtain similar help in family planning only from limited voluntary programs. This discrimination was the result of their low socioeconomic status.

Growing public pressure for governmental support of family planning services as a public health measure comes from several sources: young married couples who want financial and emotional security before venturing into parenthood, parents of large families who are overburdened and unable to break out of the poverty cycle, parents who want to give the children they already have every advantage from their limited resources, and those who are concerned about the quality of family life. Along with other professions that are responsible for enhancing family life, social work has, to a large extent, neglected to include birth control services as part of its overall task.

Problems that may occur in marital, extramarital, and premarital sexual relations require other types of professional intervention and counseling. Family planning services in themselves cannot be expected to solve these problems, but can serve both individuals and society by helping prevent the frequent result of these relationships in the birth of unwanted children. Although society is ultimately responsible for the welfare of children, much can be done through individual services to encourage and make possible responsible parenthood.

In many countries, the dual problem of excess fertility and an inadequate supply of food and other essentials has reached disaster proportions, particularly in underdeveloped countries. Especially in such areas, support of family planning by the central government or local governments frequently is sporadic or nonexistent, leaving people without access to family planning information and services. Governments in these countries lack funds and trained personnel to gather adequate demographic data, develop family planning programs, and raise their citizens' educational and employment levels to the point at which the size of families normally would begin to level off. The disparity between the world's population and the world's food supply is increasing, and famine, with all its terrible consequences, may ensue unless effective programs of family planning can be developed.

POLICY STATEMENT

A continuing partnership between the voluntary and the public sectors is necessary to assist families to plan for children. Adequate financing is necessary to make family planning programs and professional services available to all, regardless of the ability to pay. Government policies and medical programs, as well as medical programs under voluntary auspices, should ensure that potential parents have full access to the technical knowledge and resources that will enable them to exercise their right of choice about whether and when to have children. As part of the professional team operating these programs, social workers, with their underlying emphasis on and particular methods for enhancing self-determination, have a special responsibility.

The unprecedented rate of population growth, especially in the crowded urban centers, makes it vital that family planning should be accompanied by social, economic, and physical planning at the various levels of government. Freedom of choice in family planning in underdeveloped areas, within or outside our country, is especially difficult without raising socioeconomic and educational levels. A total approach to population policy should therefore include not only family planning, but improvement of socioeconomic conditions, including the provision of food and essential goods and services that are basic to the satisfaction of family needs. Without such planning and development, the democratic goals of optimum opportunity for individual achievement cannot be realized and the benefits resulting from family planning services may be nullified. Specifically, the National Association of Social Workers (NASW) endorses the following principles:

Comprehensive Services

Family planning should include a range of services relative to childbearing and child spacing to offer means that are compatible with the individual's preference. Problems of both infertility and fertility control should be given adequate attention within the context of family planning. It is especially important that individuals and families who have problems related to family planning should have access to, among others, social work, medical, psychological, and religious services.

Availability and Accessibility of Services

As a public health measure, family planning services should be available as part of the community's public and voluntary health and welfare services. Public services must be available to all without the application of a means test. No action by governmental agencies or their personnel should be permitted to limit the ready availability of these services, nor should any prohibition be placed against giving these services to individuals who want them.

Importance of Freedom of Choice

No coercion in the use or selection of a method of family planning should be permitted. People should be protected in the exercise of self-determination of whether to engage in a program of family planning that is most compatible with their personal beliefs and convictions. Clients of public and voluntary agencies should be advised clearly that their use or nonuse of family planning services will in no way affect any other benefits they are receiving through the agencies.

Governmental Support for Services, Education of Personnel, and Research

There should be active support for the development of community and statewide public voluntary health services for all methods of family planning. Government at all levels should take a vigorous and full-partnership role with other institutions of society in the broad study, planning, and programming needed to ensure that the right of all children to a family and to a world that can adequately care for them will be realized. Through its various channels, the government should provide the financial incentive and official support to public and voluntary facilities for the wide dissemination of family planning services. Such governmental support should include financing research to evaluate the effectiveness of these family planning services and to develop improved methods of preventing, postponing, or promoting conception. Governmental aid also is needed to recruit and train essential professional personnel, to staff facilities, and to provide high-quality services.

Educational Programs

Families, schools, churches, volunteer groups, and governmental health, education, and welfare agencies should educate all individuals about the rewards and responsibilities of family life. Educational efforts should include programs on the purpose and availability of family planning services.

International Responsibilities

U.S. government and voluntary American social welfare organizations should, on request, provide assistance to other countries for research, education, and the training of personnel and the operation of family planning programs. As far as possible, the U.S. government should channel its family planning assistance through agencies of the United States and other multigovernmental auspices. Because countries are at different stages of experimentation in the development of family planning and population policy, it is important to foster wide communication with regard to programs, methods, and results.

Responsibility of Social Workers

Social workers should take professional responsibility to assist clients in obtaining whatever help and information they need for effective family planning. Because social workers are knowledgeable about family and community resources in their day-to-day work, they have many opportunities to help clients obtain the desired services. Individual social workers also have a professional obligation to work with a variety of groups on the domestic and international fronts to establish family planning programs on a level that is adequate to ensure the availability and accountability of family planning services to all who want them.

Policy statement approved by the NASW Delegate Assembly, 1967; reconfirmed by the Delegate Assembly, August 1990. Referred to the 1999 Delegate Asssembly, to be combined with the policy on Abortion and renamed Family Planning and Reproductive Choices. For further information, contact the National Association of Social Workers, 750 First Street, NE, Suite 700, Washington, DC 20002-4241. Telephone: 202-408-8600 or 800-638-8799.

Family Policy

BACKGROUND

Strengthening families and providing family support are priorities of the social work profession. Because the family is the primary socializing agent in our culture, all treatment programs and policies should keep this mission in mind. Families in the United States have undergone tremendous changes in composition, structure, and roles in the 20th century. They have fewer children, and people are living longer. An increasing number of women, including women with young children, are in the work force. In addition, families have been highly mobile, moving away from parents and other natural support systems. New immigrants and refugees in this country help expand the cultural, religious, and ethnic diversity on which this nation was built. Economic and political conditions around the world, particularly in developing countries, profoundly affect the conditions in which families in the United States live.

Contemporary American families are an amalgam of many different lifestyles and many different structures. Family constructs are no longer the traditional singular model on which to base policy. Family composition may cover a range of constellations, including traditional married parents with biological children; divorced, separated, or unmarried parents who have individual, separate, or shared responsibility for the care of children; intergenerational arrangements for child or elder care; gay and lesbian couples with or without the care of children; and adoptive and foster families. Family social policy must recognize and respect this range of models and their respective specific needs.

Family is defined in its broadest sense to include two or more people who consider themselves "family" and who assume obligations and responsibilities that are generally considered essential to family life. Families are first-line providers of such services as health care, counseling, education, child care, elder care, long-term care, and income support. They may perform these functions without the adequate resources and knowledge to perform them successfully. Although most families strive for financial and social independence, many families are dependent on external support systems such as social services or social insurance entitlements. Many, however, have no guarantee that they will receive assistance when it is needed.

When families are unable to perform the roles expected of them, they may incur great stress and deep stigma before help is on the way. And when help is received, it may be too little to respond to the level of the problem that exists.

ISSUE STATEMENT

Stress of the Caregiving and Provider Roles

Profound changes in family structure have been brought about by the increase in longevity, which has resulted in many four- and five-generation families. Adult family caregivers, usually women but sometimes men, may experience five or more episodic or chronic caregiving phases—caring for children, parents, grandparents, spouses, and siblings. Family caregiving has not been compensated in this society except for families and children who receive Aid to Families with Dependent Children (AFDC) and whose incomes are below the poverty level. The caregiving role can be a financially precarious responsibility, as well as emotionally stressful and physically straining. As women increase their participation in the work force, the priority and balance of home and work responsibilities become most important.

Changes in the local, national, and world economies have brought about major shifts in livelihoods. Families may encounter multiple job changes and the lack of financial security. The loss of jobs, underemployment, the lack of health benefits, or the inability to obtain a job because of one's racial makeup or social station in life are critical factors in many contemporary families. These factors may threaten the survival of a family unit.

The lack of resources also threatens the fundamental biopsychosocial development of family members. The lack of comprehensive prenatal care is linked to low birth weight, developmental delays, and health problems. The lack of early childhood education or day care is linked to poor social development and poor performance in school. The lack of subsidy for the caregiving function of men and women may leave unattended a dependent and medically fragile child or adult. The lack of family and medical leave may create' stress in the workplace and at home.

Family-Focused Services and Practice

Increases in substance abuse, school dropouts, teenage pregnancies, suicide attempts, family violence, and stress-related health disorders may be related to family dysfunction. However, solutions often focus on single symptoms, rather than on root causes. Families may have 10 or more service providers, each addressing a different facet of their family functioning. The fragmentation of services and symptom-focused practice cannot be eliminated unless service providers reframe the presenting problems as family and community-systems issues. Moreover, practice that focuses on the individual in isolation from his or her family and primary support network may be limited in scope and effectiveness. Thus, as in child welfare and care for the elderly, the very protection of the child and elderly person depends upon effective service with family members. When empowerment is the goal of work with family members and their support systems, the practitioner depends upon these network members to reinforce, if not ensure, that the goals of practice are sustained. Social work must advocate for a family-focused model of a full range of comprehensive services, from primary prevention to treatment or rehabilitation.

In essence, even when the individual may be the central concern of the practitioner, the family support network is the action system to be mobilized and to advocate for socioeconomic changes. Family-focused practice requires community mobilization to parallel the support network. Many times, change in the family system or community institutions, such as the workplace, is a precondition for the growth and development of individuals or families.

Cultural Diversity and Support Networks

Models for child, adult, and family development and coping come from diverse communities and family systems, cultures, and ethnic groups. Differences are enriching, not deviant. As the roles of support networks become more prominent in our understanding of the strengths, resilience, and problem-solving resources of families, we need to respect the effective, kinlike relations found in various rural, ethnic, and racial communities. It is important to utilize models of successful helping networks that come from many diverse groups and cultures to build family supports. Services must be provided by individuals who are culturally aware and sensitive to ethnic, racial, and cultural diversity in working with families. A bilingual individual should be involved whenever there is a language barrier.

Economic and Social Service Infrastructure

Supports to families should encompass a comprehensive array of economic and social service entitlements to enhance family functioning. Current family problems may be as indicative of deficits in services and policy as they are of familial dysfunction. Gaps in social services and economic resources are often the root of homelessness or family violence. While the nation develops a patchwork of services, no comprehensive family support system exists.

Workplace Roles and Responsibilities

Workplace policies and practices historically have been overlooked in debates about family policy, despite their predominant role in promoting strong family stability and functioning. Employee policies, wages, and work roles are critical to the stability of families and to the development and protection of both children and adults. Therefore, the role of private-sector policies in promoting family support policies within the United States warrants attention.

POLICY STATEMENT

NASW advocates a full range of comprehensive services to families, from primary prevention to rehabilitation, across the life cycle. Strengthening families also necessitates the creation of policies that recognize the family as an intergenerational system that often includes biological, social, and psychological ties. Understanding what happens in families in terms of the flow of life over the generations, the impact of gender on family life, the family life cycle, and cultural variations in the life cycle patterns is essential. Governmental programs and policies must recognize and facilitate the cohesion of families.

Social workers can effectively develop a comprehensive national family policy by working together with other advocates, including other providers of human services and health care, law enforcement officials, criminal justice personnel, and educators. Social workers who, by virtue of their values and education, view strengths and problems in a family context may take a leadership role in this effort. Social work professionals in the United States need to consult and collaborate with social work professionals in other countries to benefit from and build upon the policy and practice experience of colleagues around the world. NASW recommends that a comprehensive family support policy be built on the following principles:

■ Family supports should encompass a comprehensive infrastructure of economic and social entitlements, including health care, income supports, employment, education, day care, elder care, housing, and social services. Comprehensive services should include a continuum that enhances functioning and prevents dysfunction and intensive intervention to alleviate problems. All these services should be provided in the spirit of respecting the integrity of the individual.

■ The civil rights of individuals, including access to needed services regardless of economic, geographic, or ethnic status, must be guaranteed.

■ The vital force of cultural diversity should be affirmed; biases by institutions or practitioners must be eliminated.

■ Supports to families should be flexible and targeted to meet the unique, diverse needs of family members. Whenever feasible, a wide array of service options should be available to the family. The family, in turn, can make an informed choice and select the most appropriate option to meet its needs. Services in the public and private sectors must demonstrate a concern for the total family, addressing the needs of parents, children, and the elderly, and must incorporate an understanding of intergenerational family functioning. Services to families should be available and accessible within communities and provided during flexible hours to those who need them. Policies must be conducive to and facilitate family functioning, as well as support the efforts of caregivers who are friends and extended family members. A family social policy extends beyond direct interventions to a wide range of practices in the public and private sectors that have a direct or indirect impact on family functioning.

■ Welfare reform efforts to enable families to achieve self-sufficiency should contain national standards that ensure the following four items:

1. educational and training opportunities including school-based options for young parents to attain high-level skills

2. sufficient choices of high-quality day care for women who are entering the work force or undertaking training and educational programs

3. the provision of transitional health and day care services

4. adequate family income supports.

■ Institutions, such as schools, workplaces, hospitals, and churches, must establish ways to help families and strengthen their functioning.

■ The media may play a role in modeling family patterns and should be encouraged to portray positive family functioning and information on parenting.

■ Services to families are complex. It is essential that these services be delivered by professionals who have the requisite skills that enable them to assess the situation and to develop and implement a plan of service that protects the integrity of the family as a functional unit. Social workers must have a background in social work education and must meet continuing education requirements.

■ The development of a partnership between families and policymakers in the public and private sectors is essential. Families need to be given a strong voice in all aspects of decision making that affect their lives. All policies of the public and private sectors must be screened and evaluated for their implicit or explicit impact on intergenerational families. Moreover, perspectives from families themselves should be deliberately sought and encouraged. Unless there is a stronger voice for families, many policies will inadvertently undercut family functioning and development.

To support these principles, it is important that the social work profession advocate policies that will provide support to families. These policies include the following:

■ full and equitable employment, including initiatives that promote permanent part-time jobs with adequate wages and benefits for adults and youths

■ early childhood and family life education addressing all aspects of caregiving and problem solving throughout the life span

■ a system of family support centers or services that promotes the development of families and that includes preventive as well as restorative services. Services can be geared toward developing a sense of community. These family support centers should be funded by the public or private sectors

■ affordable, accessible, and high-quality dependent care, including child care and elder care, in a variety of settings to meet the needs of all families. Day care in the workplace needs to be advocated

■ affordable, accessible, and high-quality housing available in all urban, suburban, and rural areas so that families may experience a high quality of life

■ family and medical leave to provide time off from work for the birth, adoption, or illness of a child or the illness of a spouse or older or disabled relative

■ comprehensive and available health, mental health, and family planning services, including strategies focused on prenatal and perinatal care for high-risk mothers

■ comprehensive services that are designed to keep family units together and to preserve the quality of life, especially when families are faced with chronic and life-threatening illnesses, such as HIV/AIDS

■ gender-equitable income supports or credits for people whose family caregiving demands impede their continuous participation in the labor force

■ supportive programs in the workplace that provide education, flexible working hours, day care facilities, counseling, and assistance to working family members

■ a comprehensive range of supportive and protective services that meet the needs of family members who are abused or neglected and also include corrective intervention services for the perpetrator.

Social workers must advocate "the family" perspective with the federal government, and should work in their states toward the development of family policy legislation. Work-incentive programs and medical care for parents and caregivers who want employment and adequate health care for their children must be advocated. Policies and programs, such as day care and pregnancy leave, to support single parents and working parents must be stressed.

The cost of investing in intergenerational family supports will be far less burdensome than is the price that the society is paying for the growing incarceration and institutionalization of dysfunctional members that are predictable by-products of the mounting dysfunction in the family and community systems. Implementation of the policy objectives and development of the needed support services to families are critical responsibilities of the social work profession. Social workers are also uniquely qualified to carry out research, program evaluations, and the administration of programs set forth from this framework. Third-party reimbursers of services must consider reimbursement for strengthening families and services given to caregivers, family members, and other people who are associated with the identified patient. The reimbursers need to pay for services to children, to parents, and to siblings as well.

Social workers need to advocate for families in society who have not been afforded their full rights, responsibilities, and benefits and to work to eradicate negative terms used to label them. The family needs to be viewed from a systems perspective to include intergenerational support, social relationship support, and community support.

As a profession, we know that taking significant initiatives will strengthen not only families, but communities, and will add vitality and meaning to the lives of people and to society. We must work to identify significant indicators that will demonstrate to the profession and to society that working to achieve the mission of supporting and strengthening families does produce significant results.

Policy statement approved by the NASW Delegate Assembly, August 1990. Referred to the 1999 Delegate Assembly for revision. This statement supersedes the policy statement on Family Policy approved by the Delegate Assembly in 1981. For further information, contact the National Association of Social Workers, 750 First Street, NE, Suite 700, Washington, DC 20002-4241. Telephone: 202-408-8600 or 800-638-8799.

Family Violence

BACKGROUND

Violence in family and primary relationships has existed throughout history but only recently has it been documented clearly and considered a social problem of enormous magnitude. Simply defined, family violence refers to physical, sexual, and emotional acts of commission and omission knowingly, purposely, or recklessly committed by and on family members. In this context, family refers to those individuals related by blood, marriage, or legal status, as well as to those who constitute primary associations, past or present. Typically, family violence includes abuse, neglect, and the exploitation of partners, parents, children, and the elderly. Little attention has been given to the problems of sibling abuse and the abuse of parents by adolescent children.

Public attention was drawn to the problem of child abuse 25 years ago by the medical profession, particularly C. Henry Kempe. In the early 1970s, the women's movement was responsible for identifying spousal abuse. Subsequently, child sexual abuse emerged as a major social problem. Unfortunately, not until the late 1970s was elder abuse "uncovered" in the field of gerontology. All these types of family violence have had a similar historical development—extreme cases were publicized, gained national prominence, and then were discounted as rare occurrences. Research later demonstrated the various gradations and widespread nature of the phenomenon.

Denial, doubt, disgust, and disbelief are the most common responses to the problem of family violence. These attitudes and beliefs are reflected in the behaviors of individuals and members of institutions and society. The result is either avoidance of the issue or a skewed perception of the problem. Most research has concluded that family violence is present in all racial, ethnic, religious, geographic, economic, political, age, and educational groups.

Incidence and prevalence data are used to measure the scope of the problem. The National Center for Child Abuse and Neglect estimates that more than 1 million children annually are physically, sexually, and emotionally abused and neglected. Approximately 2,000 children die each year as a result of abuse or neglect. Yet experts suggest that only 10 to 20 percent of the cases of child abuse in the home become known. The shame and guilt experienced by victims of child sexual abuse, as well as the level of societal denial regarding this problem, are among the reasons it is the most underreported form of child abuse. Current estimates predict that one in six children will be sexually abused before age 18. There is evidence to suggest that the majority of teenagers who run away from home and become prostitutes or drug users or both were sexually victimized by a family member.

The incidence data on spousal abuse provide only a limited picture of the scope of the problem. Only the most extreme cases are documented in the crime statistics. The Federal Bureau of Investigation estimates that a woman is battered every 30 seconds. Women who die from the actions of their partners represent one-third to one-half of all reported homicides. Because of the research problems in measuring other forms of spousal abuse and neglect, such as sexual, psychological, or emotional, researchers have focused exclusively on physical acts of violence. However, the other forms of spouse abuse and neglect are considered extensive and serious problems that affect a broad sector of the population. More recently, a few states have passed marital rape laws to protect married women from sexual violence by their mates.

Over time, the research has shown that violence escalates in frequency and severity. Fear of bodily harm and loss of financial support, as well as psychological dependence, often contribute to a woman's decision to remain in a violent relationship. It often is assumed that if the relationship ends, so will the violence. But it is well documented that violence may continue even after the wife chooses to end the relationship. Publicized cases in the 1980s demonstrate that some battered women and incest victims have resorted to the most extreme methods of escape: murdering the perpetrator of the abuse because no other alternatives seemed available.

Various forms of elder abuse and neglect have been identified by practitioners, including physical, psychological, sexual, financial, and medical. In 1979, the University of Maryland's Center on Aging undertook a study of battered elderly people and found that 4.1 percent of the elderly respondents reported being abused. If projected to a national population of elderly people, the researchers concluded that there would be nearly 1 million cases of elder abuse each year. Frail and elderly women, who are dependent on others for care and protection, are more likely to be victims of elder abuse.

Researchers and practitioners in the field of family violence attempt to identify behavioral and psychological indicators, personality profiles, family dynamics, and societal conditions as causes of the phenomenon. No one single factor causes family violence. The complexity of family violence leads most professionals to examine micro and macro issues in assessing, intervening in, and studying the problem in all its forms.

Family violence harms individuals directly and may have long-term effects on the health and well-being of families. Clearly, family violence is pervasive, because millions of children, partners, and elderly people experience it. In fact, an alarming number of children who witnessed or were victims of family violence may have learned that violence is a means of coping.

ISSUE STATEMENT

Fragmentation in the field of family violence has inhibited the development of common definitions, comparable research on incidence and prevalence, and theories of causality. Practitioners and researchers are segregated by their expertise, which is focused primarily on a particular type of family violence, such as child, spouse, or elder abuse. Also, different orientations contribute to the sharp division among professionals who work in the field of family violence. Competition for funding, rivalries among different proponents, and the emotional and political nature of family violence also have contributed to further divisions among service providers.

The prevention and treatment of family violence are difficult because the problem is denied, misunderstood, ignored, mythologized, and condoned: Sex-role stereotyping, sexist socialization, and the tradition of patriarchy perpetuate the problem. The oppression of women and children is rooted in the basic premise of patriarchal societies, which considers these individuals to be the property of men.

The acceptance of family violence as a way of life, particularly violence against women and children, is pervasive in American culture. Violence is sanctioned in child-rearing practices, as demonstrated by the Supreme Court decision to condone the use of corporal punishment in schools. Violence is presented as an acceptable form of behavior in literature, children's stories, theater, movies, athletic events, advertising, and radio and television programs.

Sex, race, and class biases by some social workers help to perpetuate the problems of family violence. Many professionals blame the victims, believing that the wife, child, or elderly individual provokes or in some way is responsible for and contributes to the violence. All social workers should recognize the complex economic, emotional, cultural, and societal factors that keep the family member in the violent situation. The social work profession has a responsibility to address the problem of family violence through needed research, the development of prevention and intervention programs, and advocacy for adequate laws and funding for protective and treatment services.

Although social workers express concern for the protection of human beings, they have been lax in adequately preparing themselves to address the problem of family violence. Given the legal liability relative to reporting child and elder abuse, students receive inadequate preparation in schools of social work to work effectively in the field of family violence. Not only does the educational system have inadequate curricula, many agencies lack sufficient policy statements, staff development, and in-service training programs to address the multifaceted aspects of family violence. The lack of sensitivity, awareness of the scope of the problem, appropriate assessment, intervention, and prevention strategies for both victims and abusers need to be addressed by the profession.

POLICY STATEMENT

NASW supports educational and prevention strategies for addressing family violence:

■ NASW encourages schools of social work to develop and implement curricula to prepare students adequately to meet the demands of mandated witnesses and work in the field of family violence. NASW encourages the development of field experiences that reflect different approaches to assessment, treatment, and prevention in this field. All social workers should be skilled in the assessment of risk factors for family violence and appropriate reporting, referral, and intervention techniques.

■ NASW promotes the development of in-service training and continuing education on all forms of family violence to increase the awareness and intervention strategies of social work practitioners. NASW encourages positive, bias-free attitudes among social workers toward the identification, assessment, treatment, prevention, and eventual eradication of family violence.

■ NASW promotes the creation of interdisciplinary training, education, and comprehensive services to link and coordinate programs with health, mental health, and protective services; the courts; schools; law enforcement agencies; the military; places of worship; workplace service providers; and social service systems for the effective treatment and prevention of family violence.

■ NASW will work to eliminate the social and structural injustices that perpetuate family violence. Specifically, NASW will work to elimi-

nate all forms of sex-role exploitation and the inequitable distribution of wealth and power in the society. NASW promotes social policies that ensure the equality of men and women.

■ NASW will work toward the elimination of sexism, racism, classism, ageism, homophobia, and other prejudices within the social work profession and in society that have an impact on family violence.

■ NASW will work to end the portrayal of violence in the media, which directly or indirectly encourages family violence.

■ NASW will develop programs to educate the public to recognize and reject common myths and stereotypes that foster family violence, be aware of the prevalence and the financial and emotional costs of family violence, hold accountable those who promote or perpetuate violence, and recognize the role that alcohol and drug abuse plays in family violence.

■ NASW supports the development of programs to teach children and adults their right to a life without violence, including prevention programs that teach children from preschool on about the integrity of their bodies and their right to say no.

■ NASW supports the development of theoretical models that encompass all forms of family violence.

■ NASW will promote research on the different forms of family violence and abuse and the dynamics involved.

■ NASW will collect and disseminate information and data to educate social workers and help them respond to and counteract a public backlash against family violence.

NASW supports legislative efforts that address family violence:

■ Each NASW chapter should work to strengthen and enforce legislation to protect individuals in the home, to provide for the legal rights of all family members, and to promote the removal of a perpetrator, rather than the victim, from the home.

■ NASW will work for legislation that funds needed programs and services for victims and perpetrators, including the necessary resources and prevention programs.

■ NASW will work for legislation to provide for the expansion of mandated treatment for perpetrators of family violence, whether in confinement or in the community after treatment.

NASW supports the funding of programs that address family violence:

■ NASW will work toward increased joint funding, by the public and private sectors, of programs that deal with all forms of family violence.

■ NASW supports funding for multilingual and multicultural shelters, telephone hotlines, drop-in centers, self-help groups, and other resources needed for crisis intervention and for long-term treatment and support of people caught up in family violence.

■ NASW will work for the expansion of agency programs to include services for victims and perpetrators of violence. Specialized treatment and preventive services should be developed in conjunction with other community resources to respond to the various forms and stages of family violence.

■ NASW will work to change policies and practices of public and private social welfare agencies to provide improved and immediate financial, residential, legal, and emotional assistance and to remove all barriers to eligibility for abused women who are employed.

■ NASW supports funding for research on all forms of family violence to examine assessment procedures, dynamics, causality, treatment, and prevention programs.

■ NASW supports adequate funding for federal programs to provide grants, to serve as a resource for information on programs and research, and to provide leadership within the federal government for changes in national policies, attitudes, and programs.

Policy statement approved by the NASW Delegate Assembly, November 1987; reconfirmed by the Delegate Assembly, August 1993. This statement supersedes the policy statement on Domestic Violence approved by the Delegate Assembly in 1979. For further information, contact the National Association of Social Workers, 750 First Street, NE, Suite 700, Washington, DC 20002-4241. Telephone: 202-408-8600 or 800-638-8799.

Foster Care and Adoption

BACKGROUND

Foster care and adoption have long served as society's way of providing alternative care to children who—on either a temporary or permanent basis and for a variety of reasons—cannot live with their families of origin. Although these services have provided needed assistance for many children, both have been subject to problems that have limited their potential for meeting children's needs.

During the past 10 years, the social service systems that provide alternative care to children have changed significantly. With the passage of P.L. 96-272 in 1980, state child welfare agencies were encouraged and, in some areas, mandated to improve their foster care and adoption programs. Since that year, the population of children in foster care diminished for a time. The decrease resulted, in part, from a new emphasis on services that prevents the removal of children from their homes and on carefully planned case review systems. Still, many children enter foster care or remain in foster care because of the lack of resources and prevention services in their communities.

In addition, the foster care and adoption populations have changed. There is an increase in the proportion of hard-to-place and special-needs children, such as children who are from minority groups; are older; are developmentally disabled; are medically needy; have AIDS or AIDS-related complex (ARC) or are HIV positive; or are emotionally disturbed.

The social work profession—considering the major role the profession plays in the development and delivery of foster care and adoption services—has a responsibility to assist in assessing public social policy and practice with regard to such services. Social workers should ensure that the services reflect the best and most current knowledge in the field to meet consistently the needs of children and of the community. Social workers who participate in the development of foster care and adoption policy and in the delivery of services must be knowledgeable about national standards in foster care and adoption and must uphold professional practice standards.

ISSUE STATEMENT

Recognition must be given to children's needs for security, continuity of parenting relationships, and nurturing in foster care and adoption services systems. In addition, families must be strengthened and supported as the primary and preferred source for meeting children's physical and psychological needs. Therefore, societal intervention into the parent–child relationship must be considered carefully so that such intervention meets the child's needs, both immediately and over time. The child's enduring ties to a family must be recognized. Child welfare practice cannot be separated from a family systems approach.

Appropriate and adequate information regarding resources, rights, and responsibilities must be available to all parties in foster care and adoption proceedings. Specifically, society's responsibility for ensuring comprehensive high-quality services, with particular attention to the special needs of high-risk children and the resources necessary to meet those needs, must be recognized. Also, the adoptee's right to know about his or her birth parents and the limits of confidentiality must be addressed for all the parties.

An emerging and growing population of children in need of services are children with AIDS or ARC and the children who test HIV positive. The complex interplay of social and medical factors that is implicit in the care of these children presents particular challenges in foster care and adoption and requires a renewed commitment to assure children with AIDS-related conditions the same opportunities to have permanent families as other children, without isolation and segregation.

Comprehensive high-quality services are of particular concern in the provision of services to children with AIDS-related conditions. All services provided to this special population must be grounded in a multidisciplinary approach and include well-thought-out medical treatment when needed.

Research, training, and evaluation of foster care and adoption delivery systems and services must be funded and disseminated. A national information system is essential for providing information for policy development and the allocation of resources.

POLICY STATEMENT

An adequate foster care and adoption policy designed to provide the best care for all children in need of such services should be predicated on four fundamental principles:

1. Every child has the right to a permanent, continuous, and nurturing relationship with a parenting person or people who convey to the child an enduring sense of love and care. The child should perceive himself or herself as a valued family member. This right shall supersede the right of birth parents to maintain legal custody when such custody is physically or emotionally harmful.

2. The opportunity to provide such a nurturing environment is the primary responsibility of the child's family. It thus becomes society's primary responsibility to provide the necessary services and supports required to safeguard and enhance, with every available means, the ability of all families to fulfill this essential role. Failing this, it becomes society's responsibility to provide for expeditious, alternative arrangements that are permanent and meet the child's physical, mental, and emotional needs.

3. Societal intervention into the parent–child relationship is an extremely serious action, which should be pursued only when the child's right to a safe, secure, and nurturing home is seriously threatened. Services should be provided with sensitivity, professional skill, regard for the legal rights of the parties involved, and a sense of the limitations and potential outcomes of such an intervention.

4. Policy and budget leaders need adequate data through a national information system for the purpose of policy development and the allocation of resources.

The four basic principles undergird an entire approach to foster care and adoption. The following includes generic principles that apply to both foster care and adoption, as well as principles that are specifically related to foster care or adoption.

Generic child placement principles include the following:

■ Both foster care and adoption services should be built on and used within an adequately financed family service system. NASW recognizes the need for such a comprehensive approach, as well as the right of people to employment opportunities or income supports or both that enable them to meet basic family needs.

■ The objective of every child's placement should be to provide a safe, nurturing, and secure alternative home when it is not possible for the child to remain with his or her family.

■ Placement decisions should reflect a child's need for continuity, safeguarding the child's right to consistent care and to service arrangements. Agencies must recognize each child's need to retain a significant engagement with his or her parents and extended family and respect the integrity of each child's ethnicity and cultural heritage.

■ The termination of parental rights, whether voluntary or involuntary, should never be undertaken lightly. Adequate information should be provided, along with the full exploration of the alternatives and due process.

■ People involved with the foster care system, adoption proceedings, or child and family services have the right to receive adequate information—from the appropriate agency, court, or community sources—especially regarding their rights, prerogatives, and responsibilities, and adequate legal representation.

■ Ongoing research and evaluation with input from clients should be used by service providers to form and guide policy and practices in foster care and adoption.

■ A child's family should receive sufficient and timely support services to prevent the need for substitute care. Neither foster care nor adoption services should be used merely because they provide a convenient choice in a difficult situation.

■ Decision makers in child placement services always should be sensitive to the inherent trauma resulting from removing a child from familiar surroundings and family members. The child's need for an improved environment must be balanced against the possible damage that could result from the separation. The decision makers also must explore alternatives to out-of-home placement and actualize the concept of "reasonable efforts to prevent removal from the home." The decision-making process must include at all times the development and implementation of a permanent plan for the child. This permanent plan can include a timely decision to terminate parental rights when it is clear that the child cannot remain in or return to his or her family. For some children, permanent planning would include preparation for independent living.

■ All independently made arrangements for children should conform to and be judged by the same principles of care established throughout this policy and should conform to national standards of foster care and adoption practices.

■ Agencies must ensure the removal of any barriers that prevent children from being placed in permanent homes. Financial barriers can be breached by the complete use and expansion of existing adoption-subsidy programs. Barriers that are unsupported by tested experience, such as resistance to using single parents, foster parents (for adoption), and nontraditional family patterns, including lesbian and gay parents, as potential foster care and adoption resources, must be removed.

■ Professional people at various levels in the government must monitor aggressively and care-

fully foster care and adoption services whether provided by the public or the voluntary sector. Professionals should have expertise in child welfare to ensure that caring, comprehensive, permanent planning and services for children are provided.

■ Patterns of funding for foster care and adoption services should guarantee high-quality services to all children, regardless of their race, language, capabilities, religion, geographic location, or socioeconomic status.

■ Foster care and adoption agencies must be administered and staffed by trained social workers. Caseloads should never exceed the ability of workers to provide reasonable, full, and careful attention to each child and his or her family.

■ The long-range advantage to society in providing high-quality family services including but not limited to foster care and adoption should be promoted. This promotion means advancing the concept of community responsibility for all children's needs and seeking to improve the public image and understanding of foster care and adoption.

■ The social work profession stresses the importance of ethnic and cultural sensitivity. An effort to maintain a child's identity and his or her ethnic heritage should prevail in all services and placement actions that involve children in foster care and adoption programs, including adherence to the principles articulated in the Indian Child Welfare Act.

Principles related to foster care include the following:

■ Foster care of children should be viewed as a support service during critical periods in the life of the family after all alternatives to out-of-home placement have been explored and tried. Foster care should not be seen as a penalty for child neglect or the inability to cope with the difficulties of raising children in a stressful world. Foster care should be viewed as a support that enables parents to resume parenting responsibilities.

■ When foster care becomes the intervention of choice, services to reunify the child with his or her family should begin immediately. These services should work toward improving the conditions in the home and facilitating the child's return. Services should be limited by time and planned. When it is clear that progress is not being made to improve conditions, a permanent plan that provides the best alternative for the child should be implemented.

■ Vigorous recruitment, mutual selection, initial and ongoing training of foster parents, and adequate financial support are seen as prerequisites to a successful foster care system. Foster parents need to be particularly sensitive to the special needs of children in their care and to be able to work with and support birth parents who are making appropriate efforts to ensure the return of their children.

■ Comprehensive and specialized training of foster parents should be required as a precondition to the licensure of foster homes, and in-service training should be required as a condition for continuing licensure.

■ Foster parents should be viewed as partners in the service delivery team. Therefore, resources are needed to assist the foster parents in providing care to the child. Resources for foster families should include day care, respite care, peer support, counseling, and parent education.

■ Liability insurance for foster parents should be the responsibility of the placement agencies.

■ The full and prompt reimbursement of maintenance costs and fees for services provided by foster parents should be viewed as an essential part of the agency's plan of care for the child and an investment in both the child and society. The agency also should acknowledge that there are children with special needs of all ages and establish a cost schedule accordingly.

■ A variety of foster care arrangements should be available to the child welfare agency, including family foster care, group home care, therapeutic foster care, day treatment foster care, and institutional care, so that appropriate placements can be made for all children who need temporary, emergency, planned long-term, and specialized foster care. The spectrum of arrangements should include supervised independent

living programs for those children who are making the transition from foster care to living on their own.

■ Child welfare agencies should ensure that each child in foster care will have a case plan. The plan should include the reasons the child was removed from the home; the special needs of the child while in and out of home care; and the services to be provided to the parents, child, and foster parents. The plan will assist in reunifying the family or, if that is not feasible, will result in permanent placement. Case plans should be reviewed periodically by the agency and the court when mandated by law.

■ The agency's periodic case review system should involve all parties, including the caseworker and supervisor, the birth parents and other relatives of the child, foster parents, and the child (if of an appropriate age). In addition, an objective party who is not involved in the management of the case or delivery of services may be involved in the review of the status of the child in care. Each party to the service planning process should be provided with a copy of the initial case plan and subsequent revised plans and agreements.

■ The recruitment of foster parents from each relevant racial and ethnic group should be pursued vigorously to meet the needs of children who require placement. Placement of choice should be within the child's family of origin, among relatives who can provide a more stable environment for the child during the period of family crisis. If no such relatives are available, every effort should be made to place a child in the home of foster parents who are similar in racial and ethnic background to the child's own family.

■ NASW will advocate policies that support the systematic involvement of child welfare agencies with foster parents. Foster parents should be trained and compensated and receive continuous support commensurate with their level of skills.

Principles related to adoption include the following:

■ All parties to adoption are individuals whose needs and rights should be respected and considered to the greatest extent possible. Full recognition must be given to a child's right to and need for ties to his or her birth family and the right of those birth parents, regardless of their condition, to the services they may need to parent their child and prevent the need for adoption. The child must, nevertheless, be seen as the primary client whose need for a permanent plan must take priority.

■ Adoption policy and practice should recognize that services should be extended to all parties who are involved in the adoption and should be made available for as long as they are needed and desired. Thus services may be provided, if needed, long beyond the legal consummation of the adoption.

■ Special attention should be given to children with special needs (children who are older; physically, intellectually, or emotionally handicapped; members of sibling groups; and of minority backgrounds), to ensure protection of their right to a caring environment. This care extends to the recruitment of appropriate families and professional services throughout the adoption process and beyond legalization.

■ Publicly funded subsidies should be available in all cases in which the cost of the child's permanent care becomes a barrier to appropriate adoptive placement. Adoption subsidies must be available to meet the child's special needs. Also, if adoption subsidies are needed through the child's minority years and transition to adulthood, the subsidies must be adequate.

■ The provision of current, viable information to all parties involved in the adoption is the responsibility of the agency. The identifying nature of the information shared is based on the law or the agreement of the parties affected. No information is to be provided to anyone other than those who are directly affected by the adoption (the adopted person, birth family, and adoptive family). Care must be taken before sharing information about a person who previously has been assured confidentiality. Efforts should be made to gain the consent of a person who had been assured confidentiality. Compelling professional reasons should allow for the sharing of identifying information. The need and right of adoptees to know their birth origin should be recognized and respected. This right extends to requests from adult adoptees for identifying information. If a reunion is requested with a birth relative, the service providers should attempt to provide counseling and intermediary services, being fully cognizant of the sensitivities of all the parties involved. Both adoptive parents and birth parents should be informed of the limits of confidentiality.

■ The social work profession, along with social agencies, has a responsibility to advocate for appropriate changes in the law and the training of social workers that would facilitate the sharing of identifying information between adult adoptees and birth parents when both parties are in agreement. When indicated, the adoptive parent should be involved in this process.

■ The recruitment of and placement with adoptive parents from each relevant ethnic or racial group should be available to meet the needs of children.

■ NASW opposes placements made by third parties who are not related to the child or who are not licensed as placement agencies. The reason for this opposition is the need to protect the rights and ensure the welfare of children through the careful preplacement selection and early monitoring of placements by qualified professionals. However, in states in which placements by third parties are legally recognized, NASW advocates that the assessment and supervision of adoptive families and children be carried out by professionally trained social workers. In such states, NASW will continue to support appropriate legislation to eliminate third-party placements.

Policy statement approved by the NASW Delegate Assembly, November 1987; reconfirmed by the Delegate Assembly, August 1993. This statement supersedes the policy statement on Foster Care and Adoption approved by the Delegate Assembly in 1979. For further information, contact the National Association of Social Workers, 750 First Street, NE, Suite 700, Washington, DC 20002-4241. Telephone: 202-408-8600 or 800-638-8799.

Full and Equitable Employment

BACKGROUND

Jobs and income are foundations for the well-being of workers, families, and communities. Although standards of living continue to improve for some, millions of Americans face a growing crisis because of rising job losses, plant closures, the demise of livelihoods and careers, and a decline in wages and benefits. Frequent recessions, technological change and automation, the shifting demands for goods and services, and the growing exportation of jobs and industries to developing nations not only increase job displacement, but impair the functioning of individuals and communities and the capacity of social welfare programs to keep pace with rising human needs. Contradictory scenarios about the future of work opportunities predict, on the one hand, surplus jobs and labor shortages by the 1990s and, on the other hand, uncertain work opportunities caused by an economy marked by a growth in joblessness.

The current restructuring of the U.S. economy has implications for the more equitable distribution of jobs, livelihoods, wages, and benefits and for workers' opportunities to use their skills and talents to achieve their full wage-earning potential. How jobs and income are allocated determines the stratification of society and shapes the quality of people's lives. Because of the strong work ethic in the United States, work takes on heightened meaning; one's occupation and employment status may define not only one's identity, but one's sense of self-worth and of value to the wider community.

In the United States, the allocation of jobs has disproportionately excluded many groups. Racial and ethnic minorities, women, the disabled, sexual minorities, youths, and older workers experience inequitable access to employment, and they may encounter discrimination in their pursuits of jobs and job mobility. Unfortunately, unemployment rates do not portray the full picture of joblessness because they exclude workers who are too discouraged or impaired by joblessness to seek work and workers who are employed only a few hours a week.

Despite proclamations and laws that have attempted to address the job gap in the United States, the fundamental practice of maintaining a surplus of workers persists. Rationales for this practice have varied through the centuries. The jobless conditions of workers and families that gave rise to the Poor Law of 1601 have recurred in recent centuries, and today these conditions have created the crisis that is displacing workers and their families from their livelihoods. In England, the economic transformation from an agrarian to a mercantile economy resulted in homelessness, starvation, looting, and begging. The first Poor Law, which created workhouses for the control and support of unemployed workers and their families, was based on the premise that a surplus of workers was necessary to keep wages low and the power of workers curbed.

Currently, barriers to full and equitable employment in the United States are based on claims, rooted in the tenets of the early Poor Laws, that full employment would be inflationary because it would give workers too much bargaining power. Although noted economists argue that targeted job generation for all who wish to work would not be inflationary, fears of full employment persist.

Calls for full employment for all who wish to work grew in the 1930s during the Roosevelt era and re-emerged after World War II; the calls culminated in the Employment Act of 1946, which called for maximum employment opportunities. The Full Employment and Balanced National Growth Act of 1978 called for reducing unemployment rates to 4 percent by 1983, but it has not been implemented. Official yardsticks for full employment have been based on unemployment rates that are pegged high enough to check inflation. Thus, in the 1960s, full employment was considered to be 4.5 percent unemployment; in the 1970s, 6 percent unemployment; and in the 1980s, as high as 8 percent unemployment. Moreover, in the past two decades, policy approaches that have deliberately used tightened monetary policies to induce recessions as curbs to inflation have resulted in stagflation, in which unemployment and inflation rise together. Therefore, the unemployment–inflation trade-off theory has been repudiated.

Gender-role segregation also excludes workers. Because society has designated the family as women's domain and women are required to be primary caregivers for family members, women have difficulty obtaining equitable access to the labor market. Primary caregiving may involve multiple episodes of intensive, round-the-clock work; child rearing; or caring for an elderly or disabled relative. These caregiving roles further exacerbate the exclusion of women because women are not compensated for them, nor can they easily delegate the tasks to others, especially given cutbacks in welfare. In some cases, the caregivers become as impaired as those for whom they are caring. Women essentially remain "on loan" to the labor market because family demands impede their continuous participation in the labor market. Because society views family work roles as women's primary duty, some employers may discriminate against women in hiring and promotion practices, as well as in wage and benefit policies. While their family work roles constitute a free labor resource to society, women as caregivers are vulnerable not only to exclusion from or occupational segregation in the workplace, but to disproportionately heavy workloads when family caregiving is combined with paid employment (women are never jobless, only "payless"). The culturally assigned status of primary caregivers also contributes to women's inequitable impoverishment, especially in their aging years. Persistent occupational segregation impedes wage and job

improvement for women who are in the labor force. In the absence of comparable worth and anti-wage-discrimination laws, women's wages are substantially below those of men.

Social workers daily address the consequences of joblessness that are costly in human and economic terms. Despite the strengths and adaptability of many jobless workers and their families, some cannot withstand the economic chaos and stresses produced by long-term or multiple spells of unemployment. Joblessness and economic insecurity may result in suicide, depression, psychiatric hospitalization, substance abuse, and stress-related health disorders. Family stress may take the form of marital conflict, separation, divorce, battering, child abuse and incest, and a weakened capacity for caregiving. Drug abuse, school dropouts, and poor achievement in school, even in the elementary grades, may be attributed, in part, to the jobless future that awaits many youths whose families, neighborhoods, and regions are afflicted by unemployment and economic stress. Some workers, who are unable to provide for themselves and their families without jobs, may exhaust their resources and life possessions and skid into the ranks of the permanently poor. In the end, they may endure homelessness, operate in a subterranean economy, and sometimes engage in criminal activities.

Although unemployment insurance is a critical aid to jobless people, it is increasingly insufficient in benefit levels and availability. Less than half the jobless people in some states currently draw benefits. When unemployment insurance is available, benefit levels may be inadequate and destabilizing because they may not cover the real living costs of workers and their families. Repossessions, utility shutoffs, and mortgage foreclosures may occur, and families may skid economically downward to welfare-benefit levels that maintain them at poverty-level subsistence.

Many of the symptoms and consequences of unemployment also are the by-products of underemployment, that is, jobs that do not use skills and abilities, that deny workers the chance to work full-time, or that are not commensurate with prior earnings. Underemployment also may affect the functioning of workers, families, and communities.

The lack of participation by workers in decisions in the workplace and in the determination of more equitable allocations of roles and opportunities in the workplace further impedes the use of workers' talents and skills. Jobs should be tools for self-development. In 1989 it was estimated that about one-third of the jobs in the United States were in the secondary sector of the labor market with dead-end futures, low pay, and unstable work careers. All workers should have more equitable access to jobs in the primary sector.

The alienation, powerlessness, and underemployment of workers waste human potential and other valuable resources. When they occur, individuals lose the ability to function appropriately in the family, the workplace, and the community. In the aggregate, there is a deterioration in the functioning of society.

ISSUE STATEMENT

The dislocation of workers from jobs and livelihoods underscores the need for the more equitable allocation of job and income entitlements. Social workers are placed in the reactive position of treating the symptoms and stresses of job displacement and exclusion. The current restructuring of national and global economies heightens the need for more equitable distribution of employment opportunities. Social workers can make major contributions by entering debates on full employment and by documenting the human costs of joblessness and the occupational segregation of workers by race, gender, age, disability, and sexual orientation.

Given the fluctuation in wages and the increase in the number of working poor and working homeless people, many workers and families are engulfed by economic insecurity that is potentially harmful even to future generations. Policy steps are needed to counter the deteriorating incomes of the working poor. One policy step is to increase the minimum wage, which has fallen in purchasing power every year since 1978 and is at its lowest level of relative purchasing power since 1949. The second policy step is to change the earned income tax credit (EITC). Designed in 1975 to encourage paid work by the very poor and last revised in 1986, EITC in 1989 provided a maximum tax credit of $910 for the

families with children who earn between $6,500 and $10,240. The size of the credit peaks at $6,500 of earnings and begins to decline at $10,240; it ends when earnings reach $19,340. If a family has an income that is too low to owe federal income tax but qualifies for a credit, the Internal Revenue Service makes the credit "refundable" and sends a check for the amount for which the family qualifies. A glaring omission in the EITC policy, however, is its lack of an adjustment for family size. The combination of a raise in the minimum wage with a family-size amendment to EITC would constitute a major step in countering the increased disparities in wages that result from the replacement of manufacturing and resource-extraction industries with a service economy.

Other steps are needed because many of the new service-economy jobs are full-time but do not offer health insurance and related benefits. Income-stabilization policies also are critical to prevent the corrosive effects of multiple layoffs, episodes of skidding on and off welfare, and the reliance on temporary contingency jobs that bring uncertain wages to the family each week.

If there are no wages for home-based caregiving, neither women nor men will have equitable access to critical family caregiving roles. Moreover, the lack of compensation for these roles will ensure that they are not considered to be work. Deinstitutionalized populations often depend upon increased family caregiving at a time when women are trying to earn more wages. Some women are forced to decide between their caregiving responsibilities and their paid jobs. Dependent-care subsidies, wages, and comprehensive benefits are some of the supports required to help relieve the double burden of work on the job and in the family and to redress the gender inequities that persist when women carry both provider and caregiver responsibilities.

Dislocated workers often are not given early warning about occupational obsolescence or sufficient retraining and job placement services; consequently, they are uncertain whether they will be recalled to their former line of work. An expectation of recall frequently preempts their job hunting and renders some permanently jobless.

The human costs of unemployment may further impede their re-employment. Early warning about plant closures and occupational-development resources may help reduce the crisis of industrial decline and relocation, as well as the permanent attrition from the labor market that increasingly has affected men during recent recessions. Locally based economic development and full employment initiatives will help to ensure that jobs and investments are tailored to the needs of local communities and that capital remains in the communities.

Intensified economic development is needed in impoverished regions, especially in rural areas where communities are deteriorating socially and economically. The redeployment of economic development resources to groups of unemployed and underemployed workers may foster the formation of cooperatives or collectives to buy out troubled businesses.

If workers, families, communities, and consumer groups do not have increased access to decisions in the workplace that affect their well-being, the high cost of grievances, lawsuits, and damages to human beings will continue to rise. Much work lies ahead to promote more democratic workplaces and to ensure more corporate social responsibility and accountability to the local communities, workforce, and their families. Without improved laws that promote nondiscrimination and enforce affirmative action, comparable worth, and democracy in the workplace, the patterns of excluding oppressed groups will persist. Current efforts to reduce the power of employee groups through union busting, lockouts, and related initiatives must be checked by a policy framework that ensures more control by workers over decisions that affect their performance, their work conditions, their wages and benefits, and the quality of their work lives.

Social workers continue to play critical roles in addressing the human costs of joblessness and underemployment for workers, their families, and communities and the inequitable access of various groups to adequate incomes and socially useful jobs. However, their effectiveness is constrained by the absence of full and equitable national employment policies.

POLICY STATEMENT

The guarantee of a safe and secure job at a decent wage should be the cornerstone of well-being for every citizen who seeks to earn a living in the United States. The right to earn a living through paid work should involve free choice of employment opportunities among socially useful jobs. Those who are unable to work for pay must be ensured an adequate standard of living. It is the policy of the NASW that full and equitable employment should be promoted as a human right in the United States through guarantees of socially useful work and wages that are sufficient for an adequate standard of living.

NASW advocates national policy that includes the following:

■ constitutionally and legally guaranteed rights to freely chosen, socially useful employment suited to individual capacity

■ constitutionally and legally guaranteed rights to an adequate income through wages, benefits, or income transfers to ensure the well-being of workers, families, and communities

■ support and compensation for critical caregiving roles in the family and the more equitable sharing by men and women of these work roles

■ the promotion of federally financed caregiving resources for all ages, including comprehensive health care, comprehensive child care, day care centers, and respite services

■ early warning systems for workers, families, and communities to prevent the unnecessary closure of businesses because of failure and to promote the retention of plants and jobs

■ legislation to require at least six months' notice of proposed plant closings so that workers and communities can plan options for dealing with the closings

■ initiatives that guarantee retraining and job-placement assistance to workers when economic forces and automation displace them from their jobs and livelihoods

■ initiatives that compel compliance with current laws that promote job rights, such as the Employment Act of 1946 and the Full Employment and Balanced National Growth Act of 1978

■ the rebuilding of the economic and employment infrastructure of regions and communities through local planning and supports for the generation of jobs

■ democracy in the workplace that promotes more equitable decision making about the allocation of jobs and the sharing of good and bad aspects of workloads and tasks

■ support for the redesign of production processes to humanize and improve the quality of work for all workers

■ initiatives, such as periodic reduction of the workweek without the loss of income, permanent part-time jobs with adequate wages and benefits, and job sharing, that promote equitable employment

■ updated employment benefits, including a minimum wage that exceeds the poverty level and parental leave time

■ assurance that the handicapped have full opportunities to compete in the job market

■ initiatives to create goal-directed programs for minority youths and young adults that ensure access to the job market, improve early experience in the workplace, and sustain the continued employability of these new workers

■ a revised Earned Income Tax Credit that includes an amount adjusted upward according to the number of children in the family

■ support for comparable-worth legislation and the concept of "equal pay for equivalent work" as part of a broader effort to close the current gender gap in income

■ legislation that prohibits discrimination in hiring and promotion policies on the basis of race, sex, sexual orientation, age, physical challenge or developmental and mental disability, and religious belief

■ cooperation with labor unions in the promotion and protection of workers' employment rights and support for the rights of workers to organize and bargain collectively on their own behalf.

Policy statement approved by the NASW Delegate Assembly, August 1990. Referred to the 1999 Delegate Assembly, to be revised and combined with the policy statement on Economic Policy. This statement supersedes the policy statement on Full and Equitable Employment approved by the Delegate Assembly in 1987. For further information, contact the National Association of Social Workers, 750 First Street, NE, Suite 700, Washington, DC 20002-4241. Telephone: 202-408-8600 or 800-638-8799.

Gender-, Ethnic-, and Race-Based Workplace Discrimination

BACKGROUND

Most analyses of wage discrimination and other workplace-related issues analyze either gender or race and ethnicity separately. However, because patterns of employment discrimination by gender and by race and ethnicity intersect and reinforce each other, it is most useful to consider them together. Doing so should not obscure the fact that African Americans, Native Americans, and Americans in each of the different Spanish-speaking and Asian ethnic and cultural groups have their own unique histories of employment on this continent and have faced their own particular forms of oppression and discrimination at different times in the history of this nation (Amott & Matthei, 1991; Glenn, 1985). In addition, men and women in each of these groups not only have shared many experiences of oppression but also have had experiences of oppression that have been unique; when it comes to employment, gender has affected patterns of work and employment-related discrimination within each of these groups. Most analysts agree that race, ethnicity, class, and gender together powerfully shape social and economic life in America (Amott & Matthei, 1991; Glenn, 1985; Rothenberg, 1995), and these "differences in race, class and gender are very costly for some and very profitable for others" (Rothenberg, 1995, p. 117).

Differences in Earnings

Although the extent to which earnings differentials by gender and race and ethnicity result from discrimination is disputed widely, research has repeatedly shown that the earnings gap between white American men and both white American women and men and women of all other racial and ethnic groups cannot be explained fully by training, education, work experience, or attachment to the labor force (Freeman, 1991). For example, "in 1992, [white] women with college degrees earned $11,721 less per year than their white male colleagues, and only $1,916 more per year than white men with only a high school diploma. . . . College educated Hispanic women actually earned less than white men who had never taken a college course" (National Committee on Pay Equity, 1995, pp. 147–148). Discrimination alone accounts for a significant proportion of the wage gap between white women and men and women of color compared with white men (Freeman, 1991; National Committee on Pay Equity, 1995).

In 1992 women constituted about 46 percent of all workers, and people classified as members of "nonwhite" racial and ethnic groups made up 14.5 percent of all workers in the civilian labor force (National Committee on Pay Equity, 1995). More people from these groups do not have access to paid employment at all; "in any given month, Hispanic unemployment is 50% higher than the rate for whites, and black unemployment is 2.5 times as high" (Business–Higher Education Forum, 1995, p. 1). Focusing on those who do work and using the somewhat limited data on race and ethnicity and earnings supplied by the U.S. Department of Labor, statistics clearly demonstrate that white American men continue to fare better in the labor market than any other group of wage earners: Median weekly earnings for full-time workers in 1992 were $518 for white men, $388 for white women, $380 for African American men, $336 for African American women, $345 for Hispanic men, and $303 for Hispanic women (U.S. Department of Commerce, 1993). Based on year-round, full-time earnings in 1992, on average African American men earned 72.1 percent and Hispanic men earned 64.6 percent of what white men earned; white women earned 69.8 percent, African American women earned 63.9 percent, and Hispanic women earned 55.3 percent of what white men earned (no data were available on Asian American or Native American men or women) (National Committee on Pay Equity, 1995). Although the specific percentage differentials between groups of workers have fluctuated over time, the basic pattern of difference has persisted for decades (Freeman, 1991; National Committee on Pay Equity, 1995). In addition, although most women are employed full-time, women predominate in part-time employment, constituting 43 percent of full-time workers and 66 percent of part-time workers (U.S. Department of Commerce, 1993).

Because of the lower earnings of women, families maintained solely by women are disadvantaged economically; in 1992, the median weekly earnings of families maintained by women of all racial and ethnic groups were $385, whereas married couple families earned $779. The figures for African American and Hispanic families headed by women were $328 and $341, respectively. As a result, although 12.8 percent of all American families had incomes below the poverty level in 1991, 34.3 percent of all female-headed families and 55.5 percent of female-headed families with children under 18 years present lived in poverty (U.S. Department of Commerce, 1993). Thus, the low earnings of women, especially African American, Hispanic, and Native American women, have major effects on children; low wages for women are a major cause of child poverty. Even without children present, being female and being a member of one of these racial and ethnic groups each contributed to the chances of being poor: Poverty rates are approximately one in 10 for white men and women, one in three for white female heads of households, one in three for Hispanic men and women, one in two for Hispanic female heads of households, one in three for African American men and women, and one in two for African American female heads of households, demonstrating that race and gender each have a powerful influence on poverty in America (Mantsios, 1995). Because 11.9 million American households are now headed by women and 67.8 percent of married women with children now

work (U.S. Department of Commerce, 1993), pay equity by gender and by race and ethnicity is essential if the suffering of children in poverty is to be eliminated.

Because the majority of American families have two earners, members of all families, including men, suffer from the low earnings of women and of people of color; a woman's earnings now constitute on average 50 percent of African American family income (Freeman, 1991), 40 percent of Hispanic family income, and 35 percent of white family income (American Association of University Women Educational Foundation, 1992). Were women in each of these groups to earn more, all families would benefit, and were African American and Hispanic men to earn more, their families, too, would benefit.

Occupational Segregation

Occupational segregation (that is, the sex-typing and racial categorization of jobs and the assignment of the lowest paying jobs to women and people of color) also characterizes the American economy. Occupational segregation is thought to be a major cause of gender-, ethnic-, and race- or ethnicity-related earnings differentials (National Committee on Pay Equity, 1995), because most of the jobs assigned to women and to people of color are in what is termed the "secondary labor market" (that is, in jobs that are characterized by lower pay, less stability, and fewer employment-related benefits).

Occupational segregation results in the "crowding" of women and of people of color into a narrow range of professions and occupations. For example, in 1992 women were 99.0 percent of all secretaries, 98.8 percent of all preschool and kindergarten teachers, and 93.5 percent of all registered nurses. Also in 1992, women were only 8.2 percent of all precision, production, craft, and repair workers and 8.7 percent of all engineers. Chicanas and Puerto Rican women living in the United States have the smallest proportion of workers with jobs in higher-level segments of the primary labor market compared with white men and with women in other racial and ethnic groups (Amott & Matthei, 1991).

In reality, not all occupations are equally open to all groups. For example, among executives, administrators, and managers in the private sector, 49 percent are white men and 36 percent are white women, whereas only 2 percent are African American men and another 2 percent are African American women (Berry, 1995). Occupational segregation results in the concentration of people from specific gender and racial and ethnic groups (except white American men) in a relatively small number of professions and occupations. This concentration has the effect of keeping wages down in the occupations with high concentrations of women or people from different racial and ethnic groups. In addition, many argue that low wages for these groups have the additional effect of keeping labor costs low in the economy as a whole (Abramovitz, 1988).

One characteristic of the occupational groups in which women who are employed are concentrated, and especially women from different racial and ethnic groups, is that many of them are involved with domestic work or service work that replaces the household work of others. Historically, social practice and social policy have rewarded and protected the unpaid family work of white middle- and upper-class women; programs such as Aid to Families with Dependent Children were originally begun so that white widows would be able to rear their dependent children without having to resort to paid employment (Miller, 1992). However, the household and child-rearing work of women from different racial and ethnic groups in relation to their own dependent children has not been so protected (Abramovitz, 1988; Glenn, 1985), although the specific ways in which this phenomenon has played out has differed for each racial and ethnic group depending on its immigration history, the forms of oppression the group as a whole has encountered in the United States, and the content of the dominant stereotypes of each group (Amott & Matthei, 1991; Glenn, 1985). In fact, some groups of women, such as African American, some Asian and Pacific Islander, and some Hispanic women, have commonly been employed to do the child-rearing and household work of affluent white women, and both men and women of color are often employed in the secondary labor market and the service sectors of the economy in devalued and poorly paid "dirty work" (Gilkes, 1990). Thus, what Abramovitz (1988) has termed "the family ethic" (p. 3) has been applied quite differently to ratio-

nalize the work of men and women and that of white Americans compared with people from different racial and ethnic groups.

It has been argued that women can obtain job and pay equity by pursuing employment in "nontraditional" occupations (that is, jobs in which men have historically outnumbered women). Considerable effort has also been expended by some to prepare and recruit people from different racial and ethnic groups to enter occupations, professions, and fields from which they have traditionally been excluded (that is, jobs in which white American men have traditionally predominated). Although these strategies may be useful, it is also important to ensure that workers are equitably compensated even if they continue to hold "female" or "minority" jobs.

Employment Benefits

An important consequence of the lower earnings and different jobs held by women and by men from different racial and ethnic groups is the effect of these patterns of employment on work-related benefits. The U.S. economy is organized in such a way that access to many economic resources in addition to income is determined by paid employment. Access to and levels of benefits from such publicly supported federal social insurance programs as unemployment insurance and Old Age and Survivors Disability Insurance benefits for workers who are older and disabled and their dependents, as well as from such state-controlled systems as workers' compensation, are determined by a person's (or their spouse's) level of compensation and tenure on the job. White American male workers have traditionally received higher levels of benefits from these programs than others because they are less likely to be underemployed or more likely to be employed in jobs with greater stability or with higher levels of compensation (Ozawa, 1989). The same is true of access to such privately funded job-related benefits as pension plans and affordable health insurance. The pattern of distribution of these noncash benefits mirrors and reinforces the pattern of earnings differences in which white American men tend to get more than women and than men from other racial and ethnic groups.

These differences in employment-related benefits affect these workers and their families not only during their years of employment but also during retirement, because retirement income programs, both public and private, are involved. Thus, these employment-related differences contribute substantially to the higher rates of poverty that white women, especially those living alone, and men and women of color suffer in old age (Crawley, 1994). For example, the median income for all older African Americans was 59.6 percent of older white Americans, and the median income of older African American women was only 67.6 percent of that for older white women (Crawley, 1994).

Family Work

One of the explanations sometimes offered for the lower earnings and different jobs of women is their greater involvement in the care of their households and their children, in what Hochschild (1989) has called "the second shift." Despite raising rates of labor force participation by women in all racial and ethnic groups in the past several decades, there has been little change in the participation of men in child rearing and other forms of housework (Hochschild, 1989). Moreover, the household tasks that men are typically involved in at home are the most flexible (that is, they are the least demanding on a daily basis and tend to interfere less with employment outside the home). However, although there is considerable evidence that women, especially women with dependent children living at home, enjoy less leisure than men because of their household responsibilities, these responsibilities interfere little, if at all, with employment or productivity on the job and cannot fully explain the lower earnings of women on the job.

Sexual Harassment

Another factor to be considered in relation to employment-related equity is harassment on the job. Sexual harassment can take two forms: (1) "quid pro quo," when sexual favors are demanded to keep or advance in a job, and (2) "hostile working environment," in which women are made to feel uncomfortable on the job through remarks and other messages from coworkers because of their gender. There is some evidence that women in nontraditional occupations face sexual harassment more commonly than other female workers do. Most women who encounter sexual harassment on the job either simply put up with it or leave their jobs (Miller, 1992), even though harassment on the job is a civil rights violation. Harassment because of race or ethnicity happens to both men and women, and there is some evidence that women of color may be more frequently targeted for sexual harassment than white women, although their responses to it may be different.

Obstacles on the Job

A major factor contributing to the lower earnings of women and of people from different racial and ethnic groups is a lack of advancement opportunities on the job, termed the "glass ceiling." The U.S. Department of Labor (1991) described the problem in corporate America as follows:

Minorities and women have made significant gains at the entry level of employment and into the first levels of management. Yet they have not experienced similar gains into the mid and senior levels of management, notwithstanding increased experience, credentials, overall qualifications, and a greater attachment to the workforce. . . . The barriers to the upper rungs of the corporate ladder for minority women appear to be nearly impenetrable. (pp. 6–7)

The Department of Labor's own study of selected major U.S. corporations showed, for example, that the companies had "a level beyond which few minorities and women had either advanced or been recruited, and minorities tended to be found at lower levels of management than women" (p. 13). These patterns seem to result from poor and limited recruitment practices; failure to afford women and workers of color the developmental experiences on the job that would prepare them for advancement, sometimes termed the problem of the "glass wall" (Lopez, 1995); and a failure to make equal opportunity a commitment of the total organization.

Even in occupations and professions in which women predominate numerically, the glass ceiling has a major effect (Mason, 1992). This situation unfortunately pertains to the social work profession as well; recent studies have shown that women are paid less compared with men and also are less likely to advance within the profession than men (Gibelman & Schervish, 1993, 1996). In addition, within the field of social work as a whole, women from different racial and ethnic groups are disproportionately found in the lowest level or paraprofessional positions (Martin & Chernesky, 1989). Although the earnings and advancement gaps in social work may be less than they are in other professions (Sokoloff, 1988), given the profession's commitment to ending discrimination in all forms and to developing diversity within the profession that will mirror the diversity in U.S. society, any gender-, ethnic-, or race-based discrimination within the profession is cause for concern.

ISSUE STATEMENT

NASW and the social work profession have long been concerned with working to eliminate discrimination in all forms. This commitment is embodied in the *NASW Code of Ethics* (NASW, 1996) and determines the major policies that NASW supports. Unfortunately, discrimination based on race, ethnicity, and gender continues to be pervasive in modern American life. Discrimination against women and people of color has an enormous and pernicious impact on the lives of the diverse clients that the social work profession and NASW members serve. It also affects NASW members who are women (the majority of members) and those who are members of diverse racial and ethnic groups. American society and social policy are organized in such a way that employment is the major means for distributing income and most other essential material social benefits, such as health insurance, public and private retirement plans, and disability insurance, as well as many nonmaterial benefits such as status and prestige. The 1993 Delegate Assembly voted to retain both a general statement on women's issues and a more specific statement on workplace discrimination. For these reasons, it is essential that NASW continue to have a strong and up-to-date policy statement addressing discrimination in the workplace to guide the association and its

members in practice, advocacy, and policy development activities.

This proposed revision improves on the previous one in several ways. Its title has been broadened to include other forms of workplace discrimination, not just wage discrimination, because wage discrimination itself is part but not all of the problem. Other discriminatory workplace policies and practices, such as those affecting advancement, training, and the working environment for those who are not white American men, limit opportunities for advancement and for participation in organizational decision making. These other forms of discrimination interact with wage discrimination to affect earnings, benefits, occupations, and personal and household income. Nevertheless, wage discrimination itself unfortunately remains part of the problem.

In the United States, wage and income disparities between women from all groups and men from different racial and ethnic groups and white American men have unfortunately been a persistent feature of economic and social life. The wages and other work-related benefits, including religious and ethnic holidays, women and men receive from other racial and ethnic groups have historically been and remain lower than those enjoyed by white men. Despite federal and state civil rights legislation, affirmative action programs, and other legislative and policy efforts to reduce these differences in the past several decades, differences in earnings and other employment-related benefits based on race and gender have not disappeared and have been only slightly reduced.

Several different explanations have been offered for the persistence of gender-, ethnic-, and race-based differences in earnings and income. One hypothesis takes a human capital approach, suggesting that many women and workers who are from different racial and ethnic groups are different from white men in their productive capacity, usually because of their level of education; experience in the labor force; or, in the case of women, role responsibilities in the family that tend to limit their productivity or commitment to employment. Another hypothesis emphasizes the occupational segregation by gender, ethnicity, and race that characterizes employment in the United States. This segregation results in the crowding of women of all groups and of men of color into a narrow range of occupations, in particular into occupations or subfields within occupations with low pay, low status, little job stability, limited opportunities for advancement, and few employment-related benefits. Sweatshops continue to exist in the United States. Employers are increasingly outsourcing menial and dangerous tasks to countries without worker protections. Of all groups, women of color are the most discriminated against: The higher the percentage of women of color in an occupation, the closer the occupation is to the lowest earning level. Whatever the explanation, differences in earnings and other employment-related benefits based on gender, race, and ethnicity affect the well-being of workers in general and social work clients in particular.

POLICY STATEMENT

Given the persistence and pervasiveness of gender-, ethnic-, and race-based workplace discrimination, pay and employment equity must remain a major policy issue for the social work profession and for the nation. The many aspects of the problem require that the solutions pursued also be multifaceted (Davis, 1994; Miller, 1992). NASW supports a number of principles and strategies for change in legislative, administrative, and educational areas.

Pay Equity

It is an essential principle of fairness that different people who do the same work be compensated equally without regard to gender, race, ethnicity, age, sexual orientation, marital status, immigration status, or physical ability. Policies to end gender-, ethnic-, and race-based employment discrimination include the following:

■ federal and state legislative measures that aim to eliminate discrimination in employment, training, compensation, and job-related benefits

■ enforcement of all laws and regulations that forbid discrimination in the workplace, including adequate funding for the federal and state agencies charged with the enforcement of civil rights and antidiscrimination laws and regulations

■ public and private affirmative action programs that aim to ensure that women of all groups and men in different racial and ethnic groups have access to employment, opportunities for advancement, nondiscriminatory working conditions, and fair compensation

■ legislative, training, and educational programs that help women from all groups and men from different racial and ethnic groups qualify for and enter occupations and fields from which they have traditionally been excluded, especially those in which white American men have predominated and that tend to offer the highest levels of compensation and benefits

■ adequate funding for social, health, and human services agencies and services so that any gender-, ethnic-, and race-based inequities in employment and compensation that exist in social work and social work agencies can be eliminated

■ elimination of all federal and state measures that unfairly limit employment and otherwise have a negative impact on immigrants and undocumented workers

■ human and civil rights measures to protect all Americans.

There is evidence that men and women of all racial and ethnic groups benefit from unionization (Institute for Women's Policy Research, 1993). Unions with a high proportion of women in their membership have also broadened the scope of their negotiations to include such issues as affirmative action, family leave, and the elimination of sexual harassment on the job (Institute for Women's Policy Research, 1993). Therefore, unionization efforts that incorporate diverse members and progressive employment policies that address gender-, ethnic-, and race-based employment discrimination into their bargaining efforts should be supported.

Comparable Worth

Principles of nondiscrimination, although essential, are not enough to ensure that gender-, ethnic-, and race-based differences in employment and earnings will be eradicated (Mason, 1992). Comparable worth strategies are based on a careful analysis of job skills and responsibilities; compensation is then based on the requirements of the position rather than on standard market forces, which undercompensate the occupations traditionally occupied by larger numbers of women and workers from different racial and ethnic groups. In such a system, the wages of white men are not lowered; rather, the wages of women and others who occupy underpaid positions are raised. However, traditional job evaluation procedures often reinforce race-, ethnic-, and gender-based evaluations of jobs and should not be used to set levels of compensation or benefits. Comparable worth principles and strategies must be included in pay equity legislation, in union negotiating, and in the administration of social work and public and private social services agencies (Freeman, 1991).

Affirmative Action

Affirmative action is another powerful tool that can be used to reduce inequities in the employment of all women and of men from different racial and ethnic groups. Affirmative action policies aim to open hiring systems and procedures and career development and advancement on the job to those who have historically been discriminated against. Affirmative action can be a powerful tool for helping men and women from different racial and ethnic groups gain access to higher paying jobs from which they have traditionally been excluded. It can also help eliminate the glass ceiling that prevents many white women and workers from different racial and ethnic groups from attaining the levels of advancement within their chosen fields that they are qualified to achieve. Affirmative action is one of the few methods identified for reducing the underrepresentation of white women and workers from different racial and ethnic groups in the highest levels of employment in America. NASW reaffirms its commitment to affirmative action in the public and private sectors and will publicize the nature and benefits of well-designed affirmative action programs. Affirmative action should also

be a consideration as employers restructure and downsize.

NASW therefore reaffirms its commitment to its own program of affirmative action within the association, which has succeeded in identifying women of all races and men of color as leaders in the profession. All social work employers, associations of social workers, and social and human services agencies should develop and implement similar affirmative action programs.

Employment-Related Measures

There are many factors that influence employment and many social programs that are influenced by work experience. Thus, policies to eliminate gender-, ethnic-, and race-based employment discrimination and to mitigate its effects must embrace other areas as well:

■ access to high-quality and affordable child care and other forms of dependent care, whether publicly or privately funded, including programs offered at the work site

■ access to the full range of educational and training opportunities for women of all racial and ethnic groups and for men of color and provision of adequate public funding for the programs that are needed to assist the more disadvantaged members of society in gaining access to employment in jobs that provide adequate compensation and benefits

■ comprehensive national and state health insurance programs so that those who do not receive health benefits through their employment and their dependent family members are not without essential health, mental health, and substance abuse services

■ well-designed federal- and state-administered social insurance programs whose benefit structures do not further penalize workers and their families who have already been disadvantaged in the labor market

■ continuing education of social workers, administrators, and social agencies, including those in public social welfare systems, about unbiased job evaluation systems and the importance of incorporating principles of comparable worth, affirmative action, client- and system-focused advocacy, and other administrative strategies that reduce gender-, ethnic-, and race-based employment discrimination

■ education of social work students about the problems of gender-, ethnic-, and race-based employment discrimination as they affect the American workforce as a whole and as they affect social work in particular, including informing them about strategies to reduce these problems

■ programs to inform legislators, administrators, and policymakers so they understand that the realization of full and equal employment opportunity is a societal problem that requires immediate action; that the human and economic costs of gender-, ethnic-, and race-based employment discrimination are unacceptable; and that, by contrast, any economic costs of achieving employment equity are fully justifiable.

REFERENCES

Abramovitz, M. (1988). *Regulating the lives of women: Social welfare policy from colonial times to the present*. Boston: South End Press.

American Association of University Women Educational Foundation. (1992). *How schools shortchange girls: A study of major findings on girls and education*. Washington, DC: Author.

Amott, T. L., & Matthei, J. A. (1991). *Race, gender, and work: A multicultural economic history of women in the United States*. Boston: South End Press.

Berry, M. F. (1995). Affirmative action: Political opportunities exploit racial fears. *Emerge, 6*(7), 29–48.

Business–Higher Education Forum. (1995). Three realities: Minority life in America. In P. S. Rothenberg (Ed.), *Race, class, and gender in the United States: An integrated study* (3rd ed., pp. 152–154). New York: St. Martin's Press.

Crawley, B. (1994). Older women: Public policy issues for the twenty-first century. In L. V. Davis (Ed.), *Building on women's strengths: A social work agenda for the twenty-first century* (pp. 159–178). New York: Haworth Press.

Davis, L. V. (1994). Why we still need a women's agenda for social work. In L. V. Davis (Ed.), *Building on women's strengths: A social work agenda for the twenty-first century* (pp. 1–26). New York: Haworth Press.

Freeman, M. L. (1991). Pay equity and social work. *Affilia, 6*, 7–19.

Gibelman, M., & Schervish, P. H. (1993). The glass ceiling in social work: Is it shatterproof? *Affilia, 8*, 442–455.

Gibelman, M., & Schervish, P. H. (1996). *Who we are: A second look*. Washington, DC: NASW Press.

Gilkes, C. T. (1990). "Liberated to work like dogs!": Labeling Black women and their work. In H. Y. Grossman & N. L. Chester (Eds.), *The experience and meaning of work in women's lives* (pp. 165–188). Hillsdale, NJ: Lawrence Erlbaum.

Glenn, E. N. (1985). Racial ethnic women's labor: The intersection of race, gender and class oppression. *Review of Radical Political Economics, 17*(3), 86–108.

Hochschild, A. (1989). *The second shift: Working parents and the revolution at home*. New York: Viking.

Institute for Women's Policy Research. (1993). *What do unions do for women?* Washington, DC: Author.

Lopez, J. A. (1995). Women face glass walls as well as glass ceilings. In P. S. Rothenberg (Ed.), *Race, class, and gender in the United States: An integrated study* (3rd ed., pp. 151–152). New York: St. Martin's Press.

Mantsios, G. (1995). Class in America: Myths and realities. In P. S. Rothenberg (Ed.), *Race, class, and gender in the United States: An integrated study* (3rd ed., pp. 131–143). New York: St. Martin's Press.

Martin, P. Y., & Chernesky, R. H. (1989). Women's prospects for leadership in social welfare: A political economy perspective. *Administration in Social Work, 13*(3/4), 117–143.

Mason, M. A. (1992). Standing still in the workplace: Women in social work and other female-dominated occupations. *Affilia, 7*(3), 23–43.

Miller, D. C. (1992). *Women and social welfare: A feminist analysis*. New York: Praeger.

National Association of Social Workers. (1996). *NASW code of ethics*. Washington, DC: NASW Press.

National Committee on Pay Equity. (1995). In P. S. Rothenberg (Ed.), *Race, class, and gender in the United States: An integrated study* (3rd ed., pp. 144–151). New York: St. Martin's Press.

Ozawa, M. N. (Ed.). (1989). *Women's life cycle and economic insecurity: Problems and proposals.* Westport, CT: Praeger.

Rothenberg, P. S. (1995). *Race, class, and gender in the United States: An integrated study* (3rd ed.). New York: St. Martin's Press.

Sokoloff, N. J. (1988). Evaluating gains and losses by black and white women and men in the professions, 1960–1980. *Social Problems, 35*(1), 336–340.

U.S. Department of Commerce. (1993). *Statistical abstract of the United States* (113th ed.). Lanham, MD: Bernan Press.

U.S. Department of Labor. (1991). *Report on the glass ceiling initiative.* Washington, DC: U.S. Government Printing Office.

Policy statement approved by the NASW Delegate Assembly, August 1996. This policy supersedes the policy statement on Elimination of Sex- and Race-Based Wage Discrimination approved by the Delegate Assembly in 1987. For further information, contact the National Association of Social Workers, 750 First Street, NE, Suite 700, Washington, DC 20002-4241. Telephone: 202-408-8600 or 800-638-8799.

Health Care Financing

BACKGROUND

NASW has taken the lead in developing a far-reaching and comprehensive proposal for national health care (*Congressional Record,* May 22, 1990). Until the proposal is implemented legislatively, social workers, by virtue of their range of expertise and responsibilities within the health care delivery system, must be involved in evaluating and improving the accessibility and quality of care for patients under prospective payment systems (PPS). The careful analysis of this method of reimbursement for the costs of hospital care is urgent and timely because PPS will continue to be used at both the state and federal levels. All-payor systems (including Medicaid and private insurance, as well as Medicare), which are based on prospective case-based pricing, are likely to affect psychiatric and medical care provided in institutional and community-based settings.

PPS, which Congress established as part of the Social Security Act Amendments of 1983, is considered the most radical change in the history of Medicare. Until 1983, Medicare reimbursed hospitals retrospectively for their costs, an action also known as cost-plus reimbursement. Attempts to contain skyrocketing costs in the 1970s through peer review or professional standards review organizations and health planning mechanisms or health systems agencies were ineffective, primarily because these programs included few sanctions. In 1983, Congress mandated prospective pricing. By basing reimbursement on a fixed rate per case, set prospectively rather than retroactively, PPS has reversed the financial incentives by which Medicare had compensated hospitals for services to patients. The rate of reimbursement is based on a system of close to 500 diagnosis-related groups (DRGs), categories of illness that are calculated

on the national average of cost per diagnosis. The national policy on Medicare PPS is set by the Health Care Financing Administration (HCFA) of the U.S. Department of Health and Human Services. It is implemented through statewide and regional peer review organizations (PROs). PROs initially were established to monitor cost containment; more recently, they were mandated to monitor the quality of care that hospitals provide.

NASW has the responsibility to ensure that the development and implementation of a health financing policy reflects social work perspectives and values. In 1979, the NASW Delegate Assembly endorsed, as part of its policy statement on national health, the development of prospective or predetermined schedules of reimbursement rates. It did so within the context of a national health care program that would ensure equal access to comprehensive services that maintain optimal health, prevent illness and disability, ameliorate the effects of unavoidable functional incapacities, and provide supportive long-term and terminal care.

In the NASW national health care proposal (*Congressional Record,* May 22, 1990), any proposals for health care financing must begin from the perspective that ensures patients the right to a comprehensive continuum of health care, regardless of race, financial status, ethnicity, religion, age, gender, sexual orientation, or geographic location.

ISSUE STATEMENT

The explicit philosophy behind PPS is cost containment of health care in hospitals and shifting the responsibility of care for nonacute patients to nonhospital settings. The former reimbursement policy, insufficiently regulated, encouraged the inefficient use of resources, unnecessary diagnostic and treatment procedures, and lengthy hospital stays; in general, the policy erred on the side of overuse or, in the extreme, abuse of the system. The current PPSs/DRG policy, without careful monitoring, encourages the opposite; in general, the policy errs on the side of too little or neglect of the system. Cost containment, although it is an acceptable goal, should not be pursued at the expense of necessary, high-quality, and comprehensive care. Reviews of the use of PPS/DRGs during the first five years have been mixed, depending upon the reviewer and the criteria used. In some areas and with some types of hospitals, shorter lengths of stay, the reduced use of services, and increased profits have resulted.

The PPS policy has been likened to the "psychiatric deinstitutionalization" policy of the past 20 years. Originally intended by progressive people to provide for a comprehensive system of community-based health services, PPS clearly has resulted in the curtailment of access to or discharge from hospitals, without an adequate continuing health care system to meet the needs of many patients. Unlike deinstitutionalized psychiatric patients, many of those who are discharged as a result of the PPS cost-containment policies are not in the public's eye. These patients tend to disappear into their own homes (however inadequate) or overstressed family systems or become the burden of long-term health care facilities. Often patients return to the acute-care hospital periodically in a more debilitated state than they were previously. This phenomenon is known as the "revolving door" syndrome.

By limiting its focus to cutting hospital costs, the PPS policy does not address a patient's total health care needs. This formal and emphatic injection of marketplace values into American medical care reflects a philosophy of retrenchment that moves in the direction of "back to the almshouse." In the past, hospitals were used to compensate for inadequate community resources and for the general lack of general preventive social and rehabilitative services. Financing patterns allowed patients to be admitted to and to stay in hospitals and encouraged the expansion of hospital-centered health care. Encouraging a more appropriate use of inpatient hospital care

through incentives is laudable, but such a policy now requires that services that were once provided in hospitals or that were neglected because their costs were not reimbursed as outpatient services be available and affordable elsewhere. Paradoxically, at a time of greater need for non-hospital-based services, cutbacks and regulatory restrictions are occurring in Medicare, Medicaid, home care, long-term care, primary care, and other related services to patients and their families.

There is increasing evidence that many patients are being denied admission to hospitals under PPS, whereas others are being admitted when they are sicker or are being discharged in a less recovered state than under the previous system. This situation is commonly referred to as the "quicker and sicker" syndrome. NASW's Commission on Health and Mental Health conducted a study during 1988–89 of the 55 NASW chapters on the impact of prospective payment systems on social work's ability to provide high-quality care to patients. The study revealed that patients, families, and the professionals who were trying to care for them encountered myriad serious problems because of shorter stays, early discharge, and the lack of adequate or affordable resources outside hospitals. Social workers reported that the quality and scope of social work services have diminished under the DRG-related pressure, although in many settings the discharge-planning function has strengthened the influence of social work inside and outside the hospital.

When the PPS strategy is combined with the situations of many elderly and poor patients, additional problems ensue. The health crises of these groups often are characterized by chronic illness, a multiplicity of interacting ailments and impairments, and fluctuating mental impairment that is exacerbated by social and economic factors. The rigid and limited disease-specific DRG formula, based on a primary diagnosis (even with age factored in) is inadequate for dealing with the needs of many patients, particularly the elderly and the poor. A far broader definition of illness is required—one that goes beyond a narrow medical assessment and acknowledges the complex interrelationship of the social and physical needs of these populations.

The PPS hospital-reimbursement formula runs counter to the principle that the health care system should provide a complex network of inter-dependent services along a continuum of care. The acute-care hospital is but one point along a continuum that must include preventive and primary care at the front end. At the other end are chronic-care hospitals, rehabilitation centers, nursing homes, hospices, and home care provided by families and a range of providers. However, at this point, reimbursement is geared only to acute-care hospitalization and is based on strict medical criteria. The effect has been the restriction of continuation of care. Responsibility for care has shifted to alternative points along the continuum with no corresponding increases in services or financing and with restrictive policies on currently reimbursable care.

Pressure from consumer and health advocates, including NASW, has resulted in some congressional protections that are designed to strengthen and safeguard patients' rights to high-quality care by establishing an elaborate appeals process for patients who are denied continued hospitalization. Some states like New York and Massachusetts have instituted even more elaborate procedures. However, the protection is limited and weak because of inadequate resources for implementation and enforcement, thereby rendering these to be empty rights. Many patients and their families are confused by or ignorant of the complex appeals system. Attempts to improve discharge planning are a step in the right direction, but they do not always ensure that timely, informed, realistic, and safe plans are professionally established or implemented by social workers. Pressure on HCFA to strengthen the monitoring function of PROs in the interest of the quality, as well as the cost, of care has resulted in some needed improvements, such as "written complaint authority" with respect to treatment in emergency rooms, nursing homes, and home health agencies, as well as in hospitals, and "intervening care review" for patients who are readmitted to hospitals within 30 days.

POLICY STATEMENT

The National Association of Social Workers (NASW) put forth in 1990 a far-reaching and comprehensive proposal for the complete reorganization of health care in this country. How-ever, until such a program is enacted, the current Medicare PPS system and similar systems at the state level must be immediately improved.

■ Congress must mandate the Health Care Financing Administration (HCFA) to define the term *social* criteria immediately, so that peer review organizations (PROs) can more appropriately and comprehensively interpret the concept of *medically necessary* care used in determining the need for continued hospitalization. The definition should include not only factors that affect medical status, such as the patient's readiness to leave, but the support and service network in place or the lack of adequate alternatives. Hospitals should not be penalized financially for the absence of available or affordable outside resources.

■ Formulation of the DRG categories must be adjusted so that PROs can assess a broader range of factors that affect the need for and length of stay in hospitals. DRG classifications should recognize the social and economic factors that affect the severity and chronicity of illness. These factors include homelessness, impaired mental functioning, and poor nutritional status, among others. Indicators need to take into consideration the severity of illnesses and the interactive nature of multiple physical ailments.

■ PROs should be expanded, with adequate staff, to monitor pre- and posthospital status, without a patient having to ask for a preadmission denial form. In addition, they must ensure that hospitals inform patients of the functions of the PROs in monitoring the quality of care. PROs also should investigate and publicly report excessive transfers of patients from private to public hospitals and other flagrant abuses of patients' rights.

■ Social workers must be included as PRO reviewers and staff to ensure that social status and social criteria are part of medical diagnosis and treatment and to promote proper discharge planning and implementation of the discharge plan. Social workers and others who perform this function are ethically and legally bound to make safe and reasonable plans, and they should be accountable for them, without being held responsible for the lack of appropriate community resources.

■ Because discharge planning—or, more appropriately, continuity-of-care planning—is mandated, it must be covered by Medicare and receive appropriate financial resources, guidelines, and support for social workers to carry out this vital professional function properly.

■ The protection-and-appeals process for patients needs strengthening, simplification, and standardization. HCFA's patients' rights message should be sent regularly to all social security–Medicare recipients to alert them to the process before they require hospitalization. The statement should be clear and available in different languages, and it should be signed by patients at the time of or shortly after their admission to hospitals. There should be no liability to the patient during an appeal.

■ Social workers and other advocates should inform clients in all health settings of their rights as defined in state health laws and hospital policies. Patients must be informed that they have the right to have all decisions about their care made on medical, not financial, grounds. Social workers should guide and support patients through the complicated review process. Penalties for deliberate and pervasive violations of patients' rights should be assessed at appropriate levels.

■ An HCFA/Medicare-funded system of patient advocates or ombudspeople should be established in the community to assist vulnerable patients and their families and to monitor the activities of hospitals and PROs. Social workers should inform patients of independent health advocacy resources that are available to patients and their families.

■ Public funds should be provided for the training and education of consumers of health care, especially the elderly. Education should stress that discharge planning is an activity that should begin before hospitalization. Social workers should help educate families on how to apply for financial benefits and community resources, as well as on the gaps in eligibility and services. Lay advocates should be trained to help families understand and use appropriate patients' rights and protections.

■ NASW will continue to pursue the attainment of its national health care proposal through congressional sponsorship and passage.

Policy statement approved by the NASW Delegate Assembly, August 1990. Referred to the 1999 Delegate Assembly, to be combined with the policy statement on Health Care. For further information, contact the National Association of Social Workers, 750 First Street, NE, Suite 700, Washington, DC 20002-4241. Telephone: 202-408-8600 or 800-638-8799.

HIV/AIDS

BACKGROUND

The human immunodeficiency virus (HIV) causes a complex, nondiscriminant infection that progresses to acquired immunodeficiency syndrome. AIDS is a specific group of diseases or conditions that impair the human body's immune system and render it vulnerable to rare and most often fatal diseases. Such conditions include Kaposi's sarcoma, *Pneumocystis carinii* pneumonia, tuberculosis, gynecological cancers, and other opportunistic infections. HIV/AIDS can also invade brain tissue, causing neurological damage and dementia.

HIV infection is contracted through behaviors that create a high risk for exposure, not through membership in a particular group. To date the only known modes of transmission for HIV infection are the exchange of blood, semen, vaginal secretions, and breast milk. Such exchanges may occur through anal, vaginal, and possibly oral sex; the use of contaminated needles or syringes and other paraphernalia for injecting drugs; contact with contaminated blood or blood products; intrauterine exposure before or during childbirth; and possibly ingestion of breast milk.

The Centers for Disease Control and Prevention (CDC) estimated that 1.5 million Americans are infected with HIV. As of December 1995 there were 513,486 reported cases of AIDS in the United States, and over 62 percent had died. Among people ages 25 to 44 years, HIV infection is the leading cause of death in men and the third leading cause of death in women (CDC, 1995).

According to the surveillance data compiled by the CDC and reported in the HIV/AIDS report published semiannually during each year of this pandemic, rates of infection have increased for all population groups. Gay men and injection drug users continue to constitute the majority of those infected with HIV/AIDS, but rates of infection have dramatically increased in the African American and Hispanic communities, in women, and in adolescents and children. People with hemophilia and other bleeding disorders are now at a decreased risk of acquiring HIV, but those exposed to contaminated blood products before 1985 are at risk for developing AIDS. In 1995 African Americans and Hispanics represented the majority of new cases reported among men (54 percent) and women (76 percent). Women accounted for 19 percent of adult and adolescent AIDS cases in 1995, the highest proportion yet reported among women. And this epidemic in women is reflected in the epidemic in children, nearly all of whom acquired HIV infection perinatally. As of December 1995 the cumulative total of children with AIDS was 6,948, and 84 percent were African American or Hispanic.

Although the psychological, social, and economic repercussions of HIV/AIDS are unique, they do have some similarities to other life-threatening, catastrophic illnesses. Social isolation, discrimination, anxiety, depression, concern about body image, loss of jobs and other financial repercussions, loss of control, and confrontation with one's own mortality are among the critical issues challenging people with HIV/AIDS. Many individuals have endured long-term economic deprivation, social oppression, and violations of their basic human and civil rights. The diagnosis of HIV/AIDS stigmatizes these individuals and contributes to their increased isolation. In addition, many people who are assumed to be infected, and those who are closely associated with them, have encountered extreme rejection and isolation resulting from the public's panic over and behavioral response to the contagion of AIDS. Because of the stigmatization of HIV/AIDS, individuals are often fearful of revealing their diagnosis to family, friends, and coworkers. The social work profession has taken a leading role in addressing some of these concerns and in confronting issues relating to education, prevention, and research efforts involving HIV/AIDS.

ISSUE STATEMENT

HIV infection and AIDS are an international public health crisis with profound socioeconomic ramifications that affect everyone. To date, initiatives undertaken to cope with this crisis, including research, education, prevention, and delivery of services, have yet to demonstrate their success in stemming the progression of this disease. In the United States there is currently a rethinking regarding the roles of government and the private sector in addressing social and economic issues. For social workers this is a time to reflect on how this rethinking may influence how we as professionals advocate on behalf of our clients and how our clients with HIV/AIDS will be served.

Several key issues provide the framework for the development of an NASW policy statement regarding services to and advocacy on behalf of people with HIV/AIDS:

■ HIV is a dynamic, complex, and evolving virus. Although combination drug therapies have show some promise in slowing the progression of the virus, neither a cure nor a vaccine is currently in sight. Current treatment programs, including nontraditional therapies, are sometimes considered experimental in nature and therefore often are not covered by insurance plans and government programs.

■ People with HIV infection and AIDS depend on the health care system for all aspects of medical care. The current system is under scrutiny, and impending changes are focused away from a system of choice and toward a system of managed care. There are concerns that managed care may have a negative impact on the inclusion of people with HIV/AIDS in clinical trials and that it may restrict diagnosis and treatment.

■ Although HIV/AIDS have some similarities to other life-threatening illnesses, no other illness currently results in such devastating feelings of social isolation, loss of jobs and other financial repercussions, and prejudice and discrimination. People with HIV/AIDS, and sometimes even those who have simply been tested for the virus, continue to face discrimination in employment, military service, housing, access to health services, social and community support programs, and basic civil and human rights.

■ The roles of the private and public sectors in funding research, education, and prevention are evolving, as are models of service delivery for people with HIV/AIDS. Questions are being raised as to who should bear the financial costs of this epidemic and the limits of the government's responsibility.

■ Education and prevention efforts continue to be severely underfunded and limited by political, religious, and cultural challenges that render them ineffective in reaching and influencing the desired audiences.

■ HIV testing continues to be offered confidentially and anonymously along with pretest and posttest counseling in most communities. With the development of over-the-counter testing kits, essential counseling is exchanged for absolute anonymity.

■ In the absence of standard statutory or regulatory guidelines, practitioners and agencies may perceive a responsibility to warn third parties of their potential for infection if their spouses, other sexual partners, or partners in intravenous drug use are HIV infected and if the partners refuse to warn them. Ethical and moral beliefs sometimes conflict with state and agency guidelines.

■ Caregivers (both professional and volunteers) families, and friends sometimes encounter the same prejudice and discrimination that people with HIV/AIDS endure.

POLICY STATEMENT

Given the high incidence of AIDS and the rapid spread of the pandemic since the late 1970s, the social work profession must take an active stand to mitigate the overwhelming psychological and social effects of HIV infection and AIDS and to assist clients in reducing their risk of infection. The social work profession must take an active role in the workplace and elsewhere to seek solutions to the complex problems that HIV infection and AIDS present to individuals and to society. Social workers have demonstrated strong leadership since the beginning of the pandemic, and they must continue to respond to the social impact of HIV infection and AIDS as mandated by the *NASW Code of Ethics* (NASW, 1996).

As the organizational arm of the profession, NASW has helped coordinate a response to HIV infection and AIDS by helping its membership recognize the need for action in a number of areas:

Research. Basic research, including epidemiological, clinical, and psychological studies, is imperative and must continue to be funded at appropriate levels by the federal government. All research efforts should be expanded to focus on the special needs of women, children and adolescents, and racial and ethnic groups. Research is also needed to assess the effectiveness of prevention and educational messages and methods.

Health Care Delivery. NASW believes that people with HIV/AIDS have a right to comprehensive and coordinated health and mental health care, choice of medical providers, quality case management, access to all necessary medication regimens specific to their needs, and comprehensive insurance through either private or government sources to pay for treatments and services. People with HIV/AIDS should receive health care services that are culturally sensitive and patient centered.

NASW believes that inmates with HIV/AIDS in federal, state, county, and local correctional facilities have a fundamental right to adequate health care services. Social work advocacy for people with HIV/AIDS in jails and prisons is critical.

Access. Comprehensive health care includes medical care, social services, and psychological services. In the absence of universal health care coverage for Americans, access to health care, clinical trials, experimental medicines, and newly approved medications that can be very costly become critical issues. Therefore, the profession of social work must commit itself to ensuring access to health care and social services for all those infected with HIV/AIDS, including all aspects of health care that will

ameliorate their condition and extend their quality of life.

Human and Civil Rights. NASW believes that people with HIV/AIDS should have the same rights as other citizens in the areas of education, employment, military service, housing, health care services, insurance, social and community support programs, and immigration services. Nondiscrimination laws should be extended and legal protection should be enforced vigorously to protect people with HIV/AIDS, those who have taken the HIV antibody test, those assumed to be at risk, and those who provide care to people with HIV/AIDS. The right to confidentiality relating to HIV/AIDS status must be ensured.

Education and Prevention. Adequate public funds must be authorized and appropriated for educational efforts among the general public to reduce the fear of HIV infection and AIDS and the stigmatization of people assumed to be at risk of infection. Adequately funded public education programs, including the promotion of behaviors to reduce the risk of HIV infection and to promote early treatment of HIV infection, should be encouraged. Proactive efforts must continually be undertaken to educate the most vulnerable populations, those who are not reached by traditional prevention and education programs. The needs of racial and ethnic groups, women, infants, children and adolescents, older people, lesbians, gay men, bisexual people, transgender individuals, injection drug users, illiterate people, and people with disabilities must be addressed. Educational efforts targeted at children and adolescents are needed in the public and private school systems, and efforts directed toward inmates should be provided in federal, state, county, and local correctional facilities. Education and prevention programs should address the needs of chronically mentally ill and developmentally disabled people. All social workers have a responsibility to educate clients about risk-reduction behaviors, including safer sexual practices, not sharing needles or other injection equipment, proper needle cleaning techniques, needle exchange programs, tuberculosis prevention, and life skills such as sexual negotiation and assertive communication. These programs may include harm reduction and needle exchange programs for injection drug users and condom distribution programs in a variety of educational, institutional, governmental, and community facilities.

Schools of social work have the responsibility to require all students to examine the ramifications of HIV infection and AIDS from the perspective of core values of the profession: human dignity, nonjudgmental attitudes, acceptance, confidentiality, social justice, cultural diversity, and self-determination. Content on the biomedical, socioeconomic, political, historical, psychosocial, legal, ethical, and spiritual aspects of the disease should be incorporated into foundation and practice courses as appropriate. Students should be exposed to the range of interventions available to people infected with or affected by HIV and AIDS, particularly those who are already stigmatized and marginalized because of their race, class, gender, drug use, or sexual orientation.

HIV Testing. All practitioners should be knowledgeable about all aspects of the HIV antibody test, including validity and risks. HIV testing should be voluntary, confidential, and performed with informed consent. In addition, anonymous testing should be available, accessible, and free. Because of the emotional stress associated with the testing process, pretest and posttest counseling by skilled practitioners is a necessary component of all testing programs. Therefore, NASW is opposed to the over-the-counter testing kits unless a pretest and posttest counseling program is provided.

Duty to Warn. Practitioners should use the strength of the client–worker relationship to encourage clients with HIV/AIDS to inform their sexual or needle-sharing partners of their status. Social workers should be familiar with applicable state law regarding duty to warn. Agencies have a responsibility to establish clear guidelines for social workers whose clients place others at risk of infection. These guidelines should be based primarily on existing standards of confidentiality, as stated in the NASW *Code of Ethics* (NASW, 1996), the "duty-to-protect" principle established by the *Tarasoff* decision in 1976, and emerging state laws concerning the notification of partners and the duty to warn them. Social workers should con-

sider legal counsel if they feel they have a duty to warn.

HIV and Tuberculosis. Because of the rise in cases of tuberculosis associated with HIV, social workers must educate themselves and others about routes of transmission and treatment options, including preventive therapy. Social work interventions must include the entire range of social work services, including advocacy, concrete needs, and counseling.

Political Action. Social workers should provide leadership and otherwise participate with other groups to lobby actively at the local, state, and federal levels on behalf of people with HIV infection and AIDS to improve the quality of their lives and to protect their civil liberties. Social workers should also advocate for increased funding for appropriate education, prevention, intervention and treatment services, and research.

Agency and Professional Accountability. The value of traditional and nontraditional families and communities and the aid and support they provide to people with HIV/AIDS must be recognized and incorporated into social work practice. Practitioners must be knowledgeable, culturally competent, trained, and sensitive. Helping professionals and appropriate licensing authorities have a responsibility to ensure that services are provided to people with HIV/AIDS, as well as their significant others, without regard to their financial or social circumstances. On the basis of the responses of members to its HIV survey (1995), NASW strongly supports the provision of initial training and continuing education for all members that cover psychosocial and legal issues, ethical dilemmas and responsibilities, medical treatment, safer sexual practices, harm reduction, community resources, and scientific and treatment developments.

REFERENCES

Centers for Disease Control and Prevention, National Center for Infectious Diseases, Division of HIV/AIDS. (1995). *HIV/AIDS surveillance report*. Atlanta: Author.

National Association of Social Workers. (1996). *NASW code of ethics.* Washington, DC: NASW Press.

Tarasoff v. Regents of the University of California, 551, P2d 334 (Calif. 1976).

Zibalese-Crawford, M., Brennan, J. P., & Stein, J. (1995). *Assessing the social work response to HIV/AIDS: A report prepared for the National Association of Social Workers Task Force on HIV/AIDS.* Washington, DC: National Association of Social Workers.

Policy statement approved by the NASW Delegate Assembly August 1996. This policy supersedes the policy statement on AIDS/HIV approved by the Delegate Assembly in 1993, the policy statement on AIDS/HIV: A Social Work Response approved in 1990, and the policy statement on Acquired Immune Deficiency Syndrome approved in 1987. For further information, contact the National Association of Social Workers, 750 First Street, NE, Suite 700, Washington, DC 20002-4241. Telephone: 202-408-8600 or 800-638-8799.

Homelessness

BACKGROUND

In 1989 the United States celebrated the 40th anniversary of the passage of the National Housing Act (Ch. 42), which set the goal of a decent home and suitable living environment for all American families (Mulroy & Ewalt, 1996). This promise remains unfulfilled. The persistence of mass homelessness is a clear indicator that poverty in America has become more extreme and that basic survival needs are a critical policy issue for the 1990s. Homelessness is a complex problem that cannot be corrected until Americans realize that it results from the culmination of past policies which have either ignored or misdiagnosed the causes and consequences of persistent poverty (U.S. Department of Housing and Urban Development [HUD], 1994). The plight of homeless people and their struggle for survival can be seen in the lives of

- young families unable to close the gap between housing costs and total household income

- individuals currently employed, either full- or part-time, with too little income to afford adequate housing

- single mothers unable to work because of child care responsibilities or the lack of skills to meet the demands of a changing labor market (Green, Johnson, Bremseth, & Tracy, 1995; North & Smith, 1993)

- youths and families of color in the inner city without the access to jobs and economic opportunities

- men, many of whom are older, and either disabled or veterans who have only the life of the street for economic and social supports

- people with mental disabilities, physical disabilities, addictions, or other disabilities who lack the social networks, health care, and other program supports to live independently in the community (Baum & Burnes, 1993; Burt, 1992).

Past and Prologue

Throughout U.S. history the approach to homelessness has mirrored the societal response to the conditions of the poorest of the poor. At the beginning of this century U.S. society focused on either homeless men or dependent children in need of care. The men were often immigrants and lived in boarding houses during the winter months until seasonal jobs resumed. Those who were classified as transients were given aid through such practices as "passing on," the forerunner to the "bus therapy" of today. Interventions by the Charity Organization Society and other groups focused on distinguishing between worthy and unworthy poor people and encouraging migration, moral treatment, and work for unworthy poor people.

During the Great Depression, U.S. society focused on families with children standing in the soup line and newly caught in the web of abject poverty. These new poor populations joined together with the transients and older beggars of the 1930s. Policy efforts were numerous and focused on structural causes rather than the personal deficits of poor people.

After World War II the focus shifted to skid row, the bowery, and the lifestyle of alcoholic older men in flophouses. Policy making focused on the housing crisis through new construction and loan programs; however, following urban renewal, residents were displaced into low-rent and single-room-occupancy hotels.

From the mid-1960s to the early 1970s, the War on Poverty and Great Society programs provided economic opportunity for poor people. Discussions of the dimensions of poverty encompassed hunger, but federal policy initiatives failed to give adequate attention to extreme poverty and the growing crisis in low-income housing (Blasi, 1994). The scope of the crisis in affordable housing that started in the early 1970s was not yet well recognized or completely understood. It was generally assumed that homelessness had diminished or could be eliminated through other reforms.

New Homelessness

Beginning in the early 1980s and continuing into the 1990s, homelessness became larger, more shocking, and in sharp contrast to the values of opportunity for all. Before the reemergence of homelessness in the 1980s, it was widely assumed that this was a social problem of either Third World countries or of an earlier and less enlightened era in the United States. However, by the mid-1980s, rising housing costs, changes in labor markets, deinstitutionalization of people mentally disabled or developmentally disabled, the return of Vietnam-era veterans, and related social forces converged to necessitate some form of response in the form of public policy.

As U.S. communities began to face the challenge of increasing numbers of homeless people on the streets and in public places, research efforts in social work and related disciplines began to document the nature and scope of the problem. Debates about the numbers, characteristics, causes, and consequences revolved around the definition of the problem as a personal crisis in the lives of individuals and families who were unable either to afford housing or to benefit from job opportunities in the emerging postindustrial economy. Media coverage focused on the plight of homeless people, and old myths about personal responsibility, worthy and unworthy poor people, and work were perpetuated by policy makers and others as a part of the public discussion. Advocacy groups were formed and focused on the need for affordable housing. Religious groups organized community kitchens, and other services, missions, public shelters, and local action groups grew in numbers and zeal.

After passage of the Stewart B. McKinney Homeless Assistance Act of 1987, initiatives

and grant-in-aid structures began to emerge. In addition to emergency shelter care, local efforts in services delivery began to include transitional housing, outreach, and case management, particularly to mentally disabled people who were homeless. However, the crisis of homelessness continued to grow, particularly among people of color, women with children, people living in overcrowded and overpriced housing, and other families unable to close the gap between affordable housing and total family income. More books and studies on homelessness were published, some with a strong undercurrent of victim blaming. Blasi (1994) noted that from 1991 to 1994, the *New York Times* and *Los Angeles Times* published more than four times as many articles about homelessness (2,146) as about poverty (469).

In 1994 the federal government published the first federal plan to break the cycle of homelessness, entitled *Priority: Home!* (HUD, 1994). The plan states that "for the most part, homelessness relief efforts remain locked in an 'emergency register'" (p. 18). Homelessness is divided into two broad categories of problems: crisis poverty and chronic disability. The plan calls for efforts to "reinvent the approach" because the "current approach is plainly not working and must be changed" (HUD, 1994, p. 4). A number of factors place people at risk for homelessness, including alcoholism; drug abuse; low education and illiteracy; sexual exploitation; chronic mental disability, developmental disabilities, or mild mental retardation; and HIV/AIDS. Our society has systematically and traditionally viewed these people as the unworthy poor.

Lessons from the Past

After almost a century of shifting definitions of the problem, denial, and neglect, the core of the homelessness problem clearly is extreme poverty. Policies on homelessness, with only a few exceptions, have emphasized the alleviation of individual needs and have ignored systemic factors that would be significant in reversing or preventing the underlying conditions of poverty. Past policy failures together with proposed changes in public assistance, housing, health care, economic opportunity, education, and affirmative action do not offer much hope that society is capable of learning from either past mistakes or accomplishments.

Far too often policy-making processes at the federal, state, and local levels have been limited to emergency measures rather than addressing the long-term structural and preventive dimensions of severe poverty and homelessness. Reoccurring themes of individual rather than communal responsibility and labels such as "bag ladies," "panhandlers," "handouts," "hobos," and "transients" have been the focus of public attention.

However, valuable lessons can be learned from the past. First, the scope of emergency measures during the Depression era did have an impact in alleviating suffering and extreme poverty. Second, long-term structural measures such as social security and the indexing of benefits, Medicare, and services to older people have been effective in protecting low-income older Americans from the risks of homelessness. Third, the failure to adequately respond to the needs of homeless individuals in the 1980s has lead to an even greater crisis in the 1990s. The new homelessness of the 1990s is a more multifaceted and entrenched problem than in earlier decades.

Clearly, the time has come to get out in front of the massive societal changes we are experiencing (Coulton, 1995) for social workers to lead the effort to eliminate homelessness (Courtney & Specht, 1994). The role of the federal government with respect to a social safety net, basic entitlements, and equality of opportunity is in danger of being dismantled. The added danger is that "the capacity to develop programs at the local level is weak and the commitment to social justice uncertain" (Coulton, 1995, p. 438).

ISSUE STATEMENT

After almost two decades of disjointed efforts to address the crisis of homelessness in America, it remains a significant issue. The reasons for this are systemic. Homelessness and poverty are inextricably linked. Being poor means living on the edge of being just an accident, an illness, or a paycheck away from living on the streets. Being poor means having limited resources to cover the necessities of housing, food, child care,

health care, and education. Housing, which absorbs a high percentage of income, is sometimes dropped when economic resources are insufficient to meet the needs of families. The cost and difficulty of trying to find low-income housing once housing has been lost can present tremendous obstacles to families. Cogent policies not supported by adequate resources contribute to the problem.

Policy making in relation to the problem of homelessness illustrates the drastic reshaping of the federal social welfare agenda in the United States during the 1980s and 1990s, but no single legislative answer will solve or significantly reduce homelessness. The dilemma of how to achieve this goal in a time of federal budget deficits, restructuring of the economy, and reduced welfare merits our attention. Social workers can and must join with the homeless to make significant changes in individual lives and in the social structures that surround them.

POLICY STATEMENT

To solve the problem of homelessness in the United States, public policies should focus on the changing social and economic conditions that foster extreme poverty and increase the risk of homelessness (Blasi, 1994). NASW advocates the following as long-term and preventive solutions to the problem of homelessness:

■ The goal of a decent home and a suitable living environment for every American (Housing Act of 1949) should be pursued (HUD, 1994).

■ Federal, state, and local housing subsidies should be available as an entitlement for all households that need them, rather than being controlled by spending caps (Grigsby, 1990).

■ The complex patchwork of housing assistance programs for low-income families should be organized into a more efficient and coordinated system that targets very poor people and households at risk of homelessness.

■ Efforts to encourage state and local communities to use mainstream programs in building a continuum of care that integrates housing, income maintenance, and supportive services should be strengthened (Kondratas, 1991).

- Education, job training, and related support services should be expanded to serve as key elements in the prevention of homelessness.

- Treatment and supportive services for special populations should be expanded and focused on innovative approaches.

- Federal, state, and local state proposals to cut expenditures and restructure social welfare programs should be examined to determine their impact on homelessness.

- The lack of bipartisan effort and consensus on policy goals to end mass homelessness continues and is a major stumbling block to federal leadership in agenda setting and appropriations. Political action strategies are needed to reverse this trend. For example, social workers need to be actively involved with state and local coalitions for the homeless; to network with or create advocacy groups for the homeless; to identify significant problems of homeless people in localities and create linkages to address and alleviate these problems; and to encourage state and local communities to use mainstream programs in building a continuum of care that integrates housing, income maintenance, and supportive services.

- A White House conference should be held to formulate strategies and build support for new directions in fighting poverty and homelessness.

Short-term program and policy changes are needed to cope with fiscal crises and the disjointed community system of emergency services for homeless individuals and families. Fiscal and programmatic recommendations contained in the 1994 federal plan (HUD, 1994) merit our attention and support. State and local communities and nonprofit and public agencies should rethink the place of shelter care within a larger continuum of care for special at-risk populations faced with crisis poverty and homelessness. Shelters have become the frontline response, and their place within a more comprehensive system of care is not well developed. Social workers should be actively involved in the development of continuity of services for children and families who are sheltered. School social workers should work as advocates for the needs of children who are part of the shelter system.

Excessive rent and other housing burdens on poor people in urban and rural communities must be alleviated. State and local resources, including voluntary efforts, must be mobilized to develop creative solutions and stopgap measures for protecting people who are precariously housed. Misconceptions about the causes of homelessness and severe poverty have contributed to the lack of public support for efforts to alleviate homelessness. Social workers in partnership with elected officials and others must lead the fight in the interests of people who are homeless. (Burt, 1992). The impact of homelessness on women and people of color in U.S. society is an important national issue and for the social work profession that must be translated into more effective efforts at coalition building.

Although more demands are being placed on shelters and emergency services for the homeless, mainstream programs for housing assistance, public assistance, and health care are being cut in the name of welfare reform. As programs become paralyzed by too many cuts, poverty becomes more severe and homelessness becomes a growing reality for the poorest of the poor.

After almost two decades of disjointed efforts to address the crisis of homelessness in America, shifts in federal and state policies are producing more homeless individuals. Five critical policy questions merit attention:

1. How can we reverse this trend toward mass homelessness?

2. What should be the goals for government policy on extreme poverty and homelessness?

3. Are we becoming too accustomed to the homeless people on the streets and in public shelters?

4. With today's political situation, what can be done to offset the impact of reduced federal and state welfare efforts?

5. How can social workers intervene to strengthen efforts at reversing and preventing homelessness?

The impact of homelessness necessitates immediate action on the part of the social work profession.

REFERENCES

Baum, A. S., & Burnes, D. W. (1993). *A nation in denial: The truth about homelessness*. Boulder, CO: Westview Press.

Blasi, G. (1994). Ideological and political barriers to understanding homelessness. *American Behavioral Scientist, 37*, 563–586.

Burt, M. (1992). *Over the edge: The growth of homelessness in the 1980s*. Washington, DC: Urban Institute Press.

Coulton, C. J. (1995). Riding the pendulum of the 1990s: Building a community context for social work research [Editorial]. *Social Work, 40*, 437–439.

Courtney, M., & Specht, H. (1994). *Unfaithful angels*. New York: Haworth Press.

Green, R. K., Johnson, A. L., Bremseth, M. D., & Tracy, E. (1995, July). *No home, no family: Homeless children in rural Ohio*. Paper presented at the 20th Annual Meeting of Social Work and Human Services in Rural Areas, Knoxville, TN.

Grigsby, W. G. (1990). Housing finance and subsidies in the United States. *Urban Studies, 27*(6), 831–845.

Kondratas, A. (1991). Ending homelessness: Policy challenges. *American Psychologist, 46*, 1226–1231.

Mulroy, E. A., & Ewalt, P. L. (1996). Affordable housing: A basic need and a social issue. *Social Work, 41*, 245–249.

North, C. S., & Smith, E. M. (1993). A comparison of homeless men and women: Different populations, different needs. *Community Mental Health Journal, 29*(5), 423–431.

Stewart B. McKinley Homeless Assistance Act of 1987, P.L. 100-77, 101 Stat. 482.

U.S. Department of Housing and Urban Development. (1994). *Priority home!* (HUD-1454-CPD[1]). Washington, DC: Author.

Policy statement approved by the NASW Delegate Assembly, August 1996. This policy supersedes the policy statements on Homelessness approved by the Delegate Assembly in 1987 and 1984. For further information, contact the National Association of Social Workers, 750 First Street, NE, Suite 700, Washington, DC 20002-4241. Telephone: 202-408-8600 or 800-638-8799.

Hospice Care

BACKGROUND

The dramatic attention accorded to hospice care in the United States during the past decade reflects the convergence of a variety of interests and needs. The issues of death and dying that have given impetus to the hospice movement include the effect on the terminally ill and their families, medical advances that enable life to be prolonged in the face of degenerative diseases and impending death, renewed attention to home care and other alternatives to hospitalization, the scarcity of resources, the emphasis on holistic health, and recognition of the rights of dying people.

The 20th century has been characterized by changing attitudes toward dying people and to the appropriate focus for their care and treatment. In the early part of the century, the family and physician provided care in the home as a matter of course. However, care gradually shifted to hospitals where diagnosis, treatment, and cure were emphasized and the focus was on the physical condition of the dying person. Social and emotional needs were largely ignored. The trauma of dying and death for both the person and the family was inadequately understood and poorly handled. It was not until Dr. Cicely Saunders traveled to the United States in the early 1960s that people began to explore the idea of specialized care for the terminally ill. Recognition of the need for special knowledge, skills, and sensitivity grew. Gradually, the institutionally oriented, medically dominated health care system has begun to recognize and become responsive to these needs.

The term *hospice* is derived from the way station or inn, which was a place of succor and rest for weary travelers in the Middle Ages. Today, the National Hospice Organization (NHO) defines hospice as "a coordinated program of palliative and supportive care (physical, psychological, social, and spiritual) for dying people and their families . . . provided by an interdisciplinary team of professionals and volunteers under a central administration" (NHO, 1987). It is a philosophy of care, not a place. Hospice serves all people perceived to be terminally ill regardless of the etiology of their disease.

Cancer patients exemplify the costs of terminal care. About half the people in the United States who develop cancer each year do not show marked improvement following major therapy—either medical or surgical. Rather, the disease recurs, progresses, and ends in death. The estimated cost of cancer in the United States in 1990 was $35.3 billion; morbidity costs (days lost from work) added $11.9 billion; and mortality costs (lost income due to premature death) added $56.8 billion for a total economic burden of cancer of $104 billion. From 1985 to 1990, direct costs of care rose by 62 percent and total costs of the economic burden rose 45 percent (Brown, 1990).

Although the cost of care in a hospice is not fully known, the benefits of hospice care increasingly are being validated. It has been recognized that such specialized care alleviates trauma for terminally ill people, family members, and the health care staff (McKell, 1978; U.S. General Accounting Office, 1979).

ISSUE STATEMENT

Traditionally, hospital care of dying people has emphasized the physical aspects of the disease process. Hospice care provides the impetus to integrate the social, emotional, and spiritual components of care into the health center. An emphasis not on cure but on care—on the control of symptoms and enhancing the quality of whatever life remains—is characteristic of the hospice approach. Other key issues include

■ the participation of dying people and their families versus professional control, including the involvement of dying people and their families in all aspects of treatment decisions that affect them

■ a continuum of care that includes bereavement counseling for families

■ a flexible and creative use of resources— professional, volunteer, familial, community based, and institutional

■ access to care at all points in the continuum of care

■ a reassessment of sociomedical values, including the use of drugs and of extreme measures to prolong life

■ the use of the treatment-team concept, with clear definitions of roles and responsibilities and equalization of team members

■ recognition of the need for specialized training for all those involved in working with dying people and their families, whether in institutions, the community, or the home

■ awareness that open communication among dying people, their families, and health care staff should be encouraged

■ understanding that the control of symptoms has medical, social, emotional, and spiritual components.

POLICY STATEMENT

NASW supports hospice care as a way of helping dying people and their loved ones to maintain their dignity and humanity while receiving optimal physical, psychosocial, and spiritual care. It is an approach, a philosophy, and an application of values, rather than a physical entity per se. The emphasis is on enabling dying people to live as fully as possible and to control their lives as much as possible. Hospice care seeks to eliminate the symptoms of illness through the control and palliation of the physical, emotional, spiritual, interpersonal, and fi-

nancial aspects of disease. It should be available to dying people and their families wherever they live.

Hospice care is part of the continuum of care and should be available to dying people and their families as a matter of choice. Toward this end, new and flexible sources of public and private financing are needed, and multiple care and other kinds of extra-institutional care, treatment, and services, furnished by a multidisciplinary team of professionals and volunteers who use nontraditional methods, must be developed and made available. Institutional care must incorporate these concepts into care of the dying. New concepts of choice by dying people and their families must be recognized. The quality of life, not merely its prolongation, should be of central concern. Accordingly, a wide range of drugs, medications, and other techniques to alleviate physical and emotional pain should be used more readily.

Effective work with dying people and their families requires special knowledge, skills, and sensitivity, which is a particular skill of social work. Moreover, the emotional demands of hospice care on both professional and lay staff and volunteers are substantial. Social workers must work to build support systems for staff. Training opportunities must be expanded and made available for students in schools of social work and for postdegree professionals through continuing education. Training methods must be reassessed and reevaluated constantly. In-service training, staff development, and other forms of training are essential. Also, realistic staffing patterns; staff/patient/family ratios; and respite for dying people, families, and staff are crucial for an effective program.

Furthermore, the role of professional social workers must be viewed as integral to hospice care. The hospice concept is the embodiment of social work values and principles. The themes of self-determination and respect for individual worth and dignity; recognition of the interplay between the dying person, the family, and the community; and concepts of the team approach and the use of natural helping networks and volunteers are central to social work training and methodology. The social worker is available to work with family members who can and want to be involved with the dying person, with family members who cannot but who want to be involved, and with family members who can but do not wish to be involved. Moreover, the special knowledge and skills of professional social workers provide direct services, skills in developing programs, professional staff development and support, administration, volunteer and staff training, help for families in case management, and utilization and coordination of community resources. All these skills are indispensable to an effective hospice program.

Social work intervention may include, but need not be limited to, planning for adaptation to a life-threatening disease, ensuring adequate support systems, facilitating communication among family members, counseling, discharge planning, ensuring continuity of care, referral to community resources, crisis intervention, advocacy, and providing information and assistance regarding financial alternatives.

REFERENCES

Brown, M. L. (1990). The national economic burden of cancer. *Journal of the National Cancer Institute*, 1811–1814.

McKell, D. (1978, September). *Hospice: A national view.* Presented at Major Addresses of the Institutes on Hospices, San Diego.

National Hospice Organization. (1987, August). *Standards of a hospice program of care.* Arlington, VA: Author.

U.S. General Accounting Office. (1979, March). *Hospice care—A growing concept in the United States* (Report to the U.S. Congress by the Comptroller General). Washington, DC: U.S. Government Printing Office.

SUGGESTED READINGS

Markman, M. (1988). An argument in support of cost-effectiveness analysis in oncology. *Journal of Clinical Oncology, 6,* 937–939.

McVie, J. C. (1988). Counting costs of care. *Journal of Clinical Oncology, 6,* 1529–1531.

Tannock, I. F. (1987). Treating the patient, not just the cancer. *New England Journal of Medicine, 317,* 1534–1535.

Tannock, I. F., & Boyer, M. B., (1990). When is cancer treatment worthwhile? *New England Journal of Medicine, 323,* 989–990.

Policy statement approved by the NASW Delegate Assembly, August 1993. This policy statement supersedes the policy statement on Hospice Care approved by the Delegate Assembly in 1981. For further information, contact the National Association of Social Workers, 750 First Street, NE, Suite 700, Washington, DC 20002-4241. Telephone: 202-408-8600 or 800-638-8799.

Housing

BACKGROUND

Housing and community environments that meet the universal need for shelter, privacy, and positive social relationships are essential for stable family life, personal development, and health and safety. Deteriorating housing and community facilities result in a four-way loss: (1) in the health and welfare of the citizens, (2) in property values and economic vitality, (3) in community morale, and (4) in housing stock. Thus, decisions regarding housing and community development cannot be left wholly to the interplay of the supply and demand of the marketplace. The private real estate market cannot be expected to adequately meet the needs of many groups, particularly those with low incomes. The general welfare requires governmental participation in housing and community development.

Throughout the 20th century, such governmental participation has increased gradually in both urban and rural areas but without fully developed principles or a philosophy. Expansion of the role of the government has been piecemeal. National policy has evolved slowly, in a patchwork manner, leaving many gaps and discrepancies that often work to the disadvantage of those who most need governmental assistance and protection. In 1949, Congress set forth a national housing goal of "a decent home and suitable living environment for every American family"—a goal, not a policy. For 30 years, progress toward this goal was measured in the statistics of dollars allocated, units planned, and housing starts—not in the quality of housing or improvements in communities. Still missing is a national policy on housing and community development that deals comprehensively with regional and demographic differences and that emanates not from concepts of property values but from concepts of human need.

In recent years, national policy has eroded financing and the efficacy of the housing programs that emerged, as well as related open housing and financing enforcement. Housing should be a national priority and a right as a basic human need. Housing affects other services and clearly illustrates the concept of mutuality. Foster care, shelters, mental and physical health, and education are affected by housing programs. When decent housing is available, the cost in financial and human terms is well documented.

ISSUE STATEMENT

Housing Supply and Affordability

The supply of suitable and affordable housing to meet the diverse needs of individuals and families in the United States is inadequate. New low- and moderate-cost housing is insufficient, and older housing stock is deteriorating rapidly because of rising operating costs and deferred maintenance.

Housing stock is being lost as more and more buildings in older areas are abandoned. The cost of energy and general inflation have had a particularly severe effect on housing and community facilities. Low- and moderate-income tenants and tenant farmers are forced to pay higher rents than they can reasonably afford and remain trapped in deteriorating housing and living environments. Only an increasingly small part of the population can afford new housing. Moderate- and middle-income tenants are threatened by the conversion of their units to cooperative apartments and condominiums priced beyond their means. It has been demonstrated that, even with low-interest-rate loan programs, low- and moderate-income families cannot afford housing without some form of rent or operating subsidies. Recipients of public assistance and Supplemental Security Income are in a particularly vulnerable position. Income allowances are insufficient to ensure choices for adequate, safe housing.

Geographic Shifts of the Population

Major long-term population shifts have not been translated into long-range planning for housing and community development on a national scale. Massive waste and tragic economic and human dislocation result from unplanned growth and development when population shifts take place from the Northeast to the Sunbelt, from urban to less populated areas, and from suburban areas back to the inner cities. Population shifts often are accompanied by the displacement of the urban or rural poor and the breakdown in the tenuous balance between economic resources and human needs.

Populations with Special Needs

In the past, governmental assistance in housing and community development programs focused largely on the traditional family in traditional housing. It failed to take into account vast portions of American society that did not fit into this pattern. During the past decade, the two fastest-growing segments of the population have been single-person households and single-parent families, especially those headed by women. For those who are poor, there are few housing options that meet their needs. With the expansion of community-based support services, many more elderly and disabled people remain in their communities and are able to live reasonably independently. A large number of youths who are too old for the child care system and an increasing number of individuals who are returning from health, correctional, or custodial institutions have few or no suitable housing options. These groups, along with others with special housing needs—immigrants, people in "isolated and depressed communities," tenant farmers, and large families who have lost their homes and are deprived

socially and economically—now are swelling the ranks of the homeless. A greater awareness of populations with special needs and the crisis of homelessness are forcing new approaches to housing.

Relationship of Housing and Social Services

The interface of housing and supportive services has been given little attention, and the relationship of housing and services has not been understood fully by planners and policymakers. Therefore, the allocation of resources that could tie together the delivery of housing with the delivery of services has been minimal and haphazard. Supportive services must be an integral part of a housing program. Conversely, the lack of suitable housing seriously impedes the effective use of social services and reduces the cost-effectiveness of both housing and service programs. Children in foster care cannot return to parents who have no homes; physically or mentally disabled individuals cannot be discharged from hospitals or treated properly without a suitable living environment; and schoolchildren cannot learn in overcrowded hotel rooms or in dangerously substandard housing. Inadequate housing undermines foster care, as well as medical, psychiatric, educational, home health care, and other human services programs.

Housing and the Community Infrastructure

In the past, there was little integrated planning for housing and the community infrastructure of facilities and services, such as transportation, schools, public services, and civic and neighborhood organizations. Such planning must be encouraged now and in the future. The current cost of energy, which circumscribes the area within which families can live suitably and meet their economic and social needs, demands the integrated planning of housing and urban or rural development.

Housing and Employment

The cause-and-effect relationship between housing and jobs has been acknowledged belatedly in the aftermath of the government-encouraged suburban expansion of the past three decades, the government's myopia regarding the flight of industry from urban centers, and the ineffectiveness of governmental efforts to develop affordable housing in areas of economic growth. Moderate-income families, and certainly poor people, consequently have been unable to take advantage of employment opportunities, because without an adequate income they are unable to meet the cost of maintaining decent housing in areas where new job opportunities have become available. Unemployed people particularly are locked in, unable to meet their housing costs and unable to relocate. The dramatic increase in both the private and governmental foreclosure rates on home mortgages and farms bears witness to this increasingly critical concern.

Integration

Despite the national policies of nondiscrimination and the goal of integration, there is a continuing trend toward "ghettoization" for ethnic minorities, minorities of color, the old and disabled, people in isolated rural communities, and poor people that only governmental policies can counteract through adequately funded enforcement mechanisms. Low-income housing opportunities in middle-income areas should be encouraged.

Housing Policy Enforcement

Open housing and gains in antiredlining policies over the years have been weakened systematically and have not been enforced. The result has been that trends in housing opportunities for minorities and the poor have been reversed.

POLICY STATEMENT

All individuals and families have the right to housing that meets their basic needs for shelter at an affordable level and provides for a rewarding community life. Both governmental and private sources must encourage the expansion of the housing supply through a wide range of innovative techniques. This housing must be designed and located so it can contribute to closer social relationships and understanding between all groups in the population. To achieve these ends, the following principles must be embodied in a national housing policy.

Providing Basic Shelter

Housing as a Social Utility and Basic Human Need. Ultimately, a national housing policy should view housing as a social utility and a basic human need for all income groups. The policy should include programs of government-sponsored or nonprofit rental housing, cooperative housing, the rehabilitation of housing, and homeownership. It should be based on an analysis of the effectiveness of existing and previous housing programs and build on their strength.

Housing as a National Resource. The federal government has the primary responsibility to take all steps necessary to ensure an adequate, affordable supply of dwellings for low- and moderate-income individuals and families. This housing must be suited to diverse physical and social requirements. It must be distributed geographically according to the housing needs of urban, suburban, and rural people, and it must be related to programs of community development that recognize changing needs and living patterns. All levels of government should adopt policies that will stimulate and support the construction of housing to meet the needs of all populations. For example, state and local governments must provide sufficient incentives for multifamily housing developments to expand the supply.

Because public-assisted housing is a vital commodity and increasingly is expensive to produce, the units that already are built should not be lost either through physical deterioration or through conversion to middle- or upper-income units. The maintenance of minimum standards of health, safety, and decency in all occupied housing should be ensured through sensitive and consistent enforcement in conjunction with the provision of low-interest loans or grants that allow for the rehabilitation of deteriorating units. Options for better utilization of existing housing stock through shared or accessory housing and single-room occupancy or congregate-living arrangements should be fostered by public initiatives, and the quality of housing and the community environment should be safeguarded. Units in the nation's inner-city neighborhoods should be maintained and improved without displacing poor and elderly people. Revitalization should be accomplished in such a way as to permit beneficial effects and to protect the interest of previous residents.

Promoting Community Life

Citizen Participation and Community Involvement. Local participation in the planning and implementation of housing and community development should be fostered by the various levels of government. Self-help groups should be supported, and community-based housing and community corporations also should be fostered. Publicly owned, nonprofit, or cooperative housing and private homes for low-to-moderate-income groups should be given priority in the allocation of housing funds. The participation of potential housing consumers, tenants, landlords, real estate and building professionals, and local community groups should be encouraged at every level of decision making in the planning and operation of housing and related facilities. Training and technical assistance should be provided to maximize citizen participation and the environment of the community.

Community Facilities, Services, and Employment. New or rehabilitated housing should dovetail with the construction of community facilities and with public services appropriate for families and individuals who are expected to reside in such housing. Planning for housing should be linked to community-based employment opportunities and job development programs. Integrated governmental policies for housing, employment, transportation, and income maintenance should be implemented by a partnership that includes the government, private enterprise, and local community residents. The government should provide incentives to the private sector to discourage disinvestments. It must encourage reinvestment in and support for older communities as well as stimulate economic development in new areas.

Equal Opportunity in Housing and Community Life. Fair-housing provisions and the integration goals of the federal government should be enforced strongly. Such enforcement will enable those people who need the status of protected-class designation to avail themselves of housing opportunities according to choice. Occupancy in decent, safe, and sanitary housing should be open to all people without discrimination because of age, color, sex, sexual orientation, disability, marital status, ethnic or religious background, family composition, source of income, or preferred place of residence.

Financing regulations and legislation that ensure equal access to financing for rehabilitation and new construction for all citizens in all geographic areas should be strengthened and enforced actively.

Recognition of Different Housing Needs. Housing that is planned for particular population groups such as the elderly, the handicapped, single-parent families, or native Americans residing on reservations should be included in a spectrum of alternative residences to meet special needs. Specialized housing whose design, location, and links to services are geared to particular groups should be promoted in the public and private sectors. Special populations should not be excluded from the general housing market, and all housing should be accessible and adaptable.

Linkage of Housing and Social Services. The linkage between housing and social services must be reinforced consistently by housing and social service policymakers and the implementers of these programs. Low-income families, the disabled, and individuals with special needs require a range of social services in varying degrees that should be accessible within their living environment or nearby community. The responsibility for providing these services and the funding mechanism must be an integral part of planning to maximize limited resources. In the context of severe reductions in resources for both housing and social service programs, it is more vital than ever that real linkages be developed and maintained in these two areas to enable individuals and families to meet their basic social and physical needs. Services must be tailored to ensure everyone's right to decent and affordable housing. Emphasis should be placed on correcting or eliminating contradictory eligibility requirements for housing, human services, and income transfer programs so the provision and delivery of services is facilitated, not hindered. Human growth requires an environment that is as supportive of one's basic needs as nutritious food is of life.

Fiscal Considerations

Fiscal Policy. Housing and community development programs must be recognized as integral to national economic growth and stability. The federal tax policy, local property taxes, and policies that foster high interest rates must be reformed to address the needs of low-income people. There should be a limit to the subsidies for the development of housing by the private sector that forces out the poor and elderly. A cap should be placed on the amount that can be deducted from federal taxes for interest payments on private homes, cooperative apartments, or condominiums. National and fiscal budgetary policies should be reassessed to ensure that

they include a consideration of the contribution that decent housing can make to the growth and stability of the nation.

Funds for Low-to-Moderate-Income Housing. Federal programs to provide funds for the capital costs of new and rehabilitated housing and the subsidies necessary to ensure affordability must be available. Without such funds, the nation will face a housing crisis of untold dimensions in supply and quality. In addition to traditional programs to provide decent, affordable, and suitable housing, the federal government should encourage new approaches to financing housing for the poor and those with special needs, such as home-equity conversion, the removal of provisions in income-transfer programs that act as disincentives to alternative living arrangements, and direct grants for the construction and rehabilitation of housing. An integrated fiscal policy and adequate funds are the backbone of a national policy that seeks to implement the 1949 legislative goal of "a decent home and suitable living environment for everyone."

Policy statement approved by the NASW Delegate Assembly, 1984; reconfirmed by the Delegate Assembly, August 1990. Referred to the 1999 Delegate Assembly, to be revised and combined with the policy statement on Homelessness. For further information, contact the National Association of Social Workers, 750 First Street, NE, Suite 700, Washington, DC 20002-4241. Telephone: 202-408-8600 or 800-638-8799.

Immigrants and Refugees

BACKGROUND

Americans have been ambivalent about immigration; we cherish our immigrant heritage, but many citizens fear new immigration. As stated by sociologist Charles Keely (1979),

> On the one hand, the country has historically been a place of refuge, a place of new beginnings, accepting and even recruiting new settlers to build the nation and its economy. On the other hand, the theme of protectionism has found recurrent expression in apprehension over the capacity of the culture and economy to absorb newcomers, in the desire to limit labor market competition and assure minimal health standards, and even in nativism and racist theories. The history of immigration policy is a dialectic of these two themes of acceptance and protection. (p. 8)

These two themes have dominated immigration policy debates since the birth of the nation. With rare exceptions, however, major changes in immigration policy have resulted when protectionism is in the ascendancy.

Immigration Policy in the Current National Debate

The overwhelming majority of immigrants and refugees come to the United States legally through a careful selection process. Undocumented immigrants account for only about 15 percent of the entire foreign-born population of the United States and for only 1.25 percent of the population in general (Kane, 1994). Annual limits are placed on the number of immigrants and refugees legally admitted to the United States. Virtually all academic and government studies show that immigrants contribute greatly to the U.S. economy and are an asset rather than a burden. For example, a study conducted by the Urban Institute found that "for the country as a whole, legal and illegal immigrants generate a $25 billion to $30 billion surplus from the income and property taxes they pay" (Gibbs, 1994, p. 47).

The admissions system to the United States is based on three American values: family, freedom, and work. One reason the United States accepts refugees and immigrants is because this nation was founded in large part by those who fled political and religious persecution. Refugee protection also serves national and international interests. As the world's lone superpower and a nation that promotes the protection of human rights as a central tenet of its foreign policy, the way in which the United States treats those who flee human rights violations sends a signal to the rest of the world.

History of Immigration Reform

The protectionist or restrictionist view of immigration seems to have almost always commanded the majority of popular opinion. In 1876, power to regulate all immigration was vested in the federal government as a result of a Supreme Court ruling; in 1906, the Bureau of Immigration and Naturalization was established. Previously, the bureau had been part of the Treasury Department and later the Department of Commerce and Labor, reflecting the prevailing view of immigration as an economic concern. As the ranks of the immigrant grew, so did the animosity felt toward them. . . . Nationalistic sentiments generated by World War I increased existing pressure to restrict immigration. Such organizations as the Immigration Restriction League often pointed to religious differences as reason enough for denying foreigners entry to the United States. Racist fears were also strong. (Morales, 1986, p. 7; see also Handlin, 1959)

By 1920 Congress had enacted a dozen major immigration laws, most of which sought to restrict certain kinds of individuals. Some of the laws were directed at specific ethnic groups and often reflected blatantly racist fears. The first of these was a series of laws, now known as the "Chinese Exclusion Acts," that were passed in response to fears in the western United States of a "yellow peril." These laws, enacted in the late 1800s and early 1900s, virtually ended immigration from Asia, prevented Asian immigrants from becoming naturalized citizens, restricted the rights of Asian immigrants to own property, and denied Asian immigrants the opportunity to reunite with family members from abroad. Another example of the growing restrictionist sentiment is the Johnson Act of 1924:

> This Act imposed a numerical limit (150,000 per year) on newcomers to the United States. The Law grew out of the notion that immigration policy should be based on racial considerations. The 1924 statute attempted to stabilize the existing ethnic balance of the country by the assignment of a quota system that obviously favored northern Europeans. (Morales, 1986, p. 7; see also Jones, 1960)

Thus, the passage of the Johnson Act of 1924 coincided with and was stimulated by fear of the new immigrant groups. Mexican Americans also have been the target of restrictionist policies:

> While no accurate record exists of the number of Mexican citizens in the territory demarcated by the Treaty of Guadalupe Hidalgo in 1848, estimates range from 75,000 to 350,000. Additional Mexicans became residents of the United States as a result of the Gadsden Purchase in 1853. These were the first Mexicans to face becoming Americans in their own land.
>
> . . . The massive land transfers, legal and illegal, from Mexican to Anglo hands, the conversion of Mexican people into a pool of cheap labor, and laws like the California "Greaser Act" of 1855 were some of the tangible effects of discrimination. (Montiel &

Ortego y Gasca, 1995, pp. 44–45; see also McWilliams, 1968; Ortego y Gasca, 1981)

In the 1930s and later in the 1950s, fears of the "wetback menace" led to the deportation of almost 4.5 million people of Mexican descent, many of whom were U.S. citizens or legal residents.

Just before World War II, anti-Semitism led to the exclusion of many Jewish refugees who were fleeing Nazi persecution. In addition, Japanese immigrants were immediately classified as enemy aliens after the attack on Pearl Harbor. Unjustified fears led to the internment of some 100,000 citizens and resident aliens of Japanese descent.

The Cold War had a strong influence on U.S. immigration policy in the 1980s:

> The fall of Cambodia and South Vietnam in 1975 created floods of refugees who were a special responsibility of the United States. . . . Washington's welcome was not universal. . . . Refugees from Communist nations were welcomed, but those from countries officially deemed "democratic," like El Salvador, got shorter shrift. So did those who were "merely" trying to escape harsh but non-Communist regimes or grinding poverty like the Haitians. (Weisberger, 1994, p. 89)

Current Wave of Immigration Reform

Since 1980 emergency circumstances in their countries of origin have prompted large numbers of people to migrate to the United States and elsewhere:

> Deeply disturbing emergencies (Iraq, Bosnia, Algeria, Haiti, Cuba, Rwanda) have forced policy makers in many countries to confront—in crisis mode—the complexities of "ethnic cleansing" and of refugee protection, asylum, and temporary safe haven. . . . In global terms, international migration movements have been large and on the rise over the past decade, and the numbers designated as refugees and displaced persons have increased sharply. . . . In many of the industrialized countries to which migrants and refugees have been moving there has been

increasing public resistance to their arrival, fueled in part by a perception that governments are no longer able to control their borders. (American Assembly, 1994, pp. 3–4)

The exoduses of Haitians and Cubans are among the most recent examples. In 1994 the U.S. government responded to two refugee flows involving Haitians and Cubans by creating a temporary holding facility at the U.S. naval base at Guantanamo Bay, Cuba. This action has far-reaching implications for the U.S. government's current and future treatment of refugees and asylum seekers at Guantanamo or other off-shore locations (for example, the Panama Canal zone). Frelick (1995), senior policy analyst with the U.S. Committee for Refugees, suggested that the prospect exists that "the U.S. government will convert Guantanamo into a permanent refugee holding facility, not limited to Haitians and Cubans nor reserved specifically for mass refugee emergencies" (p. 18). Frelick pointed out that in January 1995, a U.S. Court of Appeals ruled that "refugees in safe haven camps outside the United States do not have Constitutional rights for due process or equal protection, and are not protected against forced return by the UN Refugee Convention or the U.S. Immigration and Nationality Act" (p. 18). In addition, according to the U.S. Commission on Refugees (1996):

Under the January 1995 asylum regulations, asylum claimants in the United States are barred from work authorization for six months or until granted asylum. During this time, they are not able to gain access to public assistance. (p. 4)

U.S. asylum regulations, released by the Justice Department in December 1994,

significantly expand the possibilities of denial of asylum in the United States to refugees who have traveled to the United States from a third country. . . . The regulations lay the groundwork for a future agreement with Mexico under which asylum claimants who traveled through Mexico could be sent back, and their claims decided under Mexican law and procedure. . . . If the United States does move toward a bilateral arrangement for the return

of third country nationals to Mexico, as anticipated in the December, 1994 regulations, the key question will be whether Mexican law and procedures are "full and fair" under U.S. standards. (Gzesh, 1995, p. 36)

In its September 1994 report to Congress, the U.S. Commission on Immigration Reform stated the belief that

a credible immigration policy requires the ability to respond effectively and humanely to immigration emergencies. . . . [It must] include discussion of contingency planning, interdiction, safe havens, refugee processing, asylum procedures, temporary protected status, aid to communities experiencing emergency arrivals of aliens, and other issues. (p. 29)

During the decade from 1980 to 1990, three pieces of legislation were adopted to govern immigration policy: the Refugee Act of 1980, the Immigration Reform and Control Act of 1986, and the Immigration Act of 1990. A *refugee,* as officially defined by the Refugee Act of 1980, is a person who is outside of his or her home country and cannot go home again because of a well-founded fear of persecution on the basis of race, religion, nationality, membership in a particular social group, or political opinion. "Unlike an immigrant, who generally has the opportunity to plan and prepare to leave the native country, the refugee often flees or is forced to leave suddenly and therefore leaves with few possessions" (Drachman, 1995, p. 191).

In 1996 the 104th Congress passed landmark welfare reform legislation entitled Personal Responsibility and Work Opportunity Reconciliation Act of 1996.

The bill cuts billions of dollars of help for legal aliens, including children. Effective immediately upon enactment, legal aliens now in this country may not receive SSI or Food Stamp help (even if they currently receive these benefits). . . . At state option, as of January 1, 1997, legal aliens may also be denied welfare help, child care, social services, and non-emergency Medicaid. Legal aliens who enter the country after the date of enactment of the bill are subject to even more sweeping denials of help. During the first five years after entry, they are barred from receiving most non-emergency means-tested federal help (including child care, food stamps, SSI, and welfare). (Children's Defense Fund, 1996)

In addition, both Houses of the 104th Congress passed immigration reform measures (H2202 and S269).

Throughout American history, the changing racial and ethnic character of new immigrants has sparked widespread concern and controversy over immigration policy. It is critical that the plight of refugees and immigrants be considered on the basis of human values and needs rather than on the basis of an ideological struggle related to foreign policy.

The Immigration Act of 1990 has provided the most comprehensive change since 1965 in the legal immigration system in the United States. According to the U.S. Commission on Immigration Reform (1994), the aim of the legislation was to

■ establish overall limits on legal immigration through adoption of a flexible cap on total numbers

■ permit continued reunification of close family members

■ meet labor market needs by increasing the number of immigrants admitted for employment-based reasons and giving higher priority to the entry of professionals and others who are highly skilled

■ provide greater diversity through new opportunities for migration from countries with relatively small numbers of immigrants to the United States.

Much has changed in the United States and the world since the passage of the act; for example, the Cold War ended, many defense industries have experienced cutbacks, and new trade arrangements such as the North American Free Trade Agreement and the Global Agreement on Tariffs and Trade have been adopted. As Weisberger (1994) pointed out, "The Statue of Liberty still lifts her lamp beside the golden door, but in a time of economic downturn, there is no longer an assured consensus that the door

should be kept open very far" (p. 76). The legacy of racism and xenophobia is not to be ignored, for these same themes underlie much of the current debate about immigration reform.

ISSUE STATEMENT

Serious problems exist in the immigration policies of the United States and the implementation of those policies. The U.S. Commission on Immigration Reform, in its September 1994 report to Congress, decried hostility and discrimination against immigrants as antithetical to the traditions and interests of this country. In addition, the commission stated its concern about unfair immigration-related employment practices affecting both citizens and noncitizens that may occur as a result of the current system of employer sanctions, and it recommended that the Office of the Special Counsel for Immigration-Related Unfair Employment Practices in the Department of Justice initiate additional proactive strategies to identify and combat immigration-related discrimination in the workplace. The commission also recommended against any broad, categorical denial of public benefits to legal immigrants. However, the report went on to say that it is both a right and a responsibility of a democratic society to manage immigration so that it serves the national interest (U.S. Commission on Immigration Reform, 1994).

Social workers must take a forceful and assertive stand to ensure that policies, programs, and practices protect all individuals who reside in the United States. Efforts must be made to support budget appropriations from the federal government to reimburse states for providing public services to refugees, entrants, displaced people, and undocumented individuals that should include, at a minimum, emergency medical and social services and public education services for the children of both legal and undocumented immigrants. Opposition must be mounted to federal and state legislative initiatives and actions that discriminate against both legal residents and undocumented individuals.

The United States has a dark history of slavery, racism, and mistreatment of Native Americans. As pointed out by Morales (1995),

Many historical accounts of Puerto Rico, Latin American nations, and the United States start with Columbus's "discovery" of a "new world" in 1492. These accounts reinforce a decidedly European perspective on history and exemplify institutionalized ethnocentrism and racism by dismissing the fact that Native Americans preceded Columbus by thousands of years.

The Europeans who settled in North America brought back from Africa millions of black African natives, whom they sold as slaves in the Americas and the Caribbean. In the United States and other countries, white men justified the killing of the people they called Indians and the enslavement of Africans by viewing these populations as subhuman heathens. (p. 79)

Social workers must reaffirm that racism and ethnic discrimination have no place in U.S. immigration policy or other social welfare policies. Chang-Lin Tien (1994), Chancellor of the University of California, Berkeley, has observed:

This is a nation that has taken pride not in its homogeneity, but in its immigrant heritage. . . . The debate is now moving away from the legitimate question of how much immigration America can sustain. Instead, we're blaming immigrants for many of our most urgent problems and trying to convince ourselves that we'll solve them simply by restricting immigration. . . . Racial and cultural hostilities fanned by the present anti-immigration frenzy must cool down. (p. 19)

Social workers must demonstrate their commitment to equity and justice and must fight against the erosion of federal and state enforcement of human and civil rights and the reduction of services, resources, and entitlement programs that are available for legal refugees and immigrants as well as those whose status is undocumented. NASW must be in the forefront of the discussions on such critical issues as

■ border management policies of the United States

■ human rights and civil liberties violations both in the United States and worldwide

■ anti-immigrant violence and fear, which are at one of the highest levels in 70 years in this country, "causing a rash of violent bias crimes against anyone who is perceived as 'foreign'" (Southern Poverty Law Center, 1994, p. 1)

■ organized smuggling operations—especially the smuggling of people and goods across the U.S–Mexican border

■ discrimination in employment based on national origin and citizenship status, as well as inappropriate demands for documentation

■ policy measures that would establish a national database or registry of workers to verify citizenship and residency status

■ the need to protect the privacy of information included in any such database that threatens to undermine our constitutional right to privacy

■ inappropriate demands that all legal residents become citizens, regardless of their individual circumstances and their contributions to society

■ inappropriate and discriminate demands for all residents to speak English only

■ federal, state, or local initiatives such as California's Proposition 187 that would legislate broad, categorical denial of public benefits to immigrants and refugees, regardless of their legal status.

POLICY STATEMENT

International migration, the process of leaving one country, traveling, and arriving in another, can be either highly stressful, as in the case of refugees, or simply a planned decision about an improved lifestyle, as in the case of educated professionals migrating for career reasons. Social workers are concerned with people at the stressful end of that continuum. Social workers must give consideration to the global dynamic of immigration created by the United States, and other countries' foreign policies, including acts of aggression that are often causative factors of political and economic dislocation within most immigrant and refugee countries of origin.

Federal, state, and local actions must ensure equal protection from discrimination and exploitation for all immigrants, refugees, entrants, displaced people, and undocumented individuals who arrive and reside in the United States. NASW advocates for commitment on the part of the U.S. government to end human rights violations worldwide and for reform in immigration and refugee policy that reaffirms the contributions of immigrants to this country; provides a clear and reasonable definition of political refugee; is generous enough to permit the United States to respond humanely to victims of war, political tyranny, or persecution; and is flexible enough for officials to react to worldwide emergency situations. As stated by Winter (1995), Director of the U.S. Committee for Refugees,

> The Cold War as we knew it is long gone, though its legacy of arms and firepower haunts the world. . . . Before, the enemy was defined as the Soviet empire, or more generically, as communism. Now the enemy is more amorphous. . . . The consequences of inaction and isolationism are not only huge body counts and destabilizing as well as costly refugee exoduses, but also the rearing of the ugly, undemocratic forces that our foreign policy has supposedly been dedicated to countering all along. . . .The failure of the international community hangs like tattered rags on the meatless skeleton of Bosnia traced by a network of UN-declared safe zones, a fraud and a scandal of such enormity that all Western "leaders" should be mortified at their hypocrisy. (p. 4)

As the nation debates the critical issues surrounding immigration, NASW will actively promote sound policy that provides for fair and humane U.S. immigration laws; the development of domestic and foreign policies that help alleviate the economic and political conditions that force people to flee their homes; and a plan to ensure that victims of human conflict in the poorest, least strategically important countries of the world do not continue to be ignored.

NASW believes that federal policies and procedures must, at a minimum, include the following principles:

■ voluntary repatriation of refugees that is promoted by the United States only when conditions in the refugees' home countries do not place returning refugees at risk—ideally, repatriation should be fully voluntary, fully informed, and take place only once the conditions that gave rise to the refugees' flight no longer exist

■ commitment to and strengthening of basic human rights and civil rights policies for all refugees and immigrants, regardless of gender, race, color, religion, ethnic origin, health status, sexual orientation, or legal status

■ a plan to replace the current patchwork of immigration reform efforts with a fair, equitable, and comprehensive national plan

■ streamline application procedures for asylum with continued protection for refugees and individuals with temporary protection status

■ a more expeditious adjudication process—large backlogs of asylum cases are not acceptable

■ a plan to ensure health, education, and social services benefits to those in need, regardless of immigration status

■ adequate appropriations to reimburse states for providing public services to refugees, entrants, displaced people, and undocumented individuals that should, at a minimum, include emergency medical and social services and public bilingual and bicultural educational services for the children of both legal and undocumented immigrants

■ a plan to combat racism and immigration-related discrimination in employment that may occur under the current system of employer sanctions

■ opposition to efforts to deny all public aid to legal immigrants

■ opposition to efforts that would abolish the guarantee of citizenship to all people born or naturalized in the United States

■ opposition to efforts to make English the official language

■ opposition to efforts to force legal residents of this country to become U.S. citizens

- opposition to requirements that schools, hospitals, and police departments report suspected undocumented individuals

- opposition to efforts to limit education benefits for children of undocumented individuals

- opposition to efforts to make crimes of domestic violence, stalking, child abuse, child neglect, and child abandonment committed by people residing in this country deportable offenses under our immigration laws.

The profession must monitor all federal, state, and local immigration and refugee policies and voice objection when known abuses occur. Social workers must continue to advocate for family reunification and sanctuary from persecution and insist that due process and fundamental human rights be upheld for immigrants and refugees. The profession must promote greater education and awareness at all levels of the dynamics of U.S. and other countries' foreign policies on immigration and refugee resettlement. Finally, greater legal protection must be made available for individuals who provide sanctuary, legal aid, and support for people fleeing from persecution in their countries of origin

REFERENCES

American Assembly. (1994). *Threatened peoples, threatened borders: World migration and U.S. policy, the 86th American assembly.* Harriman, NY: Author.

Children's Defense Fund. (1996, August 8). *Analysis of welfare bill conference report, Part II.* Washington, DC: Author.

Drachman, D. (1995). Immigration statuses and their influence on service provision, access, and use. *Social Work, 40,* 188–197.

Frelick, B. (1995). Safe haven: Safe for whom? In *World refugee survey 1995* (pp. 18–27). Washington, DC: Immigration and Refugee Services of America.

Gibbs, N. (1994, October 3). Keep out, you tired, you poor. . . . *Time,* pp. 46–47.

Gzesh, S. (1995). So close to the United States, so far from God: Refugees and asylees under Mexico law. In *World refugee survey 1995* (pp. 34–40). Washington, DC: Immigration and Refugee Services of America.

Handlin, O. (1959). *Immigration as a factor in American history.* Englewood Cliffs, NJ: Prentice Hall.

Immigration Act of 1990, P.L. 101-649, 104 Stat. 4978.

Immigration Reform and Control Act of 1986, P.L. 99-603, 100 Stat. 3359.

Johnson Act, ch. 190, 43 Stat. 153.

Jones, M. A. (1960). *American immigration.* Chicago: University of Chicago Press.

Kane, P. (1994, December). *Facts and myths about immigrants and refugees.* Unpublished report, Rhode Island Coalition for Immigrants and Refugees, Providence.

Keely, C. (1979). *U.S. immigration: A policy analysis.* New York: Population Council.

McWilliams, C. (1968). *The Mexicans in America: A student's guide to localized history.* New York: Teachers College Press.

Montiel, M., & Ortego y Gasca, F. (1995). Chicanos, community, and change. In F. G. Rivera (Ed.), *Community organizing in a diverse society* (2nd ed., chap. 3, pp. 43–60). Boston: Allyn & Bacon.

Morales, J. (1986). *Puerto Rican poverty and migration.* New York: Praeger.

Morales, J. (1995). Community social work with Puerto Ricans in the United States. In F. G. Rivera (Ed.), *Community organizing in a diverse society* (2nd ed., chap. 5, pp. 77–94). Boston: Allyn & Bacon.

Ortego y Gasca, F. (1981). *Backgrounds of Mexican American literature.* Austin, TX: Caravel Press.

Refugee Act of 1980, P.L. 96-212, 94 Stat. 102.

Southern Poverty Law Center. (1994, August). Anti-immigrant violence rages nationwide. *Intelligence Report,* p. 1.

Tien, C.-L. (1994, October 31). America's scapegoats: Immigrant-bashing is hurting the native and foreign born alike. *Newsweek,* p. 19.

U.S. Commission on Immigration Reform. (1994, September). *U.S. immigration policy: Restoring credibility: A report to Congress* (Executive Summary). Washington, DC: Author.

U.S. Committee for Refugees. (1996, June). Work or welfare? Other countries provide pending asylum claimants one or the other. *Refugee Reports*, p. 4.

Weisberger, B. A. (1994, February–March). A nation of immigrants. *American Heritage*, pp. 75–91.

Winter, R. P. (1995). The year in review. In *World refugee survey 1995* (pp. 2–7). Washington, DC: Immigration and Refugee Services of America.

Policy statement approved by the NASW Delegate Assembly, August 1996. This policy supersedes the policy statements on Immigrants and Refugees approved by the Delegate Assembly in 1987 and in 1979. For further information, contact the National Association of Social Workers, 750 First Street, NE, Suite 700, Washington, DC 20002-4241. Telephone: 202-408-8600 or 800-638-8799.

The Impaired Professional

BACKGROUND

Impaired functioning is a problem for workers at all levels of our society. National statistics indicate that 10 to 15 percent of all workers are impaired because of problems such as chemical dependence, mental dysfunction, and family stress (Fitzgerald, 1983). The capacity of impaired workers to handle their problems affects not only their well-being, but their ability to perform their jobs. Social workers, no different from the rest of the population, are subject to problems of abuse, addictions, and stress. In fact, "social workers younger than age 65 experienced more suicides than the general population in that age group" (*American Medical News*, 1987). Dysfunction resulting from impairment affects the individual, his or her family, and other employees at the workplace. In addition, the impairment influences the quality and the effectiveness of service to clients.

NASW has not given high priority to impairment within the profession and assistance to impaired colleagues at the national level. When national efforts were not forthcoming, chapters began to establish programs to address the impaired professional. In 1978, New York City published *Alcoholism among Social Workers: Approaching a Colleague with a Drinking Problem*. In 1979, New Jersey established a confidential hotline. New York State created a Peer Consultation Committee that was a confidential advocacy group.

These three chapters were instrumental in preparing a national policy statement on alcoholism and alcohol-related problems within the profession that was approved by the NASW Delegate Assembly in 1979. The policy states that the social work profession can and should

assume responsibility for examining the extent of alcohol and other substance abuse problems within its own ranks, and for taking appropriate measures to protect both the ill social workers and the clients they serve. Social workers who suffer from alcoholism or other substance abuse should be assured that treatment information and appropriate health benefits and safeguards are provided by institutions and agencies that employ them, as well as by the profession of social work. (NASW, 1994, p. 39)

In 1980, Social Workers Helping Social Workers (SWHSW) was formed to provide mutual support and to assist others with impairment and related problems. The program, which has grown most rapidly in the Midwest and on the East Coast, is available to all social workers with master's degrees and to master of social work degree candidates who have experienced alcoholism in their own lives or those of their families. When John Fitzgerald, a former SWHSW chairperson, surveyed the SWHSW membership, he learned that 77 percent of the alcoholic members were never approached about their problem in the workplace, even though 87 percent indicated active abuse of a chemical during the workday. Almost all the members reported "negative behaviors" at work that passed without comment. The negative behaviors included being unable to read interview notes; using profane, insulting, or aggressive language; and making sexual overtures to a client.

It was not until 1982, under the leadership of the newly appointed National Occupational Social Work Task Force, that the plight of the impaired social worker began to receive some national attention. Chapters in Connecticut and Texas were awarded grants from the NASW Practice Advancement Fund to review guidelines for establishing programs to assist impaired social workers (for these guidelines and chapter activities, see NASW, 1987). Because of the efforts of the task force and its successor, the Occupational Social Work Planning Committee, the 1984 Delegate Assembly passed a nonbinding resolution that called upon NASW to endorse and encourage chapters' efforts to address the problems of their impaired members. The resolution stated that NASW should provide technical assistance and other resources to assist chapters in developing and implementing programs for impaired practitioners (NASW, 1984).

ISSUE STATEMENT

National and local professional health associations, including the American Dental Association, the American Medical Association, the American Nursing Association, the American Pharmaceutical Association, and the American Psychiatric Association, have adopted formal policies and procedures for addressing the needs of their impaired members, from the highest level of the organizational leadership to the individual member. In lagging behind these other organizations, NASW appears to have refused to acknowledge the needs of colleagues who are impaired. The omission of a formal NASW policy is especially glaring in light of the profession's increased activities in the workplace, where social workers are taking a lead in developing treatment and support services for employees who are impaired.

Several NASW chapters and, in some cases, affected individuals have developed programs to offer assistance to impaired social workers. Currently, a dozen chapters have colleague-assistance or impaired social worker programs. Some offer only information or education; others include confidential hotlines or referral.

Based on national statistics for the overall population, it is estimated that the work performance of at least 10 percent of professional social workers is impaired significantly by drug addiction or alcoholism. An impaired professional program is based on an understanding that alcohol and drug addictions are progressive, primary diseases. The disease is chronic because of the lifelong recovery process involved. Current knowledge of chemical dependence indicates that it becomes progressively worse. The person addicted to alcohol or other drugs must develop a lifestyle that is free from all mood-altering chemicals.

Although it is imperative that social workers do not ignore their chemically dependent colleagues, addressing the issue of impaired practice presents real dilemmas. Clients who are affected most by impaired performance generally do not recognize it. If they do, they may feel powerless to do anything about it. Unfortunately, many social workers refuse to "interfere" in the lives of their troubled colleagues and mistakenly cling to the belief that intelligence, education, and occupation exempt someone from these kinds of problems. Finally, the clinical phenomenon of denial makes it unlikely that impaired professionals will embark voluntarily upon a course of treatment for needed rehabilitation. Instead, often finding their lives in total disarray, they fear and avoid detection from colleagues who tragically find it easier to look the other way.

Any program for impaired professionals must confront inherent tensions between protection of the public, on the one hand, and confidentiality and advocacy for the distressed professional, on the other hand. Recognizing that impaired practice frequently is characterized by denial, the program first must confront the practitioner effectively and then support him or her through the recovery process.

As a profession, we must face the reality of impaired practitioners in our midst. The problem is not going to go away. Further, the problem is best handled by the profession itself. Options are available, and there is room for both compassion and firmness.

POLICY STATEMENT

As part of its responsibility to encourage the highest standards of social work practice, NASW sanctions the establishment of a colleague-assistance program for national leaders and staff and commits its support to individual chapters for the development of colleague-assistance programs. The goal of the programs will be to create a peer network through which impaired social workers may be identified, encouraged to obtain treatment, assisted toward recovery, and helped to resume and maintain safe and effective practice. By endorsing chapter programs,

NASW acknowledges its responsibility to protect consumers of social work services, to support professional responsibility among colleagues, and to continue its leadership in developing practice standards for the profession.

NASW recognizes that, although chemical dependence may be the most frequent cause of impaired practice, a wide range of psychosocial stresses and psychiatric disorders may lead to impairment. Regardless of the cause of the impairment, when an individual's practice has deteriorated to the point that it arouses concern in the practitioner, colleagues, or others, intervention is warranted. The responsibility of the intervening person or people or the committee is to ensure confidentiality, to invoke nonpunitive action, and to adhere to the *NASW Code of Ethics* (NASW, 1993). In addition, NASW encourages organizations and agencies that employ professional social workers to accomplish the following:

■ improve insurance benefits to make access to services possible

■ develop policies to protect clients or patients from poor practice

■ develop nonpunitive employment policies for dealing with colleagues who experience difficulty

■ lobby for civil immunity laws that protect potential reporters of impaired colleagues.

REFERENCES

American Medical News. (1987, January 23–30).

Fitzgerald, J. (1983, Winter/Spring). *Proposal to regulate social workers* (Testimony on H.B. 5901 before the Public Health Committee, Connecticut State Legislature).

NASW Commission on Employment and Economic Support. (1987). *Impaired social worker program resource book.* Silver Spring, MD: National Association of Social Workers.

National Association of Social Workers. (1984). *Distressed social workers.* Resolution No. 21, approved by the 1984 Delegate Assembly. (Available from NASW, 750 First Street, NE, Suite 700, Washington, DC 20002-4241)

National Association of Social Workers. (1994). Alcoholism and other substance abuse–related problems. In *Social work speaks: NASW policy statements* (3rd ed., pp. 35–39). Washington, DC: Author.

National Association of Social Workers. (1993). *NASW code of ethics.* Washington, DC: Author.

Policy statement approved by the NASW Delegate Assembly, November 1987; reconfirmed by the Delegate Assembly, August 1993. This policy statement was previously titled A Colleague-Assistance Program. For further information, contact the National Association of Social Workers, 750 First Street, NE, Suite 700, Washington, DC 20002-4241. Telephone: 202-408-8600 or 800-638-8799.

International Policy on Human Rights

BACKGROUND

The history of human rights is the history of the struggle against the exploitation of one person by another. Through the ages, the resistance to all forms of oppression has developed into the recognition, based on the concept of the inherent dignity and worth of every individual, that all people have certain basic rights.

The current status of the crusade for human rights is the recognition that such rights and obligations are necessary for all people and their social institutions. On that requirement there is international consensus, as stated in the preamble to the United Nations Universal Declaration of Human Rights (1948):

> ... recognition of the inherent dignity and of the equal and inalienable rights of all members of the human family is the foundation of freedom, justice and peace in the world. ...

Human rights are recognized specifically in the following international laws and agreements:

- United Nations Charter (signed June 26, 1945): Preamble, Articles 1, 55, and 56

- Universal Declaration of Human Rights (U.N. General Assembly, December 10, 1948)

- Convention on the Prevention and Punishment of the Crime of Genocide (U.N. General Assembly, December 11, 1948)

- International Convention on the Elimination of All Forms of Racial Discrimination (U.N. General Assembly, 1965)

- International Covenant of Economic, Social and Cultural Rights (U.N. General Assembly, 1966)

- International Covenant on Civil and Political Rights (U.N. General Assembly, 1966).

The United Nations provides oversight, investigation, and complaint bodies relative to these agreements.

Other human rights agreements of a regional or special nature now exist or are being developed. Examples of these are as follows:

- The European Convention of the Human Rights Treaty in Western Europe provides the basis for hearings and decisions of the Council of Europe's Commission on Human Rights and Court of Human Rights.

- The Treaty of the American Convention on Human Rights has set forth standards for basic human rights to be followed by members of the Organization of American States.

- The 16th Annual Conference of the Organization of African Unity called for an African Charter of Human Rights in July 1979.

- The Convention of the Elimination of All Forms of Discrimination Against Women, adopted by the United Nations in December 1979, calls on all state parties (particularly countries) to take all appropriate measures to eliminate discrimination against women in such fields as politics, law, employment, education, health care, domestic relations, and commercial transactions. The convention set up a committee on the elimination of discrimination against women to review progress made by the participating countries in this matter.

These and other agreements provide significant rules of international behavior and guidelines for progress toward the goal of full human rights for all. Nevertheless, people and their governments are far from the declared intent and goals. Gross and subtle violations of human rights are perpetrated every day against thousands of people. The phenomenon of the "disappeared," the torture of political prisoners, the increasing use of the death penalty, the extortion of confessions by physical and mental abuse, the retentions of prisoners without trial, the economic exploitation of populations and groups, and other violations are all too evident throughout the world.

Many complex factors contribute to the nature and significance of violations of human rights. The creation of new nations from the breakup of the colonial empires brought about many political struggles for power and control, often with consequent internal or external violence. The growth of transnational economic organizations has introduced different economic and social patterns throughout the world, with resultant cultural and ideological conflicts. Economic exploitation and monopolistic control of income and resources continue to produce disparities that create inevitable conflict. The increasing resort to military control by political systems has been the cause and effect of dissension and of the escalation of retaliatory measures by one group against another.

The need for an educated population in a technological society has increased intellectual independence, while communication through the mass media has escalated people's hopes and demands. Rising expectations for economic security and social justice have caused millions of people to question the prevailing social, economic, and political systems; to organize for alternative practices; and to compete for leadership in both legal and extralegal ways.

The social work profession is responsible for opposing and working to eliminate all violations of human rights. This responsibility must be exercised in the social worker's practice with individuals, groups, and communities; in the role of an agency or organizational representative; and in the role of citizen of a nation and the world. The special knowledge and understanding that is part of the education and training of the professional social worker creates an additional responsibility to educate others to respect the worth and individuality of all people and to prevent violations of human rights.

Definition of Human Rights

Human rights are those fundamental entitlements that are considered to be necessary to the development of each personality to the fullest capacity. Violations of human rights are any arbitrary and selective actions that interfere with the full exercise of fundamental entitlements. The following human rights may be regarded as a common standard and guide for all professional social workers.

Basic Rights

Every person is born free and equal and has the right of self-determination within the limits of the same right of others. Every person shall have the freedom of life, liberty, thought, speech, and security of person. Every person is entitled to his or her rights and freedom without distinction as to birth, sex, sexual orientation, race, color, language, national or social origin, property, intellect, ideology, political opinion, or other conditions.

Governance

Everyone has the right to a nationality and to governance by a government derived from the will of the people as expressed in regular and genuine secret elections that ensure universal and equal suffrage. Everyone has the right and responsibility to take part in their own governance, both directly and through freely chosen representatives. Each person shall have equal access to public services and social security in accordance with the resources of his or her national and local governments. Everyone shall have freedom of thought and communication. Everyone shall have the right of peaceful assembly without arms and to freedom of association and movement, including the right to reside, move about, or leave the country. Each person shall have the right of asylum if his or her human rights have been violated.

Justice

Every person has the right to be recognized as a person before the law and the right of fair and equitable treatment and protection. Everyone shall be free of arbitrary interference with his or her privacy, home, communications, and person and shall be subject only to the rule of democratically instituted law. Each person, when charged with violations of a law, shall be presumed innocent until proved guilty, shall be entitled to know the charges and the charging party, shall have available time and measures to prepare competent responses, shall be assured a prompt and fair trial by an objective judicial authority, and shall have the right of appeal to a higher authority.

It is important to understand the constellation of causes that brings people into conflict and that leads to punitive retaliatory measures. But it is mandatory to reject the use of brutality and to establish international agreements and practices to eliminate violations of human rights.

Professional Social Workers and Human Rights

Professional social workers have a unique role and responsibility in the struggle for human rights. As a profession that has developed in the 20th century in response to changing social conditions, social work functions to prevent or ameliorate individual, group, and community problems arising from the dysfunction between the needs of people and their societal institutions. Thus, its essential reason for being is to improve the quality of life.

The experience of social workers in recognizing and diagnosing psychosocial problems and in developing and providing social services has given them unique knowledge and convictions regarding human behavior. This practice wisdom has been distilled into certain values, such as the right to self-determination, the acceptance of differences, and the use of limits and time. Such experiences and values underpin the concept of human rights.

At the same time, the social worker's role and responsibility for helping with transactions between people and their social institutions have linked the profession with dispossessed and traumatized people and with efforts to correct deleterious conditions. As a result, social workers often are the conscience of the community or victims of human rights violations themselves. As advocates for change, they often are in the forefront of movements and actions for change and thus are subject to repression and abuse. Therefore, the value system, training, and experience of social workers require that they take professional responsibility for working for human rights.

The universal plague of human rights violations makes it even more imperative that international policy agreements between the social workers of all nations and a cooperative program of action be implemented.

POLICY STATEMENT

The social work profession, through historical, scientific, and empirical evidence, is convinced that the achievement of universal human rights for all people is fundamental to the eventual security and survival of the human race. Only through the recognition and implementation of the basic concepts of the inherent dignity, worth, and quality of each person can the world become stable and secure. The solution to individual, group, community, and societal problems is linked inextricably with the principles of equal rights and self-determination, which are subject only to recognition of and respect for the rights and freedom of others.

Each person who is found guilty of violating a just law shall be entitled to humane treatment whose purpose is the reform and social readaptation of the individual. The physical, mental, and moral integrity of the person shall be respected; no one shall be subjected to torture; to other cruel, inhumane, or degrading treatment; or to capital punishment. Differential reeducation shall be provided, depending on the person's age and physical and mental condition and the nature of the crime.

Family

The family is the natural and fundamental unit of society and the state. Every person shall be entitled to establish and maintain a family based on the free and full consent of the family members. Every family shall be entitled to security and support obtained through adequate housing, food, clothing, health care, and employment. Each family member shall have the right to measures of protection required by any special condition, such as age, sex, sexual orientation, or physical or mental limitations.

Education

Everyone has the right to education, to achieve the maximum utilization of his or her abilities in the interests of the society. Education shall be free and equal for all to the fullest extent possible in each nation. Education shall be directed not only to the acquisition of basic knowledge and vocational techniques, but to the full development of the human personality, including an understanding of individual, social, economic, political, cultural, and human rights. The educational program shall provide necessary ancillary services to achieve the educational objectives.

Work

Everyone has the right to a job, with favorable wages and safe working conditions, to allow for a standard of living adequate for the well-being of an individual and family. Everyone has the right to equal pay for comparable work, to a reasonable limitation on working hours to allow for rest and leisure, to periodic holidays and vacations with pay, and to organize or join unions to protect the conditions of employment. Everyone has the right to equal opportunities for vocational development and to have social insurance for disability, unemployment, and retirement.

Health

Everyone has the right to a life of physical and mental well-being, free from disease and in stability. Everyone is entitled, subject only to the prevailing scientific knowledge, to full measures for the prevention of ill health; to periodic diagnostic evaluation; to prompt and competent medical, psychological, and social treatment; and to participate in the means of treatment. Everyone has the right to know the state of his or her health and to make the final decision regarding the management of his or her own body.

Responsibilities

Everyone has responsibility to the community, to the nation, and to international order and development to contribute personal energy and commitment to obtain the fullest expression of human rights and social progress. Each person has a responsibility to utilize the existing social institutions to advance human rights. No person or collective of people has the right to engage in any activity that is contrary to the institution and maintenance of human rights, including propaganda to incite war, hostility, hatred, or violence.

Policy statement approved by the NASW Delegate Assembly, 1981; reconfirmed by the Delegate Assembly, August 1990. Referred to the 1999 Delegate Assembly for revision. For further information, contact the National Association of Social Workers, 750 First Street, NE, Suite 700, Washington, DC 20002-4241. Telephone: 202-408-8600 or 800-638-8799.

Juvenile Justice and Delinquency Prevention

BACKGROUND

Dean Roscoe Pound of the Harvard Law School reported in 1937 that, since its inception, the juvenile court posed a danger to the rights of children and youths (Pound, 1937). Not surprisingly, several decades later, the U.S. Supreme Court concluded that children were receiving the worst of two worlds, "bad process and bad care" (*Kent v. United States*, 1966), and a hard look at the juvenile justice system reveals that we have not eliminated these problems since the 1966 Supreme Court indictment (Orlando & Crippen, 1992). Children's rights in juvenile court remain in danger.

There is a repetitive quality to the history of juvenile justice reform (Rothman, 1984). An examination of this reform, from houses of refuge to reformatories, from probation and the juvenile court to diversion, reveals what may be viewed as well-intentioned changes that produced either dissatisfying or unknown outcomes. Examination also reveals a pattern of enthusiastic ideological support for innovations combined with an unwillingness or inability to scrutinize critically both the implementation and the performance of the innovations. The history of juvenile justice is an evolution of an ever enlarging and ever changing social control apparatus.

Juvenile Court System

Many attempts to reform the juvenile justice system have failed because of the very nature of juvenile courts, which are highly specialized and thus controlled by a small number of people in each local jurisdiction (Soler & Shauffer, 1990). Even competent counsel can become intimidated and ineffective in such a system (Feld, 1990).

In the states that sentence juveniles on the basis of their offenses, few provide jury trials and several have rejected, out of hand, the constitutional challenges that have arisen from them (Schwartz, 1992). The increased punitiveness of juvenile justice raises a dilemma of constitutional dimensions: "Is it fair, in the constitutional sense, to expose minors to adult sanctions for crimes, without granting them the same due process rights as adults?" (Private Sector Task Force on Juvenile Justice, 1987, p. 7).

In addition, the unlimited dispositional powers of local and state court systems have often proved sufficient to defeat the educational efforts of social workers to promote appropriate limits and dispositions for certain types of cases. In the name of compassion and protection, youths are too often deprived of the most basic legal rights routinely afforded to adults. Prosecutors divert youths, on whose cases they had inadequate evidence, to long terms of treatment, and, at times, it is questionable whether the parents, who concur with the court's decisions, have a youth's best interests in mind.

Despite our best intentions, there has been no dramatic change in juvenile justice since the landmark *Gault* decision in 1967, which asserted that juveniles facing adjudication were entitled to essentially the same rights to legal counsel as were adults. Prior to 1967, attorneys appeared in perhaps 5 percent of delinquency cases (Feld, 1989). In 1968, observers reported that juveniles were neither adequately advised of their right to counsel nor had counsel been appointed for them (Lefstein, Stapleton, & Teitelbaum, 1969). In most hearings in which counsel did appear, they did nothing (Ferster & Courtless, 1972). Currently, whatever the particular situation, most juveniles in most states never see a lawyer, do not waive their right to counsel, and they still confront the power of the state alone and un-aided (Feld, 1992).

Examination of the rates of secure placement and legal counsel waivers across the United States reveals patterns varying radically from one state and county to another. Secure placements in Massachusetts occur at the rate of four per 100,000 people, and in Nebraska and Nevada, at the rate of 280 per 100,000 people (Schwartz, 1989). In detention, one state has a pattern of detaining three out of every 1,000 youths, whereas another state detains 60 out of 1,000. The pattern of the waiver of counsel by and for juveniles in St. Paul, Minnesota, and three suburban metropolitan counties was less than 7 percent, whereas in Minneapolis, 48 percent waived counsel; and in one other metropolitan suburb, 93 percent waived counsel (Feld, 1989).

The efforts at reform of the juvenile justice system, encouraged by the law and social work professions, have largely involved alternatives to engagement in the court system. In view of the growing fiscal crisis in America, the use of alternatives to divert youths from the court will likely continue. If diversion is to be effective, however, researchers and diversion staff must cooperate to a greater extent when programs are planned, implemented, and studied. This partnership is crucial to avoid the frustrating cycle of sporadic and inadequate efforts at juvenile justice reform (Ezell, 1992).

Large Detention or Correctional Institutions

Between 1835 and 1970, large institutions—commonly known as training schools—were seen as the primary solution to the problem of juvenile delinquency in this country. The institutions themselves, along with their counterparts specializing in mental health and mental retardation, have been recognized as the worst of all possible choices to deal with a social problem. Brutal, violent, costly, ineffective, and often racist, training schools created graduates who now swell the populations of adult correctional institutions and figure prominently in the ranks of those who today commit heinous and violent crimes.

The number of female and minority youths currently incarcerated, held in secure institu-tional care by various juvenile justice agencies, is alarming. In general, figures show that the presence of young women in public juvenile facilities since the late 1970s has increased approximately 10 percent; and the young women were detained and committed for different and less serious offenses than young men (Federle & Chesney-Lind, 1992). The same is true for status offenders. In 1989, 36,417 African American youths were arrested and held for status offense violations (Federal Bureau of Investigation, 1990), whereas by 1992, the number increased to 40,806 (Federal Bureau of Investigation, 1993).

The youth population held in large institutional settings has been increasing steadily over the past decade, despite evidence of the ineffectiveness of institutions in dealing with the underlying problems. In fiscal year 1988, public juvenile detention centers and training schools cost taxpayers more than $1.4 billion to operate. There were nearly 500,000 admissions to juvenile detention centers in 1989, representing a 30 percent increase in the national rate of admissions during the decade (U.S. Department of Justice, 1990); and juvenile justice officials, a potent political force, increasingly are advocating "get tough" measures as a strategy for responding to the juvenile crime problem. Law enforcement officials claim that juvenile detention centers and training schools are essential in the fight against juvenile crime and that they constitute the only credible means for keeping dangerous and violent young offenders off the streets (Schwartz, Willis, & Battle, 1991). However, the argument over whether juvenile detention centers and training schools have been successful has long been settled; most scholars, even most members of the general public, now agree that these large institutions have been a costly failure (Bakal & Lowell, 1992).

Diversion Programs

With the steady reduction in available financial resources, federal, state, and local government systems have increasingly looked to the private sector to develop, build, and staff the juvenile justice systems and services for which they previously held exclusive responsibility

(Kamerman & Kahn, 1989). In fact, the private sector has been the preeminent tool for engineering the transition from training schools to community-based programs.

Diversion from both the juvenile courts and the large probation and training institutions has become increasingly popular since the 1960s, but it was not until the late 1970s that the diversion attempts began to be empirically scrutinized. Although the ability of diversion programs to reduce recidivism has received mixed reviews by researchers, it is understood that they have consistently produced a panoply of unintended consequences—positive and negative—at both the individual and system levels. Most have demonstrated a marked capability to continue the trend in larger institutions of widening the net of the justice system, extending instead of reducing the overall proportion of youths subject to some form of state control or supervision. At the same time, these programs have failed to stem the rapid increase in juvenile arrest and detention, particularly among female and minority youths.

ISSUE STATEMENT

The juvenile justice system is in such turmoil that voices across the country are suggesting that we abolish the juvenile court system. More youths currently are being confined in youth correction facilities, youth training schools, and detention centers than at any other time in our history. A recent nationwide survey revealed that at least half of all adults of voting age want juveniles who commit felonies tried in the adult criminal courts (Alcser, Connor, & Heeringa, 1991).

After five decades of struggle, the system still fails to advise youths adequately of their rights, to provide appropriate legal counsel, to allow case disposition based on individual situations, or to enable access to appropriate treatment programs.

POLICY STATEMENT

NASW recommends that the following six priority actions be considered to strengthen the juvenile justice system:

1. Develop sound systems to evaluate the problem of youth detention and incarceration within local and state jurisdictions and possible alternatives. Local jurisdictions should commission studies of the juveniles who are incarcerated within their system to determine what proportion of the youths are nonserious and nonchronic offenders who can be managed in the community without compromising public safety. Better information management systems that can be used across agency and state lines must be developed with the encouragement and guidance of the federal government.

Local juvenile justice systems should be encouraged to use research on alternatives to the use of detention and training center placements and to learn from the experiences of other jurisdictions that have successfully downsized or closed institutions in favor of community-based treatment alternatives. Furthermore, each jurisdiction should explore the potential for reallocating or redeploying existing resources from the current large institutions to smaller, more focused, and community-based treatment facilities.

2. Provide for state administrative control of all juvenile corrections programs as a means to pool available knowledge, skills, and resources and to avoid the often piecemeal and uneven provision of services at the local level.

3. Develop quality, responsive juvenile court systems. Each jurisdiction must develop well-defined "target populations" to meet the unique needs of the individuals and groups they serve.

Local courts must supply to all youths in danger of severe disposition the assistance of quality, experienced legal counsel, similar to that employed in the statewide public defender programs within adult criminal justice systems. Furthermore, a solid professional effort should be made to guide judges in communicating to youths what they need to know about their right to counsel, their right to a hearing, and their understanding of the dispositional powers of the court.

Juvenile justice systems also must provide meaningful limits to the dispositional powers of the court. Status offense case duration must be specifically stated, and the length of disposition in a misdemeanor case should not be the same as the length of disposition in a more serious case. In addition, curbs must be placed on the use of contempt proceedings to avoid enlarging a minor problem into a major crisis for a youth.

Appropriate staffing and the uniform use of quality assessment tools are mandatory. A wide option of possibilities and great discretion are needed in the matter of youth detention. Every system must be served by a trustworthy means for assessing the need for out-of-home detention.

Court officials and state diversion systems should pay greater attention to and provide for the due process rights of juveniles accused of delinquent acts.

Diversion programs should focus on meeting a limited set of service objectives required by the particular needs of their targeted group to avoid a dilution of their service effectiveness and the expansion in the number of individuals pulled into the juvenile justice service net.

Placements out of the community should be limited to only those cases deemed most severe.

Alternatives for diversion from the court process, including mediation, should be studied and implemented. It must be remembered, however, that mediation and diversion can also be dangerous for youths. In this process, there must be limits on the severity and length of dispositions, and advocates must be employed to guarantee expression of a youth's desires.

4. Promote quality case management for all youths served and provide continuous active advocacy for all needed services, including services that do not currently exist.

5. Develop and promote effective interagency service networks. Develop systems of collaboration among the various juvenile justice agencies. Jointly develop and agree on common goals; share responsibility and funding for obtaining these goals; and work together to achieve them, using the skills, resources, and expertise of each of the agency partners.

Whenever possible, blend agency staff, procedures, training, administration, and funding across agencies to enable the application of multisystemic resources. Furthermore, develop clear goals, objectives, and outcome measures to research the viability of effective interagency partnerships on the quality of services provided and the benefits ascribed to youths and their families.

6. Develop quality treatment programs. A broad array of services is required to meet the different needs of the target populations, accompanied by the elimination of categorical funding requirements, confidentiality strictures, and other statutory and regulatory barriers to coordination of those services. These include

■ A new and holistic approach to the placement and treatment of children and youth must be encouraged.

■ Treatment services must emphasize working with the entire family, rather than just the identified at-risk youth.

■ Services and placements must not serve the institutional needs over the urgent needs of the youth served.

■ Ethnic and culturally appropriate programs must be developed and funded.

■ Administrative flexibility must be encouraged. Juvenile justice administrators should examine all their options and be willing to seek solutions that break the mold of their existing treatment systems and structures.

■ New and diverse programs that focus on the individual needs of youths and that meet the requirements of public safety must be developed and implemented.

■ The state must both determine priorities and hold the providers of treatment services accountable.

An effective means must be developed for monitoring the efforts of both state facilities and private provider programs. These program assessment systems must be designed and implemented to hold systems accountable for the results of their efforts and the practices used to obtain these results. Each system should engage a program audit unit, comprising people who are expert in service delivery and able to judge the legitimacy of performance expectations. Each jurisdiction providing treatment services should require a single source case management system that will assume responsibility to network within the larger court and community systems for the youths and families served.

Except in cases in which psychiatric hospitalization is required, a unified case management system should be open to all appropriate referrals. When it is discovered that a youth cannot be served at the initial referral, a plan for needed services can be developed after 30 days and the individual can be moved to a more appropriate setting.

REFERENCES

Alcser, K. H., Connor, J. H., & Heeringa, S. G. (1991). *National study of attitudes toward juvenile crime: Final report.* Ann Arbor: Survey Research Center, Institute for Social Research, University of Michigan.

Bakal, Y., & Lowell, H. (1992). The private sector in juvenile corrections. In I. M. Schwartz (Ed.), *Juvenile justice and public policy: Toward a national agenda* (pp. 196–213). New York: Lexington Books and Macmillan.

Ezell, M. (1992). Juvenile diversion: The ongoing search for alternatives. In I. M. Schwartz (Ed.), *Juvenile justice and public policy: Toward a national agenda* (pp. 45–58). New York: Lexington Books and Macmillan.

Federal Bureau of Investigation. (1990). *Crime in America 1989: Uniform crime reports.* Washington, DC: U.S. Department of Justice.

Federal Bureau of Investigation. (1993). *Crime in America 1992: Uniform crime reports.* Washington, DC: U.S. Department of Justice.

Federle, K. H., & Chesney-Lind, M. (1992). Special issues in juvenile justice: Gender, race, and ethnicity. In I. M. Schwartz (Ed.), *Juvenile justice and public policy: Toward a national agenda* (pp. 165–195). New York: Lexington Books and Macmillan.

Feld, B. (1989). The right to counsel in juvenile court: An empirical study of when lawyers appear and the difference they make. *Journal of Criminal Law and Criminology, 79,* 1185–1346.

Feld, B. (1990). The right of counsel in juvenile court: Fulfilling *Gault's* promise. *Youth Law News, 11*(3), 20–23.

Feld, B. (1992). Criminalizing the juvenile court. In I. M. Schwartz (Ed.), *Juvenile justice and public policy: Toward a national agenda* (pp. 59–88). New York: Lexington Books and Macmillan.

Ferster, E. A., & Courtless, T. F. (1972). Predispositional data, role of counsel and decisions in a juvenile court. *Law and Society Review, 7,* 195–222.

Gault, 387 U.S. at 34–42 (1967).

Hindelang, M. J., Gottfredson, M. R., & Flanagan, T. J. (Eds.). (1981). *Sourcebook of criminal justice statistics: 1980.* Washington, DC: Bureau of Justice Statistics, U.S. Department of Justice.

Kamerman, S. B., & Kahn, A. J. (1989). *Social services for children, youth and families in the United States.* Greenwich, CT: Annie E. Casey Foundation.

Kent v. United States, 383 U.S. 541, 555 (1966).

Lefstein, N., Stapleton, V., & Teitelbaum, L. (1969). In search of juvenile justice: *Gault* and its implementation. *Law and Society Review, 3,* 491–562.

Orlando, F. A., & Crippen, G. L. (1992). The rights of children and the juvenile court. In Schwartz, I. M. (Ed.), *Juvenile justice and public policy: Toward a national agenda* (pp. 89–100). New York: Lexington Books and Macmillan.

Pound, R. (1937). Foreword. In P. Young (Ed.), *Social treatment in probation and delinquency* (p. xxvii). New York: McGraw-Hill.

Private Sector Task Force on Juvenile Justice. (1987). *Final report.* San Francisco: National Council on Crime and Delinquency.

Rothman, D. J. (1984). *Conscience and convenience: The asylum and its alternatives in progressive America.* Boston: Little, Brown.

Schwartz, I. M. (1989). In *Justice for juveniles: Rethinking the best interest of the child.* Lexington, MA: Lexington Books.

Schwartz, I. M. (1992). *Juvenile justice and public policy: Toward a national agenda.* New York: Lexington Books and Macmillan.

Schwartz, I. M., Willis, D. A., & Battle, J. (1991). *Juvenile arrest, detention, and incarceration trends: 1979–1989.* Ann Arbor: Center for the Study of Youth Policy, University of Michigan.

Soler, M., & Shauffer, C. (1990). Fighting fragmentation: Coordination of services for children and families. *Nebraska Law Review, 69,* 278–297.

U.S. Department of Justice, Bureau of Justice Statistics and Office of Juvenile Justice and Delinquency Prevention. (1990). *Juvenile detention and correctional facility census, 1988–89.* (Computer file). Ann Arbor, MI: Interuniversity Consortium for Political and Social Research (Bureau of the Census, U.S. Department of Commerce).

Policy statement approved by the NASW Delegate Assembly, August 1993. This statement supersedes the policy statement on Juvenile Delinquency and Adult Crime approved by the Delegate Assembly in 1977 and incorporates portions of Juvenile Delinquency and Adult Crime (approved in 1969) and Prisons and Jails (approved in 1971). For further information, contact the National Association of Social Workers, 750 First Street, NE, Suite 700, Washington, DC 20002-4241. Telephone: 202-408-8600 or 800-638-8799.

Lesbian, Gay, and Bisexual Issues

BACKGROUND

Social workers' awareness regarding the needs of lesbian and gay issues has been increased by the former policy statement on this diverse population. However, an important revision had to be made to improve on and strengthen NASW's policy. The addition of bisexual in the policy title and throughout this document is an attempt to make the policy more inclusive. Bisexual people are a significant population, who, like lesbian and gay people, encounter significant obstacles based on their affectional orientation.

A person's core identity incorporates many variables and is not limited simply to affectional orientation. Therefore, policy language has been changed to stress that the discourse regarding sexuality should be inclusive of the wide range of sexual expression. The policy includes added focus on negotiating relationships, exploring power dynamics, and using language describing specific behaviors. In an era when decisions regarding sexual expression can have a profound impact on health, expressions such as "gay sex" are dangerously vague and promote the assumption that specific behaviors are not part of heterosexual sexuality.

Social workers need to understand the complex issues that lesbian, gay, and bisexual people encounter within the dominant culture in order to provide services respectful of each individual. Lesbian, gay, and bisexual youths, older people, and people of color are populations that are often unnoticed and consequently underserved. Therefore, significant additions have been made to the section on education and professional development that focus on curriculum, training, and research. Additional references to recent changes in military policy and hate crime statistics also have been provided.

The recently celebrated 25th anniversary of the lesbian, gay, and bisexual rights movement marks a time when developmentally the community continues to explore questions of marriage, reproductive choices within the context of lesbian and gay relationships, and the care and safety of children. Concomitantly, as the general population ages, additional consideration must be given to lesbian, gay, and bisexual people in the development of services for older people.

Taranto, Polowy, Smith, and McHugh, counsel of record, in their *amicus curiae* brief before the Supreme Court of the United States, presented a comprehensive analysis of current professional thinking and research of the National Association of Social Workers, the American Psychiatric Association, and the American Psychological Association (*Romer v. Evans,* 1994). The *Table of Authorities* in this brief is an invaluable list of updated legal, professional practice, and research citations. The following is a summary of the evidence presented, along with others resources in relation to the nature of sexual orientation and the effects of prejudice and discrimination. Behavioral and social scientists commonly identify sexual orientation as one of several distinct but related components of human sexuality (D'Augelli & Patterson, 1995; Garnets & Kimmel, 1993; Gonsiorek & Weinrich, 1991; Shively & DeCecco, 1993; Stein, 1993). Sexual orientation refers to the tendency to experience erotic or romantic responses to men, women, or both, and the resulting sense of oneself. Sexual orientation has a number of aspects, including experiencing an ongoing attraction to people of a particular gender; developing a private personal identity or self-concept as heterosexual, gay, lesbian, or bisexual; establishing a public identity based on sexual orientation; and identifying with a community of those who share the same sexual orientation (Appleby & Anastas, in press; Herek, 1991).

Sexual orientation is distinct from sexual conduct. The fact that a person engages in same-sex sexual activity, other-sex sexual activity, both, or neither is not sufficient to determine his or her sexual orientation. Many individuals who identify themselves as gay or lesbian, or who are predominantly attracted to members of the same sex, nonetheless engage in other-sex sexual behavior (Doll et al., 1992; Kinsey, Pomeroy, Martins, & Gebhard, 1953). Like their heterosexual counterparts, all sexual or nonsexual configurations are possible (Peplau & Cochran, 1990).

Adult sexual orientation typically emerges by early adolescence, while for some by early childhood (Bell, Weinberg, & Hammersmith, 1981). Researchers have found familial patterns and biological correlates of adult homosexual orientation, suggesting that genetic, congenital, or anatomical factors may contribute to its development (Bailey & Pillard, 1991; Hamer, Hu, Magnuson, Hu, & Pattatuci, 1993; LeVay, 1991, 1993; Turner, 1995). The available studies of lesbian and gay experience indicate that same-sex attractions generally emerge by early or midadolescence (Troiden, 1989): "By the time boys and girls reach adolescence, their sexual preference is likely to be already determined, even though they may not yet have become sexually active" (Bell et al., 1981, p. 186). The scientific literature thus strongly indicates that sexual orientation is far from being a voluntary choice (Money, 1987). Lesbian, gay, and bisexual identity, however, is more complex than behaviors or orientation and include aspects of ethnicity, culture, race, and class as equally important aspects of an individual's core personal identity. Groups within the lesbian, gay, and bisexual population, including youths, older people, disabled people, and rural populations, may have additional vulnerabilities (Gonsiorek, 1993; Kanuha, 1990; Kimmel, 1993; Kurdek, 1994; Kus, 1995; Renzetti & Miley, 1996; Strickland, 1995).

The research and clinical experience of the American Psychiatric Association, the American Psychological Association, and NASW members indicate that, once established, sexual orientation is resistant to change. There is little evidence that treatment actually changes sexual attractions, as opposed to reducing or eliminating same-sex sexual behavior. There is no reliable evidence that "sexual orientation is amenable to redirection or significant influence from psychological intervention" (Haldeman, 1994, p. 149).

The mental health professions for more than a quarter of a century have viewed homosexuality as an alternative form of biopsychosocial development and not a mental disorder. The declassification of homosexual orientation as a mental disease reflects the results of extensive research conducted over 30 years showing that homosexual orientation is not a psychological maladjustment (Hart et al., 1978; Marmor, 1980). A comprehensive literature on the subject demonstrates that "theories contending that the existence of differences between homosexuals and heterosexuals implies maladjustment are irresponsible, uniformed, or both" (Gonsiorek, 1993, p. 115). Unfortunately, the social and other circumstances in which lesbians, gay men, and bisexual people live, including exposure to widespread and intense prejudice and discrimination, often cause acute distress; but there is no reliable evidence that homosexual orientation per se impairs psychological functioning or workplace functioning (Snyder & Nyberg, 1980; Swisher, 1994).

The literature also undermines negative assumptions about gay men and lesbians as parents. The most striking feature of the research on lesbian mothers, gay fathers, and their children is the absence of pathological findings. The second most striking feature is how similar the groups of gay and lesbian parents and their children are to the heterosexual parents and their children that were included in the studies. And being raised by gay parents does not appear to cause homosexual orientation (Patterson, 1994; *Romer v. Evans*, 1994).

Gonsiorek and Weinrich (1991) reported that homosexuals as a group are the first, second, or third most numerous minority in the United States, depending on which variation of the estimate is used (Singer & Deschamps, 1994). The broad variation of affectional orientation and the prevalence of homosexual behaviors in the population have been well documented (Hooker,

1957; Kinsey, Pomeroy, & Martins, 1948; Kinsey et al., 1953; Laumann, Gagnon, Michael, & Michaels, 1994; Singer & Deschamps, 1994; Strickland, 1995).

Heterosexism (the belief and concomitant assumptions that heterosexuality is the only "right" or "moral" option of sexual expression) has a serious impact on the lives of these individuals. Because of negative societal attitudes toward same-gender orientation, millions of lesbian, gay, and bisexual people are at risk of discrimination, stigmatization, and violence (Card, 1994; Comstock, 1991; Fenway Community Health Center, 1994a, 1994b; Herek & Berrill, 1992; Pesina, Hitchcock, & Rienzi, 1994). Lesbians, gay men, and bisexual people have long faced intense prejudice and discrimination based on ignorance and stereotypes. Sexual orientation not only is a fundamental facet of one's experience and sense of self but has long had immense social, and therefore personal, consequences. The experience of being gay, lesbian, or bisexual in American society today continues, to a large extent, to be defined by the requirement to cope with the negative effects of prejudice against homosexuality (Stein, 1993). Social prejudice and discrimination against lesbians and gay men have been widespread since Colonial times (Chauncey, 1994; Faderman, 1991). Lesbians, bisexual people, and gay males have been the object of some of the deepest prejudice and hatred in American society (Appleby, 1995; Melton, 1989). Berube (1991) noted that the mental health professions' adherence to an "illness model" of homosexuality supported the development of bizarre, inhumane, and sometimes brutal "treatments" and "aversion therapies" for the "sexual psychopaths" or people "afflicted with psychopathic personality or sexual deviation" (pp. 258–259).

Intense prejudice against lesbians, bisexual people, and gay men remains prevalent in contemporary American society. Public opinion studies of attitudes toward lesbians and gay men indicate that, among large segments of the public, gay people are the subject of strong antipathy (Herek & Capitanio, 1995; Kite, 1994). Verbal abuse is common (Berrill, 1992; Hunter, 1992). Discrimination based on sexual orientation in such critical areas as employment and housing remains law-

ful in most jurisdictions and appears to be widespread (Badgett, Donnelly, & Kibbe, 1992; Levine & Leonard, 1984). High rates of specifically antigay violence or "hate crimes" have been consistently documented by the National Gay and Lesbian Task Force (1996) and the Human Rights Campaign (1995).

Most heterosexuals' negative attitudes toward lesbians, bisexual people, and gay men are not based on personal experience with gay members of these groups. Only one in three Americans has a friend, relative, or acquaintance who is known by them to be lesbian or gay. Antigay attitudes have been found to be significantly less common among that one-third of the population (Herek & Capitanio, 1995; Herek & Glunt, 1993). Several studies indicate that correction of inaccurate assumptions about lesbians and gay men often leads to a reduction in antipathy (Herek, 1991). Likewise, research has shown that many people base their opinions about lesbians and gay men on an entrenched set of negative assumptions. Both gay men and lesbians are often associated with cross-sex characteristics, as mentally ill, promiscuous, lonely, insecure, and likely to be child molesters, while lesbians have been described as aggressive and hostile toward men (Appleby & Anastas, 1992; Hetrick & Martin, 1987).

These images represent crude stereotypes. While gay men are alleged by right wing family values councils to be disproportionately responsible for child abuse, there is no evidence of any positive correlation between gay orientation and child molestation (Freund, Watson, & Rienzo, 1989; Groth & Birnbaum, 1978; Jenny, Roesler, & Poyer, 1994). Despite stereotypes to the contrary, gay men and lesbians often form committed relationships that share principal elements of heterosexual marital relationships (Kurdek, 1995; McWhirter & Mattison, 1984; Peplau & Amaro, 1982).

The effects of prejudice and discrimination as summarized by Taranto, Polowy, Smith, and McHugh in 1994 are the result of institutional arrangements (*Romer v. Evans*, 1994). Oppression of lesbian, gay, and bisexual people has been expressed in religions, cultures, civil and criminal legal codes, and institutions. Such discrimination is based in homophobia, the irrational hatred, fear, and stereotyping of those whose primary sexual and affectional orientation is toward people of their own gender. Negative attitudes toward homosexuality have led to criminalization of many acts of sexual expression. Nearly half of the states have enacted sodomy laws that make same-gender sexual expression unlawful. States, cities, and counties nationwide have passed gay rights ordinances (Vaid, 1995). When prejudice against lesbians, bisexual people, and gay men takes the form of violence or discrimination, it can have such tangible consequences as physical injury or lost employment. The harmful effects of prejudice, discrimination, and violence, however, are not limited to such bodily or pecuniary consequences. The psychological effects of antigay verbal harassment from strangers, derision from family or coworkers, physical threats, or violent attacks include depression, a persistent sense of vulnerability, and efforts to rationalize the experience by viewing one's victimization as just punishment (Bard & Sangrey, 1986; Garnets, Herek, & Levy, 1990; Meyer, 1995). Lesbians, gay men, and bisexual people, like members of other groups that are subject to social prejudice, also frequently come to internalize society's negative stereotypes. Social workers and their mental health colleagues are particularly concerned about the harms that internalized social stigma can produce in lesbian, gay male, and bisexual adolescents who are newly becoming aware of their sexual orientation (Gonsiorek, 1988; Herdt & Boxer, 1993; Hershberger & D'Augelli, 1995; Remafedi, Farrow, & Deisher, 1991).

The stigma and ill treatment that attach merely to acknowledging homosexual orientation lead many people to remain "in the closet." Concealing one's sexual orientation, or attempting to avoid association with other lesbian, gay male, and bisexual people, commonly tends to compound psychological distress. The "daily need to hide an important aspect of personal and social identity operates as a corrosive denial of self-respect and self-worth" (Hetrick & Martin, 1987, p. 58). Social stigma, for some, turns into feelings of personal inferiority or self-hatred. Government measures that foster such stigma, as by pointedly foreclosing opportunities for political participation for lesbian, gay male, and

bisexual people as is the intent of the numerous antigay state initiatives (29 state initiatives in 1996), only exacerbate those psychological harms (Nava & Dawidoff, 1994). Some forms of discrimination are:

■ Despite "domestic partnership" legislation in some jurisdictions (that is, legal recognition or registration of committed lesbian and gay relationships), same-gender couples do not have the option to formalize their relationships, to marry, or to have access to the entitlement and protection that marriage affords.

■ Lesbian, gay, and bisexual people have been denied custody of their children and the right to provide foster and adoptive care.

■ Unless wills and durable powers of attorney are well executed, partners in same-sex relationships do not have the same rights of inheritance and decision making (including decisions regarding health care directives and burial requests) as do married spouses or biological next of kin.

■ People in same-sex relationships face discrimination in hospital settings. Such settings often adhere to exclusionary visitation policies in which only married spouses or biological next of kin may visit.

■ Despite antidiscrimination laws in some local or state jurisdictions, lesbian and gay people continue to suffer discrimination in housing, employment, access to adequate mental health and health care, social services, and immigration and naturalization services. Indeed, organized efforts exist to legalize discrimination against lesbian and gay people.

■ Lesbian, gay male, and bisexual people who want to serve in the armed forces are still at risk of discharge if their sexual orientation becomes known. Present policy states that military recruiters may not ask about sexual orientation. This "don't ask, don't tell" policy effectively encourages dishonesty through institutionalized "closeting," thereby silencing the voices of lesbian, gay, and bisexual people in the military.

■ Denial of legal rights reinforces and legitimizes homophobic and other acting-out behavior of those predisposed toward prejudice, discrimination, and violence.

ISSUE STATEMENT

Social workers are guided by the *NASW Code of Ethics* (1996), which bans discrimination on the basis of sexual orientation and encourages social workers to act to expand access, choices, and opportunities for oppressed people and groups.

Individual social workers, their professional associations, and their employers are not immune to cultural attitudes and values that are antithetical to those of the social work profession. Homophobia continues to give rise to multiple discriminatory practices, both individually and institutionally. Lesbians, gay men, and bisexual people frequently experience prejudice as a result of homophobia and heterosexism.

Prejudice against lesbian, gay, and bisexual people and discomfort about working with this population may lead to inappropriate, ineffective, and even damaging interventions by social workers (DeCrescenzo, 1983; Eliason, 1995; Greene, 1994; Harris, Nightengale, & Owen, 1995). Prejudice toward lesbian, gay, and bisexual social workers results in discriminatory personnel practices and unnecessary stress. It should be noted that even within the profession, lesbian, gay, and bisexual social workers do not necessarily feel safe to openly and publicly declare their sexual orientation. It is imperative, therefore, that all social workers examine their attitudes and feelings about homosexuality and their understanding of lesbian, gay, and bisexual cultures and work toward full social and legal acceptance of lesbian, gay, and bisexual people. Ongoing self-examination will ensure that social workers remain aware of the negative impact that prejudice and discrimination have on their lesbian, gay, or bisexual clients and colleagues and can minimize homophobic responses that may arise in treatment or professional settings.

POLICY STATEMENT

It is the position of NASW that same-gender sexual orientation should be afforded the same respect and rights as other-gender orientation. Discrimination and prejudice directed against

any group are damaging to the social, emotional, and economic well-being of the affected group and of society as a whole. NASW is committed to advancing policies and practices that will improve the status and well-being of all lesbian, gay, and bisexual people.

Nonjudgmental attitudes toward sexual orientation allow social workers to offer optimal support and services to lesbian, gay, and bisexual people. The profession supports and empowers lesbian, gay, and bisexual people through all phases of the coming out process and beyond. Discriminatory statutes, policies, and actions that diminish the quality of life for lesbian, gay, and bisexual people and that force many to live their lives in secrecy should be prevented and eliminated. NASW supports the right of the individual to self-disclosed sexual orientation and encourages the development of supportive practice environments for lesbian, gay, and bisexual clients and colleagues (Appleby & Anastas, 1992; Berger, 1995; D'Augelli & Patterson, 1995; DeCrescenzo, 1994; Garnets & Kimmel, 1993; Gonsiorek, 1993; Hidalgo, Peterson, & Woodman, 1985; Moses & Hawkins, 1982; Quam, 1996; Schoenberg & Goldberg, 1985; Shernoff, 1996; Woodman, 1992). The rights and well-being of the children of lesbian, gay, and bisexual people should be an integral part of all these considerations.

NASW affirms its commitment to work toward full social and legal acceptance and recognition of lesbian, gay, and bisexual people (Jones & Kosher, 1995; Nava & Dawidoff, 1994; Shawer, 1995; Stein, 1994; Sullivan, 1995; Vaid, 1995). To this end, NASW supports legislation, regulation, policies, judicial review, political action, and changes in social work policy statements and the *NASW Code of Ethics* (1996) and any other means necessary to establish and protect the equal rights of all people without regard to sexual orientation. NASW is committed to working toward the elimination of prejudice and discrimination both inside and outside the profession.

Professional and Continuing Education

■ NASW supports curriculum policies in schools of social work that eliminate discrimination against lesbian, gay, and bisexual people. In conjunction with the Council on Social Work Education, the schools of social work are expected to address the issue of discrimination; to articulate this position in curriculum policy and standards; to require course content on lesbian, gay, and bisexual cultures and concerns (Gunter, 1992; Lee, 1992); to integrate this material throughout the curriculum; to provide field opportunities for students interested in working with lesbian, gay, and bisexual people; to offer research opportunities for investigating issues of relevance to this population (while also integrating lesbian, gay, and bisexual people into general research) (Brooks, 1992; Tully, 1995); and to develop and provide training for classroom instructors, field supervisors, and field advisors regarding lesbian, gay, and bisexual issues (Goodman, 1985).

■ NASW encourages the implemention of continuing education programs on practice and policy issues relevant to lesbian, gay, and bisexual people and cultures, and human sexuality.

■ Training should focus on the complexity of power dynamics, on negotiating relationships, and on sexual behaviors.

■ NASW aims to increase awareness within the profession of oppression, heterosexism, and internalized homophobia (Appleby, 1995; DeCrescenzo, 1983; Garfinke & Morin, 1995; Peterson, 1996; Walters & Simoni, 1993). Additionally, NASW is concerned with increasing awareness of the multiple dilemmas and stigmas that lesbian, gay, and bisexual clients and social workers of color experience (Hidalgo, 1995; Lloyd & Kuszelewicz, 1995; Longres, 1996; Shernoff, 1996).

■ NASW strongly supports all social work organizations and associations in their use of inclusive, gender-neutral language and their inclusion of questions specific to lesbian, gay, and bisexual issues in social work licensing exams.

Antidiscrimination

■ NASW strives for full representation and establishment of means to affirm the presence of lesbian, gay, and bisexual people at all levels of leadership and employment in social work and in NASW.

■ NASW supports all social agencies, universities, professional associations, and funding organizations in their efforts to broaden statements of nondiscrimination to include sexual orientation.

■ NASW works in coalition with mental health and other human services professions to help enact antidiscrimination legislation at national, state, and local levels and actively campaigns against any laws allowing discriminatory practices against lesbian, gay, and bisexual people, primarily in immigration, employment, housing, professional credentialing, licensing, public accommodation, child custody, and the right to marry (NASW, 1996).

■ NASW opposes policies that exclude lesbian, gay, and bisexual people from the military and other forms of government service.

■ All social work practitioners, administrators, and educators are encouraged to take action to ensure that the dignity and rights of lesbian, gay, and bisexual employees, clients, and students are upheld and that these rights are codified in agency policies (Pierce, 1992; Terry, 1992).

Public Awareness

■ NASW supports the development of programs to increase public awareness of the discrimination experienced by lesbian, gay, and bisexual people and of the contributions to society made by lesbian, gay, and bisexual people through collaboration with educational, mental health, and research organizations serving the lesbian, gay, and bisexual communities.

■ NASW encourages the development of programs, training, and information that promote proactive efforts to end the physical and psychological violence aimed at lesbian, gay, and bisexual people.

■ NASW supports organizations that fund, develop, and provide programming that accurately portrays the lesbian, gay, and bisexual communities compassionately and accurately.

Health and Mental Health Services

■ NASW endorses policies in both the public and private sectors that ensure nondiscrimination; that are sensitive to the health and mental health needs of lesbian, gay, and bisexual people; and that promote an understanding of lesbian, gay, and bisexual cultures. Social stigmatization of lesbian, gay and bisexual people is widespread and is a primary motivating factor in leading some people to seek sexual orientation changes (Haldeman, 1994). Sexual orientation conversion therapies assume that homosexual orientation is both pathological and freely chosen. No data demonstrate that reparative or conversion therapies are effective, and in fact they may be harmful (Davison, 1991; Gonsiorek & Weinrich, 1991; Haldeman, 1994). NASW believes social workers have the responsibility to clients to explain the prevailing knowledge concerning sexual orientation and the lack of data reporting positive outcomes with reparative therapy. NASW discourages social workers from providing treatments designed to change sexual orientation or from referring practitioners or programs that claim to do so (NASW, 1992).

■ NASW strongly advocates for the availability of culturally appropriate comprehensive psychological and social support services for lesbian, gay, and bisexual people and their families (Diggs, 1993; Haldeman, 1994; Lloyd, 1992). NASW recognizes the increasing number of lesbian, gay, and bisexual people who are making reproductive choices, and it strives to establish legal, medical, and psychological supports for these families through its constituencies (Bryant & Demian, 1994; Patterson, 1994).

■ NASW continues to advocate for the implementation of programs that address the health and mental health needs of lesbian, gay, and bisexual youths, including human immunodeficiency virus (HIV) prevention, psychological stress and dysfunction prevention and treatment, and suicide prevention. This population is often denied services because without parental consent they cannot access insurance, and they often feel disenfranchised from adult lesbian, gay, and bisexual cultures (Savin-Williams, 1989, 1994; Taylor, 1994).

■ NASW recognizes the health and mental health needs of older lesbian, gay, and bisexual people and advocates for programs that address these needs (Adelman, 1991; Berger, 1995; Cruikshank, 1990; Quam, 1996).

Legal and Political Action

■ NASW and its chapters need to develop and participate in coalitions with other professional associations to lobby for the civil rights of lesbian, gay, and bisexual people and other oppressed groups; to defeat efforts to limit the civil rights of lesbian, gay, and bisexual people; and to advocate for increased funding for programs designed to eliminate hate crimes and antigay violence and to provide education, treatment services, and research that increases our understanding of the lesbian, gay, and bisexual community (Rofes, 1996).

■ NASW supports working toward implementation of domestic partnership and marriage legislation at local, state, and national levels that includes lesbian, gay, and bisexual people. It endorses the development and dissemination of model antidiscrimination and domestic partnership and/or marriage legislation that can be used in municipal, state, and national legislatures (Sullivan, 1995).

■ NASW encourages adoption of laws that recognize inheritance, insurance, same-sex marriage, child custody, property, and other rights in lesbian, gay, and bisexual relationships (Tully, 1994).

■ NASW encourages self-identified lesbian, gay, and bisexual individuals to seek election in all political jurisdictions (NASW, 1996).

REFERENCES

Adelman, M. (1991). Stigma, gay lifestyles, and adjustment to aging: A study of later-life gay men and lesbians. *Journal of Homosexuality, 20*(3/4), 7–32.

Appleby, G. A. (1995). AIDS and homophobia/heterosexism. In G. A. Lloyd & M. A. Kuszelewicz (Eds.), *HIV disease: Lesbians, gays and the social service system* (pp. 1–24). New York: Haworth Press.

Appleby, G., & Anastas, J. (1992). Social work practice with lesbians and gays. In A. T. Morales & B. W. Sheafor (Eds.), *Social work: A profession of many faces* (6th ed., pp. 347–381). Boston: Allyn & Bacon.

Appleby, G., & Anastas, J. (in press). *Not just a passing phase: Social work with lesbian, gay and bisexual people.* New York: Columbia University Press.

Badgett, M.V.L., Donnelly, C., & Kibbe, J. (1992). *Pervasive patterns of discrimination against lesbians and gay men: Evidence from surveys across the United States.* Washington, DC: American Psychological Association.

Bailey, M. J., & Pillard, R. C. (1991). A genetic study of male sexual orientation. *Archives of General Psychiatry, 48,* 1080–1093.

Bard, M., & Sangrey, D. (1986). *The crime victim's book.* New York: Basic Books

Bell, A. P., Weinberg, M. S., & Hammersmith, S. K. (1981). *Sexual preference: Its development in men and women.* Bloomington: Indiana University Press.

Berger, R. M. (1995). *Gay and gray: The older homosexual man* (2nd ed.). New York: Haworth Press.

Berrill, K. T. (1992). Anti-gay violence and victimization in the United States: An overview. In G. M. Herek & K. T. Berrill (Eds.), *Hate crimes: Confronting violence against lesbians and gay men* (pp. 19–45). Newbury Park, CA: Sage Publications.

Berube, A. (1991). *Coming out under fire: The history of gay men and women in World War Two.* New York: Basic Books.

Brooks, W. K. (1992). Research and the gay minority: Problems and possibilities. In N. J. Woodman (Ed.), *Lesbian and gay lifestyles: A guide for counseling and education* (pp. 201–216). New York: Irvington Publishers.

Bryant, A. S., & Demian, R. (1994). Relationship characteristics of American gay and lesbian couples: Findings from a national survey. *Journal of Gay and Lesbian Social Services, 1*(2), 101–117.

Card, C. (1994). The military ban and the ROTC: A study in closeting. *Journal of Homosexuality, 27*(3/4), 117–146.

Chauncey, G.A. (1994). *Gay New York: Gender, urban culture and the making of the gay male world, 1890–1940.* New York: Basic Books.

Comstock, G. D. (1991). Violence against lesbians and gay men. New York: Columbia University Press.

Cruikshank, M. (1990). Lavender and gray: A brief survey of lesbian and gay aging studies. *Journal of Homosexuality, 20*(3/4), 77–87.

D'Augelli, A. R., & Patterson, C. J. (Eds.). (1995). *Lesbian, gay, and bisexual identities over the lifespan: Psychological perspectives.* New York: Oxford University Press.

Davison, G. C. (1991). Construction and morality in therapy for homosexuality. In J. C. Gonsiorek & J. D. Weinrich (Eds.), *Homosexuality: Research implications for public policy* (pp. 137–148). Newbury Park, CA: Sage Publications.

DeCrescenzo, T. (1983). Homophobia: A study of the attitudes of mental health professionals toward homosexuality. In R. Schoenberg & R. S. Goldberg (Eds.), *With compassion toward some: Homosexuality and social work in America* (pp. 115–136). New York: Harrington Park Press.

DeCrescenzo, T. (Ed.). (1994). *Helping gay and lesbian youth.* New York: Harrington Park Press.

Diggs, M. (1993). Surveying the intersection: Pathology, secrecy and the discourses of racial and sexual identity. *Journal of Homosexuality, 26*(2/3), 1–19.

Doll, L. S., Petersen, L. R., White, C. R., Johnson, E. S., Ward, J. W., & The Blood Donor Study Group. (1992). Homosexually and non-homosexually identified men who have sex with men: A behavioral comparison. *Journal of Sex Research, 29*(1), 1–14.

Eliason, M. J. (1995). Attitudes about lesbians and gay men: A review and implications for social service training. *Journal of Gay and Lesbian Social Services, 2*(2), 73–90.

Faderman, L. (1991). *Odd girls and twilight lovers: A history of lesbian life in twentieth-century America.* New York: Columbia University Press.

Fenway Community Health Center. (1994a). *Anti-gay/lesbian incidents in Massachusetts climbed back to 1992 levels* (pp. 15, 17–18). Boston: Publication of the Fenway Community Health Center Victim Recovery Program.

Fenway Community Health Center. (1994b). *Anti-gay/lesbian violence: Massachusetts and the United States* (pp. 25, 28–29). Boston: Publication of the Fenway Community Health Center Victim Recovery Program.

Freund, K., Watson, R., & Rienzo, D. (1989). Heterosexuality, homosexuality, and erotic age preference. *Journal of Sex Research, 26,* 107–115.

Garfinke, E. M., & Morin, S. F. (1995). Psychologists' attitudes toward homosexual psychotherapy clients. *Journal of Social Issues, 34*(3), 101–112.

Garnets, L. D., Herek, G. M., & Levy, B. (1990). Violence and victimization of lesbians and gay men: Mental health consequences. *Journal of Interpersonal Violence, 5,* 366–383.

Garnets, L. D., & Kimmel, D. C. (Eds.). (1993). *Psychological perspectives on lesbian and gay male experiences.* New York: Columbia University Press.

Gonsiorek, J. C. (1988). Mental health issues of gay and lesbian adolescents. *Journal of Adolescent Health Care, 9,* 114–122.

Gonsiorek, J. C. (1993). Mental health issues of gay and lesbian adolescents. In L. Garnets & D. Kimmel (Eds.), *Psychological perspectives on lesbian and gay male experiences* (pp. 469–483). New York: Columbia University Press.

Gonsiorek, J. C., & Weinrich, J. D. (Eds.). (1991). *Homosexuality: Research implications for public policy.* Newbury Park, CA: Sage Publications.

Goodman, B. (1985). Out of the therapeutic closet. In H. Hildalgo, T. L. Peterson, & N. J. Woodman (Eds.), *Lesbian and gay issues: A resource manual for social workers* (pp. 140–144). Silver Spring, MD: National Association of Social Workers.

Greene, B. (1994). Ethnic minority lesbians and gay men: Mental health and treatment issues. *Journal of Consulting and Clinical Psychology, 62*(2), 243–251.

Groth, A. N., & Birnbaum, H. J. (1978). Adult sexual orientation and attraction to underage persons. *Archives of Sexual Behavior, 7*(3), 175–181.

Gunter, P. L. (1992). Social work with non-traditional families. In N. J. Woodman (Ed.), *Lesbian and gay lifestyles: A guide for counseling and education* (pp. 87–110). New York: Irvington Publishers.

Haldeman, D. C. (1994). The practice and ethics of sexual orientation conversion therapy. *Journal of Consulting and Clinical Psychology, 62*(2), 211–221.

Hamer, D. H., Hu, S., Magnuson, V. L., Hu, N., & Pattatuci, A.M.L. (1993). A linkage between DNA markers on the X chromosome and male sexual orientation. *Science, 261,* 321–323.

Harris, M. B., Nightingale, J., & Owen, N. (1995). Health care professionals experience, knowledge, and attitudes concerning homosexuality. *Journal of Gay and Lesbian Social Services, 2*(2), 91–108.

Hart, M., Roback, H., Tittler, B., Weitz, L., Walston, B., & McKee, E. (1978). Psychological adjustment of nonpatient homosexuals: Critical review of the research literature. *Journal of Clinical Psychiatry, 39,* 604–608.

Herdt, G., & Boxer, A. (1993). *Children of Horizons: How gay and lesbian teens are leading a new way out of the closet.* Boston: Beacon Press.

Herek, G. M. (1991). Stigma, prejudice, and violence against lesbians and gay men. In J. C. Gonsiorek & J. D. Weinrich (Eds.), *Homosexuality: Research implications for public policy* (pp. 60–80). Newbury Park, CA: Sage Publications.

Herek, G. M., & Berrill, K. T. (Eds.). (1992). *Hate crimes: Confronting violence against lesbians and gay men.* Newbury Park, CA: Sage Publications.

Herek, G. M., & Capitanio, J. P. (1995). "Some of my best friends": Intergroup contact, concealable stigma, and heterosexuals' attitudes toward gay men and lesbians. *Personality and Social Psychology Bulletin, 22,* 412–424.

Herek, G. M., & Glunt, E. K. (1993). Interpersonal contact and heterosexuals' attitudes toward gay men: Results from a national survey. *Journal of Sex Research, 30,* 239–246.

Hershberger, S. L., & D'Augelli, A. R. (1995). The impact of victimization on the mental health and suicidality of lesbian, gay, and bisexual youths. *Developmental Psychology, 31*(1), 65–74.

Hetrick, E. S., & Martin, A. D. (1987). Developmental issues and their resolution for gay and lesbian adolescents. *Journal of Homosexuality, 14*(1/2), 25–43.

Hidalgo, H. (Ed.). (1995). *Lesbians of color: A kaleidoscope.* New York: Haworth Press.

Hidalgo, H., Peterson, T. L., & Woodman, N. J. (Eds.). (1985). *Lesbian and gay issues: A resource manual for social workers.* Silver Spring, MD: National Association of Social Workers.

Hooker, E. (1957). The adjustment of the male homosexual. *Journal of Projective Techniques, 21,* 18–31.

Human Rights Campaign. (1995, Summer). Hot zones: What's happening in the trenches. *HRCF: Political News for Gay and Lesbian America,* (Premiere Issue), 8–10.

Hunter, J. (1992). Violence against lesbian and gay male youth. In G. M. Herek & K. T. Berrill (Eds.), *Hate crimes: Confronting violence against lesbians and gay men* (pp. 76–82). Newbury Park, CA: Sage Publications.

Jenny, C., Roesler, T. A., & Poyer, K. L. (1994). Are children at risk for sexual abuse by homosexuals? *Pediatrics, 94*(1), 41–44.

Jones, R. D., & Kosher, R. J. (1995). Homosexuality and the military. *American Journal of Psychiatry, 152*(1), 1621.

Kanuha, V. (1990). Compounding the triple jeopardy: Battering in lesbian of color relationships. *Women in Therapy, 9*(1/2), 169–184.

Kimmel, D. (1993). Adult development and aging: A gay perspective. In L. Garnetts & D. Kimmel (Eds.), *Psychological perspectives on lesbian and gay male experiences* (pp. 517–534). New York: Columbia University Press.

Kinsey, A. F., Pomeroy, W. B., & Martins, C. E. (1948). *Sexual behavior in the human male.* Philadelphia: W. B. Saunders.

Kinsey, A. F., Pomeroy, W. B., Martins, C. E., & Gebhard, P. H. (1953). *Sexual behavior in the human female.* Philadelphia: W. B. Saunders.

Kite, M. (1994). When perception meets reality: Individual differences in reaction to lesbians and gay men. In B. Greene & G. M. Herek (Eds.), *Lesbian and gay psychology: Theory, research, and clinical applications* (pp. 25–53). Thousand Oaks, CA: Sage Publications.

Kurdek, L. A. (1994). The nature and correlates of relationship quality in gay, lesbian and heterosexual cohabiting couples: A test of the individual difference, interdependence, and discrepancy models. In B.

Greene & G. M. Herek (Eds.), *Lesbian and gay psychology: Theory, research, and clinical applications* (pp. 133–155). Newbury Park, CA: Sage Publications.

Kurdek, L. A. (Ed.). (1995). *Social services for gay and lesbian couples.* New York: Haworth Press.

Kus, R. J. (Ed.). (1995). *Addiction and recovery in gay and lesbian persons.* New York: Haworth Press.

Laumann, E. O., Gagnon, J. H., Michael, R. T., & Michaels, S. (1994*). The social organization of sexuality: Sexual practice in the United States.* Chicago: University of Chicago Press.

Lee, J.A.B. (1992). Teaching content related to lesbian and gay identity formation. In N. J. Woodman (Ed.), *Lesbian and gay lifestyles: A guide for counseling and education* (pp. 1–22). New York: Irvington.

LeVay, S. (1991). A difference in hypothalamic structure between heterosexual and homosexual men. *Science, 253,* 1034–1036.

LeVay, S. (1993). *The sexual brain.* Cambridge, MA: MIT Press.

Levine, M. P., & Leonard, R. (1984). Discrimination against lesbians in the workforce. *Signs, 9,* 700–712.

Lloyd, G. A. (1992). Contextual and clinical issues in providing services to gay men. In H. Land (Ed.), *AIDS: A complete guide to psychosocial intervention.* Milwaukee: Family Service America.

Lloyd, G. A., & Kuszelewicz, M. A. (Ed.). (1995). *HIV disease: Lesbians, gays and the social service system.* New York: Haworth Press.

Longres, J. F. (Ed.). (1996). *Men of color: A context for service to homosexually active men.* New York: Haworth Press.

Marmor, J. (1980). *Homosexual behavior: A modern reappraisal.* New York: Basic Books.

McWhirter, D. P., & Mattison, A. M. (1984). *The male couple: How relationships develop.* New York: Prentice Hall.

Melton, G. B. (1989). Public policy and private prejudice: Psychology and law on gay rights. *American Psychologist, 44*(31), 933–940.

Meyer, I. H. (1995). Minority stress and mental health in gay men. *Journal of Health and Social Behavior, 36,* 38–44.

Money, J. (1987). Sin, sickness, or status? Homosexual gender identity and psychoneuroendocrinology. In L. Garnetts & D. Kimmel (Eds.), *Psychological perspectives on lesbian and gay male experiences* (pp. 130–167). New York: Columbia University Press.

Moses, A. E., & Hawkins, R. O. (1982). *Counseling lesbian women and gay men: A life-issues approach.* St. Louis: C.V. Mosby.

National Association of Social Workers. (1996). *NASW code of ethics.* Washington, DC: Author.

National Association of Social Workers, National Committee on Lesbian and Gay Issues. (1992). *Position statement: Reparative or conversion therapies for lesbians and gay men.* Washington, DC: Author.

National Association of Social Workers, National Committee on Lesbian, Gay, and Bisexual Issues. (1996). *NCOLGBI–Committee Charge.* Washington, DC: Author.

National Gay and Lesbian Task Force. (1996, January). *Beyond the beltway: State of the states 1995.* Washington, DC: Author.

Nava, M., & Dawidoff, R. (1994). *Created equal: Why gay rights matter to America.* New York: St. Martin's Press.

Patterson, C. J. (1994). Lesbian and gay couples considering parenthood: An agenda for research, service and advocacy. *Journal of Gay and Lesbian Social Services, 1*(2), 33–56.

Peplau, L. A., & Amaro, H. (1982). Understanding lesbian relationships. In W. Paul, J. D. Weinrich, J. C. Gonsiorek, & M. E. Hotvedt (Eds.), *Homosexuality: Social, psychological, and biological issues* (pp. 233–247). Beverly Hills, CA: Sage Publications.

Peplau, L. A., & Cochran, S. D. (1990). Value orientations in the intimate relationships of gay men. *Journal of Homosexuality, 6*(3), 1–19.

Pesina, M., Hitchcock, D., & Rienzi, B. (1994). The military ban against gay males: University students' attitudes before and after the presidential decision. *Journal of Social and Behavior and Personality, 9*, 499–506.

Peterson, K. J. (Ed.). (1996). *Health care for lesbians and gay men: Confronting homophobia and heterosexism.* New York: Haworth Press.

Pierce, D. (1992). Policies of concern for practice with lesbian women and gay men. In N. J. Woodman (Ed.), *Lesbian and gay lifestyles: A guide for counseling and education* (pp. 171–190). New York: Irvington.

Quam, J. K. (Ed.). (1996). *Social services for older gay men and lesbians.* New York: Haworth Press.

Remafedi, G., Farrow, J. A., & Deisher, R. W. (1991). Risk factors for attempted suicide in gay and bisexual youth. *Pediatrics, 87*, 869–875.

Renzetti, C. M., & Miley, G. H. (Eds.). (1996). *Violence in gay and lesbian domestic partnerships.* New York: Haworth Press.

Rofes, E. (1996). *Reviving the tribe: Regenerating gay men's sexuality and culture in the ongoing epidemic.* New York: Harrington Park Press.

Romer v. Evans. (1994, No. 94-1039, U.S. Supreme Court). Taranto, R. B., Polowy, C. I., Smith, P. M., & McHugh, J. L. *Brief Amicus Curiae of the American Psychological Association, the American Psychiatric Association, the National Association of Social Workers, Inc., and the Colorado Psychological Association.*

Savin-Williams, R. C. (1989). Coming out to parents and self-esteem among gay and lesbian youths. *Journal of Homosexuality, 18*(1/2), 1–35.

Schoenberg, R., & Goldberg, R. S. (Eds.). (1985). *With compassion toward some: Homosexuality and social work in America.* New York: Harrington Park Press.

Shawer, L. (1995). *And the flag was still there: Straight people, gay people, and sexuality in the U.S. military.* Binghamton, NY: Haworth Press.

Shernoff, M. (Ed.). (1996). *Human services for gay people: Clinical and community practice.* New York: Haworth Press.

Shively, M., & DeCecco, J. P. (1993). Components of sexual identity. In L. D. Garnets & D. C. Kimmel (Eds.), *Psychological perspectives on lesbian and gay male experiences* (pp. 80–88). New York: Columbia University Press.

Singer, B. L., & Deschamps, D. (1994). *Gay & lesbian stats: A pocket guide of facts and figures.* New York: New Press.

Snyder, W. P., & Nyberg, K. L. (1980). Gays and the military: An emerging policy issue. *Journal of Policy and Military Sociology, 8*(71), 77–79.

Stein, E. (1994). The relevance of scientific research about sexual orientation to lesbian and gay rights. *Journal of Homosexuality, 27*(3/4), 269–308.

Stein, T. (1993). Overview of new developments in understanding homosexuality. *Review of Psychiatry, 12*(9), 10–12.

Strickland, B. (1995). Research on sexual orientation and human development: A commentary. *Developmental Psychology, 31*(1), 137–140.

Sullivan, A. (1995). *Virtually normal: An argument about homosexuality.* New York: Alfred A. Knopf.

Swisher, K. (1994, October 11). Area firms lauded on gay bias policies. *Washington Post,* p. C2.

Taylor, N. (1994). Gay and lesbian youth: Challenging the policy of denial. In T. DeCresenzo (Ed.), *Helping gay and lesbian youth* (pp. 39–74). New York: Harrington Park Press.

Terry, P. (1992). Entitlement not privilege: The right of employment and advancement. In N. J. Woodman (Ed.), *Lesbian and gay lifestyles: A guide for counseling and education* (pp. 133–144). New York: Irvington.

Troiden, R. R. (1989). The formation of homosexual identities. *Journal of Homosexuality, 17*(43), 43–73.

Tully, C. T. (1994). To boldly go where no one has gone before: The legalization of lesbian and gay marriages. *Journal of Gay and Lesbian Social Services, 1*(1), 73–87.

Tully, C. T. (Ed.). (1995). *Lesbian social services: Research issues.* New York: Haworth Press.

Turner, W. L. (1995). Homosexuality, Type 1: An Xq28 phenomenon. *Archives of Sexual Behavior, 24*(2), 109–134,

Vaid, U. (1995). *Virtual equality: The mainstreaming of gay & lesbian liberation.* New York: Anchor Books.

Walters, K. L., & Simoni, J. M. (1993). Lesbian and gay male group identity attitudes and self-esteem: Implications for counseling. *Journal of Counseling Psychology, 40*(1), 94–99.

Woodman, N. J. (Ed.). (1992). *Lesbian and gay lifestyles: A guide for counseling and education.* New York: Irvington.

Policy statement approved by the NASW Delegate Assembly, August 1996. This policy supersedes the policy statement on Lesbian and Gay Issues approved by the Delegate Assembly in 1993 and 1987 and the policy statement on Gay Issues approved in 1977. For further information, contact the National Association of Social Workers, 750 First Street, NE, Suite 700, Washington, DC 20002-4241. Telephone: 202-408-8600 or 800-638-8799.

Long-Term Care

BACKGROUND

Long-term care is "a system of providing social, personal, and health care services over a sustained period to people who in some way suffer from functional impairment including a limited ability to perform the activities of daily living (ADLs) such as dressing, eating, bathing, using the toilet, cooking, shopping, or taking medicine. [Long-term care] services are required, mostly by older people, adults with developmental disabilities, people with mental illness, and people with acquired immune deficiency syndrome" (Barker, 1995, p. 218). Long-term care may consist of diagnostic, preventive, supportive, rehabilitative, habilitative, maintenance, and personal care services provided by informal caregivers, such as family or friends, or formal caregivers, such as specially trained or licensed professionals. Care can be provided in the home, in community-based programs, or in institutional settings. Long-term care is a marked departure from the traditional acute care model of health services and insurance, which is primarily designed to cure disease rather than to minimize, rehabilitate, or compensate for chronic illness or functional limitations. It also is a departure from past models of social work practice.

There has been substantial growth in the numbers of people needing long-term care. This growth is the result of a variety of demographic changes including a substantially growing aging population, a higher prevalence of chronic illnesses along the lifespan, substantial numbers of people with chronic, infectious diseases such as AIDS, dementias such as Alzheimer's, and people who are living longer as a result of medical advances (Eisenberg et al., 1991; Knight & Kaskie, 1995). It is projected that the older population needing long-term care will increase from 6.2 million to at least 9.0 million by the year 2010

(American Association of Retired Persons, 1993). A substantial portion of long-term care is provided by informal caregivers. Providers and payers offer little support for the physical, financial, and emotional stress and mental health problems of caregivers (Odell & Safford, 1992). Demand for formal long-term care is growing because of changes in family dynamics, family size, the unattended stress on informal caregivers, and the changing role of women, who have provided the majority of informal long-term care services.

The formal system of long-term care has been characterized as fragmented, inappropriate, and inadequate (Special Committee on Aging, U.S. Senate, 1993; U.S. Bipartisan Commission on Comprehensive Health Care, 1990). Most long-term care services have been institutionally based using an acute-care medical model. With the growing long-term care population and consumer and payer demands for more home- and community-based services, new providers and new services have been developed in an uncoordinated manner. This same system also has demonstrated bias and discrimination in services delivery on the basis of age, geographic location, diagnosis, race, culture, sexual orientation, or language. Home- and community-based services (for example, mental health, transportation, and adult day care) have various, fragmented funding sources and auspices and there is little effort or incentive for integration or coordination.

Examples can be found in reimbursable services funded by Medicare and Medicaid. These payer sources are based on an acute care, insurance model of providing relief from major medical costs. Medicare limits the maximum number of days for nursing home care and creates disincentives for mental health prevention, early intervention, and rehabilitation through nonparity of payments with health care (Binner, 1988; Gatz & Smyer, 1992).

In addition, Medicare's regulatory effect can be found in the prospective payment system used in hospitals, which has had severe impact on quality of care, specifically unstable conditions at discharge that lead to continued illness and dependency. Old Age Survivors and Disability Insurance contains biases in determining eligibility and disincentives to beneficiaries to return to work; it lacks early rehabilitation intervention and does not adequately consider maximum levels of independence and quality of life.

Medicaid allows for great variability in benefits for optional services such as case management, psychosocial rehabilitation, clinical services entailing outpatient therapy, partial hospitalization, and home-based personal care by nonphysician providers. Availability of these services is extremely limited, inequitable, and in some states unavailable. Medicaid services primarily have been home-based nursing care for older people with chronic, severe physical disabilities, mental illness, or dementia and have provided few additional services. Lack of services or overuse of physical restraints and psychotropic drugs has been the response of many nursing homes to those with chronic mental illness, mental retardation/developmental disabilities (MR/DD), and those who exhibit behavioral symptoms of dementia. Legislation has sought to eliminate this ineffective, custodial-oriented response with limited success (*Federal Register*, 1989). Nursing home regulations have sought to correct abusive situations by providing adequate safeguards for promoting maximization of independence, discharge planning, and patient rights through ombudsman programs and efforts to enhance the quality of life of residents.

Long-term community mental health services for older people are provided by health care, community mental health, and aging agencies. Social work has the professional responsibility to address organizational issues of collaboration, outreach, and case identification, or continuity of care. For example, less than 10 percent of community mental health center clients are elderly, and less than 5 percent of older people with mental illness are seen by private mental health practitioners (Colenda & Van Dooren, 1993).

Among those who are developmentally disabled, there is a lack of services available for elderly clients who are residents in traditional nursing home settings as well as those who are cared for at home by their families. Nursing home employees are not adequately trained to meet the specialized mental and emotional needs of this clientele. In addition, most professionals working in long-term care, including social workers, suffer from a lack of educational opportunities and lack of continuing education in gerontology (Health Resources & Services Administration, 1995). There is a need for increased field practicum opportunities in home- and community-based long-term care services, and a need to integrate aging and long-term care content into the curriculum of all bachelor and master degree programs in social work.

Current financial pressures on the health care system have resulted in the promotion of managed care programs for health services. Rapid growth in managed care (Health Insurance Association of America, 1994) has had an impact on older people and others with chronic mental and physical illnesses who are eligible for Medicare and Medicaid. Because an increasing number of employees are now covered by managed care plans, during the next decade a growing number of retirees may be in Medicare managed care plans. In addition, because of the rising costs of Medicaid, many states have opted to seek Medicaid waivers of regulatory requirements of the federal government in order to experiment with providing cost-effective services to recipients, including managed care models (Section 2175 of Omnibus Budget Reconciliation Act of 1981). Medicare experiments in several states also are attempting to enroll beneficiaries in managed care plans.

Some studies have shown that managed care organizations have made respectable attempts to provide cost-effective, quality services for people with chronic illnesses (National Conference of State Legislators, 1991). However, the philosophy of managed care is not easily adapted to optimum delivery of long-term care services. Managed care methods of intervention, although effective for many patients, are not the most effective for providing services to isolated, frail people (Knight & Kaskie, 1995), nor are they the most efficacious models of intervention for people with severe mental illnesses such as schizophrenia. Also, the managed care approach generally has not promoted outreach services to vulnerable clients, long-term care research, and training, including field instruction. Managed care, as well as block grant funding of health, mental health, and social services, has tended to exacerbate the fragmentation problem of long-term care services delivery and has not promoted the development of a continuum of care approach (Greene, 1995).

As a result of the development of managed care and the increased growth in the numbers of vulnerable, frail, and disabled people, there is a need for heightened attention to ethical and legal considerations in long-term care. Among the areas that bear attention (Fahey, 1995; Kane, 1996) are

■ fairness and adequacy of care in such areas as incentives for undertreatment

■ consumer and professional input in decision making and rationing of care decisions

■ supportive, consumer-oriented services in making end-of-life decisions

■ flexible and humane policies related to guardianship

■ accountability and protection regarding use of client and patient records

■ government responsibility for protecting vulnerable people and providing services to the economically poor.

The involvement of NASW in long-term care includes both advocacy efforts and the development of standards for the field. NASW has been instrumental in revisions to OBRA nursing home regulations and actively participated in the 1995 White House Conference on Aging. In addition, NASW supports national health care reform.

The development of professional standards includes participation in the formation of long-term care accreditation standards for the Joint Commission on Accreditation of Healthcare Organizations. NASW has created standards for social work practice in long-term care facilities

and health care settings and clinical indicators for social work and psychosocial services in nursing homes.

ISSUE STATEMENT

Long-term care services are characterized by an inadequate funding system and insufficient use of a continuum of acute and chronic care to promote maximum self-determination of clients in the least restrictive setting. Government at all levels and the private sector have failed to integrate or coordinate the growing array of available services into a viable system to meet individual and functional needs of clients, caregivers, and families. There is not a comprehensive policy that includes guiding principles as a focus for ongoing planning, policy development, and change. The increasing societal need for long-term care must be a catalyst for the health care system to reexamine its emphasis on prevention, consumer satisfaction, and cost effectiveness of services. Major problem areas within the long-term care system include access to care, eligibility and availability of services, the provision of quality care, the need for guiding principles for policy development, definition of ethical underpinnings, and the financing of long-term care services.

In response to the changes occurring in long-term care, the social work profession is faced with examining its role and function throughout the continuum of care. Social work practice approaches, such as case management, family intervention, psychosocial assessment, interdisciplinary teamwork, and outcomes-based assessment, can provide effective and efficient integration of services in long-term care. These approaches are critical to provision of services in managed care environments, which are characterized by short-term care at reduced costs. The important social work role of advocacy for appropriate, quality care and quality of life for consumers and caregivers is critical in meeting needs for consumer protection and consumer involvement. Careful consideration must be given to ethics review, which includes redefinition of roles, changes in legal perspective, and attention to self-determination and autonomy. The changing long-term care environment presents both challenge and opportunity for the profession.

POLICY STATEMENT

NASW advocates reform in long-term care that emphasizes a continuum of care services delivery model and a strengthening of the social work role within this model. Long-term care is too important for precipitous change. NASW supports the inclusion of the following principles in long-term care reform:

■ access to a variety of health and support services, based on individual needs, for people who are frail, sick, or physically and mentally challenged—these services should support habilitation and rehabilitation to enable individuals to maintain their maximum level of independence in the least restrictive environment

■ access to long-term care services for all who need them, regardless of age, income, disability, race, national origin, gender, sexual orientation, ethnicity, or geographic location

■ eligibility for long-term care services based on individual, functional need and not solely on medical necessity

■ availability of services within a continuum that links all levels of long-term care and addresses the physical, mental, cultural, and psychosocial health needs of the individual, family, and caregivers

■ availability of social work services based on individual functional need that is not solely related to medical diagnosis or the involvement of another health or mental health discipline

■ development of an adequate financing system for long-term care that preserves, increases, and redistributes revenue to increase access and provide universal coverage, relieving individuals and families of burdensome out-of-pocket costs

■ promotion of consumer self-determination in making choices and consumer participation in decisions that affect their long-term care services

■ emphasis on quality care across the continuum, including the development and delivery of services that are appropriate for a variety of ages and functional abilities and that are outcome oriented and based on quality of life

■ inclusion of social workers managed care planning teams to assure equitable use of resources in care and treatment

■ promotion of research on various client populations and on social, mental health, and substance abuse issues in long-term care with emphasis on race, ethnicity, and gender perspective

■ access to appropriately trained professional social workers

■ assurance of confidentiality and ethical considerations as a benchmark for all areas of decision making

■ expansion of education, training, and continuing education programs for all levels of social workers employed in the long-term care system.

Access to Care

Access to a variety of health and social services within the continuum of long-term care encompasses mental health, rehabilitation, nutrition, home- and community-based services (including, but not limited to, case management, senior centers, transportation services, respite care, adult day care, in-home services, and assisted living), advocacy and elder rights protections, health promotion, volunteerism, and employment. The systems in which these services are delivered include hospitals, subacute and rehabilitation facilities, partial hospitalization programs, nursing homes, assisted living facilities, group homes, board and care homes, life care communities, hospices, adult day care programs, home care systems, and community agencies. NASW promotes the use of professional social work services in all of these systems, advocates for the integration of systems of care to meet individual needs, and supports an end to declassification of social work positions.

Eligibility for and Availability of Services

Adequate long-term care services address cultural and psychosocial–behavioral health needs as well as medical needs. It is important for eligibility criteria to include individual functional need related to biopsychosocial factors. Services availability also should address the needs of informal caregivers for people who are chronically ill, so that both the caregiver and the receiver of care enjoy quality of life.

Financing

NASW promotes and encourages health care reform that provides universal, comprehensive health care coverage for people of all ages that includes affordable, quality physical and mental health care and long-term care. Benefits should be available that provide needed, reimbursable services along a continuum of care that fosters optimum independence. NASW promotes maintaining the solvency of social security, Medicare, and Medicaid programs as well as seeking alternative sources for long-term care funding. The government needs to establish consumer protection guidelines for long-term care insurance and create incentives for the purchase of this insurance. NASW promotes the use of federal and state funding for cost-effective nursing home alternative levels of care, including alternative living options, adult day care, and home care; federal and state initiatives to provide a continuum of care and programs that feature specialized care for functionally impaired individuals; and initiatives that encourage all people to plan for health care needs and retirement. Social work roles in this area include advocacy and brokering, assessment, case management, and provisions of clinical services.

Quality of Care

Quality in long-term care services can be promoted through mechanisms that involve participation of consumers and families and ensure a choice of services and providers. These mechanisms should foster self-determination for the consumer, the family, and informal caregivers.

Quality program evaluation tools could include consumer satisfaction surveys, focus groups, professional performance appraisals, evaluation and assessment of client goals, and service plans with full participation of consumers. In addition, adherence to regulatory implementation of programs and services must recognize quality of life issues. Provision of quality long-term care will support humane, effective, client-based services, inherent in professional social work values.

REFERENCES

American Association of Retired Persons. (1993). *Long-term care* (fact sheet). Washington, DC: Author, Public Policy Institute.

Barker, R. L. (1995). *The social work dictionary* (3rd ed.). Washington, DC: NASW Press.

Binner, P. (1988). Opinion: Mental health funding policy: A critical look. *Administration and Policy in Mental Health, 16,* 40–43.

Colenda, C., & Van Dooren, H. (1993). *From back wards to back streets: The failure of the federal government in providing services for the mentally ill.* Washington, DC: U.S. Government Printing Office.

Eisenberg, M., Saltz, G., Fillinbaum, G., et al. (1991). Quality of life among aging spinal cord injured veterans: Long-term rehabilitation outcomes. *Paraplegia, 29,* 514–520.

Fahey, C. (1995). The ethical underpinnings of long-term care reform. *Care Lines, 2*(4), 1.

Federal Register. (1989, February 2). (Vol. 54, pp. 5333, 5335). Washington, DC: U.S. Government Printing Office.

Gatz, M., & Smyer, M. (1992). The mental health system and older adults in the 1990s. *American Psychologist, 47,* 741–751.

Greene, R. (1995). Family involvement in mental health care for older adults: From caregiving to advocacy and empowerment. In M. Gatz (Ed.), *Emerging issues in mental health and aging* (pp. 210–230). Washington, DC: American Psychological Association.

Health Insurance Association of America. (1994). *Source book of health insurance data.* Washington, DC: Author.

Health Resources & Services Administration, Bureau of Health Professions. (1995). *A national agenda for geriatric education: White pa-*

pers, *Vol. I. Social Work Chapter*. Washington, DC: Author.

Kane, R. (1996). The ethics of health care delivery to elders in a managed care environment. *Managed Care & Aging, 3*(1), 1.

Knight, B., & Kaskie, B. (1995). Models for mental health service delivery to older adults: Implications for reform. In M. Gatz (Ed.), *Emerging issues in mental health and aging* (pp. 231–255). Washington, DC: American Psychological Association.

National Conference of State Legislators. (1991). *Report*. Washington, DC: Author.

Odell, C., & Safford, F. (1992). Working with traditional and nontraditional families of the elderly. In F. Safford & G. Krell (Eds.), *Gerontology for health professionals: A practice guide* (pp. 80–95). Washington, DC: NASW Press.

Special Committee on Aging, U.S. Senate. (1993, July 15). *Mental health and aging forum*. Washington, DC: U.S. Government Printing Office.

U.S. Bipartisan Commission on Comprehensive Health Care (Pepper Commission). (1990, September). *Call to action: Final report*. Washington, DC: U.S. Government Printing Office.

Policy statement approved by the NASW Delegate Assembly, August 1996. This policy supersedes the policy statement on Long-Term Care approved by the Delegate Assembly in 1993 and in 1979. For more information, contact the National Association of Social Workers, 750 First Street, NE, Suite 700, Washington, DC 20002-4241. Telephone: 202-408-8600 or 800-638-8799.

Managed Care

BACKGROUND

There is general agreement that the U.S. health care system is failing on at least three counts:

1.   More than 37 million Americans are not covered by any form of health care insurance and therefore have little or no access to care except for emergencies (and even emergency care is unavailable in many parts of the country). Another 50 million under-insured people are one major illness or "pink slip" away from financial ruin.

2.   The escalating costs of health care have become unacceptable to individuals, to businesses, and to governments at all levels.

3.   The quality of care varies from the best in the world to inadequate, often depending on the consumer's economic status. Basic health indicators for the U.S. population now rank the nation low among industrialized nations. (NASW has responded to the problem with its own policy on "National Health Care" [1993] and its own health care reform bills submitted to Congress.)

The federal administrations of the 1980s and early 1990s generally opposed government intervention in activities that supposedly would benefit from free-market development. The prevailing view was that competition would curb the rapid escalation of health care costs and that health maintenance organizations (HMOs) and other managed care organizations would be the major vehicle. The free marketers ignored the basic economic fact that markets require rules to ensure smooth functioning and true competition, which might lead to lowered pricing. In fact, health care has so many special characteristics that efforts at competition have had the op-posite effect from the one intended, as well as many other unintended consequences.

Managed care has become the popular phrase to signify health or mental health care delivered under controlled conditions designed to provide quality care efficiently and at lower cost than that offered in the fee-for-service professional community. Actually, there is no standard definition of managed care. Auspice, mission, financing source, and program vary from one managed care scheme to another with considerable variation in the services offered. Most managed care programs operate on a "medical model," which focuses primarily on elimination or treatment of the symptom, versus a "social health model," which views the patient from a biopsychosocial perspective. This limited medical model can fail to provide a comprehensive range of needed services.

Under managed health care, health insurance plans cut costs by monitoring access to and the quality of medical care. Insurance companies design these plans especially to oversee the use of high-priced specialists, technologies, and hospital stays. To have a particular service covered, patients must go to networks of doctors and hospitals who are affiliated with those systems. These providers often accept lower fees and stiffer regulations on their practices in exchange for guaranteed payment and high volumes of patients. Frequently, these providers are not readily accessible to the consumer.

The rapid proliferation of managed health and mental health care plans is overwhelming the ability of consumers, professionals, and governments to assess their quality and appropriateness. Managed care activities may be regulated by localities, states, or the federal government, or by agencies as diverse as insurance, health, or other departments. Or managed care may not be regulated at all except as profit-making corporations.

Significant issues unique to mental health care are of special concern to social workers. Employee assistance programs (EAPs) often substitute for conventional indemnity or managed care plans. EAPs are found in ERISA (Employee Retirement Income Security Act) plans, which are not regulated by state insurance departments but by federal law that does not have the safeguards found in most insurance laws. As a result, the EAP may act as gatekeeper or alternatively contract with a gatekeeper organization (managed care again) to determine whether a request for service is valid and to control how much service will be covered. Some corporations have developed their EAPs into sensitive instruments, with social workers helping employees obtain the most effective and appropriate services. However, many corporations use the gatekeeper function to reduce costs by limiting service. Here, and in some HMOs as well, the arbitrary withholding of services is the result of an unsubstantiated, but nationwide, perception supported by the insurance industry that sees mental health care as an expensive bottomless pit without significant results. Recent studies have shown that the reverse is true: Mental health services without restrictions lead to savings in the long run because help with emotional and other mental problems reduces the use of other health care.

Consumers and professionals must be alerted to these significant variations and the resulting care. Social workers, in particular, must develop considerable knowledge of managed care plans because they will be involved with them on a number of levels. The majority of social workers in the United States are employed in health and mental health work, offering direct services in clinics, hospitals, and in their own offices and referring clients to health and social services in their communities. Social workers work as part of primary care and hospital-based health care teams, as well as primary providers of mental health care. In managed care settings, they are preferred providers, staff professionals, administrators, case managers, program planners, and managed care advisers. Whether they evaluate a managed care setting by working with a client or work within a managed care setting, understanding the nature of managed care is essential. As in other social programs and settings, advocacy and system skills are needed in managed care.

The usual aspects of care that social workers and others address are access, range of services, cost, and quality. In managed care as in other health and mental health programs, the auspice and mission of the organization are keys to understanding the organization. Also requiring analysis is managed care's signature feature of assigning a gatekeeper who is responsible for approving the type and amount of services the patient will receive. The gatekeeping function may be performed by a primary care physician, a nurse, a social worker, or an administrator. Gatekeeping may help steer a patient to the most appropriate services, or it may be used to restrict access to services or to restrict the range of services available. The plan's mission may be to provide the best and most appropriate services, or it may be to reduce costs.

Managed care plans may be financed through full capitation (an annual payment to cover costs in advance), partial capitation, or a fee for providing management (steering) services only. Funding sources include insurance companies, employer contracts, direct payment by consumers, and the government through Medicare and Medicaid.

Managed care is a neutral concept and should not be automatically evaluated as desirable or undesirable. However, forces in the present market can and often do distort health and mental health-providing organizations, leading to inequities that should be understood and challenged:

■ *Cost containment.* To manage costs, managed care programs may intentionally or unintentionally deprive consumers of a full range of appropriate services; that is, they may create a disincentive for the use of high-priced procedures even when those procedures are needed.

■ *Capitation.* The negotiating process needed to arrive at a capitation rate may leave the managed care organization with insufficient funds to provide contracted services.

■ *Contracting.* The annual fee for enrollees is usually negotiated by surrogates—employers, government, or unions—and terms are set for eligibility and coverage that may adversely affect patient care and social work inclusion.

■ *Price escalation.* Managed care may be more efficient than other forms of organized care, but it may be as helpless as other forms of care in the face of rising prices that erode the capacity to maintain quality services.

■ *Multiple contracts.* The fact that managed care organizations do not seek the same level of services for all of their members could lead to multitiered systems with consequent confusion and potential conflict at the provider and consumer levels.

■ *Reduced services coverage.* As a result of reduced funding and higher costs, there is strong risk of a reduction in conditions covered or in services provided to people with complex medical and social conditions. As a consequence, consumers may avoid social health issues and the need for social work services.

■ *Shortages of qualified professionals.* In health care, primary and family care-trained physicians are in short supply. The impact of the shortage may result in long waits, short examination times, and fewer services for the poor.

■ *Isolated consumers.* The recipients of care rarely are involved in negotiations that determine the nature of the health and mental health services they receive from managed care organizations. The consumer is denied a real voice.

Medical care for Medicaid recipients has been characterized by lack of primary care, exploitation in "Medicaid mills," episodic uncoordinated care in emergency rooms, poor or nonexistent coordination of medications, and lack of follow-up. Care during hospitalization has usually met higher standards than care provided in ambulatory settings. Inpatient care is more expensive and more frequently needed because of the lack of adequate primary care services. Primary care services under managed care programs can be a significant step forward if they are truly accessible, comprehensive, and accountable.

Some Medicaid-eligible individuals and families are already served in managed care programs in some cities. Although their numbers are small, there is evidence that those covered by well-conceived programs achieve better health status at the same or lower cost. However, as the number of people covered increases and as new services are created, there are significant risks and potential drawbacks to these programs, the most evident ones being an insufficient number of primary care physicians and the omission of social work services. Another concern is the protection of people's right to choose their provider or provider group and their right to a strong grievance mechanism. These and other concerns are related to resources and standards.

Managed care for Medicaid-eligible people must be more than a means for cost savings. Medicaid agencies responsible for setting up managed care programs know the average cost of Medicaid per individual. Although savings may be the goal in the long run, capitation payments must be high enough to meet a defined set of care standards, including specialist services, hospitalization and long-term care (when needed), and health and mental health care. If capitation rates are set too low, access to services will be severely curtailed. If they are properly financed, and with sound accountability, Medicaid managed care programs may provide recipients with quality care.

ISSUE STATEMENT

While the United States searches for a solution to the health care problem, new delivery systems are gaining a significant foothold and are embraced as solutions by many political and media leaders. These systems, usually referred to under the rubric "managed care" or "managed competition," vary in quality and effectiveness and are frequently characterized by cost-saving measures through strict gatekeeping policies. Unable to contain costs through control of prices, managed care organizations attempt to do so by limiting subscriber access and reducing coverage.

The NASW policy statement on "Social Work on HMOs" provides a framework for developing standards for those HMOs that do not employ or contract with social workers. In these organizations, mental health services often are restricted and social workers are often locked out as providers. These issues apply to other forms of managed care, such as some EAPs in which a gatekeeping function prevents employees from obtaining needed services because decisions are based on a cost rationale. The rapid growth of the new forms of managed care pose a serious danger to the continued presence of professional social workers in health care settings.

For example, recent government initiatives based on Medicaid waivers allow the states to develop enrollment plans for people on Medicaid. The state plans provide for the enrollment of Medicaid-eligible families in HMOs and other providers through a contracting process in which saving money for the government is the goal. The providers seek to profit by cost savings and provisions that permit them to keep any surplus.

New national health policy is a top priority of congressional and White House leadership. The forthcoming debate focuses heavily on financing issues and structure. Standards must be established in managed care systems to ensure acceptable quality services based on a fundamental right to health care for all Americans. Basic standards such as universality, portability, affordability, consumer protection and involvement, and requirements for equitable coverage must be included in a national health care policy. In addition, standards for the inclusion of social health care, mental health services, and the availability of social work services are essential in reshaping health care. Given the nature of politics, it is likely we will need to engage in a continuing struggle to ensure policy and regulation that will ensure adequate universal health care for all.

POLICY STATEMENT

NASW advocates the following policy strategies related to standards, social work role, and advocacy.

Standards

When integrated community health care networks are created or contracts are made with existing ones, the specifications and contracts must respond adequately to the health care needs of the population to be served, as consumers will be constrained from using other health care resources. Standards for managed care plans at a minimum should include the following:

■ a full range of readily available services including primary care and subspecialities including mental health services and hospitalization

■ clearly maintained safeguards for confidentiality, including issues of computer technology

■ access to services that meet the needs of families, working people, older people, and people with disabilities (the emergency room will no longer be available for routine care at night or on weekends)

■ clearly drawn affiliation agreements with specialty providers, hospital pharmacies, home care agencies, and other services.

■ appropriate transitions for clients who must change health care plans or who have exhausted their benefits during the course of treatment to facilitate continuity of treatment with the current provider or provide clinically sound transition to another provider

■ emergency and urgent care procedures available on a 24-hour basis

■ medical record access to caregivers on a 24-hour basis

■ social work services basic to primary care and acute care settings in which beneficiaries have access to health and mental health services provided by social workers to receive crises intervention, assessment, prevention, health education, rehabilitation, and continuity of care

■ specialized mental health services provided by social workers to include psychotherapy and counseling practice for individuals, families, and groups and substance abuse prevention and treatment

- complaint and appeal mechanisms readily available and easy to use by all participants

- advisory boards that include consumers and that meet regularly and participate in policy and program development decisions.

Social Work Role

Social workers have been involved in all stages of the development of managed care. A number of major managed care organizations identify social workers as their founders. Many others employ social workers in key executive positions, as well as in utilization staff positions and as providers of health and mental health services. As in any host setting, it is imperative that social workers function in their organizational roles within the framework of the values and standards of the social work profession.

Social workers may play three key roles in the managed care treatment environment.

1. *Direct Provider of Services.* Social workers are fully qualified providers of health and mental health care services. Social workers are responsible for psychosocial assessments, care coordination and planning, counseling on adjustment to physical and mental illness, and counseling and treatment for individuals, families, and groups. Social workers are trained and licensed or otherwise regulated to provide prevention, assessment, and treatment of emotional and mental disorders, psychosocial dysfunction, disability, and impairment. The person-in-environment treatment perspective of social work provides a stimulus for rapid attainment of effective social functioning.

Social workers are accessible geographically and demographically. Social workers are sometimes the only mental health care providers in the community. Social workers reflect the racial and cultural demographics of U.S. society and have a history of working with culturally and economically diverse populations.

Social work is a recognized and regulated profession. All of the federal programs that provide mental health care coverage and most private insurers recognize clinical social workers as autonomous providers of mental health services.

State regulation and professional credentials provide a measure of consumer protection.

2. *Managed Care Program Staff.* In managed care organizations, social workers perform utilization management, network development and management, and operation management. Social workers bring to these roles the ability to view the client situation within the context of the person-in-environment, examining the biopsychosocial dimensions of client needs. They use the fundamentals of social work case management that provide a theoretical and technical framework for coordinating mental health and substance abuse benefits with the resources of the family and the community in the best interest of the client.

As part of this process, social workers have brought a familiarity with and a respect for multidisciplinary and interdisciplinary practice, as well as the ability to help various systems negotiate and work collaboratively.

3. *Health Care Leadership.* Social workers develop and implement service delivery models that significantly improve options for care. They present the continuum of care options that support the optimal functioning of the client in the least-restrictive environment possible, and they promote healthy community functioning.

Advocacy

Because public policy relating to managed care is embedded in federal, state, and local laws, advocacy efforts require a multitiered approach. Social workers should

- challenge managed care plans to ensure the inclusion of professional social work services

- promote state and federal legislation that supports basic standards of care that include universality, accessibility, affordability, comprehensive and adequate services, and portability

- actively work for passage of legislation that mandates professional social work services in all managed care plans, including self-insured plans

- promote legislation that mandates that utilization review be done only by a health care professional licensed in the specialty for which he or she is reviewing

■ challenge closed provider networks that restrict provider participation and consumer access

Managed care organizations and providers of services must establish mutually respectful operations to ensure that the client is neither overtreated nor undertreated. Specific standards for managed care organizations and for social workers in solo and group practice contracting with managed care organizations should include

■ provider relations

■ practice management

■ treatment planning and termination

■ confidentiality

■ provider responsibilities

■ ethical behavior.

First and foremost, NASW expects managed care organizations and all social workers involved as staff or providers to work toward the best interest of the direct consumer of service. Working together, in a client-centered context with the best talents and resources available, we can improve the health care delivery system.

There is no guarantee that any health care delivery system will be free of inequities and quality problems, but the NASW policy on national health care that calls for universal health care coverage can result in a fair and equitable system. Managed care under a national health care policy would be governed by a universally adopted set of principles applicable to all.

SUGGESTED READINGS

Anderson, M. D., & Fox, P. D. (1987). Lessons learned from Medicaid managed care approaches. *Health Affairs,* 71–86.

Borenstein, D. B. (1990). Managed care: A means of rationing psychiatric treatment. *Hospital and Community Psychiatry, 41,* 1095–1098.

Docherty, J. P. (1990). Myths and mystifications of managed care. *Journal of Mental Health Administration, 17,* 138–144.

Freund, D. A., et al. (1989). Evaluation of the Medicaid competition demonstrations. *Health Care Financing Review, 11*(2), 81–97.

Fritz, D. L. (1989). Options for providing health care for the uninsured: Opportunities for managed care. *Journal of Health and Social Policy, 1,* 61–73.

Fuchs, V. (1986). *The health economy.* Cambridge, MA: Harvard University Press.

Gray, B. H. (1991). *The profit motive and patient care: The changing accountability of doctors and hospitals* (A Twentieth Century Fund report). Cambridge, MA: Harvard University Press.

Heinen, L., Fox, P. D., & Anderson, M. D. (1990). Findings from the Medicaid competition demonstration: A guide for states. *Health Care Financing Review, 11*(4), 70–82.

Hurley, R. E., & Freund, D. A. (1988). A typology of Medicaid managed care. *Medical Care, 26,* 764–774.

Laudicina, S. (1992). *State barriers to managed care: Results of a national survey of Blue Cross and Blue Shield plans* (2nd ed.). Washington, DC: Blue Cross/Blue Shield.

Mayer, J. B., & Rubin, G. (1983). Is there a future for social work in HMOs? *Health & Social Work, 8,* 283–289.

New York State. (1991). Statewide managed care program act. *Chapter 165 of the laws 1991.* Albany, NY: Author.

Patterson, D. Y. (1990). Managed care: An approach to rational psychiatric treatment. *Hospital and Community Psychiatry, 41,* 1092–1095.

Poole, D. L., & Braja, L. J. (1984). Does social work in HMOs measure up to professional standards? *Health & Social Work, 9,* 305–313.

Prottas, J. M., & Handler, E. (1987). The complexities of managed care: Operating a voluntary system. *Journal of Health Politics, Policy and Law, 12,* 253–297.

Robinson, M. O. (1989). Relationships between HMOs and mental health providers. *Social Casework, 70,* 195–200.

Seay, J., & Vladeck, B. (1988). Mission matters. In J. D. Seay & B. C. Vladeck (Eds.), *In sickness and in health* (pp. 1–34). New York: McGraw-Hill.

Sharfstein, S. S. (1990). Impact of managed care on the private hospital: An introduction. *Journal of Mental Health Administration, 17,* 137.

Stoesz, D. (1986). Corporate welfare: The third stage of welfare in the United States. *Social Work, 31,* 245–249.

U.S. Department of Health and Human Services, Medicaid Bureau, Health Care Financing Administration. (1991). *National summary of state Medicaid coordinated care programs.* Washington, DC: Author.

Policy statement approved by the NASW Delegate Assembly, August 1993. For further information, contact the National Association of Social Workers, 750 First Street, NE, Suite 700, Washington, DC 20002-4241. Telephone: 202-408-8600 or 800-638-8799.

Mental Health

BACKGROUND

Mental disorders, characterized by a range of symptoms from depression to aberrant thought, speech, and behavior, have been noted as human problems since the earliest days of recorded history. Throughout the centuries, various civilizations have attempted to address the problem, some in a benign fashion, many with cruel and harsh treatment. Indeed, the way in which a society has addressed the problem of mental disorders has been an indicator of the level of its culture.

In 1989 it was anticipated that one of five adults in the United States would have a mental disorder during the course of the year, according to a study conducted in 1985 by the National Institute of Mental Health (NIMH), Epidemiologic Catchment Area Study. This study is the most comprehensive investigation undertaken to date of the prevalence of mental illness in both urban and rural areas of the United States.

According to this same study, only 18 percent of those adults who have mental disorders receive any specialized treatment for those disorders. Many seek treatment through the general medical care system, rather than from a mental health care practitioner. Many more neither seek nor receive the care they need.

The prevalence of emotional or mental health problems in children, although less comprehensively studied, is alarming. According to the most recent data available, approximately 12 percent, or 7.5 million, youths in the United States suffer from an emotional or mental health disorder. Studies indicate that less than 5 percent, or approximately 2.1 million, children receive treatment for these problems. Over half the youths in need of mental health services do not receive them.

National policy on the care of the mentally ill is most directly embodied in the 1963 Community Mental Health Services Act and its amendments and the 1980 Mental Health Systems Act. In addition, national mental health policy is also embodied in Titles XVIII and XIX of the Social Security Act (Medicare and Medicaid, respectively), the Education of All Handicapped Children Act, and the various yearly Budget Reconciliation Acts. This fragmentation of national mental health policy has led to conflicting priorities among public agencies that fund services for low-income people with mental illness, an uncoordinated service delivery system, and continuing stigma.

POLICY STATEMENT

NASW believes that the multidimensional consequences of mental disorders require effective treatment and prevention programs. These programs should be available to all people without regard to age, gender, ethnicity, economic status, or sexual orientation.

Mental Health Care as National Priority

NASW asserts that the incidence and prevalence of mental disorders in the United States should be reduced significantly. To accomplish this goal, it is necessary to reaffirm existing federal policy on mental health care and to reestablish mental health care and the prevention of mental disorders as a national priority.

To this end, NASW supports the following:

■ creative, visionary leadership that is receptive to new ideas and committed to building a commonality of purpose among all people who are concerned about mental health, mental disorders, and serious mental illness

■ activities by businesses, unions, employee associations, educational systems, and other organizations to promote positive mental health among their respective employees, constituencies, and their families

■ placement of the highest priority on public and private funding to support services and programs to effectively meet the needs of those with severe mental illnesses, their families, and others who are affected or are at high risk of developing mental illness

■ political action at the local, state, and federal levels to increase funding for prevention, treatment, and research and to facilitate the passage of legislation aimed at a uniform requirement that all health insurance carriers, health benefit plans, and managed care organizations provide adequate mental health benefits and include coverage for social workers as providers of mental health services

■ support for public education regarding the cause, treatment, and prevention of mental disorders aimed at reducing the negative stigma of mental illness

■ recognition of social workers as qualified clinical practitioners who are skilled in the assessment and treatment of individuals with mental health needs and who should be entitled to third-party payment

■ mental health research that includes attention to the biological, social, and psychological causes and consequences of mental illness and related conditions

■ research, with informed consent, on prevention and treatment that is conducted within the limits of ethical and humane procedures

■ funding mechanisms and enhanced coverage by corporate insurers to provide the best mental health services, regardless of insurance coverage, county of residence, or individual income, and mental health funding and services that do not require individuals to meet a certain diagnostic category to receive services

■ mental health services that are accessible, available, and affordable

■ a special effort to ensure that services meet the needs of ethnic/minority populations. Many people are unable to gain access to the mental health system because of linguistic and cultural barriers. The system must be flexible and comprehensive enough to meet the social, cultural, and care needs of ethnic/minority populations. Ethnic/minority professional staff must be increased at all levels of the mental health system, and programs must recognize and reflect differences in language, culture, and demographic and social characteristics to assure that services are effectively provided to underserved populations.

Assessment and Treatment

In the assessment and treatment of people with mental disorders, NASW affirms that the following eight areas should be considered:

1. assessment and treatment designed to meet the unique needs of individuals who are affected by mental illness that includes specified treatment goals and methods and monitored outcome criteria; treatment provided in the least restrictive environment without regard to age, gender, race, creed, sexual orientation, or social economic status; outreach to individuals with mental disorders or serious mental illnesses who are unlikely to seek care on their own behalf

2. appropriate mental health services in a continuum of care that includes community-based services, prevention, short- and long-term inpatient hospitalization, partial hospitalization, outpatient services, outreach and emergency services, and supported services to families and others who are affected by mental disorders

3. services delivered by interdisciplinary teams consisting of social workers, psychiatrists, psychologists, psychiatric nurses, and other appropriate professionals, with social workers playing a leading role

4. the provision of protection, respect, humane living conditions, and appropriate treatment for individuals of all ages

5. case management used to promote the monitoring of care, coordination of services, advocacy, and outreach to community services

that are aimed at meeting the need for shelter, housing, food, clothing, education, medical care, and vocational and rehabilitation services that maximize the possibilities of recovery and the prevention of relapse

6. treatment approaches that recognize diversity and innovation and that include methodologies that address the differential needs of individuals throughout the life cycle

7. ongoing systematic evaluation of treatment methods, community needs, and quality of care

8. the inclusion of families in the decision-making process, as appropriate, with recognition of the potential of families to provide psychosocial support and training and to improve the quality of life for family members with mental illness.

In addition, special populations, such as children and youths, people with serious mental illness, and older Americans, often present special needs.

Children and Youths

■ Mental health services must be family oriented. *Family* is defined as any group or person with whom the child lives. A family can include biological parents, a stepparent, adoptive parents, foster parents, a single parent, gay or lesbian parents, extended family members, staff of group homes, staff of institutions, or any other significant caregivers. The issues of the stages of development of the family life cycle are important when assessing the needs of children and youth for mental health treatment. Ethnicity and communication in the language the family uses must be considered when assessing the client and the family. All treatment programs should include a family treatment component.

■ Early intervention–diagnostic evaluation and treatment should be interdisciplinary, and social workers should play an integral role in evaluation and treatment teams. Treatment teams should complete comprehensive diagnostic evaluations expeditiously to develop appropriate individualized goals. The patient and

family should participate in the diagnosis, in establishing goals, and in planning treatment.

■ Short-term intensive inpatient services should be designed to serve children and adolescents who are in crisis.

■ Partial hospitalization programs that provide intensive structured treatment for children and youths who do not need 24-hour-a-day treatment or that provide a transition from residential treatment should be an option for treatment.

■ Long-term residential treatment programs should be available for those children and adolescents whose levels of functioning cannot be improved in a short-term intensive program.

■ Discharge planning and the development of an aftercare program should begin the day of admission in all mental health programs and should provide a strong treatment and support system for the child or adolescent and the family to maintain and build on the progress made in the hospital or residential treatment.

■ Outpatient services/programs must be designed to meet the individual needs of the identified patient and family members. Programs should be flexible and should include at-home, at-school, and traditional evaluations. Outpatient services should include access to 24-hour crisis intervention and respite care.

■ Day treatment services must be available to address the mental health and educational needs of children and youths.

■ The social work case manager must investigate and obtain resources, facilitate and coordinate services, and constantly review the ongoing treatment. Case managers require an understanding and familiarity with transportation, contacts in schools, the availability of treatment in mental health service facilities, local community resources, and the provision of services in public health agencies. The social work case manager's involvement should begin as soon as possible and should continue until the termination of treatment.

■ Community linkages should include, but should not be limited to, the educational system, recreational system, mental health–health systems, drug–alcohol treatment programs, services for children and youths, foster care programs, and the juvenile justice system. The appropriate use of these linkages and the networks they provide may prevent inappropriate or unnecessary hospitalizations.

■ NASW supports access to high-quality mental health services for minority and poor children and their families, as well as for children and youths with physical disabilities.

■ Comprehensive mental health for children and youths should include prevention. Research-based wellness training should be incorporated into the curricula of schools from preschool through college and may include, but should not be limited to, problem-solving skills, effective communication, peer pressure, relationships, sexuality, career planning, financial planning, and resources and treatment for mental health problems.

■ NASW places a high priority on making mental health treatment accessible to all children and their families by advocating age-appropriate educational and public relation efforts to increase awareness of the existence and availability of mental health services and working with the interest groups focused on juvenile rights to draft and encourage the passage of satisfactory legislation in this area.

Services for People with Serious Mental Illness

The major premises underlying and directing NASW policy regarding the care of children, youths, adults, and older Americans with serious mental illness are the following:

■ Research and treatment must recognize that mental illness has a biopsychosocial etiology.

■ The current understanding of serious mental illnesses, such as schizophrenia and bipolar disorder, is that they are brain diseases that require medical and social treatments.

■ Public policy and funding must differentiate acute, chronic, or serious mental illness from short-term crises, adjustment disorders, and family problems.

■ Individuals with severe, acute, or chronic mental illness must be given high priority in treatment, care, and research.

■ People with mental illness should be involved as fully as possible with the development of all aspects of their own treatment plans. Social workers should ensure that people with mental illness are not denied their rights to participate in treatment except that under no circumstances should the safety of the patient, the worker, or other people be jeopardized.

■ Individuals of all ages with severe chronic mental illnesses must be provided protection, dignity, humane living conditions, and appropriate and meaningful treatment.

■ Serious mental illness affects the economic situation of the individuals and their families. The fact that people with serious mental illness often experience extreme poverty or a reduced standard of living must be addressed by the profession and public policy.

■ Treatment programs and institutions must provide the least restrictive environment possible for individuals.

■ Services must be offered in accordance with the principles of "normalization"; that is, services should avoid stigmatizing or taking away the power and responsibility of clients or families.

■ The safety and well-being of clients shall always be placed ahead of the agency's needs and goals.

■ Rehabilitation goals shall not be established solely on the basis of the individual's capacity for employment. Treatment plans should be based on the individual's capacity to function in all areas of life.

■ Mental health systems and providers must assist with the family's and client's concrete needs, such as finances, shelter, food, child care, transportation, education, and vocational training.

■ Specific treatment and care must be provided for individuals with dual diagnoses.

■ Comprehensive rehabilitation programs for substance abuse must be available upon request.

■ Mental health delivery systems must maintain active outreach and follow-up programs for clients with serious mental illnesses.

■ Mental health systems must systematically evaluate their services, methods, the needs of the community, and the quality of providers of care.

■ Because individuals who live with similar disorders provide a major resource of support for seriously ill clients, providers should facilitate the development of self-help, support, and advocacy groups.

■ Social security must provide greater benefits to mentally ill people (for example, Supplemental Security Income, Disability Insurance, Medicare, and Medicaid).

■ Families of people with chronic mental illness must be provided access to treatment teams, treatment decisions, and community services within the constraints of client confidentiality.

■ All mental health treatment should address quality-of-life issues of people with mental illness and their families.

■ NASW calls for meaningful biopsychosocial research and community demonstration projects. Social work must provide leadership in research on the identification of high-risk populations, social prevention, improved treatment methods and programs, community housing, case management methods, measurement instruments, and delivery systems.

■ Schools of social work should require all students to gain an understanding of the biopsychosocial basis of mental illness. Social workers should be required to receive training on the biopsychosocial basis, treatment, and care of people with chronic mental illness before they obtain or renew their state social work license.

■ Every effort should be made to develop public policies that remove economic, social, and emotional burdens from family members of mentally ill people.

Services for Older Americans

Mental health care for the elderly must be provided within the context of complex social forces and the multiple medical and functional changes experienced by older patients. Therefore, NASW supports the following policy specifically addressed to the mental health needs of older people:

■ Services should be provided through community-based sites that are funded jointly by federal, state, and local money with the goals of early identification and screening, assessment, treatment interventions, and education about depression and dementia.

■ Because coexisting medical illnesses are frequently present in elderly people with mental illness, programs must integrate services to meet the physical health care needs of older people.

■ Discharge planning from psychiatric hospitals must include a comprehensive assessment and treatment plan to meet the continuing medical, educational, psychiatric, psychosocial, and functioning needs of the elderly.

■ Mental health services must be integrated into institutional care for elderly people at all levels: day care, personal care homes, assisted living, and nursing facilities.

■ Educational strategies must be developed to overcome the prejudices of professional and nonprofessional care providers toward elderly people with psychiatric disorders.

■ Community-based services must provide flexible eligibility requirements, the ability to combine private and public funding, and the integration of family supports into the service delivery system.

■ Educational initiatives must be developed to prepare and train families and the elderly to plan and arrange for their increasing and expanded need for care and decision-making responsibilities.

■ Medicare should provide reimbursement of a full range of psychiatric services for elderly people.

Policy statement approved by the NASW Delegate Assembly, August 1990. Referred to the 1999 Delegate Assembly for revision. For further information, contact the National Association of Social Workers, 750 First Street, NE, Suite 700, Washington, DC 20002-4241. Telephone: 202-408-8600 or 800-638-8799.

National Health Care

BACKGROUND

Professional social workers practice throughout the health care system and experience daily the strengths and limitations of the health system on the lives and health status of the American people. This intensive and varied fund of experience and knowledge entitles the National Association of Social Workers (NASW) to participate fully in the development and implementation of a national health policy. This responsibility is deeply rooted in the collective professional experience of the nearly 150,000 members of NASW in 1993.

History of National Health Care Reform

The federal government traditionally has provided direct care benefits to certain classes of beneficiaries. Federal health policy began in 1798, when health care for merchant seamen became a federal government responsibility. Since the 1930s, a multitude of proposals for health care have occupied major segments of legislative, administrative, and judicial processes. However, proposals for a federally financed and administered national health plan were ultimately rejected by the Roosevelt and Truman administrations. The federal government became increasingly involved in financing health care with the passage of Medicaid and Medicare in 1965. The 1960s also saw the passage of increased federal legislation and funding for a variety of social and health programs, including neighborhood health centers, migrant health centers, community mental health centers, and comprehensive health planning.

With the failure of the movement to pass a national health plan in the early 1970s during the Nixon Administration, the interest in national health policy shifted to cost containment through utilization review, professional standard review organizations, quality assurance, and prospective payment proposals. These cost-cutting policies, which also limit access, have also included the introduction of diagnosis-related groups (DRGs) classification schemes (in the early 1980s) and managed care (in the early 1990s; see the Health Care Financing policy statement).

National Health Policy in the Context of National Social Policies

In developing a national health policy, the United States must consider the interrelationship with other national policies that affect the health, security, social well-being, and functional capacities of the American people. An adequate and effective national health policy, therefore, must be accompanied by the development of other national social and economic policies, directed to the essential needs of all people and their society.

The Wave of Health Care Reform in the Early 1990s

For the first time in a number of years, a real movement to make vital changes in the health care system exists in individual states and on the federal level. Public opinion polls have indicated that nearly all Americans favor some type of national health care program and increased government spending on medical services, and a majority are willing to absorb a tax increase to obtain comprehensive care (Blendon & Donelan, 1990).

After a decade of economic and political conservatism, with a retrenchment in all entitlements by the Reagan and Bush administrations, the early 1990s saw a reemergence in the political arena of a national health care movement. The depressed economy in the early 1990s, with increasing unemployment and recession, dramatically contributed to the growing concern about health care. The number of uninsured and underinsured grew as companies cut back or eliminated their health benefits. In 1992, hundreds of bills for health care reform were introduced into Congress and state legislatures. Almost everyone, spanning the total political spectrum, climbed on the health bandwagon. With the election of President Bill Clinton, national health reform has taken center stage.

Health proposals are usually grouped in three types, from minor to major change. The least change is found in the limited small-group market health insurance plans; the middle ground is found in employers' "play or pay" proposals that require employers to either provide basic coverage for their employees or pay the government a tax to insure their employees under a public program; and the most comprehensive change is the single-payer systems that promote universal health care under one publicly financed and administered program. NASW developed a single-payer comprehensive system of reform under one program, as a way to provide comprehensive coverage to all Americans and, at the same time, constrain costs (Center for Health Policy Studies, 1990). Senator Daniel Inouye introduced the plan in the U.S. Senate in June 1992 (Inouye, 1992).

ISSUE STATEMENT

Rising Costs and Decreasing Quality

Worldwide, the United States is number one in health care spending: more than $800 billion a year as of the end of 1992, projected to be more than $1 trillion by the year 2000. Government expenditures for health care as a percentage of all federal spending increased from 12 percent ($69 billion) in 1980 to 15 percent ($191.5 billion) of the much larger 1990 budget (Iglehart, 1992). The fact that the United States ranks 17th in life expectancy and 20th in preventing infant mortality raises the question of whether the American people are getting their money's worth (American Public Health Association [APHA], 1992).

Approximately 9.1 million people were working in the health care system as of 1992, making it one of the largest U.S. industries. However, expenditures for health care continue to rise at a rate that is deemed unacceptable by a variety of interest groups, including consumers, professionals, and payers (Iglehart, 1992).

To solve the problems of high cost and access, hospitals and payers are attempting to shift uninsured patients' hospital cost to paying clients. They are trying to avoid insuring people they deem "high risk," and in many cases are succeeding, by implementing utilization reviews that greatly add to administrative costs and limit access to services. Some states are attempting to impose de facto rationing with such plans as the Oregon Medicaid waiver proposal, which covers more people but limits benefits.

Two other important developments that have occurred over the past several years make it critical to change the health delivery and financing system. First, the introduction of managed care as a cost-containment measure has diminished access to a wide range of service providers, particularly social work services for mental health. Second, there has been a proliferation of employer self-insured policies that exempt plans from statewide mandated benefits.

Inadequate and Decreasing Coverage

A public citizen survey showed that the number of Americans without insurance increased by 1.3 million between 1989 and 1990, with 74 percent of the uninsured earning more than $25,000 (Kemper & Novak, 1992). At the same time, the burden on American families to pay the major share of the national health care bill had increased to $6,535 per family by 1991. In 1991, families paid $4,296 through a combination of out-of-pocket payments, insurance premiums, Medicare taxes and premiums, and general taxes, and the rest ($2,239) was paid by employers through health insurance premiums. Health cost increases far outpaced increases in family incomes. Family income increased 88 percent since 1980, and average family-health spending had increased 147 percent as of 1991 (Families USA Foundation, 1991). In many cross-national surveys of industrialized countries, Americans are the least satisfied with their health care system (Blendon, 1989; *Health Security for All*, 1993).

Somewhere between 35 million and 38 million Americans are uninsured, and another estimated 50 million to 60 million people are underinsured. The underinsured hold limited health plans with major restrictions and uncovered services. Of the poor, 60 percent are not covered by Medicaid, and only 1 million of 30 million senior citizens have coverage for long-term health care (Foley, 1992). In 1990, about 25 percent of American women received no prenatal care. This figure has risen by 50 percent since 1980 when Reagan was elected (*Borderline Medicine*, 1991). In 1991, between 10 million and 12 million children were uninsured; these uninsured children represent more than 25 percent of all those without public or private protection (Children's Defense Fund, 1992).

Individuals with good coverage worry about rising medical costs due to increases in copayments and deductibles, and some people worry that their insurance plans no longer cover some health items. Many people are afraid to change jobs because of insurance considerations. Other individuals just fall through the cracks: workers without benefits who earn too much to qualify for Medicaid, people with preexisting conditions who cannot get insurance, workers with preexisting conditions who may lose their health insurance if they change jobs, small business owners for whom a sudden illness can put insurance premiums out of reach for the entire firm, workers who see their benefits threatened each time they go to the bargaining table, families whose emotional and financial resources are exhausted from providing long-term care to frail parents or disabled children, and uninsured pregnant women without the resources to seek prenatal care.

The lack of coverage for mental health services in the United States is especially abominable by almost any standard. The National Mental Health Association (1991) has pointed out that, of the 153 million Americans with private health insurance coverage, access to mental health services is much more restrictive than access to physical health services. Inpatient and outpatient benefits are far less comprehensive, maximum benefits are lower, deductibles and co-insurance rates are higher, and the percentages reimbursed are substantially smaller.

Gaps and Inequities in Medicare and Medicaid

The problem of access and quality health care is exacerbated for poor families with dependent children by the limits of Medicare and Medicaid. Partly because of low reimbursement rates, many providers refuse to participate or limit their participation in Medicaid (Mitchell, 1991). Benefits and eligibility requirements, which vary by state, have been cut or curtailed because of states' budgetary problems. Many low-income families with dependent children have limited or no access to health care. The lack of access is especially troubling because poor children make up half of all Medicaid recipients who obtain care because of this entitlement (Children's Defense Fund, 1992).

Coverage of the poor has been largely the responsibility of Medicaid. Unfortunately, Medicaid reaches only a fraction of the low-income population. In 1990, Medicaid covered only 42 percent of those with income below the poverty line. Nearly 25 percent are not covered by Medicaid or any other program (Levit, Lazenby, Cowan, & Letsch, 1991). Because states have failed to increase their income eligibility levels to keep pace with inflation, Medicaid programs are serving smaller proportions of the poor. The proportions of uninsured among families earning under $20,000 a year decreased from 58 percent in 1989 to 55 percent in 1990. Medicaid covered 25.3 million people in 1990 compared with 23.5 million in 1989 (Levit et al., 1991). However, 60 percent of the new recipients were children who were targeted by the expansions. In an effort to control costs, states are beginning to limit the services covered, reduce the payments made to providers for covered services, and introduce copayment and managed care without increasing the number of providers. This results in inadequate access to services, despite rising costs.

For the most part, Medicare does not cover long-term care and prescription drugs in any comprehensive manner. Although those gaps are usually a problem for the elderly, younger people with physical, developmental, and emotional impairments are also a part of this group. Approximately 7 million elderly people and almost 4 million adults and children with a disability will, at some point, need long-term care (The Pepper Commission, 1990). Despite federal government attempts to change Medicare reimbursement through a prospective system for physicians, based on resource-based relative value scales (RBRVS), there are still disincentives for physicians to participate in the Medicare and Medicaid programs.

POLICY STATEMENT

The National Association of Social Workers (NASW) advocates major reform in health and mental health care. As the nation debates the critical issues surrounding reform, NASW will actively promote sound policy that will provide comprehensive coverage to all. The following principles must be incorporated in any reform.

■ a right to health care for every American citizen and resident

■ universal access to health care for all, regardless of race, national origin, income, religion, age, gender, sexual preference, language, or geographic residence

■ comprehensive health benefits that enable people to achieve and maintain physical and mental health, maximize their potential for enhanced social and physical functioning, and sustain a meaningful quality of life

■ an integrated health delivery system that provides a continuum of care linking all levels of the health system; that addresses the physical, mental, and psychosocial health needs of the individual and the family; that promotes multidisciplinary collaboration in the delivery of services; and that reflects the demographics and sociocultural diversity of the community

■ a major emphasis on primary prevention and health promotion, with a broad range of involvement on the level of health care provid-

ers, public agencies, consumers, civic organizations, schools, employers, and unions

■ the right of consumers to participate in the decisions that directly affect their lives and in the decisions that relate to the design and implementation of health care services

■ continued commitment to and strengthening of basic health functions to provide for a safe environment, control of infectious diseases, and promotion of a healthy lifestyle and behaviors

■ a progressive financing structure that will increase access, eliminate administrative waste, and monitor the quality and cost of care.

NASW's active participation in the debate and policy development for health care and mental health care reform is based on the tenets the organization espoused in its single-payer plan. They include the following issues.

■ Replace the current patchwork of 1,500 private insurers and public programs with a single national health program administered by the states under federal guidelines.

■ Pay hospitals a negotiated annual operating budget and reimburse all independent practitioners according to a fee schedule.

■ Eliminate deductibles, copayments, and most out-of-pocket expenses.

■ Finance the program with a health premium tax on personal income, an employer-paid payroll tax, an increase in corporate taxes, and state contributions.

■ Maintain the freedom to choose any physician, hospital, or other provider.

Single-Payer Coverage and Enrollment

All people residing in the United States would be covered through a national health plan. Each person would have the freedom to choose from among any of the participating public and private providers, facilities, or care delivery options, including integrated health service plans (IHSPs). IHSPs are nonprofit, consumer-controlled plans that provide comprehensive health care services in their own facilities to an enrolled population. Individuals would enroll in the national health plan in the state in which they reside.

Coverage through employers or other privately purchased health insurance would be discontinued, although private insurance plans may provide coverage for services not covered under the national health plan.

Benefits of Single Payer

A range of benefits would include mental health services; substance abuse treatment and rehabilitation programs; inpatient and outpatient hospital services; emergency and trauma services; laboratory and radiology services; and long-term care, including home and community-based services, hospice care, prescription drugs, medical supplies and durable medical equipment, dental care, hearing and speech devices, and vision care.

Care coordination services would be used primarily for clients who require multiple services over a certain period or where such services are potentially costly.

Primary prevention and health promotion services would include comprehensive well-child care for everyone to age 21, prenatal and infant health care, routine and age-appropriate clinical health maintenance examinations for everyone older than age 21, family planning services, and school-based primary prevention programs.

Administration of a Single-Payer Plan

A new federal National Care Administration would be established as an independent agency to administer the health care plan. Policy direction would be provided by a National Health Board representing care experts and consumers. All responsibilities of the Health Care Financing Administration would be transferred to the new agency. Medicare, Medicaid, the Civilian Health and Medical Program of the Uniformed Services (CHAMPUS), and the Department of Veterans Affairs health programs would be folded into the national health care plan.

States would be provided with an annual budget for all covered health care expenditures. The global budget for each state would be based on a formula that considers population size, age, and distribution, the cost of delivery care, socioeconomic factors, and a number of key health status indicators. State global budgets would include all state health block grant funds.

The states, in accordance with federal guidelines, would ensure the implementation of all state health services, determine the distribution of health care funding, develop and administer a mechanism to pay and reimburse health care providers, work with localities and regional offices in undertaking health planning and coordination with appropriate social and human services, implement a quality assurance program, administer a consumer advocacy and information program, and license and regulate all health care providers and facilities.

Payment to Providers under a Single-Payer Plan

Hospitals would receive a prospective global budget, to be developed through annual negotiations between the designated state agency and the hospital. Global budgets would be used only for operating expenses. Separate funds for capital expansion and purchase of expensive, highly specialized equipment would be subject to approval by the state.

Other health care facilities, such as community clinics, migrant health centers, nursing homes, rehabilitation facilities, and IHSPs, would be paid on the basis of either a prospective global budget or capitation as determined by the state.

Autonomous health care practitioners and group practices would be reimbursed on the basis of fee-for-service, although group practices may choose capitation. The reimbursement rate would be based on a national fee schedule, adjusted for regional variations, and negotiated by the National Health Board and a representative organization for each category of health care practitioner. The fee schedule would be a resource-based relative value scale similar to that being implemented for physicians under Medicare.

Quality Assurance and Consumer Protection

The national health care agency would be responsible for determining guidelines; overseeing the quality assurance system, including the establishment of quality assurance standards and certification and licensing criteria for all health care providers; and developing a consumer/patient bill of rights and protection.

Peer Review Organizations (PROs) would be extended to cover all types of health care providers and services. The PROs would be responsible for utilization review and quality control. The composition of PROs must be multidisciplinary, including social workers, to reflect the types of services reviewed. Each PRO would have a consumer board to oversee the PROs, make recommendations on PRO contracts, and carry out educational programs.

The federal agency would develop a national health care database to study quality, effectiveness, utilization, and cost of care with respect to all types of health and mental health services. Federal and state consumer advocacy programs would be established to administer and monitor patients' rights and to administer ombudsman programs, hotlines for complaints, consumer information, and education programs.

Planning under a Single-Payer Plan

The national health plan would require local, state, and regional planning. At each level, the health planning function would include collecting and evaluating data to determine the supply of and demand for health resources, the distribution of such resources, and the health needs of the population in a given jurisdiction. Goals and priorities would be formulated to serve as guides to the development of health policy and programs at each level of government.

Financing a Single-Payer Plan

The national health care plan would be financed primarily from a federal-dedicated tax on personal income and an employer-paid payroll tax. Additional sources of revenue would include a state contribution based on a formula that ensures that each state pays its fair share, and an increase in the cigarette and alcohol tax.

All revenues would be placed in a National Health Care Trust Fund. All current federal appropriations for health programs would be folded into the national health program and transferred to the trust fund.

Small businesses would be protected by a cap on the amount they must contribute. New firms facing financial hardships would be protected by a reduced payroll tax rate for the first three years of operation.

Cost Sharing

There would be no deductible or copayments for health services. However, residents of nursing homes or other residential facilities would pay a modest room-and-board fee that would be waived for individuals below the poverty line.

Cost Savings from a Single-Payer Plan

NASW's health policy recognized and built in cost-containment without reducing quality and comprehensiveness. The NASW national health care proposal included a detailed cost analysis (Center for Health Policy Studies, 1990). It is estimated that implementation of this plan, including long-term care services, would initially add approximately 11.3 percent to the nation's health care expenditures. The added costs would result primarily from increased use of health care services by people who were previously uninsured or underinsured. The greater costs also reflect a projected increase in use of ambulatory care, dental care, and other professional services, including social workers and psychologists. This would be a one-time increase in costs, however, and would allow the implementation of a payment system that would contain the growth of health care costs in the future.

These cost projections, however, are conservative. They do not include what are expected to be significant long-term savings resulting from expanded health promotion and prevention activities (especially as related to prenatal and child health) and from anticipated lower rates of inflation in health care costs.

Training and Education

The health plan would include increased federal funding for a number of existing and new programs to increase the supply of needed health care personnel, encourage more health practitioners to work in underserved areas, support programs that help disadvantaged students successfully complete health training programs, provide retraining programs for those who are displaced as a result of the programs, support new approaches to continuing education programs in rural areas, and enable educational institutions to hire professionally qualified staff to teach the importance of mental and psychosocial health in prevention, treatment, and health promotion.

Research

The plan would provide funds for research efforts to develop alternative models of health delivery for special populations, study the impact of psychosocial well-being on illness and disease, develop approaches to encouraging healthy lifestyles, and study effective intervention models for the mentally impaired.

The plan would direct research efforts to examine the effect of care coordination on treatment effectiveness and efficiency. Additionally, funds would be available to continue to develop quality indicators for measuring treatment effectiveness in all types of health care settings and to develop practice guidelines for physicians and other health care providers. Research would also be directed toward reducing the number of unnecessary medical and diagnostic procedures.

REFERENCES

American Public Health Association. (1992). *The nation's health*. Washington, DC: Author.

Blendon, R. J. (1989). Three systems: A comparative survey. *Health Management Quarterly*, *11*(1), 2–10.

Blendon, R. J., & Donelan, K. I. (1990). The public and the emerging debates over national health insurance. *New England Journal of Medicine, 323*, 208–212.

Borderline medicine. (1991). Videotape available from WNET, P.O. Box 2284, Burlington, VT, 05407.

Center for Health Policy Studies. (1990). *Cost analysis of the NASW national health care proposal*. Columbia, MD: Author.

Children's Defense Fund. (1992). *The state of America's children*. Washington, DC: Author.

Families USA Foundation. (1991). *Health spending: The growing threat to the family budget*. Washington, DC: Author.

Foley, J. (1992). *Sources of health insurance and characteristics of the uninsured: Analysis of March 1991 current population survey*. Washington, DC: Employee Benefit Research Institute.

Health security for all: The single-payer answer. (1993, Summer). Washington, DC: Single-Payer Coalition.

Iglehart, J. K. (1992). The American health care system: Introduction. *New England Journal of Medicine, 326*, 962–967.

Inouye, D. K. (1992). National health care proposal (S. 2817). In *Congressional Record, 12*(81), S7697–S7716.

Kemper, V., & Novak, V. (1992). What's blocking health care reform? *Common Cause, 25*, 8–12.

Levit, K., Lazenby, H., Cowan, C., & Letsch, S. (1991). National health expenditures, 1990. *Health Care Financing Review, 13*(1), 29–54.

Mitchell, J. B. (1991). Why we need a national child health policy. *Pediatrics, 87*(1), 1–6.

National Mental Health Association. (1991). *Access to health care: NMHA speaks*. Washington, DC: Author.

The Pepper Commission. (1990, September). *A call for action* (Final Report, U.S. Bipartisan Commission on Comprehensive Health Care). Washington, DC: U.S. Government Printing Office.

Policy statement approved by the NASW Delegate Assembly, August 1993. This policy statement supersedes the policy statement on National Health approved by the Delegate Assembly in 1979. For further information, contact the National Association of Social Workers, 750 First Street, NE, Suite 700, Washington, DC 20002-4241. Telephone: 202-408-8600 or 800-638-8799.

Occupational Social Work

BACKGROUND

Occupational social work is an emerging field of professional practice that will become increasingly important in the future. It is defined in relation to the setting in which services occur and the auspices under which services are provided—corporations, small businesses, unions, hospitals, schools, military units, governments (federal, state, regional, and local), and so forth. Occupational social work includes a variety of skills and services that have traditionally been offered in other settings. What makes it unique is the impact of the organizational structure and culture on the delivery of services.

The social work profession long has been concerned about workers and the conditions of employment and unemployment. However, it was not until the late 1960s that occupational social work was conceived in response to the convergence of the following trends and social issues:

■ the reaction to the compartmentalization of life, paralleled by the renewed appreciation of the connections among work, family, and the community

■ interest in the importance of work, not only because of economic benefits, but because of its function in ascribing meaning and value to life

■ identification of the cost of personal problems, particularly chemical dependence, in terms of the productivity of workers

■ the renewed attention in the social work profession to person-in-environment as the focus of practice and interest in a nonstigmatizing approach to delivering services

■ the identification of the emotional stress and physical dangers created by the work environment, such as exposure to chemicals that are dangerous to workers

■ rapid societal and environmental changes that accentuated individual stress in the workplace and in the community

■ the entrance into the workplace of new groups with special concerns.

■ the consumer movement, the equal rights movement, and worker entitlements that resulted in such legislation as the Occupational Safety and Health Act, the Employee Retirement Income Security Act, the Age Discrimination in Employment Act, Affirmative Action in Title VII (Civil Rights Act), and Title V (Vocational Rehabilitation Act)

■ the identification by unions of job satisfaction and job security as important issues in addition to wages

■ changes in the role of women as wage earners and new family structures that lessen the separation between the workplace and the home

■ the interest of management in increasing efficiency and productivity as a way of lowering costs and raising profits

■ the interest in corporate social responsibility and its impact on the community.

Scope of Practice

Occupational social work as a field of practice incorporates a wide range of social work skills and activities, including services to individuals, families, groups, and managers, as well as organizational development, policy formulation, administration, and community organization.

Three categories of occupational social work practice can be described:

1. policy setting, planning, and administration that involve no direct counseling, such as the coordination of employee assistance programs (EAPs), functions within corporate-responsibility departments, training, the formulation of policies for career-path advancement, and the administration of affirmative action programs

2. direct practice with individuals, families, and special populations, including crisis intervention, the assessment of personal problems and the referral for treatment, counseling for chemical dependence, child care work in a company or union program, retirement counseling, and relocation services that may be under the auspices of an EAP

3. practice that combines direct service and administration-policy formulation.

Social work knowledge, skills, and experience can be used effectively in other workplace functions, such as staff development, training, organizational problem solving, planning, and corporate responsibility. Social workers can help corporations to work more effectively with communities, to determine priorities, to allocate resources through grants or other mechanisms to meet major community needs, and to develop policy implications for these directions. Services may be provided directly by the work organization, by referral for some services, or by contract with community-based service programs that are familiar with and responsive to work, workers, and work organizations, such as family service agencies and health-related services.

Social Work Perspective on Work

Work is a significant aspect of the lives of nearly 100 million employed Americans. Work is important to a person's self-esteem, economic well-being, and status in the community. Problems that occur at work have a special meaning to people and often are reflected in problems that develop at home or in the community. Conversely, concerns that arise at home may result in problems at work. The world of work is an important arena for helping individuals gain access to the helping process (counseling, advocacy, information, and referral). Managers, labor leaders, and social work practitioners are becoming more aware of the common agenda they share. This awareness has resulted in the entry of more social workers into occupational settings.

Social workers are not the only professionals who have entered the workplace to provide services. Other allied human service professionals have made and continue to make significant contributions. However, the qualifications of professional social workers are particularly suited to effective practice in this arena. Moreover, the focus on person-in-environment, which is a central element of the conceptual framework of social work practice, is basic to helping the individual at work.

Social workers actively support the development of occupational social work as a designated field of practice for many reasons. First, they recognize the critical importance of and are knowledgeable about work, work-related benefits and entitlements, and the impact of problems on the well-being of the individual, the family, and the community. They can apply their knowledge, skills, and experience to enable systems to function more smoothly, to advocate on behalf of workers, to identify new approaches to management that value employees' rights, to provide expert information about the human service needs of employees, and to link employees to a variety of services.

Second, occupational social work allows practitioners to fill the unique role of generalist. At various times, social workers will provide direct service to individuals and families, consult with managers and supervisors, assist with organizational development, train staff, and help with the administration of programs and the analysis of policies. Furthermore, they can analyze various aspects of corporate responsibility and communicate them to the community at large. In carrying out this role, social workers will use the full range of skills they have learned in school and enhanced through experience. In addition, social workers can engage in their role of social-change agents in this important environment—the workplace.

Occupational Health and Safety

There is a growing and serious incidence of occupational illnesses and conditions that result in disability and death for many of the victims. At least 15,000 chemical and physical agents currently are in use in industry, with approximately 3,000 new chemicals introduced each year. Although more than 14,000 workers are killed each year in work accidents, an estimated 100,000 workers die each year from occupational diseases. Almost one-half million workers develop "official" occupational diseases each year.

Victims often face difficulty in obtaining skilled help to consider or determine whether there is, or may be, a job-related illness or condition; to establish liability; and to obtain the overall psychosocial, medical, and financial help during what may be a critical and often is a prolonged period of time.

The workers' compensation programs work fairly well for victims of job-related injuries. However, such programs have not been the answer for those who suffer lung conditions; cancers; dermatitis; and impairment of the kidney, liver, or nervous system as a result of conditions and materials at the work site. As a result, the victims are "caught in the cracks" between the insurance companies, the compensation system, and the legal tactics used to fight the claim. It is difficult for the worker to establish the direct causal relationship between his or her illness and the work site within the time limits of the law. As a result, the victim is without support and eventually must turn to the Social Security Disability Insurance system or public assistance. This system is a poor substitute for the benefits to which the victim should be entitled.

Social workers need increased knowledge and skills to help victims and their families. Social workers in occupational settings are among those who need to be sensitized to the possibility that debilitating conditions or illnesses may be job related. Social workers must be capable of eliciting the necessary information to help determine whether further exploration or observation is indicated. They should be knowledgeable about resources, facilitate referrals for appropriate care, and ensure the continuity of appropriate social work services in settings to which they refer victims.

Occupational safety and health is an area of practice that warrants increased social work attention. This area of practice is related to the workplace and is concerned with the identification of job-related hazards and treatment of the victim for both injuries and illness.

The Bureau of Labor Statistics figures tell a dismal story of the increase in reported illness and death from accidents and toxins. Social workers need to increase their knowledge of this specific area of service in which they can make a significant contribution.

ISSUE STATEMENT

The issues that emerge in the application of social work practice to the occupational setting include the following:

■   Although some corporations, large public organizations, and unions recognize the role that social workers can play in the work setting, others do not. Therefore, to gain full acceptance, the social work profession must communicate its skills, knowledge, experience, and intentions to these organizations.

■   Social workers need to learn new skills for working in such organizations as unions or corporations whose culture, customs, and attitudes may be unfamiliar and in which the interdisciplinary team may include industrial relations staff, benefits coordinators, personnel officers, and people with whom social workers traditionally have not been associated.

■   Occupational social workers need to have a clear understanding of their own professional code of ethics as they attempt to resolve fundamental conflicts that may arise with individuals or with organizations.

■   Occupational social workers must acquire an even greater knowledge of workers' benefits, entitlements, and available resources in the work setting.

■   The issue of confidentiality has unique parameters in the workplace. The helping role may involve knowledge of situations that affect workers' relationships to each other and to their job security and advancement. Clear guidelines that ensure ethical practice are needed.

■ Occupational social workers may have a sense of isolation in an organization. Their professional identity can be enhanced through the development of a multidisciplinary team for problem solving that involves professionals from allied disciplines.

■ The problem of the absence of practice standards exists in any new field, but it is particularly complicated for occupational social work because of the variety of other professionals who already are providing services in the workplace. Social workers who seek employment in occupational settings need to correlate their level of skills with proposed job descriptions. For example, EAP staff need advanced skills in alcohol and drug abuse counseling, labor and management policies, and networking.

■ Additional resources, either internal or external to the workplace, may be needed to help an employee. To ensure that identifiable gaps in services are filled, social workers must serve as advocates in their own employment system, and the advocacy role may cause special tensions.

■ There is concern about how more services can be procured in the face of inflation. The development of occupational social work would involve the allocation of more resources for service delivery. For example, the location of child care at the workplace may be considered an effective response to the needs of parents, but organizations may be reluctant to commit extensive resources to such services.

■ Although the potential may exist for influencing the organizational policies and procedures of large corporations and business organizations, doing so will not be an easy task. For example, although many organizations may recognize that the increasing number of women in the workplace has created special needs, they still may resist implementing such efforts as flextime and job sharing. Social workers have to learn patience as well as the skills of negotiation.

■ Because there are relatively few experienced graduate social workers in occupational settings, appropriate fieldwork placements for students

may be scarce in those settings. Schools of social work should be encouraged to provide backup field instruction by faculty members and to work out other arrangements for MSW-trained field instructors.

■ In paying increased attention to the practice area of occupational safety and health, social workers must apply existing social work knowledge, skills, and experience to victims of workplace exposures and hazards, and they must develop new practice expertise. Social workers should know the symptoms of occupational illnesses, have skills in the psychosocial assessment and treatment of injured workers, and be trained in obtaining comprehensive job and work-site histories.

■ Successful practice requires a professional commitment and ability to advocate for prevention and actively promote legislation and regulations that prevent hazardous environmental conditions from continuing or developing at work sites. It requires an understanding of the workers' compensation law and other appropriate benefit systems and familiarity both with regulatory agencies that are concerned with health and safety at the workplace and with contract requirements, which may affect the worker's ability to return to work at his or her former level.

■ The practice of social work in the field of occupational health and safety also requires a commitment to comprehensive and coordinated treatment planning in the victim's environment, including working conditions. Social workers must be able to work with an interdisciplinary team of physicians, lawyers, and other specialists to provide complete services. In view of the rapid growth of clinics and outpatient hospital services under the umbrella of "occupational medicine," social workers face the challenge of using the total range of services when treating their worker-clients.

POLICY STATEMENT

Occupational social work is a legitimate field of practice with a developing focus and a body of knowledge that calls for a full range of appropriate skills. The National Association of

Social Workers (NASW) will lead in helping the profession to develop the standards needed for occupational social work practice.

Schools of social work can assume an active role in developing educational opportunities for students who are interested in the field of occupational social work, including the creation of appropriate sites for fieldwork and the development of specialized curricula that incorporate policies, programs, and approaches that are particularly suitable for effective practice in this field. In addition, schools of social work need to enrich the education about alcoholism, substance abuse, wellness, and stress-reduction programs. The nature, function, and value of work and the needs of special populations should be the core content that is generic to graduate social work education.

NASW can assume leadership to provide strategic public relations and to promote social work as industry's profession of choice for job roles related to social work skills. NASW encourages its chapters and divisions to provide continuing education related to occupational social work and to develop networks to help social workers contract with industry. NASW and schools of social work should actively collaborate with, plan, and reach out to industry to maximize opportunities for occupational social work in the immediate future.

Policy statement approved by the NASW Delegate Assembly, November 1987; reconfirmed by the Delegate Assembly, August 1993. This statement supersedes the policy statement on Occupational Social Work approved by the Delegate Assembly in 1984. For further information, contact the National Association of Social Workers, 750 First Street, NE, Suite 700, Washington, DC 20002-4241. Telephone: 202-408-8600 or 800-638-8799.

Parental Kidnapping

BACKGROUND

Parental abduction of children is integrally linked with major social changes that have affected U.S. families during the past 20 years and with single parenthood and shifting roles within families that affect child care and custody (Finkelhor, Hotaling, & Sedlak, 1991; Greif & Hegar, 1993). The number of children affected by divorce in the United States has exceeded 1 million per year since 1975, and by 1990, more than 6 million children lived with a divorced parent (Bureau of the Census, 1991). In addition to children of divorce, the more than 8 million children who live with separated or never-married parents are also potential victims of parental abduction (Bureau of the Census, 1991), along with the unknown number of children whose parents separate temporarily or consider separation.

A study sponsored by the Justice Department estimated that there are as many as 350,000 cases of parental abduction annually, when abduction is defined broadly (Finkelhor et al., 1991). The issue of definition is a central one in parental kidnapping, with legal definitions varying among states and national and international jurisdictions. Some include any parent whose actions deprive the other parent of custody or access to the child, whether the couple is married, separated, or divorced. At the other end of the continuum, some states have laws that define abduction only in terms of violating a custody order.

Recent studies that have defined parental abduction broadly identify men as the abductors in 42 percent to 55 percent of the cases (Hegar & Greif, 1991a; Janvier, McCormick, & Donaldson, 1990; Sagatun & Barrett, 1990). Older studies that considered only abductions by noncustodial parents reported a much higher proportion of male perpetrators (Agopian,

1984). Boys and girls were abducted in almost equal numbers in all of the studies reviewed, and the studies indicated that toddlers and preschoolers may be at greatest risk. The impact of parental abduction can be devastating for the left-behind parents, and the children encounter a range of experiences, from dislocation and confusion to child abuse and the trauma of repeated snatchings (Greif & Hegar, 1993; Sagatun & Barrett, 1990).

Although public awareness of parental kidnapping has grown recently because of coverage in the print and broadcast media, it is a long-standing problem that has been at least implicitly recognized in federal and state policies for decades. For almost 50 years, parents who kidnapped their children were specifically exempt from criminal prosecution under the federal Kidnapping Act. Because of the uneven nature of state laws and practices regarding child custody during this period, some parents who failed to receive custody in one state kidnapped their children and sought custody in another state (Sagatun & Barrett, 1990).

The problem of finding abducted children who were taken out of the country was particularly acute because, until the 1980s, there was no major treaty that addressed return of internationally abducted children. In two recent studies, abducted children were known or believed to have been taken out of the country in 20 percent and 40 percent, respectively, of the situations (Hegar & Greif, 1991b; Janvier et al., 1990), and approximately 4,000 cases of internationally abducted U.S. children have been reported to the U.S. Department of State (1991a; 1991b).

Significant policy developments at the state, federal, and international levels have been initiated in the past two decades. To date, most efforts to combat parental kidnapping have emphasized primarily one approach: to prevent abducting parents from going to another jurisdiction to obtain a custody order in their favor (Hegar, 1990). To that end, all states have adopted some version of the model Uniform Child Custody Jurisdiction Act and have passed additional legislation aimed at reducing parental kidnapping.

At the federal level, in 1980 the National Center for Missing and Exploited Children was founded and the Parental Kidnapping Prevention Act (1980) was enacted. However, enforcement of the act depends in part on state criminal law, because its "UFAP" (unlawful flight to avoid prosecution) provisions apply only if a state felony has been committed. The act encourages cooperation among the states and provides for Federal Bureau of Investigation (FBI) assistance in locating and returning kidnapped children (Coombs, 1990).

One Supreme Court case has interpreted parts of the Parental Kidnapping Prevention Act. In *Thompson v. Thompson* (1988), the Supreme Court established that parents generally are unable to resort to the federal courts to resolve conflicting awards of custody in state courts as a result of noncompliance with the Parental Kidnapping Prevention Act.

Civil suits (torts) arising out of loss of physical custody also are possible in many states. Some states have made or proposed statutory provisions for civil suits in parental kidnapping cases (Oberdorfer, 1991).

In 1980, participants from 29 countries, including the United States, drafted the Hague Convention on the Civil Aspects of International Child Abduction. The Hague Convention provides for children under age 16 years to be returned to their preabduction country of residence, regardless of whether a custody order is in effect. It also includes provisions concerning visitation rights across international borders.

Enforcement of the convention has been hampered by the low number of subscribing countries: 24 by mid-1992. The United States signed the convention in 1981 and ratified it in 1986, but its provisions were not implemented until July 1988 when the International Child Abduction Remedies Act took effect. That act provides specific mechanisms for the United States to comply with the convention and makes the U.S. State Department the agency in charge of enforcement (Pfund, 1990). Since 1974, approximately 4,000 internationally abducted U.S. children have been reported to the State Department (U.S. State Department, 1991a, 1991b).

Despite these policy developments on state, national, and international levels, there is evidence that U.S. state laws remain uneven in their provisions and judicial interpretations (Greif & Hegar, 1993; Sagatun & Barrett, 1990). With increasing numbers of children joining the groups at highest risk—those with separating, separated, or divorced parents—it is critical that the social work profession work with the other disciplines involved with the problem to curb and resolve parental abductions of children.

ISSUE STATEMENT

Abduction of children by their parents is a complex social and legal problem that is receiving increased public and professional attention. Many of the issues have only begun to be recognized and must be addressed in multiple arenas. Among the problems interwoven with parental abduction are the acrimony of many child custody disputes (Bautz & Hill, 1991; Bentch, 1986), dissatisfaction with custody and visitation within many separated and divorced families, high rates of domestic violence and the special difficulties of parents who take their children and flee abuse (Berliner, 1990), and the need for specialized services of all types to prevent and resolve abductions and to help the families who experience them (Greif & Hegar, 1991; Long, Forehand, & Zogg, 1991).

It is incumbent on social workers to become more knowledgeable about the problem of parental kidnapping and to participate actively in shaping policies at all levels that will prevent or reduce its occurrence. Furthermore, social workers should incorporate knowledge about parental kidnapping and its consequences for family members into their practice so they can render more effective services to those family members who have experienced such an event or who may be susceptible to its occurrence. Social workers may encounter families who are at risk or have experienced abduction in their roles in counseling couples and families; in school social work; in child protection and foster care agencies; in battered women's programs and shelters; and in forensic settings, such as police departments, prosecutors' and public defenders' offices, and prisons.

POLICY STATEMENT

In regard to the problem of parental kidnapping, it is the policy of the National Association of Social Workers (NASW) that professional social workers should do the following:

■ promote the development of social services to prevent the abduction of children by their parents and develop postkidnapping counseling and mediation services to ameliorate the effects of the kidnapping and diminish the likelihood of its recurrence.

■ advocate consensual modes, such as divorce mediation and negotiation, to work out divorce and postdivorce conflicts regarding child custody and support statutes in each state that include custody arrangements, such as joint custody, that reinforce the continued involvement of both parents in the important decisions about their children's welfare and upbringing.

■ support public education programs about the problems associated with parental kidnapping and use the print and broadcast media to educate the public and to locate abducted children.

■ alert child care providers to the potential for parental kidnapping and analyze and strengthen policies of agencies in which children usually are present, particularly schools and child care facilities, to reduce the likelihood that those agencies will become sites of parental kidnapping.

■ review, analyze, and work toward strengthening state and federal laws concerning parental kidnapping, particularly toward achieving uniform definitions of abduction.

■ recognize the potential danger to an abducted child, be mindful of the need to work toward a coordinated national network for the reunion of abducted children and their families, and encourage the full and active assistance of law enforcement agencies, particularly the FBI, in locating abducted children.

■ examine, with other concerned professionals and citizens' groups, services that are available to victims and perpetrators of parental kidnapping and encourage interdisciplinary cooperation to ensure the availability of comprehensive services.

■ work through international professional organizations to encourage adoption by more countries of the Hague Convention on the Civil Aspects of International Child Abduction.

■ advocate for state criminal statutes that allow distinction among abductions on the basis of circumstances, such as the use of force, harm done to the child, length of absence, or whether the child was concealed from the searching parent. Statutes should include a defense against the charge of parental abduction if the abductor acted to prevent or avoid harm.

REFERENCES

Agopian, M. W. (1984). The impact on children of abduction by parents. *Child Welfare, 63,* 511–519.

Bautz, B. J., & Hill, R. M. (1991). Mediating the breakup: Do children win? *Mediation Quarterly, 8,* 199–210.

Bentch, S. T. (1986). Court-sponsored custody mediation to prevent parental kidnapping: A disarmament proposal. *St. Mary's Law Journal, 18,* 361–393.

Berliner, L. (1990). Protecting or harming: Parents who flee with their children. *Journal of Interpersonal Violence, 5,* 119–120.

Bureau of the Census. (1991). *Marital status and living arrangements: March 1990* (Series P-20, No. 450). Washington, DC: U.S. Government Printing Office.

Coombs, R. M. (1990). Progress under the PKPA. *Journal of the American Academy of Matrimonial Lawyers, 6,* 59–102.

Finkelhor, D., Hotaling, G., & Sedlak, A. (1991). Children abducted by family members: A national household survey of incidence and episode characteristics. *Journal of Marriage & the Family, 53,* 805–817.

Greif, G. L., & Hegar, R. L. (1991). Parents whose children are abducted by the other parent: Implications for treatment. *American Journal of Family Therapy, 19,* 215–225.

Greif, G. L., & Hegar, R. L. (1993). *When parents kidnap: The families behind the headlines*. New York: Free Press.

Hegar, R. L. (1990). Parental kidnapping and U.S. social policy. *Social Service Review, 64*, 407–421.

Hegar, R. L., & Greif, G. L. (1991a). Abduction of children by parents: A survey of the problem. *Social Work, 36*, 421–426.

Hegar, R. L., & Greif, G. L. (1991b). Parental kidnapping across international borders. *International Social Work, 34*, 353–363.

Janvier, R. F., McCormick, K., & Donaldson, R. (1990). Parental kidnapping: A survey of left-behind parents. *Juvenile & Family Court Journal, 41*, 1–8.

Long, N., Forehand, R., & Zogg, C. (1991). Preventing parental child abduction: Analysis of a national project. *Clinical Pediatrics, 30*, 549–554.

Oberdorfer, D. (1991). *Larson v. Dunn:* Toward a reasoned response to parental kidnapping. *Minnesota Law Review, 75*, 1701–1730.

Parental Kidnapping Prevention Act, P.L. 96-611, §§ 6–10, 94 Stat. 3568, 3569 (1980).

Pfund, P. H. (1990). The Hague convention on international child abduction, the International Child Abduction Remedies Act, and the need for availability of counsel for all petitioners. *Family Law Quarterly, 24*, 35–51.

Sagatun, I. J., & Barrett, L. (1990). Parental child abduction: The law, family dynamics, and legal system responses. *Journal of Criminal Justice, 18*, 433–442.

Thompson v. Thompson, 108 U.S. 513 (1988).

U.S. Department of State, Bureau of Consular Affairs. (1991a). *International parental child abduction case statistics*. Washington, DC: Author.

U.S. Department of State, Bureau of Consular Affairs. (1991b). *Statistical report of the United States central authority for the Hague convention on the civil aspects of international child abduction*. Washington, DC: Author.

Policy statement approved by the NASW Delegate Assembly, August 1993. This statement supersedes the policy statement on Parental Kidnapping approved by the Delegate Assembly in 1984. For further information, contact the National Association of Social Workers, 750 First Street, NE, Suite 700, Washington, DC 20002-4241. Telephone: 202-408-8600 or 800-638-8799.

Peace and Social Justice

BACKGROUND

Peace is not only the absence of war but also the absence of all violence in a society, both internal and external, direct and indirect. Peace and social justice are interdependent. A superficial peace based on the denial and suppression of basic human needs and rights is built on a foundation of quicksand (Van Soest, 1992).

Lasting peace in the world can be achieved only through the fulfillment of basic human needs. In the nuclear age, the paramount requisite for "promoting the general welfare"—a goal to which the profession is committed by the *NASW Code of Ethics* (National Association of Social Workers [NASW], 1993)—is the prevention of nuclear war and the opposition to violence in all its forms. The realization of this goal will require a diversion of basic resources from the destruction of life and toward the improvement of those physical and social conditions that are basic to the support of human life.

The reliance by many nations on military force as a prime instrument of foreign policy has jeopardized the entire world. In the United States, the preoccupation with national defense so permeates the structure of society that livelihoods, civil liberties, and values have become inextricably entwined with military preparedness. The institutionalization of armed power and the development of the military–industrial complex appear inaccessible to control by citizens or the U.S. Congress.

The United States and Russia have begun to realize that reliance on military force in the nuclear age is a no-win policy, that the human and economic costs are prohibitive, and that new concepts of national security, namely "common security" and an "interdependent world,"

are emerging. The United States and Russia are to be commended for making significant progress toward reducing their nuclear and conventional military arsenals; however, this is just a beginning. Ways must be found to eliminate nuclear and other weapons, to more fully meet human needs through reductions in military spending, and to provide jobs for military and civilian personnel who depended on the military economy.

In addition to the danger of nuclear war, there is danger surrounding the actual armed conflicts that have been waged with conventional weapons in many parts of the world. The tragic loss of life, the enormous drain on the world's dwindling natural resources, and the brutalizing impact of war on all who are involved in it are antithetical to global social welfare and security, as well as to the central purpose of the social work profession.

Beyond the destruction and trauma of war is the continual drain on human and material resources—the diversion of energies and goods and services to meet military needs—while the social welfare of millions of people in the United States and abroad goes unmet. The reliance on military might had led the United States to the brink of nuclear war and to the actuality of conventional war; has sapped the nation's resources; and has resulted in the pollution of the earth and the atmosphere, which, along with other global environmental dangers, poses a threat to the world's public health and safety and to its very future. In addition to the physical, social, and economic consequences, the arms race and the threat of nuclear war pose unique psychological consequences for men, women, and children.

ISSUE STATEMENT

Since the adoption of the Peace and Social Welfare policy statement by the NASW Delegate Assembly in August 1990, a nearly universal consensus has emerged within American society that the Cold War, the stated rationale for most of their U.S. military buildup and activities for more than 40 years, has ended.

Military Spending

The United States spends about 40 percent of its military budget for the defense of Western Europe ("Two Trillion Dollars," 1987), maintains 395 military bases around the world ("U.S. Military Agenda," 1991), and retains more than 11,000 strategic nuclear warheads (Forsberg, 1992). Specifically, in 1990, according to Forsberg, the number of U.S. nuclear warheads totaled 11,658. The U.S. Defense Department has recommended that this number be reduced to 4,700 by 1997. Most of the military expenditure is for nuclear weapons and power projection around the world (Morland, 1986). Morland has estimated that the U.S. 1985 military budget comprised the following:

- 3 percent: defense of U.S. borders

- 10 percent: deterrence of unprovoked nuclear attacks

- 45 percent: Third World intervention

- 37 percent: containment of the Soviet Union

- 5 percent: miscellaneous overhead

From 1975 to 1990, real U.S. military spending increased by 50 percent (Riddell, 1990). At the same time, the poverty rate rose from 11.7 percent in 1979 to 13 percent in 1988 (Edwards, 1990). As a nation, we have not recovered from $57 billion cut from domestic programs from 1982 through 1985 (Committee for a Sane Nuclear Policy, 1986). State and local governments also lost substantial funding due to retrenchment by the federal government. Hunger, homelessness, and other social ills have increased.

Support for the military establishment constitutes a considerable burden on the taxpayer. More than half of U.S. income taxes are directly and indirectly used for military related purposes (DeGrasso, 1983; War Resisters League, 1989; Women's International League for Peace and Freedom, 1985). The War Resisters League analysis revealed that 36 percent of the budget goes for current military expenses and 24 percent for past military expenses. The following military related items do not appear in the official government military budget: half of National Aeronautics and Space Administration costs, CIA, Selective Service, Federal Emergency Management Agency, nuclear weapons (Department of Energy), veterans' benefits, and interest on the national debt due to military spending.

Economic Conversion

Various arguments have been presented against economic conversion. One is that too many jobs will be lost. Ironically, this argument is hardly plausible, given the great need to employ people in the work of ameliorating the deplorable conditions of the U.S. infrastructure, environment, and human resources—conditions that have been caused, at least in part, by military spending, manufacturing, and weapons testing.

Some people propose that the armed services be given roles that have a partial social function to enhance the military's image and to strengthen its viability. For example, troops would interdict drug supplies in other nations and intervene to prevent hunger. Other proposals stress the need to retain the military capability to enforce a new world order because the world is a dangerous place. In addition, demonization of world leaders as a tactical prelude to military intervention has been gaining increasing acceptance. However, the United States has undercut attempts to achieve collaboratively such a goal through the United Nations by stopping payments to the UN, by providing most of the military labor for some UN peacekeeping efforts, and by refusing to function in those endeavors under UN command.

These actions suggest that the United States wants to maintain a large military establishment that can promote American economic influence around the world more than it wants to establish peace through the UN. Cases in point are the CIA and military involvements that ensure the existence of foreign governments that promote economic policies favoring the United States.

The military–welfare complex often provides greater profit levels than those achievable in the more free market segments of the U.S. economy. Even now, some modest military cutbacks are being replaced by increased arms sales to other nations—even to developed nations. The recent Gulf War showcased weapons that could be marketed internationally.

More than 9 million Americans receive their paychecks from the Pentagon, and millions more are indirectly dependent on military spending (The U.S. military after the Cold War, 1989). Progress in reducing defense outlays will be difficult if there is no plan to minimize the potential job dislocation that could result. Progress is possible, however. An equally prodigious challenge was met when the United States made the transition to a peacetime economy after World War II (Borosage, 1992). According to Borosage, within three years after World War II, 24.8 million people left defense-related employment and 11 million veterans reentered the labor market thanks to the G. I. bill. Furthermore, research has demonstrated that funds create more jobs when used for civilian rather than military purposes (Anderson, 1992). A $1 billion reduction in military spending costs 24,000 jobs, but there is a gain of 31,000 jobs—a net gain of 7,000 jobs.

De-escalation of Violence

The United States is one of the most violent nations in the world, with violence rates as much as 76 times that of some other nations. We have the highest rate of incarceration in the world, having exceeded South Africa's rate in 1988.

International Cooperation

Military expenditures in the world total about $1 trillion annually (Sivard, 1988). Referring to global military expenditures, Sivard said, "In current dollars those expenditures reached $944 billion in 1987 and in 1988 appear to have set a new record high close to $1,000 billion for the year" (p. 12). Many of the world's major economic powers not only have large military budgets but also are primary sources of arms shipments to Third World nations, many of which are governed by dictatorships. For example, the United States provides weapons to 142 nations, 59 of which are authoritarian governments, such as Saudi Arabia, Indonesia, Guatemala, and Haiti (Arming dictators, 1992). Of 120 wars in the world from World War II to 1986, only one was in a developed nation (Sivard, 1986). These less-developed nations often spend sizable portions of their finances on armaments, draining funds from social needs, and engage in military actions that result in hunger and refugees. In our own country, the location of waste sites for the weapons industry causes a disproportionate health hazard to the poor, disenfranchised, and people of color.

POLICY STATEMENT

We must reduce the use of violence as a solution to domestic as well as foreign problems. This should include reducing the use of capital punishment and incarceration, which is often used for racist rather than crime prevention purposes. In addition we must demilitarize police forces and address social problems through nonviolent means, such as providing drug treatment instead of waging drug wars.

The social work profession can contribute to a redefinition of national security that includes healthy children, the prevention of poverty, an adequate education for all residents, and a productive economy. The growing reality of social disenfranchisement and frustration by those Americans who are hopeless, homeless, powerless, penniless, and ignored demonstrates an internal lack of national security that demands bold action.

As a leader in the arms race, the United States should be a forerunner in disarmament by making measured unilateral reductions in its military forces and by ending the testing of nuclear weapons before the militarization of space makes the arms race irreversible. The United States should exercise leadership toward nuclear disarmament. This leadership will require a reduction in existing nuclear weapons and opposition to the development of new weapons systems.

Military Spending

The United States should adopt a plan to reduce its military budget substantially over the next 10 years and to divert most of the savings to respond to the mounting social needs in our nation and to efforts to help military and defense industries personnel make the transition to a civilian economy.

In addition the United States should support all peaceful efforts for the nonproliferation of nuclear weapons; the abolition of nuclear weapons tests by all nations, and the eventual elimination of nuclear weapons; and the reduction of troop levels and all weapons of warfare among all nations.

Furthermore, the United States should support the abolition of all chemical warfare agents or nerve gas and a bilateral agreement between the United States and all countries to cease production of these compounds and to destroy any existing stockpiles. Also, the United States should support a UN-sponsored multinational treaty calling for the abolition of chemical warfare agents worldwide, with strong sanctions imposed against any nation that uses these weapons.

The United States should consistently emphasize cooperation in its foreign policy rather than unilateral military action. The welfare of all people and the balanced economic and social development of nations should be the goals of U.S. foreign policy.

Economic Conversion

Policies promoting economic conversion should be implemented through legislation and funding. The United States also should encourage participation at all levels of government and nongovernment organizations in studying and planning for the redevelopment of materials and personnel for the conversion of the economy from war production to peaceful pursuits. Readjustment to civilian life should be facilitated for those people who are completing

military service, especially those who are suddenly terminated because of the end of the Cold War.

International Cooperation

The United States should join other nations to reduce the production of armaments and to find more constructive and nonviolent means to deal with international conflicts. Such means include participation in the UN and other world organizations that exist primarily to foster an atmosphere of cooperation and the nonviolent resolution of conflicts.

The United States should endeavor to decrease the number of refugees by supporting democratically elected governments and by providing economic and social assistance rather than military shipments to other nations. Refugees should be granted asylum if they are faced with violence and death. Recognizing the equal worth of humans everywhere, asylum should not be based on race or other factors that are inconsistent with the UN Declaration of Human Rights. Resettlement should be done by private and governmental social agencies.

In addition the U.S. government should support the efforts of the UN, including such agencies as the UN Educational Scientific and Cultural Organization, the World Health Organization, the World Court, and other international organizations in the quest for world order, international cooperation, and disarmament.

The United States also should support implementation of the Universal Declaration of Human Rights. This declaration states that each person has the right to a standard of living that is adequate for his or her health and well-being and that the components of that standard of living, although they vary among cultures, should provide those goods and services that are essential to the social security of each individual.

Furthermore, the United States should support each country's right to political and economic self-determination, to nonintervention, and to control over its own natural resources. In considering the tragic and growing phenomena of world poverty and hunger, internationally coordinated efforts must include redistribution of global resources (such as technology transfer, reduction of Third World debt burden, reduction of over-consumption patterns of the West), improvement of women's status, and population stabilization.

The United States also should stimulate and support the use of government funds, free of military or political purposes, to promote social and economic development and protection of the environment; to meet basic human needs in education, housing, health, and welfare services; and to develop cooperative efforts with other governments through the UN to make these funds available to the people of the world.

World nations should continue the U.S. bilateral and multilateral programs for foreign aid until the needs of developing nations can be met adequately through the UN and other international programs. Such programs should be conducted in harmony with the spirit and planning of multilateral programs. Primary emphasis should be on human values and the contribution of these programs to human welfare.

Social Work Role

Qualified professional social workers should be employed in the U.S. Foreign Service and in social welfare positions in multilateral and bilateral programs of technical assistance, such as community development, social work education, and the development of social welfare services. Appropriate additional training should be provided to qualified social workers to prepare them fully for international service, including nongovernment organizations and international professional associations, such as the International Federation of Social Workers, the International Association of Schools of Social Work, the International Council on Social Welfare, and IUCUSD. In addition, stronger links must be made to the international social work community through cooperative efforts in the schools of social work, social services agencies, and hospital social work departments, to name a few. NASW's International Committee should be strengthened and made more widely known.

The United States also should continue using qualified professional social workers to serve the armed forces and military dependents, re-

gardless of their location or proximity to service. The presence of qualified social workers in the military is important to ensure that commanders give a high priority to human values and that the military establishment responds adequately to the welfare needs of military personnel and their families.

Our domestic peace and justice agenda must also include gun control legislation and the stoppage of the illegal weapons trade that brings firearms into the hands of our citizens, many of them disenfranchised young people. To prevent violence that turns communities into war zones, we must promote early and ongoing intervention through economic revitalization and educational and employment opportunities to give young people hope and direction. In addition, we must address the role of the media and other institutions in the glorification of violence and use of weapons.

Finally, in accordance with current Council on Social Work Education (CSWE) standards, the social work profession must integrate peace and justice issues into the undergraduate- and graduate-level curriculum on both the micro and macro levels. Students must be educated about the social and political aspects of social work practice from the outset and must be offered field experiences that enable them to take an active role in working for social change. Teaching the connections between direct client services and the larger sociopolitical context and providing avenues for students to learn and practice social action skills will bring social work back to its roots. As social workers, building on our activist tradition is one of the most powerful ways to carry the message of peace and justice and to help make it a reality.

REFERENCES

Anderson, M. (1992). Rebuilding America. *Boston Review, 17*, 3–4.

Arming dictators. (1992). *Defense Monitor, 21*, 5.

Borosage, R. (1992, May 20). Job blackmail: A substitute for defense cuts. *Baltimore Sun*, p. A17.

Committee for a Sane Nuclear Policy. (1986). *Fiscal year 1986 edition guide to the military budget.*

DeGrasso, R. W., Jr. (1983). *Military expansion and economic decline.* Armonk, NY: M. E. Tharpe.

Edwards, R. L. (1990, February). Poverty trend: A threat for 21st century. *NASW News,* p. 2.

Forsberg, R. (1992). Defense cuts and cooperative security in the post war world. *Boston Review, 17,* 3–4.

Morland, H. (1986). *A few billion for defense.* Washington, DC: Coalition for a New Foreign and Military Policy.

National Association of Social Workers. (1993). *NASW code of ethics.* Washington, DC: Author.

Riddell, T. (1990). Farewell to arms. *Dollars & Sense, 154.*

Sivard, R. (1986). *World military and social expenditures* (11th ed.). Washington, DC: World Priorities.

Sivard, R. (1988). *World military and social expenditures* (12th ed.). Washington, DC: World Priorities.

Two trillion dollars in seven years. (1987). *Defense Monitor, 16*(17), 3.

The U.S. military after the cold war. (1989). *Defense Monitor, 18*(8), 4.

U.S. military agenda for 1992 and beyond. (1991). *Defense Monitor, 20*(6), 3.

Van Soest, D. (1992). *Incorporating peace and social justice in the social work curriculum* (Chapter 4). Washington, DC: NASW Peace and Social Justice Committee.

War Resisters League. (1989). *Where your income tax money really goes.* New York: Author.

Women's International League for Peace and Freedom. (1985). [Title unknown.] Philadelphia: Jane Addams Peace Association.

Policy statement approved by the NASW Delegate Assembly, August 1993. This statement supersedes the policy statement on Peace and Social Welfare approved by the Delegate Assembly in 1990. For further information, contact the National Association of Social Workers, 750 First Street, NE, Suite 700, Washington, DC 20002-4241. Telephone: 202-408-8600 or 800-638-8799.

People with Disabilities

BACKGROUND

Numerous studies and polls have documented that people with disabilities, as a group, occupy an inferior status in our society and are severely disadvantaged socially, vocationally, economically, and educationally (Americans with Disabilities Act of 1990). This view of people with disabilities has relegated them to a minority status within American society. People with disabilities have been present in every society and culture since the beginning of recorded history. Yet, unlike people from other diverse groups, people with disabilities have been ostracized within their own societies and therefore have been subjected to pervasive discrimination and oppression. Western history is replete with social policies that have led to the subjugation and devaluation of people with disabilities (Longmore, 1987). Only in recent years have social attitudes and policies in the United States begun to recognize the civil rights of individuals with disabilities to be active participants in society and to control their own lives.

It is estimated that one in three people will, at some time during their lives, acquire a disability. The types of disabilities people experience vary widely and include physical, sensory, emotional, mental, cognitive, intellectual, and health-related disabilities. Some disabilities are "invisible" in that they are not readily identifiable by others. Functional limitations from disabilities range from none to profound. Some disabilities are temporary, but most are lifelong and some are life ending. People with disabilities are represented in every age group and in every segment of society.

People with disabilities have had few legal protections and in fact have been subjected to laws that have denied them rights. Longmore (1987) recounted the experiences of people with severe physical disabilities who attempted to live independently:

> Severely disabled adults. . . must spend their lives confined to families' homes or imprisoned in institutions. . . . The very agencies supposedly designed to enable severely physically handicapped adults. . . to achieve independence and productivity in the community become yet another massive hurdle they must repeatedly battle but can never finally defeat. (p. 153)

However, efforts during the past 20 years to change attitudes and beliefs have promoted the view that disability is an interaction between individuals and their environment. This view has fundamentally reshaped public policy toward disability issues and people with disabilities. Before these changes, federal "disability management" efforts focused on the individual (Vacher, 1989–1990). Examples include the Vocational Rehabilitation programs initiated in l920 and the Social Security Disability Insurance program created in 1956. Since the late 1960s, Congress has passed more than a dozen laws addressing issues related to people with disabilities. These laws range from Title VII of the Civil Rights Act of 1968, which addressed fair housing issues, to the Mental Health Bill of Rights Act of 1985, which expanded state protection and advocacy systems to cover mental illness.

Yet these laws continued to afford only limited protection to people with disabilities. For example, the Rehabilitation Act of 1973 prohibited discrimination and mandated affirmative action in employment and education for people with disabilities within the federal government and with any organizations or entities receiving federal assistance or contracts. This act also created the Architectural and Transportation Barriers Compliance Board and has been an extremely important law to people with disabilities for nearly two decades. In 1975, the Education for All Handicapped Children Act provided federal funds to states that provided appropriate and free public education to children with disabilities. In the same year, the Developmental Disabilities Assistance and Bill of Rights Act further enhanced treatment and care for people with developmental disabilities. In 1986, amendments to the Education for All Handicapped Children Act extended educational services from birth to all children with disabilities. Although these laws worked to address the inequities affecting people with disabilities, a common limitation was that they offered protection only in activities and programs involving the government.

In recent decades, people with disabilities have become an active political force in the United States (De Jong, 1979). Simultaneously, direct consumer involvement saw the disability rights movement grow with the development of the Independent Living (IL) movement in the early 1970s. IL applied a minority model to the political process of gaining civil rights for people with disabilities (Berkowitz, 1987). Whereas traditional culture and traditional models of professional treatment focused on individual pathology of people with disabilities, IL focused on discrimination of an oppressed minority and societal responses as the root of their problems. The IL movement specifically and the ever-growing disability rights movement were founded on the belief that people with disabilities have the right to participate fully both in society and in the development and implementation of social policies affecting people with disabilities.

The advocacy efforts of people with disabilities (who were joined by people without disabilities) created a sociopolitical force that resulted in the passage of the Americans with Disabilities Act of 1990 (ADA) (P.L. 101-336). With enactment of the ADA, people with disabilities for the first time were afforded rights in all segments of society. The content of the legislation is clearly addressed in the purpose of the act:

1. to provide a clear and comprehensive national mandate for the elimination of discrimination against individuals with disabilities

2. to provide clear, strong, consistent, enforceable standards addressing discrimination against individuals with disabilities

3. to ensure that the Federal Government plays a central role in enforcing the standards established in this Act on behalf of individuals with disabilities

4. to invoke the sweep of congressional authority, including the power to enforce the fourteenth amendment and to regulate commerce, in order to address the major areas of discrimination faced day-to-day by people with disabilities. (ADA, § 2, 204)

The power of the disability rights movement continues today. The Rehabilitation Act Amendments of 1992 established the purpose of Title VII as mandating the "creation of statewide networks of Centers for Independent Living," with the goal of ensuring greater involvement and authority of people with disabilities in service delivery and program management.

ISSUE STATEMENT

At least 43 million people with disabilities live in the United States today (Americans with Disabilities Act of 1990). With medical advances and an aging population, that number grows daily. Historically, society has tended to isolate and segregate individuals with disabilities, and, despite some improvements, discrimination against individuals with disabilities continues to be a serious and pervasive societal problem. Societal attitudes toward people with disabilities forced institutionalization on people with disabilities, denied them the right to enter intimate relationships and have children, subjected them to ridicule, and prohibited them from fully participating in American society.

Social workers have worked with the disability rights movement throughout the struggle, in a variety of roles, including self-advocacy. Historically, however, professionals and helpers have abrogated decision making by people with disabilities and denied them self-determination (Salsgiver & Mackelprang, 1993). The traditional models that are used to identify and work with people with disabilities tend to show such people as malfunctioning in some way. For example, the oldest definition of disability relies on the medical model, according to which disability is a chronic disease requiring various forms of treatment (Roth, 1987). Although this definition no longer is used exclusively, it still has an overwhelming effect on disability issues and on people with disabilities by inappropriately viewing them as passive, dependent, and deficient. Progressive or current models that are used to identify and work with people with disabilities view the person as participating in and contributing to society ("Communication," 1991). The minority-civil rights model identifies people with disabilities as members of a minority group, with clear civil rights and seeking legitimate political action. The cultural pluralism model identifies people with disabilities as a community of multifaceted individuals whose disability is just one trait among many ("Communication," 1991).

By identifying people with disabilities as people first, the presence of a disability is a characteristic, not the individual's sole identity. Although people with disabilities may be handicapped by environmental barriers or individual or societal attitudes, they are not handicapped people. Social work and people with disabilities must affirm the self-determination of "people first" language and practice.

POLICY STATEMENT

The National Association of Social Workers (NASW) supports the rights of people with disabilities to participate fully and equitably in society. These rights include the freedom, to the fullest extent possible, of all people with disabilities to live independently, to enjoy the rights of full societal membership, to exercise self-determination, and to have full participation in issues related to education, housing, transportation, work, health care, social services, and other public accommodations.

The *NASW Code of Ethics* (NASW, 1993) clearly defines the general principles and ethical responsibilities in work with clients and colleagues, as well as in social workers' roles as professionals and as members of society. NASW rec-

ognizes the right to self-determination and maintains that all people, with or without disabilities, have the right to control their own destiny. NASW works to ensure full participation of people with disabilities and advocates for the inclusion and full participation of people with disabilities in decision making in all arenas of social work practice, policy, and planning. NASW will work to ensure that society continues to work toward equality of opportunity, full participation, independent living, and self-sufficiency for people with disabilities. To ensure full participation of people with disabilities, NASW supports the following principles:

1. *Independent living.* People with disabilities have the right to fully participate in the decision making regarding their own living conditions and to live in environments that maximize independence and self-determination. To live independently, people with disabilities may need environmental modifications, specialized services, attendant care, or other accommodations. People who require these services should, inasmuch as possible, control how and from whom these services are provided.

2. *Public accessibility.* NASW supports the right of people with disabilities to have public access to goods and services available to others. Access is essential to full participation, and social workers should advocate for reasonable accommodations to provide ready access to people with disabilities. Physical access must be made available in all areas, including external and internal building access (for example, ramps, doors, rest rooms, drinking fountains, and elevators). In addition, access to participation includes ready access to telecommunications, alternate means of communication (such as Braille or sign-language interpreters), and modifications in service delivery. NASW is especially committed to ensuring access for people with disabilities who visit agencies and entities in which social workers work and in which social services are provided. NASW strongly supports vigorous enforcement of laws to ensure public and private accessibility in its broadest definition.

3. *Education.* NASW supports the right of every individual with a disability to obtain an education and advocates for public and private

educational entities to ensure reasonable accommodations for people with disabilities in their educational endeavors. Accommodations may be physical, environmental, or programmatic. Education must be provided in a manner that is relevant to people with disabilities and that allows them to take full advantage of educational opportunities.

NASW supports the need for social work educational programs to educate social workers to work competently with people with disabilities and to promote the opportunity to educate people with disabilities to work in all areas of social work. NASW also recognizes the need for the profession to be actively involved in producing knowledge for practice in the area of disabilities; developing disability issues curricula, including disabilities issues in programs and conferences sponsored by NASW organizations; and ensuring accessibility to people with disabilities at all NASW-sponsored or affiliated activities.

4. *Employment.* NASW supports the right of people with disabilities to pursue vocational and occupational opportunities in accessible environments and to have reasonable accommodations so that they can work toward their fullest potential. Successful employment depends on several factors, including adequate training, environmental and programmatic access, and nondiscrimination. NASW supports rigorous enforcement of laws to ensure employment access. NASW is especially dedicated to ensuring that agencies and entities that employ social workers and provide social work services are accessible and proactive in efforts to employ people with disabilities and to assist people with disabilities in obtaining employment.

When it is not possible for people with disabilities to be employed in a particular work setting, alternative work environments should be created that provide maximum opportunities for productive activities. Individualized employment plans, directed to the extent possible by the individual and focusing on matching individual strengths and abilities with employment situations, should be developed. NASW supports policy and programming that ensure that people with disabilities are afforded opportunities to engage in whatever productive activities allow for maximum contribution.

5. *Housing and transportation.* Accessible housing is critical to the independence of people with disabilities. To the maximum extent of each person's capabilities, people with disabilities should have access to reasonably priced and accessible housing. When living assistance is needed because of physical, intellectual, or other disabilities, NASW recognizes that, to the extent possible, the person with a disability should determine how and from whom care and assistance are provided. Further, NASW supports the right of all individuals to live in environments with the minimum possible restrictions; only in the most extreme situations should people with disabilities live in institutions.

A critical component of living independently is the availability of transportation. Public transportation must be easily and readily accessible to people with disabilities. NASW advocates for the availability and accessibility of other transportation options when required to ensure maximum independence.

6. *Income and health care.* Social work supports the rights of people with disabilities to affordable and accessible health care and to adequate income maintenance. Health care benefits must be comprehensive, ensuring that health and well-being are not compromised because services are unavailable, not affordable, or not accessible. Whether through employment or public funds, NASW believes a basic level of income must be maintained that allows all people with disabilities to have the necessities of life.

NASW advocates for the abolition of current policies that discourage or prohibit some people with disabilities from working because they will lose medical benefits and income (for example, Medicaid, Medicare, and SSI). These policies force people with disabilities into dependence and deny them their right to self-determination.

7. *Strengths.* NASW recognizes people with disabilities from a strengths perspective. NASW acknowledges the importance of joining forces with and seeking guidance from people with disabilities as we advocate for the rights of people with disabilities. NASW also recognizes that its own strength is enhanced by including people with disabilities in all areas of the professional organization, including policy-making boards,

staff and administrative positions, and the board of directors.

REFERENCES

Americans with Disabilities Act of 1990, P.L. 101-336, 104 Stat. 327.

Berkowitz, E. D. (1987). *Disabled policy: America's programs for the handicapped.* London: Cambridge University Press.

Communication about disability. *Rehab Brief,* 13(12), 2.

De Jong, G. (1979). *The movement for independent living: Origins, ideology and implications for disability research.* East Lansing: University Center for International Rehabilitation, Michigan State University.

Longmore, P. K. (1987). Elizabeth Bouvia, assisted suicide and social prejudice. *Issues in Law and Medicine, 3,* 141–168.

National Association of Social Workers. (1993). *NASW code of ethics.* Washington, DC: Author.

Roth, W. (1987). Disabilities: Physical. In A. Minahan (Ed.-in-Chief), *Encyclopedia of social work* (18th ed., Vol. 1, pp. 434–438). Silver Spring, MD: National Association of Social Workers.

Salsgiver, R., & Mackelprang, R. (1993, February). *Persons with disabilities and social work practice: Historical and contemporary issues.* Paper presented at the annual program meeting of the Council on Social Work Education, New York.

Vacher, R. A. (1989–1990, Winter). Employing the disabled. *Issues in Science and Technology.*

Policy statement approved by the NASW national Board of Directors, October 1993, following recommendations by the NASW Delegate Assembly, August 1993. This statement supersedes the policy statement on Handicapped Persons: Rehabilitation approved in 1967 and the policy statement on Handicapped Persons: Rights and Needs approved in 1977. For further information, contact the National Association of Social Workers, 750 First Street, NE, Suite 700, Washington, DC 20002-4241. Telephone: 202-408-8600 or 800-638-8799.

Physical Punishment of Children

BACKGROUND

Physical punishment and *corporal punishment* of children are interchangeable terms; both mean the intentional infliction of physical pain or discomfort on the body of a child as a penalty for behavior disapproved of by the punisher or as a method of modifying negative behavior. When punishment occurs in a school or custodial setting, it is generally referred to as corporal punishment. When punishment occurs in the home with the parent or caregiver as punisher, it is often described as physical punishment. This policy statement pertains to punishment in the home, as well as in schools or custodial settings. Because of the commonality of the issues in any setting, the single term *physical punishment* is used exclusively in this policy statement.

Physical punishment most commonly consists of hitting a child with the hand, but it also includes such things as washing the mouth out with soap or shaking. Physical punishment becomes abuse when the child is physically injured or placed at risk of being physically injured as a result of the adult's action. Forms of abuse that adults sometimes practice when physically punishing children include spanking with a belt, kicking, biting, arm twisting, or throwing children against a wall or floor. A study by Gelles (1978) indicated that more than 2 percent of children aged three to 17 in the United States had experienced abuse while being physically punished.

Physical punishment does not include physical restraint to prevent a child from harming himself or herself or others or to protect property, nor does it include self-defense by an adult.

The use of physical punishment in homes and schools is commonly practiced. A study by Kersey (1983) revealed that 81 percent of U.S. parents used physical punishment on their children during 1982; more than 60 percent spanked at least once a week.

Historically, schools have been viewed as having the same rights to exercise authority over the conduct and behavior of children as do parents or guardians. The exercise of authority generally is defined by states to include physical punishment, and the use of physical punishment is regulated by state law. (A growing number of states are enacting legislation prohibiting physical punishment in schools.) Thus, violence, as a method of controlling children's behavior, is commonly used by adults who have authority over children in this society.

It is significant that legal safeguards that prevent adults from being physically assaulted for infractions of rules are being systematically denied to children. Public employees (the U.S. Navy abolished corporal punishment in 1850) and convicted felons are protected from beatings by the Eighth Amendment, which deals with fair and humane punishment and due process. The U.S. Supreme Court specifically refused to extend Eighth Amendment rights to children in relation to physical punishment in schools (*Ingraham v. Wright*, 1977) because of the openness of the schools and their supervision by the community. The court further concluded that due process, as related to physical punishment in the public schools, does not require prior notice. Throughout this country, it is legal for parents to hit children, provided that the children are not injured or placed at risk of injury. Schools have this same right in the majority of states.

Since 1984, when the Delegate Assembly of the National Association of Social Workers (NASW) approved a policy opposing physical punishment of children in schools, increasing multidisciplinary attention has been given to parents' use of physical punishment. At the 1985 Surgeon General's Workshop on Violence and Public Health, both the work group on Child Abuse Prevention and the work group on Assault and Homicide Prevention recommended a campaign to abolish all physical punishment of children. Many accepted experts in the field of child development endorse this idea. A. Ellis noted that spanking engenders strong negative emotions in a child that interfere with the child's ability to learn the intended lesson (see Waters, 1983). Haim Ginott observed that physical punishment is self-defeating because it causes fear, teaches the child an aggressive mode of responding, and is not as effective as other methods for redirecting unacceptable behavior (see Orgel, 1983). Piagetians and cognitive psychologists note that corporal punishment can arrest moral development because a child is taught to avoid wrongdoing out of a fear of punishment, rather than the recognition that the wrongful action is harmful (see Dorr, 1983).

Social workers in the field of child abuse observe that, in some instances, what starts out as physical punishment becomes abuse when the adult goes too far and injures the child or places the child at risk of injury. The extreme infliction of serious injury to children is death. It is estimated that 1,000 to 5,000 children die every year because of physical abuse (Walker, 1988). In 1989, a group of researchers and representatives of national agencies and organizations, convened by the American Academy of Pediatrics Provisional Committee on Child Abuse and Neglect, the Johnson Foundation, and the University of Wisconsin–Milwaukee, issued a position statement opposing parental use of physical punishment (Johnson Foundation, 1989). Subsequently, the National Committee for Prevention of Child Abuse; National Parents Anonymous, Inc.; National Foster Parents Association; National Association of School Psychologists; and the Wisconsin Alliance for Children adopted similar statements.

Other western nations are addressing the issue of physical punishment of children as well. Sweden pioneered a law prohibiting physical punishment of children in 1979. Denmark, Finland, Norway, and Austria have since passed similar legislation. England has launched a parent-focused campaign called End Physical Punishment of Children.

ISSUE STATEMENT

Physical punishment in institutions, foster care homes, and day care settings is increasingly not tolerated by licensing authorities. Having a humane, effective, and consistent philosophy of discipline in schools, custodial settings, and homes is thought to be highly desirable by adults who are responsible for the care of children in these settings and by society in general. It is not congruent to oppose physical punishment in schools and custodial settings as being inhumane and ineffective without recognizing that the same concerns exist when physical punishment is inflicted upon children by their parents. Many parents who use some types of physical punishment are adamantly opposed to and do not engage in physical punishment that is abusive. Conversely, types of punishment that do not involve physical contact, such as denigrating statements and excessive time-outs, can also be abusive.

It is becoming increasingly clear that physical punishment of children in any setting is not an effective way to encourage desirable behavior; to enhance children's ability to learn expected skills, abilities, and attitudes that are necessary for effective interaction with others; or to develop self-esteem and a sense of morality. It is also clear that in a significant number of cases, punishment goes too far and abuse results.

Ellis pointed out that discipline is most effective when the child feels he or she is acceptable but the behavior is not (see Waters, 1983). Spanking often directs a significant amount of anger against the person of the child, perhaps resulting in the immediate control of behavior, but possibly incurring pent-up anger and resentment in the child. This interaction does not allow the parent and child to talk in a rational way about what went wrong and how it can be fixed. Losing control presents a poor model to the child who is expected to be in control.

Furthermore, physical punishment by adults models aggressive behavior as an acceptable way of resolving conflicts and thus legitimates violence. Bandura (1960) demonstrated that children who received corporal punishment at home were less aggressive at home but more aggressive in the community. Behaviorists (see, for example, Madsen & Stephens, 1983) note that physical punishment fails to help children develop positive alternative behaviors; children may simply suppress all behavior to avoid trouble.

The National Education Association's 1972 *Report of the Task Force on Corporal Punishment* emphasized the negative effects of physical punishment. It noted that physical punishment may have short-term benefits, but has to be repeated over and over, often with increasing severity, to maintain results. It does not assist children in learning to make responsible decisions about their lives. Furthermore, schools (and probably parents) that rely on physical punishment may be less creative in developing alternative forms of discipline.

Social workers and much of the general public increasingly advocate nonviolence and peace in the social, political, and economic realms. However, the quintessential hub of the peace movement may well be the early experience of peace in the family and nonviolent socialization at home and at school.

POLICY STATEMENT

The National Association of Social Workers (NASW) believes in the right of every child to a safe and nurturing environment, including home and educational experiences that are conducive to constructive learning. The use of physical force against people, especially children, is a child-rearing practice that is antithetical to the best values of a democratic society and of the social work profession. Thus, NASW opposes the use of physical punishment in homes, schools, and all other institutions, both public and private, where children are cared for and educated.

NASW affirms that all children need parental guidance and discipline and that most parents want to be able to discipline in a way that works and is helpful to children. Therefore, NASW will support parenting programs and professional social work practices that provide parents with access to training and support for learning and using nonviolent disciplinary techniques, such as positive reinforcement, time-out, and verbal problem solving, instead of physical punish-

ment with their children. Because parents who are struggling to provide their families with even the basic necessities of food, shelter, and clothing are suffering significant levels of stress that affect all types of interaction, including discipline of children, NASW will support professional social work practice, social programs, and social policies that will allow children to have their basic needs met so that parents have energy and emotional resources to use disciplinary procedures with their children.

Because of the issues of self-determination, parental rights, and family privacy, a public and professional education campaign, aided by the media, as part of the development of readily accessible and usable resources for all facets of our population is the preferred method for abolishing the physical punishment of children by their parents. These programs should be aware of and sensitive to geographic, cultural, religious, and ethnic sensitivities in child-rearing traditions. NASW favors and will actively support the passage of legislation, comparable to that already adopted in some states and some cities, that bans the use of physical punishment in schools and child care facilities and institutions. NASW will actively develop and support programs to help prepare administrators, teachers, school personnel, child care workers, and parents to use nonviolent forms of discipline. NASW will actively support research to validate its hypotheses that physical punishment is not an effective and humane way to discipline children and that alternative forms of discipline exist and are effective in changing behavior.

In adopting this policy, NASW is proud to join many other professional organizations, both national and international, that oppose the physical punishment of children in schools, institutions, and homes. In adopting this policy, NASW believes it is imperative for the social work profession, with its tradition of championing human rights, to join the effort to promote the nonviolent discipline and care of children in the United States.

REFERENCES

Bandura, A. (1960). *Relationship of family patterns to child behavior disorders.* (Progress report, research grant M-173 from the U.S. Public

Health Service). Stanford, CA: Stanford University.

Dorr, D. (1983). Overview. In D. Dorr, M. Max, & J. Bonner III (Eds.), *The psychology of discipline* (chap. 8). New York: International Universities Press.

Gelles, R. (1978). Violence toward children in the United States. *American Journal of Orthopsychiatry, 48,* 580–592.

Johnson Foundation. (1989, February 24). National group adopts statement opposing parental use of physical punishment of children. (News release). Racine, WI: Author.

Kersey, K. (1983). *The art of sensitive parenting: The ten master keys to raising confident, competent, and responsible children.* Washington, DC: Acropolis Press.

Madsen, C., Jr., & Stephens, J. (1983). Behavioral discipline. In D. Dorr, M. Max, & J. Bonner III (Eds.), *The psychology of discipline* (chap. 7). New York: International Universities Press.

National Education Association. (1972). *Report of the task force on corporal punishment.* Washington, DC: Author.

Orgel, A. (1983). Haim Ginott's approach to discipline. In D. Dorr, M. Max, & J. Bonner III (Eds.), *The psychology of discipline* (chap. 6). New York: International Universities Press.

Walker, E. (1988). *The physically and sexually abused child.* New York: Pergamon Press.

Waters, V. (1983). The rational emotive point of view of discipline. In D. Dorr, M. Max, & J. Bonner III (Eds.), *The psychology of discipline* (chap. 4). New York: International Universities Press.

Policy statement approved by the NASW Delegate Assembly, August 1990. Referred to the 1999 Delegate Assembly for revision. This statement supersedes the policy statement on Corporal Punishment of Children in Schools and Custodial Settings approved by the Delegate Assembly in 1984. For further information, contact the National Association of Social Workers, 750 First Street, NE, Suite 700, Washington, DC 20002-4241. Telephone: 202-408-8600 or 800-638-8799.

Public Child Welfare

BACKGROUND

Public child welfare services include protection services, foster care, adoption, and an array of preventive and support services that are child centered and family focused. The public child welfare agencies fulfill society's mandated commitment to help families or family substitutes care for and protect their children. The agencies provide child welfare services directly and through contacts to private agencies.

Although professional social work practice in public child welfare exemplifies the profession's values and mission to serve the most vulnerable, the recruitment and retention of professional social workers have decreased during the past decade. Social work students increasingly are interested in a more clinically oriented career. High caseloads, low pay, and poor working environments discourage new graduate social workers from entering public child welfare. Legislative efforts to declassify social work positions, as a way to save money, also have influenced qualified experienced staff to leave the child welfare field. This inability to attract and retain social workers causes concern because the tasks to be accomplished and the critical decisions that need to be made demand a high degree of professional expertise.

ISSUE STATEMENT

The lifelong effects of child welfare decisions demand highly qualified personnel in public child welfare administration and services. Decisions made by public child welfare staff are critical; they can alter the future course of a child's life and that of his or her family. Decisions such as whether or not a child was abused, should be removed from the home, or should be placed in a particular type of treatment setting or whether to petition a court for termination of parental rights are typical of those made daily by child welfare workers. Only individuals who have had professional training should be given the responsibility for such important decision making.

The social work profession needs to assert its role in public child welfare by supporting three principles:

1. An undergraduate or graduate social work degree should be required for the delivery and administration of social services in public child welfare to ensure that workers have the necessary skills, knowledge, and values to provide high-quality services.

2. The development of an educational curriculum and professional training is vital to the recruitment and retention of professional social workers in public child welfare.

3. The profession must organize at the local, state, and national levels to promote public understanding of and financial support for the public child welfare system, its services to clients, and its workers.

POLICY STATEMENT

The National Association of Social Workers (NASW) recognizes that effective services to the children and families in public child welfare demand the values, knowledge, and skills that are intrinsic to social work education. Therefore, either undergraduate or graduate social work education should be required for the delivery and administration of social services in public child welfare, depending on the practice role of the practitioner.

NASW believes that children and families who are served through public child welfare have a right to the same level and quality of services delivered by professional social workers in other fields of practice. Furthermore, because the philosophical base of public child welfare requires both rehabilitative and preventive services, skill and professionalism are needed by social workers to deliver these services under the legally mandated authority of the public agency.

The same elements that undergird all professional social work practice should guide social work practice in public child welfare. Nonjudgmental respect for the dignity of the individual child and family, the use of a helping relationship, support for family self-determination, confidentiality, and the right to culturally and ethnically sensitive service are among the essential elements in social work practice. Social workers also must address the vulnerability of women and people of color in the delivery and receipt of public child welfare services and attempt to resolve their disempowerment.

NASW advocates high standards of professional ethics and practice in foster care, group care, adoption, child protection, and child custody issues.

NASW will increase activities for the recruitment, education, training, and retention of professional social workers in public child welfare.

National and local units of NASW will work together to support and promote the use of professional social workers in state and local child welfare agencies.

Public child welfare agencies and workers face unique demands and stresses. Social workers must work with other groups and professional organizations to succeed in the following activities:

■ promoting public understanding of and financial support for public child welfare services to clients, the public child welfare system, and public child welfare workers

■ creating greater opportunities for the professional development of public child welfare workers

■ securing adequate salary levels for public child welfare workers

■ mandating a maximum caseload size according to the standards of the Child Welfare League of America

■ promoting job flexibility

■ ensuring working conditions that are suitable and professional.

Social workers should be allied with leaders in the public child welfare field to develop appropriate public policy in this arena. NASW reaffirms that professional social work practice in public child welfare exemplifies the profession's values and mission to serve the most vulnerable.

Policy statement approved by the NASW Delegate Assembly, November 1987; reconfirmed by the Delegate Assembly, August 1993. For further information, contact the National Association of Social Workers, 750 First Street, NE, Suite 700, Washington, DC 20002-4241. Telephone: 202-408-8600 or 800-638-8799.

Racism

BACKGROUND

Racism is pervasive in American society and remains a silent code that systematically closes the doors of opportunity to young and old alike. Visibly identifiable members of racial and ethnic oppressed groups continue to struggle for equal access and opportunity, particularly during times of stringent economics, strident calls for tax revolt, dwindling natural resources, inflation, widespread unemployment and underemployment, and conservative judicial opinions that are precursors to greater deprivation. Unless curbed, these conditions invariably lead to greater ethnic and racial rivalry and to greater political, social, and economic oppression.

According to the *NASW Code of Ethics* (1996), "Social workers. . . should advocate for changes in policy and legislation to improve social conditions in order to meet basic human needs and promote social justice. . . . Social workers should act to prevent and eliminate domination of, exploitation of, and discrimination against any person, group, or class" (p. 27). It is therefore appropriate that NASW assume greater leadership in developing both internal and external policies and programs to end racism in society and in the social work profession.

Education

The educational system in the United States systematically denies equal access and opportunity to children and adults of color, especially those who are poor. Adequate attention is not paid to the negative impact of societal forces such as racism, segregation, poverty, and urbanization on educational achievement. Nor is adequate attention paid to the impact of educational systems that discriminate against students of color and their families. The necessity for comprehensive multilingual and multicultural curricula is not sufficiently recognized in national policy or local practice. In higher education, people of color are not proportionately represented at staff, student, faculty, or administrative levels. Insufficient financial resources exacerbate these and other problems.

Employment

Racism is rampant in all areas of employment. For many members of oppressed racial and ethnic groups, there is always an economic depression. Often people of color are the last hired and the first fired. As a result, budget cuts, downsizing, and privatization may disproportionately hurt people of color. Furthermore, there is a growing shortage of manufacturing and other jobs that people of color have historically held. In February 1995 the unemployment rate for African Americans was 10.1 percent as compared to 4.7 percent for white Americans (Berry, 1995). The unemployment rate for adolescents of color is approximately four times that of white adolescents. Women and men of color continue to be underrepresented in decision-making and administrative positions. Affirmative action programs are not sufficiently enforced and supported and in some cases have produced conflict and polarity among employees. Tokenism, rather than genuine compliance with affirmative action and equal employment requirements, is too often the rule.

Housing

Many people of color have little choice as to where they live and pay higher rents for less adequate housing. Mortgage and lending institutions continue the illegal practice of redlining. As recently as 1994, an $11 million settlement regarding redlining mortgages in minority neighborhoods was agreed to in the Washington, DC, metropolitan area. Studies conducted by the Federal Reserve, the U.S. Department of Housing and Urban Development (HUD), and the Urban Institute have found persistent discrimination against African Americans and Hispanics by financial institutions, landlords, and real estate agencies (Congressional Black Caucus Foundation, 1995). Illegal discriminatory practices, such as steering, discourage visibly identifiable racial and ethnic group members from renting or buying in specific neighborhoods.

The maintenance of public housing continues to be a serious problem. In the 1980s housing programs were dramatically reduced. In the 1990s homeless shelters too often became the solution for housing millions of men, women, and children. The fact that African Americans and other oppressed groups are so disproportionately affected by homelessness further aggravates this inequality.

Health Care and Mental Health Services

The current dual health care systems of fees-for-service and public care are not meeting the needs of people of color. Most health care costs continue to increase, while for many the quality and accessibility of services decline. Furthermore, too many health care facilities, mental health services, and health care providers tend to be located in areas that are inaccessible to low-income urban neighborhoods and rural districts, where many people of color reside. Many cannot obtain private health or mental health care because they have neither the money nor the access to medical insurance coverage.

With the decline of free public hospitals and of public or low-cost mental health care, people of color often go without care. Public services, such as sanitation, are more likely to be neglected in low-income areas, thus creating additional health hazards. Inadequate housing and poor nutrition make chronic illness and early death common problems. For example, in the United States life expectancy for people of color is significantly less than it is for white people (Dunkel & Norgard, 1995).

Public Welfare

Public welfare is a fragmented, chaotic, and irrational system. It is an expression of the unwillingness and inability of the major beneficiaries of our "free market" economic system to accept responsibility for providing jobs to all who can work and for providing a level of income that is adequate to maintain a decent standard of life. The welfare system has been used to keep wages low and to maintain a pool of people available to work at menial, unskilled jobs. Furthermore, many unskilled jobs available in the past have disappeared. Public welfare services usually do not include coplanning for services, job training, educational, child care, family planning, or unemployment insurance services that would empower the individual to benefit from the economic system. Disregard for personal rights and human dignity, inconsistent policies, and violation of regulations have often characterized the administration and delivery of public assistance and keep visibly identifiable people of color who apply for assistance at a disadvantage.

Social Services

Social services tend to direct people of diverse racial and cultural backgrounds into a system that is designed for European Americans and serviced by workers from European American groups. Often the result is nonuse or underutilization of available services by people who confront racial, cultural, and linguistic barriers. Although desperately needed, social services often mask symptoms of larger problems, such as racism, unemployment, illiteracy, and poverty. Social workers further empower the established system when their clients are not fully informed or encouraged to use entitlements.

The need for social services often is created by economic policies and practices. Too often society "blames the victim" and focuses on adjusting the individual to existing societal conditions, disregarding the need for environmental and institutional change and responsiveness.

Political Activity

People of color are grossly underrepresented in federal and local elective and appointive positions. Thus, legislation affecting all people is produced by nonrepresentative legislative bodies. A 1991 study by Mary Sawyer found an apparent pattern of harassment against African American elected officials in the United States using tactics of Internal Revenue Service audits, surveillance, phone taps, recall movements, and so forth (Congressional Black Caucus Foundation, 1995).

ISSUE STATEMENT

Racism is the ideology or practice through demonstrated power of perceiving the superiority of one group over others by reason of race, color, ethnicity, or cultural heritage. In the United States and elsewhere, racism is manifested at the individual, group, and institutional levels. It has been institutionalized and maintained through educational, economic, political, religious, social, and cultural policies and activities. It is observable in the prejudiced attitudes, values, myths, beliefs, and practices expressed by many people, including those in positions of power. Racism is functional—that is, it serves a purpose. In U.S. society, racism functions to maintain structural inequities that are to the disadvantage of people of color.

Organized discrimination against members of visibly identifiable racial and ethnic groups has permeated every aspect of their lives, including education, employment, contacts with the legal system, economics, housing, politics, religion, and social relationships. It has become institutionalized through folklore, legal restrictions, values, myths, and social mores that are openly supported by a substantial number of people, including those who maintain control of the major institutions of American society.

The history of racism in this country began with the genocide of American Indians and includes the atrocities of slavery, colonialism, and the internment of Japanese Americans. Historically, racism has been used to justify the conquering of people of color—American Indians, African Americans, Native Alaskans, Puerto Ricans, Mexicans, and Native Hawaiians—to obtain land, forced or cheap labor, and strategic military outposts. These conquered population groups became involuntary U.S. citizens. As other people of color immigrated to the United States as legal or undocumented immigrants, especially those entering the United States after

the immigration laws of the mid-1960s, they too often faced many of the same stereotypes, myths, and prejudices that the conquered populations had faced. Among the other immigrants encountering racism are Pacific Islanders and other Asians, Dominicans, Cubans and other Latinos, and West Indians and other people of African heritage. The effects of racism are seen in poor health and health services, inadequate mental health services, low wages, high unemployment and underemployment, overrepresentation in prior populations, substandard housing, high school dropout rates, decreased access to higher education opportunities, and other institutional maladies.

Racism negatively impacts both the oppressed and the oppressor. Institutional racism has historical roots in injustices perpetrated by our ancestors on indigenous and other populations in conquering and populating this country. Recognition of historical injustices is the beginning step in combating racism. One has to acknowledge the fact that the sons and daughters are not responsible for the sins of their parents, but the sons and daughters must analyze the present reality to ascertain if as a result of the historical injustices perpetrated by our parents results in one group in society being in a more advantageous and favorable position over and at the expense of others. It is incumbent in solidarity with those groups who are subordinate to join forces together with the profession of social work to bring about a more just and equitable society in which power, status, wealth, services, and opportunities are enjoyed by all. Even those who are not consciously racist tend to accept white privilege and the benefits of discrimination against others. Racism limits and minimizes the contributions many citizens can make to U.S. society.

Social workers often hold jobs where they confront the damaging effects of racism: greater poverty, higher mortality rates, inadequate housing, higher unemployment and underemployment, more prevalent illiteracy and limited educational opportunities, greater inaccessibility to health care services, higher incidence of mental illness, disproportionate involvement in the criminal justice system, and disproportionate involvement in unpopular public welfare programs. As professional administrators, educators, organizers, planners, case managers, supervisors, consultants, caseworkers, and other practitioners, social workers have firsthand knowledge of the difficulties that many racial and ethnic group members encounter in their efforts to combat white privilege, gain access to resources, and obtain a professional education. Most social workers also witness the scarcity of racially and ethnically diverse professionals available to act as role models and to provide services to diverse client populations. Furthermore, employment opportunities in the upper echelons of the social work delivery systems have historically been elusive for African American, Latino, American Indian, Pacific Islander, and Asian social workers.

POLICY STATEMENT

NASW supports an inclusive society in which racial, ethnic, social, sexual orientation, and gender differences are valued and respected. Racism at any level should not be tolerated. Emphasis must be placed on self-examination, learning, and change to unlearn racist beliefs and practices in order to be fully competent to join others in the full appreciation of all differences.

The association seeks the enactment of public social policies that will protect the rights of and ensure equity and social justice for all members of diverse racial and ethnic groups. It is the ethical responsibility of NASW members to assess their own practices and the agencies in which they work for specific ways to end racism where it exists. The basic goal should be to involve social workers in specific, time-limited educational and action programs designed to bring about measurable changes within provider agencies and within NASW national units, chapters, and local units. This is based on the premise that to engage in constructive intraprofessional relationships and to effectively serve clients, social workers must engage in self-examination of their own biases and stereotypes and work to develop an unbiased attitude. Racism is embedded in our society and unless we identify specific instances and work to remove them we are part of the problem rather than a mechanism for the solution.

Education

NASW advocates the following:

■   adoption of a national policy calling for the development and implementation of comprehensive multilingual and multicultural curricula—such curricula must call attention to white privilege, the pain of oppression, the legacy of racism, and the contributions of racially oppressed groups

■   implementation of programs and policies designed to produce high-quality education through a range of effective approaches

■   the addressing and seeking of censure against educators and educational systems that practice discrimination against students, faculty, and staff of color and their families

■   creation of educational systems in which faculties, staff, students, administrators, and boards of education reflect the diversity of neighborhoods and the larger society

■   the upholding of the highest standard to assure that fair and adequate funding and treatment is the goal of all educational systems.

Employment

NASW advocates the following:

■   implementation of a national policy of full employment

■   development of comprehensive job training programs

■   maintenance and strengthening of affirmative action plans so that they have the necessary authority and resources to be implemented successfully as demonstrated by measurable outcomes

■   an adequate minimum wage that reflects the realities of the economy

■   effective, affordable, comprehensive, multicultural, multilingual, and accessible child care

■   establishment of workforce policies that minimize the negative impact on employees and communities of color.

Housing and Community

NASW advocates the following:

■ enactment and practice of an open housing policy designed to eliminate externally imposed segregation in housing as the result of concentrated public housing, redlining, renovation, and conversion of apartment houses to condominiums

■ establishment of government and support programs that promote revitalization in communities of people of color.

Health Care and Mental Health Services

NASW advocates the following:

■ health and mental health practitioners learn and use culturally relevant healing practices when appropriate

■ self-study of health and mental health providers to identify oppressive policies, practices, and strategies and target dates for change

■ availability and accessibility of health care facilities, mental health services, and private practitioners in all neighborhoods

■ recruitment and training of people of color as health and mental health providers, particularly social workers.

Public Welfare Services

NASW advocates the following:

■ positive regard and respect for each individual's personal rights and human dignity

■ elimination of violations of regulations and inconsistent policies in public welfare that place people of color at a disadvantage

■ the use of racial and cultural sensitivity in the development and delivery of public welfare services

■ elimination of broader problems such as unemployment, illiteracy, and poverty that create the need for social services.

Social Services

NASW advocates the following:

■ development of social services that target needs articulated by the community to be served

■ development of model social programs that emphasize empowerment of the community and stress economic independence

■ continuously addressing the underrepresentation of people of color in the social services professions and policy-making boards of social services agencies.

Criminal Justice System

NASW advocates the following:

■ fair and equitable treatment of racial and ethnic minorities involved in the criminal justice system

■ the monitoring and promoting of criminal justice policies, statutes, and laws that do not discriminate against individuals based on race, ethnicity, class, political affiliation, or place of residence

■ strive to end racism and discrimination in recruitment, hiring, retention, and promotion in employment of racial and ethnic minorities in all levels of the criminal justice system; increase the availability and accessibility of professionally trained interpreters in instances where language differences may inhibit communication.

Political Activity

NASW advocates the following:

■ passage of legislation that serves to acknowledge, maintain, or enhance the sovereign rights of indigenous populations

■ election and appointment of legislators from diverse racial and ethnic backgrounds

■ growth of public interest groups that are racially and ethnically diverse

■ passage of legislation that will have a favorable impact on people of color

- massive voter registration and education

- unseating legislators who sponsor or support bills that are racist in intent or implementation

- provision of diversity training for public officials.

Profession

NASW advocates the following:

- full representation of groups oppressed because of race, color, or ethnicity at all levels of leadership and employment—policy formulation, administration, supervision, and direct services—in social work and in NASW

- implementation of the concepts of affirmative action in all facets of the profession at both the voluntary and paid levels of service, especially in practice, education, and professional development

- development of guidelines for multicultural social work curricula that emphasize social work as a profession that strives to empower those with less power because of racial or ethnic identification.

REFERENCES

Berry, M. F. (1995, May). Affirmative action: Political opportunists exploit racial fears. *Emerge, 4,* 29–39.

Congressional Black Caucus Foundation. (1995). *The mean season for African Americans.* Washington, DC: Author.

Dunkel, R. E., & Norgard, T. (1995). Aging overview. In R. L. Edwards (Ed.-in-Chief), *Encyclopedia of social work* (19th ed., Vol. 1, pp. 142–153). Washington, DC: NASW Press.

National Association of Social Workers. (1996). *NASW code of ethics.* Washington, DC: Author.

SUGGESTED READINGS

Banton, M. (1988). *Racial consciousness.* London: Longman.

Gray, W. (1996, May). *Speech for the 100th anniversary of Plessy vs Ferguson.* Cambridge, MA: Harvard University, W.E.B. Du Bois Institute. (C-Span, August 13, 1996)

Hacker, A. (1992). *Two nations, black and white, separate, hostile, and unequal.* New York: Ballantine Books.

Kivel, P. (1996). *Uprooting racism: How white people can work for racial justice.* Philadelphia: New Society Publishers.

Swoboda, F. (1995, March 16). Glass ceiling firmly in place: Panel finds minorities, women are rare in management. *Washington Post,* pp. A1, A18.

Policy statement approved by the NASW Delegate Assembly, August 1996. This policy supersedes the policy statement on Racism approved by the NASW national Board of Directors in October 1993 following recommendations by the Delegate Assembly in August 1993. For further information, contact the National Association of Social Workers, 750 First Street, NE, Suite 700, Washington, DC 20002-4241. Telephone: 202-408-8600 or 800-638-8799.

Role of Government, Social Policy, and Social Work

BACKGROUND

The view that government contributes to the creation of social problems has a long history. It has been the conservative position of all political parties throughout American history. From Benjamin Franklin on the "poor laws" to President Franklin Pierce's veto of federal funding of psychiatric hospitals, from William Graham Sumner's social Darwinist pronouncements in the 1880s to the policies of the administrations of Coolidge and Hoover in the 1920s, conservative public leaders have reaffirmed a "hands off" policy of the federal government regarding the health and social ills of the nation.

There also have been countertrends in U.S. history to address the most extreme dimensions of poverty, inequality, and oppression. Ultimately, it was the advent of Franklin Delano Roosevelt's New Deal administration 60 years ago that changed the prevailing wisdom and firmly established the necessary role and responsibility of the federal government as an ameliorating force in a capitalistic system. For the next 40 years, the concepts of the rights of citizenship that included social, political, and economic benefits have been established and expanded at the federal level under the presidential leadership of both parties.

Leadership by the federal government in promoting an equality-of-opportunity social agenda peaked in the Kennedy–Johnson era of the 1960s. More socially progressive legislation was passed in the 88th and 89th Congresses than at any time in American history. Even under the leadership of the administration of President Nixon, this did not change appreciably. In his years as president, Nixon instituted the concept of block grants to the states, but these were implemented as part of a "new federalism" without abdicating federal leadership; more importantly Title XX sup-

port for a range of social programs was instituted during his administration. Nixon also supported the "federalization" of the categorical welfare entitlements that eventually were enacted as SSI (Supplemental Security Income) benefits. Finally, he proposed the federal takeover of Aid to Families with Dependent Children and introduced national health insurance legislation that would have extended Medicare- and Medicaid-like health coverage to everyone.

Neither the administrations of Presidents Ford nor Carter tampered much with social programs or priorities; however, the "stagflation" during the 1970s gave rise to increasing calls for limits on taxes and social spending at the state level, and a shift from universal to selective approaches to services.

The Reagan and Bush administrations in the 1980s brought with them an ideology of individualism and privatization, challenging the concept of entitlement and the government role in interfering with the marketplace and corporate profits. Their supply-side economic and tax policies demanded real cuts in social program spending, a reversal of social program priorities, and attempts to deregulate businesses. The gap between the rich and poor began increasing again. Both administrations still used the concept of a "safety net" for meeting the needs of the "truly needy" in conveying their vision of the role of the federal government. Although this safety net was a residual and minimal one with many holes, government was still considered the provider of last resort, and there was no attempt to remove federal protection for special groups, such as abused and neglected children.

After the Clinton victory in 1992, deficits were such that many members of both parties viewed the government in general, and the federal government in particular, as bloated, misguided, and inefficient. As a result, in the 1994 national elections, those supporting an antigovernment perspective won the majority of congressional seats for the first time in 40 years, and a majority of state governors were also elected on a platform of less government and lower taxes.

Together these new leaders sought a curtailed role for the federal government in social program guarantees and funding, in protection of vulnerable populations, in restricting or monitoring business and investment, and in affirmative action and other equity programs. At the same time they sought a greater social control role for government in shaping how families, and women in particular, may behave and in restricting who may come to this country and what happens when they get here.

One of the differences in the aforementioned attack on the role of the federal government from attacks at different times in the nation's history is the extreme view that Washington is the enemy of the people, not just too large, inefficient, costly, and cumbersome. There has been an important shift from a belief in at least a residual government responsibility for addressing social ills to ultimately no government responsibility at all in these matters as states also downsize and diminish their responsibilities for the welfare of their residents. This forms the basis for the elimination of all mandates, guarantees, and entitlements. There is a pervasive view that government can no longer afford to spend money on social programs, accompanied by proclamations that government programs have failed or even that they have caused problems, such as dependency and family dissolution.

These antigovernment sentiments are often accompanied by views of recipients of services which are antithetical to social work values in several ways: There is a shift from blaming to punishing victims—overtly and covertly. There is an expansion of the category of undeserving poor to include almost everyone, even those formerly exempt such as children, veterans, the elderly, and the mentally and physically ill. Greater social control measures are being promoted to control all who use public resources. There is a return to "let the buyer beware" for all people in their roles as consumers of goods, services, natural resources, and so forth. There

are renewed attacks based on stereotypical views of the personal characteristics of certain groups by virtue of their racial, ethnic, or citizenship status. Racism, ageism, sexism, homophobia, and xenophobia are justified under the guise of returning to normalcy from a perceived unnatural "political correctness." The attempt to codify this ideology into public policy and law is damaging the rights of many Americans.

Such reactionary and divisive campaigns have resulted in the implementation of a similar social agenda. Those tenets on the *economic* side include spending cuts and tax breaks for upper income groups coupled with balanced budget legislation, shifts of minimum programs back to the states without any entitlement provisions, heavy deregulation of industry, and lifting consumer and environmental protections; on the *ideological* side, they include mandates for personal responsibility legislation while, at the same time, decreasing opportunities and protections for the people of this nation.

Although many federal programs, including food stamps, Section 8 housing, Medicare, and others, have achieved their intended goals to provide a safety net or a reduction in poverty, deprivation, and hunger, conservative thinking suggests that this evidence does not warrant continuation of these programs. Yet, because of enhancements like Social Security, Medicare, and the Older Americans Act, the rate of poverty among the elderly has declined dramatically. The economic realities of the current U.S. economy are a driving force for the economically and ideologically conservative campaign. The economy has grown steadily in the 1990s. Profits have been at near record levels as stock prices have been. At the same time total compensation, which includes wages and fringe benefits, has fallen dramatically. What this means is that wages are rising slower than capital; the share of income going to workers lags behind those who own places of work. Overall, real income has dropped for 60 percent of American families over the past 25 years, and the income gap between the lowest and highest fifth income groups has widened. This has caused disaffection or withdrawal from civic life and has led some Americans to scapegoat the poor and others for their worsening situation.

In 1980, when Ronald Reagan was elected president, he claimed to have received a "mandate for change." However, this mandate was from a minority of voters. It is important to recognize he was elected president by only 26 percent of all voters, and only 39 percent of all eligible voters elected the mostly conservative 104th Congress in November 1994. With large constituencies of eligible voters unregistered, and millions of registered voters who do not vote—two thirds of whom are below the median income line—the social and political agenda is shaped by those who vote in disproportionately large numbers, predominately middle and upper income groups. Millions of dollars have been invested in the public media and grassroots organizing campaigns to promote an individual responsibility agenda. However, NASW acknowledges the interdependence among individuals, families, and communities and the responsibility of the government to assure the social welfare of its people.

Public policy is the dominant variable in determining the nature of social work practice, and it is profoundly affected by the current agenda. While social agencies and social work professionals can help shape policies and practices, the nature of the services delivery system and the legitimacy of social work as a profession are established by public social policy. Changes in government policies affect clients, their eligibility, and their ability to access benefits and services. In conclusion, restructuring and limiting government responsibility has begun to profoundly alter the availability and the delivery of social work services and the role and status of social work as a profession.

When policy is based on ideas such as the desirability of maintaining a just and humane society, social work practice can be expected to reflect that concept. For example, the addition of end stage renal disease treatment, dialysis, and transplantation in the Social Security Amendments of 1972 to the list of disabling conditions eligible for Medicare coverage included a mandate for intervention by a social worker with a master of social work degree as part of a health care team. Without this government mandate, social work services would not always be available to those with end stage renal disease. On the other hand, the role of social workers can be redefined and distorted by policy emerging from cutbacks, cost containment, and primary concern for profits. Case management, a service long considered a social work function to assist patients and clients to more effectively access resources, is increasingly used, but is too often defined by insurance companies and private providers who use it to restrict access and limit resources to reduce costs.

Clearly, when the dominant social environment becomes one of social Darwinism, social work must join in affirming and supporting the more humane and just view that emerged from the Great Depression. That view led to the Social Security Act and all the other social policies that developed to provide a safety net to safeguard Americans from the worst effects of poverty and to ensure adequate health care for children and the elderly. As the nation has built a great economic system that has benefited so many, social work must continue to identify those who have fared less well and use the social policy process to engage the government in programs that protect and assist those needing help to enjoy the full benefits of a just society.

ISSUE STATEMENT

Advances in science and technology, food production, public health, worker safety, and the environment have resulted in improvements in the quality of life undreamed of in the past. At the same time, dislocations and problems that have accompanied many of these changes have also caused considerable misery and inequities for many people and communities. For the past 60 years, the majority view of the role of government has been that of a mediating structure to modify the vagaries and inequities that may be found in the marketplace. This view has been accompanied by ideologies to create equality of opportunity to fulfill the vision of the United States of America as an open, pluralistic, and inclusive society.

For the past 60 years or more, federal government efforts have moved in the direction of sharing the benefits of economic growth among its citizens and protecting the vulnerable. Government has done this through

■ regulation and oversight

- designing and funding programs created specifically to meet its policy goals

- stimulating the economy through industrial, taxation, and other fiscal policies

- to a lesser degree, redistributing the wealth of the society as a means to accomplish the first three functions.

A combination of severe cuts in funding of social programs in order to provide tax cuts for the wealthiest citizens, deregulation of legal rights and protections, and the shift to turn programs over to states or private corporations with less funding and little or no regulation and standards with very short notice has the potential to cause great harm to our society and especially to its most vulnerable populations.

Since the beginning of social work as a profession and the inception of NASW, two basic assumptions have been made: The social ills of the nation and its citizens need public attention, resources, and solutions, and government has a major role and responsibility to meet human needs. Moreover, there has been increasing recognition that major shifts in the structure and functions of society, including demographic, economic, health, and family factors, require universal social welfare benefits and services.

In the current debate, problems are being identified as individual in origin rather than social or environmental in nature, and too often the etiology of problems in society is being characterized in moral, racial and cultural, or intellectual terms. The influence of social, economic, or political factors on community and family life has been minimized or ignored. The government is no longer regarded as a potential instrument of problem solution; instead, in some quarters, by some factions, it is portrayed as the problem or an exacerbating factor of the problem. While state governments are given more responsibility and opportunities to address these issues with fewer resources, there are yet more requirements that states meet the needs of vulnerable and oppressed populations.

POLICY STATEMENT

It is the position of NASW that federal, state, and local governments must have a role in developing policies and programs that expand opportunities, address social and economic justice, improve the quality of life of all people in this country, and enhance the social conditions of this nation's communities. NASW reaffirms its commitment to the promotion of the positive role of federal, state, and local governments as serving as guarantors of the social safety net and as the mechanisms by which people through their elected representatives can ensure equitable and accountable policies to address:

- entitlements to assist in the elimination of poverty

- access to universal comprehensive health care

- standards for public services

- enabling citizen participation in the development and implementation of social programs

- taxation that is balanced and fair

- an income floor for the working poor through earned income tax credits and other mechanisms

- adequate federal minimum wage laws

- standards and laws for the protection of workers in the workplace

- standards and laws for the protection of vulnerable populations

- product safety standards

- access to legal services

- commitment to full employment

- adequate and affordable housing

- assurance of adequate public education and educational standards for all schools

- a justice system rooted in law and administered impartially.

The key to accomplishing these policy goals is a view of government as an embodiment of and by the people, rather than an entity above and apart from its citizens. This policy calls for a renewed commitment to civic responsibility by an informed community through participation in democratic forums. It demands open debate on a wide variety of policies and programs while maintaining the basic functions listed above. As necessary, such a process would support the reform of government when it is consistent with the social work value base.

NASW reaffirms the essential role of government. The role of the federal government is to ensure uniform standards, adequate resources, equal protection under the law, monitoring and evaluating outcomes, and provision of technical assistance to state and local governments. NASW also recognizes the role of state and local governments in social programs. State governments are often in the position to understand the needs of the people in that state. As a part of a national community, states must work together to implement federal policies that support the well-being of the people of this nation. Thus, social programs are most effective when there is consistency in federal standards and guidelines with flexibility, adequate funding, and accountability mechanisms for states and localities to administer programs in ways that are best adapted to meet the needs of people, examining the effectiveness, efficiency, and accountability of specific programs necessary to ensure the success of

that role. Laws, regulations, and program guidelines need thorough review without discarding their underlying principles and intent. NASW is capable of providing significant leadership in evaluating existing programs and in designing and recommending new ones to forward the goals of the social policy it has reaffirmed.

NASW believes that social workers can be effective at all levels of government. For example, the recent Family Preservation and Support Act mandated the input of communities. It was an attempt to accommodate the input of professional social workers and the clients they serve. The recent reintroduction of block grants is another opportunity for social workers to support the collaborative efforts of government and the people. This policy asserts that government should actively and creatively guide, negotiate, and participate in cooperative efforts with nongovernmental organizations in the provision of programs that expand, support opportunity, address social and economic justice, and improve the quality of life for all people.

Policy statement approved by the NASW Delegate Assembly, August 1996. For further information, contact the National Association of Social Workers, 750 First Street, NE, Suite 700, Washington, DC 20002-4241. Telephone: 202-408-8600 or 800-638-8799.

Role of Social Work in Health Maintenance Organizations

BACKGROUND

The enactment of the Health Maintenance Organization (HMO) Act of 1973 (P.L. 93-222) was a significant step in achieving a national health policy. As a 145,000-member association and with more than 60,000 social workers practicing in health-related settings, NASW has a fund of intensive and varied experience and knowledge and a social responsibility to participate fully in the development and implementation of such policy through the legislative process as well as through clinical practice.

According to the language of P.L. 93-222, HMOs constitute an organized system of health care that directly provides or arranges for a comprehensive range of basic and supplemental health care services to a voluntarily enrolled population. Services are provided to a specific geographic area and are prepaid for a fixed period. The HMO is one of the most rapidly expanding new models of health care delivery in the country. More than 225 HMOs operate in the United States are serve approximately 8.2 million people—an increase in membership of 128 percent since 1971. Of the 225 operational HMOs, 123 are federally certified and serve more than 5.5 million people.

There are three organizational modes through which an HMO may provide services:

1. staff HMO: an HMO that delivers services through its own health professionals who are paid employees (staff of the HMO).

2. group practice: an HMO that contracts with a medical group, partnership, or corporation that is composed of health professionals who are licensed to practice medicine or osteopathy and other health professionals who are necessary for the provision of health services.

3. independent practice association (IPA): an organization that contracts with health professionals in a variety of locations. Practitioners usually are compensated by the IPA on a fee-for-service basis.

Inherent in the concept of an HMO is the provision of holistic health care in a fiscally sound operation at a reasonable cost. The HMO law and regulations embody this idea of the delivery of holistic health care. Social work as a profession is able to provide a broad range of direct services in an HMO with an emphasis on the holistic approach to health care.

Historically, social workers in medical and psychiatric settings have provided such direct services as psychosocial assessment, brief therapy, long-term-care therapy, crisis intervention, discharge planning, social histories to assist in diagnosis, and case management. Social workers in both settings have provided the indirect services of consultation, program planning, education, and coordination of community resources.

However, it is critical to note that the position and role of social workers are not specifically listed in the HMO Act as "basic health professionals." Although social workers are not listed in the HMO Act, the federal regulations have broadened the definition of basic health professionals to include social workers. Until 1981, the federal law and regulations required the provision of "medical social services" in HMOs, but no such requirement exists now.

Because there is no requirement that medical social services be provided by social workers, there are few social services departments in HMOs. This lack has had a significant impact on the effectiveness of the overall HMO health care delivery system. In practice, though, operating HMOs tend to compartmentalize into medical services and mental health services, which results in a limited emphasis on medical social services. Those HMOs with social services departments have increased the effectiveness of the overall health care delivery system because of their emphasis on coordination, continuity of care, appropriate diagnosis, and use of community resources.

The federal HMO law and regulations include the provision of services that have been traditionally the concern of social workers. They are as follows: shorterm evaluative or crisis intervention mental health services, referral services for the abuse of or addiction to alcohol or other drugs, and grievance procedures for hearing and resolving grievances between the HMO and the members of the HMO.

The importance of the potential role of social workers in HMOs can only increase in the next decade. The national HMO developmental strategy through 1988 (P.H.S. 79-50111) is to increase services to medically underserved rural or inner-city populations, including Medicare and Medicaid recipients. Currently, less than 2 percent of the total number of Medicare and Medicaid beneficiaries are enrolled in HMOs. Consequently, there will be a real increase in the number of programs and people being served by HMOs.

ISSUE STATEMENT

Few HMOs have authorized departments of social services that are responsible for the social services needs of their subscribers, especially those in high-risk categories. The lack of professional social services departments has limited the research on cost–benefits and the provision of social services in HMOs.

The lack of legislation and regulations that require the provision of HMO social services by master's- and baccalaureate-level social workers who have graduated from an accredited school of social work has resulted in the underemphasis of the social services needs of the HMO population. The existing structure of HMOs creates a split in function for the profession. Medical and psychiatric social work services are defined as distinct entities with a lim-

ited overlap of services and therefore operate counter to the holistic approach to health care. Administrative and planning bodies of HMOs frequently ignore the benefit of social workers who are trained in clinical services and community organization.

The social advocacy experience that is traditionally ascribed to social workers often is underutilized legally by administrators of HMOs even in the mandated grievance procedures. The role of social workers in primary prevention, an area critical to the function of HMOs, is underdeveloped n both academic settings and practicing HMOs. The scarcity of graduate social work programs with concentrations in social work in the health care system limits the acceptance and function of social workers in health care settings in general and in HMOs in particular.

POLICY STATEMENT

The policy of NASW in relation to the role of social workers in HMOs is the following:

■ Social work has a definite and substantial role in HMOs. That role should encompass therapy, case management, patient advocacy, inpatient planning, primary prevention, consultation and liaison services, and coordination with community resources.

■ NASW should encourage the employment in staff positions of master's- and baccalaureate-level social workers who have graduated from accredited schools of social work. Supervisory and administrative positions should require the ACSW certification or licensure at the equivalent level.

■ HMOs should be encouraged to develop departments of social work. The function of these departments is to ensure the quality of professional services, accountability, and research and the development of more effective social work roles.

■ Social workers should be included as part of the professional bargaining group.

■ Master's- and baccalaureate-level social workers should be necessary members of the mental health and medical units on the administrative, supervisory, and service levels.

■ Master's- and baccalaureate-level social workers should assume the responsibility of membership on all HMO planning boards.

■ There should be an increase in the number of health care concentrations in graduate schools of social work. These programs should include field practicums in HMO settings.

■ More research that focuses on the cost-effectiveness of social workers in prevention and intervention should be supported.

■ Interprofessional cooperation should strive for the maintenance of adequate mental health and alcoholism benefits in HMOs.

■ Social workers should develop planning groups to coordinate meetings and workshops and to educate peers in the areas of practice in an HMO setting.

■ Social workers should be involved actively with HMO planning committees on the national, state, and local levels in focusing on, among other things, the service needs of subscribers and the definition of professional roles.

Policy statement approved by the NASW Delegate Assembly, 1981; reconfirmed by the Delegate Assembly, August 1990. Referred to the 1999 Delegate Assembly, to be revised and combined with the policy statement on Health Care. For further information, contact the National Association of Social Workers, 750 First Street, NE, Suite 700, Washington, DC 20002-4241. Telephone: 202-408-8600 or 800-638-8799.

School Dropout Prevention

BACKGROUND

One in four students does not graduate from high school in the United States (Ranbom, 1986). The problem is especially acute in the inner cities, where about half of students fail to complete high school and where the dropout rate for African American and Hispanic students is particularly high. During the 1992–1993 school year, the dropout rate for African American students increased even as the overall dropout rate among inner-city students declined ("Dropout Rates," 1994). As U.S. schools continue to enroll children from diverse and disadvantaged populations or who suffer from a number of growing social problems (living in poverty, being homeless, suffering from the human immunodeficiency virus or acquired immune deficiency syndrome, or affected by substance abuse), the number of potential dropouts will continue to increase.

Rumberger (1987) claimed that although the present national dropout rate of 25 percent is objectively better than at any other time in U.S. history, it is "subjectively worse than ever" (p. 101). Before the 1950s, a labor-intensive economy, the military service, and the agricultural sector could absorb those who did not finish high school (LeCompte, 1987). The labor force, however, changed dramatically during the 1960s and 1970s as a result of a sharp rise in the number of potential workers (that is, the entry of increasing numbers of youths and women in the workforce) and a decrease in the number of unskilled and semiskilled positions. This combination of factors forced "high school dropouts to compete with more and more graduates for fewer and fewer entry-level jobs" (Larsen & Schertzer, 1987, p. 163). Three of four jobs in the United States require educational or technical training that goes beyond a high school diploma (Smith & Lincoln, 1988).

Why do students drop out of school? The dropout process is multidimensional, interactive, and cumulative in nature. At-risk students enter schools with multiple social and emotional needs that affect their ability to perform the academic and social tasks expected of them within the school environment. This mismatch between the capabilities of vulnerable groups of students in interaction with the demands of the school environment results in school failure and dropouts. Carnahan (1994) stated that "this discrepancy exists on school entry, and continues to widen, until the fit between the child and school is so poor that the child drops out" (p. 107). Unfortunately, this "mismatch" will only continue to grow as linguistically, culturally, economically, and racially diverse children enter a U.S. public school system that is designed to serve "a monolingual, White, Anglo, middle-class culture" (First, Kellog, Almeida, & Gray, 1991, p. 212). NASW supports bilingual education as being an integral part of public education as this plays an important role in dropout prevention.

Research has shown a number of school, family, economic, and personal factors to be predictive of and associated with the process of dropping out. Poverty is the overwhelming demographic predictor of dropping out (Paulu, 1987). Children of low socioeconomic status are five times more likely to fail to complete high school than are children from middle- and upper-class families (Smith & Lincoln, 1988). Dropout rates are higher for members of racial, ethnic, and language minorities (Archer & Dresden, 1987; Pallas, 1986; Peng & Takai, 1983; Rumberger, 1987), and more males than females drop out (Rumberger, 1987). Teenage pregnancy and subsequent parenting responsibilities are the most common reason for females to drop out

(Hahn, 1987). Only three in 10 adolescent mothers earn a high school diploma by age 30 years (Maynard, 1996). On an annual basis, adolescent child bearing is directly responsible for 30,000 young women not completing high school. For males, an inability to get along with teachers, receiving suspensions and expulsions (Ekstrom, Goertz, Pollack, & Rock, 1986), and providing financial support for their families (Mann, 1986) contributed to their dropping out of school. According to the National Educational Longitudinal Survey: 88 Dropout Study, having friends who are dropouts or being in a drug or alcohol rehabilitation program may contribute to dropping out (McPartland, 1994). Youth are increasingly vulnerable to dropping out of school as they become involved in gang activity. Furthermore, statistics indicate that gay and lesbian youth and children of gay and lesbian parents, who are exposed to a negative school environment because of institutional homophobia, are at a higher risk of dropping out.

The recent school reform movement, with increasing academic demands of all students at every grade level, has increased pressure on students who are already at risk of school failure and dropout (Hamilton, 1986; LeCompte, 1987; Mearoff, 1988). Other powerful predictors of early school leaving include low scores on tests of basic skills (Smith & Lincoln, 1988), low grades (Rumberger, 1987), grade retention (Hammack, 1986), and school suspensions (DeRidder, 1990). School failure and truancy or frequent absenteeism are markers that predict dropout at the elementary school level. In fact, children at risk of school failure can be identified as early as third grade (Carnahan, 1994). Academic "tracking" also contributes to the dropout process because "disadvantaged students are much more likely to be assigned to the lower tracks and ability groups within their schools, where teacher expectations often are low and other learning resources weak" (McPartland, 1994, pp. 260–261).

Family factors that contribute to the dropout process include families in which parents and older siblings have dropped out and where support for educational goals is low (Howell & Frese, 1982; Rumberger, 1983; U.S. General Accounting Office, 1986). Nearly three-fourths of recent dropouts "had high school–aged brothers or sisters who had also dropped out"

(McPartland, 1994, p. 260). Families that are excessively stressed, have moved and changed schools frequently, or in which the father is absent also have been cited as contributing to the dropout process (Ziesemer, 1984).

Most federal government efforts to prevent school dropouts focus on the prevention of school failure through remedial and compensatory education for at-risk children. Most federal funding in this category is spent on Head Start early childhood programs (Smith & Lincoln, 1988). The Follow Through Program disseminates exemplary compensatory education model programs for children from low-income families and bilingual and vocational education programs (Smith & Lincoln, 1988). Chapter 1 is the largest federal education program targeting students at risk of school failure (Letgers & McDill, 1994). Indeed, "the size and scope of Chapter 1 make the program an important bellwether for change in educational programs for youth at risk" (Letgers & McDill, 1994, p. 25). The Hawkins–Stafford Elementary and Secondary Education Act Amendments of 1988 allowed schools with 75 percent or more students eligible for free lunch to use Chapter 1 funds for schoolwide programs (LeTendre, 1991, as cited in Letgers & McDill, 1994). The amendments also provide funds for a variety of Chapter 2 block grants to states and localities, including programs for at-risk children from preschool through secondary school and programs for educationally deprived children, bilingual education, drug abuse prevention programs, and programs for gifted and talented students (Hare, 1988).

The 1994 reauthorization of the Elementary and Secondary Education Act (ESEA) included a reformulation of Title I (formerly Chapter 1) programs "to provide a greater proportion of resources to poorer school districts, and to demand that these children, like other students, will attain high standards of performance" (Hare, 1994a, p. 4). As a result of NASW advocacy, the final bill incorporates the term "pupil service personnel" to ensure that school social workers are eligible for the development of local plans for Title I schoolwide and targeted assistance programs; training designed to increase and improve parental involvement in Title I programs; and professional development activities (Hare, 1994a). In addition, the Education of the

Handicapped Act Amendments of 1986 provide early intervention services to preschoolers and infants and toddlers with developmental delays. The amendments were extended in 1988 to provide services to young children "deprived of full educational opportunity for a variety of other reasons such as poverty and language and cultural differences" (Hare, 1988, p. 230). A major piece of recent legislation provides a framework for addressing the needs of students who are at risk of school failure and dropping out as we enter the next century. Goals 2000: Educate America Act, passed by Congress on March 31, 1994, legislates eight national educational goals that "promote the research, consensus building, and systemic changes needed to ensure equitable educational opportunities and high levels of educational achievement for all students" (Hare, 1994b, p. 2). Goal 2 focuses on the nation's high dropout rate by stating: "By the year 2000, the high school graduation rate will increase to at least 90 percent." The objectives under this goal state that "75 percent of the students who do drop out will successfully complete a high school degree or its equivalent [and] the gap in high school graduation rates between American students from minority backgrounds and their non-minority counterparts will be eliminated" (National Education Goals Panel, 1994, p. 8). Social workers are included under "related services" in this act and, as such, can participate as members of the National Education Standards and Improvement Council and State Improvement Plan Panels to provide leadership in grassroots efforts at restructuring and improving elementary and secondary education (Hare, 1994b).

Five major categories of programs have been developed to promote student learning and prevent dropout in school districts across the United States: (1) alternative schools, which include both separate schools and "schools within a school"; (2) vocational–technical schools; (3) teen–parent programs; (4) volunteer community service programs—an emerging trend in preventing school failure and dropping out is the increasing use of collaborative models within local communities; and (5) school social work services in schools. These collaborative models include school–community partnerships (for example, Cities-in-Schools, the New Futures initiative, and the

Walbridge Caring Community), school–business partnerships (for example, the Boston Compact), and university–school partnerships (for example, the Stay-in-School Partnership Project) (Dryfoos, 1994). Regardless of their approach, all successful dropout prevention programs "share a low teacher-to-student ratio (ranging from 5:1 to 11:1) and a 'coach' model of teacher–student relationships that is caring, supportive, and encouraging" (Carnahan, 1994, p. 117). Of particular interest to social workers is the Schools of the Future project, which "places a full-time project coordinator (a social worker) in a community to establish links and partnerships between the schools and health and human services providers and to involve parents and teachers in program activities" (Dryfoos, 1994, p. 73). This project also involves graduate social work students who provide crisis intervention, conduct home visits, and work with child protective services and economic services.

The prevention of school dropouts is and will continue to be a priority concern of NASW. NASW has been actively involved in advocating for the needs of children and youth who are at risk of school failure and dropping out. *The Human Factor: A Key to Excellence in Education* (Mintzies & Hare, 1985), an NASW publication, was a response to the educational excellence movement in the United States and documented the major human, social, and interpersonal factors that inhibit the achievement of educational excellence. This publication also contained recommendations for programmatic and policy changes to overcome these barriers to academic excellence. *Achieving Educational Excellence for Children at Risk* (Hawkins, 1986), another NASW publication, contained papers from NASW's Third National School Social Work Conference that addressed a number of barriers facing children at risk in the quest for educational excellence. In 1986 school social workers participated in a nationwide series of "information exchanges" sponsored by the National Education Association (NEA) to identify how to prevent students from dropping out. Through its involvement, NASW played a significant role in the development by NEA of *A Blueprint for Success*, which identifies key ingredients of effective dropout prevention programs, including school social work services. Programs and policies to support student learning and prevent school dropout are even more important now than they were in November 1987, when the original policy statement was adopted by the Delegate Assembly of NASW.

ISSUE STATEMENT

Preventing school dropout must become a priority social policy issue. The public and private sectors share equally in providing leadership, resources, and solutions to this important problem. Dropping out is the quiet killer of the American dream (National Foundation for the Improvement of Education, 1986). An estimated 5 million U.S. students are at educational risk because of limited English proficiency, poverty, race, geographic location, or economic disadvantage (Strauss, 1994).

More children are living in poverty and will enter schools with health and learning difficulties that are a direct result of inadequate prenatal care or the effects of substance abuse. These conditions may contribute to dropping out of school before completion of secondary education. Additionally, current welfare changes are likely to increase poverty and homelessness and inevitably place more children at risk. When a student drops out of school it poses lifelong challenges for the individual and concomitant costs for society. Consequently, the need for effective action in the area of school dropout prevention has never been greater.

To support student learning, NASW's policy on school dropout prevention is consistent with its mission of enhancing the functioning of individuals, families, and society at large, particularly in light of current social and funding trends. These trends include increasingly complex demands on schools that have limited resources. Schools are experiencing a diminished ability to provide for students who require educational services beyond the conventional; a competitive labor market that requires entry-level employees to have not only basic skills, but also advanced technical abilities; increasing political pressure for decreasing and redirecting funding for government educational and social welfare assistance; and imposing financial penalties on those who are poor.

Dropout prevention programs assist individuals in obtaining self-sufficiency and dignity. These programs help an individual to compete in the global marketplace and therefore are cost-effective as well as humane. The projected loss in human capital of youths not completing high school is staggering. Dropouts are more likely than high school graduates to be unemployed and are more likely to be incarcerated. The unemployment rate for dropouts in 1992 was nearly twice that of high school graduates who did not attend college, and the median income of dropouts was about half the income of high school graduates (Center for the Study of Social Policy, 1994). Dropouts are more likely to have a criminal record than youths who graduate from high school. In 1992, 50 percent of the prison population in the United States were dropouts compared with about 25 percent of the general population (Kirsch, Jungeblut, Jenkins, & Kolstad, 1993).

Dropping out is a multidimensional, interactive, and cumulative "process" that involves school, family, economic, and personal factors. Past dropout prevention efforts have focused too much attention at changing children rather than at changing children's environments. Although several innovative, exemplary programs to prevent school dropout have been developed, most current dropout prevention programs do not adequately focus on those school conditions that contribute to the "dropout process." McPartland (1994) stated, "It seems that most current programs are add-on or supplemental approaches that do not get at the basic structures and characteristics of schools that can turn off many students" such as tracking, grading, and promotion practices (p. 270). To address these limitations, dropout prevention efforts must be both comprehensive and preventive (Dupper, 1993). Comprehensive dropout prevention programs must target those factors in schools, families, and communities that contribute to or exacerbate the dropout process. In addition to providing direct services to high-risk youth, interventions must include school-based reform efforts and organizational changes that are designed to reduce the detrimental impact of school factors on vulnerable children and youth that include classroom environment, teaching styles, and methodology.

The role of prevention must be emphasized in dropout prevention policies and programs. A prevention approach allows early identification of potential risk and protective factors within individuals, schools, families, and communities. *Risk factors* are those factors in people or environments that place individuals at a heightened probability for the subsequent development of a disease or disorder (Schroeder & Gordon, 1991). According to Mrazek and Haggerty (1994), "risk factors can reside with the individual or within the family, community, or institutions that surround the individual" (p. 127). Risk factors within the individual include poor self-esteem and an external locus of control (Schroeder & Gordon, 1991); risk factors within the family or environment include limited financial or material resources and a poor social support network (Schroeder & Gordon, 1991); risk factors within schools include punitive or inadequate attendance policies and punitive discipline policies (Wheelock & Dorman, 1988).

Protective factors are defined as "those personal, social, and institutional resources that can promote successful development or buffer the risk factors that might otherwise compromise development" (Garmezy, Masten, & Tellegan, cited in Morrison, Furlong, & Morrison, 1994, p. 245). Examples of protective factors within individuals include high self-esteem and an internal locus of control (Schroeder & Gordon, 1991), protective factors within the family or environment include adequate child care resources and adequate financial resources (Schroeder & Gordon, 1991), and protective factors within schools include programs that support the establishment of strong relationships between the teacher and child and an appropriate degree of environmental structure and control (Rutter, 1979).

Dropout prevention programs and services must be provided before the cumulative impact of these various risk factors results in school failure and dropping out. Prevention approaches allow the reduction of the at-risk status of vulnerable populations by focusing on increasing the protective factors and working to minimize the risk factors within these various systems. Many dropout prevention programs include activities that are best performed as a result of the training and expertise of school social workers.

School social workers are skilled in assessing the issues that lead to excessive absences, a primary predictor of school dropout. Among education professionals, school social workers are uniquely qualified to offer innovative and comprehensive strategies that go beyond individualistic approaches to the problem and take into account the "social environment" of potential dropouts. Consequently, school social workers must take a greater leadership role in advocating, developing, and implementing dropout prevention programs and policies that are comprehensive and preventive.

POLICY STATEMENT

It is the policy of NASW to promote comprehensive services to enhance each student's opportunity to successfully complete school. The following points outline the policy of NASW regarding school dropout prevention:

■ To implement prevention programs, each school should have fully funded and staffed student service teams that include school social workers.

■ At-risk students should have access to alternative education programs with an adequate number of school social workers to address the myriad problems that this population presents. Appropriate ratios for school social work staff to students depend on the characteristics of the student population to be served (NASW, 1992, Appendix A). NASW believes that these schools within a school, or separate alternative programs, are to be regarded as a student's right and not a punishment for unproductive and disruptive behaviors.

■ To alleviate the issue of at-risk students, schools and communities must recruit adults as mentors, advocates, or tutors for potential dropouts. It is particularly important that African American and Hispanic men be recruited as such mentors.

■ School social workers should play a substantial role in empowering parents of at-risk students to participate more fully in decision making about school programs and services.

■ Public schools should be more responsive to the needs of at-risk students and should incorporate policies and practices that are respectful of differences among people, including race, gender, cultural heritage, sexual orientation, and socioeconomic status.

■ Steps must be taken to make schools safe, particularly those located in increasingly violent urban settings.

■ To prevent school dropout, and support student learning, services to at-risk students and their families must be delivered in a collaborative, integrated manner because the needs of potential dropouts and their families cannot be addressed by our public schools alone. The multiple and interconnected needs of at-risk children and their families demand that health, social, and economic services be delivered in a "timely, coordinated, and comprehensive fashion" (Behrman, 1992, pp. 4–5).

■ School-linked, integrated service programs should be established to meet the varied needs of at-risk students and their families. These integrated and coordinated health and social services should be offered on or near the school campus and/or the child's community and involve school social workers in coordination and services delivery.

■ At the elementary school level, early screening and assessment procedures should be developed that identify risk and protective factors in order to provide prevention services to students, families, and schools.

■ Schools must provide more opportunities for at-risk students to increase their attachment to and connectedness with their school while simultaneously working to decrease their alienation and disengagement from school.

■ Social workers, in recognizing the increasing demands on educators to meet the social and emotional needs of students, should provide support, consultation, and education, when needed, to assist educators with the complexities of this difficult task.

■ Social workers should initiate, direct, and participate in evaluating the effectiveness of dropout prevention programs. Findings should be reported to policy makers so that the most successful dropout prevention programs can be replicated.

REFERENCES

Archer, E. L., & Dresden, J. H. (1987). A new kind of dropout: The effect of minimum competency testing on high school graduation in Texas. *Education and Urban Society, 19,* 269–279.

Behrman, R. E. (1992). Introduction. *The Future of Children, 2*(1), 4–5.

Carnahan, S. (1994). Preventing school failure and dropout. In R. J. Simeonsson (Ed.), *Risk resilience and prevention: Promoting the well-being of all children.* Baltimore: Paul H. Brookes.

Center for the Study of Social Policy. (1994). *Kids count data book: State profiles of child well-being.* Washington, DC: Author.

DeRidder, L. M. (1990). How suspension and expulsion contribute to dropping out. *The Education Digest, 56,* 44–47.

Dropout rates for minority students keep rising in cities (1994, September 28). *The New York Times,* p. B8.

Dryfoos, J. G. (1994). *Full service schools: A revolution in health and social services for children, youth, and families.* San Francisco: Jossey-Bass.

Dupper, D. R. (1993). Preventing school dropouts: Guidelines for school social work practice. *Social Work in Education, 15,* 141–149.

Education of the Handicapped Act Amendments of 1986, P.L. 99-457, 100 Stat. 1145.

Ekstrom, R. B., Goertz, M. E., Pollack, J. M., & Rock, D. A. (1986). Who drops out of high school and why? Findings from a national study. *Teachers College Record, 87,* 356–373.

Elementary and Secondary Education Act of 1965, P.L. 103-252, 108 Stat. 649 (1994).

First, J., Kellog, J. B., Almeida, C. A., & Gray, R. (1991). *The good common school: Making the vision work for all children.* Boston: National Coalition of Advocates for Students.

Goals 2000: Educate America Act, P.L. 103-227, 108 Stat. 125.

Hahn, A. (1987). Reaching out to America's dropouts: What to do? *Phi Delta Kappan, 69,* 256–263.

Hamilton, S. F. (1986). Raising standards and reducing dropout rates. *Teachers College Record, 87,* 410–429.

Hammack, F. M. (1986). Large school systems' dropout reports: An analysis of definitions, procedures, and findings. *Teachers College Record, 87,* 324–341.

Hare, I. R. (1988). School social work and its social environment. *Social Work in Education, 10,* 218–234.

Hare, I. R. (1994a). The elementary and secondary Education Act (ESEA) includes "pupil services personnel." *School social work information bulletin* (Spring, p. 4). Washington, DC: National Association of Social Workers.

Hare, I. R. (1994b). Goals 2000: Educate America Act (PL 103-227) signed into law. *School social work information bulletin* (Spring, pp. 2–4). Washington, DC: National Association of Social Workers.

Hawkins, M. T. (Ed.). (1986). *Achieving educational excellence for children at risk.* Silver Spring, MD: National Association of Social Workers.

Hawkins–Stafford Elementary and Secondary Education Act Amendments of 1988, P.L. 100-297, 102 Stat. 302–319.

Howell, F. M., & Frese, W. (1982). Early transition into adult roles: Some antecedents and outcomes. *American Educational Research Journal, 19,* 51–73.

Kirsch, I. S., Jungeblut, A., Jenkins, L., & Kolstad, A. (1993). *Adult literacy in America: A first look at the results of their national adult literacy survey* (Report prepared by Educational Testing Service under contract with the National Center for Education Statistics, U.S. Department of Education). Washington, DC: U.S. Government Printing Office.

Larsen, P., & Shertzer, B. (1987). The high school dropout: Everybody's problem? *School Counselor, 34,* 163–169.

LeCompte, M. D. (1987). The cultural context of dropping out: Why remedial programs fail to solve the problems. *Education and Urban Society, 19,* 232–249.

Letgers, N., & McDill, E. L. (1994). Rising to the challenge: Emerging strategies for educating youth at risk. In R. J. Rossi (Ed.), *Schools and students at risk: Context and framework for positive change* (pp. 23–47). New York: Teachers College Press.

Mann, D. (1986). Dropout prevention: Getting serious about programs that work. *NASSP Bulletin, 70,* 66–73.

Maynard, R. A. (Ed). (1996). *Kids having kids: A Robin Hood Foundation special report on the costs of adolescent childbearing.* New York: The Robin Hood Foundation.

McPartland, J. M. (1994). Dropout prevention in theory and practice. In R. J. Rossi (Ed.), *Schools and students at risk: Context and framework for positive change* (pp. 255–276). New York: Teachers College Press.

Mearoff, G. I. (1988). Withered hopes, stillborn dreams: The dismal panorama of urban schools. *Phi Delta Kappan, 69,* 632–638.

Mintzies, P., & Hare, I. (1985). *The human factor: A key to excellence in education.* Silver Spring, MD: National Association of Social Workers.

Morrison, G. M., Furlong, M. J., & Morrison, R. L. (1994). School violence to school safety: Reframing the issue for school psychologists. *School Psychology Review, 23,* 236–256.

Mrazek, P. J., & Haggerty, R. J. (1994). *Reducing risks for mental disorders: Frontiers for preventive intervention research.* Washington, DC: National Academy Press.

National Association of Social Workers. (1992). *NASW standards for school social work services.* Washington, DC: Author.

National Education Goals Panel. (1994). *The national education goals report: Building a nation of learners 1994.* Washington, DC: U.S. Government Printing Office.

National Foundation for the Improvement of Education. (1986). *A blueprint for success.* Washington, DC: Author.

Pallas, A. M. (1986). School dropouts in the United States. In J. D. Stern & M. F. Williams (Eds.), *The condition of education* (pp. 158–170). Washington, DC: U.S. Government Printing Office.

Paulu, N. (1987). *Dealing with dropouts: The urban superintendent's call to action.* Washington, DC: Office of Educational Research and Improvement, U.S. Department of Education.

Peng, S. S., & Takai, R. T. (1983). *High school dropouts: Descriptive information from high school and beyond.* Washington, DC: National Center for Education Statistics.

Ranbom, S. (1986). *School dropouts: Everybody's problem.* Washington, DC: Institute for Educational Leadership.

Rumberger, R. W. (1983). Dropping out of high school: The influence of race, sex, and family background. *American Educational Research Journal, 20,* 199–220.

Rumberger, R. W. (1987). High school dropouts: A review of issues and evidence. *Review of Educational Research, 57,* 101–122.

Rutter, M. (1979). Protective factors in children's responses to stress and disadvantage. In M. W. Kentand & J. E. Rolf (Eds.), *Primary prevention of psychopathology: Social competence in children* (Vol. 3, pp. 49–74). Hanover, NH: University Press of New England.

Schroeder, C. S., & Gordon, B. N. (1991). *Assessment and treatment of childhood problems: A clinician's guide.* New York: Guilford Press.

Smith, R. C., & Lincoln, C. A. (1988). *America's shame, America's hope: Twelve million youth at risk.* Chapel Hill, NC: MDC.

Strauss, V. (1994, October 6). 2 schools to study "at-risk" education. *Washington Post,* pp. DC1–DC2.

U.S. General Accounting Office. (1986). *School dropouts: The extent and nature of the problem* (Briefing report to congressional requesters HRD 86-106 BR). Washington, DC: U.S. Government Printing Office.

Wheelock, A., & Dorman, G. (1988). *Before it's too late: Dropout prevention in the middle grades.* Carrboro, NC, and Boston: Center for Early Adolescence and Massachusetts Advocacy Center.

Ziesemer, C. (1984). Student and staff perceptions of truancy and court referrals. *Social Work in Education, 6,* 167–178.

Policy statement approved by the NASW Delegate Assembly, August 1996. This policy supersedes the policy statement on School Dropout Prevention approved by the Delegate Assembly in 1987. For further information, contact the National Association of Social Workers, 750 First Street, NE, Suite 700, Washington, DC 20002-4241. Telephone: 202-408-8600 or 800-638-8799.

Social Services

BACKGROUND

Social services has its roots in the charitable-voluntary agencies and limited government institutions that were created to fill perceived societal needs and reduce problems. The charitable–voluntary institutions have largely evolved into the private nonprofit agencies of today, and continue to be reflected in community fundraising and allocation entities, such as the United Way. The limited government influence has evolved into a pervasive government involvement because of greater societal needs and the necessity of a broader economic base to meet those needs. A system of laws also has evolved to ensure equal opportunity and access to and availability of services, as well as mandates for the operation of certain services (Brieland, 1987; Leiby, 1987).

A complementary relationship between private and public resources is necessary to sustain the web of services that are essential to maintain, encourage, develop, and promote family and individual well-being (Kahn, 1987; Maroney, 1987; Wenocur, 1987).

Social services is defined in the *Social Work Dictionary* (Barker, 1991) as

> the activities of social workers and other professionals in promoting the health and well-being of people and in helping people to become more self-sufficient; preventing dependency; strengthening family relationships; and restoring individuals, families, groups, to communities or successful *social functioning*. Specific kinds of social services include helping people obtain adequate financial resources for their needs, evaluating the capabilities of people to care for children or other dependents, *counseling*, and *psychotherapy*, *referral* and *channeling*, *mediation*, advocating for social causes, informing organizations of their obligations to individuals, facilitating health care provisions, and linking clients to *resources* (p. 221; italics in original).

An assessment of current patterns of providing social services indicates a wide disparity between the needs of people and the services provided to meet those needs, among the public bureaucracies and the private nonprofit agencies created to provide those services, and between the available funding base and the need for services. The public agencies are funded by fluctuating tax dollars, and the private nonprofits depend on ephemeral government contracts, private fundraising efforts, and community resources. Program development becomes focused on those areas that currently are in vogue, that is, fundable. The competition for available financial resources, particularly in recessionary times, becomes a struggle for the survival and maintenance of existing programs that do not fit the current focus. Furthermore, the lack of direction and the confusion in planning and service provision stem from a fundamental ambivalence resulting from the need to provide services and the need to control and account for the allocation of financial resources (Loarenbrack & Keys, 1987).

The heightened demand for accountability and program evaluation has provided the impetus for more social work research and for refinements in evaluation measures and design. It has focused attention on discovering what works and how to generalize that information. It has also focused attention on cost-effectiveness as related to program outcome (Holland & Petschers, 1987; Tripodi, 1987).

Results can be immediately demonstrated in short-term programs with limited goals and objectives. It is more difficult and more complex to demonstrate any immediate results in long-term programs that are designed to affect multiple problems within individuals and families. Community organization projects have a similar difficulty, as well as additional environmental factors that would further complicate cause and effect. Neighborhood groups that have mobilized to find their own solutions and develop programs to meet their unique needs get caught in the bureaucratic tangle. As a result, the continuum of services that is implicit in the definition of social services becomes further eroded (Austin, 1987; Coulton, 1987; Tropman, 1987).

The public–private partnership of service provision and resource allocation is unresponsive to the needs of the whole person, the family as a unit, or the unique needs of the community. The lack of direction, comprehensiveness, and continuity in service provision and planning creates an environment in which the needs of the bureaucracy seem to supersede the needs of the individuals and communities it is meant to serve (Morris, 1987; Yankey, 1987).

Social policy is defined in the *Social Work Dictionary* (Barker, 1991) as

> the activities and principles of a society that guide the way it intervenes in and regulates relationships between individuals, groups, communities, and social institutions. These principles and activities are the result of the society's values and customs and largely determine the distribution of *resources* and level of well-being of its people (p. 220; italics in original).

In a democratic society, the social services system exists to assist families and individuals in making optimal use of existing resources and opportunities to sustain and enhance their social functioning in a highly complex social and physical environment. Historically, social work has developed from a social reform orientation and individual-oriented change. This has given the profession its unique perception of the individual in the context of family and environment. The traditional base of social work practice, casework, group work, and community organiza-

tion reflects those interrelationships (Gilbert & Specht, 1987; Maroney, 1987).

Social work education and training have expanded to include other theoretical models and methods in response to family and individual needs and societal change. Social work should play a paramount role in the provision and planning of social services (Austin, 1987; Yankey, 1987).

ISSUE STATEMENT

There is a glaring absence of a national policy defining the need, significance, and role of social services in the United States. These activities form a complex system that is continuously influenced and bounded by social, economic, and political forces on the national, state, and local levels, and the social services system is in a chronically reactive position to these forces.

Services are established and provided in an unsystematic, fragmented manner; individuals and families become compartmentalized by problems; and resources are allocated by categories. Implicit decisions are made as to who is eligible for service, under what circumstances services are to be offered, and the duration of services. Self-determining families and individuals with the equal right to succeed or to fail have the right to accept or reject services. Because income is often used as an eligibility criterion, services are not uniformly available or accessible. (Accessibility includes the ability of a client to physically reach the service provider. This issue is central to any policy and planning because it often is a major barrier [Kahn, 1987; Morris, 1987].)

Within such context, social services are provided at the point of breakdown, and prevailing knowledge and concepts on prevention are improperly used. Emphasis is placed on short-term solutions, demonstration projects, and discrete programs. There is a continuing debate on the definitions of prevention and the efficacy of treatment, as if each were totally independent. Core services that provide the foundation for a comprehensive system are seriously impaired by funding cuts and inconsistent policy decisions that are sometimes at cross-purposes (Kahn, 1987; Yankey, 1987).

The objective, then, is the development of a new comprehensive social services system in the United States that will assist families and individuals efficiently to sustain and enhance their social functioning in a given community.

POLICY STATEMENT

Social services are services provided through therapy, case management, resource management, and interventions that address the identified needs of any individual as a member of a family within a community. Services empower individuals, groups, and communities to achieve self-sufficiency and interrelatedness so that the family and community function to establish a quality of life that sustains the society's ability to renew itself (Kahn, 1987; Morris, 1987).

NASW advocates the following principles:

Right to Services

Social services shall be available to all people as a right. Eligibility for social services is present when a reasonable request is made to a practitioner who, or social services agency that, possesses required skills to meet the request, subject to the willingness of the recipient to make a reasonable investment in the service. Availability of services may be subject to community priorities when the community has identified them as recommended or discretionary. However, when services are imposed by courts, considered mandatory, or based on needs that may result in significant life changes for an individual or family, such services shall be available in a timely manner and according to best practice standards. Appropriate private administrative review and reasonable subsidy shall be available in instances in which the service is imposed by court action or mandated by public law.

Comprehensive Services

The social services system must develop a broad spectrum of public and private services to meet the short- and long-term services requests and needs of individuals, groups, or families. No single service or continuum of services shall be prescribed or mandated as the sole option when services are imposed. Alternatives for consumers, access and movement from one service to another, and specific competency to fulfill defined purposes should be included in services systems that are supported by public funds to any degree. Informed consent and consumer participation in selection of services must be ensured.

Universality

Services must be accessible, attainable, and offered in a way that encourages voluntary use. No arbitrary criteria, including gender, marital status, sexual orientation, disability, religion, political views, race, and ethnic and national origin, shall be exercised to limit services access. Services shall be connected through proficient referral mechanisms to comprehensive services programs to prevent the fragmentation of services delivery and to ensure availability of all services to such special target groups.

Consumer Sovereignty

The use of social services presumes some appropriate dependency by the consumer. Mechanisms must assure that each consumer has informed self-determination regarding choice of services, protection of individuality, and ability to participate in policy matters, if not directly, then through selected or assigned advocates. Confidentiality is not absolute but dictates that sharing of information is done at all times in the best interest of those served.

Accountability

The social services system must contain the mechanisms to provide maximum accountability. Funding sources, policy-making bodies, administrators, service personnel, and consumers should obtain regular and precise information about the operations, trends, problems, and results of the services that are delivered.

Provisions for the rapid retrieval of data to monitor the quality, quantity, and impact of services are necessary to achieve accountability. However, they should not be used at the expense of the consumer's right to service. Social workers must take a more active leadership role in developing accountability systems.

Simplicity and Efficiency

Systems to establish accountability for social services must be designed to ensure simplicity of procedures and administration. Required documentation should be limited to what is essential. Systems for accountability should not become ends in themselves.

Establishment of Policies and Priorities

Establishment of policies and priorities for the social services system must include active participation of social work professionals. Policy design and standard setting must include consumers and the community at large, in addition to organizational representatives. Social workers should take the initiative in facilitating broad participation in the design of policy, and priority setting in the social services should reflect the principle of full participation.

Planning and Evaluation

To ensure competent and responsible delivery of social services, guarantee accountability, and meet developing needs, the planning and evaluation processes must involve social work professionals, agency managers, the community, and the consumer.

Advocacy

Social workers should support ombudspersons and other advocacy mechanisms. The client is entitled to service, and social workers should participate in assuring that services are appropriately provided.

Multiple Providers: Public, Private, and Voluntary

The social services system must include multiple types and levels of providers, as well as prominent roles for federal, state, and local governments, to meet various needs. The professional expertise of social workers must be integrated into the decision-making process at all levels.

Financing

Financing of the social services system is the joint responsibility of all citizens and all levels of government. Public–private partnerships should be facilitated to enhance these services. It is essential that social workers advocate for adequate funding.

Coordinated Services

Applicants and clients should be informed of available services and resources. Providers of services should collaborate with input from recipients of services to assure that appropriate nonduplicated services are provided.

REFERENCES

Austin, D. M. (1987). Social planning in the public sector. In A. Minahan (Ed.-in-Chief), *Encyclopedia of social work* (18th ed., Vol. 2, pp. 620–625). Silver Spring, MD: National Association of Social Workers.

Barker, R. L. (Ed.). (1991). *The social work dictionary* (2nd ed.). Washington, DC: NASW Press.

Brieland, D. (1987). History and evolution of social work practice; In A. Minahan (Ed.-in-Chief), *Encyclopedia of social work* (18th ed., Vol. 1, pp. 739–754). Silver Spring, MD: National Association of Social Workers.

Coulton, C. J. (1987). Quality assurance. In A. Minahan (Ed.-in-Chief), *Encyclopedia of social work* (18th ed., Vol. 2, pp. 443–445). Silver Spring, MD: National Association of Social Workers.

Gilbert, N., & Specht, H. (1987). Social planning and community organization. In A. Minahan (Ed.-in-Chief), *Encyclopedia of social work* (18th ed., Vol. 2, pp. 602–619). Silver Spring, MD: National Association of Social Workers.

Holland, T. P., & Petschers, M. K. (1987). Organizations: Context for social service delivery. In A. Minahan (Ed.-in-Chief), *Encyclopedia of social work* (18th ed., Vol. 2, pp. 204–214). Silver Spring, MD: National Association of Social Workers.

Kahn A. J. (1987). Social problems and issues: Theories and definitions. In A. Minahan (Ed.-in-Chief), *Encyclopedia of social work* (18th ed.,

Vol. 2, pp. 632–644). Silver Spring, MD: National Association of Social Workers.

Leiby, J. (1987). History of social welfare. In A. Minahan (Ed.-in-Chief), *Encyclopedia of social work* (18th ed., Vol. 1, pp. 755–777). Silver Spring, MD: National Association of Social Workers.

Loarenbrack, G., & Keys, P. (1987). Settlements and neighborhood centers. In A. Minahan (Ed.-in-Chief), *Encyclopedia of social work* (18th ed., Vol. 2, pp. 556–561). Silver Spring, MD: National Association of Social Workers.

Maroney, R. M. (1987). Social planning. In A. Minahan (Ed.-in-Chief), *Encyclopedia of social work* (18th ed., Vol. 2, pp. 593–602). Silver Spring, MD: National Association of Social Workers.

Morris, R. (1987). Social welfare policy: Trends and issues. In A. Minahan (Ed.-in-Chief), *Encyclopedia of social work* (18th ed., Vol. 2, pp. 664–681). Silver Spring, MD: National Association of Social Workers.

Tripodi, T. (1987). Program evaluation. In A. Minahan (Ed.-in-Chief), *Encyclopedia of social work* (18th ed., Vol. 2, pp. 366–379). Silver Spring, MD: National Association of Social Workers.

Tropman, J. E. (1987). Policy analysis: Methods and techniques. In A. Minahan (Ed.-in-Chief), *Encyclopedia of social work* (18th ed., Vol. 2, pp. 268–283). Silver Spring, MD: National Association of Social Workers.

Wenocur, S. (1987). Social planning in the voluntary sector. In A. Minahan (Ed.-in-Chief), *Encyclopedia of social work* (18th ed., Vol. 2, pp. 625–632). Silver Spring, MD: National Association of Social Workers.

Yankey, J. (1987). Public social services. In A. Minahan (Ed.-in-Chief), *Encyclopedia of social work* (18th ed., Vol. 2, pp. 417–426). Silver Spring, MD: National Association of Social Workers.

Policy statement approved by the NASW Delegate Assembly, August 1993. This statement supersedes the policy statement on Social Services approved by the Delegate Assembly in 1975. For further information, contact the National Association of Social Workers, 750 First Street, NE, Suite 700, Washington, DC 20002-4241. Telephone: 202-408-8600 or 800-638-8799.

Social Work in Home Health Care

BACKGROUND

Home health care has a rich history of providing nursing and auxiliary services to the sick and dying in their own homes. In 1966, the implementation of Title XVIII legislation, under which the Medicare program developed, resulted in the creation of certified home health agencies nationwide. The legislation also provided a structure in which these participating providers of home health care would be reimbursed for skilled care given to eligible beneficiaries according to specific guidelines. In addition to Medicare (a primary coverage for the majority of patients receiving home health care), Medicaid and private health insurance companies also reimburse certified home health agencies on a per visit basis for eligible individuals. Certified home health agencies can provide skilled nursing, physical therapy, occupational therapy, speech pathology, medical social work services, home health aide services, and auxiliary services. Under the present home health care system, medical social work service is not considered a primary skilled service independently reimbursable by Medicare and other health insurances.

In June 1986, NASW established the Home Health Care Work Group, a subgroup of the NASW Commission on Health and Mental Health. In doing so, NASW took a definitive stand on the importance of social work as an integral and key component of home health care.

As of July 1, 1989, Medicare regulations identified family counseling, when related to the improvement of the patient's medical condition, as a reimbursable activity of social workers in home health care. This regulation was the result of intensive and coordinated efforts by NASW and the Home Care Work Group to influence and change the Health Care Finance Administration's position and interpretation of the Medicare regulation. This joint effort illustrates the leadership that social workers must continue to take in setting standards and developing policies that will ensure consumers equitable access to and participation in home care services.

Home care social workers are in a unique position to address, and perhaps bridge, the gap between the issues of quality and cost in the delivery of health care services. Too often, patients, particularly elderly people, tend to rely on expensive medical intervention in an attempt to resolve related social and emotional problems. By addressing the psychosocial needs of the patient that interfere with the treatment plan or the patient's rate of recovery, home care social workers are able to prevent unnecessary medical costs.

■ Data suggest that early social work assessment and intervention in home care expedite shorter periods of skilled nursing and other medical services.

■ Social work services, which address the social and emotional problems that negatively affect the patient's response to treatment, increase the patient's ability to stay at home, thus preventing rehospitalization or other costly types of institutionalization.

■ Social work services that strengthen the family and other support systems and provide a link to needed community resources stabilize the caregiver system and further promote recovery in the home.

The goal of medical social work services in home health care is to improve or maintain the social, emotional, functional, and physical health status of the patient; to enhance the capabilities and coping skills of the family and other caregiver systems; and to ensure that the patient's needs are being met in the home environment. The social worker is uniquely qualified to take leadership as a primary, not ancillary, deliverer of home care services.

The role and responsibilities of the home care social worker include the following:

■ *Assessment of social and emotional factors:* skilled assessment of social and emotional factors related to the patient's illness, need for care, response to treatment, and adjustment to care, followed by care plan development

■ *Counseling for long-range planning and decision making:* assessment of the patient's need for long-term care, including evaluation of the home and family situation, requirements for enabling the patient and family to develop an in-home care plan, and arrangement for placement

■ *Community resource planning:* the promotion of community-centered services, including education, advocacy, referral, and linkage

■ *Short-term therapy:* goal-oriented intervention directed toward management of a terminal illness, reactions and adjustment to illness, strengthening the family's support system, and the resolution of conflict related to the chronicity of illness

■ *Other:* other medical social services related to the patient's illness and his or her need for care and to problems associated with indicators of high risk that endanger the patient's mental and physical health, including abuse or neglect, inadequate food or medical supplies, and high potential for suicide.

The professional social worker, by training and perspective, can offer leadership in the entire case management process. Health services, social supports, counseling, and the like should be seen as core services; social work should function in a primary, reimbursable, and managerial role.

ISSUE STATEMENT

Medicare

Three problems severely impede the effective provision of home care social work services to eligible Medicare patients. These problems limit the availability of needed services to the population currently receiving home health care and, if unresolved, promise to affect an even greater population. The diagnosis-related group (DRG) payment system in Medicare promotes the earlier discharge of hospitalized Medicare patients; consequently, a growing number of Medicare patients require home health care. Furthermore, the growing population of elderly people demands increased provision of home health services.

1. *Relationship to qualifying service.* Home care social work services may be provided only after the opening of a case by a qualifying service, that is, nursing, speech pathology, or physical therapy. Also, the services must be terminated before the closing of the qualifying service.

The historical failure of the Medicare program and other health insurances to recognize medical social services as independently reimbursable in home health care has had serious social, financial, and professional implications for both beneficiaries and providers. With the July 1990 amendment to Medicare, Part B, recognizing social work as a reimbursable service, positive change seems possible, but the full effects remain unclear at this time.

■ Patients receive fractured services because the social worker's entrance into a case is delayed. Services also suffer from premature and, at times, unplanned termination.

■ Because of the pressure of home care agencies to limit service, social workers are not always able to facilitate the provision of supportive services in the time allowed. Worse yet, referrals for social work intervention are not made at all. As a result, the linkage of patients to entitlements and community resources often is not completed.

■ Because homebound patients cannot gain access to home care, community clinics and community agencies are severely limited in their ability to provide in-home counseling. Therefore, patients often are hospitalized for primarily psychosocial, not medical, reasons, and the costs of their medical care are increased.

■ For isolated, frail elderly people, the home care social worker is often the only link to community services. If long-term needs are not met, the patient will not continue to be as independent as possible and will again require more frequent medical services.

■ Qualifying services, particularly nursing, are pressured to postpone the discharge date of patients so that social workers can complete their interventions, thus adding additional costs. Conversely, qualifying services often are forced to open cases so the social worker can intervene for identified social problems, not medical ones, again adding to the costs.

■ The secondary-service status for home care social work jeopardizes professional values. Home care workers are in the challenging position of attempting to straddle the growing gap between the increased needs of the home care population and the decreased availability of community support services. Medicare's secondary-service designation for social work is yet another impediment to the home care worker's ability to address patients' needs effectively. Home care social workers are struggling to adhere to social work values and maintain their professionalism against unrelated reimbursement factors that impinge and even threaten their practice.

2. *Contradictions about reimbursable services.* State and regional intermediaries provide contradictory definitions of *legitimate,* and therefore, reimbursable home health social work services. The lack of clarity and uniformity in the reimbursement of home health social work services under Medicare creates confusion among providers and affects the provision of needed services to home care patients.

■ This inconsistent interpretation of reimbursable social work services in home health care has led to increased denials of reimbursement for social work activities and to a defensive posture by provider agencies that fear that social work services will not be reimbursed. Fearing denials,

agencies minimize the involvement of social workers or expect nurses to perform social work tasks.

■ Intermediaries have made arbitrary determinations of the types of home health social work services that may be reimbursed by Medicare. In some parts of the country, they have imposed arbitrary limits on the number of visits a social worker may make per home health case. (In some instances, intermediaries have restricted the visits to as few as one to two per case.) These decisions severely limit the services to which the Medicare beneficiary is entitled.

3. *Contradictions about "assessment only" visits.* Some intermediaries are reimbursing or denying Medicare reimbursement for "assessment only" visits by home health social workers. An "assessment only" visit is defined as a one-time visit in which the social and emotional needs and functioning of the patient and support system are evaluated and recommendations for services are made. Beyond the skilled assessment activity, the social worker provides no other services and makes no follow-up visits.

■ In some cases, an initial assessment visit by the social worker will identify potential problems before they have an effect on the patient's medical condition. Early detection and response to environmental, social, and emotional problems are preventive; therefore, they are effective and economical in the long run.

In addition, the Health Care Finance Administration published a notification that Medicare will not reimburse medical social workers for time spent in helping clients complete Medicaid application forms. This provision, which impedes the home care social workers' ability to assist their clients in obtaining needed community resources, should be revoked.

Medicaid

Although the Medicare program recognizes the role of social work services in home health, approximately 95 percent of the states do not reimburse social work services in home care funded through Medicaid. Medicaid law does not include a specific benefit for medical social services. However, the current waiver provision for home and community-based care under Medicaid does suggest the allowability of these services:

(4) A waiver under this section may, consistent with paragraph (2), provide medical assistance to individuals for case management services, homemaker/home health aide services and personal care services, adult day health services, respite care, and other medical and social services that can contribute to the health and well-being of individuals and their ability to reside in a community-based care setting. (Section 1915 (d) (4), Social Security Act).

State Medicaid agencies have indicated that they think it is impossible for them to cover home care social work services because there is no federal provision for the coverage. In addition, a federal Medicaid guideline reportedly states that coverage of home care social work would be a duplication of services already provided by state agencies. (In some states, the state suggests that "social workers" with the state's Department of Human Resources should provide these services. The problem is that state agencies often use the term *social worker* to refer to individuals who are not professionally trained as social workers. Furthermore, "social workers" from state agencies do not work in multidisciplinary health care teams. In contrast, Medicare regulations specifically identify a qualified social worker, for the purposes of home health care, as an individual who has a master's degree in social work from an accredited program and possesses one year of experience in a health care setting.)

The ideal remedy for the problem would be for the Medicaid statute to specify which medical social services benefits are to be provided by qualified social workers. An alternative would be to include report language in the Medicaid statute indicating that medical social services are, indeed, allowable in home health care under Medicaid and that these services should be provided by a qualified social worker. Although the alternative is not as strong as an insertion in the law itself, it should enable advocates at the state level to encourage states to provide the services.

POLICY STATEMENT

Resolving the identified problems that interfere with the effective provision of home care social work services will serve to support patients and their caregiver systems who wish to continue health care in the home. Resolving the problems also will promote the cost-effective provision of home health care. NASW recommends that these problems be resolved by

■ granting skilled status to medical social work services under Medicare, thus establishing social work intervention as a qualifying service in home health

■ specifying a clear and uniform delineation of home health social work services that are reimbursable under Medicare

■ recognizing assessment and follow-up services, including case management by a home health social worker, as a skilled, reimbursable service under Medicare

■ recognizing medical social work services as a reimbursable benefit under Medicaid

■ Monitoring implementation of the July 1990 amendment to Medicare, Part B, and advancing professional autonomy for home care social workers.

Social workers should provide increased support and advocacy to ensure the successful passage of federal legislation addressing these needs. Home care social workers must be allowed to provide the level of professional care that home care patients require.

Policy statement approved by the NASW Delegate Assembly, August 1990. Referred to the 1999 Delegate Assembly, to be revised and combined with the policy statement on Health Care. This policy statement supersedes the policy statement on Social Work in Home Health Care approved by the Delegate Assembly in 1981. For further information, contact the National Association of Social Workers, 750 First Street, NE, Suite 700, Washington, DC 20002-4241. Telephone: 202-408-8600 or 800-638-8799.

Social Work in Rural Areas

BACKGROUND

Social work has its roots in urban America. Opportunities for casework, group work, and community organization practice came as a result of increased industrialization and urbanization and in response to social reformers who abhorred the effect of the city on people. Early social work educational programs were located in institutions and major population centers. Rural areas were considered "pristine" and "folksy."

The stereotype of rural areas was predominant until the Great Depression, when workers in the Federal Emergency Relief Administration/Works Progress Administration and the Agricultural Assistance Administration helped dispel many of the myths about rural "bliss." In 1967, the National Advisory Commission on Rural Poverty issued *The People Left Behind*. The Great Society and the War on Poverty programs of the 1960s further developed an awareness of the needs of rural people.

Despite the orientation of new governmental programs toward minority and low-income people in urban areas, few human service jobs were included for rural areas. The Community Mental Health Act of 1964 and the upgrading of the social services section of the Public Welfare Law also increased opportunities for social services practitioners in rural areas, although the involvement of professional social work continued to be limited.

Thus, the underlying social problems of rural America were ignored in favor of the more visible problems of the cities. As a consequence, small towns and nonmetropolitan areas continue to have hard-core social problems, some of which (poverty, poor health care, and lack of adequate housing) are more prevalent in rural than in metropolitan areas.

Although federal concern over rural areas increased in the late 1970s, policies more frequently addressed the "rediscovered countryside" and have not been substantially more effective in resolving rural problems. The Agricultural Extension Service often has been considered the "helping hand" and "watchful eye" of rural areas, but the literature documents that the Agricultural Extension Service has benefited wealthy groups in rural areas and the big corporate sector involved in agriculture at the expense of the small farmer, poor people, and rural minorities.

Rural America is just as diverse in its racial and ethnic composition as is metropolitan America. Rural areas contain a significant number of African Americans, primarily in the rural South; many Hispanics, primarily Chicanos, outside metropolitan areas in the Southwest and West, and primarily Puerto Ricans, in rural areas of the East; and Native Americans, who have always been a predominantly rural minority. Furthermore, Asian Americans are beginning to settle in rural areas. Migrant farmworkers constitute what might be called another rural minority group, and the special conditions of women in rural areas make this group a minority group as well. Naturally, rural America has always counted a large number of white ethnic groups who also differ from each other in their history, culture, religion, and characteristics.

In the 1970s, social work decried the lack of federal attention to rural issues on various legislative fronts. Since then, the situation has improved significantly as a result of a variety of indigenous rural groups working vigorously for new and better legislation. The 1980 amendments to the Rural Development Act of 1972 established the position of undersecretary of agriculture for small community and rural development. Rurally oriented groups at the national and local levels should be able to continue to exert influence and improve conditions for rural people through these newly created avenues. Social workers must become alert to these developments and work, preferably through coalitions with other groups, on behalf of their rural constituencies.

In addition, national events, particularly those related to energy and natural resources, are making rural development a key area of interest and concern. Social work has the potential for looking at such development, not just from an economic perspective but from a cultural and social perspective, as well.

Rural America is rapidly changing, and new population migrations from urban to rural areas will soon transform rural life. Social work can no longer limit itself to addressing the neglect of rural issues, but must become involved in questions of conservation and responsible development of the rural areas of this country.

ISSUE STATEMENT

Services and Education

An increasing number of social services jobs are becoming available in small towns and nonmetropolitan areas. Yet, the design of these programs and their administrative regulations often are based either on an urban bias or on a misrepresentation of the reality of rural life. Furthermore, in rural employment, social work is often an unknown profession. Many rural areas are still unaware of the roles played by social workers who have master of social work (MSW) and bachelor of social work (BSW) degrees or are unable to compete for qualified personnel. Thus, social services personnel in rural areas often are not professional social workers. Social work has a responsibility to identify for public and private employers the skills that well-trained social workers at all levels can bring to jobs.

Social workers who find positions in rural areas usually come from urban areas; sometimes they are unable to offer their reluctant employers significant expertise in rural issues. These social workers require continuing education and

retraining to make significant contributions to the rural milieu. The rural practice setting is markedly different from urban settings in the areas of tasks, clients' characteristics, social and physical environments, and the roles of social workers. Experience has shown that urban-trained social workers have difficulty applying their knowledge to rural practice and must adapt their practice model significantly to do a credible job in rural areas. Conversely, urban social workers are often not prepared to deal with problems of people from rural areas who move to cities. Although rural outmigration is now abating, there will continue to be pockets of rural people in the large cities for years to come.

Although a few schools of social work have recently developed an educational focus on rural areas, the constrictions on accredition by the Council on Social Work Education and other impediments have tended to stagnate rurally oriented curricula that are aimed at specific locales and are rich in relevant rural material. Social workers should encourage the identification and inclusion of rural content in both BSW and MSW programs.

Health Care

The rural and urban health care delivery systems require great modifications. Although urban health care is often inadequate, rural systems frequently do not exist. Medical, nutritional, home care, and other health services are less accessible to rural residents. Dental care is a major problem for the rural poor because only large dental schools run dental clinics and many counties in rural states provide no dental care for the rural poor.

Transportation

Federal and state transportation policies always have shown a marked bias for urban areas. Attention and funding have been focused primarily on urban mass transit systems; a paucity of attention has been given to the unique transportation needs of rural areas. Gasoline shortages and costs limit the access to services and facilities even for the rural car owner. Those who, for reason of poverty, physical or mental impairment, age, or other reasons, do not have immediate access to an automobile or other forms of transportation suffer serious deprivations. The elderly population continues to grow in rural areas; hence, innovative ways must be found for transporting senior citizens. For example, other countries have been successful in using government-owned or subsidized transportation to remedy the mobility problems of the rural poor. Ways must be found to gather national resources of this country on behalf of the rural dweller without transportation.

Housing and Land Ownership

Rural residents always have had housing problems because of the unavailability of and ill repair of housing. The new flood of migrants from urban areas has caused the price of land and property to rise, to the further disadvantage of the rural poor. The ability of the poor, especially minorities, to purchase and retain ownership of land is an ever-increasing dilemma, severely aggravated by the introduction of new tax structures and the rising influence of agribusiness.

The rental and ownership of mobile homes, which have been viewed as an answer to the rural housing shortages since World War II, continue to be plagued by difficulties. Often, there are no regulations regarding conditions in trailer parks. The Department of Housing and Urban Development and state housing authorities should be encouraged to develop regulations that set a minimum standard for mobile homes.

Schools and Post Offices

It has been amply documented that rural schools, shops, and post offices are not only services but also social centers that are crucial to the life of communities. The closing and consolidating of rural schools, shops, and post offices for financial and technical reasons is eroding the quality of life in and capacity to survive of many communities. Social workers must recognize publicly the complementarity of social institutions. Bigger is not always better, and development does not always mean progress.

Women

Rural women often have been overlooked when social work has formulated goals and policies regarding women. In addition to the different class and cultural concerns of urban and rural women, rural women are faced with a variety of other environmental problems. Geographic isolation, a lack of resources, and expensive and frequently inadequate transportation, to name a few, combine to make the needs and desires of rural women different. Social work must be finely tuned to the cultural and local mores of women in a variety of geographic settings.

Economic Policy

Public policy continues to spur industrial development in rural areas to improve economic opportunities and meet the demands of market forces for material resources. Still, rural populations have not obtained the expected advantages because large-scale nonindigenous industries do not necessarily draw from local labor pools. The problems are compounded by the fragmented policies and programs of the federal government that often hinder local capacity-building efforts because they represent excessive administrative burdens and costs at the local level, a lack of flexibility to respond to local needs and opportunities, and a limited ability to involve private individuals and groups in developmental efforts. (The goals of economic policy in rural communities should include a flexible regulatory approach by the government, recognition of the contribution of traditional local economies, and support for community-based organizations.)

Energy

Rural communities in every region bear a special burden as energy resources (such as coal, shale oil, and water) are developed. Boom towns are of special concern because they are ill prepared to manage rapid growth. Moreover, they are not receiving adequate assistance from state and federal governments, energy companies, universities, and professional organizations and are bearing a disproportionate amount of the burden created by the energy crisis. Therefore, fiscal and professional aid in planning for and coping with such growth should be provided by federal and state governments.

In addition to the rising cost of transportation, the rural poor are paying a disproportionate share of their income for fuel, particularly in those climates where fuel for heat can be an issue of survival. The poor, the aged, and hard-to-reach groups in rural areas are often uninformed about energy-saving devices. Although federal programs have addressed the energy crisis in areas such as "weatherization," the funding for technical assistance and educational and outreach services has been grossly inadequate.

Employment

According to the U.S. Department of Labor, employment in farm areas continues to decline sharply, whereas employment in rural nonfarm areas is rising, but more slowly than for the nation as a whole. In most of rural America, industrial development and demographic trends have not increased the prospects for rural employment. Moreover, federal policy still emphasizes income transfer strategies, rather than job creation for low-income rural people. Public policy should support local job creation strategies in rural communities and attendant job training. Steady long-term economic development, a priority for rural populations, should capitalize on local small-scale industry, crafts, home-based employment, tourism, and whatever other resources can be tapped at the local level.

Mental Health

Most of rural America is unserved and underserved by mental health programs. Because values are an integral part of a culture, the emotional experience of illness in a rural area requires a different type of intervention from what is needed in urban communities. Low population density, combined with a shortage of trained health, mental health, and human services personnel, hinders the effective delivery of services. It is important for the social work profession to identify natural helping networks, to consider them an important resource, and to work with them in the delivery of services. Mental health legislation should foster a sensitivity to the rural environment, rural people, and rural needs. The focus of the Mental Health Systems

Act on giving priority to the unserved and underserved is an important step toward promoting the organization of mental health programs in rural areas.

Rural Minorities

Rural America is as diverse in its racial and ethnic composition as is metropolitan America. Racial and ethnic minorities and lesbian and gay people in rural areas have particular difficulty in obtaining full access to the goods and services that exist in their communities. In addition, specialized services focusing on the unique needs of these groups in rural areas are extremely limited.

POLICY STATEMENT

NASW continues to lobby for recognition of and the delivery of services to racial and ethnic minorities, migrant workers, women, people with disabilities, lesbian and gay people, older people, and other people at risk who have been left out of the mainstream of existing services delivery systems or funding patterns. In the 1990s, social work should play an important role as advocate for the empowerment of people in rural areas.

The profession must influence the public policies of the federal, state, and local governments that affect the development and reorientation of the services delivery system in rural areas. Social work must stress the unique needs of local communities and work for legislation and regulations whose administration is flexible and can be adjusted to the specific needs of a locality. The profession also must continue to work for the development of legislation on licensing in rural states and for the implementation of the requirements for continuing education in licensing.

NASW supports rural social work educators' efforts to incorporate rural content into the curricula of schools of social work, within the context of the present or future accreditation requirements of the Council on Social Work Education. The content of this curricula should additionally address the unique needs of physically and mentally impaired, ethnic and cultural minorities, women, lesbian and gay people, older people, religious minorities, people who are unmarried, children, those who live alone, and those with language barriers in the rural environment.

Social work should continue to work for appropriate and broadly based legislation and regulations on health care, transportation, employment, and housing for rural America. Social work must develop further expertise in and become more involved in issues related to the ownership and retention of land. It must advocate for the needs of disadvantaged rural populations on these issues. Moreover, the profession must refine its position vis-à-vis rural development, taking into account social issues and the survival of rural lifestyles, as well as those of economic growth. Thus, it is incumbent on the profession to have appropriate knowledge of the diverse needs, norms, and values of rural men, women, and children.

Policy statement approved by the NASW Delegate Assembly, August 1993. This policy statement supersedes the policy statement on Social Work in Rural Areas approved by the Delegate Assembly in 1981. For further information, contact the National Association of Social Workers, 750 First Street, NE, Suite 700, Washington, DC 20002-4241. Telephone: 202-408-8600 or 800-638-8799.

Social Work Practice in the Health Care Field

BACKGROUND

Health care, in its broadest sense, is the largest field of social work practice. According to the 1987 NASW Membership Data Bank Survey, about half the members of NASW work in this field. Social workers have been involved in this field since before the turn of the century. The profession's earliest concerns were with making health care services available to the poor and improving social conditions associated with the breeding of infectious diseases, such as tuberculosis. Later, social work's role expanded. By the 1950s, when the delivery of health care services became comprehensive, social workers took their place beside other health care professionals who were concerned with the delivery of high-quality services. Today, social workers can be found in every area of the health care system.

NASW has issued public policy statements on health care, as well as professional-issue statements on social work practice in health care. These statements have included a comprehensive public policy statement on national health policy; professional-issue statements about the role of social workers in such health care settings as long-term care, health maintenance organizations, and home health care, or with physically or mentally vulnerable groups such as people with disabilities, deinstitutionalized mentally ill people, and others; and the *NASW Standards for Social Work in Health Care Settings.*

The rise of nontraditional therapies and growing feelings of territoriality among health care professionals create pressure on social workers to define how their particular education and values contribute to the quality of the care they provide. Social work's historical advocacy skills and commitment to the interests and participation of clients are crucial to assure clients' rights of autonomy, self-determination, and access to care. Furthermore, in social work, as in all professions in the health care field, there has been a proliferation of subspecialists. These subspecialists include, for example, the hospice worker, the health planner for maternity and infant care programs, and the alcoholism–drug counselor. To guide the future development of subspecialties, the profession needs an integrated and comprehensive statement that draws together their ethics, standards, and practice functions. NASW must assume leadership in defining the role of social workers in health care and the value of social work to society.

ISSUE STATEMENT

The issues to be addressed are the following:

■ a description of social work in health care that is broad enough to describe the commonalities of practice in related settings

■ an enumeration of common social work roles and functions in the health care field, spanning practice in institutional and noninstitutional settings.

POLICY STATEMENT

Social Work's Commitment to and Involvement in Health Care

The well-being of all Americans is determined, in large measure, by their health status. The fulfillment of each person's potential usually depends on maintaining good physical and mental health or in having the necessary supports to compensate for disability. Because of their commitment to such goals, social workers have been active participants in the development of health policy and health care programs since the inception of the profession in the nineteenth century. Social workers recognize the need for a social environment that supports all people, regardless of income, race, ethnicity, religious adherence, gender, sexual orientation, or disabling condition. They recognize the right of all people to adequate health care, as well as to adequate income, housing, and food. Therefore, social workers who practice in a variety of settings in which their efforts are directed to helping individuals, families, and communities realize their personal and social aspirations and contributing to the common good.

Good physical and mental health is the product of an environment that is free of toxicity and the availability of personal health care services for maintaining and restoring health. Good health begins with prevention: a supportive environment, opportunity for optimum development in utero and after birth, adequate nutrition, wellness training, and support for the loss of functioning in the frail elderly. When necessary, personal health care services to overcome illness and the effects of accidents maintain health at an optimum level. When loss of function because of physical or mental disability results in impairment, the individual requires care and services to maintain functional and social capacity.

Social Component in Health Care and the Role of Social Work

The ability of people to maintain health, recover from illness, and overcome disabling conditions depends on their strength and capacity to use their social and physical environment. These two elements—strength and capacity (rather than pathology)—and the social context are critical to maintaining health and overcoming illness. The assessment of strengths and of social supports are the major tools of social workers who are strategists in prevention and health care. The unique role of social workers is to help people understand and use their strengths, their relationships, and their social environment to maintain and enhance their

autonomy, social roles, and optimum functional capacity.

The social work profession is committed to action for those who are vulnerable or powerless. At the same time, social workers appreciate the complexity of the person-in-situation equation and provide necessary planning and services to clients, regardless of their social status. Discharge planning, which facilitates effective aftercare, is essential to the future of any person who is admitted to a hospital or specialty care facility for physical or mental illness. Thus, social workers are an integral part of the health care and mental health care delivery systems, which include, but are not limited to, acute, transitional, long-term, and rehabilitative care and services.

Discharge Planning

The discharge-planning process incorporates the specialized skills of many disciplines. However, social work's unique person-in-situation perspective, clinical skills, and systems expertise propels the profession into a central leadership role.

NASW recommends that social work practitioners with advanced degrees and experience in health care settings should manage and supervise discharge-planning functions in all health care settings.

NASW strongly recommends that organizations recruit, select, and retain professional social workers to assume discharge-planning responsibilities. NASW recognizes that the discharge-planning process requires skilled clinicians to address the complexity of psychosocial issues that emerge during that process. In areas where there is a shortage of professionally trained social workers, NASW recommends that qualified and experienced social work professionals act as consultants to and developers of programs until professional social workers can be recruited to serve as principals in the discharge-planning process.

NASW strongly urges schools of social work, at both the baccalaureate and graduate levels, to include in their curricula the specific knowledge, methods, and techniques of the continuity-of-care model that is reflected in sound discharge planning.

New Technologies and the Implications for Social Work

The range of human problems and needs addressed by the health care system is ever expanding as new discoveries and technology increase society's capacity to maintain health and improve functioning. These discoveries and technology frequently result in new areas of specialization for providers of care. Although social workers serve in a variety of new specialty areas, their basic role, responsibilities, and method of delivering services must remain consistent with accepted social work practice. To this basic role they will need to add knowledge and skills to serve the particular needs and demands of specialized populations and specialty areas.

NASW supports social work research activities that will break new ground, advance the social work professional's knowledge and skills, and contribute to the education of other health professionals, consumers, and legislators.

These same new discoveries and technologies give rise to new ethical dilemmas and challenges. Social workers must address these often-conflicting values by incorporating social work principles.

Social Work's Contribution to the Health Care Field

Social workers contribute to the care of patients, the development and administration of programs, research, and expanded public understanding about meeting health care needs. They also advocate on behalf of patients and for a better health care delivery system. This collective professional experience is refined through NASW programs and is returned to the profession through formal and informal educational channels.

The social work profession uses this expanded knowledge and these refined skills to promulgate standards of practice, recommend health policy, improve social health programs, and ensure sound practice. The following are examples of such activities:

■ *Practice standards: NASW Standards for Social Work in Health Care Settings* were approved by the NASW Board of Directors in 1981. These stan-

dards are reviewed and updated regularly to address emerging issues and concerns. For example, in 1987, specialized standards were added for treatment settings for home health care.

■ *Health policy:* Social workers are involved in activities to support policies that seek to create a healthful environment and services that promote and maintain health for all people.

■ *Health care programs and policies:* Health care is delivered in a variety of institutional and community settings, as well as in the home, and is financed through a variety of mechanisms. As socially oriented professionals working in health care settings and programs, social workers have a responsibility to ensure that the quality of life of patients is not compromised by inadequate or insufficient health care. Health care should be affordable, humane, accessible, coordinated, and comprehensive. One function of social workers is to advocate for high-quality health care for vulnerable populations. Social work promotes public and professional awareness of health care delivery policies and practices that are detrimental to the well-being of clients.

The advantages of health care must be available to all people. However, there are numerous barriers—economic, political, demographic, language, and cultural—that result in the denial of adequate health care. Furthermore, the health status of an increasing number of people is endangered by environmental hazards. Social workers carry significant responsibility for advocating on behalf of those affected by these continuing problems.

■ *Social work services in the health care delivery system:* Health care services require social work services to ensure that all patients have the opportunity to retain or regain their social roles and functional capacities within the limits of their mental and physical condition.

Existing and future health care programs must include social work services if patients and their families are to have the opportunity to receive the maximum benefits from this care. Social work services are required for disadvantaged or vulnerable clients to achieve equity as members of this society. The rights to appropriate decision making of those involved in care that requires the most recent life-sustaining technology necessitate the availability of social work services. The values and skills of social workers are vital for preserving the humane aspect of health care in an increasingly technologically and economically driven system.

Policy statement approved by the NASW Delegate Assembly, August 1990. Referred to the 1999 Delegate Assembly, to be revised and combined with the policy statement on Health Care. This policy statement supersedes the policy statement on Social Work Practice in the Health Care Field approved by the Delegate Assembly in 1984. For further information, contact the National Association of Social Workers, 750 First Street, NE, Suite 700, Washington, DC 20002-4241. Telephone: 202-408-8600 or 800-638-8799.

Tax Reform

BACKGROUND

Overview of Tax Policy

Customs duties provided most of the necessary revenues to fuel the Republic until the Civil War, when Congress passed federal excise taxes on alcohol and tobacco, the individual income tax, and estate and gift duties. Even so, heavy borrowing was necessary to finance the war, and the war taxes were continued into the 1870s to repay the debt (Ippolito, 1990). The federal income tax was briefly revived in 1894, but declared unconstitutional in 1895 (*Pollock v. Farmer's Loan & Trust Co.*).

By 1913, the Sixteenth Amendment to the Constitution provided that the "Congress shall have power to lay and collect taxes on incomes, from whatever source derived,"–just in time for World War I. The initial tax structure exempted the first $4,000 of income, which included just about everyone, and then imposed a 1 percent tax; for the new industrialists with incomes of more than $500,000, the marginal tax rate rose to 7 percent. However, during the war, the top marginal rate was highly progressive, up to 77 percent of taxable income. The tax policy was driven by revenue needs and was not redistributive in intent (Ippolito, 1990).

In the 1920s, Secretary of Treasury Andrew Mellon drastically reduced the progressive tax structure, cutting the top marginal rate by two-thirds. His arguments anticipated the supply-siders of the 1980s. High taxes, he said, produce negative economic and revenue effects. High rates do not raise more revenue, because the rich engage in tax evasion, or direct their capital into nontaxable, or tax-favored investments (Ippolito, 1990). Secretary Mellon repealed the excess-profits tax on corporations, but retained a high corporate income tax.

President Franklin D. Roosevelt, by his "wealth tax" bill in 1935 during the Great Depression, restored progressivity to the tax system, with a top marginal rate of 79 percent (on incomes above $5 million). Corporate income taxes and estate and gift taxes were increased, and a new tax on corporate dividends was passed (Ippolito, 1990).

Roosevelt's tax policy aim was redistribution, requiring the upper brackets to bear the tax burden and exempting most workers. Unanticipated at the time, the 1935 Social Security Act's payroll financing mechanism for the social insurance would, 40 years later, prove regressive to active workers (but not to retirees or other beneficiaries).

During World War II, the federal government initiated tax withholding, and Congress approved steep marginal tax rates (23 percent to 94 percent). An enduring change during World War II was the creation of a mass tax base. Seventy-five percent of the labor force filed tax returns during World War II, contrasted with 15 percent during World War I (Ippolito, 1990). Today, about 115 million people file individual income tax returns. In 1990, they paid a tax liability of $471.1 billion (U.S. Department of the Treasury, 1992, p. 126).

The Truman and Eisenhower administrations retained the progressive rate structure and the mass-tax base. Furthermore, they resisted congressional initiatives for tax reductions. Instead, the two presidents, one a Democrat, the other a Republican, insisted that taxing and spending be kept in budget balance (Ippolito, 1990).

The environment of tax stability changed in the Kennedy-Johnson years. Instead of balanced budgets, Kennedy courted short-term deficits to stimulate growth (Revenue Act of 1964). He lowered the top marginal rate to 70 percent and inaugurated an investment tax credit. Congress added a new minimum standard deduction for low-income taxpayers. The timing of the combination of tax policy changes in the mid-1960s led to an "extraordinary economic expansion," later reframed and applied in a very different economic environment by supply siders in the Economic Recovery Tax Act (ERTA) of 1981, with disastrous results (Ippolito, 1990, pp. 41–43).

President Johnson, following Kennedy, used the fiscal surplus to launch a War on Poverty and to escalate defense spending in the Vietnam War. The economic growth imperative gave way to a tax policy driven by spending. A badly timed tax surcharge failed to check inflation, and by 1969, two-thirds of all taxpayers found themselves in higher tax brackets, paying higher taxes ("bracket creep"), although real incomes had not kept pace.

The scene was set for the destabilizing 1970s, with tax policy objectives at cross-purposes. Tax preferences and tax expenditures proliferated. Pechman (1989) has defined *tax expenditures* as "revenue losses attributable to special provisions that deviate from the normal tax structure" (p. 78). The tax base shrank. Social security payroll taxes rose during the decade from a wage base of $7,800 and a tax rate of 4.8 percent in 1970 to a 6.13 percent tax rate on a wage base of $22,900 in 1979 (U.S. House of Representatives, 1991).

The revelations in a 1969 Department of Treasury study that the wealthy were practicing "tax avoidance" sparked a concern about tax equity or the fairness of the tax system (Ippolito, 1990). In 1978, a full-fledged taxpayer revolt broke out in California with the passage of Proposition 13, which placed a cap on local property tax increases.

By 1974, both President Nixon and the congressional watchdog of the House Ways and Means Committee, Chairman Wilbur Mills, had left government. In the same year, democratic congressional reforms, opening committees to new leadership more responsive to the public temper, ironically weakened the coherence and discipline of tax policy and its basic revenue-producing function (Ippolito, 1990). The ERTA of 1981 under Reagan, with its massive tax cuts,

and the "revenue-neutral" Tax Reform Act (TRA) of 1986 finally completed the uncoupling of the traditional relationship between balanced budgets and calibrated revenue and spending goals. The tax process lost its moorings in the 1980s, deficits piled up to defund the transfer programs of the next generation, and "no new taxes" became the slogan of successful political candidates of the Reagan-Bush era.

Fairness

A leading tax authority (Pechman, 1989, p. 2) has argued that the overall tax system in the United States is "mildly progressive" if one assumes, as he does, that the corporate income tax and property taxes "are borne by owners of capital and the payroll tax is borne by workers."

Most federal tax revenue derives from the individual income tax. The individual income tax is a tax only on income, regardless of how it is allocated. It provides an automatic flexibility, responding immediately to income change. It is the best measure of ability to pay (Pechman, 1989).

Vertical equity concerns the "distribution of tax burdens among persons in different economic circumstances" (Pechman, 1989, pp. 41–42). Progressive taxation assumes that the tax burden should increase with income and that upper-income classes have the ability to pay more. If marginal tax rates become too proportional or "flat," they violate that assumption.

Data from the Congressional Budget Office from 1977 to 1991 indicate that effective federal tax rates (the average percentage of a family's income paid in taxes) among quintiles of the population are still progressive. But within each quintile, the tax burden has decreased for the top fifth and the bottom fifth of the population over this period, whereas the tax burden has increased over time for the middle class (Kettl, 1992).

Horizontal equity is "the tax treatment of persons in essentially the same economic circumstances" (Pechman, 1989, pp. 41–42). Yet, in the tax code, great emphasis is placed on the differentiation of tax liability among people in similar circumstances, justified for societal reasons. For instance, the personal exemption provision considers family responsibilities, thereby increasing the number of exemptions. The TRA of 1986 raised the personal exemption substantially to remove some low-income classes from the tax rolls. To this degree, large personal exemptions favor low-income groups and moderate the tax burden at higher levels if family size is large. Special exemptions favor vulnerable groups or compensate groups society deems meritorious, such as veterans or the aged (Pechman, 1989).

Income groups in similar circumstances are treated differentially in the tax code, according to the source of their income. For instance, until 1986 capital gains received preferential tax treatment (lower rates), thus benefiting upper-income groups whose assets include capital gains. In 1986, the TRA reclassified capital gains income as "ordinary income," subject to the same tax rates as ordinary income.

Middle-class and upper-income groups who hold stocks and bonds and receive dividend income are not subject to income withholding under the tax laws, whereas salary income is subject to withholding. Employer-paid fringe benefits are not taxed, nor is the imputed rental value of owner-occupied homes, a tax break for the middle class. Low-income working families may receive a payroll tax offset in the form of a refundable earned income tax credit, but a working couple with no children present would be ineligible (Pechman, 1989; Hoffman & Seidman, 1990).

The tax code also provides differential treatment of people in similar circumstances on the basis of the use to which income is put. For example, the TRA of 1986 preserved deductions for interest on home mortgages, usually the greatest asset of middle-class families, but there are no deductions for renters. Charitable deductions remain, but deductions for credit card interest charges have been phased out.

Individual retirement accounts that permit middle- and upper-income groups to shift savings from taxable to nontaxable accounts were eliminated for most groups in the TRA of 1986, although there is strong pressure to restore them.

Tax-sheltered income, passive losses (real estate was a favored shelter for the wealthy), and investment tax credits were eliminated or phased out in the TRA of 1986 to flatten the tax rates, broaden the tax base, and preserve revenue neutrality. Barely six years later, strong congressional pressures may restore them.

The Gini coefficient of inequality (0 = perfect equality, 1 = perfect inequality) increased from .399 for all households in 1967 to .428 in 1991 (U.S. Department of Commerce, 1991, p. 5). It confirms the subjective sense of greater life-style gaps among income classes, despite the leveling in the TRA of 1986. A bright spot is a degree of progressivity at the lower end of the income distribution scale, represented by earned income credit.

ISSUE STATEMENT

Tax policy underwent dramatic changes in the 1980s. The first Reagan administration tax bill, the ERTA of 1981, lowered top marginal tax rates from the Vietnam War era (14 percent to 70 percent) and World War II highs (23 percent to 90 percent), to a top bracket amount of 50 percent, and instituted rapid depreciation writeoffs for the purchase by businesses of new plants and equipment (the accelerated cost recovery system).

The new supply-side economics, temporarily displacing the Keynesian orthodoxy stemming from the Great Depression, promised to attack the high inflation/high unemployment stagflation legacy of the late 1970s with a new set of remedies. High tax rates, economists argued, cost the government revenue because of the perverse effects on individual incentives: If people could not keep most of what they made by hard work, they either slacked off or hid their extra work effort, evading the higher marginal tax rate, "the rate that individuals pay on the last dollars they earn" (Kettl, 1992, p. 60). Businesses, through corporate income taxes, economists argued, also experienced perverse disincentives, which reduced corporate profits and led to slow economic growth.

Thus, the 1980s introduced a new microeconomic focus on factors that influenced individual decisions to work, save, and invest; a focus on manipulating interest rates and tax rates to stimulate businesses to risk and innovate and become more efficient; and a focus on reducing the size of government by cutting back the rate of spending on nonmarket transfer programs, specifically the entitlements social workers associate with the social services state (Lindsey, 1990, pp. 3–7).

Subsequent tax acts (the Tax Equity and Fiscal Responsibility Act of 1982 and the Deficit Reduction Act of 1984) checked the huge revenue loss from the ERTA tax cuts. The 1981 tax cuts enacted over three years, along with the deepest recession (1981–1983) since the Great Depression, contributed to the buildup of a $4 trillion debt, the largest in the history of the United States.

The other dramatic change in tax policy in the 1980s was the TRA of 1986, a major correction in tax policy supported by both liberals and conservatives. The long-term commitment to progressivity in the tax code was permanently shifted toward more proportional tax rates (15 percent to 28 percent, with a 5 percent surtax on higher incomes). Many tax shelters and tax preferences were eliminated or phased out, the acceleration of depreciation deductions by businesses was reduced, and the tax base was broadened.

The major issues that the tax policy changes of the 1980s pose are related to the reduction of progressivity (taxing according to ability to pay) in the tax code. What effects do these changes have on society? On revenue production? On economic growth? On deficit reduction? On social goals?

What effect do the changes have on specific income groups? Recent government, advocacy, and think-tank reports sound areas of concern. A Children's Defense Fund Report found that young families with children in 1990 had real incomes one-third less than similar families in 1973, a generational decline in the life chances of children today (De Parle, 1992). Studies by the Annie E. Casey Foundation ("Report Says," 1992), the Center for the Study of Social Policy, and the Economic Policy Institute traced similar trends: the erosion of the wage base, poorer families becoming poorer, and the life chances of children, measured by quality-of-life indicators, becoming more dismal (Greenhouse, 1992).

On the other hand, the top 1 percent in the income distribution increased its pretax income by 77 percent from 1977 to 1989, a change from a $325,000 to a $559,800 average annual income for families in this percentile. Their posttax incomes in the same period increased 60 percent, according to tax data from the Internal Revenue Service and Congressional Budget Office, used in a study by Paul Krugman of the Massachusetts Institute of Technology (Nasar, 1992a and 1992c).

The assets of the top 1 percent of wealthholders in the 1979–1989 decade present the sharpest concentration of wealth since the 1920s. Their share of the nation's wealth increased from 20 percent in 1979 to 36 percent in 1989. In the 1992 presidential campaign, the Midas touch took on a human face as one of the 71 reported billionaires in 1991, Ross Perot, ran for president and personally financed his own campaign. (Federal Reserve Board data, reported by Harvard professors Claudia Goldin and Bradford De Lang, and New York University economist Edward Wolff in Nasar, 1992b).

Without question, the marked increase in inequality in American society in the 1980s will rise to the top of the political agenda in the 1990s, and tax policy will be a major instrument of redress.

POLICY STATEMENT

NASW supports a tax policy that

■ treats groups fairly

■ restores a greater degree of progressivity to the tax structure

■ reduces the middle-income tax squeeze

■ reestablishes the link between spending targets and revenue-generating capacity

■ promotes economic growth, jobs, infrastructure renewal, new housing stock, educational access, universal health care, a guaranteed minimum income, and a reduction in poverty

■ retains the broad tax base and the gains made by the elimination of special preferences in the Tax Reform Act of 1986

■ continues the earned income tax credit wage supplementation for low-income working families, sufficient to raise them above the Official Poverty Threshold.

NASW specifically endorses the following new initiatives:

■ a refundable child tax credit in the range of $800 to $1,000 per child

- extension of the earned income tax credit to low-income working people, regardless of whether children are present

- an increase in the social security wage base to the median income level of the top quintile in the income distribution

- a tax surcharge on incomes in the upper 1 percent of the income distribution

- income withholding on interest and dividends

- elimination of the tax exemption on state and municipal bonds

- elimination of income-splitting and restoration of the marital deduction.

REFERENCES

Deficit Reduction Act of 1984, P.L. 98-369, 98 Stat. 494.

De Parle, J. (1992, April 15). Incomes in young families drop 32 percent in 17 years, study finds. *New York Times*, p. D27.

Economic Recovery Tax Act of 1981, P.L. 97-34, 95 Stat. 172.

Greenhouse, S. (1992, September 7). Income data show years of erosion for U.S. workers. *New York Times*, pp. A1, A20.

Hoffman, S. D., & Seidman, L. S. (1990). *The earned income tax credit: Antipoverty effectiveness and labor market effects.* Kalamazoo, MI: W. E. Upjohn Institute.

Ippolito, D. (1990). *Uncertain legacies: Federal budget policy from Roosevelt through Reagan.* Charlottesville: University of Virginia.

Kettl, D. F. (1992). *Deficit politics: Public budgeting in its institutional and historical context.* New York: Macmillan.

Lindsey, L. (1990). *The growth experiment: How the new tax policy is transforming the U.S. economy.* New York: Basic Books.

Nasar, S. (1992a, March 5). The 1980s: A very good time for the very rich. *New York Times*, pp. A1, C13.

Nasar, S. (1992b, August 16). The rich get richer, but never the same way twice. *New York Times*, p. A3.

Nasar, S. (1992c, July 20). The rich get richer, but the question is by how much? *New York Times*, p. D1.

Pechman, J. A. (1989). *Tax reform, the rich and the poor* (2nd ed.). Washington, DC: Brookings Institution.

Pollock v. Farmer's Loan & Trust Co., 157 U.S. 429 (1895).

Report says poor children grew poorer in 1980s. (1992, March 24). *New York Times*, p. A22.

Tax Equity and Fiscal Responsibility Act of 1982, P.L. 97-248, 96 Stat. 324.

Tax Reform Act of 1986, P.L. 99-509, 100 Stat. 1951, 1964, 1965, 1995.

U.S. Department of Commerce, Bureau of the Census. (1991). *Money income of households, families, and persons in the U.S.: 1990* (Series P-60, No. 174). Washington, DC: U.S. Government Printing Office.

U.S. Department of the Treasury, Internal Revenue Service. (1992, Summer). *Statistics of income (SOI) bulletin* (Vol. 12, No. 126). Washington, DC: U.S. Government Printing Office.

U.S. House of Representatives, Committee on Ways and Means. (1991). Overview of entitlement programs. In *1991 green book*, (p. 124). Washington, DC: U.S. Government Printing Office.

Policy statement approved by the NASW Delegate Assembly, August 1993. This statement supersedes the policy statement on Tax Reform approved by the Delegate Assembly in 1975. For further information, contact the National Association of Social Workers, 750 First Street, NE, Suite 700, Washington, DC 20002-4241. Telephone: 202-408-8600 or 800-638-8799.

Third-Party Reimbursement and Consumer Choice

BACKGROUND

Today, clinical social workers are regarded as fully qualified mental health professionals. Clinical social work shares with all social work practice the goal of enhancing and maintaining the psychosocial functioning of individuals, families, and small groups. Clinical social work practice is the professional application of social work theory and methods to the treatment and prevention of psychosocial dysfunction, disability, or impairment, including emotional and mental disorders. It is based on knowledge of one or more theories of human development within a psychosocial context.

The perspective of person-in-situation is central to clinical social work practice. Clinical social work includes interventions directed to interpersonal interactions, intrapsychic dynamics, and life-support and management issues. Clinical social work services consist of assessment; diagnosis and treatment, including psychotherapy and counseling; client-centered advocacy; consultation; and evaluation. The process of clinical social work is undertaken within the objectives of social work and the principles and values contained in the *NASW Code of Ethics* (NASW, 1993).

For many years, a major initiative of NASW has been to achieve legal regulation of all clinical social workers in all states and jurisdictions and, concomitantly, to pass vendorship or consumer-choice laws that enable consumers of mental health services to be treated by qualified mental health practitioners of their choice. NASW also supports standards of practice to ensure that social workers are all working in conditions that promote professional standards of service and care for clients.

Currently, the social work profession is legally regulated in 50 states, as well as in the District of Columbia, Puerto Rico, and the Virgin Islands. In addition, 24 states and the District of Columbia have enacted laws that provide for the reimbursement of clinical social work services under insurance policies that cover their beneficiaries for mental health services.

The autonomy and cost-effectiveness of clinical social work services also have been recognized by the Civilian Health and Medical Program of the Uniformed Services and the Federal Employees Health Benefits Program. Both of these programs, covering millions of federal employees and military dependents, ensure reimbursement for clinical social workers as autonomous professional providers of mental health services. In 1990, Medicare and some Medicaid programs recognized social workers as independent providers.

ISSUE STATEMENT

Clinical social work has made enormous strides in professional recognition and parity with other mental health service providers. However, the social work profession continues to be faced with the need to achieve broader societal recognition and respect and to be remunerated for clinical social work and mental health services on a parity with other providers of mental health services.

In addition to securing much needed protection for the public, legal regulation of mental health services has provided legal status and recognition for the social work profession. The next logical step is to advocate for and gain passage of consumer-choice or vendorship legislation that would require insurance companies to allow beneficiaries to choose the qualified licensed mental health service providers they wish to use. Vendorship and consumer choice open the market in a healthy competitive fashion.

Several major issues require a change in NASW's strategy to achieve full recognition of clinical social work by all sectors of our society. These issues relate to the method of paying for the United States' seriously escalating health care costs, which have risen recently at twice the rate of inflation. Mental health costs, which represent only a part of these increases, have risen for several reasons, including increased use of costly inpatient and residential treatment services, and increased marketing by the for-profit mental health sector. In fact, care management can add to the cost of providing mental health care. Media attention to mental health concerns has increased public awareness and acceptance of treatment. Currently, several approaches are being used by companies in an effort to contain costs.

Self-Insured Plans

The purchase of commercial indemnity health plans has become increasingly expensive. Therefore, an increasing number of companies, particularly larger ones that cover many employees, have turned to self-insured plans. Often, they contract with commercial insurance carriers to administer their health and welfare plans because these carriers have existing systems and expertise. These self-insured plans, however, are covered by the federal Employee Retirement Income Security Act of 1974 (ERISA) that specifically preempts state laws. Therefore, even in states with social work regulation and consumer-choice laws, these employers are not constrained to include reimbursement for clinical social workers in their health plans.

Some employers with self-insured plans, however, have voluntarily included social workers as mental health providers. Education and marketing efforts should be directed toward increasing other employers' understanding of the value and need of mental health services for their employees and the benefits of including clinical social workers in their health plans.

Third-Party Reimbursement Systems

In a parallel effort to contain the costs of health care, companies increasingly are providing health care for their employees through a vari-

ety of health maintenance organizations, managed care, and capitation payment systems. The NASW policy statement, *The Role of Social Work in Health Maintenance Organizations*, revised in 1990, defines the role of social workers through such organizations.

The social work profession must address new issues, such as full and equal reimbursement of clinical social workers, either as employees or as independent providers of services. In addition, social workers must work within these systems to promote high-quality mental health treatment services for all clients.

The social work profession must recognize the impact of these health care delivery systems on clients and on the ability of social workers, who are employed in these systems, to deliver care that meets the profession's standards of ethics and quality. In addition to the exclusion of diverse and skilled providers, limitations on authorized services can place constraints on professionals in a number of disciplines that affect the quality of care they can provide. These constraints on care often affect vulnerable populations, such as those with chronic mental illness, whom the profession is committed to serving.

Quality Assurance and the Freedom to Exercise Professional Judgment

Many managed care programs involve external evaluators who make decisions regarding the reimbursement of treatment. Social workers are entitled to peer review, but some third-party payers use nonprofessional staff or staff from other disciplines to make initial decisions about reimbursement. The required paperwork and telephone documentation process can be excessive and time-consuming. Some third-party payers set up clearly adversarial relationships with their providers. Given these conditions, it is imperative that social workers

■ assess the goodness-of-fit between their practice and theoretical orientations and the parameters of the payer contract

■ carefully review proposed contracts with third-party payers to ensure that the provider is not left with total legal liability should the client suffer as a result of reduced care

- understand provisions for payer access to and auditing of records

- understand provisions or limitations that will affect social worker–client confidentiality or the ability of therapists to thoroughly exercise their clinical judgment

- avoid situations in which the therapist's actions might be compromised, or the therapist penalized for exercising appropriate clinical judgment (for example, referring a client for impatient hospitalization).

Social workers should consult relevant resources, such as social policy statements on related issues, the *NASW Code of Ethics* (NASW, 1993), and NASW guidelines for assistance in dealing with emerging issues.

Exclusion of Certain Diseases and Treatment Modalities

Guidelines for third-party coverage may exclude certain conditions, such as schizophrenia, bipolar disorder, personality disorders, or substance abuse/addiction. These conditions can be successfully managed or remediated through good professional care.

Many payers do not cover important treatment modalities, such as family, couple, group, and collateral treatment, which are commonly accepted in the field. Employers, carriers, and third-party administrators need to be educated about the efficacy of different modalities and urged to include such services in the policies they develop. In addition, services that are central to the social work profession, such as case management, are vital in working with many kinds of clients. Social workers performing these services should be reimbursed for their time and specialized skill. Brief therapies should be used only when appropriate and not as a substitute for more appropriate forms of care.

Consumer Choice

The availability of treatment services is often reduced by third-party payers using closed panels. Closed means that therapists not already in the company's provider network may not be used by the client if the client wishes to use the company's coverage. A change to a closed panel system can result in a client no longer being able to use coverage to pay for treatment already underway.

Consumer choice also enhances clients' access to a diverse group of culturally sensitive providers and increases the likelihood that they will be able to obtain services from a provider with the specialized knowledge and training that they need.

Developing health care packages should provide for a range of health and mental health services and include social workers as fully reimbursable providers. In fact, unless clinical social workers are included as providers, there may not be enough providers of service available to meet the need for mental health care.

POLICY STATEMENT

NASW reaffirms its commitment to achieve full legal regulation and recognition of the social work profession throughout the entire health care system. Furthermore, NASW advocates full and equal reimbursement by all third parties for mental health services provided by clinical social workers in all settings, including such federal programs as Medicaid and Medicare, as well as fee-for-service, capitation, and self-insured programs; health maintenance organizations; preferred provider organizations; and all other managed health care systems.

To accomplish these goals, NASW and its members will

- develop materials related to these issues that provide substantive support for chapters and members to work toward achieving parity for licensed or certified clinical social workers with other mental health professionals

- educate consumers, employers, and carriers on how timely mental health care can eliminate the need for more costly medical care

- advocate with employers, insurers, managed care systems, and with legislative bodies for clients' right to choose their providers from the range of qualified mental health providers

- advocate for social work peer review in the third-party payer system and work to eliminate poorly prepared or nonprofessional staff from the decision-making process related to the authorization of benefits or treatment

■ encourage social workers to be accountable for their treatment of clients by adequately documenting treatment goals and outcomes without compromising client confidentiality

■ advocate for reasonable reimbursement of expenses in reporting to third-party payers, and work to eliminate excessive paperwork, reporting, and documentation

■ develop and promote model contracts with third-party payers for licensed or certified clinical social workers and social work consortiums

■ consider pursuing class action legal remedies for social workers excluded from third-party reimbursement

■ work to educate employers, carriers, and third-party payers regarding the value of family, couple, group, and collateral therapies, as well as case management services, including the value of the social work perspective and training in the provision of these services

■ actively seek coalition with other organizations and interdisciplinary groups to effect these goals

■ work to change the federal regulations covering self-insured groups so that all third-party payers who offer coverage must meet the insurance regulations of any state in which they do business

■ ensure that all third-party reimbursement systems in all states include a low-cost appeals process, clearly defined and advertised, that clients can access in cases of denial of coverage or benefits

■ explore the feasibility of NASW forming provider networks to assist members, who are regulated clinical social workers, to negotiate with third-party payers.

Because the provision of high-quality care is a primary value of the profession, NASW will assume leadership to ensure that access to appropriate mental health and clinical social work services will be available to all consumers, regardless of their ability to pay or the payment system under which they receive care. NASW will continue to work for universal comprehensive health care coverage that includes adequate mental health and substance abuse benefits and will monitor federal legislation and use available opportunities to ensure that social workers, along with other mental health providers, have equal access to mental health reimbursement.

REFERENCES

Employee Retirement Income Security Act of 1974, P.L. 93-406, 88 Stat. 829.
National Association of Social Workers. (1993). *NASW code of ethics*. Washington, DC: Author.

Policy statement approved by the NASW Delegate Assembly, August 1993. This policy statement supersedes the policy statement on Insurance Reimbursement and Consumer Choice approved by the Delegate Assembly in 1990. For further information, contact the National Association of Social Workers, 750 First Street, NE, Suite 700, Washington, DC 20002-4241. Telephone: 202-408-8600 or 800-638-8799.

Volunteers and Social Services Systems

BACKGROUND

Volunteers are a primary national resource of the United States. Volunteers nurture our children, mentor our youths, comfort those in trouble, care for our elders, and fuel much of the activity that makes our country the democracy that it is. Were we to lose volunteers, we would simultaneously lose the Boy Scouts, Girl Scouts, 4-H, Parent–Teacher Associations, Foster Grandparents, the American Red Cross, and a multitude of other community, church, and school activities. The Peace Corps would fade from the international horizon, and VISTA would vanish from our inner cities.

Volunteer participation in community service is a phenomenon deeply rooted in the American ethos. Early volunteers, mostly affluent, often expressed their religious convictions and feelings of social concern through direct gifts and service to those who were less fortunate. Over the years, volunteerism expanded to recognize those with time as well as money to contribute. In the 1960s, the application of the principles of citizen participation and maximum feasible participation brought a sharp upsurge of volunteer activity by poor people and by consumers of services. Society has begun to view volunteer service as having benefits for those who give as well as those who receive.

In the 1990s, the practice of giving and serving continues. Former U.S. President George H. Bush's "1,000 Points of Light" and U.S. Senator Edward M. Kennedy's National and Community Service Act both found a place in the nation's domestic program lexicon (*Changing the Paradigm*, 1992). A 1990 Gallup Poll (Gallup Organization, 1990a) commissioned by Independent Sector revealed that about two of five Americans volunteer (98.4 million) and that more than 25 million give five or more hours per week.

"In 1974 the typical American volunteer was a married, white woman between 25 and 44 who held a college degree and was in the upper-income" (Manser, 1983, p. 169). According to the Gallup survey (Gallup Organization, 1990a), the demographic profile of volunteers has changed. Men and women volunteer in almost identical proportions: male, 52 percent, and female, 56 percent. Moreover, although those aged 25 to 44 years still have the highest rates of volunteerism, other age groups are not far behind: 43 percent of those between the ages of 18 and 24 years volunteer; 56 percent of those aged 45 to 54 years; 51 percent of those aged 55 to 64 years; and nearly half of those older than 65 years. The Independent Sector also discovered through another survey (Gallup Organization, 1990b) that about 13 million teenagers volunteer (a rate of about 58 percent) and give an average of about 3.9 hours per week. No longer is volunteerism the sole province of the well-to-do. In 1990, one-third of those with annual incomes below $10,000 volunteered.

Realizing the importance of volunteer service, both the public and private sectors provide benefits for volunteer activity (Kurtz & Small, 1988). These benefits include provision of tax allowances, certain kinds of insurance benefits, and reimbursement for out-of-pocket volunteer expenses, such as child care and transportation. In December 1990, President Bush announced initiatives to protect volunteers from unwarranted exposure to legal liability and to make insurance to protect against such liability more affordable. A clear rationale for such measures is to provide equal access to volunteer opportunities without regard to income, race or ethnicity, gender, age, or disability, while protecting all from undue financial risk in our increasingly litigious society.

But as our nation's enthusiasm for volunteerism continues to grow, and although we encourage it, human services professionals must be careful to temper that enthusiasm with realism. Volunteers nurture our children but they cannot replace professional child care workers; they mentor and tutor our young but nevertheless are no substitute for professional educators. Although volunteers can play vital roles in the human services, they must not be perceived as viable substitutes for professional care.

Similarly, although volunteers are vital to the fabric of national and community service, they must not be left holding this country's social safety net. In terms of national policy, there is no substitute for federal domestic leadership. If we add 2 million volunteers to our roster in a given year only to create, through their service, more and better homeless shelters and soup kitchens, we ultimately fail the poor and hungry of this nation.

ISSUE STATEMENT

The social work profession operates under the assumption that volunteers are an integral part of our human services programs (National Assembly of National Voluntary Health and Social Welfare Organization, 1989). NASW should continue to formulate policies to guide social work practice in the interactive roles of professionals and volunteers working together in policy making, advocacy, and direct service roles.

Policy is also needed to guide professional practice in encouraging, activating, and administering volunteer programs in such a way as to make volunteers collaborators with—but not replacements for—professional social workers. Volunteers can make special contributions to social services at every level of practice that may not be possible for paid staff because of public and client perceptions of professional roles and interests. Likewise, professionals are trained and educated to make contributions that are neither possible nor advisable to expect of lay volunteers.

Implementation of such policies depends on making work with volunteers integral to professional education and training through class, field, and in-service training.

POLICY STATEMENT

NASW will advance policies and standards that facilitate the optimum participation of volunteers at all levels to enhance the development and delivery of human services. NASW supports and encourages local human services agencies to support the following:

■ legislation requiring volunteer involvement in publicly financed programs at the federal, state, and local levels

■ reimbursement of out-of-pocket expenses, including meals, transportation, and child care

■ legislation that provides a tax deduction for out-of-pocket expenses by volunteers providing human services through public or voluntary "(501)(c)(3)" organizations when such expenses are not reimbursed

■ performance standards that measure the benefits to clients from volunteer activities

■ enrichment of programs through the broadest possible citizen involvement

■ insurance coverage for volunteers and support for volunteer protection legislation

Integration into Agency Structures

Volunteer roles should be integrated into official social agency structures, emphasizing collaboration in the delivery of community service. Within human services organizations, there should be a positive vision—clearly articulated, widely shared, and openly discussed—concerning the role of volunteers.

Institutionalizing the status, position, and visibility of volunteers within agency organizational structures ensures that volunteers have credibility. Task or role descriptions should delineate and make clear differences in the work performed by paid and volunteer staff. There should be a clear focal point of leadership for volunteer coordination, but volunteer management should be well integrated at all levels and in all parts of the organization.

As volunteer contributions become part of the official agency structure, questions pertaining to liability, labor management codes, and reimbursement of volunteer expenses must be answered. In addition, the issue of insurance coverage for professional people working with volunteers should be addressed.

Increased Opportunities

Through volunteer activities in direct service, policy making, and advocacy, individuals within communities should have increased opportunities to contribute to and to influence the systems of decision making that affect their lives.

Traditional direct service volunteer activities that provide satisfaction and rewards other than money are important and should be expanded. But participation in policy development and community decision making have too often been the domain of small affluent groups. Volunteer opportunities in policy development and community decision making must also be expanded to include the full spectrum of citizens of all ages and socioeconomic backgrounds, along with training to enable effective participation.

Nondiscrimination

Nondiscrimination should be practiced in every phase of the volunteer structure of social services systems. A policy of nondiscrimination regarding income, age, gender, ethnicity, and disability should be maintained. People from all socioeconomic levels should be represented in all phases of the volunteer structure of social services systems, and representatives of groups previously denied participation need to be recruited and trained to assume volunteer roles.

Volunteer and Professional Distinctions

Volunteers should not supplant or decrease the availability of suitably qualified, regularly employed professional staff. Written policies of agencies should include the following:

■ a clear differentiation of the functions and activities appropriate for volunteer and professional staff

■ task or role descriptions for each category of volunteer

■ procedures for monitoring, evaluating, and measuring volunteer activities and contributions.

Education and Training Programs

Agencies should institute education and training programs for social workers on the effective involvement of volunteers in policy making, advocacy, and direct service. NASW and other continuing education providers should offer curricula on volunteer administration and citizen participation and should plan workshops and seminars for social work practitioners.

Volunteer Services Coordinators

Agencies that use many volunteers should develop a volunteer services position. Volunteer services coordinators can provide volunteer recruitment, interviewing, orientation, and supervision on a systematic basis. These professional positions should be at the supervisory or management level, and job specifications should include a training component.

Volunteer Experience and Work Equivalence

Potential employers and educational institutions should include volunteer experience as well as paid experience on application forms. Employers should consider volunteer experience—properly defined, supervised, recorded, and evaluated—and assess its suitability for work equivalence. Universities seeking to evaluate life-experience equivalences should develop standards for assessing volunteer experience.

REFERENCES

Changing the paradigm: The first report. (1992). Washington, DC: The Points of Light Foundation.

Gallup Organization. (1990a). *Giving and volunteering in the United States 1990.* Washington, DC: Independent Sector.

Gallup Organization. (1990b). *Volunteering and giving among American teenagers 14–17 years of age.* Washington, DC: Independent Sector.

Kurtz, D. L., & Small, J. A. (1988). *Nonprofit organizations 1988: Current issues and developments*. Washington, DC: Practicing Law Institute.

Manser, G. (1983). Volunteers. In S. Briar, A. Minahan, E. Pinderhughes, & T. Tripodi (Eds.), *Encyclopedia of social work* (17th ed., 1983–1984 suppl., pp. 169–176). Silver Spring, MD: National Association of Social Workers.

National Assembly of National Voluntary Health and Social Welfare Organization. (1989). *A study in excellence: Management in the nonprofit human services*. Washington, DC: Author.

Policy statement approved by the NASW Delegate Assembly, August 1993. This policy statement supersedes the policy statement on Volunteers and Social Services Systems approved by the Delegate Assembly in 1977. For further information, contact the National Association of Social Workers, 750 First Street, NE, Suite 700, Washington, DC 20002-4241. Telephone: 202-408-8600 or 800-638-8799.

Voter Participation

BACKGROUND

Citizen participation in national elections has declined steadily. In 1988, only 50.1 percent of eligible voters cast ballots, the lowest rate in 64 years. This downturn follows the midterm 1986 election, when barely one in three adults voted. These elections are not isolated instances; rather, they represent the continuation of a decades-long trend toward decreased voter participation. In many cases, public officials are being elected to office by the votes of less than 25 percent of the eligible electorate.

Citizens vote if they are registered. Even in presidential elections with overall low turnouts, 80 to 90 percent of registered voters participate. In 1988, 86.2 percent of citizens who were registered actually voted, according to the U.S. Department of Commerce (1989) census statistics.

The United States is the only Western democracy that does not automatically register its citizens to vote. A recent comparison of voter participation among 24 democratic nations showed that the United States ranked 23rd in the percentage of eligible voters who actually voted in national elections.

Nonvoters in the United States include disproportionate numbers of low-income, minority, young, and less-educated adults. There continue to exist in this country organized efforts by certain groups to keep people of color and other oppressed people from voting by use of intimidation and other means. The lack of involvement by certain sectors of society in the most basic civic responsibility both erodes the principles of a representative democracy and renders individuals powerless to influence governmental decision making.

Advances in exit-polling technology have made it possible to predict accurately the out-come of an election before all votes are cast. After the 1980 and 1984 presidential elections, many citizens in western states complained that the early projections of winners by the television networks had discouraged them from going to the polls. Predicting the outcome of an election before all the polls are closed has serious consequences, including decreased participation and a sense of disenfranchisement for voters in the West.

ISSUE STATEMENT

One of the guiding principles of the social work profession is the commitment to individual empowerment and self-determination. NASW has worked to expand the involvement of social workers in the electoral process. In addition, many social workers have been leaders in local community efforts to register voters and to make government at all levels more accessible and responsive to the average citizen. Given this tradition of commitment and involvement, it is imperative that NASW speak to the issue of the reform of national voter-registration laws.

Currently, states exercise the authority to prescribe the methods of voter registration, to maintain voting lists, and to establish election-day voting procedures. In many states and local jurisdictions, it is still difficult for citizens to register to vote. Local election officials often have considerable discretion under state law; therefore, practices vary widely from jurisdiction to jurisdiction. In recent years, civil rights and civil-interest groups have joined forces to persuade governors, mayors, and state legislators to make voter registration services available at government offices serving the public. In addition, nonprofit health and welfare agencies have been asked to offer registration services to clients on a routine basis. These grassroots efforts have increased public awareness of the relationship between the barriers to registration and low turnout of voters and consequently have fueled interest in and support for the reform of national voter registration laws.

POLICY STATEMENT

In supporting the reform of voter registration laws and voting practices, NASW is guided by the following principles:

■ Voting is a basic right, and citizens should be assisted, not obstructed, in exercising that right.

■ Government at all levels is responsible for ensuring that eligible citizens are enrolled on the voter registration lists.

■ To the extent possible, voting laws and practices should be standardized nationally and within each state.

■ Every effort should be made to improve access to registration facilities and polling places for handicapped and elderly individuals and to prevent any action that denies access or intimidates people of color or other minority voters.

NASW supports federal voter registration reforms that increase access to the electoral system for all citizens, including disadvantaged, disabled, or minority citizens. These reforms should include the following:

■ Registration by mail and in person should be possible at all federal, state, county, and municipal agencies that serve the public directly and at all nonprofit agencies that receive grant-in-aid funds and serve the public (for example, automatic voter registration when a driver's license is issued).

■ Election-day registration should be allowed when the voter can provide appropriate identification.

■ Limitations should be set on purging for not voting so that citizens may maintain their registration with a valid driver's license or other authorized identification.

■ Adequate funding must be provided for voter registration and election-day services, including transportation.

■ Federal registration standards, reporting requirements, and enforcement authority must conform to federal election practices.

■ Voting by mail should be made possible.

■ A single, simultaneous, national poll-closing time for presidential elections should be established.

REFERENCE

U.S. Department of Commerce, Bureau of Census. (1989). *Current population reports* (Series P-20, No. 435). Washington, DC: Author.

Policy statement approved by the NASW Delegate Assembly, August 1990. Referred to the 1999 Delegate Assembly for revision. For further information, contact the National Association of Social Workers, 750 First Street, NE, Suite 700, Washington, DC 20002-4241. Telephone: 202-408-8600 or 800-638-8799.

Women in the Social Work Profession

BACKGROUND

Social work often is described as a "women's profession," and in fact, the proportion of women within the NASW membership has increased consistently over the past 30 years, from 68 percent in 1961 to more than 77 percent in 1994 (Gibelman & Schervish, 1993b). The U.S. Department of Labor's Bureau of Labor Statistics (1961, 1993) indicated that women held 57 percent of all social services positions in this country in 1960 and 69 percent in 1992. This trend can be expected to continue in the near future. During the 1992–1993 academic year, more than 86 percent of bachelor's of social work degree (BSW) graduates and 82 percent of master's of social work degree (MSW) graduates were women (Lennon, 1994). Given that most NASW members, professional social workers, and social work students are women, employment issues that disproportionately affect women social workers are of grave concern to the membership of NASW.

Salary

According to the U.S. Department of Labor's Women's Bureau (1990), women social workers earned 85 percent of what male social workers earned in 1989. A recent survey of salaries of NASW members also shows evidence of widespread gender discrimination in salary and advancement in the profession. At the salary mean, women earned 89.4 percent of the salaries reported by men (Gibelman & Schervish, 1995). About 47 percent of women and only 28 percent of men earn salaries at or below the median for the membership as a whole: $30,000 (Gibelman & Schervish, 1993b). On the other hand, men were disproportionately represented at the higher salary levels at all levels of experience and for all functions (direct service, supervision,

and management), and this differential increased with function and experience (Gibelman & Schervish, 1995). Gibelman and Schervish also found that gender accounted for more of the differential in primary income of the 1991 membership of NASW than did auspices, setting, practice, function, ethnicity, or geography.

A 1983 study of social workers in North Carolina found that gender explained more of the difference in women's and men's salaries than did years of work experience, job position, or education (York, Henley, & Gamble, 1987). Fortune and Hanks (1988) found that although the salaries of people with MSWs in their first jobs did not differ for men and women, differences did begin to emerge as they changed jobs. Even when factors such as experience, age, additional education, and type of position were controlled, men's salaries were significantly higher than women's. More recently, Lambert (1994) reported similar findings, and Huber and Orlando (1995) found that for people with MSWs, men's incomes were consistently higher than women's across various fields of practice, and the gender gap was more pronounced in administrative positions than in direct practice positions. The Ridgewood Financial Institute's annual Fee and Practice Survey indicated that male social workers in private practice earned median incomes of $57,273 compared with $47,000 for women social workers in private practice (Landers, 1992).

Since the 1970s, several studies of social work faculty members have reported salary inequities between men and women (Harper, 1991). Although earlier investigations reported that gender played a greater role in these inequities than did variables such as rank, education, and experience (Gould & Kim, 1976), more recent studies suggest that this gap may be closing for faculty within each rank (Harper, 1991; Rubin, 1988). Gender inequities that persist may be a product of differential rates of promotion, which also may reflect gender discrimination rather than gender per se.

The fact that social work is a women-dominated profession numerically contributes to low salaries overall in the profession (Sokoloff, 1992). Social work is one of the most underpaid occupations in the United States (National Committee on Pay Equity, 1987). Sorensen's (1994) review of 18 studies of men's and women's salaries, as well as her own investigations (Sorensen 1991, 1994), found that workers employed in jobs predominantly held by women earned less than other workers, even after differences in productivity were taken into account. This discrepancy has changed little in recent times; for full-time employees, women's pay relative to men's was only 6 percent higher in 1991 (70 percent of men's salary) than it was in 1955 (Sorensen, 1994). This factor may be particularly troublesome for African American women, who tend to be even more segregated into lower-paying women-dominated occupations than white women (Sokoloff, 1992).

All women social workers would benefit if they were to be paid what they are worth compared with other occupations that have similar training and skill requirements. Comparable worth initiatives, which demand that jobs requiring comparable skill, effort, responsibility, and working conditions get equal pay, have been used primarily in the public sector and have resulted in reductions in pay differentials between women and men (Sorensen, 1994).

Career Advancement

Sokoloff (1988, 1992) called attention to the segregation of men and women and of African American people and white people not only by different occupations but also by different employment settings and different job titles within settings. As Dressel (1987) stated, "the numerical dominance of women in social work has not translated into authority, power, and pay equity or equality" (p. 297). Lambert (1994) demonstrated that participation in administrative tasks early in one's social work career is significantly related to one's later position in the organization

and control over critical resources. Men are more likely than women to enroll in the macro practice tracks of MSW programs (Dressel, 1987; Fortune & Hanks, 1988). Men take on administrative tasks and move into administrative positions more often and at a much faster rate than women, with significant differences appearing within three to 10 years after receiving the MSW (Austin, Kravetz, & Pollock, 1985; Fortune & Hanks, 1988; Gibelman & Schervish, 1993a; Lambert, 1994; Zunz, 1991).

Harper (1991) found in a 1983 study that female directors of BSW programs were more likely than their male counterparts to be untenured and to hold a lower academic rank. Her 1988 study of BSW directors found that women were being appointed as directors at a faster rate than men; however, they were not being promoted to the rank of professor at the same rate as men. Rank and tenure were found to be better predictors of salary than was gender, supporting Rubin's (1988) argument that in academia, the access of women to promotional opportunities is a more important issue than salary equity per se.

Prater (1992) reported that only 3 percent of executive and managerial positions in social work are held by women of color. In a study of one state's public employees, it was found that African American women were represented in supervisory positions at only half the level of their representation among workers in the system as a whole (Martin & Chernesky, 1989). However, women of color are overrepresented in paraprofessional positions (Martin & Chernesky, 1989). Within academic settings, there is evidence that the gender gap between African American women and men has widened over the past two decades. Schiele (1992) found that significantly more African American women than male faculty members held the rank of assistant professor (a low rank) and that a greater percentage of men had been members of editorial boards of journals and were tenured. The first two findings held true even when only faculty members who held doctorates were considered.

Conflicts between Work and Family Life

Social work, as a primarily women's profession, needs to address the conflicts between work and family. Women continue to fulfill the role of primary caregiver for children more often than men (Gray, Lovejoy, Piotrkowski, & Bond, 1990; Hochschild, 1989). Between 1959 and 1983, the collective number of hours that women spent in the labor market nearly doubled, whereas the number of hours they devoted to child care and housework decreased by only 14 percent. However, the total combined hours that men worked in the labor market and at home fell by 8 percent (Fuchs, 1986). Corporate studies indicate that about one-half of women employees and one-third of male employees say child care responsibilities interfere with their work in some way (Shellenbarger, 1993a). Employed women are more likely than men to use sick leave to care for children and other family members (Schultz, 1994); one study found that women with children in out-of-home care were up to 65 percent more likely to be absent than other employees (Shellenbarger, 1993a). Although more than 93 percent of women social workers in Marshall and Barnett's (1991) study reported some gains from combining work and family life, more than half of them were concerned about the impact of this situation on their children. Sixty-eight percent of black and 58 percent of white social workers acknowledged feeling some strain because of this "double shift." The limited availability of programs and policies that support employed mothers contributes to this strain (Marlow, 1991). According to an article in *The Wall Street Journal*, many women avoid taking advantage of "family-friendly" employment policies when they are offered because they believe that it would inhibit their opportunities for advancement (Sharpe, 1994).

Women are more likely than men to be the primary caregivers for dependent adults and to provide more intensive care for these adults (Anastas, Gibeau, & Larson, 1990; Brody, 1990; Scharlach, Lowe, & Schneider, 1991). Although being employed reduces the number of hours of help given by sons to their older parents, it does not significantly reduce the amount of help provided by daughters (Scharlach et al., 1991; Stoller, 1983). Most caregivers report that they receive satisfaction or personal growth from their fulfillment of this role (Scharlach, 1994). However, 33 to 77 percent of employees providing elder care report elevated rates of work-related outcomes such as absenteeism, reduced productivity, tardiness, missed advancement and training opportunities, reduction in work hours, quitting work, and increased job stress, as well as a variety of personal difficulties such as diminished social contacts and leisure time, depression and other emotional problems, physical fatigue, and financial strains (Brody, 1990; Scharlach, 1994; Scharlach et al., 1991; Shellenbarger, 1993a). Women report a greater level of burden associated with caregiving (Barusch & Spaid, 1989; Brody, 1990) and a higher degree of conflict between work and caregiving demands than do men (Anastas et al., 1990).

Women are more likely than men to be providing care for multiple generations simultaneously (Brody, 1990; Shellenbarger, 1993b). A recent study suggested that African American women may be particularly vulnerable to the resulting strain of role overload because they begin to provide care for other family members at an earlier age than white women, are more often single parents, are often caregivers for parents and grandchildren as well as their own children, and are less likely than white women to use corporate support programs (Shellenbarger, 1993b).

Sexual Harassment and Violence

The social work profession has an unacceptably high level of sexual harassment in the workplace. Women are more likely than men to experience sexual harassment in the workplace and less likely to be its perpetrators (Kaplan, 1991). A study of NASW members in Iowa found that 35 percent of the women respondents and 14 percent of the males had been victims of sexual harassment by supervisors or administrators, coworkers, and clients (Maypole, 1986). In another study, 44 percent of women who held administrative positions reported having been sexually harassed on the job by superiors, coworkers, board members, and members of funding sources (Kravetz & Austin, 1984). A study of MSW-level field instructors reported that 38 percent of the respondents (49 percent of the women and 17 percent of the men) had experienced unwelcome sexual advances (Judd, Block, & Calkin, 1985). Eighty-five percent of the reported incidents involved a man harassing a woman. Fifty-four percent of the 83 deans and directors of MSW programs in Singer's (1989) study reported that they had had reports of sexual harassment of students by faculty members and field supervisors within the previous five years. The majority of victims were women, and all of the perpetrators were men.

These studies and others reveal that harassment often has negative repercussions on the victim's emotional and social well-being and on work performance and career advancement (Kaplan, 1991). On the other hand, most of the harassers experience no concrete consequences because most incidents are not reported within the workplace (Judd et al., 1985; Kaplan, 1991).

Physical violence has dramatically increased in our society. Physical violence is an increasing problem for social workers in carrying out their duties with clients. Women social workers are especially vulnerable to physical violence by clients. The Centers for Disease Control found that homicide is the number one cause of death at the workplace for women, outnumbering heart attacks and job-related accidents. The federal Occupational, Safety, and Health Administration identified social workers as being at high risk for violence in the workplace. Education, precautions, and procedures need to be developed for the protection of women social workers.

NASW's Response

NASW has responded directly to some of these issues since its formation. In the 1950s, NASW initiated efforts to recruit men into social work "to overcome its female image and to raise the status of the profession" (Scotch, 1971, p. 6). The unintended consequence, however, seems to have been that the newly recruited men advanced upward more often and more quickly than women (Sutton, 1982).

The *NASW Code of Ethics* (1996) states that social workers should act to prevent and eliminate discrimination in the employing organization and in society as a whole. In 1973 NASW adopted a policy to address the elimination of sexism and sex discrimination in society and the profession. An affirmative action plan was initiated to ensure that the voluntary leadership in NASW would reflect the racial and gender composition of the membership and that women

and people of color would have equal employment opportunities within the association. The association has yet to meet all of these goals. For fiscal year 1994–1995, the goal for women was met for the national Board of Directors and Committee on Nominations and Leadership Identification, elected positions in 76 percent of the 51 chapters reporting data, and appointed positions in 82 percent of the 50 reporting chapters. The goal was not met for new appointees to national volunteer positions, total national appointments, elected positions in 24 percent of the chapters, and appointed positions in 18 percent of the chapters. In 1994 the national NASW staff employment goal was exceeded in all three organizational centers, but the goal for higher staff grades was met in only one.

The National Committee on Women's Issues was mandated as a standing committee of NASW in 1975 to encourage and monitor association activities aimed at the elimination of sexism within the association, the profession, and society. The 1977 NASW Delegate Assembly adopted a policy statement on women's issues. It was superseded by the 1987 women's issues policy that, among other things, expressed a commitment to increase women's leadership within professional organizations and social services agencies and to ensure equal pay for men and women with similar qualifications and responsibilities (NASW, 1994). The 1993 Delegate Assembly approved a resolution entitled "NASW Personnel Policies on Sexual Harassment" that addressed the need for educational materials and personnel policies and procedures to protect NASW employees and social workers in general from sexual harassment. The NASW *Standards for Social Work Personnel Practices* (1990) addressed issues of discriminatory hiring and personnel actions, comparable worth, and employer's support of the family responsibilities of caregivers. NASW has made considerable progress in addressing these issues within the organization; however, there has been far less advancement in ending discrimination of women social workers in the workplace in general.

ISSUE STATEMENT

Attention to women's issues in the profession is essential because inequities and discrimination continue in the social work profession. Women social workers perform the majority of the profession's work. While economic, political, social, and cultural forces contribute to the inequities in the social work profession, the existence of these forces does not excuse the discrimination against women. These inequities manifest themselves in areas such as lack of comparable pay, occupational and setting segregation, reduced advancement options, sexual harassment, and conflicts between the demand of work and family responsibilities. These disadvantages affect the personal, economic, spiritual, social, and physical well-being of women professionals and their families. In addition, certain groups of women—women of color, women who head single-parent households, women who care for children and older people, older women, lesbians, and disabled women—often face even greater discrimination and disadvantage than do other women social workers.

Continuing efforts to develop workplace and employment-related practices and policies that better meet the needs of women social workers remain essential for enhancing their well-being and for allowing the profession to fully utilize one of its greatest resources: its own women members. For more than two decades, NASW has taken specific actions directed toward the elimination of sexism and gender discrimination in society and the profession. The *NASW Code of Ethics* (NASW, 1996) mandates that individual social workers do the same. This stance is a particularly meaningful one for a profession in which the majority of practitioners, including association members, and of consumers are women.

POLICY STATEMENT

NASW recognizes the wide range of issues that negatively affect women in the profession of social work and is committed to advancing policies and practices that will improve the status and well-being of all women social workers. Policy concerns of the association cover a range of areas, and action is needed at the federal, state, and local government bodies in the workplace, in social work education, and in program development and design.

Salary

NASW supports the following:

■ all legislative and administrative strategies that address pay equity for women in social work, including measures that allow women social workers who are discriminated against in employment and compensation to seek full legal and fiscal compensation

■ comparable worth initiatives for women social workers in both the public and the private sectors

■ research regarding the effects of various pay equity approaches for women social workers and dissemination of findings to policymakers in both the private and public sectors

■ participation in coalitions that focus on pay equity issues for women social workers.

Career Advancement

NASW supports the following:

■ efforts to eliminate barriers that limit the upward mobility of women in social work and their advancement to positions of greater reward and power in both public and private employment

■ affirmative action programs as effective tools to help women and to address issues of diversity in gaining access to higher positions within the social work profession

■ research and dissemination of findings regarding the barriers to advancement of women in social work and the outcomes of strategies designed to eliminate them.

Conflicts between Work and Family Life

NASW supports the following:

■ initiatives that maximize the flexibility of working conditions in order to support the needs of social workers who provide care to family members, most of whom are women

■ employee services that support women social work staff's caregiving roles

- employee benefits that financially help caregiving women social workers

- flexibility in the design of benefit packages and the inclusion of women social work employees in the development of their own benefits plans

- agency, community, state, and national initiatives that address the need for accessible and affordable child care that meets high standards of quality.

Sexual Harassment and Violence

NASW supports the following:

- policies and procedures designed to eliminate sexual harassment and violence against women social workers in all workplaces

- research to document the extent of sexual harassment, violence against women social workers, and the outcomes of educational and intervention efforts.

REFERENCES

Anastas, J. W., Gibeau, J. L., & Larson, P. J. (1990). Working families and eldercare: A national perspective in an aging America. *Social Work, 35,* 405–411.

Austin, C. D., Kravetz, D., & Pollock, K. L. (1985). Experiences of women as social welfare administrators. *Social Work, 30,* 173–179.

Barusch, A. S., & Spaid, W. M. (1989). Gender differences in caregiving: Why do wives report greater burden? *The Gerontologist, 29,* 667–676.

Brody, E. M. (1990). *Women in the middle: Their parent-care years.* New York: Springer.

Dressel, P. (1987). Patriarchy and social welfare work. *Social Problems, 34,* 294–309.

Fortune, A. E., & Hanks, L. L. (1988). Gender inequities in early social work careers. *Social Work, 33,* 221–226.

Fuchs, V. (1986). Sex differences in economic well-being. *Science, 232,* 460–472.

Gibelman, M., & Schervish, P. H. (1993a). The glass ceiling in social work: Is it shatterproof? *Affilia, 8,* 442–455.

Gibelman, M., & Schervish, P. H. (1993b). *What we earn: 1993 NASW salary survey.* Washington, DC: NASW Press.

Gibelman, M., & Schervish, P. H. (1995). Pay equity in social work: Not! *Social Work, 40,* 622–629.

Gould, K. H., & Kim, B. C. (1976). Salary inequities between men and women in schools of social work: Myth or reality? *Journal of Education for Social Work, 12,* 50–55.

Gray, E. B., Lovejoy, M. C., Piotrkowski, C. S., & Bond, J. T. (1990). Husband supportiveness and the well-being of employed mothers of infants. *Families in Society, 71,* 332–341.

Harper, K. V. (1991). Gender issues in academia: A second look at BSW directors. *Affilia, 6*(1), 58–71.

Hochschild, A. (1989). *The second shift: Working parents and the revolution at home.* New York: Viking Press.

Huber, R., & Orlando, B. P. (1995). Persisting gender differences in social workers' incomes: Does the profession really care? *Social Work, 40,* 585–591.

Judd, P., Block, S. R., & Calkin, C. L. (1985). Sexual harassment among social workers in human service agencies. *Arete, 10*(1), 12–21.

Kaplan, S. J. (1991). Consequences of sexual harassment in the workplace. *Affilia, 6*(3), 50–65.

Kravetz, D., & Austin, C. D. (1984). Women's issues in social service administration: The views and experiences of women administrators. *Administration in Social Work, 8,* 25–38.

Lambert, S. J. (1994). A day late and a dollar short: Persistent gender differences amid changing requirements for organizational advancement. *Journal of Applied Social Sciences, 18*(1), 89–108.

Landers, S. (1992, April). Survey eyes therapy fees. *NASW News,* pp. 1, 8.

Lennon, T. (1994). *Statistics on social work education in the United States: 1993.* Alexandria, VA: Council on Social Work Education.

Marlow, C. (1991). Women, children and employment: Responses by the United States and Great Britain. *International Social Work, 34,* 287–297.

Marshall, N. L., & Barnett, R. C. (1991). Race, class, and multiple role strains and gains among women employed in the service sector. *Women and Health, 17*(4), 1–19.

Martin, P. Y., & Chernesky, R. H. (1989). Women's prospects for leadership in social welfare: A political economy perspective. *Administration in Social Work, 13*(3/4), 117–143.

Maypole, D. E. (1986). Sexual harassment of social workers at work: Injustice within? *Social Work, 31,* 29–34.

National Association of Social Workers. (1990). *Standards for social work personnel practices.* Washington, DC: NASW Press.

National Association of Social Workers. (1994). *Social work speaks: NASW policy statements* (3rd ed.). Washington, DC: NASW Press.

National Association of Social Workers. (1996). *NASW code of ethics.* Washington, DC: Author.

National Committee on Pay Equity. (1987). *Pay equity: An issue of race, ethnicity and sex.* Washington, DC: Author.

Prater, G. S. (1992, July). *The cross-cultural emergence of women in management.* Paper presented at the World Assembly, NASW's annual conference, Washington, DC.

Rubin, A. (1988). Gender and salary in graduate schools of social work: An outworn issue? *Affilia, 3*(3), 63–82.

Scharlach, A. E. (1994). Caregiving and employment: Competing or complementary roles? *The Gerontologist, 34,* 378–385.

Scharlach, A. E., Lowe, B. F., & Schneider, E. L. (1991). *Elder care and the work force: Blueprint for action.* Lexington, MA: Lexington Books.

Schiele, J. H. (1992). Disparities between African-American women and men on social work faculty. *Affilia, 7*(3), 44–56.

Schultz, E. E. (1994, September 27). Your money matters: "Time-off bank" lets employees choose. *The Wall Street Journal,* p. C1.

Scotch, C. B. (1971). Sex status in social work: Grist for women's liberation. *Social Work, 16,* 5–11.

Sharpe, R. (1994, March 29). Women in management: Family friendly firms don't always promote females. *The Wall Street Journal,* p. B1.

Shellenbarger, S. (1993a, June 21). Work and family (a special report): No action; data gap: Do family-support programs help the bottom line? The research is inconclusive. *The Wall Street Journal,* p. R6.

Shellenbarger, S. (1993b, December 17). Work and family. *The Wall Street Journal,* p. B1.

Singer, T. L. (1989). Sexual harassment in graduate schools of social work: Provocative dilemmas. *Journal of Social Work Education, 25*(1), 68–76.

Sokoloff, N. J. (1988). Evaluating gains and losses by black and white women and men in the professions, 1960–1980. *Social Problems, 35,* 36–53.

Sokoloff, N. J. (1992). *Black women and white women in the professions: Occupational segregation by race and gender, 1960–1980.* New York: Rutledge.

Sorensen, E. (1991). *Exploring the reasons behind the narrowing gender gap in earnings.* Washington, DC: Urban Institute Press.

Sorensen, E. (1994). *Comparable worth: Is it a worthy policy?* Princeton, NJ: Princeton University Press.

Stoller, E. P. (1983). Parental caregiving by adult children. *Journal of Marriage and the Family, 45,* 851–858.

Sutton, S. A. (1982). Sex discrimination among social workers. *Social Work, 27,* 211–217.

U.S. Department of Labor, Bureau of Labor Statistics. (1961). *Salaries and working conditions of social welfare manpower in 1960.* Washington, DC: U.S. Government Printing Office.

U.S. Department of Labor, Bureau of Labor Statistics. (1993). Employed civilians by detailed occupation, sex, race, and Hispanic origin. *Employment and Earnings, 40*(1), 195.

U.S. Department of Labor, Women's Bureau. (1990). *Facts on working women.* Washington, DC: U.S. Government Printing Office.

York, R. O., Henley, H. C., & Gamble, D. N. (1987). Sexual discrimination in social work: Is it salary or advancement? *Social Work, 32,* 336–340.

Zunz, S. J. (1991). Gender-related issues in the career development of social work managers. *Affilia, 6*(4), 39–52.

Policy statement approved by the NASW Delegate Assembly, August 1996. For more information, contact the National Association of Social Workers, 750 First Street, NE, Suite 700, Washington, DC 20002-4241. Telephone: 202-408-8600 or 800-638-8799.

Women's Issues

BACKGROUND

In 1990, 51.3 percent of the population of the United States was female, and women outnumbered men by 6.2 million. In the second half of this century, the proportion of women in the paid labor force has risen dramatically from 38 percent in 1960 to almost 46 percent in 1993. By 1992, 42 million women were employed full-time (that is, 43 percent of full-time and 66 percent of part-time workers were women). The greatest increase in the labor force participation of women has been among married women with children under age 6; in 1960, only 18.6 percent of such women worked, whereas by 1992, 59.9 percent of them were employed (U.S. Department of Commerce, 1993). This increase in the labor force participation of women has had and will continue to have profound effects on the workplace and on family and community life.

Women's increased rates of labor force participation have not been matched by equivalent increases in earnings. In 1990, women working full-time had median weekly earnings that were 72 percent of those for men; compared within different racial and ethnic groups, these proportions were 71 percent for white women, 86 percent for African American women, and 87 percent for Hispanic women. Median weekly earnings for full-time workers in 1992 were $518 for white men, $388 for white women, $380 for African American men, $336 for African American women, $345 for Hispanic men, and $303 for Hispanic women. White women and women and men from racial and ethnic groups lagged far behind white men in earnings (U.S. Department of Commerce, 1993).

These differences in earnings are related both to occupational segregation and the crowding of women into a small number of gender-typed occupations that pay less than the occupations typically occupied by men and to gender discrimination in wages and opportunities for promotion. Occupations are also racially segregated, and the jobs traditionally held by women of color in the United States have been among the lowest paid and least stable of all (Glenn, 1985); thus, for example, African American women, especially those with little education, are concentrated in a small number of poorly paid jobs (Burbridge, 1992). Similarly, all women face obstacles to promotion and advancement at work, but women of color face even greater barriers to advancement in the corporate world than white women (U.S. Department of Labor, 1991). For these reasons NASW has consistently supported legislation and significant court cases that seek to combat discrimination against women in the workplace.

Because of the lower earnings of women, families maintained by women are disadvantaged economically and are more likely to be among those living in poverty; in 1992, the median weekly earnings of families maintained by women were $385 while married couple families earned $779. The figures for African American and Hispanic families maintained by women were $328 and $341, respectively. As a result of lower earnings and income maintenance programs that do not support families at a level above the poverty line, although 12.8 percent of all American families had incomes below the poverty level in 1991, 34.3 percent of all "female-headed" households and 55.5 percent of those "female-headed" households with children under age 18 present lived in poverty (U.S. Department of Commerce, 1993). However, because the majority of American families have two earners, the lower earnings of women affect all households not only those in which the woman is the sole earner or "head of household"; a wife's earnings now constitute 50 percent of black family income, 40 percent of Hispanic family income, and 35 percent of white family income (American Association of University Women Educational Foundation, 1992).

In addition to providing income, employment in the United States is also a major vehicle for the provision of both private benefits, such as health insurance and retirement income through pensions, and public social insurance benefits such as Old Age and Survivors Disability Insurance, the major public source of income for workers who are retired or have disabilities and their dependents. Although women's labor force participation has been increasing, rates of employment are still lower for women than for men. In 1992, 57.8 percent of white women and 76.4 percent of white men, 58.0 percent of African American women and 69.7 percent of African American men, and 52.6 percent of Hispanic women and 80.5 percent of Hispanic men were employed (U.S. Department of Commerce, 1993). Some benefits, such as retirement income, are specifically anchored to earnings. Thus, those who earn less also tend to have lower levels of benefits, especially retirement income (Ozawa, 1995). In addition, to the extent that women may work part-time or interrupt their paid labor force participation over the life course, their eligibility for employment-related benefits at present and in retirement is compromised, especially if they have never married. These facts help explain why older women who live alone have the highest rates of poverty among older Americans (U.S. Department of Commerce, 1993).

Women who are employed outside the home are also generally responsible for a "second shift" at home (Hochschild, 1989). Changes in the division of unpaid labor at home, particularly the care of children and dependent adults, including those with disabilities and older family members, have not kept pace with changes in labor force participation. These dual roles—of earner and family care provider—carry both strains and gains for women, often depending on the quality of the roles (Barnett & Baruch, 1987). As the population ages, women in their middle years, sometimes referred to as the "sandwich

generation" (Brody, 1981), can find themselves giving care both to children and to older family members whether or not they are employed. Both community-based and workplace services, such as quality day care, extended school day services, adult day health services, eldercare services, family medical leave, dependent care benefits, and flextime on the job, contribute to the well-being of the women who give care as well as to their family members who use the services. The caring work that women do within families has long been recognized by social workers not only as important for survival but also as an essential part of what children and other dependent family members need to grow, develop, and function at their full potential. However, women who do this essential family work require access to the full range of community-based social and human services to assist them.

Education is not only a means for enhancing human development but also a major vehicle for preparing people for the workforce. Despite Title IX of the Education Amendments of 1972, which makes it illegal to discriminate on the basis of gender in any program that receives federal funding, there is considerable evidence that American public schools continue to "shortchange girls" (American Association of University Women Educational Foundation, 1992). In addition, girls from racial and ethnic groups and those from families with low socioeconomic status face even greater difficulties (American Association of University Women Educational Foundation, 1992). Although gender gaps in achievement in reading and mathematics may be narrowing, girls in need of special education services to enhance their learning are often underidentified; and girls still lag far behind boys in participation and achievement in science. Although American girls in general and African American girls in particular are more likely to complete high school and go on to college than are comparable boys, adolescent pregnancy remains a major barrier to school completion for many girls, in part because of the practices of schools (American Association of University Women Educational Foundation, 1992). Women are also underrepresented in American higher education; based on 1992 data, although more young women than men graduate from high school, 15 percent of men and only 13 percent of women earn a bachelor's degree, and 9.0 percent of men but only 5.6 percent of women earn an advanced degree (U.S. Department of Commerce, 1993). Clearly, American schools must do a better job of preparing all women and girls to function competently and confidently in the increasingly technological workforce of the future.

Schools may be inhospitable to women in a number of ways. The curriculum materials that girls and boys are exposed to are often gender biased; young women of color in particular may find the experiences of people like them invisible (American Association of University Women Educational Foundation, 1992). Also, research shows that the ways in which women learn and grow cognitively differ from those of men (Belenky, Clinchy, Goldberger, & Tarule, 1986), but this knowledge has been slow to influence teaching. In addition, evidence is mounting that girls of all ages are subjected to sexual harassment at school, which has a corrosive effect on their learning and their self-esteem (Stein, Marshall, & Tropp, 1993).

Women's health concerns generally have not received the attention they deserve despite recent federal legislative and administrative efforts to change the situation (Olson, 1994). Infant mortality rates in the United States are currently 24th among industrialized nations (U.S. Department of Health and Human Services, 1993), and women of color, especially African American women, suffer much higher infant and maternal mortality rates than white women (U.S. Department of Commerce, 1993) and have less access to adequate prenatal care. These high infant and maternal mortality rates have been linked to the problems associated with poverty, such as lack of adequate nutrition, lack of education, exposure to danger and disease, and lack of access to prenatal care (Olson, 1994). The impact of the acquired immune deficiency syndrome epidemic on women, especially women in ethnic and racial communities, has only recently been recognized (Dicks, 1994; Kaplan & Krell-Long, 1993). Breast cancer is on the increase for reasons that are not well understood, and lesbians and women of color are at increased risk of developing and dying from the disease (Bricker-Jenkins, 1994).

Access to the full range of family planning services and to safe, legal abortion remains a challenge, especially for women who must rely on Medicaid for their medical insurance, and those who use and provide these services, including abortion services, must be protected from harassment and harm. Although new reproductive technologies can offer a much-wanted pregnancy to infertile women, the economic costs, ethical dilemmas, and danger of exploitation of women inherent in some of these procedures are a continuing concern (Boston Women's Health Book Collective, 1992). More than half a million hysterectomies are performed annually in the United States, many of which are not medically necessary (Doress-Worters & Siegal, 1994). The research available to guide midlife and older women and their health care providers in the decision about long-term hormone additive therapy during or after menopause is currently confusing and contradictory (Notelovitz & Tonnessen, 1993). Finally, while women tend to live longer than men, for older women chronic illness and disability in addition to the burdens of caring for a spouse, partner, or an even older parent can be major problems. Thus, women tend to be in the majority of those elders who must turn to institutional or home-based long-term care, a system that can impoverish families and in which younger women are the majority of its underpaid workers.

There are also certain mental health problems that have special salience for women. More women than men are diagnosed with and treated for depression and other affective disorders (Regier et al., 1988; Wetzel, 1994). The fact that married women with young children at home are at special risk of depression, for example, illustrates that women's vulnerability to certain kinds of mental health problems can be related to their social circumstances, such as low income, and the stresses that their gender roles place on them. Although the diagnosis of most mental illnesses still seems to be more common among women than among men (Barker, Mandersheid, Hendershot, Jack, Schoenborn, & Goldstrom, 1992; Regier et al., 1988), women's mental health issues have not been given adequate attention (Blanch & Feiden-Warsh, 1994). African American, Asian American, and Latina women face greater barriers to accessing mental health services than either males or white women (Amaro & Russo, 1987; Fugita, 1990; Ruiz, 1990). Older women are also underserved. In addition, women have for years been underserved in programs to prevent or treat problems of substance use and abuse, and many current treatment programs do not meet the needs of women well, especially women with children or pregnant women (Abbott, 1995). Nevertheless, there have been persistent attempts to criminalize the use of illegal drugs by pregnant women despite strong evidence that this approach drives women away from needed prenatal care and violates their civil rights (Andrews & Patterson, 1995; Gustavsson, 1991; Norton Hawk, 1994).

Violence is a major problem affecting women of all ages, races, ethnicities, and sexual orientations and bearing on both health and mental health. Although violence is often seen as a problem that occurs in the streets, much of the violence that women suffer occurs at home or at the hands of someone they know well. Statistics show that every 15 seconds, a woman is beaten by her husband or partner (Boston Women's Health Book Collective, 1992). It is estimated that between 21 percent and 34 percent of women will be physically assaulted by an intimate adult partner in their lifetimes (Goodman, Koss, Fitzgerald, Russo, & Keita, 1993). Every six minutes a woman is forcibly raped (Boston Women's Health Book Collective, 1992), and the rate of reported forcible rape is increasing 4.5 percent per year (U.S. Department of Commerce, 1993). Sexual harassment, a form of sex discrimination that can range from the creation of a hostile working environment to verbal attacks to forcible sexual assault, is a problem that affects 50 percent of women at some point in their lives at work or in school (Goodman et al., 1993).

Violence against women is a crime, but it is also a health problem. It has been estimated that more than 20 percent of hospital emergency department surgical visits by women result from violence (Browne, 1993). Incidents of battering often occur when a woman is pregnant, endangering not only herself but her fetus (Browne, 1993). More than half of women murdered were killed by a partner (Browne, 1993). Lesbian women may suffer verbal, physical, or sexual assault because of their sexual orientation (Koss, 1993). Abuse of older women is also a major problem, often in their own families. In addition, surveys suggest that one-fourth or more of women have experienced sexual abuse as children, most often by an older male family member, and these rates are much higher among those women receiving inpatient or outpatient mental health and substance abuse services. Both the aftereffects of these traumas on the surviving victim and the pervasive fear of violence that most women experience can have long-term major social and mental health consequences (and on any children these women may have). In particular, posttraumatic stress disorder is now understood to be a common syndrome in women who have been subjected to physical or sexual assault, but this diagnosis can only be made if the history taking reveals that a trauma has occurred (Browne, 1993).

Finally, social welfare policies, even those intended to benefit women, have had the effect of enforcing gender norms of behavior (Abramovitz, 1988; Miller, 1992). In addition, history shows that although the family responsibilities of middle-class and affluent European American women have been to some extent protected and honored, there has been no policy support for the family work and childrearing responsibilities of women of color or women who are poor (Glenn, 1985). Thus, social programs such as Aid to Families with Dependent Children; family planning, adolescent pregnancy, abortion, and other reproductive health services; funding for day care; child custody and child support; and other programs and policies from which women and children primarily benefit often prove to be hotly debated because they are intimately related to ideologies about women's roles and the control of women and their bodies. Women living in rural areas also tend to experience limited access to resources because social policies are largely developed in large urban areas and are frequently insensitive to the unique needs of women in smaller communities (Caputo & Gray, 1996). In addition, social policies are still generally made by white men because, despite some impressive gains made by women seeking elective office and other positions of power, men still predominate in legislatures and executive offices in both the public and the private sector and thus in the development of social and organizational policy.

ISSUE STATEMENT

Women make up a majority of the population and of the clients social workers serve, and continued attention to women's issues is essential because of the disadvantages and discrimination women still face in many aspects of their lives (Davis, 1994). Women perform the majority of the world's work but control a disproportionately small share of its resources. Although women in the more prosperous Western nations fare better in life circumstances than women in many of the less wealthy nations of the world, economic, political, social, and cultural forces in all societies operate to the disadvantage of women and girls. These disadvantages affect education; health care, including reproductive and mental health; crime, especially as victims of violence; employment; and social welfare, especially income maintenance programs. These disadvantages affect the well-being of women and their families at all stages of the life cycle, from girlhood through old age. In addition, certain groups of women—women of color, women who are poor, women who maintain households, younger or older women, lesbians, and women who are mentally and physically challenged—often face even greater discrimination and disadvantage than other women do.

The social work profession has a long-standing commitment to the elimination of all forms of discrimination against women—in society, as clients, and as social work professionals. Many efforts have been made to reduce the disadvantages and discrimination women face in all societies. However, continuing efforts to develop social work practices, social policies, and health and human services that better meet the needs of women remain essential for enhancing the health, development, and well-being of all American women, especially our clients and others at greatest risk, at all stages of life.

POLICY STATEMENT

NASW recognizes the wide range of issues that affect women and is committed to advancing policies and practices to improve the status and well-being of women of all ages. NASW actively advocates for remedies to gender inequity at all levels of traditional social work intervention: at the macro level through federal and state legislation and in the executive branches of government; at meso levels in communities and organizations; and at micro levels in direct practice with individuals, families, and groups. Action is needed not only to ensure access to all institutions and services but to ensure equality of value of women's knowledge base, experience, work, and ideas.

Employment

NASW supports the following:

■ legislative and administrative strategies that address pay equity for women

■ measures that allow women who are discriminated against in employment and compensation to seek full legal and fiscal compensation

■ comparable worth initiatives for increasing women's wages in both the public and private sectors

■ improving women's earnings as a necessary part of any strategy to reduce poverty

■ breaking the "glass ceiling" that limits the upward mobility of women and their advancement to positions of greater power and reward in both public and private employment

■ initiatives related to improving women's economic development to support entrepreneurial efforts

■ providing women and girls education and on-the-job training opportunities for job entry, high-wage work, and career advancement

■ ending sexual harassment wherever it occurs

■ initiatives that maximize the flexibility of working conditions in order to support the needs of women who provide care to family members

■ agency, community, state, and national initiatives that address the need for accesible and affordable child care

■ supporting affirmative action programs that help women gain access to educational opportunity and more highly paid jobs and to advance in whatever occupations or careers that they choose—NASW itself as an organization has used affirmative action effectively in both its staffing and its volunteer leadership to increase the numbers of women in positions of leadership in the association, and thus serves as a model for other human services and professional organizations showing that affirmative action works

■ public and workplace policies that support the economic and social value of the unpaid work that women do in caring for children and families

■ payment for the caregiving work of women

■ training and compensation for women who are paid providers of hands-on care—in health care, long-term care, child care, and home care—that reflects the true value of the work they do.

Income Maintenance and Other Public Welfare Systems

NASW supports the following:

■ adequate funding of public social insurance and income maintenance programs that are designed in such a way that women benefit from them to the same degree that men do—the continuing efforts to "reform" the Aid to Families with Dependent Children program, for example, must not be used in a way that is really designed to "reform women" (Axinn & Hirsch, 1993)

■ programs that afford women an adequate standard of living as well as respect and dignity

■ access to the workforce without jeopardizing resources such as quality child care and health insurance benefits

■ programs for the enforcement, collection, and distribution of child support that are universally available

■ programs and policies that recognize housing as a basic human need, that end homelessness, and that provide adequate affordable housing.

Education

NASW supports the following:

■ ending gender discrimination in education and training in all forms and at all levels

■ accessibility to special education, vocational education, and the full range of courses for all girls, especially those from ethnic and racial minority groups

■ curriculum that includes women's issues and experiences, especially in social work education

■ adequate support for education and training for poor women.

Health and Mental Health

NASW supports the following:

■ initiatives to reduce teen pregnancy, as it has been demonstrated that, intended or unintended, adolescent motherhood truncates the educational, vocational, and economical lives of young women

■ adequate funding for health and mental health services that address the needs of women, including adolescent women, poor women, women of color, lesbians, older women, and women with long-term disabilities

■ access to adequate health and mental health services regardless of financial status, race and ethnicity, or age

■ research on the health problems and mental health needs of women, especially women of color, poor women, and both adolescent and older women

■ reproductive freedom and safe access to the full range of reproductive health services for all women, including those who must depend on public health insurance systems—self-determination will be a reality only when all of those who deliver and make use of reproductive health services, including abortion services, are safe and free from harassment

■ school-based health services for adolescents that include access to sanitary hygiene products, reproductive health information, and the prevention information needed to protect young women from human immunodeficiency virus infection in particular and sexually transmitted diseases in general

■ more and improved research, services, and treatment for women with human immune deficiency virus and acquired immune deficiency syndrome

■ improved substance abuse programs that meet the full range of women's needs with regard for the interests of both the women and their children

■ continued efforts to combat violence against women of all ages as well as adequate health, mental health, and social services for women and girls who are the victims of violence in all forms

■ professional education of men and women, especially social work education, that makes clear the extent of violence against women and girls, how to prevent it, and how to respond to it effectively

■ educational programs that help boys and girls learn that violence is not acceptable and how to maintain nonviolent relationships

■ efforts to seek out, study, develop, and disseminate theories of psychosocial development and models of services delivery that recognize and do not pathologize the unique developmental patterns of women—such theories and models recognize the diversity of women's experiences, situations, cultural and ethnic identifications, and sexual orientations

■ efforts to empower women in the planning, monitoring, and design of health and mental health services.

Human Rights

The 1995 United Nations Fourth World Conference on Women recognized women's rights are inherently human rights. Therefore, NASW supports

■ ratification by the United States of the Convention to Eliminate All Forms of Discrimination against Women

■ recognition that changing national and international economic and structural arrangements are resulting in the exploitation of women

■ recognition that some religious traditions may victimize women.

REFERENCES

Abbott, A. A. (1995). Substance abuse and the feminist perspective. In N. Van Den Bergh (Ed.), *Feminist practice in the 21st century* (pp. 258–277). Washington, DC: NASW Press.

Abramovitz, M. (1988). *Regulating the lives of women: Social welfare policy from colonial times to the present*. Boston: South End Press.

Amaro, H., & Russo, N. F. (1987). Hispanic women and mental health: An overview of contemporary issues in research and practice. *Psychology of Women Quarterly, 11*(4), 393–407.

American Association of University Women Educational Foundation. (1992). *How schools shortchange girls: A study of major findings on girls and education*. Washington, DC: Author.

Andrews, A. B., & Patterson, E. G. (1995). Searching for solutions to alcohol and other drug abuse during pregnancy: Ethics, values, and constitutional principles. *Social Work, 40*, 55–64.

Axinn, J. M., & Hirsch, A. E. (1993). Welfare and the "reform" of women. *Families in Society, 74*(9), 563–572.

Barker, P., Mandersheid, R., Hendershot, G., Jack, S., Schoenborn, A., & Goldstrom, I. (1992). Serious mental illness and disability in the adult household population. *Advance Data, 218*, 1–12.

Barnett, R., & Baruch, G. K. (1987). Social roles, gender and psychological distress. In R. C. Barnett, L. Bienecke, & G. K. Baruch (Eds.), *Gender and stress* (pp. 122–143). New York: Free Press.

Belenky, M. F., Clinchy, B. M., Goldberger, N. R., & Tarule, J. M. (1986). *Women's ways of knowing: The development of self, voice and mind*. New York: Basic Books.

Blanch, A. K., & Feiden-Warsh, C. (1994). Women's mental health services: The need for women in mental health leadership. *Jour-*

nal of Mental Health Administration, 21(4), 332–337.

Boston Women's Health Book Collective. (1992). *The new our bodies, ourselves: A book by and for women*. New York: Simon & Schuster.

Bricker-Jenkins, M. (1994). Feminist practice and breast cancer: "The patriarchy has claimed my right breast...." In M. M. Olson (Ed.), *Women's health and social work: Feminist perspectives* (pp. 17–42). New York: Haworth Press.

Brody, E. M. (1981). Women in the middle and family help to older people. *The Gerontologist, 23*, 471–480.

Browne, A. (1993). Violence against women by male partners: Prevalence, outcomes & policy implications. *American Psychologist, 48*(10), 1077–1087.

Burbridge, L. C. (1992). *New economic trends for women's employment: Implications for girls' vocational education* (Working Paper Series No. 247). Wellesley, MA: Wellesley College Center for Research on Women.

Caputo, R., & Gray, S.W. (1996, July). *Women and rural poverty: A national study*. Paper presented at the 21st Annual Conference of Social Work and Human Services in the Rural Environment, University of Western Michigan, Kalamazoo, MI.

Davis, L. V. (Ed.). (1994). *Building on women's strengths: A social work agenda for the twenty-first century*. New York: Haworth Press.

Dicks, B. A. (1994). African-American women and AIDS: A public health/social work challenge. In M. M. Olson (Ed.), *Women's health and social work: Feminist perspectives* (pp. 123–144). New York: Haworth Press.

Doress-Worters, P. B., & Siegal, D. L. (1994). *Ourselves, growing older: The new book for women over forty (updated)*. New York: Simon & Schuster.

Education Amendments of 1972, P.L. 92-318, 86 Stat. 235.

Fugita, S. (1990). Asian/Pacific mental health: Some needed research in epidemiology and service utilization. In F. Serafica et al. (Eds.), *Mental health of ethnic minorities* (pp. 66–84). New York: Praeger.

Glenn, E. N. (1985). Racial ethnic women's labor: The intersection of race, gender and class oppression. *Review of Radical Political Economics, 17*(3), 86–108.

Goodman, L. A., Koss, M. P., Fitzgerald, L. F., Russo, N. F., & Keita, G. P. (1993). Male violence against women: Current research and future directions. *American Psychologist, 48*(10), 1054–1058.

Gustavsson, N. S. (1991). Pregnant chemically dependent women: The new criminals. *Affilia, 6*(2), 61–73.

Hochschild, A. (1989). *The second shift: Working parents and the stalled revolution at home*. New York: Viking.

Kaplan, M. S., & Krell-Long, L. (1993). AIDS, health policy and ethics. *Affilia, 8*(2), 157–170.

Koss, M. P. (1993). Rape: Scope, impact, interventions, and public policy responses. *American Psychologist, 48*(10), 1062–1069.

Miller, D. C. (1992). *Women and social welfare: A feminist analysis*. New York: Praeger.

Norton Hawk, M. A. (1994). How social policies make matters worse: The case of maternal substance abuse. *Journal of Drug Issues, 24*(3), 517–526.

Notelovitz, M., & Tonnessen, D. (1993) *Menopause and midlife health*. New York: St. Martin's Press.

Olson, M. M. (Ed.). (1994). *Women's health and social work: Feminist perspectives*. New York: Haworth Press.

Ozawa, M. N. (1995). The economic status of vulnerable older women. *Social Work, 40*, 323–331.

Regier, D. A., et al. (1988). One-month prevalence of mental disorders in the United States. *Archives of General Psychiatry, 45*, 977–986.

Ruiz, D. S. (Ed.). (1990). *Handbook of mental health and mental disorder among Black Americans*. New York: Greenwood Press.

Stein, N., Marshall, N. L., & Tropp, L. R. (1993). *Secrets in public: Sexual harassment in our schools*. Wellesley, MA: Center for Research on Women, Wellesley College.

U.S. Department of Commerce. (1993). *Statistical abstract of the United States* (113th ed.). Lanham, MD: Bernan Press.

U.S. Department of Health and Human Services. (1993). *Health United States and healthy people 2000 review—1992.* Hyattsville, MD: Author.

U.S. Department of Labor. (1991). *A report on the glass ceiling initiative.* Washington, DC: U.S. Government Printing Office.

Wetzel, J. W. (1994). Depression: Women-at-risk. In M. M. Olson (Ed), *Women's health and social work: Feminist perspectives* (pp. 85–108). New York: Haworth Press.

Policy statement approved by the NASW Delegate Assembly, August 1996. This policy supersedes the policy statement on Women's Issues approved by the Delegate Assembly in 1987 and in 1977. For further information, contact the National Association of Social Workers, 750 First Street, NE, Suite 700, Washington, DC 20002-4241. Telephone: 202-408-8600 or 800-638-8799.

Youth Suicide

BACKGROUND

Although suicide among young adults and adolescents is not a new or recent phenomenon, interest in and the classification of this event as a significant social problem is relatively recent. Within the past 15 years, attention has centered on increasing rates of youth suicide and, more recently, on dramatic increases in suicide among those ages 14 and younger. With more sophisticated methods of surveillance and analysis of mortality data, it is apparent that suicide is currently among the leading causes of death among children and youth in the United States. However, the research on youth suicide is limited because much of the data are usually from psychological autopsies and are retrospective rather than prospective. Control groups have consisted of psychiatric inpatients, suicidal youths, or suicides from older age groups. Research using youths in the general population as control subjects is lacking and may again reflect the discomfort that exists in confronting the prevalence of youth suicide. This deficit in the research makes it difficult to determine the importance of identified risk factors and their relative risk values in the context of the general youthful population (Holinger, Offer, Barter, & Bell, 1994).

Despite the inability of previous research to definitively identify causes of youth suicide and the conditions that result in greater susceptibility for some youths than others, ongoing research continues to explore the range of factors associated with youth suicide. Although a definitive answer to the question of causation is slow to emerge, current research is probing a combination of risk factors. Some of the identified indicators are genetic susceptibility; previous family history of suicide; depression and other mental health problems; impulsivity; learning disabilities; physical and sexual abuse; de-

mographic pressures; social changes; unwanted pregnancy; the use of drugs; disrupted family relationships; the role of popular culture, including music and television; suicide clusters and contagion; and the availability of lethal weapons (Berman & Jobes, 1991).

Sexual identity issues, including homosexuality and bisexuality, appear to represent a risk factor for youth suicide. There is consistent evidence that homosexual people of both sexes attempt suicide more often than heterosexual people (Alcohol, Drug Abuse, and Mental Health Administration, 1989b). Conflicts of youths with family members or within themselves over homosexuality and "coming out" are identified as periods of greater risk for suicide for gay men, lesbians, and bisexual people. Personal and family stress are compounded by a society and culture that is organized for heterosexuality and that, at times, reflects heightened hostility toward gay, lesbian, and bisexual people (Harry, 1989).

Firearms in the homes of potentially suicidal adolescents have been shown to markedly increase their risk for suicide. In 1992 firearm-related deaths accounted for 64.9 percent of suicides among people under age 25 (Centers for Disease Control and Prevention, 1995). In addition, a clustering effect, also known as a contagion effect, has been observed in communities, in which the death of one young person may be followed by the suicide of several others (Davidson, Rosenberg, Mercy, Franklin, & Simmons, 1989). Because of this, other community identities, such as the media, need education regarding intervention and postvention of youth suicides. Furthermore, because of the stigma of suicide, the social supports ordinarily present when a loved one dies, especially a child, may not be readily offered to the families of those who attempt or complete suicide.

According to the *Report of the Secretary's Task Force on Youth Suicide* (Alcohol, Drug Abuse, and Mental Health Administration, 1989a), prior suicidal behavior of any kind is a strong risk predictor for adolescents. Other behaviors that may be precursors to suicide and that appear consistently in the histories of adolescents who attempt or complete suicide include academic difficulties; disciplinary problems; truancy; antisocial behavior, including assaultiveness; social isolation; impulsive behavior; running away; suggestibility; and imitation. Although these factors alone may not suggest suicidal risk, when combined with family history and thorough diagnostic assessment, they may signal the need for further diagnostic inquiry and, if indicated, implementation of prevention services. In addition, it should be noted that different behavioral indicators of suicide exist for children age 14 and younger than for older adolescents.

Programs exist in many communities to intervene early and provide a continuum of services to youth at risk of suicide and their families. These programs include public information and education campaigns, peer counselor and mentoring programs in public schools, the development of integrated prevention curricula that emphasize protective factors for youth, special education and training for teachers and others who work with youth, suicide prevention centers, and 24-hour youth crisis lines.

Presently at both the federal and state levels, positive momentum to establish programs and services to prevent youth suicide may be slowed by reductions in health and human services funding. Furthermore, reductions in a range of health and human services funding may result in fewer community services for families or more stringent eligibility standards, thereby exacerbating conditions that are associated with increased risk of youth suicide.

ISSUE STATEMENT

The phenomenon of youth suicide should be viewed as a complex problem that involves multiple physical, psychological, and social factors (Berman & Jobes, 1991). From the social work perspective, crucial interventions include supporting the family, teaching children and adolescents coping skills, and developing humane social policies that support a healthy, safe environment for all youth. Specifically, the various services delivery systems in our society must develop programs designed to identify children and youth who are at risk and provide effective intervention strategies geared to the multiple needs of these youngsters and their families. Furthermore, suicide should not be viewed in isolation from other problems involving children and adolescents.

Social workers and others in health and human services, such as school social workers, school counselors, individual and family therapists, physicians, nurses, and psychologists, may have specialized training in the etiology and treatment of children and youth at risk of suicide (Leenaars & Wenckstern, 1990). However, the institutional structures, policies, and procedures necessary to increase interdisciplinary cooperation, communication, information exchange, and coordination of services are not widely and consistently available to address the risk factors that contribute to youth suicide and that are necessary for early identification, prevention, and intervention.

POLICY STATEMENT

NASW views the current high rate of child and adolescent suicide as a national tragedy. To address the complex and multiple social and health issues related to youth suicide, NASW supports the following:

■ social workers assuming a leadership role in ensuring that the staff of all agencies is prepared to recognize the risk factors associated with children and adolescent suicide and that policies are in place that allow for the provision of intervention services or referral of youths and their families for appropriate services

■ provision of a range of professional prevention, intervention, and postvention services for families and others affected by the suicide of children and youths

■ public and private funding of multidisciplinary research to extend and verify knowledge of youth suicide and social work institutions and educational facilities using the most current and well-researched standards of practice

■ social workers involvement in the development of policies, procedures, and protocols that facilitate interdisciplinary collaboration in the provision of early identification, intervention, and postvention services, including educating the media about responsible reporting and the contagion effect

■ educational and legislative measures that restrict access of youths to firearms, the use of which is a major method of achieving youth suicides

■ use of the best current research regarding the unique risk factors and special needs of various groups of youths, such as white males ages 14 to 20; ethnically diverse youths, particularly African American and Native American youths; and youths who experience problems with sexual identity, especially gay, lesbian, and bisexual youths

■ school social workers in providing an active role in suicide prevention and intervention programs in the schools and community and providing training to teachers, staff, and student peers to detect and refer youths with self-destructive behavior and other problems that may lead to suicide.

REFERENCES

Alcohol, Drug Abuse, and Mental Health Administration. (1989a). *Report of the secretary's task force on youth suicide: Volume 2. Risk factors for youth suicide* (DHHS Publication No. ADM 89-1622). Washington, DC: U S. Government Printing Office.

Alcohol, Drug Abuse, and Mental Health Administration. (1989b). *Report of the secretary's task force on youth suicide: Volume 3. Prevention and interventions in youth suicide* (DHHS Publication No. ADM 89-1623). Washington, DC: U.S. Government Printing Office.

Berman, A. W., & Jobes, D. A. (1991). *Adolescent suicide: Assessment and intervention.* Washington, DC: American Psychological Association.

Centers for Disease Control and Prevention. (1995). Suicide among children, adolescents, and young adult—United States, 1980–1992. *Morbidity and Mortality Weekly Review, 44*(15), 289–291.

Davidson, L. E., Rosenberg, M. R., Mercy, J. A., Franklin, J., & Simmons, J. T. (1989). An epidemiologic study of risk factors in two teenage suicide clusters. *Journal of the American Medical Association, 262,* 2687–2692.

Harry, J. (1989). Sexual identity issues in alcohol, drug abuse, and mental health administration. In Alcohol, Drug Abuse, and Mental Health Administration, *Report of the secretary's task force on youth suicide: Volume 2. Risk factors for youth suicide* (DHHS Publication No. ADM 89-1622, pp. 131–142). Washington, DC: U.S. Government Printing Office.

Holinger, P. C., Offer, D., Barter, J. T., & Bell, C. C. (1994). *Suicide and homicide among adolescents.* New York: Guilford Press.

Leenaars, A. A., & Wenckstern, S. (Eds.). (1990). *Suicide prevention in schools.* Washington, DC: Hemisphere.

Policy statement approved by the NASW Delegate Assembly, August 1996. This policy supersedes the policy statement on Youth Suicide approved by the Delegate Assembly in 1987. For further information, contact the National Association of Social Workers, 750 First Street, NE, Suite 700, Washington, DC 20002-4241. Telephone: 202-408-8600 or 800-638-8799.

NASW CODE OF ETHICS

NASW Code of Ethics

PREAMBLE

The primary mission of the social work profession is to enhance human well-being and help meet the basic human needs of all people, with particular attention to the needs and empowerment of people who are vulnerable, oppressed, and living in poverty. A historic and defining feature of social work is the profession's focus on individual well-being in a social context and the well-being of society. Fundamental to social work is attention to the environmental forces that create, contribute to, and address problems in living.

Social workers promote social justice and social change with and on behalf of clients. "Clients" is used inclusively to refer to individuals, families, groups, organizations, and communities. Social workers are sensitive to cultural and ethnic diversity and strive to end discrimination, oppression, poverty, and other forms of social injustice. These activities may be in the form of direct practice, community organizing, supervision, consultation, administration, advocacy, social and political action, policy development and implementation, education, and research and evaluation. Social workers seek to enhance the capacity of people to address their own needs. Social workers also seek to promote the responsiveness of organizations, communities, and other social institutions to individuals' needs and social problems.

The mission of the social work profession is rooted in a set of core values. These core values, embraced by social workers throughout the profession's history, are the foundation of social work's unique purpose and perspective:

- service
- social justice
- dignity and worth of the person

- importance of human relationships
- integrity
- competence.

This constellation of core values reflects what is unique to the social work profession. Core values, and the principles that flow from them, must be balanced within the context and complexity of the human experience.

PURPOSE OF THE NASW CODE OF ETHICS

Professional ethics are at the core of social work. The profession has an obligation to articulate its basic values, ethical principles, and ethical standards. The *NASW Code of Ethics* sets forth these values, principles, and standards to guide social workers' conduct. The *Code* is relevant to all social workers and social work students, regardless of their professional functions, the settings in which they work, or the populations they serve.

The *NASW Code of Ethics* serves six purposes:

1. The *Code* identifies core values on which social work's mission is based.
2. The *Code* summarizes broad ethical principles that reflect the profession's core values and establishes a set of specific ethical standards that should be used to guide social work practice.
3. The *Code* is designed to help social workers identify relevant considerations when professional obligations conflict or ethical uncertainties arise.
4. The *Code* provides ethical standards to which the general public can hold the social work profession accountable.

5. The *Code* socializes practitioners new to the field to social work's mission, values, ethical principles, and ethical standards.

6. The *Code* articulates standards that the social work profession itself can use to assess whether social workers have engaged in unethical conduct. NASW has formal procedures to adjudicate ethics complaints filed against its members.[1] In subscribing to this *Code*, social workers are required to cooperate in its implementation, participate in NASW adjudication proceedings, and abide by any NASW disciplinary rulings or sanctions based on it.

The *Code* offers a set of values, principles, and standards to guide decision making and conduct when ethical issues arise. It does not provide a set of rules that prescribe how social workers should act in all situations. Specific applications of the *Code* must take into account the context in which it is being considered and the possibility of conflicts among the *Code*'s values, principles, and standards. Ethical responsibilities flow from all human relationships, from the personal and familial to the social and professional.

Further, the *NASW Code of Ethics* does not specify which values, principles, and standards are most important and ought to outweigh others in instances when they conflict. Reasonable differences of opinion can and do exist among social workers with respect to the ways in which values, ethical principles, and ethical standards should be rank ordered when they conflict. Ethical decision making in a given situation must apply the informed judgment of the individual social worker and should also consider how the issues would be judged in a peer review process where the ethical standards of the profession would be applied.

Ethical decision making is a process. There are many instances in social work where simple answers are not available to resolve complex ethical issues. Social workers should take into consideration all the values, principles, and standards in this *Code* that are relevant to any situation in which ethical judgment is warranted.

Social workers' decisions and actions should be consistent with the spirit as well as the letter of this *Code*.

In addition to this *Code*, there are many other sources of information about ethical thinking that may be useful. Social workers should consider ethical theory and principles generally, social work theory and research, laws, regulations, agency policies, and other relevant codes of ethics, recognizing that among codes of ethics social workers should consider the *NASW Code of Ethics* as their primary source. Social workers also should be aware of the impact on ethical decision making of their clients' and their own personal values and cultural and religious beliefs and practices. They should be aware of any conflicts between personal and professional values and deal with them responsibly. For additional guidance social workers should consult the relevant literature on professional ethics and ethical decision making and seek appropriate consultation when faced with ethical dilemmas. This may involve consultation with an agency-based or social work organization's ethics committee, a regulatory body, knowledgeable colleagues, supervisors, or legal counsel.

Instances may arise when social workers' ethical obligations conflict with agency policies or relevant laws or regulations. When such conflicts occur, social workers must make a responsible effort to resolve the conflict in a manner that is consistent with the values, principles, and standards expressed in this *Code*. If a reasonable resolution of the conflict does not appear possible, social workers should seek proper consultation before making a decision.

The *NASW Code of Ethics* is to be used by NASW and by individuals, agencies, organizations, and bodies (such as licensing and regulatory boards, professional liability insurance providers, courts of law, agency boards of directors, government agencies, and other professional groups) that choose to adopt it or use it as a frame of reference. Violation of standards in this *Code* does not automatically imply legal liability or violation of the law. Such determination can only be made in the context of legal and judicial proceedings. Alleged violations of the *Code* would be subject to a peer review process. Such processes are generally separate from legal or administrative procedures and insulated from

---

[1]*For information on NASW adjudication procedures, see* NASW Procedures for the Adjudication of Grievances.

legal review or proceedings to allow the profession to counsel and discipline its own members.

A code of ethics cannot guarantee ethical behavior. Moreover, a code of ethics cannot resolve all ethical issues or disputes or capture the richness and complexity involved in striving to make responsible choices within a moral community. Rather, a code of ethics sets forth values, ethical principles, and ethical standards to which professionals aspire and by which their actions can be judged. Social workers' ethical behavior should result from their personal commitment to engage in ethical practice. The *NASW Code of Ethics* reflects the commitment of all social workers to uphold the profession's values and to act ethically. Principles and standards must be applied by individuals of good character who discern moral questions and, in good faith, seek to make reliable ethical judgments.

ETHICAL PRINCIPLES

The following broad ethical principles are based on social work's core values of service, social justice, dignity and worth of the person, importance of human relationships, integrity, and competence. These principles set forth ideals to which all social workers should aspire.

Value: *Service*

Ethical Principle: *Social workers' primary goal is to help people in need and to address social problems.*

Social workers elevate service to others above self-interest. Social workers draw on their knowledge, values, and skills to help people in need and to address social problems. Social workers are encouraged to volunteer some portion of their professional skills with no expectation of significant financial return (pro bono service).

Value: *Social Justice*

Ethical Principle: *Social workers challenge social injustice.*

Social workers pursue social change, particularly with and on behalf of vulnerable and oppressed individuals and groups of people. Social workers' social change efforts are focused primarily on issues of poverty, unemployment, discrimination, and other forms of social injustice. These activities seek to promote sensitivity to and knowledge about oppression and cultural and ethnic diversity. Social workers strive to ensure access to needed information, services, and resources; equality of opportunity; and meaningful participation in decision making for all people.

Value: *Dignity and Worth of the Person*

Ethical Principle: *Social workers respect the inherent dignity and worth of the person.*

Social workers treat each person in a caring and respectful fashion, mindful of individual differences and cultural and ethnic diversity. Social workers promote clients' socially responsible self-determination. Social workers seek to enhance clients' capacity and opportunity to change and to address their own needs. Social workers are cognizant of their dual responsibility to clients and to the broader society. They seek to resolve conflicts between clients' interests and the broader society's interests in a socially responsible manner consistent with the values, ethical principles, and ethical standards of the profession.

Value: *Importance of Human Relationships*

Ethical Principle: *Social workers recognize the central importance of human relationships.*

Social workers understand that relationships between and among people are an important vehicle for change. Social workers engage people as partners in the helping process. Social workers seek to strengthen relationships among people in a purposeful effort to promote, restore, maintain, and enhance the well-being of individuals, families, social groups, organizations, and communities.

Value: *Integrity*

Ethical Principle: *Social workers behave in a trustworthy manner.*

Social workers are continually aware of the profession's mission, values, ethical principles, and ethical standards and practice in a manner consistent with them. Social workers act honestly and responsibly and promote ethical practices on the part of the organizations with which they are affiliated.

Value: *Competence*

Ethical Principle: *Social workers practice within their areas of competence and develop and enhance their professional expertise.*

Social workers continually strive to increase their professional knowledge and skills and to apply them in practice. Social workers should aspire to contribute to the knowledge base of the profession.

ETHICAL STANDARDS

The following ethical standards are relevant to the professional activities of all social workers. These standards concern (1) social workers' ethical responsibilities to clients, (2) social workers' ethical responsibilities to colleagues, (3) social workers' ethical responsibilities in practice settings, (4) social workers' ethical responsibilities as professionals, (5) social workers' ethical responsibilities to the social work profession, and (6) social workers' ethical responsibilities to the broader society.

Some of the standards that follow are enforceable guidelines for professional conduct, and some are aspirational. The extent to which each standard is enforceable is a matter of professional judgment to be exercised by those responsible for reviewing alleged violations of ethical standards.

1. SOCIAL WORKERS' ETHICAL RESPONSIBILITIES TO CLIENTS

1.01   Commitment to Clients

Social workers' primary responsibility is to promote the well-being of clients. In general, clients' interests are primary. However, social workers' responsibility to the larger society or specific legal obligations may on limited occasions supersede the loyalty owed clients, and clients should be so advised. (Examples include when a social worker is required by law to report that a client has abused a child or has threatened to harm self or others.)

1.02   Self-Determination

Social workers respect and promote the right of clients to self-determination and assist clients in their efforts to identify and clarify their goals.

Social workers may limit clients' right to self-determination when, in the social workers' professional judgment, clients' actions or potential actions pose a serious, foreseeable, and imminent risk to themselves or others.

1.03   Informed Consent

(a) Social workers should provide services to clients only in the context of a professional relationship based, when appropriate, on valid informed consent. Social workers should use clear and understandable language to inform clients of the purpose of the services, risks related to the services, limits to services because of the requirements of a third-party payer, relevant costs, reasonable alternatives, clients' right to refuse or withdraw consent, and the time frame covered by the consent. Social workers should provide clients with an opportunity to ask questions.

(b) In instances when clients are not literate or have difficulty understanding the primary language used in the practice setting, social workers should take steps to ensure clients' comprehension. This may include providing clients with a detailed verbal explanation or arranging for a qualified interpreter or translator whenever possible.

(c) In instances when clients lack the capacity to provide informed consent, social workers should protect clients' interests by seeking permission from an appropriate third party, informing clients consistent with the clients' level of understanding. In such instances social workers should seek to ensure that the third party acts in a manner consistent with clients' wishes and interests. Social workers should take reasonable steps to enhance such clients' ability to give informed consent.

(d) In instances when clients are receiving services involuntarily, social workers should provide information about the nature and extent of services and about the extent of clients' right to refuse service.

(e) Social workers who provide services via electronic media (such as computer, telephone, radio, and television) should inform recipients of the limitations and risks associated with such services.

(f) Social workers should obtain clients' informed consent before audiotaping or videotaping clients or permitting observation of services to clients by a third party.

1.04 Competence

(a) Social workers should provide services and represent themselves as competent only within the boundaries of their education, training, license, certification, consultation received, supervised experience, or other relevant professional experience.

(b) Social workers should provide services in substantive areas or use intervention techniques or approaches that are new to them only after engaging in appropriate study, training, consultation, and supervision from people who are competent in those interventions or techniques.

(c) When generally recognized standards do not exist with respect to an emerging area of practice, social workers should exercise careful judgment and take responsible steps (including appropriate education, research, training, consultation, and supervision) to ensure the competence of their work and to protect clients from harm.

1.05 Cultural Competence and Social Diversity

(a) Social workers should understand culture and its function in human behavior and society, recognizing the strengths that exist in all cultures.

(b) Social workers should have a knowledge base of their clients' cultures and be able to demonstrate competence in the provision of services that are sensitive to clients' cultures and to differences among people and cultural groups.

(c) Social workers should obtain education about and seek to understand the nature of social diversity and oppression with respect to race, ethnicity, national origin, color, sex, sexual orientation, age, marital status, political belief, religion, and mental or physical disability.

1.06 Conflicts of Interest

(a) Social workers should be alert to and avoid conflicts of interest that interfere with the exercise of professional discretion and impartial judgment. Social workers should inform clients when a real or potential conflict of interest arises and take reasonable steps to resolve the issue in a manner that makes the clients' interests primary and pro-

tects clients' interests to the greatest extent possible. In some cases, protecting clients' interests may require termination of the professional relationship with proper referral of the client.

(b) Social workers should not take unfair advantage of any professional relationship or exploit others to further their personal, religious, political, or business interests.

(c) Social workers should not engage in dual or multiple relationships with clients or former clients in which there is a risk of exploitation or potential harm to the client. In instances when dual or multiple relationships are unavoidable, social workers should take steps to protect clients and are responsible for setting clear, appropriate, and culturally sensitive boundaries. (Dual or multiple relationships occur when social workers relate to clients in more than one relationship, whether professional, social, or business. Dual or multiple relationships can occur simultaneously or consecutively.)

(d) When social workers provide services to two or more people who have a relationship with each other (for example, couples, family members), social workers should clarify with all parties which individuals will be considered clients and the nature of social workers' professional obligations to the various individuals who are receiving services. Social workers who anticipate a conflict of interest among the individuals receiving services or who anticipate having to perform in potentially conflicting roles (for example, when a social worker is asked to testify in a child custody dispute or divorce proceedings involving clients) should clarify their role with the parties involved and take appropriate action to minimize any conflict of interest.

1.07 Privacy and Confidentiality

(a) Social workers should respect clients' right to privacy. Social workers should not solicit private information from clients unless it is essential to providing services or conducting social work evaluation or research. Once private information is shared, standards of confidentiality apply.

(b) Social workers may disclose confidential information when appropriate with valid consent from a client or a person legally authorized to consent on behalf of a client.

(c) Social workers should protect the confidentiality of all information obtained in the course of professional service, except for compelling professional reasons. The general expectation that social workers will keep information confidential does not apply when disclosure is necessary to prevent serious, foreseeable, and imminent harm to a client or other identifiable person or when laws or regulations require disclosure without a client's consent. In all instances, social workers should disclose the least amount of confidential information necessary to achieve the desired purpose; only information that is directly relevant to the purpose for which the disclosure is made should be revealed.

(d) Social workers should inform clients, to the extent possible, about the disclosure of confidential information and the potential consequences, when feasible before the disclosure is made. This applies whether social workers disclose confidential information on the basis of a legal requirement or client consent.

(e) Social workers should discuss with clients and other interested parties the nature of confidentiality and limitations of clients' right to confidentiality. Social workers should review with clients circumstances where confidential information may be requested and where disclosure of confidential information may be legally required. This discussion should occur as soon as possible in the social worker–client relationship and as needed throughout the course of the relationship.

(f) When social workers provide counseling services to families, couples, or groups, social workers should seek agreement among the parties involved concerning each individual's right to confidentiality and obligation to preserve the confidentiality of information shared by others. Social workers should inform participants in family, couples, or group counseling that social workers cannot guarantee that all participants will honor such agreements.

(g) Social workers should inform clients involved in family, couples, marital, or group counseling of the social worker's, employer's, and agency's policy concerning the social worker's disclosure of confidential information among the parties involved in the counseling.

(h) Social workers should not disclose confidential information to third-party payers unless clients have authorized such disclosure.

(i) Social workers should not discuss confidential information in any setting unless privacy can be ensured. Social workers should not discuss confidential information in public or semipublic areas such as hallways, waiting rooms, elevators, and restaurants.

(j) Social workers should protect the confidentiality of clients during legal proceedings to the extent permitted by law. When a court of law or other legally authorized body orders social workers to disclose confidential or privileged information without a client's consent and such disclosure could cause harm to the client, social workers should request that the court withdraw the order or limit the order as narrowly as possible or maintain the records under seal, unavailable for public inspection.

(k) Social workers should protect the confidentiality of clients when responding to requests from members of the media.

(l) Social workers should protect the confidentiality of clients' written and electronic records and other sensitive information. Social workers should take reasonable steps to ensure that clients' records are stored in a secure location and that clients' records are not available to others who are not authorized to have access.

(m) Social workers should take precautions to ensure and maintain the confidentiality of information transmitted to other parties through the use of computers, electronic mail, facsimile machines, telephones and telephone answering machines, and other electronic or computer technology. Disclosure of identifying information should be avoided whenever possible.

(n) Social workers should transfer or dispose of clients' records in a manner that protects clients' confidentiality and is consistent with state statutes governing records and social work licensure.

(o) Social workers should take reasonable precautions to protect client confidentiality in the event of the social worker's termination of practice, incapacitation, or death.

(p) Social workers should not disclose identifying information when discussing clients for teaching or training purposes unless the client has consented to disclosure of confidential information.

(q) Social workers should not disclose identifying information when discussing clients with consultants unless the client has consented to disclosure of confidential information or there is a compelling need for such disclosure.

(r) Social workers should protect the confidentiality of deceased clients consistent with the preceding standards.

1.08 Access to Records

(a) Social workers should provide clients with reasonable access to records concerning the clients. Social workers who are concerned that clients' access to their records could cause serious misunderstanding or harm to the client should provide assistance in interpreting the records and consultation with the client regarding the records. Social workers should limit clients' access to their records, or portions of their records, only in exceptional circumstances when there is compelling evidence that such access would cause serious harm to the client. Both clients' requests and the rationale for withholding some or all of the record should be documented in clients' files.

(b) When providing clients with access to their records, social workers should take steps to protect the confidentiality of other individuals identified or discussed in such records.

1.09 Sexual Relationships

(a) Social workers should under no circumstances engage in sexual activities or sexual contact with current clients, whether such contact is consensual or forced.

(b) Social workers should not engage in sexual activities or sexual contact with clients' relatives or other individuals with whom clients maintain a close personal relationship when there is a risk of exploitation or potential harm to the client. Sexual activity or sexual contact with clients' relatives or other individuals with whom clients maintain a personal relationship has the potential to be harmful to the client and may make it difficult for the social worker and client to maintain appropriate professional boundaries.

Social workers—not their clients, their clients' relatives, or other individuals with whom the client maintains a personal relationship—assume the full burden for setting clear, appropriate, and culturally sensitive boundaries.

(c) Social workers should not engage in sexual activities or sexual contact with former clients because of the potential for harm to the client. If social workers engage in conduct contrary to this prohibition or claim that an exception to this prohibition is warranted because of extraordinary circumstances, it is social workers—not their clients—who assume the full burden of demonstrating that the former client has not been exploited, coerced, or manipulated, intentionally or unintentionally.

(d) Social workers should not provide clinical services to individuals with whom they have had a prior sexual relationship. Providing clinical services to a former sexual partner has the potential to be harmful to the individual and is likely to make it difficult for the social worker and individual to maintain appropriate professional boundaries.

1.10 Physical Contact

Social workers should not engage in physical contact with clients when there is a possibility of psychological harm to the client as a result of the contact (such as cradling or caressing clients). Social workers who engage in appropriate physical contact with clients are responsible for setting clear, appropriate, and culturally sensitive boundaries that govern such physical contact.

1.11 Sexual Harassment

Social workers should not sexually harass clients. Sexual harassment includes sexual advances, sexual solicitation, requests for sexual favors, and other verbal or physical conduct of a sexual nature.

1.12 Derogatory Language

Social workers should not use derogatory language in their written or verbal communications to or about clients. Social workers should use accurate and respectful language in all communications to and about clients.

1.13 Payment for Services

(a) When setting fees, social workers should ensure that the fees are fair, reasonable, and commensurate with the services performed. Consideration should be given to clients' ability to pay.

(b) Social workers should avoid accepting goods or services from clients as payment for professional services. Bartering arrangements, particularly involving services, create the potential for conflicts of interest, exploitation, and inappropriate boundaries in social workers' relationships with clients. Social workers should explore and may participate in bartering only in very limited circumstances when it can be demonstrated that such arrangements are an accepted practice among professionals in the local community, considered to be essential for the provision of services, negotiated without coercion, and entered into at the client's initiative and with the client's informed consent. Social workers who accept goods or services from clients as payment for professional services assume the full burden of demonstrating that this arrangement will not be detrimental to the client or the professional relationship.

(c) Social workers should not solicit a private fee or other remuneration for providing services to clients who are entitled to such available services through the social workers' employer or agency.

1.14 Clients Who Lack Decision-Making Capacity

When social workers act on behalf of clients who lack the capacity to make informed decisions, social workers should take reasonable steps to safeguard the interests and rights of those clients.

1.15 Interruption of Services

Social workers should make reasonable efforts to ensure continuity of services in the event that services are interrupted by factors such as unavailability, relocation, illness, disability, or death.

1.16 Termination of Services

(a) Social workers should terminate services to clients and professional relationships with them when such services and relationships are no longer required or no longer serve the clients' needs or interests.

(b) Social workers should take reasonable steps to avoid abandoning clients who are still in need of services. Social workers should withdraw services precipitously only under unusual circumstances, giving careful consideration to all factors in the situation and taking care to minimize possible adverse effects. Social workers should assist in making appropriate arrangements for continuation of services when necessary.

(c) Social workers in fee-for-service settings may terminate services to clients who are not paying an overdue balance if the financial contractual arrangements have been made clear to the client, if the client does not pose an imminent danger to self or others, and if the clinical and other consequences of the current nonpayment have been addressed and discussed with the client.

(d) Social workers should not terminate services to pursue a social, financial, or sexual relationship with a client.

(e) Social workers who anticipate the termination or interruption of services to clients should notify clients promptly and seek the transfer, referral, or continuation of services in relation to the clients' needs and preferences.

(f) Social workers who are leaving an employment setting should inform clients of appropriate options for the continuation of services and of the benefits and risks of the options.

2. SOCIAL WORKERS' ETHICAL RESPONSIBILITIES TO COLLEAGUES

2.01 Respect

(a) Social workers should treat colleagues with respect and should represent accurately and fairly the qualifications, views, and obligations of colleagues.

(b) Social workers should avoid unwarranted negative criticism of colleagues in communications with clients or with other professionals. Unwarranted negative criticism may include demeaning comments that refer to colleagues' level of competence or to individuals' attributes such as race, ethnicity, national origin, color, sex, sexual orientation, age, marital status, political belief, religion, and mental or physical disability.

(c) Social workers should cooperate with social work colleagues and with colleagues of other professions when such cooperation serves the well-being of clients.

2.02   Confidentiality
Social workers should respect confidential information shared by colleagues in the course of their professional relationships and transactions. Social workers should ensure that such colleagues understand social workers' obligation to respect confidentiality and any exceptions related to it.

2.03   Interdisciplinary Collaboration
(a) Social workers who are members of an interdisciplinary team should participate in and contribute to decisions that affect the well-being of clients by drawing on the perspectives, values, and experiences of the social work profession. Professional and ethical obligations of the interdisciplinary team as a whole and of its individual members should be clearly established.
(b) Social workers for whom a team decision raises ethical concerns should attempt to resolve the disagreement through appropriate channels. If the disagreement cannot be resolved, social workers should pursue other avenues to address their concerns consistent with client well-being.

2.04   Disputes Involving Colleagues
(a) Social workers should not take advantage of a dispute between a colleague and an employer to obtain a position or otherwise advance the social workers' own interests.
(b) Social workers should not exploit clients in disputes with colleagues or engage clients in any inappropriate discussion of conflicts between social workers and their colleagues.

2.05   Consultation
(a) Social workers should seek the advice and counsel of colleagues whenever such consultation is in the best interests of clients.
(b) Social workers should keep themselves informed about colleagues' areas of expertise and competencies. Social workers should seek consultation only from colleagues who have demonstrated knowledge, expertise, and competence related to the subject of the consultation.

(c) When consulting with colleagues about clients, social workers should disclose the least amount of information necessary to achieve the purposes of the consultation.

2.06   Referral for Services
(a) Social workers should refer clients to other professionals when the other professionals' specialized knowledge or expertise is needed to serve clients fully or when social workers believe that they are not being effective or making reasonable progress with clients and that additional service is required.
(b) Social workers who refer clients to other professionals should take appropriate steps to facilitate an orderly transfer of responsibility. Social workers who refer clients to other professionals should disclose, with clients' consent, all pertinent information to the new service providers.
(c) Social workers are prohibited from giving or receiving payment for a referral when no professional service is provided by the referring social worker.

2.07   Sexual Relationships
(a) Social workers who function as supervisors or educators should not engage in sexual activities or contact with supervisees, students, trainees, or other colleagues over whom they exercise professional authority.
(b) Social workers should avoid engaging in sexual relationships with colleagues when there is potential for a conflict of interest. Social workers who become involved in, or anticipate becoming involved in, a sexual relationship with a colleague have a duty to transfer professional responsibilities, when necessary, to avoid a conflict of interest.

2.08   Sexual Harassment
Social workers should not sexually harass supervisees, students, trainees, or colleagues. Sexual harassment includes sexual advances, sexual solicitation, requests for sexual favors, and other verbal or physical conduct of a sexual nature.

2.09   Impairment of Colleagues
(a) Social workers who have direct knowledge of a social work colleague's impairment

that is due to personal problems, psychosocial distress, substance abuse, or mental health difficulties and that interferes with practice effectiveness should consult with that colleague when feasible and assist the colleague in taking remedial action.

(b) Social workers who believe that a social work colleague's impairment interferes with practice effectiveness and that the colleague has not taken adequate steps to address the impairment should take action through appropriate channels established by employers, agencies, NASW, licensing and regulatory bodies, and other professional organizations.

2.10   Incompetence of Colleagues

(a) Social workers who have direct knowledge of a social work colleague's incompetence should consult with that colleague when feasible and assist the colleague in taking remedial action.

(b) Social workers who believe that a social work colleague is incompetent and has not taken adequate steps to address the incompetence should take action through appropriate channels established by employers, agencies, NASW, licensing and regulatory bodies, and other professional organizations.

2.11   Unethical Conduct of Colleagues

(a) Social workers should take adequate measures to discourage, prevent, expose, and correct the unethical conduct of colleagues.

(b) Social workers should be knowledgeable about established policies and procedures for handling concerns about colleagues' unethical behavior. Social workers should be familiar with national, state, and local procedures for handling ethics complaints. These include policies and procedures created by NASW, licensing and regulatory bodies, employers, agencies, and other professional organizations.

(c) Social workers who believe that a colleague has acted unethically should seek resolution by discussing their concerns with the colleague when feasible and when such discussion is likely to be productive.

(d) When necessary, social workers who believe that a colleague has acted unethically should take action through appropriate formal channels (such as contacting a state licensing board or

regulatory body, an NASW committee on inquiry, or other professional ethics committees).

(e) Social workers should defend and assist colleagues who are unjustly charged with unethical conduct.

3.   SOCIAL WORKERS' ETHICAL RESPONSIBILITIES IN PRACTICE SETTINGS

3.01   Supervision and Consultation

(a) Social workers who provide supervision or consultation should have the necessary knowledge and skill to supervise or consult appropriately and should do so only within their areas of knowledge and competence.

(b) Social workers who provide supervision or consultation are responsible for setting clear, appropriate, and culturally sensitive boundaries.

(c) Social workers should not engage in any dual or multiple relationships with supervisees in which there is a risk of exploitation of or potential harm to the supervisee.

(d) Social workers who provide supervision should evaluate supervisees' performance in a manner that is fair and respectful.

3.02   Education and Training

(a) Social workers who function as educators, field instructors for students, or trainers should provide instruction only within their areas of knowledge and competence and should provide instruction based on the most current information and knowledge available in the profession.

(b) Social workers who function as educators or field instructors for students should evaluate students' performance in a manner that is fair and respectful.

(c) Social workers who function as educators or field instructors for students should take reasonable steps to ensure that clients are routinely informed when services are being provided by students.

(d) Social workers who function as educators or field instructors for students should not engage in any dual or multiple relationships with students in which there is a risk of exploitation or potential harm to the student. Social work educators and field instructors are responsible for setting clear, appropriate, and culturally sensitive boundaries.

3.03 Performance Evaluation

Social workers who have responsibility for evaluating the performance of others should fulfill such responsibility in a fair and considerate manner and on the basis of clearly stated criteria.

3.04 Client Records

(a) Social workers should take reasonable steps to ensure that documentation in records is accurate and reflects the services provided.

(b) Social workers should include sufficient and timely documentation in records to facilitate the delivery of services and to ensure continuity of services provided to clients in the future.

(c) Social workers' documentation should protect clients' privacy to the extent that is possible and appropriate and should include only information that is directly relevant to the delivery of services.

(d) Social workers should store records following the termination of services to ensure reasonable future access. Records should be maintained for the number of years required by state statutes or relevant contracts.

3.05 Billing

Social workers should establish and maintain billing practices that accurately reflect the nature and extent of services provided and that identify who provided the service in the practice setting.

3.06 Client Transfer

(a) When an individual who is receiving services from another agency or colleague contacts a social worker for services, the social worker should carefully consider the client's needs before agreeing to provide services. To minimize possible confusion and conflict, social workers should discuss with potential clients the nature of the clients' current relationship with other service providers and the implications, including possible benefits or risks, of entering into a relationship with a new service provider.

(b) If a new client has been served by another agency or colleague, social workers should discuss with the client whether consultation with the previous service provider is in the client's best interest.

3.07 Administration

(a) Social work administrators should advocate within and outside their agencies for adequate resources to meet clients' needs.

(b) Social workers should advocate for resource allocation procedures that are open and fair. When not all clients' needs can be met, an allocation procedure should be developed that is nondiscriminatory and based on appropriate and consistently applied principles.

(c) Social workers who are administrators should take reasonable steps to ensure that adequate agency or organizational resources are available to provide appropriate staff supervision.

(d) Social work administrators should take reasonable steps to ensure that the working environment for which they are responsible is consistent with and encourages compliance with the *NASW Code of Ethics*. Social work administrators should take reasonable steps to eliminate any conditions in their organizations that violate, interfere with, or discourage compliance with the *Code*.

3.08 Continuing Education and Staff Development

Social work administrators and supervisors should take reasonable steps to provide or arrange for continuing education and staff development for all staff for whom they are responsible. Continuing education and staff development should address current knowledge and emerging developments related to social work practice and ethics.

3.09 Commitments to Employers

(a) Social workers generally should adhere to commitments made to employers and employing organizations.

(b) Social workers should work to improve employing agencies' policies and procedures and the efficiency and effectiveness of their services.

(c) Social workers should take reasonable steps to ensure that employers are aware of social workers' ethical obligations as set forth in the *NASW Code of Ethics* and of the implications of those obligations for social work practice.

(d) Social workers should not allow an employing organization's policies, procedures, regulations, or administrative orders to interfere with their ethical practice of social work. Social workers should take reasonable steps to ensure that their employing organizations' practices are consistent with the *NASW Code of Ethics*.

(e) Social workers should act to prevent and eliminate discrimination in the employing organization's work assignments and in its employment policies and practices.

(f) Social workers should accept employment or arrange student field placements only in organizations that exercise fair personnel practices.

(g) Social workers should be diligent stewards of the resources of their employing organizations, wisely conserving funds where appropriate and never misappropriating funds or using them for unintended purposes.

3.10   Labor–Management Disputes

(a) Social workers may engage in organized action, including the formation of and participation in labor unions, to improve services to clients and working conditions.

(b) The actions of social workers who are involved in labor–management disputes, job actions, or labor strikes should be guided by the profession's values, ethical principles, and ethical standards. Reasonable differences of opinion exist among social workers concerning their primary obligation as professionals during an actual or threatened labor strike or job action. Social workers should carefully examine relevant issues and their possible impact on clients before deciding on a course of action.

4.   SOCIAL WORKERS' ETHICAL RESPONSIBILITIES AS PROFESSIONALS

4.01   Competence

(a) Social workers should accept responsibility or employment only on the basis of existing competence or the intention to acquire the necessary competence.

(b) Social workers should strive to become and remain proficient in professional practice and the performance of professional functions. Social workers should critically examine and keep current with emerging knowledge relevant to social work. Social workers should routinely review the professional literature and partici-

pate in continuing education relevant to social work practice and social work ethics.

(c) Social workers should base practice on recognized knowledge, including empirically based knowledge, relevant to social work and social work ethics.

4.02   Discrimination

Social workers should not practice, condone, facilitate, or collaborate with any form of discrimination on the basis of race, ethnicity, national origin, color, sex, sexual orientation, age, marital status, political belief, religion, or mental or physical disability.

4.03   Private Conduct

Social workers should not permit their private conduct to interfere with their ability to fulfill their professional responsibilities.

4.04   Dishonesty, Fraud, and Deception

Social workers should not participate in, condone, or be associated with dishonesty, fraud, or deception.

4.05   Impairment

(a) Social workers should not allow their own personal problems, psychosocial distress, legal problems, substance abuse, or mental health difficulties to interfere with their professional judgment and performance or to jeopardize the best interests of people for whom they have a professional responsibility.

(b) Social workers whose personal problems, psychosocial distress, legal problems, substance abuse, or mental health difficulties interfere with their professional judgment and performance should immediately seek consultation and take appropriate remedial action by seeking professional help, making adjustments in workload, terminating practice, or taking any other steps necessary to protect clients and others.

4.06   Misrepresentation

(a) Social workers should make clear distinctions between statements made and actions engaged in as a private individual and as a representative of the social work profession, a professional social work organization, or the social worker's employing agency.

(b) Social workers who speak on behalf of professional social work organizations should accurately represent the official and authorized positions of the organizations.

(c) Social workers should ensure that their representations to clients, agencies, and the public of professional qualifications, credentials, education, competence, affiliations, services provided, or results to be achieved are accurate. Social workers should claim only those relevant professional credentials they actually possess and take steps to correct any inaccuracies or misrepresentations of their credentials by others.

4.07   Solicitations

(a) Social workers should not engage in uninvited solicitation of potential clients who, because of their circumstances, are vulnerable to undue influence, manipulation, or coercion.

(b) Social workers should not engage in solicitation of testimonial endorsements (including solicitation of consent to use a client's prior statement as a testimonial endorsement) from current clients or from other people who, because of their particular circumstances, are vulnerable to undue influence.

4.08   Acknowledging Credit

(a) Social workers should take responsibility and credit, including authorship credit, only for work they have actually performed and to which they have contributed.

(b) Social workers should honestly acknowledge the work of and the contributions made by others.

5.   SOCIAL WORKERS' ETHICAL RESPONSIBILITIES TO THE SOCIAL WORK PROFESSION

5.01   Integrity of the Profession

(a) Social workers should work toward the maintenance and promotion of high standards of practice.

(b) Social workers should uphold and advance the values, ethics, knowledge, and mission of the profession. Social workers should protect, enhance, and improve the integrity of the profession through appropriate study and research, active discussion, and responsible criticism of the profession.

(c) Social workers should contribute time and professional expertise to activities that promote respect for the value, integrity, and competence of the social work profession. These activities may include teaching, research, consultation, service, legislative testimony, presentations in the community, and participation in their professional organizations.

(d) Social workers should contribute to the knowledge base of social work and share with colleagues their knowledge related to practice, research, and ethics. Social workers should seek to contribute to the profession's literature and to share their knowledge at professional meetings and conferences.

(e) Social workers should act to prevent the unauthorized and unqualified practice of social work.

5.02   Evaluation and Research

(a) Social workers should monitor and evaluate policies, the implementation of programs, and practice interventions.

(b) Social workers should promote and facilitate evaluation and research to contribute to the development of knowledge.

(c) Social workers should critically examine and keep current with emerging knowledge relevant to social work and fully use evaluation and research evidence in their professional practice.

(d) Social workers engaged in evaluation or research should carefully consider possible consequences and should follow guidelines developed for the protection of evaluation and research participants. Appropriate institutional review boards should be consulted.

(e) Social workers engaged in evaluation or research should obtain voluntary and written informed consent from participants, when appropriate, without any implied or actual deprivation or penalty for refusal to participate; without undue inducement to participate; and with due regard for participants' well-being, privacy, and dignity. Informed consent should include information about the nature, extent, and duration of the participation requested and disclosure of the risks and benefits of participation in the research.

(f) When evaluation or research participants are incapable of giving informed consent, social workers should provide an appropriate explanation to the participants, obtain the participants' assent to the extent they are able, and obtain written consent from an appropriate proxy.

(g) Social workers should never design or conduct evaluation or research that does not use consent procedures, such as certain forms of naturalistic observation and archival research, unless rigorous and responsible review of the research has found it to be justified because of its prospective scientific, educational, or applied value and unless equally effective alternative procedures that do not involve waiver of consent are not feasible.

(h) Social workers should inform participants of their right to withdraw from evaluation and research at any time without penalty.

(i) Social workers should take appropriate steps to ensure that participants in evaluation and research have access to appropriate supportive services.

(j) Social workers engaged in evaluation or research should protect participants from unwarranted physical or mental distress, harm, danger, or deprivation.

(k) Social workers engaged in the evaluation of services should discuss collected information only for professional purposes and only with people professionally concerned with this information.

(l) Social workers engaged in evaluation or research should ensure the anonymity or confidentiality of participants and of the data obtained from them. Social workers should inform participants of any limits of confidentiality, the measures that will be taken to ensure confidentiality, and when any records containing research data will be destroyed.

(m) Social workers who report evaluation and research results should protect participants' confidentiality by omitting identifying information unless proper consent has been obtained authorizing disclosure.

(n) Social workers should report evaluation and research findings accurately. They should not fabricate or falsify results and should take steps to correct any errors later found in published data using standard publication methods.

(o) Social workers engaged in evaluation or research should be alert to and avoid conflicts of interest and dual relationships with participants,

should inform participants when a real or potential conflict of interest arises, and should take steps to resolve the issue in a manner that makes participants' interests primary.

(p) Social workers should educate themselves, their students, and their colleagues about responsible research practices.

6. SOCIAL WORKERS' ETHICAL RESPONSIBILITIES TO THE BROADER SOCIETY

6.01 Social Welfare

Social workers should promote the general welfare of society, from local to global levels, and the development of people, their communities, and their environments. Social workers should advocate for living conditions conducive to the fulfillment of basic human needs and should promote social, economic, political, and cultural values and institutions that are compatible with the realization of social justice.

6.02 Public Participation

Social workers should facilitate informed participation by the public in shaping social policies and institutions.

6.03 Public Emergencies

Social workers should provide appropriate professional services in public emergencies to the greatest extent possible.

6.04 Social and Political Action

(a) Social workers should engage in social and political action that seeks to ensure that all people have equal access to the resources, employment, services, and opportunities they require to meet their basic human needs and to develop fully. Social workers should be aware of the impact of the political arena on practice and should advocate for changes in policy and legislation to improve social conditions in order to meet basic human needs and promote social justice.

(b) Social workers should act to expand choice and opportunity for all people, with special regard for vulnerable, disadvantaged, oppressed, and exploited people and groups.

(c) Social workers should promote conditions that encourage respect for cultural and social diversity within the United States and globally.

Social workers should promote policies and practices that demonstrate respect for difference, support the expansion of cultural knowledge and resources, advocate for programs and institutions that demonstrate cultural competence, and promote policies that safeguard the rights of and confirm equity and social justice for all people.

(d) Social workers should act to prevent and eliminate domination of, exploitation of, and discrimination against any person, group, or class on the basis of race, ethnicity, national origin, color, sex, sexual orientation, age, marital status, political belief, religion, or mental or physical disability.

Index

Abandonment, 344
Abduction, parental. *See* Parental abduction
Abortion
    access to, 325
    background on, 3
    free speech restrictions and, 54, 58
    policy statement on, 3
Achieving Educational Excellence for Children at Risk (Hawkins), 277
Acknowledgment of credit, 349
Acquired immune deficiency syndrome (AIDS). *See* HIV/AIDS
Adjudication
    background of, 4–5
    issue statement on, 5–6
    policy statement on, 6–7
Adolescent pregnancy
    background of, 8–9
    issue statement on, 9
    policy statement on, 9–11
    school dropout rate and, 8, 275–276
Adolescents. *See also* Children; Juvenile justice system
    health care for, 9, 10
    parenting services for, 9–10
    school dropout rate among, 8, 275–279
    sex education for, 10, 110
    sexual relationships between, 8–9
    suicide among, 332–334
Adoption
    background of, 136
    issue statement on, 136–137
    policy statement on, 137–140
Adoption Assistance and Child Welfare Act of 1980, 45
Affirmative action
    background of, 12
    in education, 12
    in employment, 12, 13, 152
    in housing, 13
    issue statement on, 13–14
    policy statement on, 14
African Americans
    adolescent pregnancy and, 8
    affirmative action and, 12–14
    with HIV/AIDS, 159
    economic status of elderly, 17
    incarceration of, 52
    income of, 146–148, 323
    life expectancy for, 16
    opportunities for, 65
    poverty among, 25, 149
    school dropout rate among, 275
    workplace discrimination and. *See* Workplace discrimination
Aging. *See* Elderly individuals

Aid to Families with Dependent Children (AFDC)
    adolescent pregnancy and, 8
    background of, 23–25, 148
    issue statement on, 25–28
    policy statement on, 28–29
Alcohol abuse. *See also* Substance abuse
    among elderly individuals, 18
    among social workers, 185–187
    extent of, 32
Alternative work patterns
    background of, 39–40
    issue statement on, 40
    policy statement on, 40
American Psychiatric Association, 198, 199
American Psychological Association, 198, 199
American Red Cross, 91
Americans with Disabilities Act of 1990 (ADA), 251
Architectural and Transportation Barriers Compliance Board, 251
Assisted suicide
    physician-, 59–60
    social worker involvement in, 61–62
Audiotaping, 340–341
Authorship credit, 349

Bartering arrangements, 344
Billing practices, 347
Bisexuals
    background of, 198–201
    issue statement on, 202
    policy statement on, 202–203
    public awareness of issues related to, 203–204
A Blueprint for Success (National Education Association), 277
Brown v. Board of Education, 12

Cancer, economic costs of, 169
Caregivers
    of elderly individuals, 127–128
    use of physical punishment by, 255–257
    women as, 142
Case management
    background of, 42–43
    issue statement on, 43
    policy statement on, 43–44
    restrictions imposed on, 269
Center for the Study of Social Policy, 46
Child Abuse Prevention and Treatment Act Amendments, 46
Child Abuse Prevention and Treatment Act (CAPTA), 45
Child abuse and neglect
    background of, 45–46
    extent of, 326
    within families, 132, 133
    issue statement on, 47

physical punishment as, 256, 257
policy statement on, 48–49
Child custody
homosexuals and, 201
parental abduction and, 240–241
Child Support Enforcement Law, 23
Child welfare services, 259–260
Children. *See also* Adolescents
deinstitutionalization of dependent, 85
foster care or adoption of, 136–140
with HIV/AIDS, 159
living in poverty, 23, 25, 66, 103, 278
mental and emotional problems in, 223
mental health services for, 225–226
parental abduction of, 240–242
Children's Defense Fund, 46
Children's Trust Funds, 45–46
City of Richmond v. Croson, 53
Civil liberties. *See also* Social justice
background of, 50
issue statement on, 50–55
policy statement on, 55–58
Civil Rights Act of 1964, 12
Civil Rights Act of 1966, 53
Civil Rights Act of 1968, 250
Client records
access to, 343
documentation in, 347
responsibilities related to, 347
storage of, 347
transfer or disposal of, 343
Clients
abandonment of, 344
commitment to, 340
deceased, 343
definition of, 337
dual or multiple relationships with, 341
illiterate, 340
interruption of services to, 344
involuntary, 340
lacking decision-making capacity, 344
payment issues and, 343–344
physical contact with, 343
privacy and confidentiality of, 341–343
referral of, 345
respect for dignity and worth of, 339
sexual harassment of, 343
sexual relationships with, 343
social diversity of, 341
termination of services to, 344
transfer of, 347
use of derogatory language to, 343
Clinical social workers
function of, 306
professional recognition of, 306, 307
Collaboration, interdisciplinary, 345
Colleagues. *See also* Social workers
assistance programs for, 186–187
confidential information shared by, 344–345
consultation between, 345
disputes involving, 345
impairment of, 185–187, 345–346, 348
interdisciplinary collaboration between, 345
referrals to, 345
respect for, 344
sexual harassment of, 345

sexual relationships with, 345
unethical conduct of, 346
Commission on Health and Mental Health (NASW), 156
Commitment
to clients, 340
to ethical principles, 339
Community development
background of, 63–65
housing and, 66, 172, 175
issue statement on, 65
policy statement on, 65–66
Community Mental Health Act of 1964, 292
Community Mental Health Services Act of 1963, 223
Comparable worth strategies, 151–152
Competence
area of, 340, 346
of colleagues, 346
cultural, 341
protecting clients who lack, 344
standards for, 341
Computer data banks, confidentiality and, 55, 70
Confidentiality. *See also* Privacy rights
adoption and, 140
background of, 68–69
client records and, 343
computer data banks and, 55, 70
couple or marital counseling and, 342
of deceased clients, 343
drug testing and, 95
in evaluation and research, 350
family, group, and marital counseling and, 342
group counseling and, 342
HIV/AIDS and, 160–162
issue statement on, 69
limitations to, 342
policy statement on, 69–71
responsibility to clients regarding, 341–343
shared by colleagues, 344–345
third-party payers and, 342
workplace and, 237
Conflict of interest
responsibilities in order to avoid, 341
sexual relationships as, 345
Consent, informed, 340–341, 349
Constitutional Amendments
affirmative action and, 12
First Amendment, 53–54, 56–57
Fifth Amendment, 56
Eighth Amendment, 255
Fourteenth Amendment, 52, 54, 55
Sixteenth Amendment, 301
Consultants and consultation
colleagues as, 345
confidentiality and, 343, 345
Continuing education, 347
Corporal punishment. *See* Discipline; Physical punishment
Council on Social Work Education (CSWE), 75, 296
Couple or marital counseling, 342
Crime, 32
Criminal defendants, 55–56
Criminal justice system
access to justice and, 52–53, 56
civil liberties and, 51–52
juvenile, 192–196. *See also* Juvenile justice system
racism in, 265–266
reform of, 55–56

Cultural competence
    background of, 75–76
    Code of Ethics and, 341, 350–351
    issue statement on, 76–77
    policy statement on, 77
Cultural diversity
    background of, 72–73
    community development and, 64
    competence in dealing with, 75–77
    family policy and, 128
    foster care or adoption and, 138, 139
    issue statement on, 73
    policy statement on, 73–74
    promotion of conditions to encourage, 350–351
    respect for, 339
    understanding of, 341

Death and dying. *See also* End-of-life decisions; Suicide
    attitudes toward, 169
    hospice care and, 169–171
Death penalty
    abolition of, 55
    extension of, 51–52
Deceased clients, 343
Deception, 348
Declassification
    background of, 79–81
    issue statement on, 81
    policy statement on, 81–83
Deinstitutionalization
    of dependent children, 85
    of developmentally disabled individuals, 84
    of elderly individuals, 85–86
    issue statement on, 86
    of juvenile offenders, 85
    of mentally ill individuals, 84–85, 156
    policy statement on, 86–87
Derogatory language, 343
Developmental Disabilities Assistance and Bill of Rights Act of
    1975, 251
Developmentally disabled individuals, 84. *See also* Individuals
    with disabilities
Diagnosis-related groups (DRGs), 155–157, 228
Dignity of person, 339
Disabled individuals. *See* Individuals with disabilities
Disasters
    at-risk populations for, 88–90
    definitions of, 88
    issue statement on, 91–92
    management of, 90–91
    policy statement on, 92–93
    research on human services aspects of, 90
    stages associated with, 88
Discharge planning, 298
Discipline. *See also* Physical punishment
    effectiveness of, 256
    physical punishment as, 255–257. *See also* Physical punish-
        ment
    in schools, 109, 113
Discrimination. *See also* Racism
    affirmative action and, 12–14
    criminal justice system and, 52, 55
    against elderly individuals, 20–21
    against homosexuals and bisexuals, 200–204
    against immigrants and refugees, 180–182
    against individuals with disabilities, 251

social worker responsibilities regarding, 348
    against women, 188, 327
    workplace, 53, 146–153, 347. *See also* Workplace discrimina-
        tion
Dishonesty, 348
Disputes, with colleagues, 345
Dissent, right to, 56–57
Diversion programs, 193–195
Divorce. *See* Parental abduction
Drug abuse. *See* Substance abuse
Drug testing. *See also* Substance abuse
    background of, 95–96
    issue statement on, 96–97
    opposition to, 57
    policy statement on, 98–99
    requirements for, 52, 55
Dual or multiple relationships
    with clients, 341
    with educators, 346
    with field instructors, 346
    with supervisors, 346
Due process issues
    NASW position on, 56
    in schools, 113
Duty-to-protect principle
    confidentiality and, 342
    HIV/AIDS and, 162

Early childhood care
    background of, 100
    issue statement on, 100–101
    policy statement on, 101–102, 112
Earned income tax credit (EITC), 25, 145
Economic policy and issues
    background of, 103
    elderly individuals and, 16–20
    full and equitable employment, 141–145
    housing and, 176
    issue statement on, 103–105
    policy statement on, 105–107
    in rural communities, 294
    social program funding and, 270
    tax reform, 301–305
Education. *See also* Schools; Social work education and training
    AFDC reform and, 27
    affirmative action in, 12
    aid for, 108
    alternative, 109–110
    bilingual and bicultural, 73–74
    changing labor force requirements for, 65–66
    components of, 111–113
    of females, 324–325, 328
    health and mental health education, 112–113
    of high-risk students, 109
    of individuals with disabilities, 252–253
    issue statement on, 111
    need for changes in, 108
    policy statement on, 111–114
    racism and, 261, 264
    relationship of federal government to, 108–109
    right to, 191
    sex, 10, 110
    of students with disabilities, 108
    vocational, 112
Education for All Handicapped Children Act, 108, 223, 251
Educators

confidentiality and, 342–343
    dual or multiple relationships with, 346
    responsibilities as, 346
Eighth Amendment, 255
Elderly individuals
    abuse of, 132, 133, 326
    deinstitutionalization of, 85–86
    demographics of, 16, 63–64
    economic issues and, 16–17
    family caregiving and, 127–128
    issue statement on, 18–19
    long-term care for, 210, 211. *See also* Long-term care
    mental health care for, 18, 22, 227
    policy statement on, 19–22
    poverty among, 16–17, 26, 149, 268
    social characteristics of, 17
    societal response to, 18
    vulnerability of, 17–18
Electoral politics. *See also* Political activity
    background of, 115–118
    explanation of, 116
    issue statement on, 118
    policy statement on, 118–119
Electronic media
    confidentiality and, 342
    services via, 340
Elementary and Secondary Education Act (ESEA), 276
Emergencies, 350
Employee assistance programs (EAPs), drug testing and, 95, 97, 98
Employee Retirement and Income Security Act (ERISA), 217, 307
Employment
    conflict between family life and, 317–318, 320–321
    full and equitable, 141–145
    of individuals with disabilities, 253
    racism in, 261, 264–265
    right to, 191
    in rural areas, 295
Employment Act of 1946, 141–142, 144
Employment issues. *See also* Labor force; Workplace
    affirmative action and, 12, 13, 152
    alternative work patterns and, 39–41
    elderly individuals and, 20–21
    family support policies and, 129
    housing and, 173–174
    wages and benefits as, 106–107, 146–149
    workplace discrimination, 53, 146–153. *See also* Workplace discrimination
Employment programs, 27
End-of-life decisions. *See also* Death and dying
    background of, 59–60
    issue statement on, 60–61
    policy statement on, 61–62
Energy issues
    background of, 120–121
    issue statement on, 121–122
    policy statement on, 122
Energy resources, 294–295
English-Only movement, 72–73
Epidemiologic Catchment Area Study (NIMH), 223
Equal protection, 57
Equitable employment. *See* Full and equitable employment
Ethical decision making, 338
Ethical principles, 339–340
Ethical responsibilities

to broader society, 350–351
    to clients, 340–344
    to colleagues, 344–346
    in practice settings, 346–348
    as professionals, 348–349
    to social work profession, 349–350
Ethnic diversity, 339, 341. *See also* Cultural diversity
Euthanasia. *See* End-of-life decisions
Evaluation
    of performance, 346–347
    responsibilities related to, 349–350
Executive Order No. 11063, 13
Executive Order No. 11246, 12
Executive Order No. 12892, 13

Fair Housing Act of 1968, 13
Families. *See also* Fathers; Mothers; Parents
    change in structure of, 64, 127
    child abuse and neglect and, 47
    human rights and, 190–191
    parental abduction and, 240–242
    relationship between schools and, 110
    substance abuse within, 33
Family planning
    access to, 325
    background of, 124–125
    policy statement on, 125–126
Family policy
    background of, 127
    issue statement on, 127–129
    policy statement on, 129–131
Family Preservation and Family Support Services Act, 46
Family Support Act of 1988
    impact of, 24–25, 27
    provisions of, 23–24
Family violence
    background of, 132–133
    issue statement on, 133–134
    policy statement on, 134–135
Fathers, adolescent, 11. *See also* Families; Parents
Federal Emergency Management Agency (FEMA), 90
Federal government
    development of family policy legislation by, 130–131
    housing and, 174–176
    NASW and role of, 271
    preventive measures for school failure by, 276
    relationship to education, 108–109
    social policy and, 267–271
Fees. *See* Payment for services
Field instructors, 346
Fifth Amendment rights, 56
First Amendment rights
    restrictions on, 53–54
    support for, 56–57
Flex-time employment, 39, 40
Foster care
    background of, 136
    issue statement on, 136–137
    policy statement on, 137–140
Fourteenth Amendment rights, 52, 54, 55
Fraud, 348
Free speech rights, 57
Freedman's Bureau Bill of 1865, 12
Full and equitable employment
    background of, 141–143
    issue statement on, 143–144

policy statement on, 144–145
Full Employment and Balanced National Growth Act of 1978, 142, 144

Gag rule, 54, 58
Gault decision, 192
Gays
    background of, 198–201
    with HIV/AIDS, 159
    issue statement on, 202
    policy statement on, 202–203
    public awareness of issues related to, 203–204
Glass ceiling, 149–150
Government, 267–271. *See also* Federal government
Griswold v. Connecticut, 54
Group counseling, 342

Habeas corpus, 56
Hague Convention on the Civil Aspects of International Child Abduction, 241, 242
Hand, Learned, 53
Handicapped individuals. *See* Individuals with disabilities
Harris, Dorothy, 5
Health care. *See also* Managed care; Mental health care; National health care
    for adolescents, 9, 10
    background of, 297
    cost and quality of, 229
    for elderly individuals, 18, 21, 22
    financing of, 155–158
    home, 288–291
    for homosexuals and bisexuals, 204
    in hospices, 169–171
    for individuals with disabilities, 253
    for individuals with HIV/AIDS, 161
    issue statement on, 297
    policy statement on, 297–300
    racism in, 262, 265
    right to, 191
    in rural areas, 293
    social component in, 298
    substance abuse and, 34
Health care reform. *See* National health care
Health education, 112–113
Health insurance. *See also* Health maintenance organizations (HMOs); Managed care; Third-party reimbursement
    civil liberties and, 55, 57
    individuals covered by, 216, 229–230
    self-insured plans, 307
    substance abuse coverage by, 35
Health issues
    for elderly individuals, 17–18
    self-determination and, 59–62
    substance abuse and, 32
    terms related to, 59–60
    for women, 325, 328–329
Health maintenance organizations (HMOs)
    explanation and types of, 272–273
    issue statement on, 273
    policy statement on, 273–274
Helfer, Ray E., 46
Hispanics
    economic status of elderly, 17
    with HIV/AIDS, 159
    housing and, 13
    immigration policies affecting, 178, 179

income of, 146, 147
    poverty among, 26
    school dropout rate among, 275
HIV/AIDS
    background of, 159–160
    foster care or adoption of children with, 136–137
    issue statement on, 160
    policy statement on, 160–162
    testing for, 55, 58, 160, 162
Holmes, Oliver Wendell, 53
Home health care
    background of, 288–289
    issue statement on, 289–291
    policy statement on, 291
Home Mortgage Disclosure Act, 13
Homelessness
    background of, 164–165
    failure of policies dealing with, 165–166
    housing issues and, 173
    issue statement on, 166
    policy statement on, 166–168
Homosexuals. *See* Bisexuals; Gays; Lesbians
Hospice care
    background of, 169
    issue statement on, 169–170
    policy statement on, 170–171
Housing. *See also* Homelessness
    affirmative action and, 13
    background of, 172
    as basic shelter, 174–175
    community development and, 66, 172, 175
    community infrastructure and, 173
    community life and, 175–176
    elderly individuals and, 17, 22
    employment and, 173–174
    eviction of tenants and, 58
    fiscal considerations and, 176
    geographic shifts and, 173
    for individuals with disabilities, 253
    racism and, 261–262, 265
    rural, 294
    segregation and, 174
    social services and, 173, 175–176
    special needs populations and, 173
    supply and affordability of, 172–173
Housing and Community Development Act of 1967, 13
The Human Factor: A Key to Excellence in Education (Mintzies & Hare), 277
Human immunodeficiency virus (HIV). *See* HIV/AIDS
Human rights
    background of, 188–190
    definition of, 189
    policy statement on, 190–191

Illiterate clients, 340
Immigrants
    current wave of, 178–180
    demographic change and, 64, 76
    federal policy regarding, 177–178, 182, 183
    issue statement on, 180–181
    language use and, 72, 73
    policy statement on, 181–183
Immigration Act of 1990, 180
Impairment, of colleagues, 185–187, 345–346, 348
Incarceration
    of African Americans, 52

of youths, 193, 194. *See also* Juvenile justice system
Income
    disparities in, 103–105, 146–147. *See also* Workplace dis-
        crimination
    of female social workers, 316–317, 320
    individuals with disabilities and, 253
    recommendations for equity in, 151
    of women, 104, 142, 146–148
Incompetence, of colleagues, 346
Independent living, individuals with disabilities and, 251, 252
Individuals with disabilities
    background of, 250–251
    deinstitutionalization of, 84–86
    education of, 108
    housing and, 173
    issue statement on, 251–252
    part-time work for, 40
    policy statement on, 252–254
Informed consent
    for evaluation and research participants, 349
    responsibilities related to, 340–341
Ingraham v. Wright, 255
Integrity, 339, 349
Interdisciplinary collaboration, 345
International Child Abduction Remedies Act, 241, 242
Interpreters, 340
Interruption of services, 344
Involuntary clients, 340

Job performance, 57
Johnson-Reed Act of 1924, 178
Judicial appointments, 56
Juvenile justice system. *See also* Criminal justice system
    diversion programs of, 193–194
    issue statement on, 194
    large institutions in, 193
    policy on, 194–196
    reform in, 192–193
Juvenile offenders, 85

Keely, Charles, 177
Kempe, C. Henry, 45, 132
Kent v. United States, 192
Kidnapping. *See* Parental abduction

Labor force. *See also* Employment issues; Workplace
    changing education and skill requirements for, 64
    women in, 39, 64, 104, 323, 324
Labor–management disputes, 348
Land use, 66
Least-restrictive environment, 111–112
Legal aid services, 52, 56
Legal issues and legislation
    adolescent pregnancy, 10–11
    affirmative action, 12, 13
    child abuse and neglect, 45–46
    Code of Ethics and, 342
    criminal justice system and, 51–52
    disasters and, 90, 91
    immigrants and refugees, 177–180
    individuals with disabilities and, 250–251
    linguistic diversity and, 72–74
    long-term care and, 212
    privacy rights and, 68–71. *See also* Confidentiality; Privacy
        rights
    sexual orientation and, 203, 204

Lesbians
    background of, 198–201
    issue statement on, 202
    policy statement on, 202–203
    public awareness of issues related to, 203–204
Linguistic diversity. *See also* Cultural diversity
    background of, 72–73
    issue statement on, 73
    policy statement on, 73–74
Long-term care. *See also* Hospice care
    background of, 210–212
    for elderly individuals, 21
    issue statement on, 212
    Medicare and, 231
    mental health, 211
    policy statement on, 213–214
Los Angeles v. Lyons, 53

Managed care
    background of, 216–218
    explanation of, 216–217
    issue statement on, 218–219
    long-term care and, 211–212
    policy statement on, 219–221
Marriage, same-sex, 201
Media, 342
Medicaid
    elderly individuals and, 21
    gaps in, 230–231
    home-care services and, 290–291
    long-term care and, 210, 211, 214
    managed care and, 218
    passage of, 228
    services available under, 211
Medical insurance. *See* Health insurance
Medicare
    gaps in, 230–231
    home-care services and, 289–290
    long-term care and, 210–211, 214
    passage of, 228
Mental health
    disaster effects and, 90, 92
    education issues and, 112–113
    substance abuse and, 32
    women and, 325–326, 328–329
Mental Health Bill of Rights Act of 1985, 250
Mental health care
    background of, 223
    for children, 225–226
    for elderly individuals, 18, 22, 227
    for homosexuals and bisexuals, 204
    insurance coverage for, 230. *See also* Health insurance
    issues unique to, 217
    as national priority, 223–224
    racism in, 262, 265
    in rural areas, 295
Mental Health Systems Act of 1980, 223
Mentally ill individuals
    assessment and treatment of, 224–225
    deinstitutionalization of, 84–85, 156
    national policy on care of, 223
    services for, 226–227
Meyer, Carol, 79
Military issues
    economic conversion as, 245–247
    expenditures as, 245, 247

homosexuals and, 201, 203
Minimum wage, recommendations for, 105–106, 143
Minorities. *See also* African Americans; Hispanics; Women
    demographics of, 64, 76
    full and equitable employment for, 141
    incarceration of, 52, 193
    in rural areas, 295
    services for elderly, 20
    workplace discrimination and, 146–153
Minority Enterprise Program (Small Business Administration), 13
Miranda rights, 55
Misrepresentation, 348–349
Mothers, adolescent, 8, 275–276. *See also* Families; Parents
Moynihan, Daniel Patrick, 23
Multiple relationships. *See* Dual or multiple relationships

NASW Chapter Guide for Adjudication of Grievances (NASW), 4
NASW Code of Ethics (NASW)
    client interests and, 95
    compliance with, 347
    cultural competence and, 77
    ethical principles in, 339–340
    ethical standards in, 340–351
    political action and, 115, 261, 350–351
    preamble of, 337
    privacy rights and, 69
    professional standards in, 4
    purpose of, 337–339
    requirements of, 50, 319
    use of, 338
    violations of, 6–7
NASW Standards for Social Work in Health Care Settings, 297
NASW Standards for Social Work Personnel Practices, 4–5, 319
National Association of Social Workers (NASW)
    adjudication procedures of, 6–7
    affirmative action committee of, 14
    Commission on Health and Mental Health, 156
    disaster services and, 91
    electoral politics and, 116, 117
    health care reform and, 155, 212, 214, 228, 231. *See also* National health care
    jurisdiction of, 5, 6
    legal regulation of clinical social workers and, 306
    peace and social welfare policy of, 245
    physical punishment and, 255–257
    policy statement on HMOs, 219
    role of federal government and, 271
    self-determination and, 252
    sexual orientation and, 198, 199, 202–204
National Center for Missing and Exploited Children, 241
National Center for Social Policy and Practice (NASW), 80
National Center on Child Abuse and Neglect (NCCAN), 45–46
National Committee on Inquiry (NCOI), 5, 7
National Committee on Women's Issues (NASW), 319
National health care. *See also* Health care
    background of, 228
    in early 1990s, 228–229
    issue statement of, 229–231
    NASW support for, 155, 212, 214, 228, 231
    policy statement on, 231–234
National health care proposal (NASW), 155, 157
National Housing Act, 164
National Occupational Social Work Task Force, 185, 186
Native Americans, 180–181
Neglect. *See* Child abuse and neglect

No-knock entry, 51

Occupational social work
    background of, 235
    health and safety issues and, 237
    issue statement on, 237–238
    perspective on work and, 236
    policy statement on, 238–239
    scope of, 235–236
Occupational Social Work Planning Committee, 186
Office of Federal Contract Compliance Programs (OFCCP) (U.S. Department of Labor), 13
Old Age and Survivors Disability Insurance, 148, 211, 324
Older Americans Act, 19, 268

Parental abduction
    background of, 240–241
    issue statement on, 241–242
    policy statement on, 242
Parental Kidnapping Prevention Act of 1980, 241
Parenting services
    for adolescents, 9–10
    for foster parents, 139
Parents. *See also* Families; Fathers; Mothers
    abduction by, 240–242
    child abuse and neglect by, 47
    relationship between schools and, 110
    use of physical punishment by, 255–257
Part-time employment, 39–40
Patients' Self-Determination Act of 1990, 60
Patterson v. McLean Credit Union, 53
Payment for services, 343–344
Peace
    background of, 244
    de-escalation and, 246
    economic conversion and, 245–247
    international cooperation and, 246–248
    military spending and, 245, 247
    promotion by social workers of, 248
Peer review process, 338
Performance evaluation, 346–347
Personal Responsibility and Work Opportunity Reconciliation Act of 1996, 179–180
Personnel standards, 4, 5
Physical contact, 343
Physical punishment
    background of, 255–256
    issue statement on, 256–257
    policy statement on, 257
    in schools, 109, 113, 255–256
    Supreme Court and, 133
Plessy v. Ferguson, 12
Police authority, 56
Political Action for Candidate Election (PACE), 81, 116–118
Political activity. *See also* Electoral politics; Voter participation
    NASW Code of Ethics and, 115, 261, 350–351
    racism and, 263, 266
    of social workers, 115, 116, 118, 119
Pound, Roscoe, 192
Poverty. *See also* Welfare reform
    adolescent pregnancy and, 8
    changes in rate of, 103–104
    children living in, 23, 25, 66, 103, 278
    elderly individuals living in, 16–17, 26, 149, 268
    homelessness and, 164–167
    women living in, 25

Practice settings, 346–348
Preamble of *NASW Code of Ethics*, 337
Pregnancy. *See also* Reproductive issues
    adolescent, 8–11
    substance abuse and, 32–33
Preventive detention, 51
Privacy rights. *See also* Confidentiality
    client records and, 347
    drug testing and, 95–96
    responsibilities related to, 341–343
    restrictions on, 54–55
    support for, 57–58
Private conduct, 348
Pro bono services, 339
Prospective payment system (PPS), 155–157
Public access, individuals with disabilities and, 252
Public child welfare services, 259–260
Public emergencies, 350
Public participation, 350
Public schools. *See* Schools
Public welfare law, 292
Pupil services teams, 111

Quicker and sicker syndrome, 156

Racism. *See also* Discrimination
    background in, 261, 263
    in criminal justice system, 265–266
    in education, 261, 264
    in employment, 261, 264–265
    explanation of, 263
    in health care and mental health care services, 262, 265
    in housing, 261–262, 265
    issue statement on, 263–264
    policy statement on, 264–266
    political activity and, 263, 266
    in public welfare services, 262, 265
    in social services, 262, 265
Reclassification. *See* Declassification
Records. *See* Client records
Referrals, 345
Refugees, 179, 182. *See also* Immigrants
Regular Education Initiative, 108
Rehabilitation Act Amendments of 1992, 251
Rehabilitation Act of 1973, 250–251
Religious beliefs, 57
Report of the Task Force on Corporal Punishment (National Education Association), 257
Reproductive issues
    abortion, 3, 325, 328
    adolescent pregnancy, 8–11, 275–276
    civil liberties and, 54–55
    family planning, 124–126, 325, 328
    substance abuse and, 32–33
Research
    dual or multiple relationships with participants in, 350
    responsibilities related to, 349–350
    on substance abuse, 36
Respect
    for clients, 339
    for colleagues, 344
    for diversity, 339
Revolving door syndrome, 156
Reynolds, Bertha, 63
Roe v. Wade, 54, 58

Rural areas
    elderly individuals in, 20
    energy issues in, 120–121
    social work in, 292–296
Rural Development Act of 1972, 292–293
Rust v. Sullivan, 54, 58

School dropout rate
    adolescent pregnancy and, 8, 275–276
    background of, 275
    issue statement on, 278–279
    policy statement on, 279–280
    preventive measures for, 276–278
    reasons contributing to, 275–276
Schools. *See also* Education
    environment in, 109, 325
    health services in, 329
    home, community, and, 110
    physical punishment in, 109, 113, 255–257
    rural, 294
    social workers in, 110–111, 113–114, 279, 280
Segregation. *See also* Affirmative action
    in housing, 174
    occupational, 142, 147–148, 323
Self-determination
    abortion and, 3
    client, 339, 340
    in end-of-life decisions, 59–62
    right to, 189, 252
Self-incrimination, 56
Sex education, 10, 110
Sexual abuse, 132–133. *See also* Family violence
Sexual harassment
    of clients, 343
    of colleagues, 345
    extent of, 326
    of female social workers, 318–319, 321
    occupational, 149
Sexual orientation. *See also* Bisexuals; Gays; Lesbians
    adolescent suicide and, 332
    conversion therapies to change, 204
    emergence of, 199
    explanation of, 198–199
    extent of variations in, 199–200
    issue statement on, 202
    policy statement on, 202–203
    prejudice and discrimination and, 200–204
Sexual relationships
    among adolescents, 8–9
    with clients, 343
    with colleagues, 345
Sixteenth Amendment, 301
Small Business Administration, Minority Enterprise Program, 13
Smoking. *See* Tobacco abuse
Social action, 350–351
Social diversity, 341, 350–351. *See also* Cultural diversity
Social justice. *See also* Civil liberties
    background of, 50
    issue statement on, 50–55
    NASW Code of Ethics and, 244, 337, 339
    peace and, 244–248
    policy statement on, 55–58
Social Security Act, Titles XVIII and XIX, 223
Social Security Act Amendments of 1939, 68
Social Security Act Amendments of 1983, 155

Social services
    AFDC reform and, 27–28
    background of, 283–284
    declassification issues and, 79–83
    for elderly individuals, 20–22
    explanation of, 283
    for families, 128–130
    issue statement on, 284–285
    policy statement on, 285–286
    privacy rights and, 57–58
    racism in, 262, 265
    relationship between housing and, 173, 175–176
    volunteers in, 310–312
Social work education and training
    in child abuse and neglect, 48
    in child welfare services, 259
    in community development, 66
    continuing, 347
    development of cultural awareness through, 74
    in disabilities, 253
    in family violence issues, 134
    in HIV/AIDS, 162
    NASW position on, 80
    in occupational social work, 239
    in peace and social justice issues, 248
    rural content in, 295–296
    in sexual orientation issues, 202–203
    in substance abuse, 35, 99
    trends in, 80
Social work profession
    case management in, 42–44
    cultural competence in, 75–77
    ethical responsibilities to, 348–349
    impact of new technologies on, 299
    integrity of, 349
    mission and core values of, 337
    social worker responsibilities to, 349–350
    women in, 316–321
    workplace discrimination in, 150
Social work services
    via electronic media, 340
    ethical principle regarding, 339
    interruption of, 344
    payment for, 343–344
    pro bono, 339
    referral for, 345
    right to refuse, 340
    termination of, 344
Social worker responsibilities
    to broader society, 350–351
    to clients, 340–344
    to colleagues, 344–346
    in practice settings, 346–348
    as professionals, 348–349
    regarding evaluation and research, 349–350
    to social work profession, 349–350
Social workers. *See also* Colleagues
    as administrators, 347
    alternative work patterns for, 40
    assisted suicide and, 61–62
    clinical, 306
    confidentiality and, 68–71. *See also* Confidentiality; Privacy
        rights
    educational background of, 79. *See also* Declassification
    as educators or trainers, 346

    ethical principles of, 339–340
    ethical responsibility to society of, 96
    family planning services by, 126
    in health care, 297–300
    HMOs and, 272–274
    home care, 288–291
    human rights and, 190
    impairment of, 185–187, 345–346, 348
    licensing and certification of, 81
    managed care role of, 220
    need for gerontological, 18–19
    occupational, 235–239. *See also* Occupational social work
    perception of profession by, 4
    political activity by, 115, 116, 118, 119
    promotion of peace by, 248
    in public schools, 110–111, 113–114
    in rural areas, 293
    in schools, 279, 280, 333, 334
    substance abuse among, 31
    as supervisors, 346
Social Workers Helping Social Workers (SWHSW), 185
Special-needs populations, 173. *See also* Individuals with disabilities; *specific special-needs groups*
Spergel, Irving, 63
Spousal abuse. *See also* Family violence
    background of, 132–133
    extent of, 326
Sterilization, 58
Students
    dual relationships with, 346
    evaluation of performance of, 346–347
Substance abuse. *See also* Drug testing
    among elderly individuals, 18
    among social workers, 185–187
    background of, 31
    explanation of, 31
    impact on family of, 33
    issue statement on, 34
    policy statement on, 34–36
    practice wisdom regarding, 33–34
    research on, 36
    scope of, 31–33
Suicide
    among adolescents, 332–334
    among elderly individuals, 18
    among social workers, 185
    physician-assisted, 59–60
    social worker involvement in assisted-, 61–62
Supreme Court, U.S.
    appointments to, 52–53
    corporal punishment and, 133
    parental abduction and, 241
    on physical punishment in schools, 52–53

Tarasoff decision, 162
Tax reform
    background of, 301–303
    issue statement on, 303–304
    policy statement on, 304–305
Termination
    of practice, 342
    of services, 344
Third-party reimbursement
    background of, 306
    confidentiality and, 342

issue statement on, 306–308
policy statement on, 308–309
Thompson v. Thompson, 241
Tien, Chang-Lin, 181
Tobacco abuse, 32. *See also* Substance abuse
Trainers
    confidentiality and, 342–343
    responsibilities as, 346
Transfer
    of client records, 343
    of clients, 347
Translators, 340
Transportation services
    for elderly individuals, 22
    for individuals with disabilities, 253
    in rural areas, 293–294
Tuberculosis, 162

Underemployment, 142–144
Unemployment
    accuracy in rates of, 106, 141, 142
    economic and social consequences of, 142–144
Unemployment insurance, 142, 148
Unethical conduct, 346
United Nations Universal Declaration of Human Rights, 188
Universal Declaration of Human Rights, 247

Values
    ethical decision making and personal, 338
    ethical principles based on core, 339–340
    of social work profession, 337
Videotaping, 340–341
Violence. *See also* Child abuse and neglect; Family violence
    directed toward social workers, 319, 321
    physical punishment as, 256–257. *See also* Physical punishment
    toward women, 326, 329
    U.S. rate of, 246
Vocational education, 112
Volunteers
    background of, 310–311
    issue statement on, 311
    policy statement on, 311–312
Voter participation. *See also* Political activity
    background of, 314
    issue statement on, 314–315
    policy statement on, 315

Webster v. Reproductive Health Services, 54
Welfare reform
    AFDC and, 23–29. *See also* Aid to Families with Dependent Children (AFDC)
    developments in, 23–25
    family self-sufficiency and, 129–130
    recommendations for, 26–28
Women
    abuse of elderly, 133
    AFDC reform and needs of, 27
    alternative work patterns among, 39–40
    discrimination against, 188, 327
    economic status of elderly, 17
    education of, 324–325, 328
    equitable employment for, 141, 142
    health issues for, 325, 328–329
    with HIV/AIDS, 159
    household and caregiving tasks of, 149, 324
    incarceration of, 193
    income maintenance for, 328
    income of, 104, 142, 146–148, 323
    in labor force, 39, 64, 104, 323
    living in poverty, 25, 323
    in rural areas, 294
    substance abuse and, 32
    workplace discrimination against. *See* Workplace discrimination
Workers' rights, support for, 57
Workplace. *See also* Employment issues; Labor force
    confidentiality and, 237
    drug testing in, 95–99. *See also* Drug testing
    health and safety of, 237
    social workers in. *See* Occupational social work
Workplace discrimination
    background of, 146
    Code of Ethics and, 347
    employment benefits and, 148–149
    family work and, 149
    income disparities and, 103–105, 146–147
    issue statement on, 150–151
    job obstacles and, 149–150
    judicial decisions regarding, 53
    occupational segregation as, 142, 147–148, 323
    policy statement on, 151–153
    sexual harassment and, 149